DYNAMIC ECONOMI

BARRY BRUNT, PATRICK O'T

What you need to study for Leaving Certificate Geography:

Higher Level students must cover *six* sections of this book:

1. The Physical Environment (chapters 1-17)
2. Regional Geography (chapters 18-36)
3. Maps and Photographs (chapters 37-38)
4. Economic Activities (chapters 39-63)
5.a Global Interdependence (chapters 64-78)
   or
5.b Geoecology (chapters 79-84)
6. Fieldwork Investigation (chapter 85)

Ordinary Level students must cover *five* sections of this book:

1. The Physical Environment (chapters 1-17)
2. Regional Geography (chapters 18-36)
3. Maps and Photographs (chapters 37-38)
4. Economic Activities (chapters 39-63)
5. Fieldwork Investigation (chapter 85)

DYNAMIC ECONOMIC GEOGRAPHY

BARRY BRUNT, PATRICK O'DWYER & CHARLES HAYES

GILL & MACMILLAN

Gill & Macmillan Ltd
Hume Avenue
Park West
Dublin 12
with associated companies throughout the world
www.gillmacmillan.ie

© Barry Brunt, Patrick O'Dwyer & Charles Hayes
Authors:
Patrick O'Dwyer: chapters 1-17, 37-38, and chapter 85.
Barry Brunt: chapters 18-36 and 39-63.
Charles Hayes: chapters 64-84.

Artwork by Design Image, Dublin

978 07171 4193 7

Colour reproduction by Typeform Repro, Dublin
Print origination in Ireland by Design Image, Dublin

The paper used in this book is made from the wood pulp of managed forests. For every tree felled, at least one tree is planted, thereby renewing natural resources.

CONTENTS

Maps and Photographs

Economic Activities

Acknowledgments

The authors are especially appreciative of the many people who were directly involved in the preparation, design and publication of this book. Special thanks are due to Hubert Mahony, Aoileann O'Donnell and Helen Thompson of Gill & Macmillan, to Picot Cassidy who was a critical and effective editor and to Kristin Jensen for proofreading. Dara O'Doherty and her team at Design Image are thanked for their creative design of the book.

Thanks are also due to geography teachers from many schools throughout Ireland who offered valuable insights on and inputs to the text. In particular, the authors acknowledge the contributions of Ms Una Nation, St Mary's High School, Midleton, Co. Cork in revising the content and layout of this book.

Patrick O'Dwyer would like to thank the Department of Geography at Maynooth and Edel Carmody at St Joseph's Secondary School, Doon, Co. Limerick for their advice and support.

Charles Hayes would like to thank the members of the AGTI, whose advice and support have been invaluable. Sincere thanks also to Baby Milk Action, Jacinta Brack, Sandra Carroll, Christian Aid, Citizen Traveller, Comhlamh, Concern, Corporate Watch, Debt and Development Coalition (Ireland), *The Ecologist* (London), East Cork Area Development Ltd, Fairtrade Mark (Ireland), Eugene Fraser, *The Independent* (London), International Baby Food Action, *The Irish Examiner*, *The Irish Times*, Irish Traveller Movement, Catherine Joyce, Joe Kelly of IRD Kiltimach Ltd, Anne Kinsella, Tom McGrath, Marine Current Turbines, John Mulcahy, *Multinational Monitor* (Boston), *New Internationalist*, Finbarr O'Connell, Kevin O'Dwyer, Crissie O'Sullivan, Pavee Point, Kathleen Regan, Conor Ryan, Jill Ryan, Martyn Turner, Richard Wilson, *Time*, Traveller Visibility Group and Trócaire.

Barry Brunt wishes to thank his colleagues in the Department of Geography and the staff of the Official Publications Section of the Library at UCC for their advice and support in researching and writing this text.

In addition, many other individuals and institutions provided access to a range of essential data and information. Included in this are: Bord na Móna; Bord Iascaigh Mhara; Central Statistics Office; Coillte; Cork and Dublin City Councils; Departments of Agriculture and Food, Education and Science, Finance, Foreign Affairs, Justice, Marine and Natural Resources; Electricity Supply Board; Fáilte Ireland Tourism; Ford Ireland; Forfás and IDA Ireland; and Wyeth Medica (Ireland).

THE PHYSICAL ENVIRONMENT

CHAPTER 1
THE PLANET EARTH

 **KEY IDEA!** The ability of the earth's crust to move about produces forces that create different rock layers within the earth.

The planet earth is some 4.6 billion years old. It formed from a cloud of dust that became molten from the impact of meteorites crashing into it. As the earth cooled, heavier materials sank and lighter materials stayed at the surface, forming the different layers of the earth's crust. **The earth is still cooling, and its molten rock continues to rise from its core to the crust.** This liquid rock brings heat to the surface to be released, so the earth does not overheat.

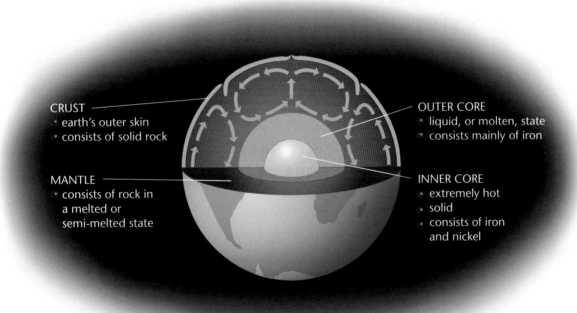

CRUST
* earth's outer skin
* consists of solid rock

MANTLE
* consists of rock in a melted or semi-melted state

OUTER CORE
* liquid, or molten, state
* consists mainly of iron

INNER CORE
* extremely hot
* solid
* consists of iron and nickel

Fig. 1.1 A section through the earth.

The rising molten rock forms **convection currents** that create earthquakes, volcanoes and mountain ranges that shape our lands and seas. Convection currents move slowly through the underlying mantle rock. Over millions of years, rock can flow like glacier ice, and it moves about as fast as our fingernails grow.

convection currents

Fig. 1.2 Convection currents in a heated pot.

The Earth's Crust

The earth's crust has two parts:

- The continental crust, which is formed of light rocks called sial.
- The ocean floor, which consists of basalt and is called sima.

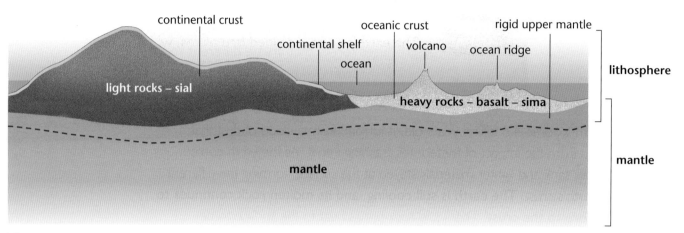

continental crust
oceanic crust
rigid upper mantle
continental shelf
volcano
ocean ridge
ocean
lithosphere
light rocks – sial
heavy rocks – basalt – sima
mantle
mantle

Fig. 1.3

Rocks are cooler, stronger and more rigid in the lithosphere than in the mantle. According to the theory of plate tectonics, the lithosphere is broken into plates. The plates are much like segments of cracked eggshell.

Crust 0–50 km

Lithosphere

Continental Crust

The continental crust is **thick**. It averages between 35 and 40 km thick and is up to 70 km in thickness under the mountain ranges. The rocks that form the continental crust are **light** in weight.

Ocean Crust

The ocean crust is **thin**; it averages 8 km in thickness, but may be as thin as 3 km in some places. The rock forming the ocean crust is basalt, which is **heavy**.

Rigid Upper Mantle 50–100 km

The upper mantle is made up of rigid (inflexible) rocks. The continental crust + ocean crust + rigid upper mantle = lithosphere.

Mantle

Mantle 100–2,900 km

The mantle lies between the crust and the core. It consists of semi-molten (melted) rock that moves in convection currents. The plates of the earth's crust are carried about on these slow-moving convection currents.

Core

Core

At the centre of the earth is the heaviest of the three layers, the **core**. The core is composed mainly of **iron** with some **nickel**.

CHAPTER 2
GLOBAL CRUSTAL PLATE MOVEMENT

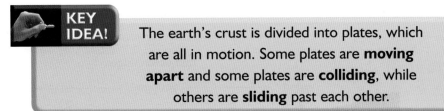

KEY IDEA! The earth's crust is divided into plates, which are all in motion. Some plates are **moving apart** and some plates are **colliding**, while others are **sliding** past each other.

There are two types of plates:
- **Ocean plates,** which form the deep ocean floors.
- **Continental plates,** which form the continents and continental shelves.

These huge crustal plates of rock at the surface **float** on the layer of **heavier,** 'plastic-like' rock underneath, called the mantle. The plates on the surface move in relation to each other, carried along by **convection currents** within the mantle. To us, this movement may seem slow, but in terms of geological time it is fast. These movements cause **folding, faulting, volcanic activity** and **earthquakes**. This concept is known as **plate tectonics** and was first proposed by Alfred Wagner in 1915.

> What three parts form the lithosphere? Explain your answer.

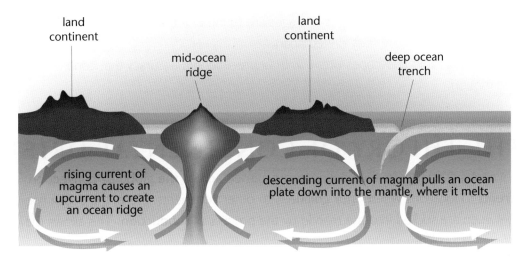

> On average, the ocean crust is about 8 km thick, while continents are between 35 and 40 km thick.

Fig. 2.1 Convection currents make the plates of the earth's crust move about.

Plate tectonics involves two theories:
- Sea floor spreading.
- Continental drift.

SEA FLOOR SPREADING

This suggests that ocean floors widen as **new rock** is formed at **mid-ocean ridges,** where continents were split apart originally. This new rock is then carried away from the ridge by **convection currents** within the mantle.

Fig. 2.2

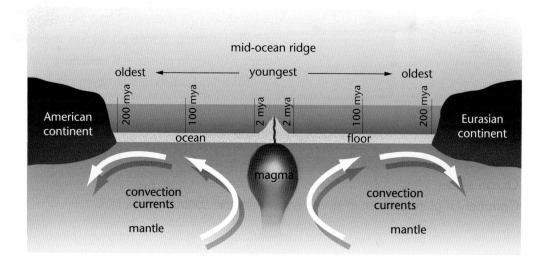

When hot magma cools on the sea floor at mid-ocean ridges, it adds new rock in equal proportions to both plates.

Some Proof of Sea Floor Spreading

- The existence of mid-ocean ridges.
- The varying ages of the sea floor – the age of the sea floor is youngest where new rock is formed along mid-ocean ridges and oldest along continental edges.
- Glacial deposits of similar types and ages are found in the areas where continents were attached before they drifted apart.
- Lasers and radio telescopes prove with unprecedented accuracy that continents are in motion.

THE THEORY OF CONTINENTAL DRIFT

Continental drift suggests the continents are carried **across the globe** by **convection currents** to locations where they **collide** with other continents. Here, the ocean floors in between are sucked into the mantle by the process of **subduction**. This allows the continents to collide.

Hot rock rises slowly from deep inside the earth and it cools, flows sideways and sinks. The rising hot rock and its sideways flow are believed to be the factors that control the positions of oceans and continents.

The Process of Subduction

Fig. 2.3

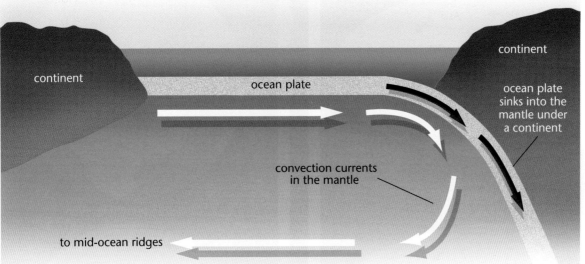

Activity
In your exercise book, write a detailed account of the processes at work in Fig. 2.3.

Proof of Continental Drift
- Matching rocks found on continents that are thousands of miles apart.
- Matching fossils that are found in precise locations in South America and Africa where the continents were once joined together.
- Matching edges of continents along the edges of the continental shelves that fit together like a jigsaw puzzle (for example, South America fits into West Africa).
- Mountains that were once part of the same mountain range are now found in North America, Greenland, Scandinavia, Britain and Ireland.

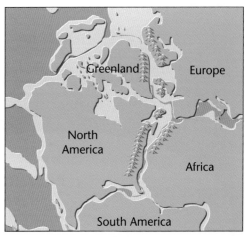

Fig. 2.4 Landmasses fit when they are placed in their pre-drift position.

The Movement of Continents and Ireland Over Time

The theory of continental drift suggests that the continents have moved great distances on the earth's surface and are still moving today. According to the theory, the continents once formed part of a single landmass, called Pangaea, which was surrounded by the world's single ocean, called Panthalassa. About 200 million years ago, Pangaea began to break apart. The formation of the present continents and their drift into their present positions took place gradually over millions of years (see Fig. 2.5).

Ireland's position on the globe has also changed over time. It was originally in two parts that eventually collided about 2 million years ago to form Britain and Ireland. Since then, it has migrated northwards from the southern hemisphere to its present location in the northern hemisphere.

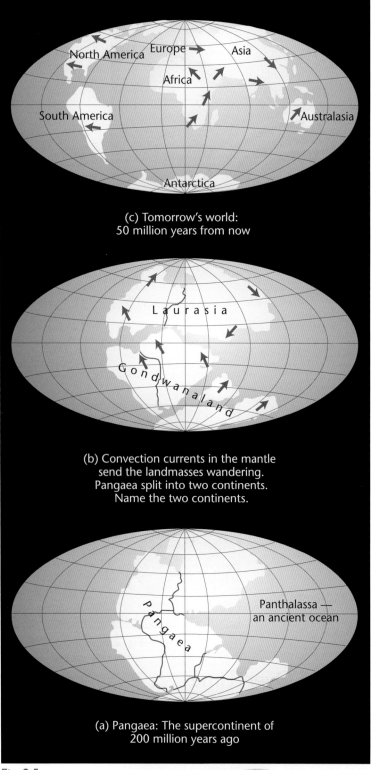

(c) Tomorrow's world:
50 million years from now

(b) Convection currents in the mantle
send the landmasses wandering.
Pangaea split into two continents.
Name the two continents.

(a) Pangaea: The supercontinent of
200 million years ago

Fig. 2.5

Ireland's present location

350 million years ago

west and northwest Ireland

south and east Ireland

500 million years ago

Fig. 2.6

Continents continue to
split apart today. Africa
is splitting apart along
the African Great Rift
Valley fault line.

The Global Distribution Of Plates

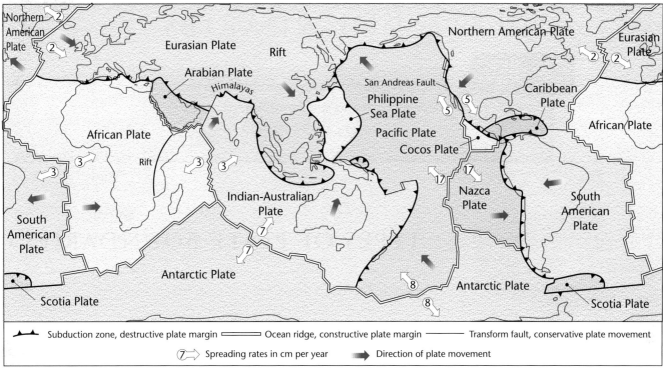

Fig. 2.7

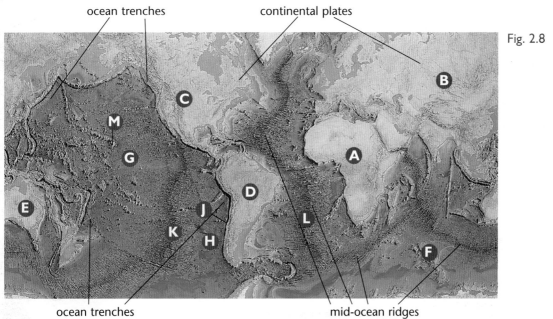

Fig. 2.8

ocean trenches   continental plates

ocean trenches   mid-ocean ridges

Activity

1. In which direction is each of the following plates moving?
   a. Eurasian Plate
   b. African Plate
   c. Pacific Plate
   d. Indian-Australian Plate

2. State the speed at which the following plates are moving apart.
   a. North American and Eurasian Plates
   b. Indian-Australian and Antarctic Plates
   c. Pacific and Nazca Plates

3. Identify:
   a. the continental plates A–E
   b. the ocean plates F–H
   c. the landforms J, K, L and M.

7

CHAPTER 3
PLATE BOUNDARIES

Forces within the earth create, change and destroy rock and landforms where plates collide and separate.

See the school video *Written in Stone*.

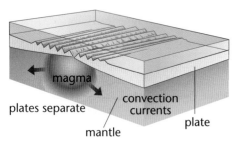

plates separate — magma — convection currents — plate — mantle

1. constructive

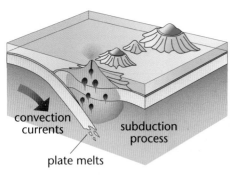

convection currents — subduction process — plate melts

2. destructive

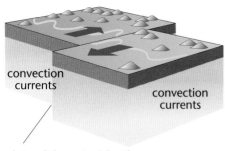

convection currents — convection currents

plates slide past each other along the transform fault

3. passive

Fig. 3.1

TYPES OF PLATE BOUNDARIES

At plate boundaries, rock and rock structures are formed, changed or destroyed. There are three types of plate boundaries.

Boundaries of Construction (Divergent Boundaries)

Here, new rock is formed to create mid-ocean ridges. Plates formed from this new rock separate and move away from each other. Example: The Mid Atlantic Ridge.

Boundaries of Destruction (Convergent Boundaries)

Here, rock is **destroyed** or **changed**. There are three types of destructive boundaries:

● Where two ocean plates collide, called **ocean-ocean**.
● Where an ocean plate and a continental plate collide, called **ocean-continent**.
● Where two continental plates collide, called **continent-continent**.

Where destruction occurs, an ocean plate sinks into the mantle beneath the other plate and melts. A deep **sea trench** is formed on the sea floor. This process is called **subduction**. Example: West coast of South America.

Passive Boundaries

Land is neither created nor destroyed at these boundaries. Plates simply **slide past each other.** Example: The San Andreas Fault.

Activity

1. With the aid of diagrams, explain why boundaries of construction are different from boundaries of destruction.
2. Explain why passive boundaries are different from both boundaries of construction and destruction.
3. Draw a labelled diagram to explain what happens when any two plates collide.

CONSTRUCTIVE PLATE BOUNDARIES
The Process of Rifting

The process of rifting includes continental break-up and the formation of mid-ocean ridges, new sea floor and new oceans.

A. A hot current of magma, called a plume, rises from the mantle towards the surface, stretches the crust of the continent and splits the continent. New volcanoes appear along the cracks at the surface. An example of this process in action is the East African Rift Valley, in eastern Africa.

B. Only two of the cracks widen and the continent splits into two new continental plates. Sea water floods into the new valley that forms in between. Hot magma rises from the mantle in the middle of the valley and cools quickly, forming basalt rock when it meets the cold sea water. This basalt forms the new sea floor, or ocean crust, and a mid-ocean ridge directly over the rising magma.

C. The plates continue to separate, widening the sea to form an ocean. As the continents move apart, their edges are no longer supported and they dip into the sea, forming shallow continental shelves.

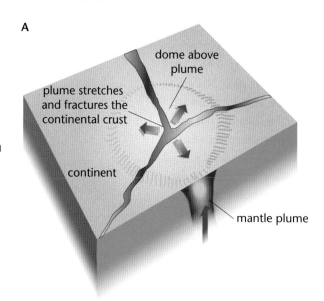

A

dome above plume

plume stretches and fractures the continental crust

continent

mantle plume

Fig. 3.2 Rifting of a continent.

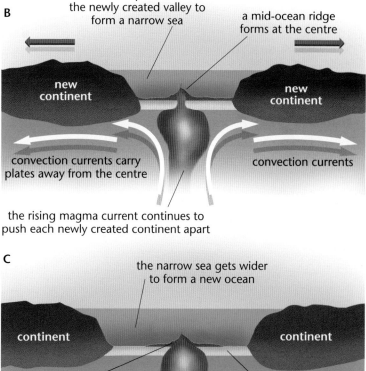

B

ocean water spills in and fills the newly created valley to form a narrow sea

a mid-ocean ridge forms at the centre

new continent

new continent

convection currents carry plates away from the centre

convection currents

the rising magma current continues to push each newly created continent apart

C

the narrow sea gets wider to form a new ocean

continent

continent

a mid-ocean ridge forms along cracks on the sea floor

a new sea floor is created as the rising magma forms basalt rock at the mid-ocean ridge

Fig. 3.3 Stages in the formation of a new sea floor, mid-ocean ridge and ocean.

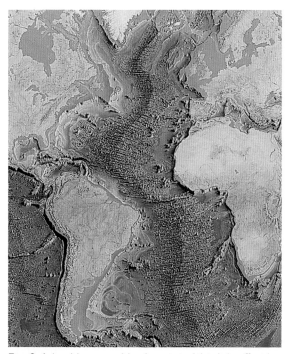

Fig. 3.4 A mid-ocean ridge is not straight. It is offset by transform faults that allow newly created crust to adjust to the spherical (curved) shape of the earth.

DESTRUCTIVE PLATE BOUNDARIES
Ocean-Ocean Boundaries

Where two ocean plates collide, one plate is pulled under the other.

Volcanic island arcs form where two ocean plates meet. The Lipari Islands near Sicily, in Italy, also form an arc. The islands of Japan were formed when many volcanoes joined along an ocean-ocean boundary.

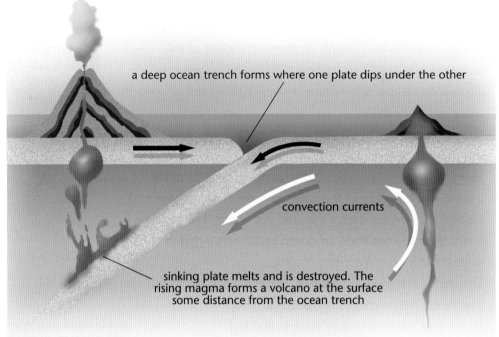

a deep ocean trench forms where one plate dips under the other

convection currents

sinking plate melts and is destroyed. The rising magma forms a volcano at the surface some distance from the ocean trench

Fig. 3.5

Student's Note:
Answers should always be written in the form of **significant relevant points (SRPs)**.

An **SRP** is a **significant relevant point**, or **statement of fact**. For example:
When two ocean plates collide, one plate sinks under the other and melts.
or
A deep ocean trench forms where one ocean plate sinks under another ocean plate.

- The descending plate bends downwards, forming a deep, curved ocean trench. As the plate descends, it melts because:
  – Heat radiates from the hot magma in the mantle.
  – Heat increases due to compression (being squeezed).
- Because the descending plate is saturated with water, it melts quickly.
- Magma then rises and forms volcanic cones on the ocean floor. Dry land eventually emerges from the ocean depths to form an island arc, a curved string of islands parallel to the ocean trench.

Activity
1. Explain what happens when one ocean plate is pulled under another ocean plate.
2. What landform develops because of this process?
3. There are many island arcs in the Pacific Ocean. Name them.
4. Write six SRPs to explain how volcanoes occur at this type of boundary.

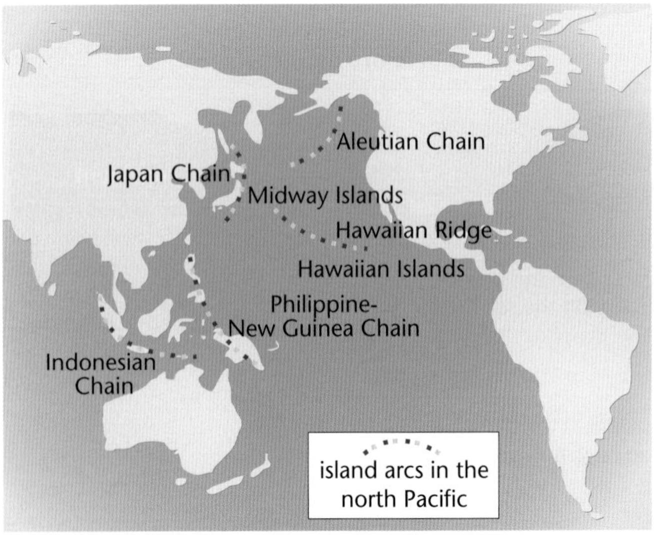

Aleutian Chain
Japan Chain
Midway Islands
Hawaiian Ridge
Hawaiian Islands
Philippine-New Guinea Chain
Indonesian Chain

island arcs in the north Pacific

Fig. 3.6 Island arcs in the Pacific Ocean.

Ocean-Continent Boundaries
Case Study: How the Rockies Were Formed

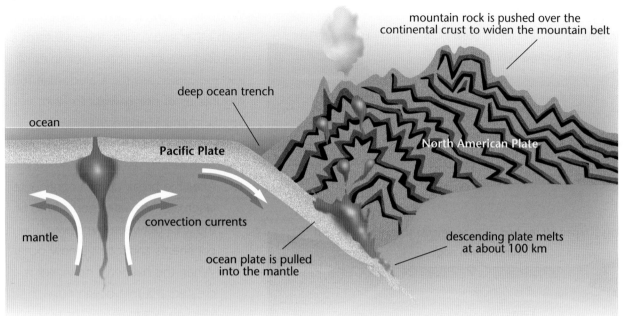

Fig. 3.7

mountain rock is pushed over the continental crust to widen the mountain belt

deep ocean trench

ocean

North American Plate

Pacific Plate

convection currents

mantle

ocean plate is pulled into the mantle

descending plate melts at about 100 km

When an ocean plate and a continental plate collide, the heavy ocean plate is pulled under the lighter continental plate. The ocean plate sinks into the **mantle** and **melts** at a depth of about 100 km. Magma rises to create volcanoes at the surface.

Meanwhile, the continental plate scrapes layers of sediment and islands off the descending ocean floor to form layers of rock along the seaward edge of the continent. Eventually these layers of rock are **compressed** (squeezed) and **folded** (buckled) to form fold mountains. In some places rock is **metamorphosed** (heated and changed). This has happened in the Rocky Mountains in North America, in the Andes in South America and in counties Donegal, Galway and Wicklow in Ireland.

Squeezing caused by the colliding plates causes **faulting**. Constant pressure over millions of years cracks the rock (faulting) and pushes some of it forward either horizontally or at a low angle for many kilometres, thus increasing the width and the thickness of the mountain belt. The faults created by this action are called **thrust faults** (see Chapter 8, page 50). Faults like these are found in the mountains of **Donegal**, such as the **Gweebarra Fault**, and the Rockies in North America.

MYA means millions of years ago.

intrusive
'Intrude' means 'enter by force'. Formed within the earth's crust.

Some ocean plates sink beneath other ocean plates.

Activity
1. Which two plates have collided to form:
    a. the Rockies
    b. the Andes?
2. What is a thrust fault?
3. How are some fold mountains formed? Explain using a labelled diagram.
4. Write six SRPs to explain the process that occurs at this type of boundary.

11

Continent-Continent Boundaries
Case Study: The Formation of Caledonian Fold Mountains 400 MYA

Stage 1

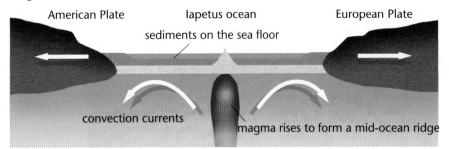

Stage 2

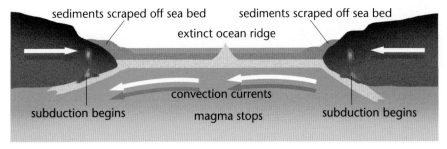

Stage 3

volcanic activity
folded sediments form mountains
volcanic activity
convection currents

Stage 4

buckled and folded sediments form high mountain range

batholiths in Donegal, Mayo and Connemara
batholiths in Down and Wicklow
collide
American Plate
European Plate

Fig. 3.8 The Iapetus Ocean disappeared and the Caledonian mountains were formed. These mountains included the mountains of Connemara, Mayo, Donegal, Down and Wicklow, the Scottish Highlands and the Scandinavian Highlands. These mountains tend to run north-east to south-west.

When two continental plates approach each other and collide, they will form a high fold mountain chain. Examples of fold mountains are the **Caledonian fold mountains of north-west Ireland, Scotland and Scandinavia** (see the activity on page 53.)

1. After the break-up of a continental landmass, seawater pours in to fill the area between the new continents and forms a new ocean. When this happens, new rock is created at a mid-ocean ridge to form an ocean floor, thus pushing the continents apart. Also, a thick wedge of sediment from erosion is deposited along each coastline.

2. For reasons not yet understood, at some stage the ocean basin begins to close. The continents approach each other and the ocean floor is pulled into the mantle. This starts a long period of volcanic activity and the creation of batholiths (see Fig. 5.9, page 29).

3. Eventually the continents collide. This event buckles, deforms or metamorphoses the rocks and trapped sediment washed in by rivers to form **fold mountains**. **Faulting and folding** of the trapped sediments occur in the fold mountains.

Activity
1. Explain what happens when continents approach each other.
2. Name two fold mountain chains that formed when continents collided.
3. Write eight SRPs explaining how the Caledonian fold mountains formed.

Passive Boundaries

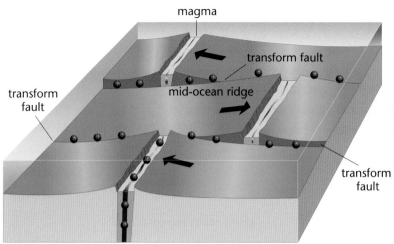

Fig. 3.9 Transform faults at a mid-ocean ridge allow the earth to retain its spherical shape.

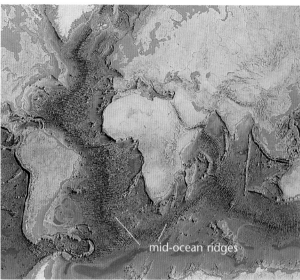

Fig. 3.10 A mid-ocean ridge and numerous transform faults in the Indian Ocean.

● *Can you identify the Mid Atlantic Ridge?*

Only earthquakes occur at passive boundaries. Passive boundaries occur where plates slide past each other without crust being created or destroyed, and there is no subduction. The line along which the plates slide is called a fault line.

These faults are called **transform faults** and they provide the means by which the ocean crust created at a mid-ocean ridge can be carried to a boundary of destruction. Most transform faults are located under the oceans, but a few, including the San Andreas Fault in California, are situated within continents.

A mid-ocean ridge is not straight. Many transform faults are offset and cross the mid-ocean ridge at right angles, so that new rock may fit on the curved surface of the earth (see Fig. 3.9).

Activity

1. Explain why there are no volcanoes along transform faults.
2. Name two regions of the world where transform faults are located.
3. Use a diagram to explain the purpose of transform faults at mid-ocean ridges.

The San Andreas Fault is clearly visible on a satellite photo of the earth's surface. Some rock is deformed along the San Andreas Fault.

CHAPTER 4
VOLCANIC ACTIVITY

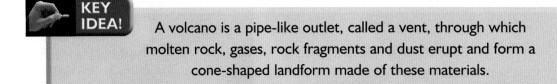

KEY IDEA!

A volcano is a pipe-like outlet, called a vent, through which molten rock, gases, rock fragments and dust erupt and form a cone-shaped landform made of these materials.

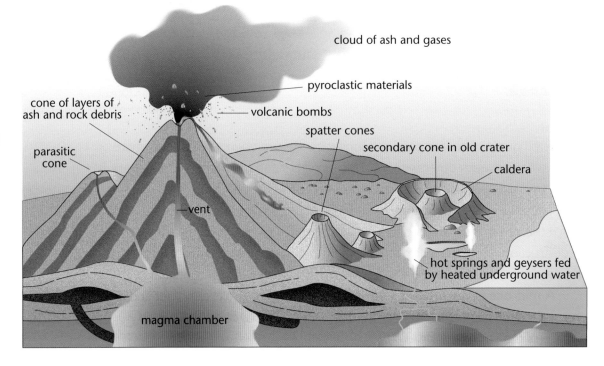

Fig. 4.1 A volcanic landscape (not to scale) showing some of the major features commonly associated with volcanic activity.

cloud of ash and gases

pyroclastic materials

cone of layers of ash and rock debris

volcanic bombs

spatter cones

secondary cone in old crater

caldera

parasitic cone

vent

hot springs and geysers fed by heated underground water

magma chamber

Volcanic activity occurs where plates **separate** and **collide,** but most volcanoes occur at **subduction zones** along the Pacific Ring of Fire where ocean plates are pulled into the mantle. They also occur at **hot spots.**

Fig. 4.2 Most volcanoes occur around the rim of the Pacific Ocean.

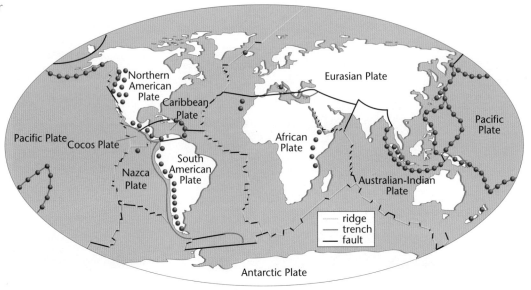

Northern American Plate

Caribbean Plate

Eurasian Plate

Pacific Plate

Pacific Plate

Cocos Plate

African Plate

Nazca Plate

South American Plate

Australian-Indian Plate

ridge
trench
fault

Antarctic Plate

Volcanoes are found at the following locations:

- At mid-ocean ridges.
- At subduction zones.
- At hot spots.

Magma also reaches the surface through long cracks called **fissures**. When magma reaches the surface, it is called **lava**. When lava and other volcanic materials reach the surface, they are called **extrusive** materials.

Materials that are pushed into the coast are called **intrusive** materials. Later, they may be exposed at the surface by erosion of the overlying rocks.

Both extrusive and intrusive materials are called **igneous rocks**.

> There are three types of volcanoes:
> - **Active:** Currently erupting, e.g. **Mt Etna**.
> - **Dormant:** Has not erupted for some time, e.g. **Mt Vesuvius**.
> - **Extinct:** Has not erupted for millions of years, e.g. **Slemish** mountain in Antrim.

WHY DO VOLCANOES EXPLODE?

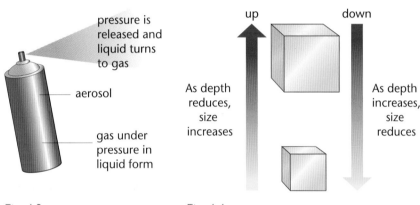

Fig. 4.3   Fig. 4.4

1. As magma rises, **gases** dissolved in the magma **expand** and bubble off, as water does when it is boiled. The resulting froth creates tremendous outward pressure that forces the magma upward.
2. As the magma meets groundwater near the surface, the volcano becomes like a **pressure cooker**.
3. The volcanic **mountain bulges**. Finally, the expanding gases push through cracks in the volcano. When they reach the surface, the pressures are suddenly released, the **bubbles expand dramatically** and the volcano erupts in an explosion of ash and molten rock.

> **Silica** is a material formed from silicon and oxygen. It makes lava thick, or stiff. It **traps gases** within magma. The more silica in magma, the more gases it traps and the more likely the volcano will **explode violently**. Volcanoes at **subduction zones** contain a lot of silica, so they are **highly explosive** and dangerous.

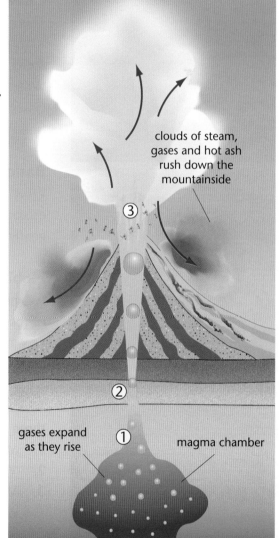

Fig. 4.5 Why a volcano explodes.

Pyroclasts are rock particles blasted from a volcano during an eruption. They include:

- **Cinders:** When the pyroclasts are the size of peas.
- **Lapilli:** When they are the size of walnuts.
- **Blocks:** When they are made of hardened lava.
- **Bombs:** When they are ejected as red-hot lava.
- All pyroclastic debris is called **tephra.**

MATERIALS EJECTED FROM VOLCANOES

These include volcanic ash, which may be carried great distances from a volcano by the force of the eruption, by wind or both. Other materials, such as rock fragments, are called pyroclasts.

A lava fountain displays pyroclasts being blasted into the air.

Lava
There are two types of lava: acid and basic.

Acid Lava
When lava is high in silica (over 70 per cent), it is thick and does not flow far. Gases are trapped until the volcano explodes violently. It forms **steep cones** (see Fig. 5.3 on page 26).

Basic Lava
When lava is low in silica (45 to 55 per cent), it is very fluid (runny). Gases escape freely, and they push the lava forward, making it flow quickly. It forms **gently sloping cones**, such as Hawaii (see Fig. 5.2 on page 26).

Mobility of Lava
Gas helps lava flow. The mobility and cooling of lava depend on the **amount of gases** dissolved within the lava. In Hawaii, lava flows containing a lot of gas have remained mobile until they cooled at 850°C far from the volcano's vent. Other lavas with less gas have cooled at 1,200°C close to the vent.

When lava cools, it may take a number of forms. Some of these forms have Hawaiian names because of the research carried out there. **There are three main forms of lava.**

1. When lava is runny and has a **ropy texture**, it is called **pahoehoe lava.**
2. When lava has a **lumpy texture**, it is called **Aa lava.**
3. When lava appears under the sea, it comes out as rounded **blobs** and is called **pillow lava.**

Activity					
Identify the types of lava in photos A, B and C and write the name in the box.					
A		B		C	

HOT SPOTS

Some volcanic activity occurs **away from plate boundaries.** It is localised and confined to specific spots on the earth's crust, such as in Hawaii or the Canary Islands. These places are called hot spots. Some hot spots are located at plate boundaries, e.g. in Iceland.

The Pacific Ring of Fire, the largest earthquake and volcano zone, lies around the edge of the Pacific Ocean.

Distribution of Hot Spots

Most evidence indicates that hot spots remain stationary. Only about twenty of the 120 hot spots that are believed to exist are near plate boundaries.

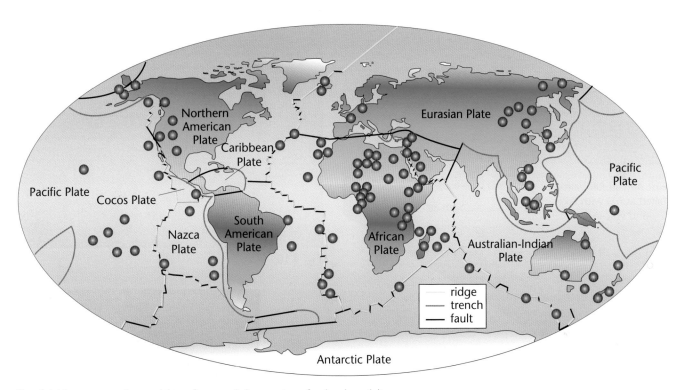

Fig. 4.6 Hot spots at the earth's surface; each is a centre of volcanic activity.
● *Which spot represents Hawaii?*

What Are Hot Spots?

Hot spots are unusually hot areas found deep within the earth's mantle. Some geologists believe that narrow columns of hot magma, called **plumes,** rise through the mantle to the surface in the way smoke rises through a chimney. These plumes can **split continents** (see page 9) or **create volcanoes,** as in Hawaii.

   A hot spot under Iceland is thought to be responsible for the regular volcanic activity on the island, which is sited on the Mid Atlantic Ridge. Another hot spot is believed to exist beneath the Canary Islands.

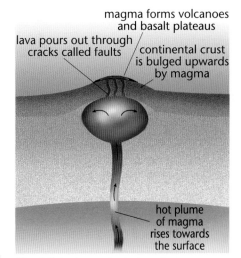

Fig. 4.7 A plume at a hot spot may cause rifting of a continent.

Activity
1. Why are volcanoes that form near deep ocean trenches the most dangerous?
2. Why are some volcanoes not as explosive as others?
3. Write six SRPs to explain how volcanoes occur at hot spots.

Fig. 4.8

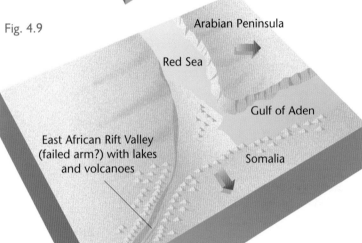

plume stretches and fractures the continental crust

dome above plume

continent

the third fracture fails to open wide

mantle plume

Fig. 4.9

Arabian Peninsula

Red Sea

Gulf of Aden

East African Rift Valley (failed arm?) with lakes and volcanoes

Somalia

Hot Spots and the Process of Rifting

Scientists believe a continent may initially be split apart by rising magma at a hot spot. The rising magma creates a bulge that stretches the crust. This fractures the surface in a three-pronged, or Y-shaped, pattern.

Geologists suggest that rifting like this created the **Red Sea,** the **Gulf of Aden** and the **African Rift Valley.**

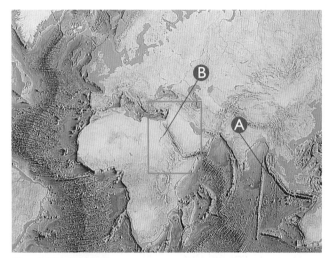

Fig. 4.10

Activity

1. In Fig. 4.10, identify:
   a. the Red Sea
   b. the Gulf of Aden
   c. India.
2. Identify the type of boundary at A and B.
3. Explain the process at one of these boundaries and name the plates involved (see Fig 2.7 on page 7 and Fig. 3.1, page 8).

Activity

Carefully examine the satellite image of the Middle East, then use your atlas to answer the following question.

1. Draw a sketch map of this region and on it mark and name the following.
   a. The Red Sea
   b. The Gulf of Aden
   c. The Gulf of Iran
   d. The Black Sea
   e. The Caspian Sea
   f. The Mediterranean Sea
   g. Saudi Arabia
   h. Yemen
   i. Egypt
   j. Sudan
   k. Eritrea
   l. Djibouti
   m. Somalia

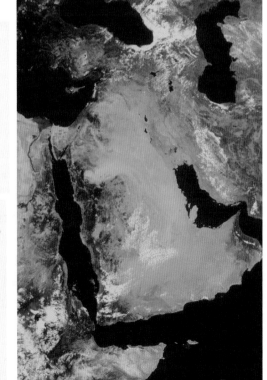

A satellite image of the Red Sea and the Gulf of Aden.

18

Case Study: Hawaiian Islands at a Hot Spot in the Pacific Ocean

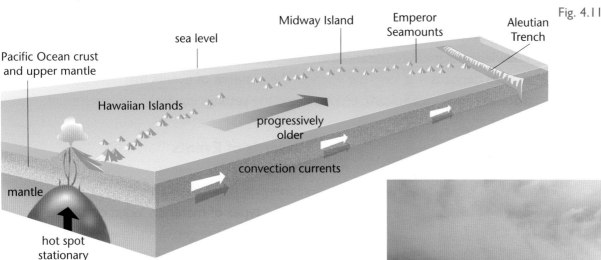

Fig. 4.11

Scientists discovered that the Hawaiian Islands in the Pacific Ocean are older the closer they are to Alaska. The probable explanation is that each volcano formed over the stationary hot spot over which Hawaii is now situated and then moved away from the hot spot as the sea floor spread to the north and then the north-west. As the ocean crust cooled, the sea floor deepened and the volcanic islands were submerged.

The Hawaiian Islands were created at a hot spot.

Other Forms of Volcanic Activity

Hydrothermal areas occur at sites of past volcanic activity where moisture is trapped and heated by the magma as it cools near the surface. These areas include geysers, hot springs and black smokers.

- **Geysers** are **jets of hot water** and **steam** that shoot into the air, often rising 30 to 60 m, at regular intervals. The most famous geyser in the world is Old Faithful in Yellowstone National Park in the US.

- **Hot springs** occur when groundwater circulates **at great depths** and becomes **heated**. If the water rises to the surface, it may emerge quietly as a hot spring. Hot springs are common in Iceland and Italy.

- **Black smokers** are **chimney-like openings** at mid-ocean ridges where super-hot water of **700°C** gushes out through vents on the new ocean floor from the mantle, and can be as tall as 30 m (see page 27).

- **Fumaroles** are small vents on the slope of a volcanic cone that emit steam or gas, such as sulphur.

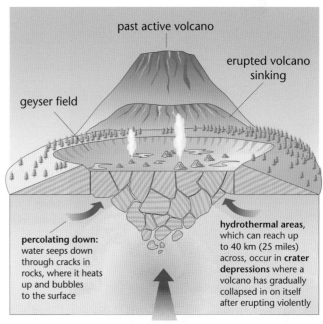

what is left of old magma chamber still produces a lot of energy

Fig. 4.12

How Volcanoes and Their Effects Can Be Predicted

Many steps are involved in forecasting volcanic eruptions and their effects. Firstly, geologists (people who study rock and rock structures) draw on their **background knowledge** of the way volcanoes are formed, how they are composed, the **type and date of deposits** that form the volcano, the **patterns of events** that have been associated with past volcanic eruptions and the **settings** in which volcanoes erupt.

Some geologists take great risks with their personal safety so that we can increase our knowledge of volcanoes and magma.

Geologists study rock samples around a volcano.

An erupting volcano. Column of ash, hot gases and pulverised rock.

A geologist installs a seismograph to detect earthquakes.

Patterns of Events

The type, date and patterns of deposits are useful information to geologists.

- The **types of materials** found on the sides of volcanoes help geologists to work out the power and explosive nature of past eruptions. **Dating** these deposits helps to establish a rhythm – whether the volcano erupts regularly, every 100 years, or once every 1,000 years.
- The **distribution of ejected material** and its relation to the local landscape is studied. This suggests where ejected material is likely to collect and helps geologists to **pinpoint the places most likely to be affected** by an eruption.

Minor Earthquakes

There is often an increase in the frequency of **minor earthquake tremors** (mild shaking of the ground) before a volcanic eruption.

- Having decided that a volcano may erupt in the foreseeable future, geologists set up a number of **seismographs** (instruments that measure earthquakes) around the sides of the summit of the volcano. These help to track the **location, strength and frequency** of earthquakes.
- Geologists also install **tiltmetres** to detect if there is ground swelling or other movements.

Activity

1. Why are volcanoes on some Hawaiian islands extinct, while on other islands they are active? Explain.
2. What are hydrothermal areas?
3. Identify three types of hydrothermal activity.

Other Patterns

Other signs that are monitored include:

- Changes in the quantity and type of gases escaping from the vent.
- Changes in the heat escaping from the crater.
- Changes in local groundwater.
- The appearance of geysers, hot springs or steam vents in the region.

By integrating this information, geologists hope to improve their forecasting abilities.

Past Volcanic Eruptions

Knowing the effects of volcanoes that erupted in the past in a certain area helps to **warn** people or to evacuate residents **who may be affected** if a new eruption is likely in that place. These effects include the following.

Lahars

Lahars are mud flows created by the sudden melting by hot ash and lava of ice on elevated, ice-capped volcanic cones. Earlier lahars may indicate where other lahars are most likely to occur again.

Nuée Ardente

When expanding hot, poisonous gases and glowing ash are ejected from a volcano, they may produce a heavy, fiery, grey cloud called a nuée ardente. Also referred to as glowing avalanches, these devastating clouds of steam, poisonous gases and ash flows, which are heavier than air, race down steep volcanic cones at speeds up to 200 km per hour and travel more than 100 km from their source.

Poisonous gases, such as sulphur (which is yellow), escape from the sides of some volcanoes.

Lahars cause great damage to towns and villages.

Nuée ardentes regularly cause loss off life during volcanic eruptions.

Activity

1. Explain the causes and effects of:
   a. a lahar
   b. a nuée ardente.
2. From your history studies at Junior Certificate, explain the type of volcanic processes that covered Pompeii in AD 79 and killed many of its citizens.

PEOPLE AND VOLCANIC ACTIVITY – OTHER NEGATIVE EFFECTS

Global Warming

Rising sea levels caused by global warming could trigger hundreds of volcanic eruptions around the world this century, wreaking havoc with the climate.

Deciding that the best way to predict the future behaviour of volcanoes was to study their distant past, scientists found that rises in sea levels caused by periods of global warming have almost all been followed by a surge in volcanic activity.

① The present sea level is very low, caused by billions of tonnes of water being locked up in the ice caps. Global warming is melting the ice and experts predict a rise of up to a metre in sea levels over the next few decades.

② About 90 per cent of volcanoes are close to or surrounded by sea. As water rises, it begins to erode the lava. The rising water also causes landslides, triggering **tsunamis**.

③ These **landslides** weaken the outside rock. Eventually, the mountain becomes unable to withstand the internal pressure of the magma and erupts.

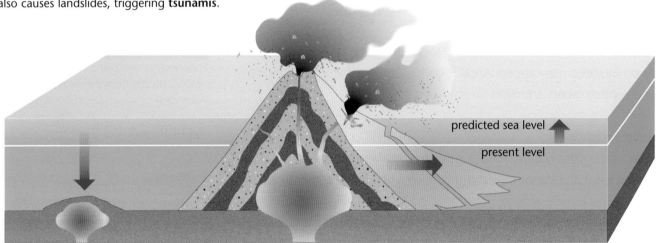

④ Huge magma reservoirs often lie close to the sea bed, held in check by the water pressure above. If levels change, the sea bed may crack, allowing the magma to come out and forming new volcanoes.

Fig. 4.13

PEOPLE AND VOLCANIC ACTIVITY – POSITIVE EFFECTS

Soils

Soil that forms from weathered lava in hot regions is called **laterite soil**. It is rich in minerals and is often called **terra rossa** (red soil). Cities such as Naples in southern Italy are surrounded by precious volcanic soils for growing vegetables. In Brazil and Central American countries, cash crops such as coffee are produced on terra rossa soils. Brazil is the largest exporter of coffee in the world.

Laterite soil developed in Antrim millions of years ago when lava was weathered during long intervals between lava flows. It was mined for:

- **Bauxite** (aluminium ore) during World War II. During this time, aluminium needed for aircraft manufacture was in short supply.
- **Iron** ore during the nineteenth century.

Tourism

Tourism is a major industry based directly on volcanic structures such as craters, volcanic cones or geysers. Every year, **Mt Vesuvius** attracts hundreds of thousands of tourists, who pay a fee to climb this dormant volcano. Nearby historical sites such as **Pompeii,** which was devastated when Vesuvius erupted in AD 79, also attract many visitors. Local spin-off industries, such as hotel and catering, souvenir manufacture and local guides and shops, all benefit from this kind of tourism.

Geothermal Energy

Geothermal energy is the use of natural steam to generate electricity. This type of energy source is available in areas where rock temperatures are high due to relatively recent volcanic activity.

Using water warmed by volcanic rocks, Icelanders heat their houses, grow tomatoes in hothouses and swim all year round in naturally heated pools, even though the temperatures outside may be below freezing. They also generate most of the electricity they need by using volcanically produced steam.

In Iceland, geysers are used to generate energy.

Geothermal Energy from Dry Rocks

Energy may also be generated where hot rocks lie close to the surface. Cold water pumped through fractures at the bottom of a deep well becomes heated, then flows back up to the geothermal power plant, where this energy is converted to electricity.

Mineral Deposits

Many mineral deposits form from mineral-rich fluids that escape from magma. These fluids are very hot and under tremendous pressure as they escape through cracks or faults in the crust. Some fluids cool along these cracks, or faults, and form **mineral veins**. Others are 'sweated' into rocks, where they form **mineral ores,** such as **copper ore** or **zinc ore**. Zinc ore is found at Lisheen in Co. Tipperary and at Navan in Co. Meath.

New Land

Volcanoes create new land in the sea. Many islands like this, as in Japan, are among the most densely populated regions on earth.

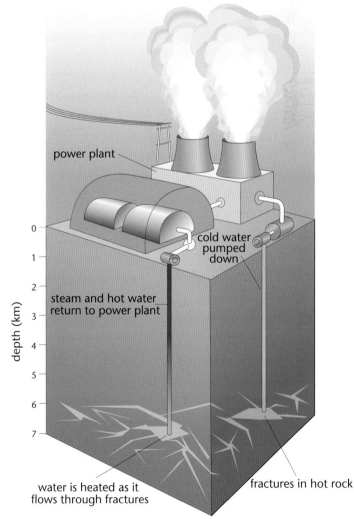

power plant

0
1
2
3
4
5
6
7

depth (km)

cold water pumped down

steam and hot water return to power plant

water is heated as it flows through fractures

fractures in hot rock

Fig. 4.14 The process of obtaining geothermal energy from dry rocks.

Activity

Short-answer Questions

1. Name the most volcanically active region in the world.
2. What is a volcanic arc?
3. What are pyroclasts?
4. Name four types of pyroclasts.
5. Name two types of lava based on silica content.
6. What is pahoehoe lava?
7. What is Aa lava?
8. Where would you locate new pillow lava?
9. What is the difference between magma and lava?
10. What is a hot spot?
11. Name one hot spot in the Pacific Ocean.
12. What is rifting?
13. Name one continent where rifting is splitting the crust.
14. Name one sea area that has only recently formed from rifting.
15. Identify one type of hydrothermal that occurs on the sea floor at mid-ocean ridges.
16. Name five signs that a volcanic eruption may be imminent.
17. What is laterite?
18. Name four ways that volcanic activity can be of benefit to people.

Multi-part Questions

1. Volcano, Mid-ocean ridge, Subduction zone.
    A. Select any **two** of the above features, and for each one you select:
        i.   name **one** example in the world
        ii. describe and explain, with the aid of a diagram, how it was formed.   [20 marks]
    B. Describe one process that each of the above three features have in common.
                                                                                            [30 marks]
    C. Explain, with the aid of diagrams, the relationship between each of the above features and the theory of plate tectonics.   [30 marks]
2. A. Using a diagram, name and label the processes and landforms at any boundary of destruction.   [20 marks]
    B. Explain the processes involved in the formation of any mountain system that you have studied.   [30 marks]
    C. 'Many examples of island arcs are found in the Pacific Ocean.' Explain this statement.   [30 marks]
3. A. 'Ireland's location on the globe has changed over time.' Explain this statement.   [20 marks]
    B. Explain, with the aid of a labelled diagram or diagrams, the process of crustal plate movement as it is currently understood.   [30 marks]
    C. Explain why some volcanoes explode massively. In your answer, refer to one world example.   [30 marks]

CHAPTER 5
VOLCANIC AND PLUTONIC LANDFORMS

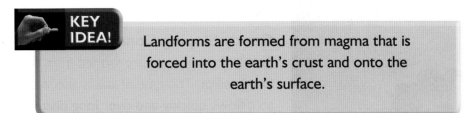

KEY IDEA! Landforms are formed from magma that is forced into the earth's crust and onto the earth's surface.

Fig. 5.1 Volcanic and plutonic landforms.

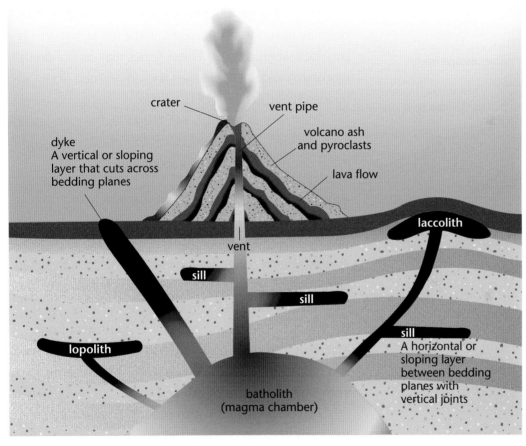

Volcanic means 'formed on the earth's surface'. Plutonic means 'formed within the earth's crust'. Both may now be on the surface after millions of years of weathering and erosion.

Extrusive means 'formed outside the earth's crust'. Intrusive means 'formed within the crust'. Volcanic rocks are extrusive and plutonic rocks are intrusive.

VOLCANIC LANDFORMS

There are two types of opening through which magma reaches the crust and the earth's surface.

Vent

A vent is a pipe-like opening through which magma rises close to or onto the earth's surface. Vent eruptions create volcanic cones.

Fissure

A fissure is a long crack, or fault, through which sheets of lava pour out onto the surface. Fissure eruptions create basalt plateaus.

Volcanic Cones

Examples: Mt Vesuvius in Italy
           Mauna Loa in Hawaii

There are two types of volcanic cones: gently sloping and steeply sloping.

Gently Sloping Cones

Gently sloping cones are formed from **basic lava,** which is very **low in silica**. This type of lava is also very hot (about 1,000°C), so it **flows quickly and over long distances**. This lava has a smooth or ropy surface and is called **pahoehoe lava**.

Expanding **gas bubbles escape** rapidly and, as they do, they drive the lava forward, and it forms thin sheets of lava rock when it cools. These cones may be hundreds of kilometres wide at their bases and are formed from hundreds of thousands of lava flows.

Magma is driven high into the air as the gases escape from the vent. This is particularly dramatic at night, and these displays are called **lava fountains**.

Steeply Sloping Cones

Example: Mount St Helens in the US

Steeply sloping cones are formed from viscous lava. It is **high in silica,** so it is stiff and **flows slowly and over short distances**. This helps to make the cones steep.

Because the lava is viscous, it is **explosive. Rock materials** from explosive volcanoes fall **around the vent,** also helping to make the cones steep. These cones form from alternate **layers of ash and lava**.

All volcanic cones within mountain ranges are steep and form from viscous lava and ash. They are located over subduction zones.

Pahoehoe lava is fluid and travels long distances.

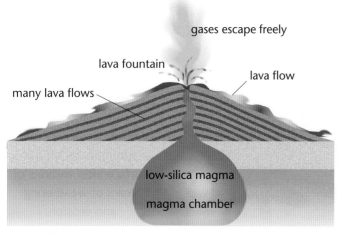

gases escape freely

lava fountain

many lava flows

lava flow

low-silica magma

magma chamber

Fig. 5.2 These gently sloping cones form the Hawaiian Islands.

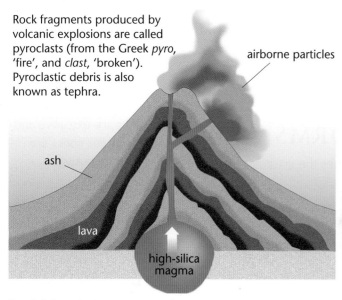

Rock fragments produced by volcanic explosions are called pyroclasts (from the Greek *pyro,* 'fire', and *clast,* 'broken'). Pyroclastic debris is also known as tephra.

airborne particles

ash

lava

high-silica magma

Fig. 5.3 Steeply sloping cones are formed from viscous lava.

This is a satellite image of an erupting, steep-sided cone in Japan formed from viscous lava.

Basalt Plateaus
Case Study: The Antrim Plateau
World example: The Deccan Plateau in India

About **65 million years ago** the American and European plates were still joined over what is now the Norwegian Sea. A new hot spot in this region caused **rifting,** and the Mid Atlantic Ridge extended northwards. The crust was stretched and lava poured out through this new mid-ocean ridge extension to form the Norwegian Sea region.

In Antrim, this stretching created **fissures** (cracks), and lava poured out red hot and liquid onto the surface. Each successive lava flow cooled quickly to form a layer of **basalt** rock. Eventually, the basalt layers built up to form a **high, flat-topped upland** called the **Antrim Plateau.**

Where there were long periods between lava flows, the surface basalt weathered to form **laterite** soil. This may be seen as a horizontal **red band** between the basalt layers in Antrim.

● *Can you identify the laterite soil layers on this cliff face in Antrim?*

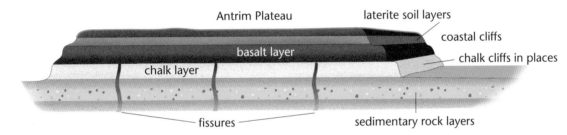

Fig. 5.4 The formation of the Antrim Plateau.

Black Smokers

Black smokers are **chimney-like openings** at mid-ocean ridges, where super-hot water (**700°C**) with minerals dissolved in it gushes out from the mantle through vents on the new ocean floor. The **mineral-rich water** is highly toxic, but wildlife at the vent site has adapted uniquely by surviving on bacteria that flourish in this environment.

These smokers were first discovered in 1977 and can be as tall as **30 m.** The **minerals** dissolved in the super-hot water **solidify and build up a pipe-like chimney around the vent.**

Fig. 5.5

PLUTONIC LANDFORMS
Laccoliths, Sills and Dykes of Basalt Rock

In some places in Antrim, the magma was unable to find its way to the surface and so it squeezed its way into cracks (faults) and along bedding planes of sedimentary rock within the crust. Here it cooled to form **plutonic** landforms.

When magma moves between bedding planes, it forms a sill. When magma cuts across bedding planes, it forms a dyke.

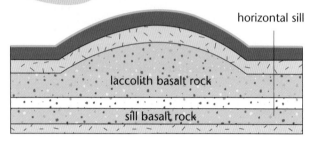

horizontal sill

laccolith basalt rock

sill basalt rock

Fig. 5.6

Laccolith

A laccolith is a small, **dome-shaped** mass of igneous rock **close to the surface**. It forms when a mass of magma forces the overlying layers of rock up into a dome, producing a low hill directly above the magma mass.

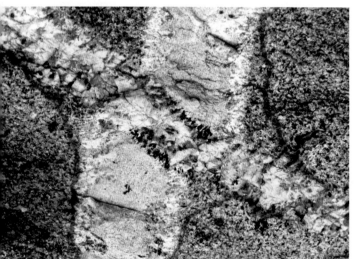

the term 'sill' is given to igneous rock which forces itself between other rock layers

low escarpment

sloping sill

basalt

bedding planes

Fig. 5.7

Sill
Example: The Grotto, Pallas Grean, Co. Limerick.

When a sheet of magma squeezes **along a bedding plane**, it hardens to form a sill. Some sills form **horizontal** layers, while others are **sloping** due to a tilt in the bedding planes.

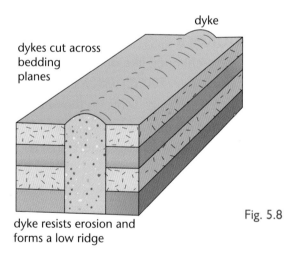

dyke

dykes cut across bedding planes

dyke resists erosion and forms a low ridge

Fig. 5.8

This is an igneous dyke in rock in Thailand.

Dyke
Irish example: Site of Carrickfergus Castle, Co. Antrim

When a sheet of magma **cuts across bedding planes**, it hardens to form a dyke. Dykes form when magma rises through **vertical**, or near-vertical, fissures and cools to form igneous rock.

Activity
1. Explain **how** and **why** the Antrim Plateau formed.
2. Explain, with the aid of diagrams, the difference between a laccolith and a sill.

Batholith

Case Study: The Leinster Batholith

A batholith is a dome-shaped mass of **granite** rock that cooled from magma deep within the earth's crust during a period of **mountain building**. Batholiths form from magma over **subduction zones,** where ocean plates sink under continents into the mantle and melt.

As in Leinster, the batholiths may also form from **continental crust** that has been buckled and **pushed down so deep** near the mantle that it melts to form magma. Magma is hot and lighter than surrounding rock, so it rises back up into the buckled continental crust. Here, it cools slowly to form huge masses of **granite**.

The Leinster Batholith formed within the **Caledonian mountains** when the American and European plates collided some **400 million years ago** (see the case study on page 12). This huge batholith stretches from Sandycove in Dublin through Wicklow to Thomastown in Co. Kilkenny. It includes the Dublin Mountains, the Wicklow Mountains and the Blackstairs Mountains.

This granite batholith is now exposed at the surface because weathering and erosion for over 400 million years have removed the overlying rock layers. Batholiths are also found in **Connemara,** in Co. Galway, and in Co. **Donegal** and Co. Down as well as in **Devon** and **Cornwall** in southern England.

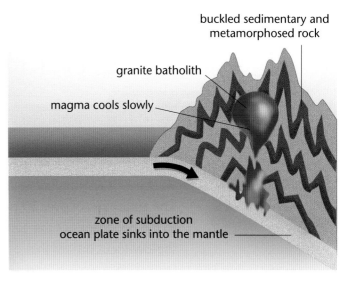

Fig. 5.9

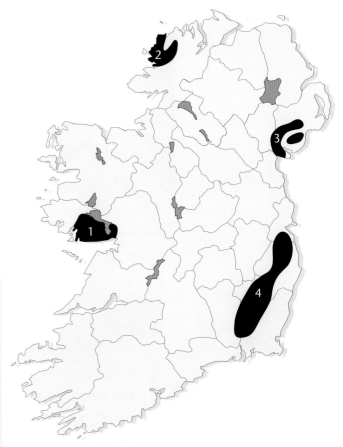

Fig. 5.10

Activity

1. Volcanic cone, Batholith, Basalt plateau, Dyke
   Select any **three** of the above landforms and for each one you select:
   i. Name one example of the landform.
   ii. Describe and explain, with the aid of a diagram, how it was formed.
2. Rifting in the northern region of the North Atlantic created major volcanic landforms in north-eastern Ireland. Select **one volcanic** and **one plutonic** landform in Antrim formed as a consequence of this rifting. For each one you select:
   i. Name one example of the landform.
   ii. Describe and explain, with the aid of a diagram, how it was formed.
3. Name the various counties where each batholith 1–4 or part of batholith is located on the map in Fig. 5.10.
4. What type of rock is found at each of these locations?

CHAPTER 6
EARTHQUAKES

KEY IDEA!

Earthquakes are caused by structures and processes that have resulted from the operation of the tectonic cycle.

The epicentres of over 99 per cent of the earthquakes that occur each year are confined to the boundaries of the earth's crustal plates. Ninety per cent of all earthquakes are shallow-focus quakes that occur close to the earth's surface.

DISTRIBUTION, CAUSES AND BOUNDARIES WHERE EARTHQUAKES OCCUR

Fig. 6.1

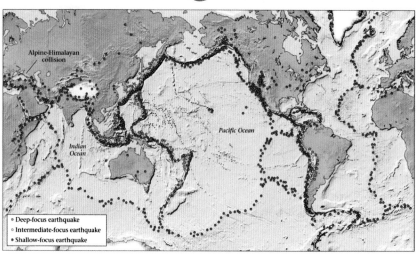

Fig. 6.2 Rifting.

Rifting over a hot spot splits a continent into new plates. As the plates separate, **tension cracks,** or faults, form. Rift valleys appear as **land drops** along parallel faults. Earthquakes occur **along the faults**.

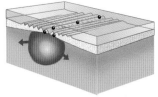

Fig. 6.3 Plates separate.

As plates separate, new **rock** at mid-ocean ridges **splits**. Most of these earthquakes occur under the oceans. **Transform faults** also create earthquakes here, as **new sea floor adjusts** to the curved shape of the earth.

Fig. 6.4 Plates subduct.

- **Shallow quakes** occur because the sinking plate jams and then suddenly releases.
- **Intermediate quakes** occur when the plate melts.
- **Deep quakes occur** due to chemical changes and mineral changes.
- Earthquakes occur along the **Wadati-Benioff Zone.**

Fig. 6.5 Plates slide past.

As they **slide past** each other, **plates get stuck**. **Compression** builds up until the jammed plate suddenly frees and adjusts to its new position.

Other Causes of Earthquakes

Ice Age

Earthquakes may be associated with the melting of the great ice sheets that covered much of North America, Europe and Asia for over 2 million years. Melting relieved the load that pushed down the crust. This caused **rebounding of the crust** and strain on old faults created earthquakes.

Ancient Faults

Less than 1 per cent of all earthquakes occur away from plate boundaries, but some of these have caused great destruction to populated areas. Geologists believe that these devastating earthquakes may be related to a **renewal of ancient faults** that are buried deep in the earth's crust.

Case Study: Earthquakes on the San Andreas Fault Line

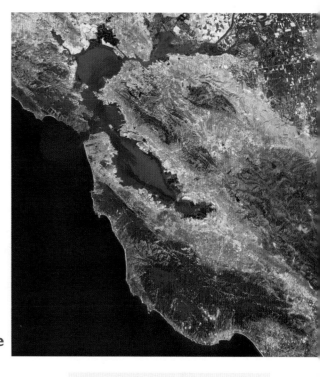

What is the focus?
What is the epicentre?

Activity

1. Identify the region of the world in this satellite image above.
2. Why is this region associated with earthquakes?

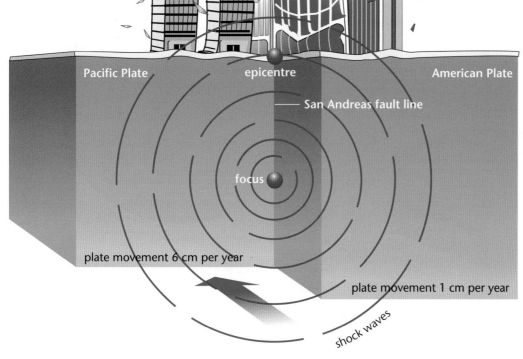

Pacific Plate   epicentre   American Plate

San Andreas fault line

focus

plate movement 6 cm per year

plate movement 1 cm per year

shock waves

The American Plate and the Pacific Plate slide past each other on the San Andreas Fault Line in California. Because the Pacific Plate is moving faster than the American Plate, it gives the impression that the plates are moving in opposite directions.

Fig. 6.6

31

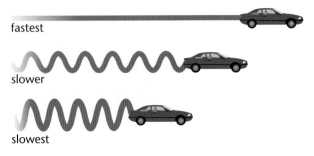

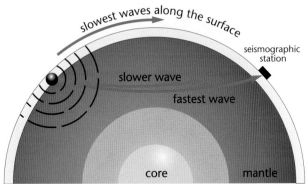

Fig. 6.7 (a) Different seismic waves travel at varying velocities, like cars racing at different speeds. (b) Different waves arrive at different times at seismograph stations. P-waves arrive first, then S-waves, and finally surface waves. The difference in speed explains the seismograph in Fig. 6.9.

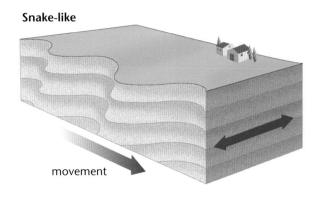

Fig. 6.8

Earthquake Waves

An earthquake releases two classes of vibrations, or seismic waves:

- **Body waves,** which travel through the interior of the earth. The body waves that travel through the interior of the earth are in turn divided into two types:
  - Fastest waves.
  - Slower waves.
- **Surface waves,** which travel close to the surface.

What Happens to the Crust During an Earthquake?

Some waves make the ground undulate in a rolling motion, like the surface of the sea. Other waves cause the ground to undulate laterally (sideways in a snake-like movement).

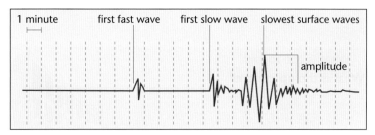

Fig. 6.9 Typical earthquake vibrations on a seismograph. The arrival times of shock waves from at least three recording stations are used to locate the quake's epicentre. See also Fig. 6.10.

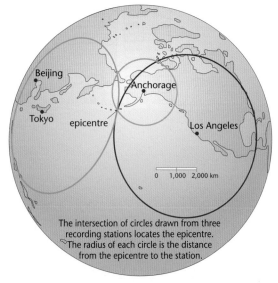

Fig. 6.10 How epicentres are located.

Activity

1. Describe what is happening to the ground during an earthquake as shown in Fig. 6.7 and Fig. 6.8.
2. How do experts locate the epicentre of an earthquake at their recording stations? See Fig. 6.9 and Fig. 6.10.

Damage Caused by Earthquakes

The extent of the damage and loss of life caused by an individual earthquake depends on a number of factors:

- The magnitude (size) of an earthquake and its location.
- The depth of the focus.
- The types of rock and soil through which the waves travel.
- How close the epicentre is to cities.
- The buildings and utilities (water supply, gas pipes, etc.) affected.
- The time it happens, i.e. day or night, rush hour, etc.

An earthquake's **size** and its **location** indicate the potential damage that the earthquake will cause.

Estimating the Size of an Earthquake

The Richter Scale

The Richter Scale is an indication of the size, or magnitude, of an earthquake. A magnitude 2 is a mild quiver, undetectable by all but the most sensitive instruments. By contrast, a magnitude 7 is a major earthquake.

The size of an earthquake of 7 on the Richter scale is ten times more powerful than one of 6 and 100 times more powerful than one of 5. It is ten times less powerful than one of 8.

The Mercalli Scale

The Mercalli Scale measures earthquake damage on a 12-point scale: 1 means no damage, while 12 indicates complete devastation.

Finding the Location of an Earthquake

Once it has been established where an earthquake has occurred and what its magnitude (size) is, it is vital to estimate the damage created by an earthquake. For example, if an earthquake occurs in the middle of the Sahara Desert, it is unlikely to cause any great damage or loss of life because very few people live in this area. If the earthquake has occurred in a city in India, however, enormous damage and tens of thousands of deaths could have resulted. Locating and recording the size of an earthquake is vital to estimate potential damage and to arrange for **emergency aid** for the region. Local communications systems may be 'down' and there may be no way of contacting the population affected. The earlier help arrives, the greater the number of lives that may be saved.

A toppled train and burnt-out homes show some effects of an earthquake in Japan.

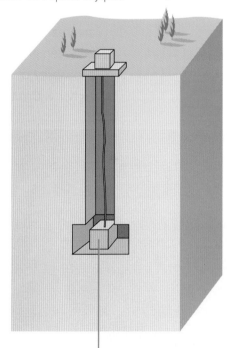

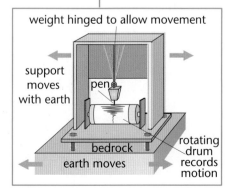

weight hinged to allow movement

support moves with earth

pen

bedrock

earth moves

rotating drum records motion

Fig. 6.11 A seismograph measures earth tremors.

How Earthquakes and Their Effects Can Be Predicted

Long-range earthquake forecasts are based on the idea that earthquakes are repetitive. As soon as one earthquake is over, the movement of the earth's plates builds strain until this is released by another quake along a fault line. This has led seismologists (scientists who study earthquakes) to study the history of earthquakes in an area and to search for patterns so that the occurrence of earthquakes might be predicted.

Seismic Gaps

Places along fault lines that have been 'quiet' for a long time are called seismic gaps. According to recent studies, quiet segments of a fault bordered by the places (epicentres) of recent earthquake activity are the **most likely places** to look for the next great earthquake.

Dating

In order to forecast the future, it is important to know the past pattern of earthquakes in an area. For example, it was found in one region that there was an interval of 150 years between great earthquakes, and if the last one occurred about 120 years ago, the probability of a great earthquake occurring within the next thirty years is high, even higher within the next forty years and so on.

Other Methods

Small changes can warn us if **strain is building up** and close to snapping. These include:

- **Increased uplift of land:** Land levels are recorded over a long time. If there is a noticeable change in movement of the surface level, it is a sign of increased stress on rocks. This stress can be measured using **creep meters, bore-hole strain meters** and **tiltmeters.**
- **Movement of rocks: Lasers** can measure the slightest movement of rocks across a fault line. Again, this could indicate a build-up of strain in rocks on one or both sides of the fault.
- **Foreshocks:** Many **seismographs** are installed in an area to record **foreshocks** (tiny earthquakes that occur before a great earthquake). It has been observed that a pattern of numerous small quakes occurs over days, weeks or months before a major earthquake.

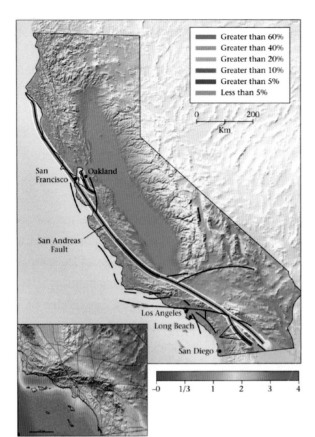

Greater than 60%
Greater than 40%
Greater than 20%
Greater than 10%
Greater than 5%
Less than 5%

Fig. 6.12 This map forecasts the probability, as a percentage, of a strong to great earthquake occurring along segments of the San Andreas Fault during the next thirty years.

Activity

Carefully examine the earthquake forecast map in Fig. 6.12 and look in your atlas, then answer the following.

1. Name the American state in the map.
2. Identify the region of greatest earthquake probability.
3. Identify the region of least probability.
4. Which one of these regions you have named is a seismic gap? Explain.
5. Identify the fault line that creates these earthquakes in this region.
6. Explain the plate movements that create this fault line.
7. Identify the type of fault marked in the diagram.

Other Effects of Earthquakes

Liquefaction

Earthquakes can create a phenomenon called liquefaction which occurs when a great thickness of silt or sand is saturated with water. Under these conditions, for 15 seconds or so what had been a stable foundation soil turns into a thick liquid that is no longer able to support buildings. Buildings, especially multi-storey buildings, simply sink into the ground. Underground objects, such as storage tanks and sewer pipes, may float to the surface.

Because **Mexico City** has been built on a lake bed, it is likely that some parts of the city will suffer from liquefaction during an earthquake.

Landslides

The shaking of an earthquake can cause ground on steep slopes or ground with weak sediment underneath it to give way. This movement results in landslides, the tumbling and flow of soil and rock downslope. Landslides destroy everything in their path – buildings, trees and roads.

Landslides caused great damage in **Kashmir in 2005**. During an earthquake, roads on steep slopes through this mountainous region in the Himalayas were destroyed by landslides, cutting off access to isolated communities.

A building sinks due to liquefaction.

A landslide in action.

35

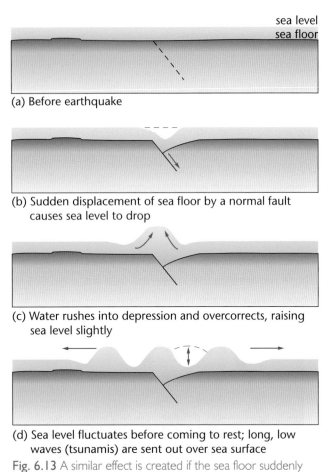

(a) Before earthquake

(b) Sudden displacement of sea floor by a normal fault causes sea level to drop

(c) Water rushes into depression and overcorrects, raising sea level slightly

(d) Sea level fluctuates before coming to rest; long, low waves (tsunamis) are sent out over sea surface

Fig. 6.13 A similar effect is created if the sea floor suddenly rises due to a thrust fault movement set off by an earthquake.

Tsunamis

How a Tsunami Forms

If a **sea floor falls or rises suddenly** due to plate movement along a fault, it may generate a wave in the water above it. If it falls due to normal faulting, the water level above suddenly sinks, and water rushes in from the sides to fill the space. If the sea floor rises as a result of reverse, or thrust, faulting, the water level suddenly rises and water rushes off the uplifted area (see Fig. 6.13).

In either case, the sudden movement of the sea surface creates waves that radiate out from the epicentre across the ocean surface and may cause damage and loss of life even thousands of kilometres from where they originate.

Similar waves may be created by coastal landslides or by volcanic eruptions at sea. Such waves are called **tsunamis**, a Japanese word meaning 'harbour wave'. A wave like this may travel at speeds up to 80–100 km an hour. As the tsunami approaches the shore, it '**touches bottom**' and the water builds up to form a monster wave up to **30 m high**. If the wave funnels into a narrow estuary or harbour, it may reach heights of 70 m.

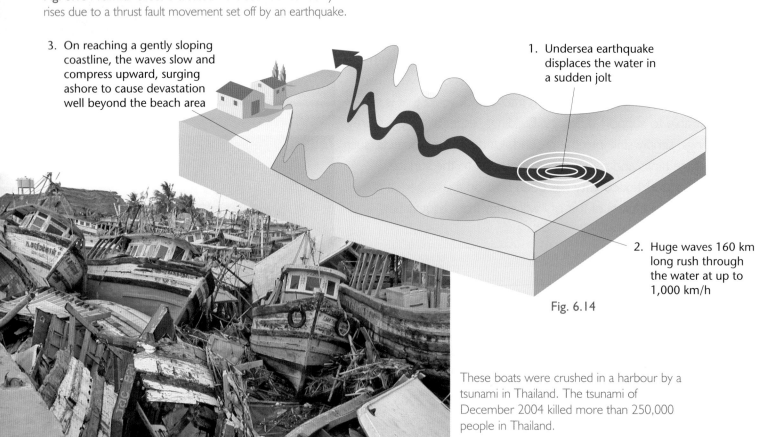

3. On reaching a gently sloping coastline, the waves slow and compress upward, surging ashore to cause devastation well beyond the beach area

1. Undersea earthquake displaces the water in a sudden jolt

2. Huge waves 160 km long rush through the water at up to 1,000 km/h

Fig. 6.14

These boats were crushed in a harbour by a tsunami in Thailand. The tsunami of December 2004 killed more than 250,000 people in Thailand.

Case Study: The 2005 Earthquake in Kashmir

The Kashmir earthquake in October 2005 measured 7.6 on the **Richter scale,** the same strength as the 1906 earthquake in San Francisco. Over 79,000 people died and more than 3.3 million people were left homeless, only weeks before the start of the winter snows.

The **epicentre** was located in the Pakistan-administered region of Kashmir, a territory disputed with India that is by far the most earthquake-prone region in the mountains. Kashmir lies in the area where the Eurasian and Indian **tectonic plates** are colliding. Out of this collision, the Himalayas began uplifting 50 million years ago, and continue to rise by about 3 mm per year. The **focus of the earthquake** was located at a depth of 26 km below the surface. About 50 million people are at risk from Himalayan quakes.

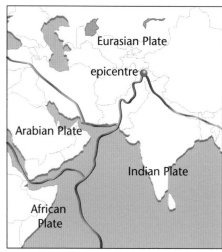

Fig. 6.15 The collision of the Indian and Eurasian plates creates earthquakes in the Himalayas.

The earthquake caused widespread destruction in northern Pakistan, as well as damage in Afghanistan and the Kashmir valley in northern India. As the earthquake struck on a Saturday and this is a normal schoolday in the region, most students were at school at the time. Many were buried under collapsed school buildings. Many other people were trapped in their homes and, because it was also the month of Ramadan when most people were taking a nap after their pre-dawn meal, they did not have time to escape during the quake. Reports confirmed that entire towns and villages were completely wiped out in northern Pakistan, with other surrounding areas suffering severe damage.

Landslides block roads in mountainous regions such as the Himalayas.

Mountainsides collapsed, sweeping away houses and terraced fields. Some landslides collapsed into river valleys, creating mountains of rock and mud over 100 m high that changed the courses of some rivers. Thousands of people in villages were cut off from relief supplies by the landslides. There were multiple landslides on one road. The landslides were so big they had to be cleared by blasting them with explosives. Over much of the region, the only choice was to bring in supplies by air.

Some isolated communities suffered from outbreaks of diseases such as cholera. Blue canvas tents dotted the hillsides, where families camped beside their damaged homes. These tents and other supplies, such as blankets and food, formed part of the relief efforts by various agencies such as the Red Cross and the US, Indian and Pakistani armies.

Activity

1. Explain the terms Richter scale, epicentre, focus, tectonic plates.
2. Why is Kashmir an earthquake-prone region?
3. On Fig. 6.15, which shows the tectonic boundaries of this region, draw arrows showing the direction of the plates' movements (see Fig. 2.7 on page 7).
4. Landslides are part of which type of surface process? (see Fig. 11.1 on page 65.)
5. Using a diagram, explain how landslides occur (see page 70).
6. Why did so many landslides occur during the 2005 Kashmir earthquake?
7. Describe and explain the damage caused by the landslides.
8. Explain why so many buildings collapsed during the quake.
9. What type of aid was given to the people affected? Explain.
10. What is Ramadan? Explain.
11. Do all people of this region take part in Ramadan? (See Chapter 76 on religions of the world.)

Why Do Most Earthquakes and Volcanoes Occur Along the Pacific Ring of Fire?

Write four SRPs explaining the processes that occur in each of the diagrams in Fig. 6.16.

- The Atlantic Ocean, the Indian Ocean and the Pacific Ocean all have ocean ridges where new crust is being created. To balance this, there are corresponding locations where old crust is being recycled and sucked into the mantle.
- Most of this recycling, called subduction, occurs around the edges of the Pacific Ocean where ocean plates sink under continental plates and other ocean plates.
- Most earthquakes and volcanoes occur around the Pacific Rim at these **subduction** zones.
- These volcanoes are **highly explosive** because they have thick, **viscous magma,** high in silica, which traps gases.

What Happens at Subduction Zones Along the Pacific Rim?

**A. Ocean-ocean destructive boundary –
example: Japan Islands and the Philippines**

**B. Ocean-continent destructive boundary –
example: Rockies and Andes**

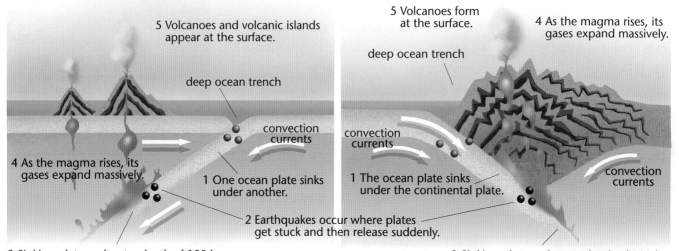

Fig. 6.16 Note that the intermediate and deep-focus earthquakes occur only within the sinking slab of the ocean plate. This is called the Wadatti-Benioff zone.

The earthquakes occur along the descending plates only. This is called the Wadatti-Benioff Zone. There are two types of subduction zones around the Pacific Rim:

- Diagram A represents an **ocean-ocean** boundary. This represents the **island arcs** of Japan, Indonesia and the Philippines in the western Pacific Ocean.
- Diagram B represents an **ocean-continent** boundary that matches the North American coast and the **Rockies,** and the South American coast and the **Andes** in the eastern Pacific Ocean.
- Each of these boundaries create **both earthquakes and volcanoes**.
- At each of these locations, an ocean plate is pulled into the mantle.
- These descending plates regularly get stuck, leading to earthquakes along their Wadatti-Benioff zones.
- All the descending plates eventually melt, creating volcanoes at the surface.

Sample Questions and Answers

Why Is Ireland Regarded as *Relatively* Safe from Destructive Earthquakes?

- Ireland is located far from its nearest existing plate boundaries. These are the Mid Atlantic Ridge to the west and the African-European Plate boundary to the south.
- Earthquake waves decrease in strength with distance from an epicentre. Most of the earthquake epicentres closest to Ireland are located on these distant plate boundaries.
- Ice sheets disappeared from the Irish landscape over 10,000 years ago. Most rebounding of the land that could cause earthquakes due to squeezing by overlying ice sheets has already occurred since the end of the Ice Age.
- When earthquakes have occurred over the past 300 years, they are generally small and are associated with rebounding rather than plate collision or transform boundaries, where most destructive earthquakes occur.

Why Are There No Active or Dormant Volcanoes in Ireland?

- Ireland is located far from its nearest existing plate boundaries. These are the Mid Atlantic Ridge to the west and the African-European Plate boundary to the south, where the closest volcanoes are located.
- Ireland lies on a passive margin where plate activity is absent. It lies on the stable continental shelf of the European Plate.
- Ireland has no hot spot activity beneath its surface. This creates a stable crust, free from volcanic activity.
- The most recent volcanic activity in Ireland occurred about 60 million years ago when rifting caused magma to pour out onto the surface to form the Antrim Plateau. No volcanic activity has occurred since that time.

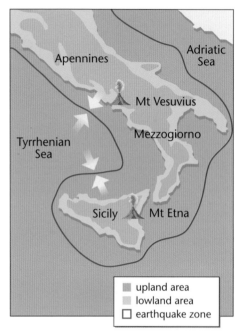

Fig. 6.17 Southern Italy is called the Mezzogiorno.

Why Do Earthquakes Occur in Southern Italy?

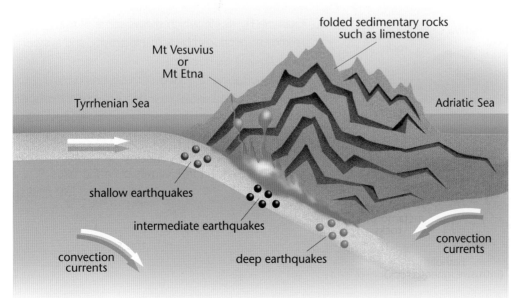

Fig. 6.18

The floor of the Tyrrhenian Sea slips under the toe of Italy. Earthquakes always **occur along the path of this descending plate**, as it dips into the mantle. In addition, limestone sediment from the sea floor is squeezed and buckled up to form the Apennines (fold mountains). This is why the land in southern Italy is steep. It is dry because any rain that falls on land quickly disappears through the limestone rock.

See Activities on Irish earthquakes in *Dynamic Geography Core Workbook*, pages 24–27.

Multi-part Questions

1. **A.** Name one active volcano and explain why it is active. [20 marks]
    B. 'Earthquakes and volcanoes occur in quite predictable locations on the globe.' Examine the theoretical basis for this statement. [30 marks]
    C. The frequency of occurrence of earthquakes and volcanic eruptions is much more difficult to predict than their location. Assess the accuracy of this statement with reference to examples you have studied. [30 marks]

2. **A.** Draw a map of the world and mark the names of regions of regular earthquake activity on it. [20 marks]
    B. With the aid of a diagram, describe the different types of seismic waves associated with earthquakes. [30 marks]
    C. Explain how loss of life and destruction of property differs between earthquake-prone regions of advanced and developing countries. [30 marks]

3. **A.** Explain the meaning of plate tectonics. [20 marks]
    B. Explain how plate tectonic theory has helped us to understand the world distribution of:
       i. fold mountains **AND**
       ii. volcanic island arcs. [30 marks]
    C. i. Another of the consequences of the movement of crustal plates is the occurrence of earthquakes. With reference to appropriate examples, describe the impact which a major earthquake can have on a human population.
       ii. Briefly examine attempts to lessen that impact.

4. **A.** Name and explain **one** example of each of the following:
       i. convergent margin
       ii. divergent margin
       iii. a transverse (transform) margin
       iv. a mid-plate volcanic island arc. [20 marks]
    B. Explain why most volcanoes and earthquakes occur around the Pacific Ring of Fire. [20 marks]
    C. Explain how people benefit from the occurrence of volcanic activity. [30 marks]

5. **A.** 'A study of patterns in the worldwide distribution of volcanoes and earthquake zones can help us to understand the causes of these events.' Examine this statement with reference to examples which you have studied. [50 marks]
    B. Describe two effects on human societies of the occurrence of: (a) a volcanic eruption (b) a major earthquake in populated areas. [20 marks]
    C. Explain how a tsunami forms. [30 marks]

6. Examine Fig. 6.19, which shows some of the landforms produced by volcanic activity, and answer the following questions.
    A. In the case of any **two** of these landforms, describe and explain the processes which shaped them. [20 marks]
    B. Briefly examine ways in which volcanic activity can be of economic benefit to people. [30 marks]
    C. Briefly explain three causes of earthquakes. [30 marks]

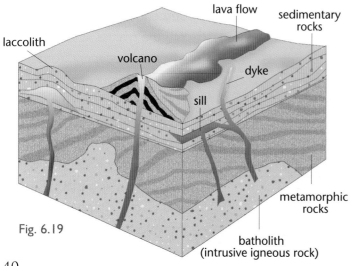

Fig. 6.19

CHAPTER 7
THE ROCK CYCLE

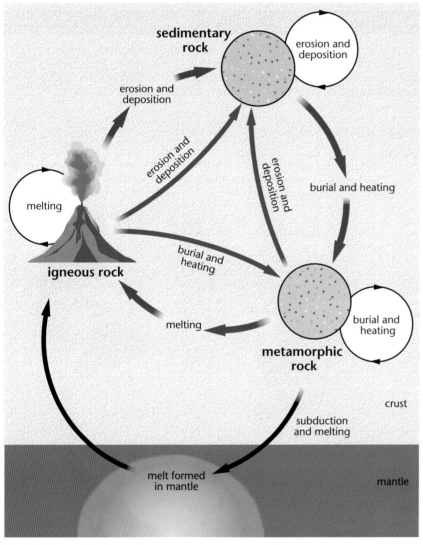

Fig. 7.1 The rock cycle.

Igneous activity and plate tectonics create mountain regions. Weathering breaks up the rock that forms these mountains, and erosion removes the rock particles to lowlands and seas where they form many types of sedimentary rock.

Plate tectonics may then buckle and raise some of these sedimentary rock layers to form mountains where denudation (weathering and erosion) repeats the cycle.

During new mountain-building periods, more of the sedimentary rock layers may be compressed, heated and then cooled to form metamorphic rock. Sometimes the cooled metamorphic rock may itself be changed by increased heat and pressure to form different types of metamorphic rock.

In some instances during mountain-building periods, the sedimentary rock layers may be pushed down into the crust so far that they melt to form magma. If this magma cools, it will form igneous rock within the crust. This is called plutonic rock. If instead the molten rock or magma rises, it may reach the surface to form volcanic rock, such as basalt, lava or pyroclastic rocks.

Activity
Carefully examine the diagram in Fig. 7.1 and use your studies so far to answer the following.
1. How does sedimentary rock become metamorphic rock?
2. How does metamorphic rock become (a) igneous rock (b) sedimentary rock?
3. What other type of rock can metamorphic rock become other than (a) and (b) above?
4. Explain the processes that cause igneous rock to change to other rock types.
5. List the various processes mentioned in this flow chart.

SETTINGS WHERE IGNEOUS, SEDIMENTARY AND METAMORPHIC ROCKS FORM

KEY IDEA!

Rocks are formed in different environments. Some are formed within the earth. Others are formed on the earth's surface, either on land or in water environments. These environments greatly affect the type of minerals that make up the rock.

Group	How Formed	Examples
IGNEOUS	They were formed when hot, molten rock matter cooled and became solid.	granite, basalt, lava, pyroclasts
SEDIMETARY	They were formed from the **crushed-together remains** (sediments) of animals, plants and other rocks	limestone, coal, sandstone, shale
METAMORPHIC	They were once igneous or sedimentary rocks, which were **changed by great heat or pressure.**	marble, quartzite, slate, schist

Activity

1. Using Fig. 7.2, identify the counties where the following rock types are located:
   a. granite
   b. basalt
   c. quartzite and some other metamorphics
   d. slates and shales
   e. sandstones only
   f. limestone only (four counties).
2. According to Fig. 7.2, which county has:
   a. only granite and quartzites and other metamorphics
   b. mostly basalt
   c. mostly sandstone
   d. only limestone at the surface?
3. Which region(s) has the most granite, quartzite and other metamorphics?

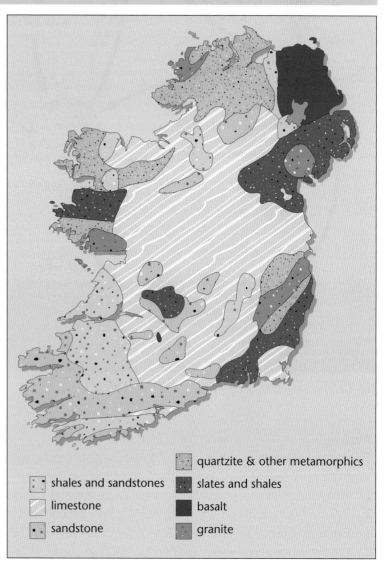

quartzite & other metamorphics
shales and sandstones
slates and shales
limestone
basalt
sandstone
granite

Fig. 7.2 Surface rock in Ireland.

IGNEOUS ROCKS

Igneous rocks were formed from magma either inside the earth's crust (called intrusive, or plutonic, rock) or on the earth's surface (called extrusive, or volcanic, rock).

All igneous rocks have crystals. The **largest crystals** are found in the rocks that cooled **slowly deepest** in the crust. The **smallest crystals** are found in the rocks that cooled **quickly on the surface**. Generally, crystal size in igneous rock decreases towards the surface.

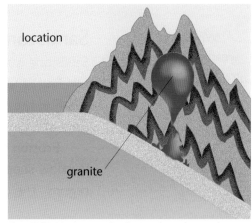

location

granite

Fig. **7.3** Where granite forms.

Plutonic Rock

Plutonic rocks (also called intrusive rocks) are formed when magma cools within the earth's crust. The most common plutonic rock is granite.

Formation of Granite in Batholiths

Granite formed from masses of magma **deep within fold mountains.** These are destructive boundaries where the ocean crust is subducted into the mantle.

- Large masses of magma rise from the sinking plate into the buckled and folded rock to form **batholiths.**
- This magma **cools very slowly** over millions of years and creates **large crystals of mica, feldspar and quartz.** These three minerals form granite.
- The overall colour of granite can vary from pink with dark spots to black and white (looking something like a firelighter). The quartz grains are clear and glassy, the feldspars vary from white to pink, and crystals of mica are black or silvery.

Some varying colours of granite.

Volcanic Rock

Formation of Basalt

Basalt is a volcanic rock that cooled quickly **on or near the surface.** It has **tiny crystals** visible only under a microscope. It forms where magma **pours out quietly** from a crack, or **fissure,** on the surface and covers the surrounding landscape with a thick lava layer that cools quickly. These layers or sheets of basalt cover all humps and hollows and create a level surface. These flows are often 5 to 6 m thick.

- If the liquid lava is trapped to form **deep pools,** such as in a blocked river valley, the cooling rock cracks to form **five or six-sided columns** of basalt. Columns like these can be seen at the Giant's Causeway in Co. Antrim and at Linfield Quarry in Pallas Grean, in Co. Limerick.
- Basalt is a **dark heavy rock** when it forms. It may have **rusty spots** due to its high iron content. It may also have some **tiny holes** where gases escaped while cooling. If it is exposed at the surface, however, it may become coated with a whitish or other litchen that varies the appearance of the basalt.

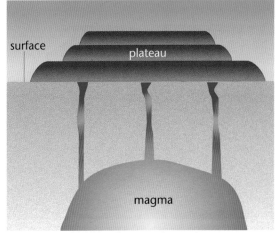

surface

plateau

magma

Fig. **7.4** Where basalt forms at the surface.

43

SEDIMENTARY ROCKS

Sandstone

When granite weathers, the quartz grains are transported to form sandstone. The mica and feldspar weather to form clay and mud.

Sandstone is a hard rock that **resists erosion**. The most common type of sandstone is Old Red Sandstone. Approximately 350–400 million years ago, Ireland was located **20° south of the Equator**. The Kalahari Desert is at this latitude today, and it has the same **semi-arid climate** with seasonal rainfall as Ireland had at that time.

Erosion of the Caledonian mountains of Mayo, Connemara, Donegal and Wicklow **supplied sediments** carried in large rivers to huge deserts and lakes in lowland regions. The quartz grains from the eroding mountains were laid down in layers by the seasonal river waters to form thousands of metres of sandstone. The sandstone grains were compressed by the weight of overlying layers. They were **cemented together** by an iron cement, which was dissolved in groundwater that seeped through the rock. This iron cement also coloured the rock red, so it is called Old Red Sandstone.

The **mountains of Munster** are formed from this sandstone, which is over 6 km thick in places. (See page 51.)

Sandstone also formed from **delta deposits** in **river channels** and **floodplains**, and from **beach sand** and **sand dunes** at this time.

Many sandstones form from sand deposits in river channels.

Conglomerate

Conglomerate was formed from **gravel** in **alluvial fans** or **river channels** at the foot of steep slopes **within the Caledonian mountains**. The large particles, or clasts, were not eroded much because they were **not carried far** from their source in the mountains. These were deposited by **flash floods** in the same semi-desert conditions as the Old Red Sandstones. These may be seen on the **Devil's Bit** in Co. Tipperary.

Conglomerate forms from poorly sorted particles.

Shale

Shale forms in the sea from **fine particles of mud or clay**. These fine particles are so light they are carried far from their source in mountain regions. They are the last particles to be deposited by rivers that erode the mountains. This is why they are found on continental shelves and enclosed estuaries.

Shale is made up of numerous **thin layers** of sediment. Each layer represents a period of deposition that was separated from the next by a period of time when no deposition took place. Shale is easily broken and so is a **soft rock**.

Shale forms from the lightest rock particles (clay particles).

Limestone
The Setting When Ireland's Limestones Were Formed

1. Most of Ireland was submerged beneath a warm, equatorial sea. The Caledonian mountains of Connemara, Mayo, Donegal, Down and Wicklow stood as islands above the sea.

2. The great mass of Carboniferous rock that covers the plains of Ireland today must have originally been some thousands of metres thick.

3. The coalfields of Ireland, Britain and Europe were laid down in swamp-filled depressions at this time.

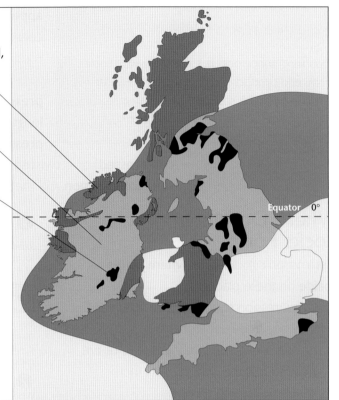

Fig. 7.5 Where limestone forms.

Activity
Look at Fig. 7.5. Why is there little limestone rock in Donegal, Galway, Mayo, Down and Wicklow?

	dry land
	mountains
	warm seas
	coal swamps

Equator 0°

Limestone is formed from the mineral calcium carbonate or calcite. It formed in two ways:
- **Calcium carbonate** from seawater collected around tiny sand grains floating in shallow lagoons near the Equator.
- **Billions of shells** and **skeletons** from tiny and large organisms, such as corals, which lived in the **tropical seas**.

Ireland's limestone formed when Ireland was **near the Equator 300–350 million years ago**. It is mostly composed of compressed shells, the remains of shellfish and coral skeletons that were abundant in the seas, so it has many **fossils**.

During this time there was an **explosion in new forms of sea life,** and many types of small, soft, slow-moving sea creatures **developed hard shells** to protect themselves from predators. They all lived in warm seas, coral reefs and shallow lagoons in the tropics. When they died, their shells and skeletons built up on the sea floor and were compressed by their own weight and the weight of later rocks to form solid limestone rock.

Because a lot of coal (which initially developed as peat in shallow swamps in delta areas at this time) became buried in the limestone, this period of time is called the **Carboniferous period.**

Ireland's limestone was formed in a setting of coral reefs similar to this photograph.

METAMORPHIC ROCKS OF IRELAND

In a simple way, metamorphism is something like baking. When you bake, what you get to eat depends on what you start with and on the cooking conditions. It is the same with rocks: the end product is controlled by the initial make-up of the rock and by the metamorphic conditions (baking = the amount of heat).

Igneous and sedimentary rocks may change both in their **appearance** (physically) and in their **make-up** (chemically) as a consequence of heat or pressure, or both. This process of change is called **metamorphism**.

Factors that contribute to the end product include the **presence and amount of liquid** within the changing rock, the **length of time** a rock is subjected to **high temperature** or **high pressure**, and **whether** the changing rock is simply squeezed (**compressed**) or is **twisted**. These three basic factors all contribute to metamorphism: **heat, compression** and the **presence of liquids**.

Where Do Metamorphic Rocks Form?

Metamorphic rocks form **where plates collide**. In these places:

- Compression squeezes rock layers and they begin to heat and change.
- Rock layers come in contact with or are close to magma, which heats them intensely, causing change.
- Heating makes mineral atoms vibrate, and some break away. Liquids seeping through the heated rock carry the breakaway atoms to other locations, where they cluster to form new minerals.

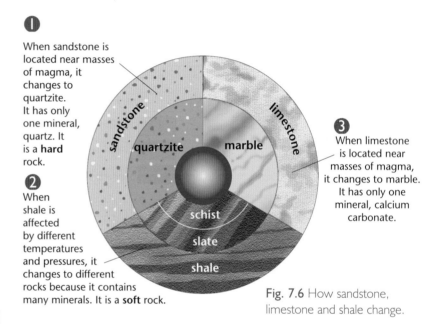

① When sandstone is located near masses of magma, it changes to quartzite. It has only one mineral, quartz. It is a **hard** rock.

② When shale is affected by different temperatures and pressures, it changes to different rocks because it contains many minerals. It is a **soft** rock.

③ When limestone is located near masses of magma, it changes to marble. It has only one mineral, calcium carbonate.

Fig. 7.6 How sandstone, limestone and shale change.

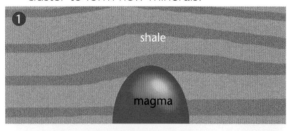

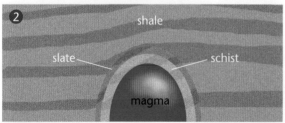

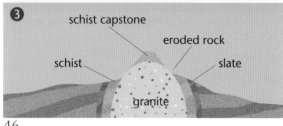

Case Study: Metamorphic Rocks in Leinster

The metamorphic rocks of Leinster formed when the European and American plates collided. Magma heated the buckled shale rock and changed it to schist or slate. In other places it changed sandstone rock to quartzite.

Fig. 7.7

① Layers of shale were buckled and folded during collision. Then magma rose up into the shale.

② The magma heated and changed the shale. The hottest shale changed to schist. Farther out, with less heat, the shale changed to slate. The remaining shale was unchanged.

③ After millions of years, most of the overlying schist, slate and shale has been removed by weathering and erosion. Because schist resists erosion, it still protects some peaks, such as Lugnaquilla.

ACTIVE AND TRAILING PLATE MARGINS

A continent's active margin occurs where an ocean plate sinks under the continental plate. On its western edge the American Plate is **colliding with or sliding past** plates such as the **Juan de Fuca Plate** and the **Pacific Plate**. This boundary is America's **active plate margin,** where faulting, earthquakes, volcanoes and high mountains are located. Because this plate margin is active, America's **newest igneous and metamorphic** rocks are forming here.

America's east coast has a wide **continental shelf**, just as Ireland has, where rivers from eroding mountains have built up **great depths of sedimentary rock**. This region is **not tectonically active**. No major earthquakes occur here and there are no active or dormant volcanoes. This is America's **passive, or trailing plate,** margin.

Which margin of the Eurasian Plate is:
a. an active margin?
b. a passive margin?

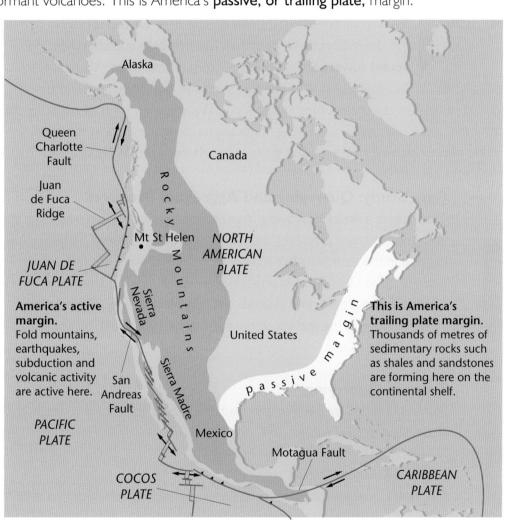

Fig. 7.8

Activity

Look at Fig. 7.8 and answer the following questions.
1. Which margin of the North American plate is (a) an active margin (b) a passive margin?
2. Name two major transform fault lines along the American west coast.
3. Name one ocean plate that is being subducted under the American Plate.
4. Name one active volcano along America's active margin.
5. Explain, with the aid of a diagram or diagrams, why this volcano is active.
6. Name one region that is regularly prone to earthquakes along this active margin.
7. Why is America's east coast a passive margin?

HOW PEOPLE INTERACT WITH THE ROCK CYCLE

Case Study: Extracting Building Materials

Most **buildings** are built from rock, such as **limestone, sandstone** or **granite**, or rock compounds, such as **concrete blocks** or **clay bricks**. To reinforce buildings or **pre-cast concrete** units, some metals, such as iron and steel, are included.

Stone Age people – Paleolithic, Mesolithic or Neolithic, as we now classify them – were so called because **tools** they used were made from stone. **Iron Age** people (Celts) used stone as a foundation for their forts and lake-side crannog settlements and extracted metal from stone (smelting) to manufacture their **weapons** of iron.

Early Christian monks built beehive **cells** and **churches** and **round towers** to protect them from attacks by the Vikings. The Normans, and later the Irish chieftains, built huge castles and defended settlements to protect their lands. Today, stone is used for road surfacing and in domestic house construction, for filling, foundations (concrete), blocks for **walls**, concrete **tiles** or **slates** for roofing, and gypsum for **plaster** in ceilings and walls.

Stone masons and sculptors create designs by working stone.

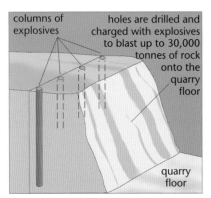

columns of explosives

holes are drilled and charged with explosives to blast up to 30,000 tonnes of rock onto the quarry floor

quarry floor

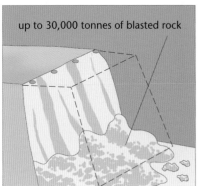

up to 30,000 tonnes of blasted rock

Fig. 7.9

Case Study: Quarrying and Aggregate Products

Quarrying is a method of taking large, solid blocks or broken masses of stone from the earth and preparing them for construction projects. A quarry is a large pit in the earth's surface from which stone is taken out (extracted). The types of stone taken from quarries include basalt, granite, limestone, marble, sandstone and slate. Some quarries are dug into the sides of mountains. Most are open at the surface. A quarry may be over 30 m deep and many times as wide as that.

Types of Quarrying

Stone is quarried by the plug and feather method, the explosive method or channelling by machinery.

Plug and Feather Method

Drill holes, wedges (plugs) and steel rods are used to split rock into thin slabs.

Explosive Method

The explosive method is used to break off huge masses of rock from a rock face.

Channelling by Machinery

Huge slices of rock are cut off a rock edge by a large rotating disc. These slices are taken away for cutting into various sizes.

The Economic Impact of Quarrying in Ireland

- Aggregates are an essential requirement for construction.
- About 90,000 people are employed in the construction industry.
- Over 40,000 housing units are built each year.
- About 7 tonnes of aggregates are used per 1,000 tonnes of building work.
- About 50,000 tonnes of aggregates are required each year.
- Ireland has over 200 active pits and quarries.

Two major quarrying companies in Ireland include **Roadstone** at Bunratty, Co. Clare and **Ready Mix** at Tullamore, Co. Offaly. Private quarrying companies include Kelly and Gleeson at Donohill, Co. Tipperary.

Carrara Marble Quarries In Tuscany, Italy

Carrara has been famous for its marble since Roman times. Stone from these quarries was used in Rome at the time of Emperor Augustus (27 BC–AD 14). Later, Carrara's finest pure white marble was made famous by the great sculptors, Leonardo da Vinci and Michelangelo. Marble quarries surround the town of Carrara and it is one of the world's major centres for marble production and export. The port of Marina di Carrara handles marble almost exclusively.

Marble is used extensively in the construction of buildings, especially in warm countries, such as Italy. It creates a **cool interior** atmosphere and so is used for **floors** in **airports** and other **public buildings**. Because it can be polished at quarries to produce a smooth surface, it is used for **walls and bathroom floors in domestic houses throughout the world**.

Negative Effects of Quarrying

Quarrying can have a negative impact on the landscape. Some impacts include:

- Airborne dust that can affect nearby homes and farmland.
- The generation of silt into rivers that affects water quality and fish spawning grounds.
- Noise and vibration from blasting and machinery.
- Damage to roads between the quarry and construction sites.
- Disused quarries scar the landscape and have regularly been reused as rubbish pits.

> About 60 hectares of land are used each year to extract 35 million tonnes of rock and 15 million tonnes of sand and gravel. This annual land usage by the whole Irish quarrying industry amounts to less than 0.001 per cent of the total land area of Ireland.

> Quarrying for sand and gravel is carried out in almost every county in Ireland. Most of this material is found in esker ridges that were deposited as the ice sheets melted about 10,000 years ago.

Carrara

> Limestone rock in Ireland is a major economic resource. Explain three ways that limestone is used in the construction industry and farming.

- *How was marble formed?*
- *What are its uses today?*

49

CHAPTER 8

SEDIMENTARY LANDFORMS CREATED BY EARTH MOVEMENTS

 **KEY IDEA!**

Sedimentary landforms are created by earth movements.

The rocks of an anticline crack and open. This allows the forces of weathering and erosion to attack and erode the anticline quickly.

LANDFORMS CREATED BY FOLDING

Folding is caused by **compression**. It is associated with the **closing of an ocean**. On the ocean floor, thousands of metres of sediment are compressed by their own weight into solid rock. Once the ocean closes, these sedimentary rocks are crushed between the colliding continents. The **layers of sediments are compressed, folded and pushed up (and sometimes down)** to form fold mountains.

Fold Types	Formation	Fold Types	Formation
Symmetrical fold (simple fold)	Both limbs have similar slopes.	Over fold	One limb is pushed over the other limb.
Asymmetrical fold	One limb is steeper than the other.	Thrust fault	When compression is great , a fracture (crack) occurs in the fold. One limb is then pushed forward over the other limb at a very low angle along the fault line. This limb may be displaced for a distance of a few kilometres.

Fig. 8.1

When bedding planes run parallel, as in Fig. 8.2, Diagram A, it indicates that all the rock layers were folded at the same time. It also indicates that the surface layers are younger than the lower layers. These layers are said to 'conform'.

Fig. 8.2

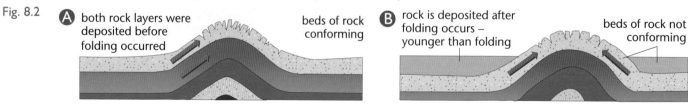

Ⓐ both rock layers were deposited before folding occurred — beds of rock conforming

Ⓑ rock is deposited after folding occurs – younger than folding — beds of rock not conforming

In Fig. 8.2, Diagram B, surface rock on the lowland does not follow the original folds, so it does not conform. It is clear, then, that this rock was deposited on the lowland after the folding took place.

THE ARMORICAN FOLDINGS IN MUNSTER 300 MYA

Sandstone and Limestone Rock Layers

Only 50 million years after their formation, the **Caledonian** mountains were worn down to sea level across the Irish **Midlands** and **Munster**. Their eroded materials were deposited in these regions to form layers of sandstone rock. At this time, Ireland had a hot, dry climate with seasonal rainfall.

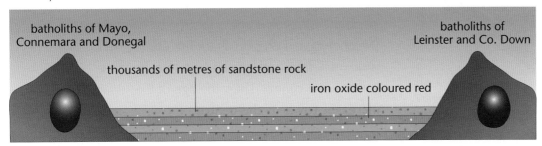

batholiths of Mayo, Connemara and Donegal

batholiths of Leinster and Co. Down

thousands of metres of sandstone rock

iron oxide coloured red

Fig. 8.3

Then, about **350 million years ago,** Ireland and its level sandstone layers sank beneath a warm equatorial sea. Great depths of **limestone formed on top of the sandstones from the shells and skeletons of sea creatures.**

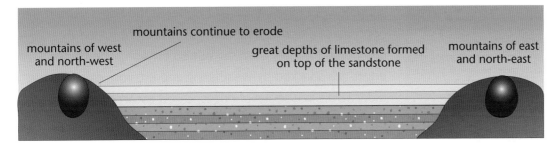

mountains continue to erode

mountains of west and north-west

great depths of limestone formed on top of the sandstone

mountains of east and north-east

Fig. 8.4

Suddenly Africa crashed into Europe, and all the other continents were now welded into a single continent, Pangaea. The Appalachians in the US and the Pyrenees, the Urals and many mountains in Germany were buckled upwards.

Ireland was dry land once more, and its **limestone and sandstone rock layers were buckled and intensely folded in Munster,** forming **east-west ridges and valleys** because they were closest to the African-European boundary. They are the Armorican fold mountains.

Two types of rock were involved in the folding:

- **Old Red Sandstone**, the older rock, and so the lowest layer.
- **Limestone**, the younger rock, and so the surface layer.

Since then the **softer limestone** has **eroded faster** than the harder sandstone, so the **sandstone** stands out as **ridges,** while the limestone covers the valleys.

Some mountains have a distinctive **trend**. This means their ridges and valleys run in a definite direction.

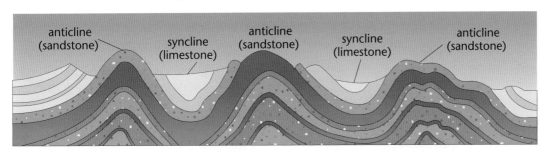

anticline (sandstone)

syncline (limestone)

anticline (sandstone)

syncline (limestone)

anticline (sandstone)

Fig. 8.5 Munster's ridges and valleys.

LANDFORMS CREATED BY DOMING, SAGGING AND TILTING

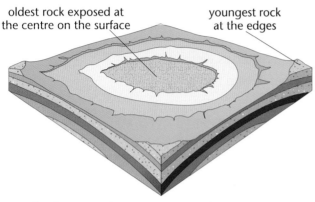

oldest rock exposed at the centre on the surface

youngest rock at the edges

Fig. 8.6 Dome landform in the Weald of southern England.

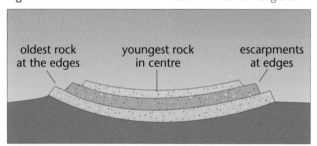

oldest rock at the edges

youngest rock in centre

escarpments at edges

Fig. 8.7 The Paris Basin is a dish-shaped structure.

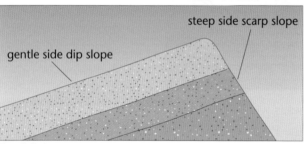

steep side scarp slope

gentle side dip slope

Fig. 8.8 An escarpment has dipping rock layers.

Doming

Example: The Weald in Sussex, in England, formed after the Alpine foldings

A dome is a structure in which the beds of rock dip away from a central point. The beds are like upturned saucers, one inside the other. A dome is formed by compression. Weathering and erosion attack the uplifted rock. Over time, wind, rain, frost and ice combine to expose the older rock layers in the centre. Thus, the **age** of the surface rock **increases towards the centre**.

Sagging

Example: The Paris Basin

When horizontal rock layers sag, they create a saucer-shaped basin, lower in the centre and higher at the edges. This is the opposite of a dome. The rock layers are first folded by compression. They then sag due to erosion. The higher edges are attacked by weathering and erosion, exposing the older rocks in a series of ridges, called **escarpments**. Thus, the **age** of rocks **reduces towards the centre**.

Tilting

Example: The Dartry-Cuilcagh Uplands

When horizontal rock layers are gently tilted by uplift or sagging, a structure with uneven slopes is formed. One slope, called the scarp slope, is steep. The other is gentle and is called the dip slope. This landform is called an **escarpment**. When the surface rock layer of the escarpment is sandstone, it will resist erosion and protect the underlying softer rock. Over time, surrounding rock may be eroded, leaving the escarpment to dominate the surrounding region.

LANDFORMS CREATED BY FAULTING

The following are some features that have been formed by vertical and horizontal rock movement.

Fig. 8.9 Landforms created by vertical movement.

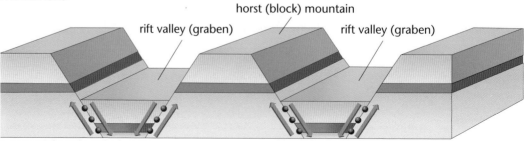

horst (block) mountain

rift valley (graben)

rift valley (graben)

potential earthquake locations

Definitions of Faults and Landforms

Reverse Faults
Example: The Ox Mountains in Co. Sligo

A reverse fault occurs due to **compression** from destructive plate movement. Pressure causes the rock to fracture and there is an **upward** movement of land between parallel faults. Reverse faulting creates **block mountains.**

Normal Faults
Example: The Rift Valley of Scotland

A normal fault occurs when bedrock is stretched due to tension until it fractures along a fault line. There is a **downward** movement of land between parallel faults. Normal faulting creates **rift valleys.**

Block Mountains (Horst)
Example: The Ox Mountains in Co. Sligo

Block mountains are upland regions that were pushed upward between parallel faults due to compression (bedrock being squashed from two opposite directions).

Rift Valleys (Graben)
Example: The Rift Valley of Scotland

Rift valleys are lowland regions that were dropped down between parallel faults due to tension (bedrock being stretched or pulled apart).

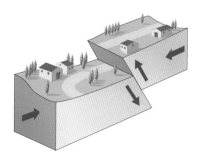

Reverse fault

Normal fault
Fig. 8.10

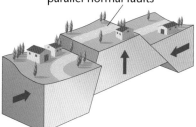

long, narrow block uplifted between parallel normal faults

Block mountain (horst) – compression

Fig. 8.11

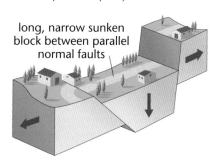

long, narrow sunken block between parallel normal faults

Rift valley (graben) – tension

The Victoria Falls in Zimbabwe are created by a fault line where the African Plate is being split apart. A rift valley has formed.

Activity
Carefully study the Ordnance Survey map of the Derryveagh Mountains in Co. Donegal on page 54, then answer the following.
1. What is the direction, or trend, of the Derryveagh Mountains?
2. Why do these mountain ridges run in this direction?
3. What influence does this trend have on the:
    a. local river pattern   b. local routeways?
4. What processes were responsible for the creation of this mountainous landscape? In your answer, refer to:
    a. internal forces (endogenic)   b. external forces (exogenic).

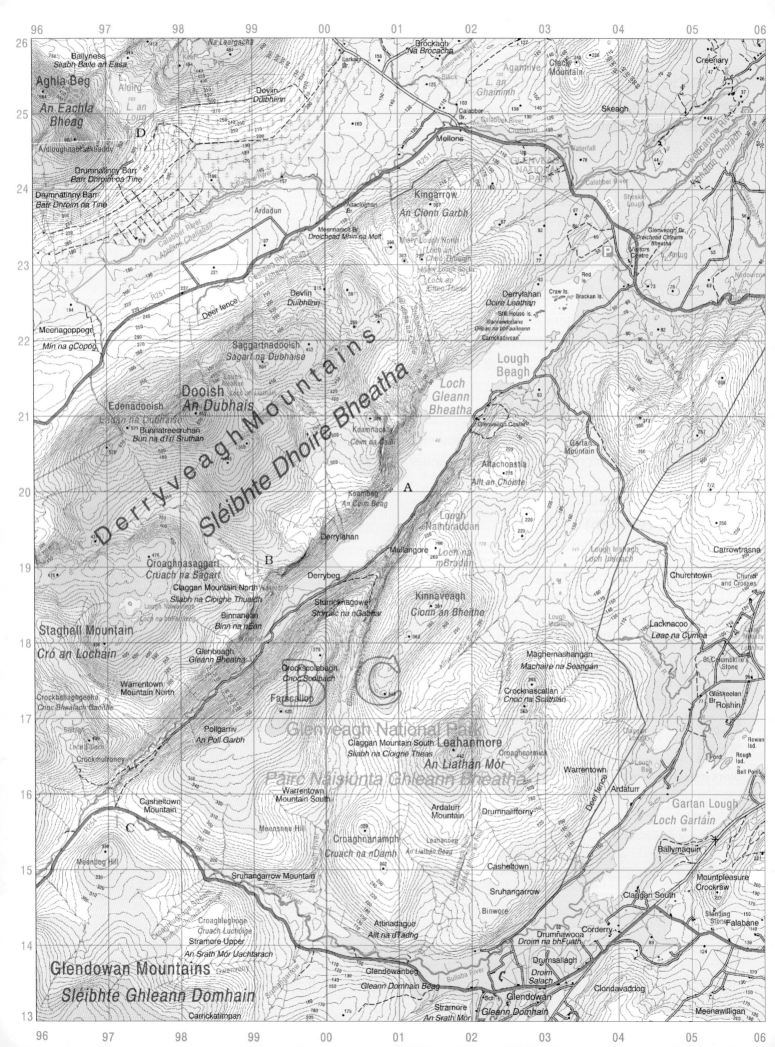

CHAPTER 9
WEATHERING PROCESSES AND LANDFORMS

When rock is placed in a different environment from which it formed originally, it becomes unstable and so is prone to rapid change by the elements of weathering and erosion.

Weathering is the breaking down or decay of rocks that lie on or near the earth's surface. There are two types of weathering: mechanical and chemical.

MECHANICAL WEATHERING

Mechanical weathering involves rocks breaking up into smaller fragments. Mechanical weathering in Ireland is caused by:

- Joint formation, onion weathering and exfoliation.
- Freeze-thaw action.
- Plants and animals.

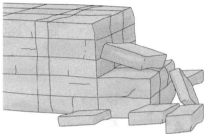

Fig. 9.1 Joints in rock aid the processes of weathering.

Joint Formation (Jointing)

Rock buried deep beneath the ground surface is subjected to enormous confining pressure. This is **weight that squeezes the rock** from all sides. As **erosion** wears away the surface, the weight of the overlying rock and the **pressure is reduced.** This is called **pressure-release,** or **unloading. Joints** then form and these can break rocks into large or small rectangular blocks, or pillar-like columns.

Once formed, the joints act as passageways for rainwater to enter a rock. This increases the rate of further physical and chemical weathering.

Well-jointed granite.

Sheeting of Granite Batholiths

Typically, granite batholiths split into **onion-like sheets** along joints that lie parallel to the surface of the rock. This is due to **unloading** and is called **exfoliation**.

Sheeting of surface granite.

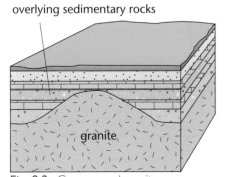

overlying sedimentary rocks

granite

Fig. 9.2a Compressed granite.

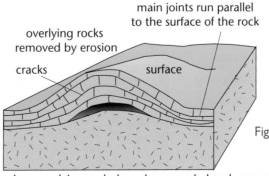

overlying rocks removed by erosion

cracks

surface

main joints run parallel to the surface of the rock

Fig. 9.2b Pressure removed from granite.

when overlying rocks have been eroded and removed, pressure is reduced from the granite and cracks appear

trapped water freezes during winter at night on high mountains

Fig. 9.3 Surface water fills cracks in rock.

ice expands by about 9% and lengthens joints

Fig. 9.4 Freeze-thaw action shatters rock.

Freeze-Thaw Action

Freezing water bursts pipes and shatters bottles because water expands when it freezes and pushes the walls of the container apart. This also happens in rock. When the **water trapped** in a joint freezes, it **forces the joint open** and may cause the joint to lengthen. This is particularly active in temperate climates where water periodically **freezes and thaws**. This process shatters rock. The shattered rock collects at the foot of steep slopes, forming scree.

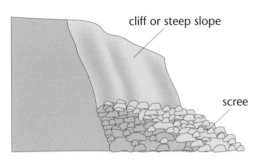

cliff or steep slope

scree

Fig. 9.5 The shattered rock at the foot of steep slopes forms scree.

scree

Joints, Freeze-Thaw and Unloading

Some rocks break up into large rectangular-shaped blocks under the action of mechanical weathering. This is called block disintegration. It may be due partly to frost action and partly to expansion due to unloading and the creation of joints. This increases the surface area that is exposed to weathering.

joints are opened by both frost action and expansion due to unloading

Fig. 9.6 Joints help rock disintegration.

Plant Roots

Seeds germinate in cracks in rock to produce plants. The plant roots then **penetrate into the cracks and crevices** in the rock, **widening these** as they grow larger and causing sections of rock to split apart.

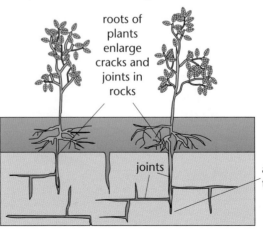

roots of plants enlarge cracks and joints in rocks

joints

Fig. 9.7 Plant roots enlarge joints in bedrock.

as the root grows, the joint is opened up

Surface Flaking

Water solutions containing minerals seep some distance into pores in some rocks like sandstone. The solutions dry out in hot weather and leave minerals behind that form crystals. Over time, this process helps the **crystals** to **grow**. These crystals **push out** neighbouring grains to form flaking at the surface.

Surface flaking has damaged many urban buildings in recent decades.

CHEMICAL WEATHERING

Water and water solutions are the principal agents of chemical weathering. The effects of chemical weathering are greatest where the climate is **hot and wet**.

Most rocks are composed of two or more minerals. Exposure to chemical weathering weakens or breaks these bonds, causing disintegration of the rocks. The most important types of chemical weathering are:

- Carbonation.
- Oxidation.
- Hydration.
- Hydrolysis.

Carbonation

Rainwater falling through the air joins with small amounts of carbon dioxide to form a weak **carbonic acid**. As it reaches and trickles through limestone joints and bedding planes, it weathers the limestone. Weathering changes the calcium carbonate mineral that forms limestone into **calcium** and **bicarbonate minerals**. These are **soluble in water,** so they are carried away in solution.

Oxidation

This is simply the **rusting** of some minerals. Minerals, such as iron, become oxides in the presence of oxygen. This creates a **red** or **yellowish colouring** that is carried away by groundwater. When the mineral dries it becomes a cementing agent (a new mineral) in sedimentary rocks, such as sandstone. **Iron oxide** (haematite and magnetite) discoloured the quartz grains of sandstone to a brownish or reddish colour to form Old Red Sandstone.

Carbonation has increased and damaged many important monuments and buildings in recent decades.

Hydration

Some minerals **absorb water**. When they do, they expand. If a rock contains these kinds of mineral, the wet, expanding minerals **create stresses** within the rock and over time shatter the rock. 'Tiny' **freeze-thaw** within wet minerals also helps shatter rock particles, leading to them breaking up.

Hydrolysis

This is the most important chemical process in the break-up of rock. It involves a chemical reaction between some rock minerals and water.

In granite, for example, it joins with **feldspar** minerals to form **clay** minerals. But as the feldspar minerals were the **cement** that held the other minerals (the micas and quartz) together, the rock crumbles.

Iron oxide tinted sandstone a reddish or yellow colour.

DISTINCTIVE LANDSCAPES AND LANDFORMS

KEY IDEA! When some rock types are weathered, they produce distinctive landscapes.

Granite tors on Dartmoor create a distinctive landscape.

Granite Landscapes

Granite rises to the surface when **overlying rock is removed** by weathering and erosion in fold mountain regions. The pressure of surrounding rock is no longer present and this **loss of weight** allows the granite to **expand**. This creates cracks, or **joints**, in the granite. Joints are enlarged through chemical weathering and this causes **the edges** of the blocks to **become rounded**. These rounded blocks of granite separated by joints are called **tors**.

Weathered granite forms gently sloping uplands. This combination of **gently sloping uplands** of fields for cattle and sheep grazing, **with tors on top,** creates a distinctive landscape. **Dartmoor,** in south-west England, has a distinctive granite landscape. The **Wicklow Mountains** have some tors on their summits (see **Mechanical Weathering and Chemical Weathering,** pages 55–7).

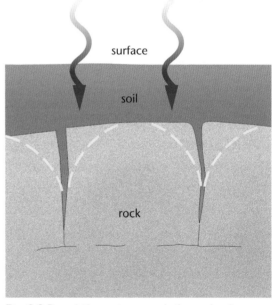

Fig. 9.8 Percolating water rounds the rock edges.

Quartzite Landscapes

Examples: The Great Sugar Loaf in Co. Wicklow
Croagh Patrick in Co. Mayo

Quartzite is found **near granite regions**. Unlike granite, quartzite is very resistant to chemical weathering, but it is **prone to frost action**. This **freeze-thaw** action breaks off long, angular slabs of the quartzite. This process creates the distinctive **pointed peaks** in quartzite regions.

Quartzite resists erosion and forms pointed peaks like Croagh Patrick in Mayo.

CHAPTER 10
DISTINCTIVE LIMESTONE LANDSCAPES AND LANDFORMS

The distinctive landscape and landforms of limestone regions are directly influenced by the mineral composition of the limestone rock.

The Burren, Co. Clare

Karst is a term used worldwide to describe the distinctive landforms that develop on limestone rock that is easily dissolved by water. Some Irish karst regions include the following:

Fig. 10.1 The Burren in Co. Clare.

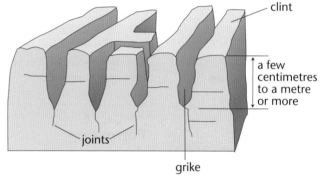

Limestone Pavement

Irish examples: Near Black Head in the Burren, Co. Clare
Marble Arch Uplands in Co. Fermanagh

Formation

Limestone pavement forms in regions of medium to heavy rainfall with a warm to temperate climate. It also forms because limestone:

- Is composed of one mineral, calcium carbonate. This creates **even weathering** of the rock surface, so forming level land.
- Reacts with rainwater, so dissolving the rock.
- Has regular joints caused by unloading of overlying rock through erosion.
- Is pervious, which means rainwater is able to pass freely through its vertical joints and horizontal bedding planes.

Rainwater is a weak acid, called **carbonic acid**. This acid forms as rain falls through the air and absorbs **carbon dioxide**. When the rainwater lands on bare limestone rock, it creates a chemical reaction. The hydrogen in the carbonic acid separates the calcium carbonate of the limestone rock into separate **calcium and bicarbonate atoms,** which are both soluble in the groundwater. In this way the limestone is dissolved and removed, so the rock is worn away.

Limestone pavement in the Burren.

The parallel **vertical joints** in the limestone allow the water to trickle through the rock. These cracks are widened and deepened through solution. These widened cracks are called **grikes.** The wider the **grikes** become, the faster the water is able to sink through the limestone. In the **Burren** these grikes mostly run in a **north-south** direction.

The parallel grikes create **flat ridges of rock** between them, called **clints.** This combination of grikes and clints form a distinctive level surface that is only found in limestone regions.

Limestone reacts with rainwater somewhat like the way soluble aspirin does when it is put in a glass of water.

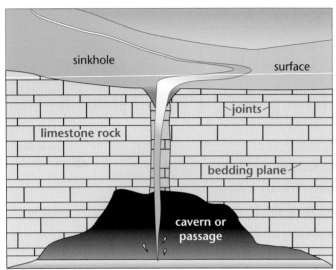

sinkhole • surface

limestone rock • joints

bedding plane

cavern or passage

Fig. 10.2 Limestone pavement in the Burren.

Sinkholes

Example: Poulnabunny in Co. Mayo
The Cradle Hole in the Cuilcagh Uplands

A sinkhole is an opening in the bed of a river through which a river disappears underground in a limestone region. It is also called a swallow hole, a slugga or a sink.

Sinkholes may form at the surface where the roofs of underground caverns collapse, such as at Winter Garden in Florida, USA.

Formation

Rainwater is a weak acid, called **carbonic acid**. This forms as rain falls through the air and absorbs **carbon dioxide**. When the rainwater lands on bare limestone rock, it creates a chemical reaction. The hydrogen in the carbonic acid separates the calcium carbonate of the limestone rock into separate **calcium** and **bicarbonate atoms,** which are both soluble in the groundwater. In this way the limestone is dissolved and removed, so the rock is worn away.

As rivers flow across limestone regions, some of the rainwater trickles down through the joints and bedding planes on the riverbed. The joints and bedding planes are widened, also allowing more **surface water and any sediment** that the flowing water is carrying to go underground.

Underground, the flowing **groundwater dissolves** the limestone and the **sediment erodes** the rock through abrasion along these lines of weakness. These processes create underground **passages** that originate under the riverbed.

The joints and bedding planes divide limestone into blocks. These blocks become unstable where the rock beneath has been eroded. Where some **blocks fall** from the ceiling of the passages, this eventually leads to a collapse of the rock on the riverbed. This creates **an opening from the surface to the underground passage,** through which the river plunges vertically downwards.

The opening that swallows up the river is called a sinkhole. The remaining river valley downstream of the sinkhole becomes dry and so is called a **dry valley**. If the river floods, the underground passage may be unable to carry all of the river's volume. In this case, some water will pass through the dry valley again and temporarily occupy its original channel.

The opposite of a sinkhole is a **resurgence**. At a resurgence, a river appears from underground. It is not a spring; it is the location where a river that had gone underground at some upstream location **reappears on the surface**.

A **turlough** is a seasonal lake. It appears during long, wet spells when underground passages fill up. It dries out when the water table falls.

60

Caverns

Example: Marble Arch Cave in Co. Fermanagh
Mammoth Cave in Kentucky, USA

A cavern is a subsurface landform.

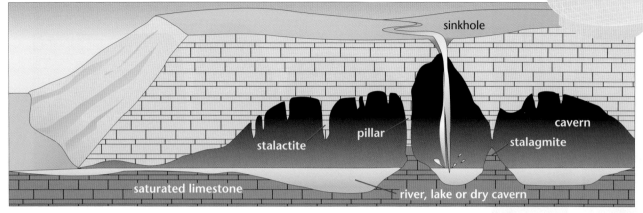

Fig. 10.3
A sinkhole.

Labels in figure: sinkhole, pillar, cavern, stalactite, stalagmite, saturated limestone, river, lake or dry cavern

Formation

The formation of most caverns takes place in the **zone of saturation**, at or below the water table in limestone regions. Some caverns, such as Marble Arch Caves, were formed by flowing water that came from the surface rivers.

When rain falls on the ground, it trickles through the soil and bedrock until it meets an **impermeable rock layer**. It cannot go down, so its level rises and it saturates the porous, or pervious, rock above so that all pore spaces between the rock grains and joints and bedding planes are filled with water.

This underground water is not stationary, as it constantly **seeps and flows through the bedrock**. This water is acidic because it dissolved carbon dioxide from the air and from organic matter as it trickled down through the soil. It is **carbonic acid** and it creates a chemical reaction with limestone. The hydrogen in the carbonic acid separates the calcium carbonate of the limestone rock into separate **calcium and bicarbonate atoms, which are both soluble in groundwater**. In this way the limestone is dissolved and removed, so the rock is worn away.

This process creates huge cavities that become enlarged by other processes over time. **Sediment** in flowing groundwater erodes the rock by **abrasion**. **Collapsing** limestone **blocks** from small cavern ceilings increase the height of the caverns.

Meltwater from melting ice sheets and glaciers at the end of the last Ice Age increased the flow of water through some underground passages and caverns. This vast release of meltwater carried sand, rocks and boulders into these underground channels through sinkholes and enlarged the channels into enormous caverns.

Many of these caverns are dry due to a fall in the water table or tectonic uplift.

Mammoth Cave in Kentucky is world famous.
● *What features can you identify in this cavern?*

Stalactites and stalagmites sometimes join to form pillars or columns.

Speleothems or Dripstone Formations

Examples: Marble Arch Caves in Co. Fermanagh

Mitchelstown Caves in Co. Tipperary

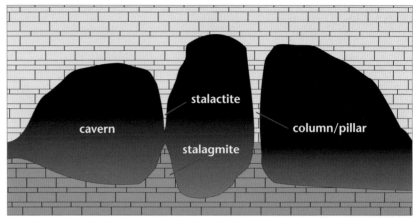

Fig. 10.4 A cavern.

Formation

Speleothems, or dripstone formations, include **stalactites, stalagmites, pillars or columns, and curtains.** They are all formed of the mineral **calcite**. Calcite is calcium carbonate and in its purest form it is white.

These landforms develop in caverns that are dry or partially dry due to a lowering of the water table by a stream or tectonic uplift. The drop in the water table exposes the underground chambers to the air, which in turn plays its part in the formation of the calcite landforms.

The calcite landforms form by the continuous deposition of calcite, where water drips from cavern ceilings. Some form on the ceiling, while stalagmites develop on the sides or floor of caverns. Groundwater in limestone regions is saturated in dissolved **calcium atoms** and **bicarbonate atoms**. It is also **supersaturated in carbon dioxide**. When the water that trickles down through vertical cracks reaches the cavern ceiling, the carbon dioxide escapes into the air and it **reverses the solution process**. Calcite is deposited where the water drops from the ceiling.

Initially, calcite builds around the outside of the drip, forming a delicate, hollow stalactite, called a **soda straw**. Eventually the hollow **fills up** or **gets blocked** with grit, and water seeps around the hanging stem to form a more massive solid **stalactite**.

Where the drip hits the floor, it splashes, and the resulting calcite builds up to form an upward-pointing cone, called a **stalagmite.** If this process continues over a very long time, the stalagmites and stalactites join to form limestone **columns, or pillars.**

If this process occurs along a crack in the ceiling, it builds a vertical **curtain-like** sheet of calcite that hangs from the cavern roof.

If the groundwater flows along the surface of a wall, it drapes the wall with **cloth-like** sheets of calcite called **flowstone**. Thin sheets of flowstone tend to be translucent when lit from behind.

Limestone caves are great tourist attractions. Can you name some?

Tower Karst Landscape

This dramatic landscape has inspired many Chinese artists and photographers.

Formation

Example: Guangxi, in south-west China, and north-east Vietnam

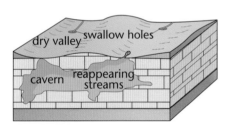

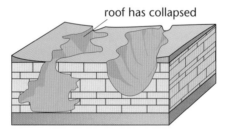
roof has collapsed

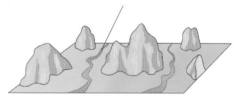
surface drainage returns as underground passages are filled with sediment

Fig. 10.5 Tower karst.

Tower karst consists of **isolated tower-like hills** separated by **flat areas of alluvium**. It represents the **late stage** of weathering of a limestone landscape.

- In the **early stage of karst formation**, weathering and erosion dissolve and erode away the surface limestone. **Joints and bedding planes** are widened, creating a limestone pavement of **grikes and clints**. Streams disappear through sinkholes into underground passages and caverns.
- The **middle stage** involves the **collapse of cavern and passage roofs,** creating large depressions, called **poljes**, surrounded by higher ground, as in the Burren in Co. Clare.
- In the **late stage** there is **large-scale collapse** of the underground landforms. This creates tower-like hills of limestone throughout the landscape. Sediment builds up in sinkholes and blocks underground drainage. **Surface rivers flow** once more, creating **flat floodplains of alluvial** soils between the towers.

In an exam, include the process of the chemical weathering of limestone as part of your answer. (See page 57.)

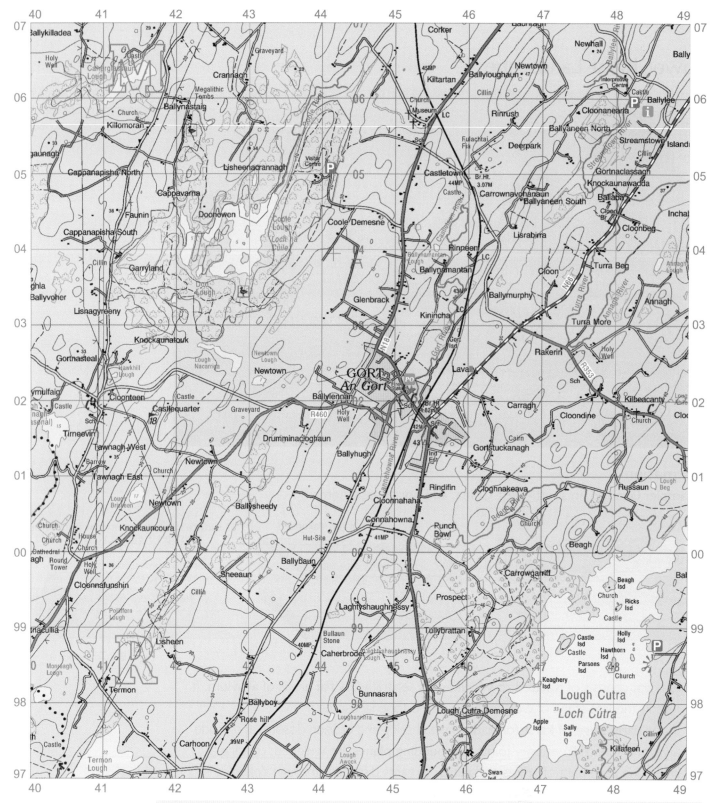

Activity

1. In which direction does the Beagh River flow?

2. Explain what happens to this river at the Punch Bowl at grid reference M 458 003.

3. Name and identify the type of lake at grid reference M 40 01. Explain.

4. Describe the course of the Gort River. Explain why the river ends at the town.

5. In which direction is the Coole River flowing? Explain fully.

6. There is a visitors centre at Coole Demesne, grid reference M 439 049. Explain the purpose of this centre. Explain your answer, using evidence from the map only.

7. From your rock and landform studies so far, classify this type of landscape. Use evidence from the map to explain your answer.

8. Is the landform at grid reference M 475 062 a sinkhole or a resurgence (see page 60)? Explain.

CHAPTER 11
MASS MOVEMENT, PROCESSES AND LANDFORMS

KEY IDEA! Mass movement describes all downhill movements of material (regolith), including soil, loose stones and rocks, in response to gravity. It excludes movements where the material is carried by water, ice or wind. The result of this movement is called mass wasting.

Although by definition mass movement does not include water, in reality, water is usually present and assists downhill movement. **Speed of movement and the amount of moisture present** are used as a basis to distinguish between the various types of mass movement.

Some mass movements are slow – almost impossible to notice – and continue over a long time. Others, usually on a large scale, act suddenly, rapidly and sometimes catastrophically. Some are caused by the results of weathering, others by erosion. Some rapid movements may be due to the influence of people's activity.

Factors that Influence Mass Movements
Angle of Slope (Gradient)
The steeper the slope, the faster and more likely that movement will occur.

Material
Loose material, rather than compacted or bonded material, is more prone to movement.

Water Content
The greater the water content, the greater the likelihood of movement. Porous bedrock and low rainfall reduce the risk of high water content at the surface.

Vegetation Cover
Roots bind surface soil particles and so help to reduce movement, but bare regolith (bedrock) on gentle or steep slopes is prone to movement.

Tectonic Activity
Earthquake tremors and volcanic eruptions create many types of mass movements.

People's Activities
Road or trench construction as well as farming practices can lead to mass movements.

Study all the processes and landforms in chapters 11 to 14. Learn in detail the formation of landforms from ONE of these chapters.

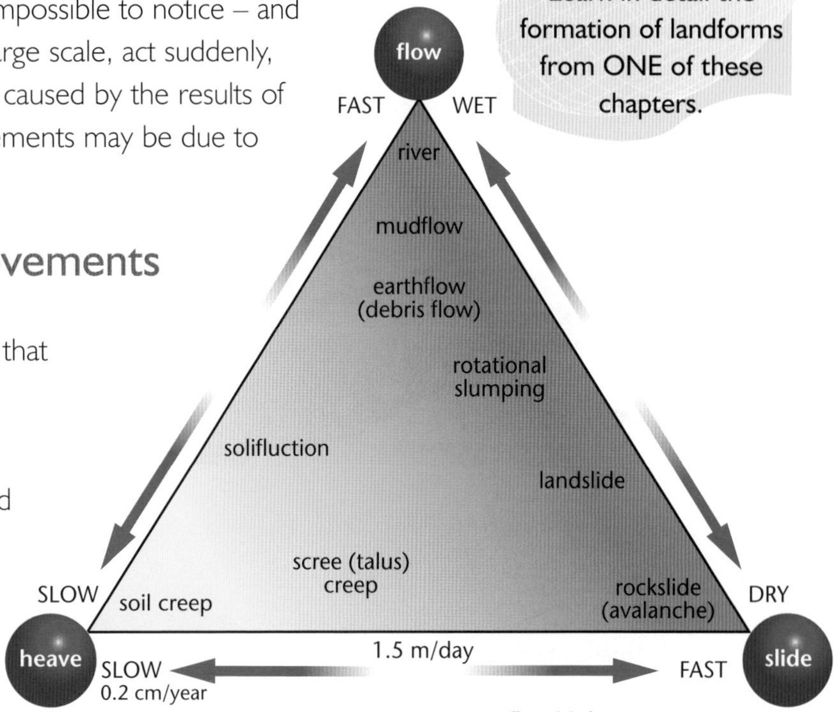

flow

FAST   WET

river

mudflow

earthflow (debris flow)

rotational slumping

solifluction

landslide

scree (talus) creep

rockslide (avalanche)

SLOW   soil creep

DRY

heave

SLOW
0.2 cm/year

1.5 m/day

FAST

slide

Fig. 11.1

Activity
Use Fig. 11.1 to identify the following types of mass movement:
a. fast and wet
b. fast and dry
c. fast and moist
d. slow and moist
e. very slow.

TYPE AND SPEEDS OF MASS MOVEMENTS

Fig. 11.2

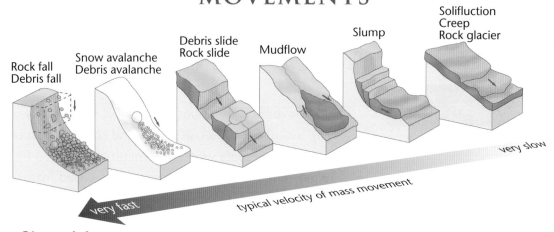

Slow Movements

Soil Creep

Examples: Steep slopes in Ireland

Solifluction on slopes in Alaska, USA

Soil creep is the slowest type of mass movement. We cannot see it happening, but we can see the effects of it on the landscape, especially on steep slopes.

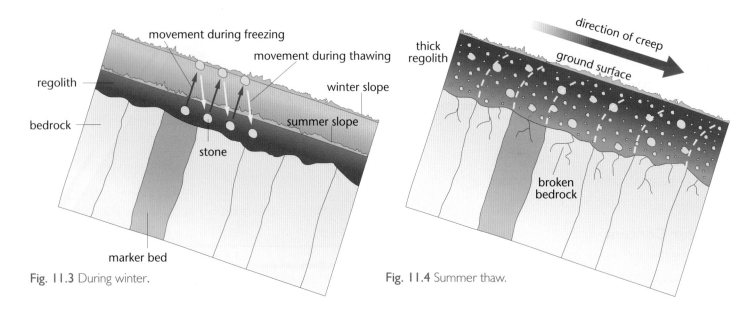

Fig. 11.3 During winter.

Fig. 11.4 Summer thaw.

Temperate Climates

Regions like Ireland have moist, cool winters. The upper few centimetres of ground freeze during very cold spells in winter, only to thaw again some days later. Because water expands by about 9 per cent when it freezes, the water-saturated soil and underlying fractured rock expand outward. Particles in the regolith **are pushed out at right angles to the slope**.

When the soil **thaws**, regolith ice changes back to water, and gravity makes the **particles sink vertically** and migrate downslope slightly. This gradual movement of regolith downslope is called creep. It creates a ribbed or stepped pattern that develops across the slope, called **terracettes**. The rate of movement is less than 1 cm per year.

Terracettes on the Galtees.

Solifluction flows in Alaska.

Arctic or High Mountain Climate

At high latitudes or in high mountains, **regolith freezes solid to a great depth** during the winter. During the short summer, only the uppermost 1 to 3 m of the ground thaws. Because the lower ground remains frozen (it is called the **permafrost layer**), the meltwater cannot seep downwards, and the uppermost, thawed **regolith** becomes **soggy** and weak and flows slowly downslope in **overlapping, tongue-like sheets**. This is called **solifluction**.

As well as adding to the weight of the material, water also causes some soil particles to swell. This swelling causes nearby particles to move and it lubricates the soil, making it more likely to move downslope.

Solifluction is slightly faster than creep and averages movement of between 5 cm and 1 m per year.

Slumping

Example: Slumps at Garron Point in Co. Antrim

A slump is a type of slide that occurs when blocks of rock that are intact or loose debris slide downwards **along curved planes** in response to **gravity.** The blocks tend to tilt backwards during the slump, so that rotation as well as downward movement take place.

Slumps generally occur on:

- Hills thickly covered with soil.
- Steep coastal cliffs made of loose or poorly cemented materials.
- River banks of incised meanders.

This happens because the forces that bind particles of soil together fail, causing a slump. This is called **shear failure**. As in all mass movement, slumps are most common on slopes that are over-steepened, water-saturated and undercut by rivers, ice, waves or human activities.

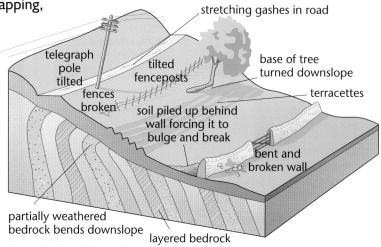

Fig. 11.5 The effects of soil creep.

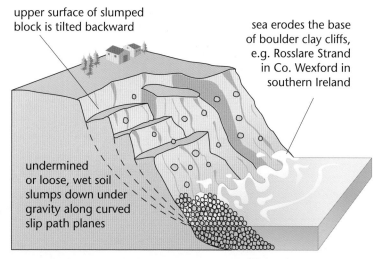

Fig. 11.6 The effect of slumping.

Case Study: Rotational Slumping on the Antrim Coast

The Glenariff Valley is a spectacular example of a glaciated U-shaped valley. The steep sides and its U-shape were created by the erosive action of a glacier. The valley floor is formed of soft mudstone, while the valley sides are made of chalk at the base, with basalt on top. Nearby at Garron Point, the same glaciers removed some of the mudstone and undermined the chalk. Consequently, when the ice melted, the **chalk and basalt cliffs** here slumped as large blocks shifted in a curved movement called rotational slumping.

In other places, the sea has undermined coastal cliffs, creating landslides and rock falls along the coast.

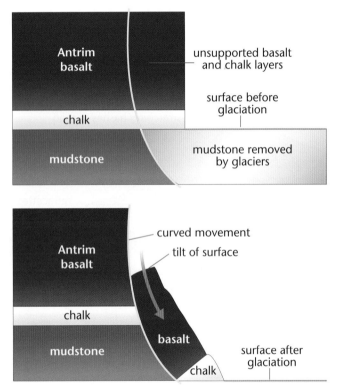

Fig. 11.7 Slumping at Garron Point.

Sloping cliffs due to slumping at Garron Point, Co. Antrim.

Slumping is also common on unconsolidated coastal cliffs. Expensive homes along the coast at **Malibu**, a region of steep coastal cliffs near Los Angeles **in southern California,** have been lost due to the collapse of unstable sediments. Here, slumping was caused by **earthquakes**. Slumping regularly occurs here because the San Andreas Fault is close by.

Slumping occurs regularly along the California coast near Malibu Beach due to erosion by the sea or earthquakes.

Bog Bursts
Example: Derrybrien in Co. Galway

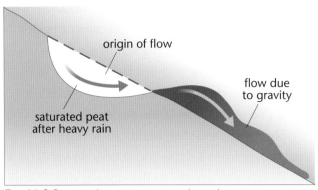

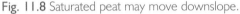

Fig. 11.8 Saturated peat may move downslope.

Bog bursts occur in upland regions of blanket bog.

A bog burst is a type of earthflow. Earthflows occur **on sloping ground** in regions of heavy rainfall where rock is deeply weathered. These deep soils become mobile when saturated with water and may suddenly slip downslope in response to **gravity.** This action leaves a curved-shaped scar where the slip begins and a bulge at the base of the slope.

The peat in bogs contains **95 per cent water** and **5 per cent solids,** so even in its normal state it may become unstable on steep slopes. This risk increases after periods of heavy rain. Some bog bursts may move slowly. Others that are completely saturated with water may move quickly. A slope of 4 degrees is sufficient for a burst to take place, but it may occur on a slope of as little as 2 degrees.

Whether the bedrock under the peat is **permeable or impermeable** will also affect the likelihood of flow. Impermeable bedrock will not soak up water, and the bog surface becomes saturated easily and quickly. The **quality and amount of vegetation** on the bog surface also has an important bearing on the eventual outcome. Roots from heathers, plants such as rhododendron and trees such as birch or pines help to prevent downslope movement of bog material.

Periods of very **heavy rain followed by** unseasonably long spells of **hot, dry weather** create the most risk of bog burst. During hot, dry spells, the intricate root system of the upper layer of bog, which under normal conditions acts as an anchor for the bog, starts to shrink and die back. With nothing left to anchor the bog, the peat mass may flow downslope.

- **Human activity** on the bog surface may also encourage a burst. Industrialised **peat harvesting, sheep grazing** and the removal of peat from hilltops for **wind farm construction** also encourage flow. This flow may take the form of a slow-moving mass or a free-flowing avalanche of soil that can often resemble a lava flow by the sheer force of its movement.

- Recent bog bursts include one at **Derrybrien**, in the Slieve Aughty Mountains, in Co. Galway in 2003. A bog burst in **Doon** in east Limerick in 1708 killed three families, twenty-one people in total. Their three dwellings were destroyed by a burst that was 7 m deep, 1.5 km long and 1 km wide. The bog burst travelled several kilometres, crossed several roads and demolished many bridges.

Gravity and saturation of peat causes a bog burst.

Peat contains 95 per cent water and 5 per cent solids.

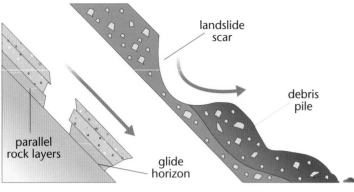

Fig. 11.9a Rock slide.   Fig. 11.9b Landslide.

Landslides

Geologists refer to a sudden movement of rock and debris down a non-vertical slope as a landslide. If the mass consists only of rock, it is called a **rock slide**. If it consists only of regolith, it is called a **debris slide**. Once a landslide has occurred, it leaves a **landslide scar** on the slope and forms a **debris pile** at the base of the slope.

Slides happen when bedrock, or regolith, breaks away from a slope and shoots downhill on a **glide horizon** (slope angle) roughly parallel to the slope surface. Slides may move at speeds up to 300 km an hour. They are particularly fast when a cushion of air gets trapped beneath the moving mass. In this case, there is hardly any contact between the moving mass and the ground surface, so the mass moves something like a hovercraft. Sometimes rock and debris slides move so fast they have sufficient energy to climb the opposite side of the valley.

Rock slides occur due to gravity on slopes where bedding planes of rock layers that lie parallel to the surface are undercut or become too heavy. The rock mass moves downslope when the weight of the surface layers is too great for the slope to support.

Landslides occur on a variety of scales. Most are small, involving blocks up to a few metres across. Some, however, are large enough to be catastrophic. **Earthquakes** in mountain regions cause **landslides**. Many such slides occurred in **Kashmir** in Pakistan in **2005** when an earthquake shook this region. They restricted access for getting emergency relief to the wounded and isolated communities in the mountainous region in the Himalayas.

A landslide in Taiwan devestated the village of Wu Feng.

Case Study: Vaiont Dam Disaster, Italy

The **Vaiont Dam** was **built** in the **Italian Alps in the 1960s**. It **rose 260 m** above the valley floor, with a concrete wall as high as an **85-storey building** forming a large reservoir above the dam. The slopes of the reservoir lake were formed of **dipping limestone and shale layers** that lay parallel to the valley side and curved under the reservoir lake.

As the reservoir lake filled, the rock cracked, shook and rumbled. Several days of rain then added to the weight of rock on the slope. The mountain shook, but no one ordered the evacuation of the town of **Longarone** that was in the valley below the dam. That same day, 600 million tonnes of rock broke from the valley side and slid down into the reservoir. The displaced water poured over the dam, rushed down the valley and wiped out the town and its 1,500 inhabitants.

Destruction in the town of Longarone.

Lahars and Mudflows

Examples: Lahar: Armero in Colombia

Mudflow: Sarno, near Naples in Italy

Mudflows

Mudflows occur when **deep soils become saturated with water** and move due to **gravity.** Soil particles expand rapidly and are separated by water molecules. **Grain-to-grain contact is lost,** and the saturated layer turns to slurry, which flows downhill. The steeper the slope and the greater the water and soil content, the greater the speed of the flow.

Gravity plays a major role in mudflows. Hot regions that often have **prolonged torrential downpours** are particularly prone to mudflows. In southern Italy, for example, the slopes of the Apennines are steep and have deep volcanic soils in some places. Vegetation is scarce because the original forest cover of pines has been cut down for farming activity. Grasses are scarce, and some surfaces have little vegetation cover. A lot of unrestricted construction has also disturbed the surface in places where buildings should not have been constructed.

A mudflow may cause great loss of life and destruction in built-up areas far from its origin.

- In 1998, at **Sarno near Naples**, forty-eight hours of torrential rain created mudflows on local hillsides. Rivers of mud burst into the town centre, tearing apart houses and bridges, covering people and cars, while other inhabitants were sent running for their lives. Over 100 people died. This region has experienced over 630 landslides over the past seventy years.

Lahars

Lahars are **mudflows caused by volcanic eruptions**. Many volcanic cones are so high that they are **permanently capped with snow**. The most dangerous lahars occur on volcanic cones in fold mountain regions that have been dormant for a long time. Over the years, great depths of snow and ice accumulate on the slopes of these cones. Their slopes are also composed of loose **ash and pyroclastic layers.**

When eruptions occur in these volcanoes, vast quantities of **hot ash** are **ejected** from the crater because the magma is **viscous** (thick). Viscous lava traps expanding gases. The hot ash lands on the surrounding ice fields and instantly melts the ice and snow. The vast quantities of water released rush downslope, gathering ash and pyroclasts as they go. This creates liquid mud that moves through the valleys at the base of the mountain, carrying along rocks, trees, houses and everything else it can root up on its journey.

- On 13 November 1985, a lahar descended the 5,400 m slope of **Nevado del Ruiz** in Colombia, in South America. It reached the town of **Armero**, which was 48 km from the summit, and approximately **20,000 residents** were buried alive in the mud. This disaster should never have happened. Soil studies later showed that many lahars had occurred there before in the distant past. Today, the authorities prevent people from building on that part of the valley.

- *Identify this type of mass movement.*

71

Multi-part Questions

1. Examine Fig. 11.10, which classifies mass movement, and answer the following questions.

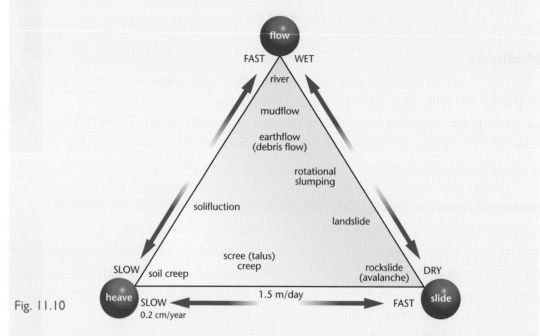

Fig. 11.10

A. Identify **one** type of fast and **one** type of slow mass movement. In each case, name one Irish region where it occurs or occurred. [20 marks]

B. With reference to examples that you have studied, fully explain **one** example of slow and **one** example of fast mass movements. [30 marks]

C. Examine **two** ways in which human activities can accelerate mass movements. [30 marks]

2. Soluble limestone or karst regions, such as the Burren, contain a great variety of landscape features, both over and under the surface.

A. Name any **three** of these features and in each case name an Irish example. [20 marks]

B. For **two** of the features named above, describe and explain how they were formed. [30 marks]

C. The Burren is Ireland's best-known soluble limestone region. Briefly explain its importance, referring to each of the following:
   i. heritage
   ii. tourism. [30 marks]

3. Limestone pavements, Swallow holes, Limestone caves, Dry valleys.

A. Limestone caves have interesting geographical features. Name any **four** features and identify the processes that formed them. [20 marks]

B. Select **two** of the above features and, using a diagram, describe how they were formed. [20 marks]

C. 'Weathering can be caused by physical **or** chemical action.' Explain this statemet, using one physical and one chemical process in detail. [30 marks]

4. As a result of pressure from tourism, karst regions have vulnerable environments.

A. Examine **one** example of this vulnerability. [20 marks]

B. 'The processes of weathering, together with gravity, are important factors in shaping landscapes.' Explain this statement, referring to **two** weathering processes. [30 marks]

C. Examine how human activities can accelerate or intensify any **one** of the weathering processes referred to above. [30 marks]

CHAPTER 12
GLACIAL PROCESSES, PATTERNS AND LANDFORMS

 **Landforms are created by glacial processes.**

During the last Ice Age that **began about 2 million years ago** and **ended about 10,000 years ago**, highland and lowland areas were covered by a layer of ice thousands of metres thick. Only some high mountain peaks, called **nunataks**, were exposed and subjected to severe frost action, so they became pointed. They are called pyramidal peaks. While ice increased in thickness in mountain areas, some ice moved down river valleys to form rivers of ice, called **glaciers**. When the glaciers reached the lowland, they joined to form **ice sheets** that completely blanketed the land.

Glaciers still exist today in Iceland, the Alps, the Rockies, the Andes and the Himalayas. By studying these glaciers and ice sheets, we can understand the various processes of ice action and how they created landforms of erosion and deposition.

Snowflakes are crystals of moisture. When they gather on the ground, they do not fit well together and so this snow contains about 90 per cent air and has a white colour. As snowflakes become buried, they are squeezed and change into grains of ice that fit together better. Only 25 per cent air remains trapped between the grains. This ice is called **firn**. With a little more pressure, it contains only about 20 per cent air trapped as air bubbles. This ice has a **bluish colour** and is called **glacier ice**.

The Matterhorn in Switzerland is a pyramidal peak that formed due to frost wedging (freeze-thaw action).

PROCESSES OF ICE ACTION
Processes of Ice Movement

Ice moves for one or a number of the following reasons.

Gravity

Ice moves downslope in response to gravity. The steeper the slope, the greater the pull of gravity and the faster the movement.

Basal Sliding

Meltwater exists at the base of some glaciers, and some sediment particles are also present. Together, these form a type of slush that the glacier slides on to move downslope.

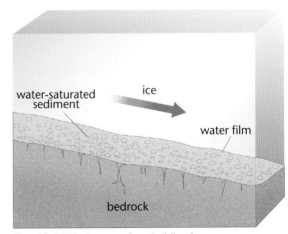

Fig. 12.1 Wet bottom (basal slidings).

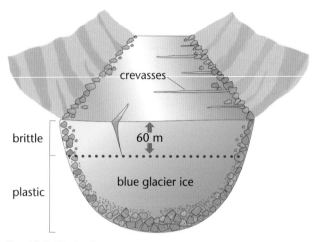

Fig. 12.2 Glacier ice.

Internal Flow

Below a depth of about 60 m, ice acts like plastic. It can **bend and twist** without cracking (a process called fracturing). Crystals of glacier ice **alternately melt and refreeze** to squeeze their way through valleys or around obstacles as the glacier moves along. The top 60 m of ice is brittle and cracks, forming deep chasms called **crevasses**.

The centre of a glacier moves about five times faster than its edges, and the top of a glacier moves faster than its base. Glaciers move at average speeds of tens of metres to hundreds of metres a year.

Plucking

The water slick between the bedrock and the ice regularly freezes. This causes freeze-thaw action in the bedrock surface. Once the ice starts to move, it **plucks** the loosened chunks of rock from the ground and carries them downslope. This process is especially effective where the rock is already jointed or faulted.

Abrasion

The plucked rocks become part of the base and sides of the glacier. As the glaciers or ice sheets move, these rocks **scour, polish and scrape** the surface over which they pass (much as rough sandpaper acts on wood), leaving deep grooves and scratches called **striations** on the rock landscape.

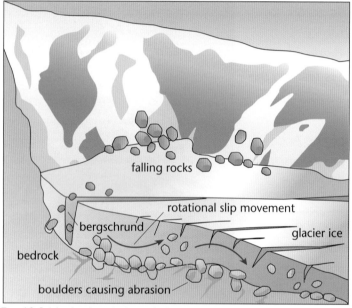

Fig. 12.3 Moving ice plucks and abrades the bedrock.

Other Factors

The amount of plucking and abrasion often depends on other factors.

- **The weight of ice:** Erosion increases with the weight of the overlying ice. Glaciers were often over 600 m thick in Ireland during the Ice Age.
- **The hardness of rock:** The softer the rock, the greater the amount of erosion and the more rounded the upland peaks. Evidence of rounded hilltops and mountaintops may be seen in the uplands of southern Ireland, such as the Slieve Felim Mountains in Co. Tipperary.

A glacier is a river of ice in a mountain valley.

Zones of Accumulation and Ablation

Ice gathers in high regions. This is the **zone of accumulation**. Ice melts in the zone of **ablation**. The **process of calving** occurs in the zone of ablation when large blocks of ice break off the edge of a glacier or ice sheet.

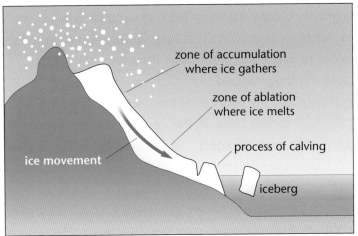

Fig. 12.4 The process of calving.

Calving occurs where blocks of ice break off glaciers and ice sheets.

SOME LANDFORMS OF GLACIAL EROSION

Landform: Cirque

Example: Devil's Punch Bowl in the Macgillicuddy's Reeks

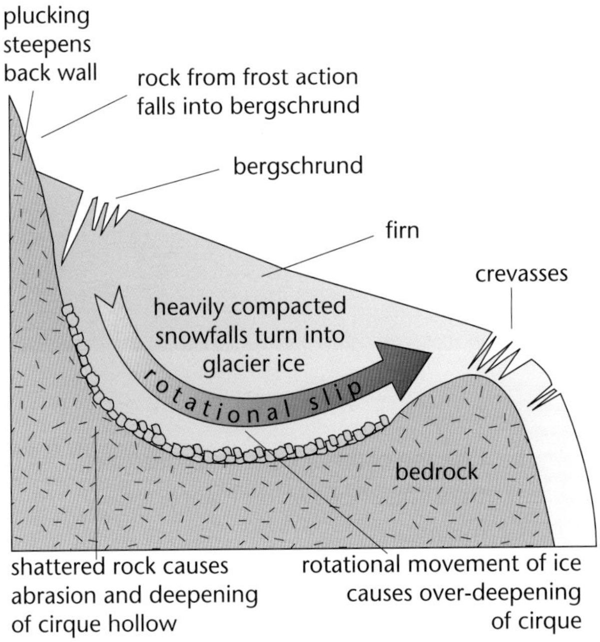

You must include the processes when you are writing out your landform feature.

plucking steepens back wall

rock from frost action falls into bergschrund

bergschrund

firn

heavily compacted snowfalls turn into glacier ice

rotational slip

crevasses

bedrock

shattered rock causes abrasion and deepening of cirque hollow

rotational movement of ice causes over-deepening of cirque

Fig. 12.5

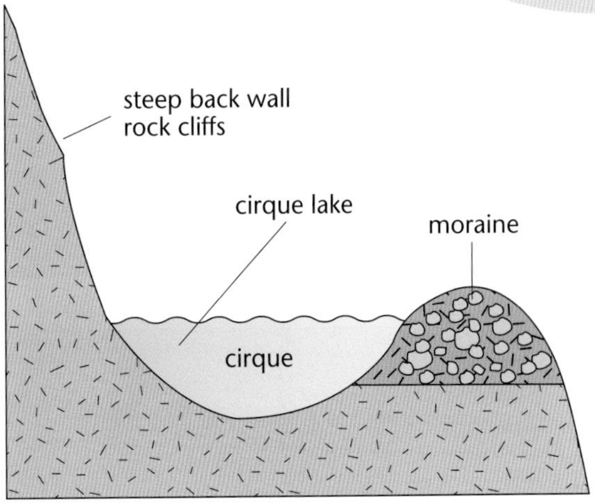

steep back wall rock cliffs

cirque lake

moraine

cirque

Fig. 12.6 Cirques are regularly found on north-facing slopes.

Formation

Cirques began as slight hollows in mountain areas in the **zone of accumulation,** where snow gathered to form an **ice field**. Each snowfall added more weight so that the bottom snowflakes were squeezed to become **firn ice**. Great depths of ice built up until the hollow overflowed and ice began to move downslope.

This downslope pull due to **gravity** caused the ice in the hollow to **slide** in a process called **rotational slip** that lasted throughout the Ice Age. Gravity also caused the **ice** at the upslope side of the hollow **to crack** and break away from the rock surface. This created a deep **crevasse** called the **bergschrund**.

Meltwater seeped between the ice and the bedrock in the hollow. This water regularly froze, which shattered the rock surface beneath the ice. As the rock moved due to rotational slip, it **plucked** out large **rock boulders** and **abraded** the bedrock, thus **deepening** the hollow to form rock basins over time.

These basins are **amphitheatre-shaped** with three steep sides, and sometimes **vertical rock walls** on all sides except the one facing down the valley. Cirques are more common on **north-facing** and north-east-facing slopes.

At the end of the Ice Age many of these rock basins filled with water to form cirque lakes. These cirques are also called **corries, cooms, cums** and **tarns**.

Lakes with names beginning with 'coum' or 'coom' are cirque lakes.

Cirques are surrounded by cliff-like slopes on three sides.

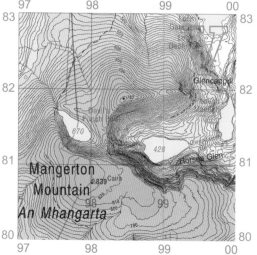

Activity

1. Use the contour pattern to describe the cirque hollows on Mangerton mountain.
2. Identify the glacial landform at grid reference V983 812.

Landform: U-Shaped Valley
Example: Glendalough in Co. Wicklow

Formation

From **snowfields** in the zone of accumulation high in the mountains, ice moved downslope under **gravity** through **river valleys.**

Meltwater seeped between the base of the ice and the bedrock, and mixed with sediment to form a type of slush. This allowed glaciers to slide downslope in a process called **basal sliding.** The meltwater regularly **froze** when the **ice stopped** moving. Freeze-thaw action then occurred, **shattering the rock** surface beneath the ice.

When the glacier moved again, it **plucked** large boulders and rocks from the bedrock surface and used them to **abrade** and **deepen** the valley. The **higher slopes** of the valley above the glacier were also exposed to frost wedging. **Shattered rock** fell onto the **glacier edges** and became **embedded** in the ice. Combined with other plucked rocks from the side of the valley, they **widened** and **straightened** the sides.

The processes of freeze-thaw and abrasion created **truncated spurs** by **eroding the interlocking spurs** of the original river valley through which the glacier travelled. These form **short cliff ledges** along glaciated valleys.

These processes also created **rock basins,** where shattered rock or patches of **soft rock** existed on the valley floor. These **long, deep hollows** later filled to form **ribbon lakes.** Where a stream joined the hollows together in a string, they are called **paternoster lakes**

Very deep glaciated valleys with vertical sides are called **glacial troughs.** If, after the Ice Age, the valleys were **flooded** by the sea, **fjords** were formed.

Hanging valleys formed where **smaller glaciers** entered the main valley. The **less erosive power** of these tributary glaciers caused them to 'hang' into the valley once the ice had gone.

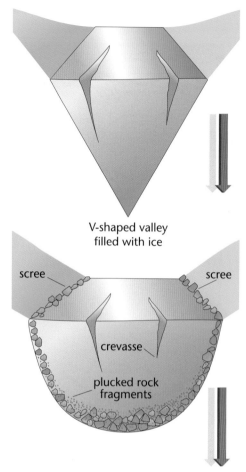

V-shaped valley
filled with ice

scree   scree

crevasse

plucked rock
fragments

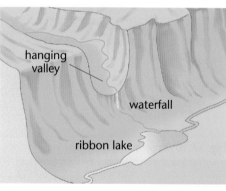

hanging
valley

waterfall

ribbon lake

Fig. 12.7 Cirques are regularly found on north-facing slopes.

Activity

1. Use the contour pattern in the map to describe:
   a. the valley sides in Glendalough
   b. the valley floor in Glendalough.
2. Identify:
   a. The land use at T 115 977. Suggest one reason for the land use at this location.
   b. The tourist facility at T 122 968. Give two reasons for the facility in this area.

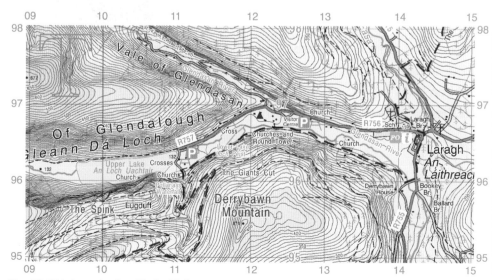

Fig. 12.8 V-shaped valley filled with ice.

OTHER LANDFORMS OF EROSION

Fig. 12.9 Identify the landforms A–D.

Landform: Pyramidal Peaks

Example: Carrauntoohil in Co. Kerry

A mountain peak in the shape of a pyramid is a pyramidal peak. These peaks formed when mountaintops **stood above** the surrounding snowfields and **ice sheets**. They became pointed when:

● They were subjected to severe and continuous **freeze-thaw action** for a long time.
● Three or more cirques formed back to back in a process called **headwall recession**.

Landform: Arête

Example: The Devil's Punch Bowl on Mangerton Mountain

An arête is a **knife-edged ridge** between two cirques or two valleys. When two cirques erode back to back or side by side, they may create a very narrow, knife-edged ridge between them. This sharp ridge is an arête.

Fig. 12.10 A roche moutonnée.

Landform: Roche Moutonnées

Example: Owenreagh Valley, near Killarney

Large rock outcrops on a valley floor or on plains were obstacles to the movement of valley glaciers. As the ice passed over the rock surface, it smoothed and polished the upstream side of the rock. **Plucking** occurred on the downstream side, leaving it irregular and angular.

Rock Basins and Ribbon Lakes

Example: Lough Beagh in Co. Donegal

Rock basins formed by **freeze-thaw action** and **plucking**, where shattered rock or patches of soft rock existed on a valley floor. **Long, deep lakes called ribbon lakes** formed when the hollows later filled with meltwater. If a number of these lakes are linked by a stream, they are called **paternoster lakes**.

Fjords

Example: Killary Harbour in Co. Galway

Some glacial valleys were over-deepened by erosion. When the Ice Age ended, **sea levels rose** again and some of the deep valleys that opened onto the sea became **flooded**. These fjords have **steeply sloping, parallel sides**. The Norwegian coast has many fjords.

Deep rock basins form ribbon lakes.

● *What are the physical characteristics of these fjord inlets?*

SOME LANDFORMS OF GLACIAL DEPOSITION

The area where the ice melted and materials were deposited is called the **zone of ablation**. There are many landforms of deposition.

Drift is the term used to refer collectively to all glacial deposits. These deposits include boulders, gravels, sands and clays, and may be **subdivided** into **till**, which includes all material deposited directly by ice, and **fluvioglacial material**, which is the debris deposited by meltwater streams. **Till** consists of **unsorted material**, whereas **fluvioglacial** deposits have been **sorted**. Deposition occurs both in upland valleys and across lowland areas.

In this section, till is divided into separate landforms:

- Moraines.
- Boulder clay.
- Drumlins.

Deposition
When world temperatures increased, glaciers and ice sheets melted. As they did, they deposited large amounts of material that they had eroded from highland areas on lowlands. This material is called **till, or boulder clay**.

In addition, the water from the melting ice formed rivers under the lowland ice sheets and, as it flowed, it deposited huge amounts of sand and gravel in tunnels and on lowland areas in front of the ice sheets. This material is called **fluvioglacial deposits**.

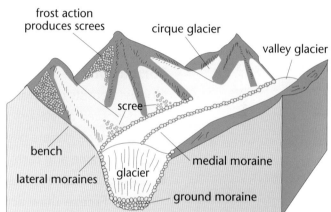

Fig. 12.11 The source of glacial material is generally in upland regions.

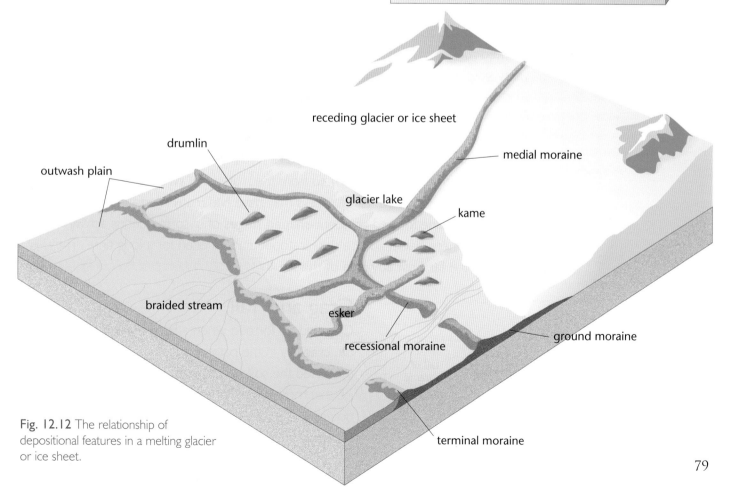

Fig. 12.12 The relationship of depositional features in a melting glacier or ice sheet.

Landform: Moraine
Example: In the Gap of Dunloe in Co. Kerry

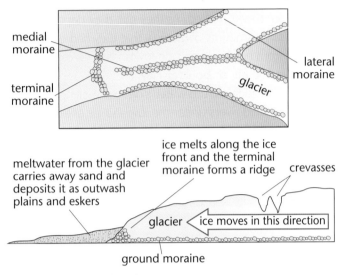

Fig. 12.13 Moraine deposits.

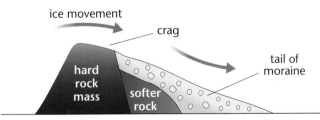

Unsorted material deposited by a glacier. Many of the rocks are angular.

Formation

Moraine consists of **unsorted debris** of rounded and angular boulders, stones, soil and sand deposited by glaciers. This material was **plucked** or **abraded** from the landscape over which the glaciers passed. It may be divided into three main types: **lateral moraine, medial moraine and terminal moraine.**

- **Lateral moraine** formed **long, sloping ridges** of material deposited along **valley sides. Freeze-thaw action** on the unglaciated **benches** above the ice caused angular rocks of all sizes to fall onto the glacier edges below. As the ice moved downslope, it became embedded in the glacier ice. As the glacier edges moved downslope, they **plucked** rocks from the valley sides. This removed the interlocking spurs and the valley sides were straightened and deepened by **abrasion.**

    Much of this eroded debris was deposited along the valley edge when all the ice had melted. It is recognisable as a **lesser slope** than the valley walls, or as a rocky, sloping surface.

- **Medial moraine** is an uneven, long ridge of similarly unsorted material that runs along the centre of valleys. It formed from the material of **two lateral moraines** when two glaciers **joined**. Large valleys may have had many medial moraines.

- **Terminal moraine** formed **crescent-shaped ridges** of unsorted debris across valleys and plains where glaciers or ice sheets stopped and melted for a long time. They represent the **farthest advance of the ice.**

Crag and Tail

Crag and tail formed when a **hard mass of rock**, called the **crag**, lay in the path of oncoming ice. The hard crag protected the softer rock in its lee from erosion by the ice that moved over and around the crag. On the downstream side, deposition by the ice created a **tapering ridge of moraine**. This is called the tail.

Fig. 12.14 Crag and tail.

Landform: Drumlins

Example: Hills in Cavan and Islands in Clew Bay

Formation

Drumlins are **rounded**, **oval-shaped hills** of ground moraine. They usually occur in clusters or swarms. They are especially well developed in Ireland, for example in **Clew Bay** in Co. Mayo.

Drumlins are mainly formed of **boulder clay**. This **unsorted material** consists of rocks, pebbles, gravel, sand and clay mixed up together. It represents the ground moraine of ice sheets. This debris came mainly from rocks that were **plucked** from the bedrock over which the ice passed and broken into stones, clay and sand.

Drumlins may have formed in a number of ways.

- The debris was deposited by moving ice sheets when they were **overladen** with material. As the ice moved over this material, it formed rounded hills with a **steep end facing the oncoming ice** and a low, tapered side in the direction of ice movement.

- When a glacier pushed forward over a terminal moraine, if the till was **dry**, it moulded the debris into long, streamlined hills. The **long axis** of a drumlin indicates the **direction of ice** movement. These hills range from small mounds just a few metres long to larger hills a few kilometres or more in length and as much as 100 m high.

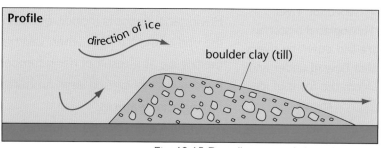

Fig. 12.15 Drumlins are oval-shaped hills.

Drumlins form basket-of-egg scenery in Strangford Lough.

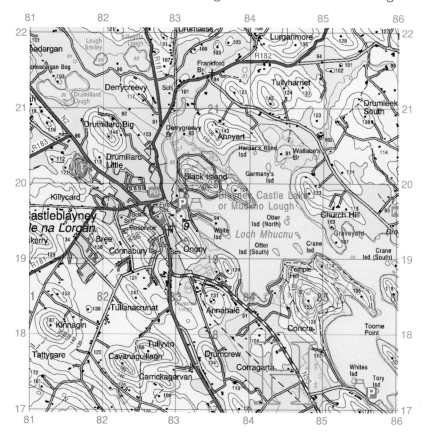

Fig. 12.16 Glacial deposits of Ireland's last ice advance.

Activity

Carefully study the Ordnance Survey map extract and answer the following questions.

1. Look at the island in Muckno Lough at grid reference H 847 192. Is this a drumlin? Explain your answer.

2. In which direction did the ice pass over this area? Was it:
   a. north-west to south-east
   b. south-east to north-west
   c. neither?

3. Have the drumlins in this area affected the shape of Castleblaney? Explain.

4. a. Where in Ireland are most drumlins located? (See page 82.)
   b. Explain, with the aid of a diagram, how drumlins form.

PATTERNS OF FLUVIOGLACIAL DEPOSITS

Fluvius is the Latin word for 'river'. Fluvioglacial materials are laid down by rivers that flowed under and from the front of ice sheets.

Fluvioglacial deposits include outwash plains and eskers. These features formed towards the end of the Ice Age, when vast quantities of meltwater were released from the melting ice as a result of rising temperatures. The many rivers that flowed from the melting glaciers carried large amounts of sand and gravel and deposited them to form **fluvioglacial features**.

Irish ice developed a number of ice domes, or ice caps. Ice sheets spread from these areas across the country, where they deposited moraine, drumlins, kames and eskers. The moraines, kames and eskers have since provided plentiful supplies of rocks, gravel and sand for the construction industry.

The two charts below show the location and direction of the ice that created these glacial deposits.

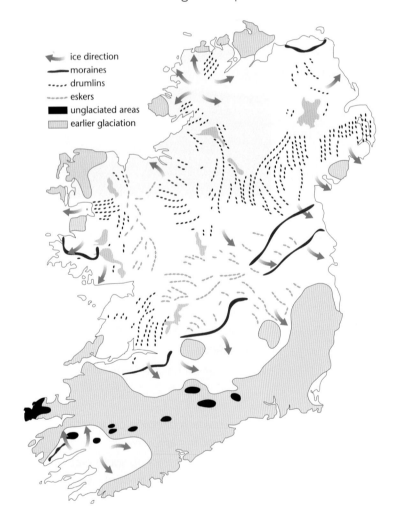

ice direction
moraines
drumlins
eskers
unglaciated areas
earlier glaciation

many moraine and esker deposits overlap in this area because ice sheets meet along an east-west line from Galway towards Dublin

many moraine and esker deposits overlap in this area because ice sheets meet along a north-south line from just north of Galway through Mayo

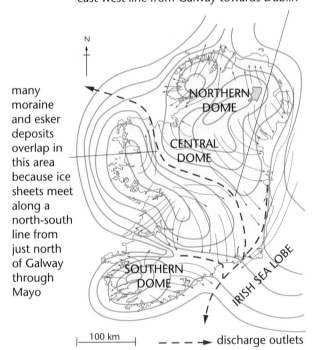

100 km ⊢———⊣ – – – → discharge outlets

Fig. 12.17 Domes of ice that created Ireland's ice sheets.

Outwash Plain

The melting ice sheet caused many rivers to flow from the front of the ice (see Fig. 12.12 on page 79). The meltwater flushed sand, gravel and clay through the terminal moraine to form an **outwash plain**. The Curragh in Co. Kildare is this type of feature.

Landform: Esker

Example: Eiscir Riada at Clonmacnoise, Co. Offaly

Fig. 12.18

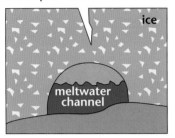

1. As ice melts, meltwater channels form under the ice.

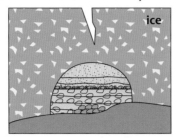

2. Sand, gravel and boulders are deposited, depending on the speed of meltwater flow.

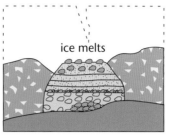

3. Meltwater channel fills with deposits as the ice melts.

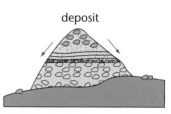

4. After the ice has melted, esker slopes stabilise, leaving a ridge of sand, gravel and boulders.

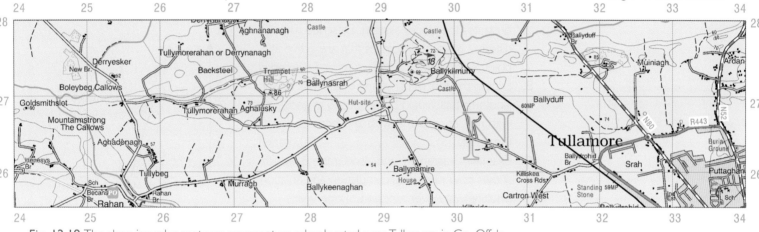

Fig. 12.19 The close irregular contours represent an esker located near Tullamore in Co. Offaly.

Formation

Melting ice sheets produced vast amounts of **meltwater**, some of which flowed through **tunnels** under the ice. The pressure of the water enclosed within the tunnels was considerable and caused the water to flow quickly.

The **fast flow** of the water allowed it to pick up **large quantities of sediment** from the ground moraine beneath the glacier. It washed and cleaned the sediment and carried it along, some in **suspension**, some by **saltation** and more by **traction** (see page 86). The **silt and clay particles** were carried far from their source to lakes or to the sea, while the **sand and gravel** particles were laid down in **alternate sorted layers** on the beds of the enclosed rivers and streams. Layers of fine sediment, such as **fine sand**, were deposited during times of **low water**, while **gravels** were laid down during periods of **rapid ice melt**, such as in summer.

These sub-glacial rivers formed a **winding course** across level plains beneath the ice, just as rivers do when they **meander** in their late stage of development. The deposits they made today form winding ridges of sand and gravel across lowland regions.

Once the esker ridges were exposed after the Ice Age, they were subjected to **weathering and erosion** forces. Parts of them may have **slumped** due to **gravity,** and over time they took on the more pointed ridge-like form they have today.

Esker ridges wind and twist across level lowland.

Transportation of Sediment
- Suspension – float
- Saltation – bounce
- Traction – roll

Multi-part Questions

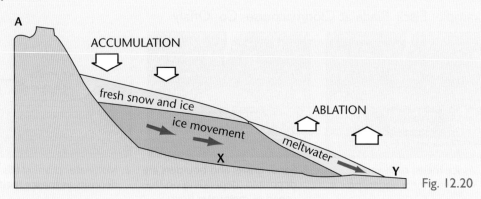

Fig. 12.20

1. **A.** Examine Diagram A in Fig. 12.20, which illustrates the glacier system. Describe the different physical processes that are active at point X and point Y. [20 marks]
   B. Explain the formation of any **one** characteristic landform that would be produced at each point, with reference to the surface processes that formed it. [30 marks]
   C. Examine Diagram A, and also Graph B, which shows how rates of accumulation and ablation (melting) vary over a period of one year. Describe and explain what this information tells us about how the glacier system changes over time. [30 marks]

2. **A.** Identify **two** glacial landforms, one formed by glacial erosion and one by glacial deposition. In the case of **one** landform, describe and explain the processes involved in its formation. [20 marks]
   B. Explain how urban water supplies and tourism have been enhanced by glacial erosive action. [30 marks]
   C. The melting of ice masses at the end of the last glacial period released great quantities of meltwater that created landforms in lowland regions. With reference to **one** such landform, explain how it was formed [30 marks]

3. **A.** Cirque, Ribbon lake, Hanging valley, Fjord.
   With reference to any **one** of these landforms, explain how the processes of ice action led to its formation. [20 marks]
   B. Explain the basic conditions of climate and of topography that are necessary to bring about a period of widespread glaciation of a landscape. [30 marks]
   C. Explain the formation of any two landforms that were formed at or beyond the ice front. [30 marks]

4. Study the Ordnance Survey map of Ballyconnell in Co. Cavan on page 97, then answer the following questions.
   Drumlins are low, rounded hills of boulder clay created by glacial deposition. An example of a drumlin is at grid reference H 235 172. The low-lying areas around these hills have a coating of clay, also deposited by the ice. Carefully study similar contour shapes on the map that indicate drumlin hills. Explain how these hills:
   A. were formed
   B. have affected drainage on the map
   C. have affected land patterns in this region. [30 marks]

CHAPTER 13
RIVER PROCESSES, PATTERNS AND LANDFORMS

KEY IDEA! Rivers perform three basic functions: they erode, transport and deposit material. The energy of a river depends on its volume and its speed, or velocity.

The material that a river transports is called its **load**. Most of the river's energy is used up in transporting this load. **As a river's volume increases, so does its load**.

A river carries its greatest load, and its largest particles, when it is in flood after heavy rain. When in flood, a river's water turns brown due to the high content of soil particles that it carries in suspension. When a flood subsides and normal water levels return, the brown colour disappears and only tiny particles can be moved.

Torc Waterfall in Killarney.

PROCESSES OF RIVER EROSION
Hydraulic Action

Hydraulic action is the force of moving water. By rushing into cracks, the force of moving water can sweep out loose material or help break up solid rock. Turbulent (very disturbed) and eddying (swirling) water may undermine (cut under) banks on the bend of a river. This process is called **bank caving** (see photo below).

Erosion also occurs because of **cavitation**. Cavitation takes place when **bubbles of air collapse** and form tiny **shock waves** against the banks. These tiny explosions loosen soil particles and are particularly effective on banks of clay, sand or gravel.

Over time, hydraulic action breaks solid rock.

A river undercuts a bank when it is in flood, causing bank caving and slumping.

Abrasion

Abrasion is the way the river **uses its load to erode**. The greater the volume and speed of a river, the greater its load and the greater its power to erode. A river reaches its **greatest erosive power** during times of **flood**, when riverbanks are most likely to collapse.

Abrasion is seen most effectively where rivers flow over layers of rock. Pebbles are whirled round by eddies in hollows in the riverbed. This action forms potholes (deep pools), which are regularly found in mountain streams.

Pebbles and rocks become rounded as they hit off each other on the riverbed.
● *Name this process.*

Attrition

As a river carries its load, the **particles** are constantly **in collision** with each other and with the bed of the river. As these particles move downstream, they get progressively smaller. Boulders and pebbles in a river are always **rounded and smooth** to touch.

Solution

Solution is chemical erosion. **Rocks, such as limestone and chalk, dissolve** when water flows across their surface. As rainwater seeps through soil, it becomes more acid than rain. When it meets limestone or chalk, it reacts with them (it fizzes) and dissolves them. It then carries these dissolved particles away in solution.

PROCESSES OF TRANSPORTATION

The river's load is carried in the following ways (see Fig. 13.1).

Suspended Load

Most particles, including fine clay and silt, are carried in suspension by a river. Water action may initially cause fine particles to be lifted from the riverbed, but once in suspension the turbulence of the water keeps them up and the particles are transported downstream.

Solution

Rivers that flow over soluble rock, such as limestone or chalk, will carry some matter in solution.

Saltation

Some particles are light enough to be bounced along the riverbed. They are lifted from the riverbed by **hydraulic action**. Because they are too heavy to form part of the suspended load, they fall back onto the riverbed to be picked up once more. This process is repeated and so the pattern of bouncing stones is achieved.

Traction (Bedload Drag)

The volume and speed of a river is greatly increased during times of flood. Pebbles, large stones and sometimes huge boulders are rolled along the riverbed during these periods of high water. This process is often referred to as **bedload drag**.

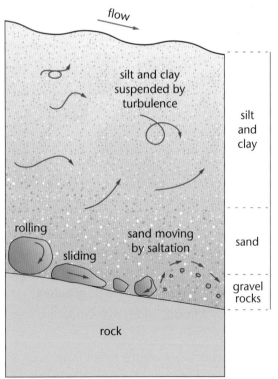

Fig. 13.1 Materials are moved along a river's course by processes of transportation.

Drainage Basins

Rivers generally rise in mountain regions and flow downslope into the sea. On its journey, a river is joined by smaller streams, called tributaries. The area drained by a river and all its tributaries is called its **basin.** Each river basin is separated from neighbouring basins by areas of high ground called **watersheds.** All precipitation that falls within a drainage basin will eventually find its way into the main river. The name of the river gives its name to its drainage basin, e.g. the **Shannon Basin.**

Some drainage basins are small while others are large. The Amazon and the Mississippi basins are huge. The Mississippi Basin drains all the interior of the United States (except Alaska).

The Shannon Basin drains all the Midlands of Ireland, so it has many tributaries and lakes. As an exercise, use your atlas to draw a sketch map of the Shannon Basin and on it mark and name the River Shannon, its main tributaries and its main lakes.

Alluvial Fans

In mountain areas during periods of heavy rain or during **flash floods,** some water torrents pour over steep edges onto lower ground, or emerge from narrow valleys into more open ground. There, the water torrents deposit large and small broken rock particles, including pebbles and boulders in steeply sloping fan-shaped mounds. These landforms are called **alluvial fans.** This is where most **conglomerate rock** forms.

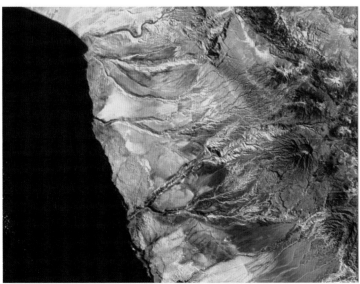

Alluvial fans form within mountain regions.

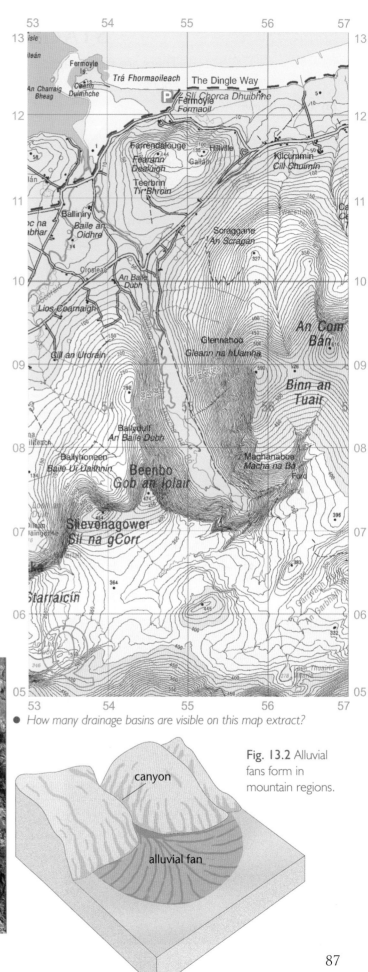

● *How many drainage basins are visible on this map extract?*

Fig. 13.2 Alluvial fans form in mountain regions.

canyon

alluvial fan

STAGES IN A RIVER'S COURSE

There are three stages in the course of a river: upper course, middle course and lower course.

(a) Upper course

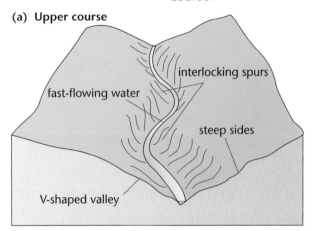

The river flows around the interlocking spurs.

(b) Middle course

Interlocking spurs are cut away in a mature floodplain.

(c) Lower course

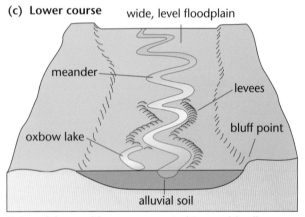

Oxbow lakes and levees are created in an old valley.

Fig. 13.3 The three stages in a river's course.

Rivers in their upper courses flow quickly within narrow, steep-sided V-shaped valleys.

Landform: V-Shaped Valley

Valley: Devil's Glen in Co. Wicklow

Formation

V-shaped valleys form on mountain slopes. The water from many **gullies** and streams joins to form substantial rivers in mountain regions. This water finds the easiest route downhill by **winding and twisting** its way around obstacles of **hard rock**.

The flowing water becomes a **current** that tends to flow **strongest** on the **outside** of the bends in the river. **Abrasion** by the river's load and the **hydraulic action** of the fast water at these locations make the bends more pronounced. The projections down the sides of the valley are called **interlocking spurs**.

Rainfall on the steep valley sides, the action of **freeze-thaw** in winter and **gravity** (creating soil creep) cause downhill movement of material into the river channel. Over time, the river moves this material to lowland areas.

Erosion is greatest in times of **flood**. The **increased speed** and **load** of the river allow the water to transport large rock particles by **traction** and **saltation**, as well as sand and pebbles, so increasing the river's erosive power. This erodes the riverbed and makes the **valley deeper**.

Landform: Waterfall

Example: Torc Waterfall near Killarney

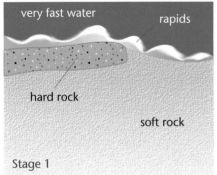

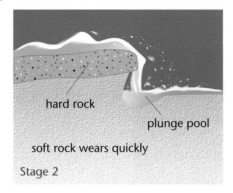

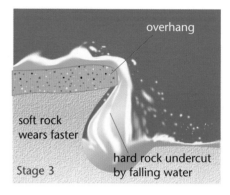

Fig. 13.4 The formation of a waterfall.

Formation

A waterfall usually occurs in the upper course of a river. It forms where a layer of **hard rock** that lies across the riverbed is **horizontal** or **tilted upwards**.

Uneven hardness of the bedrock leads to **differential erosion**. The softer rock is eroded at a faster rate than the hard rock layer. The river finds it difficult to remove the hard rock. Generally, this process is represented by a stretch of **rapids** above the hard rock. The rushing water forces its way into the **joints** in the hard rock, creating an uneven surface.

Directly downstream from the rapids, the softer rock undergoes severe erosion due to **hydraulic action** and **abrasion**. This causes a vertical drop on the riverbed, where the hard rock ends and the softer rock begins.

As the falling water strikes the soft rock on the riverbed, its erosive power gouges out a deep pool, called a **plunge pool**. This pool is gradually deepened with the **eddying** or swirling action of the water and its **load**, creating **abrasion** within the pool.

The mist created by the falling water rots the soft rock underneath the hard rock cap. This soft **rock crumbles** and the hard rock is undermined. Large **chunks** of the hard rock **break away** from the front of the waterfall and fall to the base of the waterfall as a result of undermining or opening up of its joints by hydraulic action.

In some regions where extremely cold conditions are experienced and the river **freezes** over, some freeze-thaw may result in these rock chunks being loosened. In this way the **waterfall retreats** upstream, leaving a deep, steep-sided narrow channel downstream from the waterfall. This landform is called a **gorge**.

Yosemite Falls in Yosemite National Park in California,
● *Suggest one reason why this waterfall formed here.*

Activity
1. Name one example of a waterfall in Ireland.
2. Explain, with the aid of diagrams, how a waterfall forms in a young river valley.
3. Explain, using examples, how waterfalls are used to encourage economic development.

89

Landform: Floodplain
Example: Blackwater Valley near Fermoy

Erosion occurs on the outside of a bend. Deposition occurs on the opposite side where water is slower-moving.

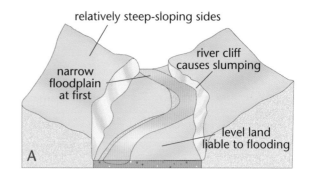

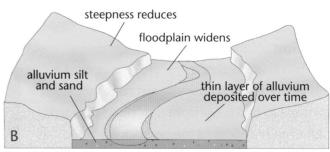

Fig. 13.5 A floodplain widens over time and the sides reduce in steepness.

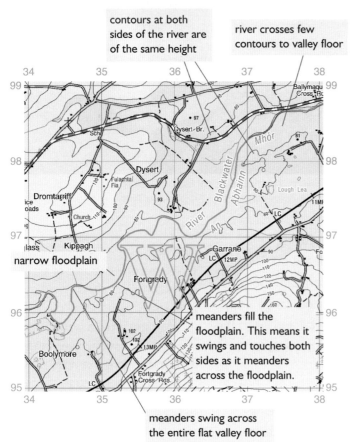

contours at both sides of the river are of the same height

river crosses few contours to valley floor

narrow floodplain

meanders fill the floodplain. This means it swings and touches both sides as it meanders across the floodplain.

meanders swing across the entire flat valley floor

Formation

When a river reaches lowland areas, it **slows down** and starts to swing from side to side. This creates **lateral erosion** and begins the process of removing the river's interlocking spurs. The processes of hydraulic action, cavitation and abrasion are very active at this stage.

As the river flows around a bend, it **erodes** most strongly on the **outside** of the bend, forming a **river cliff**. The bank is **undercut** and parts of it **slump** into the river.

Little erosion occurs on the inside of the bend, but there is often deposition, forming a gravel beach or a **point bar**. The lateral (side to side) wandering of the river is called **divagation**.

Over time, a wide and flat valley floor is created. During times of flood, the rivers **overflow** their channels and spread across the flat valley floor. Away from the river's channel, the floodwater is calm and it has lots of fine sediment, such as silt and fine sand, in suspension. This is deposited on the level surface of coarse deposits and is called **alluvium**. Over thousands of years each successive flow builds up a thick blanket of alluvium to form extremely fertile, level land, called a **floodplain**, suited to growing cereal or cattle grazing.

Landform: Oxbow Lake

Example: River Shannon at Leitrim town

Formation

Oxbow lakes are relic river channels where looping meanders were cut off from the main river and are no longer active. Their waters are stagnant and their levels rise and fall with the water table. Oxbow lakes form where a river makes huge sweeping or **looping meanders** as it flows across a wide, flat floodplain in the river's middle or especially in its **lower stage**.

Lateral erosion of a river's channel causes meanders to move across its floodplain and also to move downstream. This is called the process of **divagation**.

Constant **erosion** on the **outside** of a meander bend leads to a sweeping loop forming in the river's course. This process creates a 'peninsula' of land with a narrow neck trapped by the looping river's channel. As the river sweeps around this looping bend, the zone of highest speed within the channel swings towards the outer bank. There is great water **turbulence** where the river strikes the bank, which is formed of sediment previously deposited by the river.

The **abrasive action** of the river's load, the collapsing of air bubbles (called **cavitation**), causing shock waves, and the **hydraulic** force of the water combine to cause **undercutting** of this soft material. The undercutting causes **slumping** of the bank into the river.

Meanwhile, along the inner side of each meander loop, where the water is shallow and slow-moving, coarse sediment (such as gravel and sand) builds up to form a beach, called a **point bar**. During a flood, the river cuts through the neck of land and continues on a straighter and easier route, leaving the cut-off to one side. **Deposition** occurs at **both ends** of this cut-off to form an oxbow lake. After a long time, the oxbows fill with silt from floodwater and eventually dry up. When this happens, they are called **meander scars**, or **mort lakes**.

Practise these drawings over and over again.

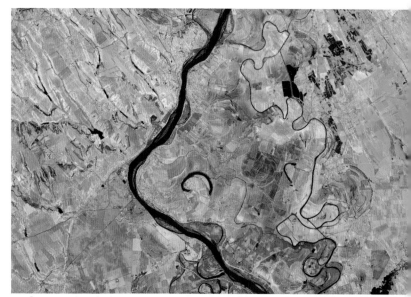

● *Can you identify the oxbow lakes in this satellite photograph of the Danube?*

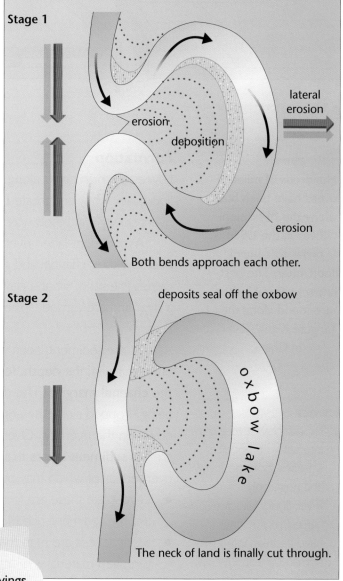

Fig. 13.6 The formation of an oxbow lake.

Landform: Levee

Example: Mulkear River in Co. Limerick

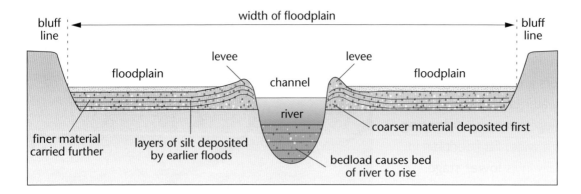

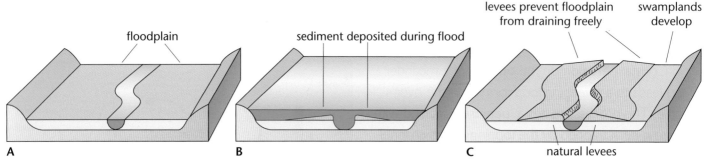

A   B   C

Fig. 13.7 The formation of levees.

Hundreds of miles of levees have been built along the Mississippi River in the US in order to control floodwater. The best-known natural levees are found along the Yangtze Kiang (River) in China.

Formation

Levees are high banks along the edges of a river's channel, raised above the floodplain. They are created naturally along the edges of **large, silt-laden rivers** as the rivers slowly wind their way across flat floodplains to the sea.

As sediment-laden rivers flood during prolonged spells of heavy rain, their waters overflow their channel and spread across the floodplain. At this lower stage the river carries fine sand, silt and clay particles in suspension. These are the lightest particles in a river and are carried farthest from their source in the mountains where the river rises.

As the sediment-laden waters flow out from their completely submerged channel during a flood, the **depth, force** and **turbulence** of the water **decreases sharply at the channel margins**. This decrease results in the fine sand and coarse silt suddenly being dropped along the edges of the channel. A thick sediment deposit is also laid down on the riverbed. Over hundreds of thousands of years, **repeated flooding** creates **sediment layers** that build up high banks parallel to the river's channel and a riverbed, all of which may be well above the level of the surrounding floodplain.

- Levees like these are found along delta distributaries, such as in a bird's foot delta like the sediment-rich Mississippi River estuary in the Gulf of Mexico.
- Some levees are man made to prevent flooding of farmland or an urban area. Dredged material is dumped along the channel edges by machines. These levees, however, are narrow and not as stable as naturally occurring ones.

Activity

1. Explain how levees may interact with people's activities, both positively and negatively.
2. River floodplains are natural regions that have been adapted for human benefit. Discuss.

Landform: Delta

Example: Clohoge River Delta in Lough Tay, Co. Wicklow

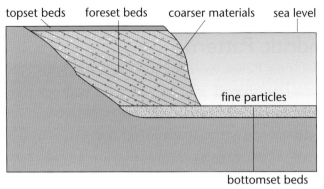

Fig. 13.8 Delta deposits.

This is a satellite image of the Mississippi Delta.

- *What type of delta does this river form? Explain.*

Formation

A delta forms at the **mouth of a river** if the river carries a heavy load as it enters calm waters in a lake or enclosed estuary. If the delta forms in a lake, it is a **lacustrine** delta. If it forms on the coast, it is a **marine delta**.

The materials that build up to form a delta are composed of **alternate layers** of **coarse and fine deposits** that reflect times of high and low water levels, respectively. On the coast the meeting of freshwater and salty seawater produces an electric charge that causes the silt and clay particles to 'clot' and settle on the seabed.

These materials are classified into three categories:

- Fine particles, such as clay, are carried out to sea and deposited in advance of the main delta. These form the **bottomset beds**.
- Coarser materials, such as silt and very fine sand, form **sloping layers** over the bottomset beds and gradually build outwards, each one on front of and above the ones before, causing the delta to advance. These are the **foreset beds**.
- Sediments of various grain sizes, ranging from sand to fine silt, are deposited **between distributary channels**. These build out a flat surface, so extending the floodplain. These deposits are called the **topset beds**.

There are three types of marine deltas: arcuate, estuarine and bird's foot.

- An **arcuate delta** has a triangular shape, like the Greek letter 'delta'. The apex of the triangle points upstream. Arcuate deltas are formed mostly of coarse sands and gravels where coastal sea currents are relatively strong, e.g. the Nile Delta.
- **Estuarine deltas** form at the mouths of submerged river estuaries. The deposits form long, narrow, flat or sloping banks along both sides of the estuary, e.g. the Shannon Estuary.
- **Bird's foot deltas** form where rivers carry heavy loads of fine materials to the coast. These impermeable deposits cause the river to break up into a few large distributaries. Levees develop along these distributaries, so long 'fingers' project into the sea, making a shape like a bird's foot, e.g. the Mississippi Delta.

Activity

1. Deltas develop at various stages along the courses of some rivers.
   a. Identify two locations where deltas form.
   b. Explain how the sediments at each of these locations may differ considerably.
2. Use the diagram in Fig. 13.8 to explain three categories of sediments that are found in a delta.
3. Study the OS map extract on page 90. Explain the influence of the River Blackwater on settlement patterns in the area.

93

PATTERNS OF DRAINAGE

There are four patterns of drainage: **dendritic**, **trellised**, **radial** and **deranged**.

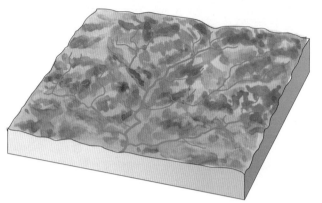

Fig. 13.9 Dendritic drainage pattern.

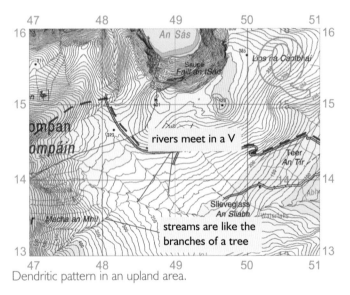

rivers meet in a V

streams are like the branches of a tree

Dendritic pattern in an upland area.

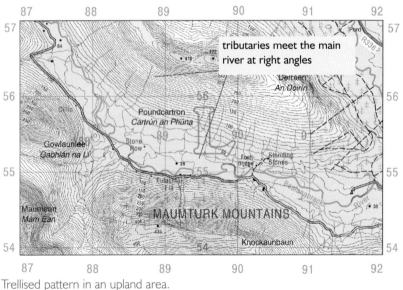

tributaries meet the main river at right angles

Trellised pattern in an upland area.

Dendritic Pattern

Dendros is the Greek word for 'tree', so a dendritic pattern is **tree-shaped**. In areas where the **bedrock** is of **equal hardness**, a river and its tributaries will erode evenly to provide a **tree-shaped river pattern**. The main river, because of its greater volume, will erode the most and so has the widest and deepest valley. The tributaries have less water, so their erosive power is less than the main river. Their valleys are therefore smaller and not as deep.

Each tributary **flows with the slope of the land** and meets the main river or other tributaries at an **acute angle** (an angle of less than 90°). This is why every tributary appears to consist of a main trunk, fed from a variety of branches, each one running into a valley proportional to the river's size.

Trellised Pattern

A trellised pattern forms when tributaries flow into the main river at right angles. This pattern forms when the bedrock of an area is of unequal hardness. Some areas have **soft rock**, while other adjoining areas have **hard rock**. The hard rock is resistant to erosion, while the soft rock erodes quickly.

In Munster, for example, the bedrock consists of alternate parallel layers of sandstone, which is hard, and limestone, which is soft. The limestone has eroded quickly and forms valleys. The more resistant sandstone stands out as parallel ridges that separate the valleys (see page 51).

Trellised patterns also develop in **steep-sided valleys**, such as glaciated U-shaped valleys. Tributary water rushes down the steep slopes of the sides and enters the main river at **right angles**.

Activity

Describe the patterns of drainage on each of the Ordnance Survey maps on this page.

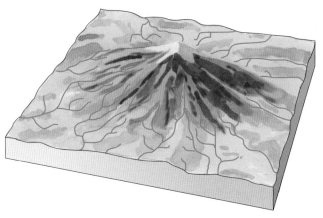

Fig. 13.10 Radial pattern in an upland area.

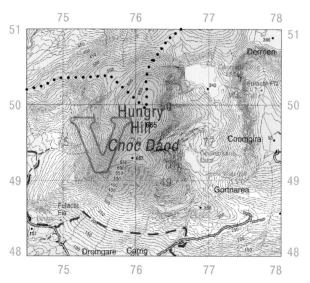

Radial pattern in an upland area. When several streams flow outwards (radiate) in all directions from a mountain or hill, they form a radial pattern of drainage.

Radial Pattern

Rivers which radiate outward from a mountain form a radial pattern. This is best displayed in well-defined circular or oval-shaped upland areas. Some of these rivers may in fact display a different drainage pattern from one another, but together they may radiate outward (north, south, east or west) from a central elevated area. They all share a common watershed at their highest source streams.

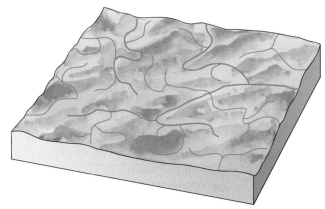

Fig. 13.11 Deranged pattern in a lowland area.

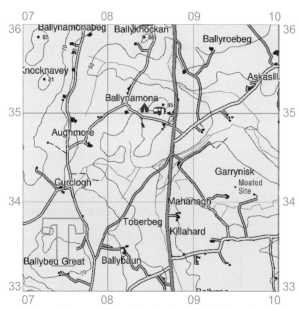

Deranged pattern in a lowland area. This is a river pattern which generally develops in a lowland area where glacial drift exists. The rivers have a chaotic appearance.

Deranged Pattern

Deranged drainage generally develops in a lowland area. Rivers have a chaotic appearance, with streams intersecting each other and flowing in no apparent direction. Deranged drainage usually develops as a result of widespread deposition of glacial material, through which post-glacial streams have had to find a route. An example of deranged drainage can be found on the coastal plain west of Cahore Point in Co. Wexford.

Multi-part Questions

Carefully study the Ordnance Survey map of Ballyconnell in Co. Cavan on page 97, then answer the following questions.

1. River processes have affected this region in Co. Cavan over time. Using evidence from the map, identify **two** landforms that have been created by these processes. In each case:
   A. i.   name the landform
      ii.   locate the landform on the map
      iii. give another Irish example. [20 marks]
   B. Explain the processes that led to the formation of one of these landforms. [30 marks]
   C. Explain two ways that people have attempted to manage or control the natural processes that operate in river valleys. [30 marks]

2. Carefully study the Ordnance Survey map of Ballyconnell in Co. Cavan on page 97, then answer the following questions.
   A. Name and locate three types of drainage patterns. For any **two** of these patterns, describe how and why they formed. [20 marks]
   B. Describe, using evidence from the map, the stage of formation of the Woodford River. [30 marks]
   C. Draw a sketch map of the area on the map.
      i.   On it, mark and name two distinct physical regions.
      ii. Explain how any one of these regions affects the development and pattern of routeways. [30 marks]

3. V-shaped valley, Oxbow lake, Delta, Levees, Interlocking spurs, Waterfall.
   A. **Each** of the above features found along the course of a river, state whether it is formed by erosion or deposition. [20 marks]
   B. Select any **two** of these features and, with the aid of a diagram, describe how each was formed. [30 marks]
   C. 'Large-scale flooding by rivers has caused enormous problems for local communities.'
      Discuss this statement. [30 marks]

4. Carefully examine the hydrograph showing a river's discharge after a downpour in Fig. 13.12, then answer the following questions.
   A. i.   At what time of day did the river's water level rise initially?
      ii. What was the lag time, i.e. the length of time between maximum rainfall and peak discharge? [20 marks]
   B. Did this river flood the surrounding landscape, i.e. did it overflow its banks? Explain. [30 marks]
   C. How long did it take for the floodwaters to recede?
   D. Give one reason why the lag time is so fast.
   E. Would you think the falling limb suggests a heavily vegetated drainage basin that has a less rapid run-off rate? Explain. [30 marks]

> The lag time varies according to conditions within the drainage basin, e.g. slope and size of the basin, number of tributaries, type and amount of vegetation and water already in storage.

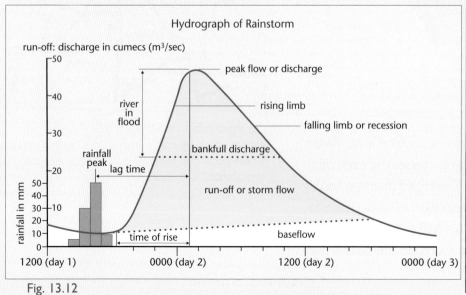

Fig. 13.12

KEY TO DIAGRAM

- **Approach segment** shows the discharge of the river before the storm.
- **Rising limb** shows the rapid increase in discharge in response to rainfall. (The steeper the rising limb, the faster the water flows off the landscape into the river.)
- **Peak discharge** shows when the river reaches its highest level.
- **Lag time** is the period between the maximum rainfall and peak discharge.
- **Falling limb** shows when discharge is decreasing. Dense vegetation reduces run-off rate.
- **Bankfull discharge** occurs when a river's water level reaches the top of the river bank. Any further increase results in flooding of surrounding land.
- **Base flow** is the normal water level released by the ground surface.

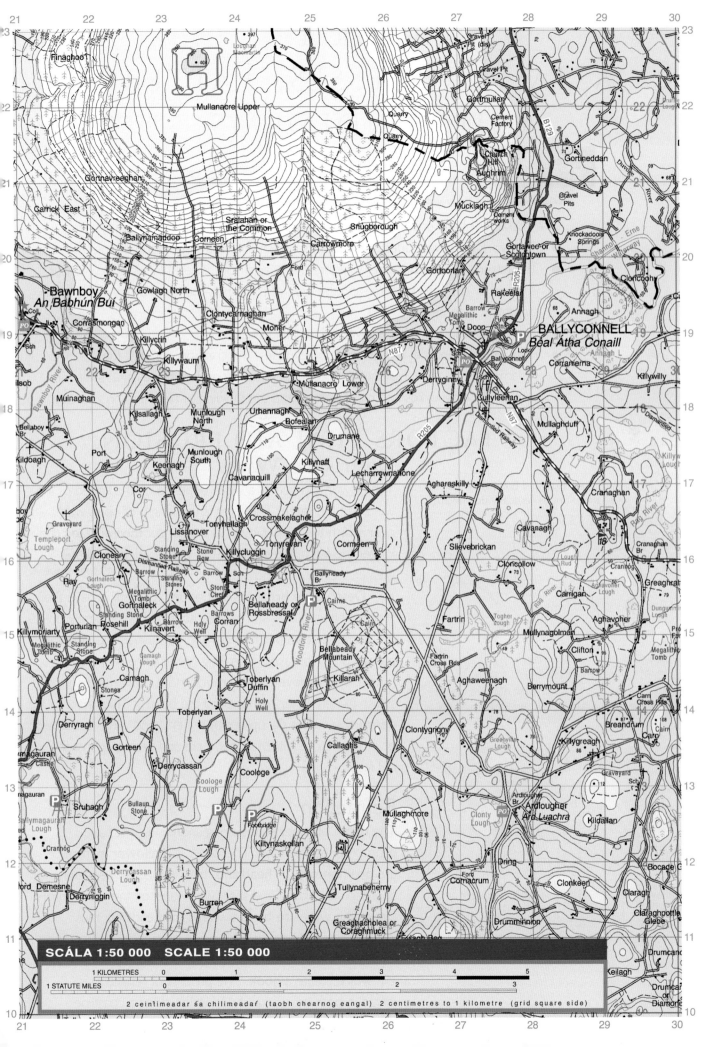

CHAPTER 14
COASTAL PROCESSES, PATTERNS AND LANDFORMS

 **KEY IDEA!** Landforms are created by coastal processes.

The character of any coastline depends on a number of factors. These include:

- The **work of waves, tides and currents**, which erode, transport and deposit materials.
- The **nature of the coastline**: whether the coastal rock is resistant or not; whether it is varied or even in character and the type of coastline – highland or lowland, even straight or indented.
- The **changes** in the relative **levels** of land and sea.
- **Human interference**: the dredging of estuaries; the creation of ports; the reclamation of coastal marshes; the construction of coastal defences against erosion, such as groynes, dykes and breakwaters; and the building of piers and promenades.

FACTORS THAT AID EROSION

Destructive Waves

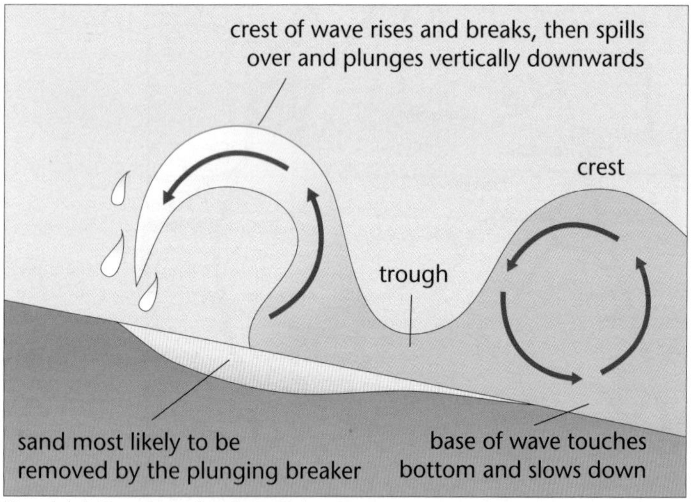

The power and size of a wave depends on the speed of the wind and the **fetch**. The fetch is the length of open water over which the wind blows. The stronger the wind and the longer the fetch, the stronger the waves will be and the greater their erosive power.

  Destructive breakers that pound a coastline have their greatest effect during storms. Because of the frequency of the waves (twelve per minute) and because of the **vertical plunge** of the breakers (breaking waves), the backwash (when waves move back) is much more powerful than the swash (when water rushes onto the beach). Thus these destructive waves dig up beach material and carry it seaward or pick up loose material near a cliff and bash it against the cliff face.

Refraction

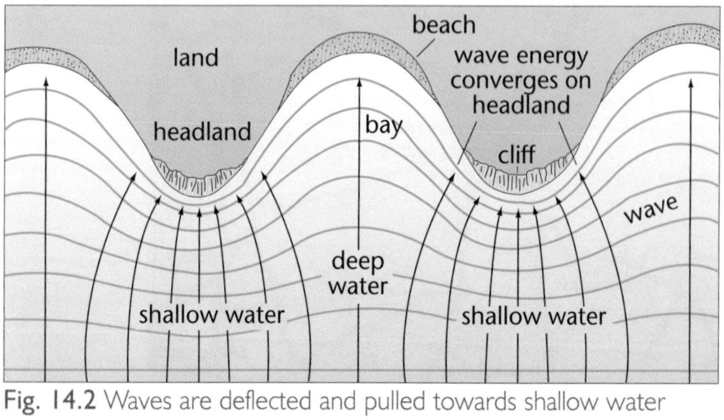

The depth of water varies along shorelines that have promontories and bays. The water is **shallower** in front of the **promontory,** or **headland,** than in the bay. As waves approach the shore, the shallower water off the promontory causes the waves **to bend** towards the headland, thus increasing erosion there. This wave **refraction**, or bending, also occurs when waves pass the end of an obstacle, such as a spit, which create a **hook.** The process of refraction is involved in both erosion and deposition along a coastline.

Fig. 14.1 Process of a destructive wave.

crest of wave rises and breaks, then spills over and plunges vertically downwards

crest

trough

sand most likely to be removed by the plunging breaker

base of wave touches bottom and slows down

Fig. 14.2 Waves are deflected and pulled towards shallow water along headlands.

beach

land

wave energy converges on headland

headland

bay

cliff

wave

deep water

shallow water

shallow water

PROCESSES OF COASTAL EROSION

These processes include:

- Hydraulic action.
- Compression.
- Abrasion.
- Attrition.

Fig. 14.3 Hydraulic action.

Hydraulic Action

When strong waves crash against a coast, they have a **shattering effect** as they pound the rocks. Waves crashing against the base of a cliff **force rocks apart,** making them more prone to erosion. Cliffs of boulder clay are particularly affected, as loosened soil and rocks are washed away.

Compression

Air filters into joints, cracks and bedding planes in cliff faces. As incoming waves crash against the coast, the **air is trapped**. The trapped air is compressed by the waves squeezing their way into the air-filled cavities. When the wave retreats, it results in a **rapid expansion** of the compressed air, creating an **explosive effect** that widens the cracks (fissures) and shatters the rock face.

Abrasion

When boulders, pebbles and sand are pounded against the foot of a cliff by waves, fragments of rock are broken off and **undercutting** of the cliff takes place. The amount of abrasion depends on the ability of the waves to pick up rock fragments from the shore. Abrasion is most active during storms and at high tide, when **incoming waves throw water and suspended rock material** high up the cliff face and sometimes onto the cliff edge.

Attrition

Fragments that are pounded by the sea against the cliff and **against each other** are themselves worn down by attrition, creating sand and shingle.

The ability of waves to pick up rocks and lash them against a coast is many, many times greater than waves during periods of calm weather.

Wave action creates caves and inlets on Ireland's west coast.

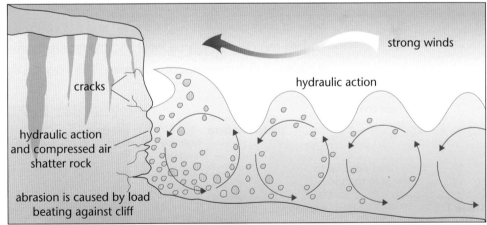

strong winds

hydraulic action

cracks

hydraulic action and compressed air shatter rock

abrasion is caused by load beating against cliff

Fig. 14.4 Storm waves bash rocks and boulders against a coast. These rocks are also reduced in size as they shatter upon hitting the cliff face.

Water-rolled rocks are rounded and smoothed as they roll back and forth on top of each other.

LANDFORMS OF COASTAL EROSION
Landform: Cliff
Example: Cliffs of Moher in Co. Clare

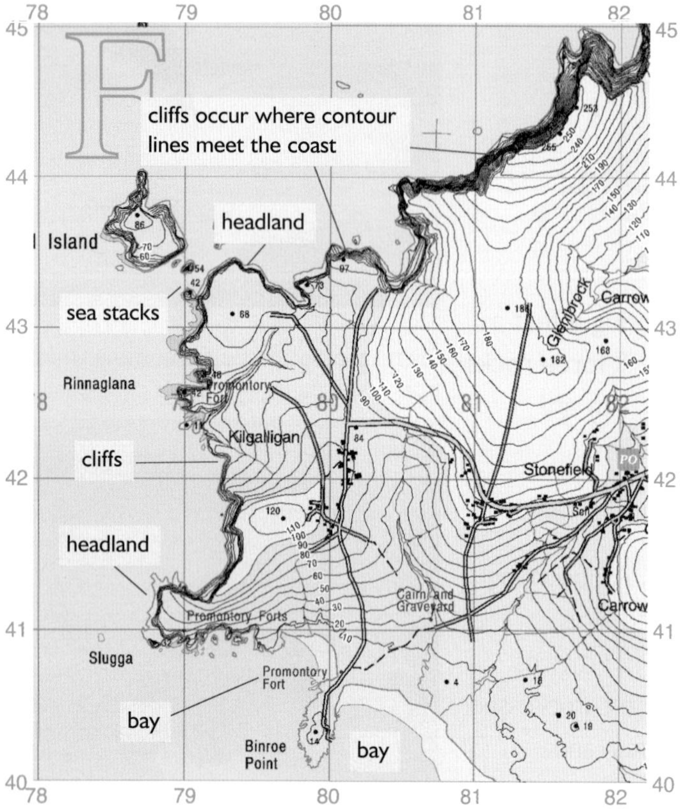

The map shows labels including:
- cliffs occur where contour lines meet the coast
- headland
- Island
- sea stacks
- Rinnaglana
- cliffs
- headland
- bay
- Slugga
- Kilgalligan
- Promontory Fort
- Stonefield
- Glenbrock
- Carrow
- Promontory Forts
- Cairn and Graveyard
- Promontory Fort
- Binroe Point
- bay

Formation

Wave action cuts a **notch** on any new land surface that is exposed to the force of the sea. This notch is eroded by the processes of hydraulic action and abrasion. When joints and bedding planes in rock surfaces are exposed to wave action, air is forced into them. The **air is trapped** and **compressed** by the force of incoming waves. This is called **hydraulic action**. As each wave retreats, the air instantly expands and this **'explosive' expansion** enlarges the cracks and eventually **the rock shatters** into small and large blocks and boulders. The rock particles are removed by the crashing waves and fall to the seabed. **Strong waves** pick up these shattered rock particles and bash them off the coast. Most of this action takes place at or below high tide level. This process is called **abrasion**.

The combined processes of hydraulic action and abrasion eventually cut a notch in the coast that creates an **overhanging rock ledge**. When this notch lengthens, the overhanging rock mass becomes too heavy to be supported and **collapses** into the sea. This creates a vertical 'wall' of rock along the water's edge and it is called a cliff.

As the cliff 'retreats', a level rock surface is formed at the base of the cliff. This surface is called a **wave-cut platform**. This may be exposed at low tide in some places.

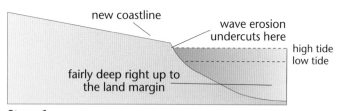

Stage 1

- new coastline
- wave erosion undercuts here
- high tide
- low tide
- fairly deep right up to the land margin

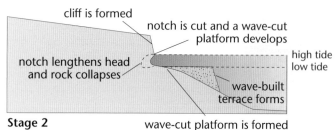

Stage 2

- cliff is formed
- notch is cut and a wave-cut platform develops
- notch lengthens head and rock collapses
- high tide
- low tide
- wave-built terrace forms
- wave-cut platform is formed

Fig. 14.5 A wave-cut platform.

● *What features indicate that this is a wave-cut platform?*

Landform: Sea Stack
Example: Sybil Point in Co. Kerry

Formation

Sea stacks form in areas of active erosion, where a **large joint** in a cliff or a **faulted zone** or a **soft rock area** may allow severe wave erosion at a particular spot on a promontory or headland. First a cave forms, then an arch and finally a stack.

Air is **forced into joints** and bedding planes in the rock surface. The air is trapped and compressed by the force of incoming waves. This is called **hydraulic action**. As each wave retreats, the escaping air instantly 'expands' and the **explosive expansion** enlarges the cracks and eventually the rock shatters into small and large rock particles and boulders. The rock particles are removed by the crashing waves and fall to the seabed. Strong waves pick up these rock particles and boulders and bash them off this same rock surface. This process is called **abrasion**. Eventually both processes create a **cave**.

The **force of the waves** themselves also erodes part of the cave surface. Over time all these processes **lengthen the cave** until it cuts through the promontory or headland. A **sea arch** then forms.

Continual erosion of hydraulic action and abrasion increases the width and height of the cave until the roof becomes too wide and heavy to be supported. The **roof collapses, cutting off** a part of the promontory or headland from the coast. This cut-off rock structure is called a **sea stack**.

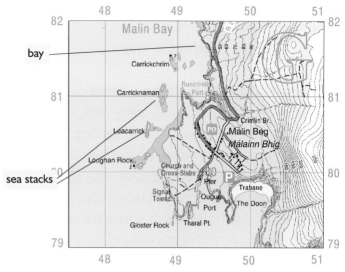

When this sea arch collapses it will leave a sea stack cut off from the coast.

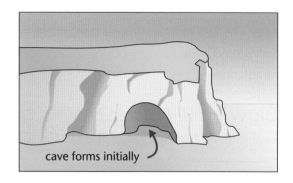

cave forms initially

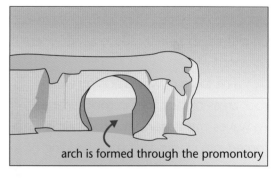

arch is formed through the promontory

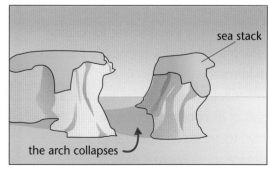

sea stack

the arch collapses

Fig. 14.6 Stages in the formation of a sea stack.

101

Bays and Headlands

Examples: Clew Bay in Co. Mayo

Erris Head in Co. Mayo

Coasts are composed of **alternate bands** of rock that vary in hardness and structure. Some rock, such as shale, is **soft** and has many closely spaced bedding planes that are easily shattered by hydraulic action. It is eroded quickly by destructive waves. Boulder clay coasts are also quickly eroded and may retreat by as much as 1–2 m a year. Other coastal stretches may have **harder rock,** such as sandstone, that resists erosion.

The way in which coasts do not erode uniformly is called differential erosion. This is especially noticeable on coasts where areas of hard and softer rock lie side by side. The less resistant rock erodes more rapidly and forms **bays**. The harder rock resists erosion and forms **headlands**.

Blow Hole (Gloup)

Example: At the Bridges of Ross in Co. Clare

Blow holes form at weak points, or **faults,** in coastal rock along the coastline. They form in **wave-cut platforms** or on **cliff edges** directly above caves where the roofs have collapsed.

The force of waves acts on weak rock areas or fault lines in rock surfaces. As waves crash against the rock, **air is forced** into cracks, fault lines, bedding planes and joints. When each wave retreats, the escaping air expands instantly and the **explosive expansion** enlarges the cracks. Eventually the rock shatters and a cave is created.

Over time, the cave lengthens and part of its **roof may collapse** into the cave to create an opening to the surface some metres away from the cliff edge or water's edge. During storms, **surf and foam** may be forced upward to the surface through this opening.

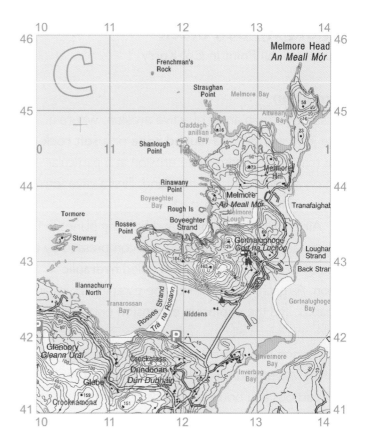

Activity

Identify:

a. four bays and four headlands in the map extract above
b. the landforms A–E in the photo below.

PROCESSES OF COASTAL TRANSPORT AND DEPOSITION

These processes include:

- Longshore drift.
- Wind action.

Longshore Drift

Longshore drift refers to the movement of material, such as sand and shingle, along a shore. When waves break obliquely onto a beach, pebbles and sand are moved up the beach by the **swash** at the same angle as the waves. The **backwash** drags the material down the beach at right angles to the coast, only to meet another incoming wave. As the process of swash and backwash in longshore drift is repeated, material is moved along the shore in a zigzag way.

Wind Action

As beaches dry at low tide, some dry sand is blown up the beach, and it gathers above high tide level in large heaps or small hills that get more extensive over time. These hills are called sand dunes.

Breaking Waves and Surf

On reaching a shore, waves are said to **break**. The way this happens is of fundamental importance to coastal processes. Shallow water causes incoming waves to steepen, the crest spills over and the wave collapses. The turbulent water created by breaking waves is called **surf**. In the landward margin of the **surf zone**, the water rushing up the beach is the **swash;** water returning down the beach is the **backwash**. The swash moves material up the beach, and the backwash **may** carry it down again.

As well as destructive waves, there are **constructive waves**. They break slowly, and more material is left on the beach.

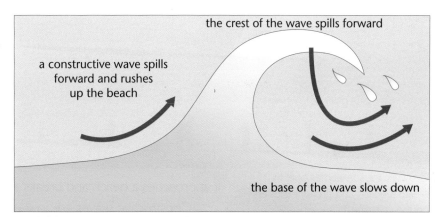

Fig. 14.7 The process of longshore drift.

Fig. 14.8 A constructive wave: spilling breaker.

Waves break as they approach a shore.

103

Landform: Beach
Example: Tramore Beach in Co. Waterford

Fig. 14.9 The profile of a beach.

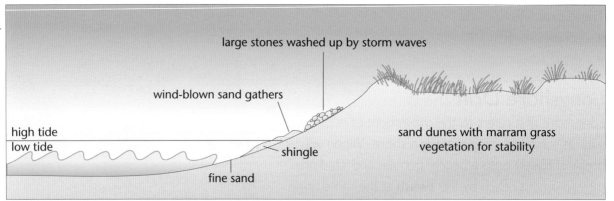

large stones washed up by storm waves

wind-blown sand gathers

high tide
low tide

shingle

sand dunes with marram grass vegetation for stability

fine sand

Groynes are sometimes built to create a beach and prevent erosion on the coastline.

yellow indicates a beach

Formation

A beach is formed by the process of **longshore drift**. This refers to the **zigzag movement** of beach material, such as sand and shingle, along a shore. Every constructive wave that approaches a shore carries some of this sand and shingle with it and will eventually deposit some of it on a beach.

As a constructive wave approaches a shore, part of the wave 'touches ground' and slows down, while the remainder of the wave in deeper water continues at a faster speed. This makes a wave tend to **bend** as it approaches a beach and breaks at an **oblique angle**.

Constructive waves are low waves and when they 'break' they are called **spilling breakers**. Because they commonly occur on **beaches with a low angle**, they have a wide area to cross and so their swash loses its energy quickly, leaving a weak backwash. In this way, sand and shingle are slowly but continually moved up the beach.

With constructive waves, little material is pulled down the beach by the **backwash**. The force of the backwash is called the **undertow**. Constructive waves have a gentle undertow and so are not dangerous to people.

During storms, sea level is higher than normal due to low atmospheric pressure. Waves are also stronger and they regularly throw **large rocks**, broken shells and driftwood up on the shore above normal high tide levels. This forms the **backshore**, or **storm beach**.

The **foreshore** is composed of **fine sand** and small shell particles. It has a gentle gradient and is covered regularly by the tide each day. Some beaches may be crescent-shaped in pocket bays or coves. Others are long and narrow and run parallel to the shore.

Landform: Sand Spit
Example: Inch Strand in Co. Kerry

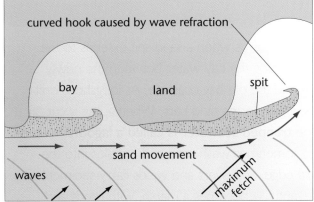

Fig. 14.10 Longshore drift of sand can form spits.

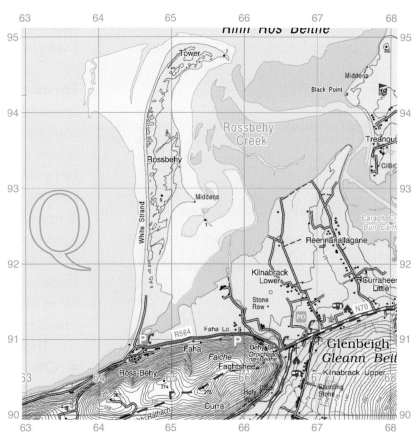

Formation

A sand spit is a beach that extends out across a bay or a river estuary. It is formed by the processes of **longshore drift** and **deposition**. A spit develops where a coastline **changes direction sharply** and longshore drift is unable to continue its zigzag movement of sediment along the shore.

Initially, **sand, shingle** and **pebbles** are deposited in the **slacker water** in the **lee of the headland** or the changing shoreline. These build up to the level of the sea surface, and this forms a foundation for deposits of finer material to be carried a little farther out into the bay by longshore drift.

As the spit continues to grow, incoming **constructive waves** pass over this extended shore, depositing fine sand and shingle on its base of coarser material. **Storm waves** throw some **larger material** above the high water mark, making the spit more permanent. Fine sand is added by **surface winds** blowing it from the beach to create **sand dunes** on the landward side of the spit. **Marram grass** then grows and its long roots stabilise the dunes.

Many spits develop a **hooked,** or **curved, end**. This is generally formed by wave refraction where waves bend around the end of the spit. A change in prevailing winds for an extended period or a storm may also aid the development of a spit.

Spits rarely join up with the opposite side of a bay where a **river estuary** keeps a channel open and free from sediment due to **scouring action** after high tide.

A sand spit projects into the bay at Glenbeigh in Co. Kerry.

Activity

1. Look at the Ordnance Survey map and photograph above. What human activities in this region relate directly to the natural processes at work in this coastal area? Explain.
2. Choose two coastal landforms and explain how the processes of erosion and/or deposition have formed them.
3. What do the irregular contours on the sand spit at Q 647 928 refer to?

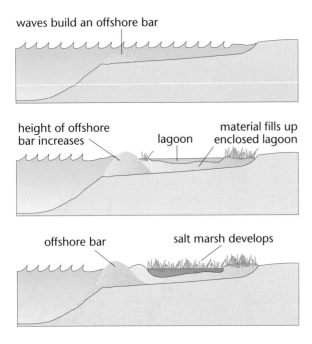

waves build an offshore bar

height of offshore bar increases

lagoon

material fills up enclosed lagoon

offshore bar

salt marsh develops

eventually the sand dunes move over the salt marsh

sand dunes

finally the marsh becomes an area of sand dunes

Fig. 14.11 The life cycle of a lagoon.

A baymouth bar cuts off Lady's Island Lake from the sea in Wexford.

Landform: Sand Bars and Lagoons
Example: Lady's Island Lake and sand bar in Co. Wexford

Formation

Generally, a sand bar forms when a sand spit extends to the opposite shore, trapping the bay water between the newly formed sand bar and the old bay coastline. As longshore drift forms sand spits, it also forms sand bars. When a bay is cut off from the sea, the **trapped seawater is called a lagoon**. In times of storm, waves sometimes wash sand and pebbles into the lagoon's seaward edge, and rivers and winds carry sediment into it. The lagoon eventually becomes a marsh, with reeds and coarse vegetation growing in the sediment. Finally, the combined forces of waves, wind and rivers turn the marsh into an extensive area of sand dunes.

There are two main types of sand bars:

- **Offshore bars** are ridges of sand or glacial till lying parallel to the shore and some distance out to sea. Sometimes these offshore bars are pushed along in front of the waves until finally they may lie across a bay to form a baymouth bar (see Fig. 14.12). Bartragh Island in Killala Bay is an offshore bar.

- **Baymouth bars** form from offshore bars, as mentioned above, but generally they form when sand spits grow across a bay to the far shore. In this way they cut off the original bay from the sea to form a lagoon.

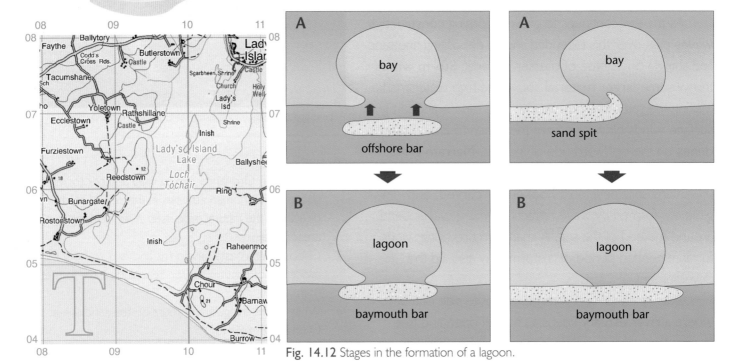

Fig. 14.12 Stages in the formation of a lagoon.

Landform: Tombolo
Example: Omey Strand in Co. Galway

Formation

This landform is created when either a spit or a bar links an island or a sea stack to the mainland. If two tombolos join an island from opposite directions, they may enclose seawater between them and create a lagoon. Tombolos are regularly formed along rugged coastlines, such as the west coast of Ireland.

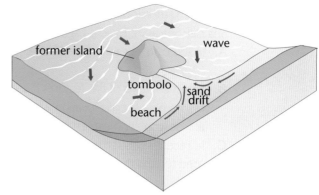

Fig. 14.13 A single tombolo may join an island to the mainland.

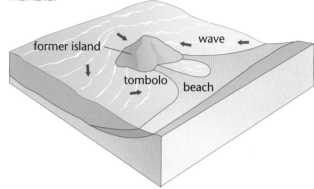

Fig. 14.14 Two tombolos may create a lake between them as they join an island to the coast.

A tombolo joins this island with Castle Tioram to the mainland in Scotland.

Activity

Study the OS map of the Omey Island region on the right, then answer the following questions.

1. Carefully examine the contour pattern in Omey Island, then suggest how Fahy Lough may have formed. Explain.
2. Omey Strand is a tombolo. Explain why this feature may have formed at this location.
3. The term 'midden' is marked at four locations on this map. Explain its significance to Ireland's history of human settlement and patterns (see Chapter 50).

Multi-part Questions

1. Sea cliff, Sea arch, Beach, Lagoon, Blow hole, Sand spit.

    A. In the case of **each** of the above coastal features, state whether it is the result of erosion or deposition.

    [20 marks]

    B. Select any **two** of the features listed above and in the case of **each**:

    i. name a specific location where the feature may be found

    ii. describe and explain, with the aid of a diagram, how it was formed.   [30 marks]

    C. In recent years, coastal erosion has caused enormous damage to coastal areas. Describe **two** methods used to limit this damage.   [30 marks]

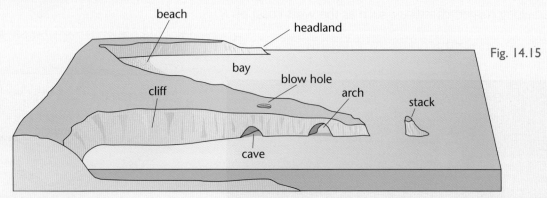

Fig. 14.15

2. The diagram in Fig. 14.15 shows an area where marine erosion has been active.

    A. With reference to any **one** major landform which is evident in the diagram, describe and explain how marine erosion has shaped it.   [20 marks]

    B. Identify any **two** landforms of marine deposition.

    i. In each case name **one** Irish example.

    ii. Explain the processes involved in the formation of any **one** of these landforms.   [30 marks]

    C. 'Materials produced by erosion at one part of a coastline are transported to other parts and deposited. Human action is sometimes taken in order to interfere with these natural processes.' Explain this statement.   [30 marks]

3. Examine the OS map on page 109, then answer the following qusetions.

    NB: DO NOT use tracing paper when answering this question.

    A. On a sketch map based on the map, mark and label:

    i. the coastline

    ii. the network of roads

    iii. **four** different coastal landforms.   [20 marks]

    B. With reference to **one** landform mentioned above, describe and explain how the processes of erosion and/or of deposition affect coastlines.   [30 marks]

    C. 'Conflict is inevitable between the different ways in which people make use of coastal areas like this.' Examine this statement.   [30 marks]

4. The shaping of coastal landforms involves interaction between three forces: waves, currents and tides.

    A. Examine this statement with reference to **three** landforms that are typical of coastal regions.   [20 marks]

    B. With reference to the map on page 109, describe fully how Keel Lough, the golf course and Trawmore Beach formed.   [30 marks]

    C. Growth of urban settlement in coastal areas regularly changes the quality of the local environment over time. With reference to the map, explain how this might occur.   [30 marks]

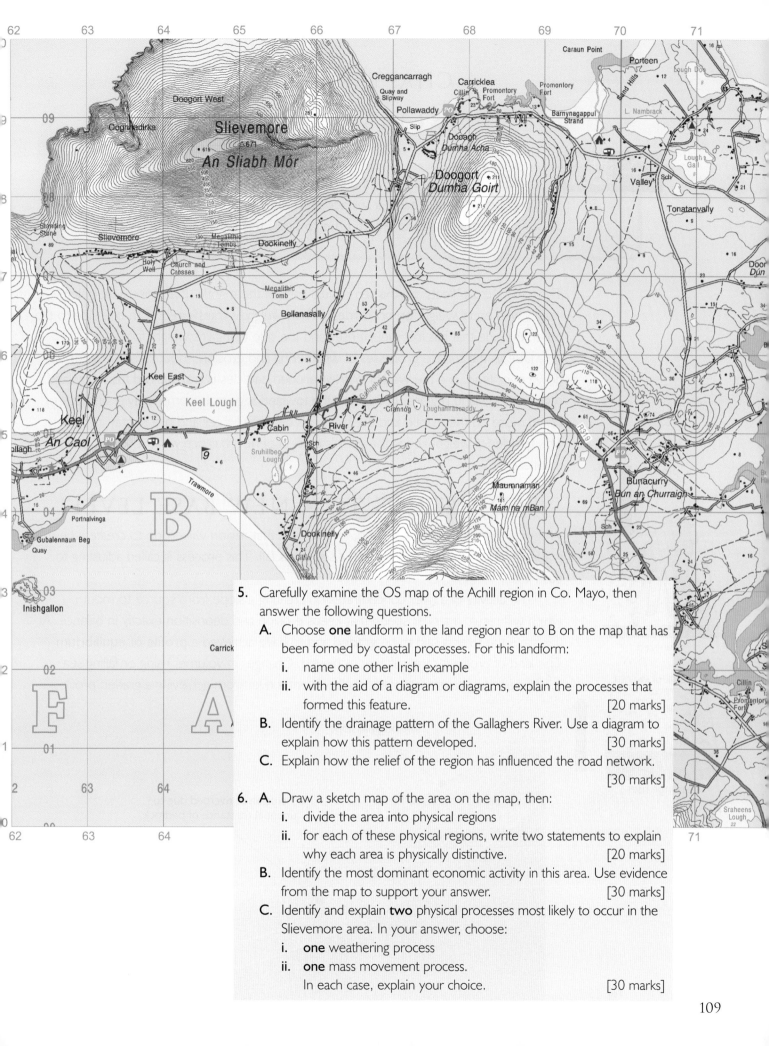

5. Carefully examine the OS map of the Achill region in Co. Mayo, then answer the following questions.

A. Choose **one** landform in the land region near to B on the map that has been formed by coastal processes. For this landform:

   i.   name one other Irish example

   ii. with the aid of a diagram or diagrams, explain the processes that formed this feature. [20 marks]

B. Identify the drainage pattern of the Gallaghers River. Use a diagram to explain how this pattern developed. [30 marks]

C. Explain how the relief of the region has influenced the road network. [30 marks]

6. A. Draw a sketch map of the area on the map, then:

   i.   divide the area into physical regions

   ii. for each of these physical regions, write two statements to explain why each area is physically distinctive. [20 marks]

B. Identify the most dominant economic activity in this area. Use evidence from the map to support your answer. [30 marks]

C. Identify and explain **two** physical processes most likely to occur in the Slievemore area. In your answer, choose:

   i.   **one** weathering process

   ii. **one** mass movement process.

      In each case, explain your choice. [30 marks]

CHAPTER 15
ISOSTASY

All landforms represent a balance between forces of erosion and deposition on the earth's surface and other forces within the earth's crust and mantle. From time to time, this balance changes.

The earth's crust 'floats' on the semi-liquid rock of the mantle. It acts like a weighing scales, with equal weight on both sides. When weight is transferred from one side to the other, the side that has lost weight rises and the side that gains weight falls.

Due to the surface processes of weathering and erosion, mountains are worn down over time, and the **weight** of their eroded particles **is transferred** from highland regions to lowland regions. In this way the lowland regions become heavier and push down more on the mantle and the highlands become lighter and rise to stay in balance. This transfer of weight keeps the earth's crust in perfect balance while it floats on the mantle.

ADJUSTING TO A NEW BASE LEVEL

When earth movements raise land, the rivers in that region will erode to create a new graded profile. This can also happen if sea levels fall. This process is called adjusting to base level.

The activity of a river concentrates on creating a slope from source to mouth, which will result in a river speed that keeps erosion and deposition exactly in balance. At this stage the river is said to be **graded** and to have achieved a **profile of equilibrium**. This kind of profile is rarely, if ever, achieved. Changes in volume, rising or falling sea level or unequal resistance of rocks all prevent a river from achieving a graded profile.

press down

squeezed

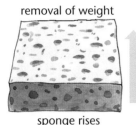

removal of weight

sponge rises

Fig. 15.1

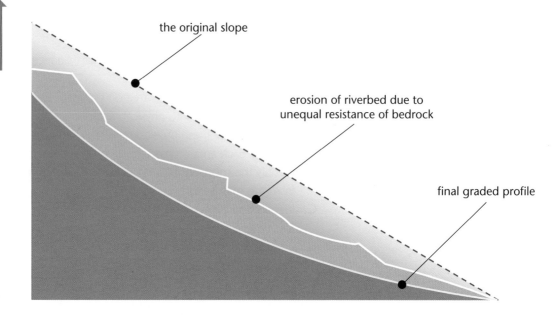

the original slope

erosion of riverbed due to unequal resistance of bedrock

final graded profile

Fig. 15.2

REJUVENATION

When land rises due to uplift, sea level falls and rivers get a new base level. Then the middle and lower courses of rivers begin a new phase of vertical erosion. This change is called **rejuvenation** (literally 'being made young again'). Many Irish river valleys display evidence of rejuvenation.

During the last Ice Age, Donegal in north-west Ireland had a cover in excess of a thousand metres of ice, pressing down on the land and 'squeezing' it like weight on a sponge. The loss of this weight about 10,000 years ago has allowed the land to rise, and the rivers now cut their way to the sea to create new river channels and new profiles.

Evidence of Rejuvenation in Ireland
Raised Beaches

Coastlines are particularly prone to changes of level. There is evidence that even since the end of the last Ice Age the level of the land in Ireland, relative to the sea level, has altered more than once. Traces of **old shore lines**, called raised beaches, are found along the coast some metres above high tide levels. Examples of these are found in Co. Donegal and Co. Antrim.

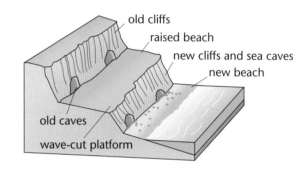

Fig. 15.3

Knick Point

When land rises relative to the sea, a rejuvenated river will cut upstream from its estuary. This creates a new base level. The change from the old to the new base level is marked by a sudden **change in the gradient** of the river. This is called the knick point and is represented by a waterfall or rapids. Over time, the knick point gradually moves upstream, until a completely new profile is achieved.

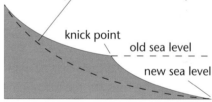

Fig. 15.4 The effect of rejuvenation on a river's profile.

Incised Meanders

On a rejuvenated river, vertical erosion begins again, so a meandering river that has been rejuvenated will cut deeply into its floodplain while maintaining its winding course. This process creates incised meanders. The River Nore has incised meanders in its valley.

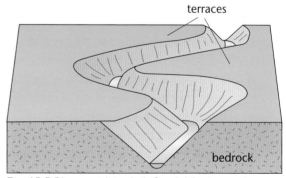

Fig. 15.5 Rivers cut into their floodplains to create incised meanders.

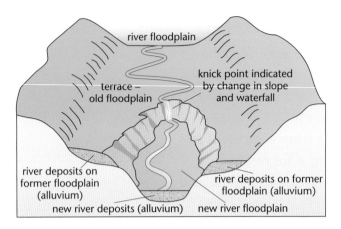

Terraces

Once incised meanders form, they begin to erode laterally and form a new floodplain at a lower level than the old one. The remnants of the old floodplain above the new level form terraces and are evidence that the river was rejuvenated.

Some river valleys display terraces at various levels. This suggests that the river was rejuvenated on a number of occasions in the past.

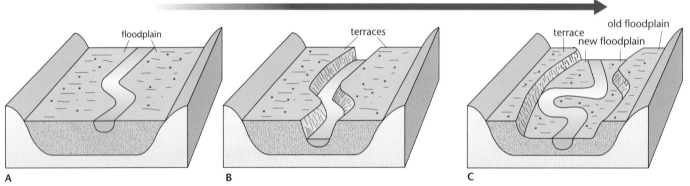

A　　　　　　　　　　**B**　　　　　　　　　　**C**

Fig. 15.6 The creation of terraces.

Activity

1. Explain the processes at work due to rejuvenation in diagrams A, B and C in Fig. 15.6.

2. Carefully examine the Ordnance Survey map on the next page, then answer the following questions.

   a. Does the River Barrow flow south through upland or lowland?

   b. Is the river following a straight or a meandering course?

   c. How would you describe the bend at S 72 35?

   d. At first glance, does this course suggest an upper, middle or lower stage of maturity?

   e. Look at the contour pattern at grid ref. S 73 36 along the river's edge. Does this suggest a V-shaped valley or a floodplain? Explain.

   f. From your studies of isostasy and adjustment to base level, explain possible reasons for the river's winding course and the contour pattern that borders the river.

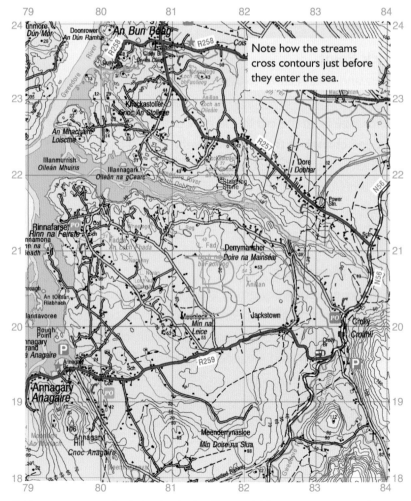

Note how the streams cross contours just before they enter the sea.

Evidence on maps of rejuvination in Co. Donegal. Rivers cross contours just before they enter the sea.

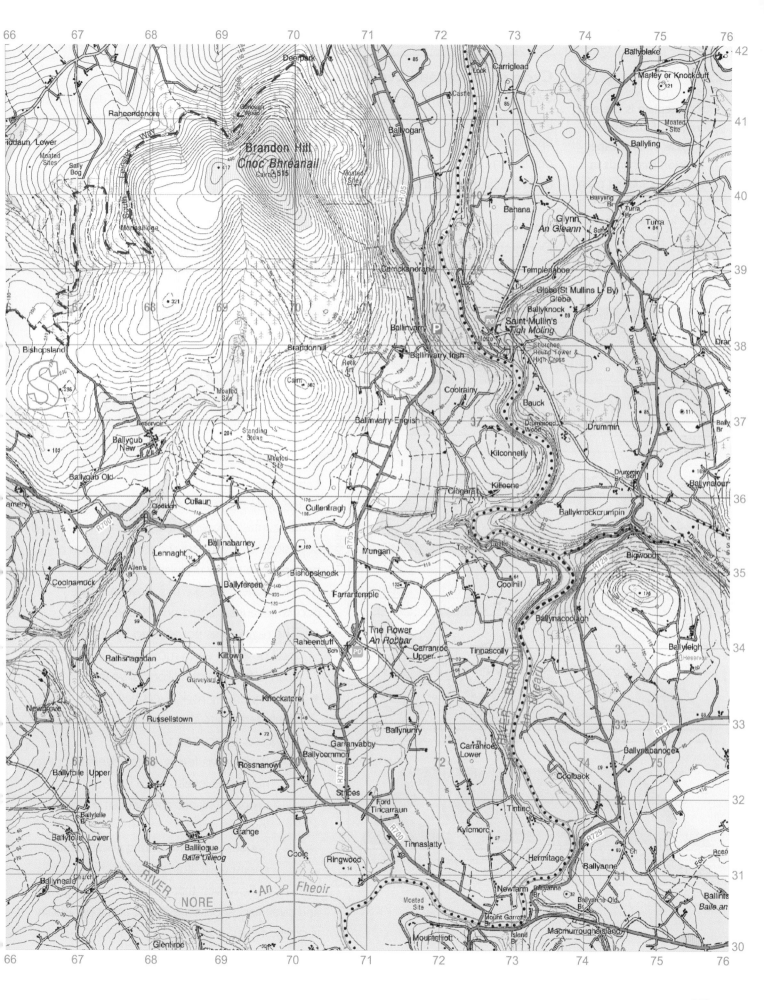

113

Cycle of Landscape Evolution

While streams are cutting their valleys, they are really sculpting the land. To describe this unending process, we have to visualise a beginning. For this, think of a relatively flat upland area with a wet climate, such as Ireland's. In this landscape, lakes and ponds will occupy any hollows that exist. As streams form and cut their valleys, they will eventually drain the lakes or fill them with sediment.

A peneplain is the end result of an idealised cycle of landscape erosion that ends in a gently undulating plain almost at sea level, e.g. the Munster Peneplain.

Early Stage

During the early stage, the landscape retains its **relatively flat surface**, interrupted only by narrow stream valleys.

Middle Stage

As vertical erosion (downcutting) continues, relief increases and the flat landscape is changed into one of **hills and valleys**. This is the middle stage. Eventually, some of the streams will approach base level. Downcutting will be replaced by lateral erosion, creating floodplains and lowering watersheds.

Later Stage

As the cycle nears the later stage, the effects of flooding, mass movement and lateral erosion and deposition by rivers will reduce the land to a **peneplain** (a gently undulating plain).

A simple cycle like this, however, rarely occurs because it could only happen if:

- The region was not affected by any additional local or global earth movements or climate change for tens of millions of years.
- The underlying rock layers had similar characteristics to the upper rock layers.
- No ice age occurred to:
  - Reduce sea levels, or for rivers to cut to new base levels.
  - Erode highlands and deposit materials on lowland.
  - Squeeze the land during glaciation and create uplift after glaciation.

We know, however, that change occurs regularly and over very short time spans, and a peneplain is rarely, if ever, achieved.

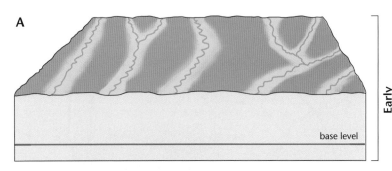

A

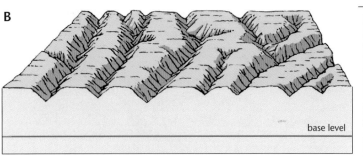

B

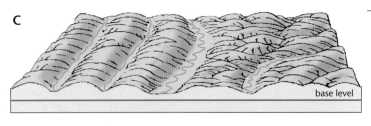

C

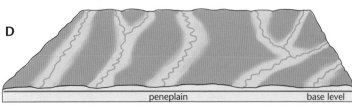

D

Fig. 15.7

Early

Middle

Later

CHAPTER 16
HOW PEOPLE INTERACT WITH SURFACE PROCESSES

 **KEY IDEA!** People's activities can affect the process of mass movement.

MASS MOVEMENT AND PEOPLE'S IMPACT

The Impact of Overgrazing

At moderate densities, when farm animals graze land, they encourage plants to grow by manuring the soil and clipping off the tops of plants, just as pruning encourages new growth on fruit trees or roses. With a high density of animals, the **vegetation is eaten faster than it can grow,** plant cover is reduced and soil may be washed away or blown away by the wind.

The number of animals that can be supported on farmland varies from region to region. In areas with moderate to high rainfall evenly distributed throughout the year, such as Ireland, cattle can be maintained at high densities (about three cattle per hectare). For arid and semi-arid regions, the density drops greatly. In Arizona, in the US, it takes between 17 to 25 hectares to support one animal.

Over the past few hundred years throughout peninsular Italy, **sheep and goats have overgrazed the slopes of the Apennines.** Soils that once supported these animals were exposed to summer thunderstorms and winter rains and were washed downslope into rivers. Sediment **clogged the water channels,** and swamps and **marshes** were created. An example of this is the Pontine Marshes, south of Rome. Malarial mosquitoes bred in these warm swamplands, leading to widespread **malaria** among rural families and working conditions that made farming uneconomic.

Students need study only **one** of the following:
People's activities and their impact on:
- Mass movement processes.
- River processes.
- Coastal processes.

Overgrazing by too many sheep has led to severe soil erosion in the Galtee Mountains.

Erosion of Irish Mountainsides

Overgrazing has occurred on some Irish mountainsides. Two examples include the Galtee Mountains in Co. Tipperary and the Mweelrea Mountains in Co. Mayo. **Overgrazing by sheep** has been the main cause of this problem. Farm subsidies for sheep led to a rapid increase in sheep numbers on mountainsides. The land became overstocked, and the grasses and heather were overgrazed. Mountain **soil was exposed to heavy rains** and localised landslides became commonplace (see the photo of the Galtees on page 115).

The Dust Bowl in the US. The soil was literally blown away.

The Impact of Overcropping

One of the worst examples of overcropping occurred in the **Dust Bowl** region of North America between 1934 and 1936. The worst affected areas were parts of **western Kansas, Nebraska, Oklahoma** and **Texas**. Overcropping happened when wheat was planted in semi-arid grazing areas because grain was fetching high prices and the region appeared to be moist enough to produce crops. The years of sufficient rain were then followed by several years of very low rainfall. The tilled soil was exposed to the strong winds of these level lands and was literally blown away, leaving only sand and gravel particles.

Many **farmers abandoned their farms and their homes** and headed west with their belongings. They went to California to become penniless fruitpickers, like the people who were immortalised in *The Grapes of Wrath,* a novel by American writer John Steinbeck.

A family uses a raft made from banana shoots to reach their home in the state of Assam, in India, which borders Bangladesh.

The Impact of Deforestation

Deforestation has happened throughout the world and on every continent. Today, it continues where population numbers are increasing rapidly. Most of these regions are in the tropics.

Forests are a global resource, so cutting forests in one country may severely affect another. For example, **Nepal in the Himalayas**, one of the most mountainous countries in the world, lost more than half its forest cover between 1950 and 1980. Little forest cover now remains in Nepal, and the loss of it has increased flooding in Bangladesh.

Cutting down forests **removes the vegetation** (trees and plants) that protects the soil. Killing the **tree and plant roots** that **bind** the soil particles together **exposes the soil** to heavy monsoon rains, and the rate of **landslides increases**.

116

Large quantities of **soil** are **washed downhill** into streams and river channels that flow into India and Bangladesh. This sediment **clogs the river channels,** which in turn causes widespread flooding, bringing death and destruction to the delta lowlands.

Other reasons for felling trees include the use of wood for firewood and the sale of timber for construction and paper pulp. Slightly more than half of all wood used in a year is used for **firewood.** In developed countries, it forms less than 1 per cent of energy used, but in Africa it generates more than half.

Desertification in Rajasthan and Gujarat in India's North-West

Fig. 16.1 The Thar Desert lands in India.

In India there are about 2.34 million square kilometres of hot desert called the **Thar**. It is an extremely arid region that receives only between **100 and 500 mm** of rain annually between July and September. Most of this rainfall filters quickly through the poor, sandy soils that are low in humus and mineral matter.

The Thar is a very hostile environment for living in, yet it is a densely populated tillage farming (crop-growing) region. The land is owned by **poor farmers** whose **traditional farming practices** restrict efficient conservation programmes.

Satellite images have proved that this region was once a rich agricultural area. The over-exploitation of land and water resources since earliest times has turned it into desert.

Problems

- The Thar desert suffers from **high winds, huge shifting sand dunes, high temperatures** by day and cold at night, **intense sunshine** and **high evaporation rates.**
- The cutting of wood for fuel and fodder production for cattle, the two basic necessities of life for the desert people, destroy the natural ground cover and aid desertification.
- Some regions have been grazed clean, and shrubs have been eaten down to extremely low levels.

Solutions

- The **Indira Ghandi Canal** was constructed to divert water from the Himalayan rivers to the desert region. This canal has dramatically changed the lands bordering the canal into an evergreen forest ecosystem.
- Because native trees in the region were few in number and also slow-growing, newer, **faster-growing species** were introduced from isoclimatic (similar) regions of the world. Each new species was chosen to suit individual environments, for example *Acacia tortilis* from Israel was ideal for stabilising sand dunes. Other species were chosen for biomass production and fodder.

Desertification has created major erosion problems in parts of India.

- **Shelter belts** and tree screens were grown as windbreaks to reduce wind speeds and to reduce erosion rates.
- **Seeding** from helicopters in association with the Indian military and manual seeding of dunes was also carried out.
- **Rooted grasses** were transplanted and **hedges** were established.

117

RIVER PROCESSES AND PEOPLE'S IMPACT ON THEM

The Impact of Hydroelectric Dams

Examples: Ardnacrusha on the River Shannon

Pollaphuca Dam on the River Liffey

KEY IDEA!

People's activities can interfere with the processes that operate in river valleys.

Dams are constructed across a river's channel to generate hydroelectric power. The dams **interrupt the natural flow of rivers and reduce the ability of rivers to carry sediment** from their upper valleys to their floodplains and their estuaries in lowland areas.

Hydroelectric dams are designed to block and use the flow of rivers. Water builds up behind the dams to form lakes, called **reservoirs**. The depth of a reservoir is regulated by allowing some water to flow through pipes in the dam, called penstocks, to generate **hydropower**.

Building hydroelectric dams may have **some positive results.** These include:

- Providing over 6 per cent of the world's energy needs.
- Providing reservoirs for irrigation and water supply.
- Regulating floodwaters to reduce flooding in lowland areas.

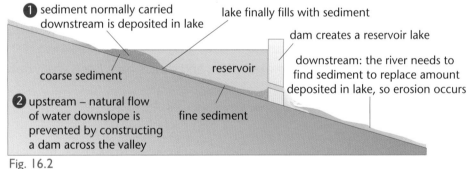

① sediment normally carried downstream is deposited in lake

lake finally fills with sediment

dam creates a reservoir lake

coarse sediment

reservoir

downstream: the river needs to find sediment to replace amount deposited in lake, so erosion occurs

② upstream – natural flow of water downslope is prevented by constructing a dam across the valley

fine sediment

Fig. 16.2

Dams are used to:

- Control floods.
- Store fresh water.
- Generate hydroelectricity.
- Supply water to industry and to people's homes, and for irrigation.

Activity

1. Carefully examine the aerial photograph on the left.
2. Identify the main landscape feature A.
3. Name the structure B.
4. Name the landforms C and D.

The way dams interfere with rivers' natural processes creates **some negative effects.**

Trapping of Sediment

The trapping of sediment in the reservoir lake reduces the silt and clay particles that are usually transported to the alluvial lowlands of floodplains and deltas. This reduces the fertility of the land and increases the need to apply expensive fertilizer.

As flowing water enters a reservoir, it drops its coarser sediment first, farthest from the dam. The finest material is dropped closest to the dam. The rapid build-up of coarse sediment may quickly build up a floodplain extending into the new lake and there may be flooding of settlements on the lake shores.

The fine silt may be removed at intervals to allow the dam to operate efficiently. This may lead to the reservoir having to be emptied and valuable water being lost as well as being a very costly operation.

The mass of the reservoir water may lead to faulting in regions prone to earthquakes. One fear of geologists for the new Kalabagh Dam in Pakistan is that this region is already tectonically active. This could lead to dam failure and a devastating outpouring of the lake waters from the dam.

Submergence of Land

Submergence of ecosystems, farmland and settlements occurs above dams. People are moved from their traditional homes and lands. As well as the **farmland** and **settlements, people's unique identity** is lost forever.

Reduced Volume

Reduced river flow out of dams proposed for the Indus in Pakistan could contribute to very low levels of water reaching the river's delta region. This would allow seawater to filter back into the delta lands and **poison the fragile freshwater ecosystem,** which includes wildlife, as well as turning fertile districts into waterlogged salt marshlands.

The Impact of Canalisation

Canalisation has been developed for:

- Improved water transportation.
- The transfer of water.

Improved Water Transportation

Canalisation may increase flooding. The River Rhine is Europe's most important navigable waterway. Ocean-going ships may go as far as Cologne, in Germany, and large barges may reach Basle, in Switzerland. Because of canalisation, however, meanders in the Rhineland have been straightened and floodwaters move too quickly downstream. This leads to flooding of towns and farmland in the lowlands of the Rhine.

The Transfer of Water

The need to transport water is growing as the world's population grows. But drawing water from source areas may have serious consequences if it is not managed carefully.

These consequences include the following.

Pore Collapse and Subsidence

When water fills the pore space of a rock in an aquifer (saturated rock layer below the water table), it holds the grains of the rock apart because water cannot be compressed. When too much water is taken for irrigation, air replaces the water. Air can be compressed, so the rock grains become packed more closely. This can have two effects:

- The ability of the rock to hold as much water as before may be reduced and so reduces its value as an aquifer.
- The surface level of the ground sinks. This is called subsidence and may cause the ground and the foundations of buildings to crack. Buildings may also tilt, such as the Leaning Tower of Pisa, or they may sink, such as happens in Venice.

> An aquifer is a body of permeable rock or regolith saturated with water and through which groundwater moves.

Increased Salt Content

Groundwater contains dissolved minerals, called **salts.** Within normal limits these help crops to grow, but in regions of intensive irrigations practices, such as the San Joaquin Valley in California, the evaporation rates cause increased salt content that may poison land.

Destruction of Ecosystems

The reduction in outflow of the Sacramento River is due to diversion of water to the San Joaquin Valley. This has allowed seawater to replace freshwater along the river's estuary and to poison its ecosystem.

Case Study: The Aral Sea

The water of the two largest rivers, the **Amu** and **Syr,** which provide fresh water for the Aral Sea, were diverted through canals to irrigate 7 million hectares of cotton, rice and melons for the former Soviet Union. The loss of this water to the sea has had the following effects:

- The Aral Sea has greatly reduced in size. Some ships that once transported goods or fished its waters are now beached on a dry seabed.
- The salt content of the sea has increased from 10 per cent to 40 per cent. This has changed the sea from being a freshwater lake to a saltwater lake.
- Many fish species have been wiped out.
- Summer temperatures near the lake have risen at times up to 45°C. Winter temperatures have become colder.

> The Aral Sea has been shrinking for the past thirty years because of the effects of canalisation.

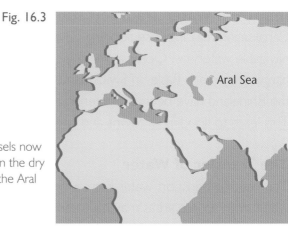

Fig. 16.3

Fishing vessels now stranded on the dry seabed of the Aral Sea.

Aral Sea

Flood Control Measures

Dam Construction

Dams are an efficient way to control floodwaters. The building of the Aswan High Dam in Egypt prevented annual flooding on the Nile downstream and allowed farmers to produce many crops in a single season.

Building Levees

Example: Mulcair River in Co. Limerick

Levee comes from the French word *'lever'*, which means 'to raise'. In the United States, the term is used to describe walls or dykes built along the southern part of the Mississippi River to retain floodwaters. The levees on the Mississippi are over 10 m high.

A river and its nearby flat floodplain together make up a natural system. In most untouched natural river valleys, the water flows over the riverbanks and onto the floodplain every year or so.

There are a number of natural processes that occur because of flooding:

- Water and nutrients are stored on the floodplain.
- Silt deposits on the floodplain increase the mineral content of the soil.
- Undeveloped land absorbs water and holds the excess until it can drain off naturally.
- Wetlands on the floodplain provide a natural habitat for many birds, animals, plants and other living organisms.

The construction of levees has a negative effect on all of these processes.

Floodplains are natural regions that absorb and store floodwaters until the water drains away naturally. Natural flooding is not a problem until people choose to build homes and other structures on floodplains. These structures are prone to damage and loss when flooded. People have chosen to build on so many floodplains that flooding is the **most universal natural hazard** in the world. The 1993 flood of the Mississippi took over fifty lives and caused over US$10 billion in damage when about 70 per cent of the levees failed. They simply were not designed to withstand a flood that lasted over two months.

The Mississippi floods vast regions of farmland and cities when its levees cannot retain its water.

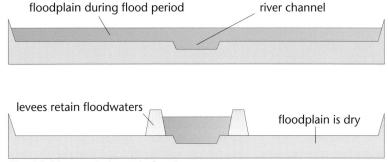

floodplain during flood period   river channel

levees retain floodwaters   floodplain is dry

Fig. 16.4 Levees help retain floodwaters.

Levees retain floodwaters of the Mississippi River.

121

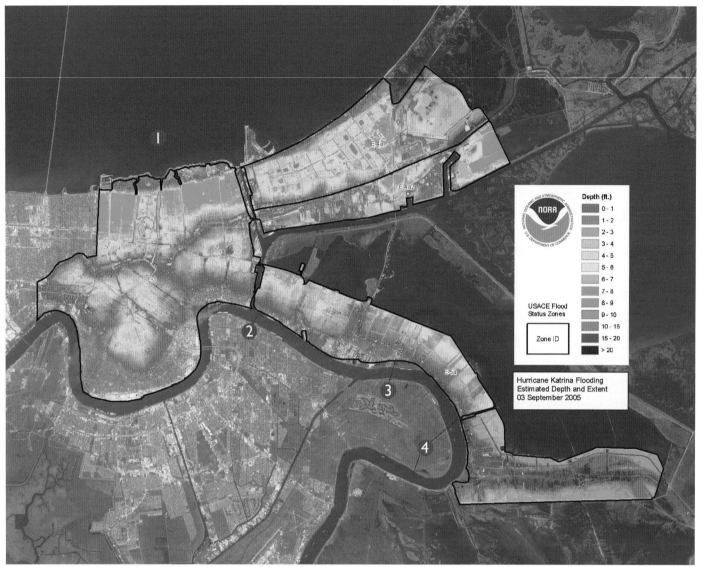

This is a satellite image of New Orleans in flood. Hurricane Katrina created such high water levels that its levees failed. New Orleans was flooded and many of its inhabitants died.

Activity

Carefully examine the satellite image, then answer the following questions.

1. Name:
   a. the sea area at 1
   b. the river at 2
   c. the landform at 3
   d. the landform at 4.
2. Identify the stage of maturity of this river in New Orleans. Explain.
3. What type of atmospheric pressure is associated with a hurricane?
4. What type of weather is associated with a hurricane? Explain.
5. What is the greatest depth of the floodwaters?
6. With the aid of diagrams, explain the formation of levees.
7. Explain why you think the levees may have failed.
8. Why do levees form along this part of the river?
9. Identify and explain the formation of the type of delta that is associated with this river.

COASTAL PROCESSES AND PEOPLE'S IMPACT ON THEM

 **KEY IDEA!** People's activities can interfere with coastal process.

Recreational Pressures

Extensive construction of hotels, mobile home sites, golf courses, marinas and holiday homes along Irish and global coastal regions has increased pressure on fragile coastal environments in a number of ways.

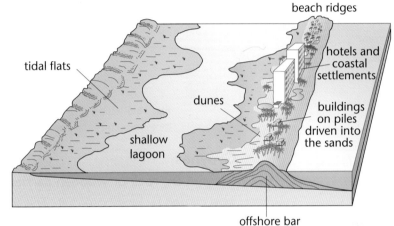

Fig. 16.5 Offshore barrier island bars are developed as coastal resorts, with hotels and holiday complexes along much of the east coast of the United States.

In Ireland

- The **visual impact on the landscape** of hotels, mobile homes, golf courses and marinas has changed some regions dramatically. In addition, holiday homes, most of which are unoccupied for most of the year, have altered the character of some local communities.

- Increased tourism has created a difficulty with the **quality of coastal water** in seaside towns and with local sewage systems that struggle to cope with demand during the peak holiday season. Low funding from local authorities to improve these services adds to the difficulty. As settlements grow, their sewage discharges increase dramatically, especially during summer when towns that may have only 400 residents during winter swell to 25,000 in July and August.

- **The Environmental Protection Agency** and local authorities regularly monitor the quality of seawater and the maintenance of beaches at coastal resorts.

In Other Parts of the World

- **Access to beaches** has been restricted in places such as Malibu in California and around the Mediterranean where private dwellings and hotels form continuous development along the coast.

- The **location of coastal developments** on low-lying sand bars and spits make them vulnerable to storm damage. Coastal developments in the Caribbean and Florida have suffered severe damage during the hurricanes that regularly affect these regions.

Coastal developments have altered many coastlines in warm regions.

123

The Impact of Coastal Defence Work

Sand dunes have suffered from severe erosion in some places in recent years. Here, **chestnut fencing** is used to trap sand and prevent erosion.

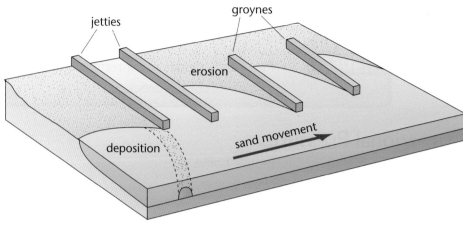

Fig. 16.6 Jetties, groynes and breakwaters interrupt the movement of sand by beach drift and longshore currents. Beach erosion often results downcurrent from the site of the structure.

Groynes

Groynes are **rock or wooden barriers placed at right angles** to the seashore to trap sand carried by longshore drift. This trapped sand eventually creates a beach that allows waves to lose their energy when they crash onshore. Groynes have to be carefully managed, as they reduce the amount of sediment carried further along the coast and this may lead to the erosion of other beaches.

The **location and spacing** of groynes is essential to make sure that the correct level of sediment is trapped by the groynes so that the need for protecting the area is balanced with the requirements of the zones further along the coast.

Breakwaters

Offshore breakwaters are **long, parallel mounds of rubble or rock that are built parallel to the shore to reduce erosive wave action.** Like groynes, breakwaters are designed to suit each individual site of coastal erosion.

Concrete sea walls and honeycomb rock are used to protect urban areas from erosion.

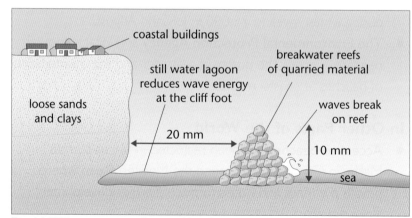

Fig. 16.7 There are many forms of breakwater.

The effect of wave change around the breakwater is to set up new currents that trap sediment in the sheltered side of the structure. The sediment deposited in the lee of the breakwater may result in either an increase in the beach width at the shoreline or a sandbar reaching to the breakwater in the form of a tombolo. The formation of the tombolo will depend on local factors, such as the tidal current, the storm frequency or the shape of breakwater.

Breakwaters are sometimes attached to the shore. These include long walls built across a harbour to protect fishing trawlers and ferries that are moored to a quayside. Leisure craft are sometimes moored away from industrial port areas and also need the protection of breakwaters from storm waves.

Fig. 16.8

[figure labels: eroded rocks, collapsing cliff, original narrow beach, breakwater, new tombolo accumulations of sand]

Leisure craft, such as sailing boats, are often protected by breakwaters in coastal areas.

Conservation and Management Measures

In recent decades, it has been recognised that **a coastline is a valuable natural resource that needs careful and sensitive management.** This is especially so in the case of Ireland, where the shores are subjected to severe storm waves from the Atlantic every year and to human interference from the recent rapid developments of golf courses and coastal holiday homes and mobile home sites.

A code of practice for coastal management and conservation has been established on the **basis of pilot projects and by gathering expert knowledge** of individual coastal areas. The code of practice is called **ECOPRO – Environmentally Friendly Coastal Protection**. The objectives of ECOPRO are to:

- Develop monitoring methods suited to various types of coastline.
- Develop a sensitivity index to grade a coastline's susceptibility to erosion.
- Present an evaluation of various coastal protection and management methods.
- Present case histories of some of these methods.

Beach Management

The **principle** behind the code of practice **is to maintain** as far as possible **the protection created by the natural features** of the coast. For example, a beach is nature's way of reducing the energy of sea action. The objective should be to keep beaches in place. Beaches and sand dunes are valuable coastal resources that should be protected.

Straw bales and jute matting placed behind rocks to project beach sand from erosion.

Marram grass planted to stabilise sand dunes.

Concrete sea walls and rock armour are used to protect coastline areas from erosion.

Because the depth of sand on beaches may naturally fluctuate (increase or decrease) from season to season, the beach must be allowed to do this without interference. The dunes at the back of beaches form an integral part of the system, so they must also be allowed to fulfil their function. While sand dunes are valuable for leisure activities, it is necessary to regulate how they are used. It is important to note that a valuable resource may be easily and permanently destroyed by inappropriate management.

Where there is erosion, the new management policy must first:

- Deal with an assessment of the erosion problem. The aim is to determine the nature of the problem: whether there is continuous erosion, or erosion caused by a single storm or a few storms over a short period, such as a month or two. The aim is also to identify the causes, whether they were natural or man-made.
- Identify suitable solutions and assess how these solutions have worked in other areas.

Beach Nourishment

Beaches sometimes lose their sand covering during storms. Beach nourishment is simply **pumping new sand** onto eroded beaches to change wave movement from being destructive to being constructive. The presence of a renewed beach allows the swash to filter into the sand, while at the same time, depositing new sand in the process. The additional sand is usually obtained by offshore dredging, although in certain cases sand quarries are used for small schemes. Great care is taken in choosing **sand grain size** and its **distribution** so that it suits the site.

A beach nourishment programme was undertaken in Rosslare Strand from October 1994 to January 1995. Over a quarter of a million cubic metres of sand was dredged from a site 6 km offshore and pumped onto the beach. A rock groyne system helps to retain sand on the beach. In this case, beach nourishment was carried out for coastal defence work as well as for recreational use.

Causes of Erosion

Coastlines are constantly receding because they are being worn away by the forces of nature. The causes of erosion may be classified into two groups:

- Erosion caused by people.
- Erosion caused by nature.

Erosion Caused by People

Human interference includes removing sand directly (for building and other uses), or indirectly by interfering with natural processes such as longshore drift.

The coastal engineer must aim to strike a balance between preventing erosion and interference with natural processes that may destabilise the coastline.

Erosion Caused by Nature

Natural causes include:

- The erosion-deposition balance, which may be affected by climatic change (such as increased storm frequency).
- The rise or fall of sea level due to earth movements.
- Natural changes in sediment supply.

Sand Dune Management

Recreational activites, such as pedestrian traffic, cars, caravan parks, horse riding and motorbike scrambling, can seriously damage dune vegetation and increase the rate of sand loss through wind erosion. This loss of sand could directly affect the amount of sand on the beach and the size of the sand dunes.

Some Effects of Recreational Activities

- The trampling of vegetation by pedestrian traffic is the most widespread form of damage to sand dunes by people. This occurs where human activity is concentrated in small areas and a fan-shaped network of paths and tracks develop leading from caravan parks, car parks and other areas of public access to the coast. As vegetation is damaged, erosion begins and the wind attacks the exposed sand, eventually forming gullies and gaps called blow-outs. Paths across the tops of dunes are most at risk, as wind speeds are greater there and path slopes are often steeper. Gullies created in cliffs of boulder clay can lead to cliff slumping.
- Ideally, vehicles, horse riding and motorbike scrambling should be banned from beach areas because they can devastate sand dune systems. If 200 vehicles per year pass over sand dunes, it can reduce vegetation cover by 50 per cent. Where these activities are allowed on dunes, paths for them should run at right angles to the direction of the prevailing winds.

Protection of Natural Wildlife Habitats

Sandflats and **mudflats** in tidal areas, such as river estuaries, hold dense populations of marine worms, shellfish and other invertebrate life. These are the foods that attract large numbers of wintering migrant birds. Some of these birds include the oystercatcher, curlew, redshank, ducks (such as teal), waders and geese. **Salt marsh areas** attract birds to hatch and rear their young. One of the best-known wildlife habitats is in Dublin Bay, off **Dollymount Strand**. Usually, the greatest abundance of life is close to land and so is under constant threat of pollution and habitat destruction. Careless dredging, dumping of waste or coastal defences could pollute these areas or remove them due to changes in coastal currents. To protect these areas, some inshore areas are designated as **Natural Heritage Areas.**

Migrating birds seek tidal flats for their food supply.

Activity
1. Why are beaches important for controlling coastal processes?
2. Explain why evaluating and recording natural coastal processes is essential for balanced human interaction in coastal areas.
3. Describe the positive and negative effects of some engineering structures designed to reduce erosion.
4. Beaches are natural regions that are essential for coastal and human processes. Discuss.

127

CHAPTER 17
WEATHER CHARTS AND SATELLITE IMAGES

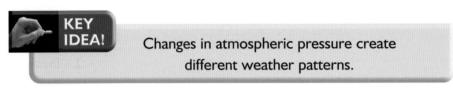

KEY IDEA!

Changes in atmospheric pressure create different weather patterns.

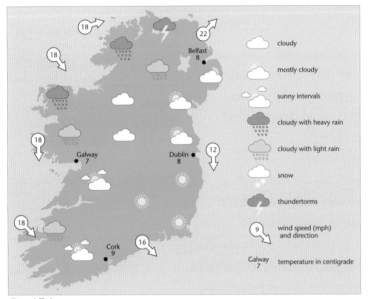

cloudy

mostly cloudy

sunny intervals

cloudy with heavy rain

cloudy with light rain

snow

thundertorms

wind speed (mph) and direction

temperature in centigrade

Fig. 17.1

A weather map is also called a **synoptic chart**. It shows weather for a particular area at one specific time. It is the result of collecting and sorting a considerable amount of information at numerous weather stations. This information is then refined by computers and plotted on a map, using internationally accepted **weather symbols**.

Weather maps are produced for different purposes and at various scales:

- The **daily weather map** as seen on TV or in the newspaper. This gives a clear but very simplified impression of the weather.
- At a higher level, a synoptic chart shows certain weather characteristics for specific weather stations. These characteristics generally include six elements: temperature, pressure, cloud cover, present weather (type of precipitation), wind direction and wind speed.
- At **the highest level,** weather maps show trends of pressure change, types of cloud at various levels and the dew point.

Forecasters now use satellite images that show a **simulated three-dimensional model** including present weather conditions and a short forecast.

The most typical weather patterns that develop over the north Atlantic Ocean include high pressure systems called **anticyclones** and low pressure systems called **cyclones**, or **depressions**.

Fig. 17.2

CLOUD		WEATHER		WIND SPEED			
Symbol	Cloud amount (eighths)	Symbol	Weather	Symbol	Speed (knots)	Force	3°Celsius
	0	=	mist		calm	0	
	1/8 or less or 1 octa	=	fog				Pressure is shown by isobars and is measured in millibars
	2/8 or less or 2 octas	,	drizzle		5	2	
	3/8 or less or 3 octas	;	rain and drizzle				
	4/8 or less or 4 octas	•	rain		10	3	
	5/8 or less or 5 octas	*	rain and snow				———1012———
	6/8 or less or 6 octas	*	snow		15	4	
	7/8 or less or 7 octas	▽	rain shower	For each additional half-feather add 5 knots			mean sea level pressure
	8 octas or overcast	* ▽	snow shower				L = centre of an area of low pressure
	sky obscured by fog	△ ▽	hail shower	WIND DIRECTION			
	missing or doubtful data	⌐	thunderstorm	Indicates a north-westerly wind direction at 15 knots			H = centre of an area of high pressure

128

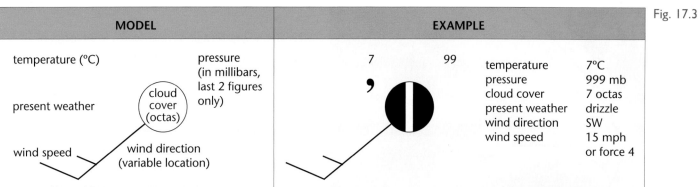

Fig. 17.3

During a Depression or Cyclone

- Warm air is forced to rise into the atmosphere, so creating low pressure.
- This creates **cooling** of the warm air, and cloud forms along the boundary of the warm and cold air masses.
- These boundaries are called **fronts**.

Within a depression there are two fronts:

- A **warm front** represented by this symbol ⬤⬤⬤ on a weather map.
- A **cold front** represented by this symbol ▲▲▲ on a weather map.

Further cooling creates precipitation. The cloud or mist particles join to form water droplets. When the rising air is unable to suspend the droplets in the air, they fall as precipitation.

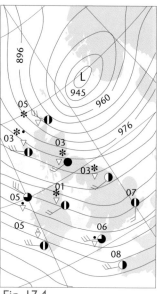

Fig. 17.4

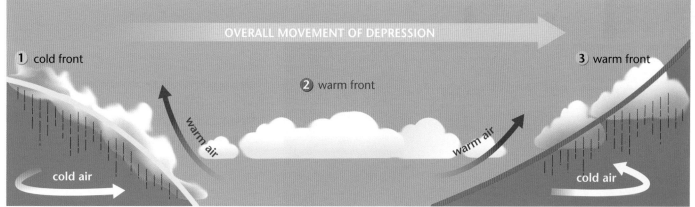

A wedge of cold air cuts under the warm, humid, tropical air. The warm air is forced to rise, so it cools, condenses and clouds form along the cold front. Precipitation falls, mostly in the form of heavy rain. **Strong winds blow.**

The warm air continues to rise slowly until the cold wedges of air finally meet. Broken stratus clouds fill the sky. Some sunny spells occur. Drizzle sometimes falls. Gentle winds blow.

The warm tropical air is forced up over the cold polar air. Cooling and condensation of the rising air creates clouds along the warm front. Precipitation forms mostly as showers. **Strong winds blow.**

Fig. 17.5

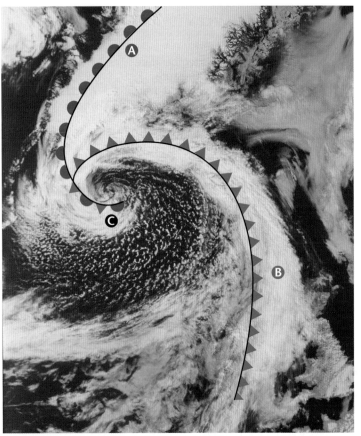

North Atlantic depression. Ireland and the UK are located in the bottom right. At top centre is the ice cap of Greenland. The frontal system is the swirling mass of cloud to the left of centre, with a low pressure area at the centre of the spiral. Low-level clouds are shown as yellow or pink. High-level clouds are white.

Activity

1. Over which region is the warm front located?
2. Over which country is the cold front located?
3. Describe the general weather conditions at A, B and C.
4. Look at the weather chart on page 128, then answer the following questions.
   a. Describe the weather conditions over the north Kerry/Dingle region.
   b. Does this type of weather system bring stable or unstable conditions? Explain.
   c. Is this weather system a cyclone or an anticyclone?

Activity

Examine the satellite image of a weather system below, then answer the following.

1. Identify this type of weather system.
2. Identify the land region on the top left and centre left.
3. Describe the weather conditions associated with such a weather system in this region.
4. At what time of year are these weather systems most frequent in this region? Explain.

Activity

This is a satellite image of a cyclone, or hurricane, in the tropics. Use the internet to learn about hurricanes that strike the Florida and Gulf coastal states in the US.

During an Anticyclone

- Heavy, cold air high in the atmosphere falls towards the earth's surface. It presses down, **squeezing** the air near the ground and creating **high pressure.**
- Winds blow outwards from the centre of the high pressure.
- Due to the **Coriolis force,** these winds blow in a **clockwise** movement.
- Increasing pressure heats the air, so it is able to hold more moisture. The air has little or no cloud, so it is **sunny** and **dry.**

Slack Winds

Anticyclones bring **light winds, or calm** conditions. When wind does exist, it will blow outwards in a **clockwise** movement due to the **Coriolis force. Isobars** are **widely spaced** to represent light or calm conditions.

Less Cloud

Descending air increases pressure, which has the effect of **increasing air temperature**. Warming air is able to **hold more moisture** than cooling air, so it is **dry** and creates **little or no cloud**. Little or no cloud results in **sunny** weather.

Dry Weather

Descending air gets warmer and holds its moisture in the **form of gas**. Even though the air may have lots of **water vapour,** little condensation occurs and there is little cloud.

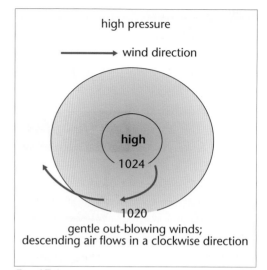

high pressure

→ wind direction

high
1024

1020

gentle out-blowing winds;
descending air flows in a clockwise direction

Fig. 17.6

Activity

Study the satellite image of weather systems over the north Atlantic in June, then answer the following questions.

1. Identify the type of weather system:
   a. over Ireland
   b. over north-east Canada and Greenland.
2. a. Describe the weather conditions over Ireland at this time.
   b. Explain the type of airflow one should expect during these atmospheric conditions.
   c. Is this type of weather over Ireland created by high or low atmospheric pressure? Explain.

REGIONAL GEOGRAPHY

CHAPTER 18
WHAT IS A REGION?

KEY IDEA!

A region is an area on the earth's surface that has a different identity from surrounding areas.

The Concept of a Region

What Is a Region?

A region is an area of the earth's surface that has human and/or physical characteristics that give it an identity and make it different from all the areas around it.

Table 18.1 illustrates some of the different types of region that we can study. These are highlighted and explained in the following chapters.

Table 18.1

Examples of Different Regions	
Region Type	**Example**
Climate region	Cool Temperate Oceanic (Chapter 19)
Physical region	The Burren (Chapter 20)
Administrative region	*Départments* in France (Chapter 21)
Cultural region	The Gaeltacht (Chapters 21; 33)
Core region	Paris region (Chapter 28)
Peripheral region	The Mezzogiorno (Chapter 27)
Industrial declining region	Sambre-Meuse Valley (Chapter 24)
Urban region	Dublin (Chapters 25; 34)

Activity

Study Table 18.1 and answer the following questions.
1. Suggest the main characteristic(s) which gives each regional example its distinctive identity.
2. Provide another example for each of the regional types.

Regions and Differences of Scale

There are many sizes of region. Some, such as the subcontinent of India, are huge, while others, such as the Gaeltacht regions in the West of Ireland, are small. The size of a region and **scale** of map used to define a region depend on the reason for studying it.

Figs. 18.1 and 18.2 show this with maps of two regions drawn at different scales. The first map, in Fig. 18.1, is drawn at a large scale to show the region of Europe. Not much detailed information can be shown at this scale. In contrast, Fig. 18.2 is drawn at a much smaller scale and allows for more detailed study of the Greater Cork Area.

Fig. 18.1 The countries of Europe.

Activity

Look at the maps in Figs. 18.1 and 18.2.

1. Do maps drawn at large scales show more details than maps drawn at small scales?

2. For **each** map, suggest two advantages of studying the region at the scale shown on the map.

3. What could be a disadvantage of studying each region at the scale shown?

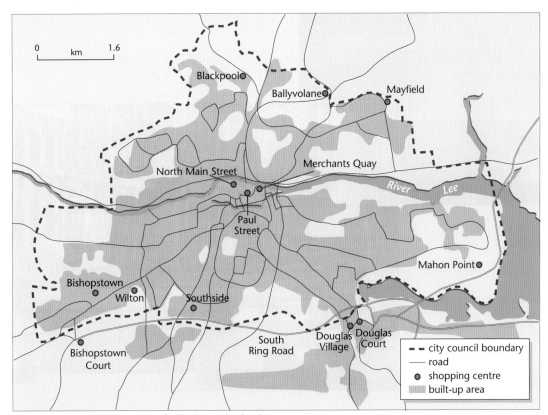

Fig. 18.2 Shopping centres in Cork city and suburbs.

General Characteristics of a Region

Although regions can be defined in different ways, some factors are the same for all regions:

- **Area:** Regions occupy an area of the earth's surface that can be identified as being different from surrounding areas.
- **Boundaries:** Regions are enclosed by boundaries that separate them from surrounding regions. Some boundaries are easily identified on the earth's surface, such as the crest of a mountain range or the course of a river. Most boundaries used by people, however, are not so easily recognised in the landscape, such as local government boundaries.
- **Image:** For most people, mentioning the name of a region often creates a perception or image of that region for them. These images are usually based on someone knowing about or being familiar with a region.
- **Change:** Regions change over time. At the start of the twentieth century, the Dublin urban region was quite small. Today, modernisation of transport systems has resulted in Dublin's urban region extending to 80 km or more from the city centre (see Chapter 34).

Different images of Ireland.
- *Which would be the image for a person living in Ireland as opposed to an American tourist planning a visit to Ireland?*

CHAPTER 19
CLIMATIC REGIONS

KEY IDEA! A climatic region is an area with an identity that comes from regular weather patterns over a long period of time. These weather patterns affect vegetation and soils in a region.

Climatic regions are areas that have their own distinct climate and are separated from each other by boundaries. In some areas these boundaries are sharply defined, while in others they are not as well defined because one climate area blends into another. Within a climate region, the unique weather system and its temperature, precipitation, seasons, soil and vegetation make it completely different from all the surrounding regions.

Some climate regions are huge, for example the equatorial climate region that includes the Amazon Basin in South America, the Congo Basin in Africa and the Indonesian islands.

Remember from your Junior Certificate how climate affects soil. Cold boreal climate areas have **podzol** soils and hot climates have **laterite** soils.

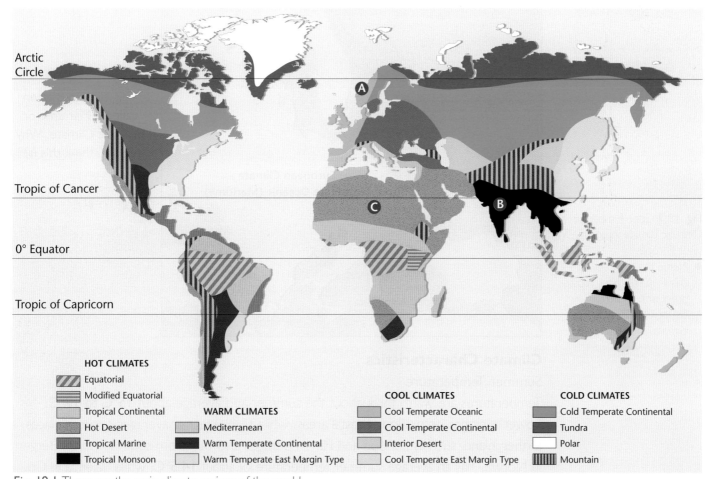

HOT CLIMATES
- Equatorial
- Modified Equatorial
- Tropical Continental
- Hot Desert
- Tropical Marine
- Tropical Monsoon

WARM CLIMATES
- Mediterranean
- Warm Temperate Continental
- Warm Temperate East Margin Type

COOL CLIMATES
- Cool Temperate Oceanic
- Cool Temperate Continental
- Interior Desert
- Cool Temperate East Margin Type

COLD CLIMATES
- Cold Temperate Continental
- Tundra
- Polar
- Mountain

Fig. 19.1 These are the main climate regions of the world.
- Identify the climates at A, B and C.

A cloud-covered Dingle Peninsula.
- *Suggest reasons for the high frequency of cloud cover and high rainfall experienced in such areas.*

Other climate regions are tiny. These are called **microclimates**. The physical presence of a city affects the local climate, and as a city changes, so does its climate. The bigger the city becomes, the more polluted the air is and the warmer its temperature. Buildings absorb and release heat, while the dust in the air traps and reflects heat back into the city, making the urban area warmer than its surrounding areas. This is called an urban microclimate. Microclimates may vary from one side of a rock to another, or from one side of a tree to another.

Case Study: Climate of North-West Europe: Cool Temperate Oceanic Climate

This climate region occurs as a narrow coastal zone in Western Europe that stretches from northern Norway to north-west Spain. It includes the whole of Britain and Ireland.

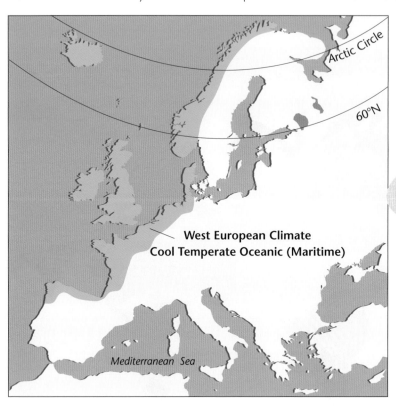

Fig. 19.2 Cool Temperate Oceanic climate in north-west Europe.
- *Name the countries on this map that have coastal areas with a Cool Temperate Oceanic climate.*

This climate is often called a Maritime or Oceanic Climate. Why do you think this is?

Climate Characteristics

Summer Temperature

Temperatures are warm throughout the summer and average about **15°C to 17°C**. Lower averages occur along coastal areas, while slightly higher averages occur in places further inland, such as London and Paris. Averages also vary from south to north. Bergen in Norway has an average summer temperature of about **14.5°C**, while Valentia in Co. Kerry averages about **15°C**. Daytime temperatures may reach **23°C** or more on hot days.

Winter Temperature

Temperatures are mild through winter months, and January temperatures may average about **4°C to 5°C**. The warm North Atlantic Drift that flows from the Gulf of Mexico to the west coast of Europe influences all the sea areas. Blowing over this warm water surface are the South-West Anti-Trade Winds that bring warm air to coastal areas throughout the year. This is most noticeable during winter, as temperatures are generally above **4°C** and so make the weather mild and moist.

Precipitation

The one certainty about precipitation (rainfall) in this climate region is that it may fall at any time of year. Most rain, however, falls in winter. It is mostly associated with depressions or cyclones that travel from a south-west to north-east direction across the North Atlantic and bring changeable weather to this coastal region.

Relief rain also occurs, and highland and upland areas, such as the mountains of the West of Ireland, the Scottish Highlands and the Scandinavian Highlands, receive more rain than lowland areas. Some precipitation falls as snow. The total rainfall can vary from as little as 500 millimetres (mm) in lowland areas to 2,500 mm in highland areas.

The Climate of Ireland

Ireland is located in north-west Europe and so has a Cool Temperate Oceanic or Maritime climate. Its prevailing winds are the South-West Anti-Trades that blow from the Atlantic Ocean. These winds and the presence of mountains along Ireland's coastline cause Ireland to be divided into **two climatic regions**. They are the wetter West of Ireland and the drier eastern Ireland.

■	over 2,000 mm	▨	1,000–1,200 mm
■	1,600–2,000 mm	▨	800–1,000 mm
■	1,400–1,600 mm	▨	less than 800 mm

Fig. 19.3 Annual rainfall totals in Ireland.

Activity

Look at Fig. 19.3 and answer the following.
1. Using a diagram, explain why Ireland's heaviest rainfall occurs along the western coast.
2. Explain why the Dublin region in the east of the country has the least rainfall. Think about relief rain and rain shadow.

CHAPTER 20
PHYSICAL REGIONS

A physical region is an area with an identity that comes from its surface characteristics being different from all its surrounding areas.

Remember how landforms of karst landscapes were explained in Chapter 10, page 59.

Physical regions have surface characteristics that make them different from all the areas around them. The physical differences may be due to height and relief, the rock types, drainage pattern or internal rock structure, or a combination of these factors.

Karst Landscapes

Karst landscapes are regions formed by chemical weathering.

Case Study: The Burren in Co. Clare

The Burren is an upland, terraced limestone region in Co. Clare. The beds of rock dip gently to the south. In some places the limestone is covered by shale. Some of the soil cover was eroded by glaciers, while tilling the land by early farmers exposed the remaining soil to strong coastal winds.

Most of the Burren today has no soil cover and weathering has created a karst landscape. Large expanses of limestone pavement with grikes and clints dominate the area. There are few surface streams. Most disappear underground through sinkholes (swallow holes) and flow through underground passages and caverns.

Karst landscapes occur in many areas in Ireland, such as the Dartry-Cuilcagh Uplands in Co. Fermanagh and Co. Cavan (see Chapter 8, page 52). The best example in Ireland is the Burren in Co. Clare.

Formation

The Burren was formed when the African and European plates collided. This collision also formed a huge mountain chain across Europe, of which the Galtees, the Macgullicuddy's Reeks and the ridges of Munster are remnants.

● *What evidence in the photograph suggests that the Burren in Co. Clare is a karst region?*

Munster Ridge and Valley Region

This natural region is explained in Chapter 8, page 51.

The North European Plain Region

The North European Plain is a lowland region that extends from west to east across Europe from Ireland and Britain to the countries around the Black Sea, such as Romania and the Ukraine (see Fig. 20.1).

Formation

The forces that created the ridge and valley region of Munster and the Burren Upland in Co. Clare also rippled the seafloor that now forms the foundation of the North European Plain. Later, after the Alps and surrounding uplands were formed, sediments were washed down or blown by wind onto the plain from the weathered and eroded mountains and levelled it. The final result was the North European Plain. Slight warpings have made it undulating rather than flat.

During the last great Ice Age, an enormous ice sheet squeezed down this lowland region of north-west Europe. When the ice melted and raised the level of the sea, much of the land that had subsided was submerged beneath the North and Baltic Seas. In this way, Britain and Ireland were cut off from mainland Europe. Rivers flowed northwards and formed deltas along the coasts of the Netherlands, Belgium and northern Germany. As the great weight of ice was removed, the land started to rise again. This process continues today and is noticeable in the raised beaches found along the coast of Northern Ireland, Scotland and the Baltic coastline.

Remember isostasy in Chapter 15 on page 110.

The North and Baltic Seas are shallow because their floors were once part of the North European Plain.

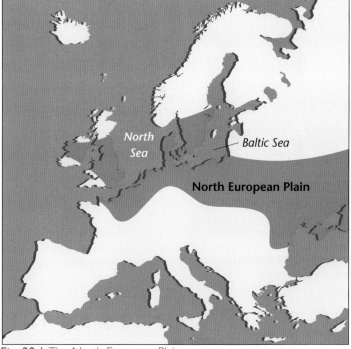

Fig. 20.1 The North European Plain.

Activity

Look at Fig. 20.1 and name some of the countries that are in this lowland region.

CHAPTER 21
ADMINISTRATIVE REGIONS

There are many types and sizes of administrative regions.

ADMINISTRATIVE REGIONS AT DIFFERENT SCALES

One of the most basic forms of region are administrative units such as county and city councils. Most governments divide their national space into a hierarchy of local and regional areas. This allows them to administer development more effectively.

Administrative areas need to be large enough to allow for providing services efficiently; an example of this is the Health Service Executive Areas (Fig. 21.5). The areas also need to be **small** enough to work effectively and reflect community interests, for example local school districts.

The links between various levels of administration generally take one of two forms (see Figs. 21.1 and 21.2).

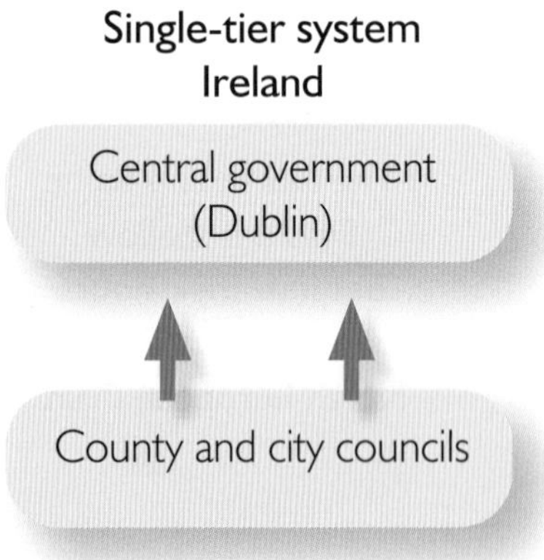

Why do communities prefer small and more localised forms of administration?

Multiple-tier system France

Central government (Paris)

22 regional governments

92 *départements* (local government)

Single-tier system Ireland

Central government (Dublin)

County and city councils

- **Single-tier system:**
  Each administration area has direct access to central government, for example, Ireland.

- **Multiple-tier system:**
  Local authorities work with central government through a bureaucracy (system of government officials and departments) of one or more regional levels, e.g. France.

Fig. 21.1 A single-tier system of government.

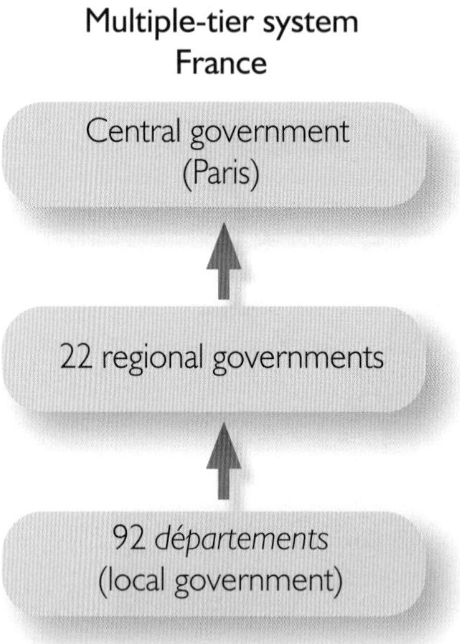

Fig. 21.2 A multiple-tier system of government.

ADMINISTRATIVE UNITS IN IRELAND
The Counties of Ireland

Following their invasion in 1169, the Anglo-Normans introduced new forms of administration or adapted existing forms to allow them to control the territory they conquered in Ireland. The **county** was the central part of this system.

By the mid-thirteenth century, the settled parts of Ireland had been divided into eight counties. The number of counties gradually increased, and from 1606 to 1994, twenty-six counties made up the Republic of Ireland (Fig. 21.3). In 1994, however, Co. Dublin was subdivided into three new counties – Dublin, Fingal and Dun Laoghaire-Rathdown – to reflect the complexity of this capital city region.

Many counties are defined by major physical features such as the River Shannon, or mountain ranges such as the Blackstairs Mountains. Counties also bring to mind powerful images of distinctive cultural and physical landscapes.

People identify strongly with their county and have a pride in and loyalty to their county. This is often expressed by the support and intense rivalries generated at GAA matches at county level and between neighbouring counties, such as Cork-Kerry, Dublin-Meath, Tipperary-Kilkenny.

● While the landscape may not change dramatically when moving from one county to another, would you **feel** you were entering a different part of Ireland? Why?

Urban-based Administrative Units

With the growing role of urbanisation in Ireland, three types of administrative units are based around urban centres:

● City councils.
● Borough councils.
● Town councils.

City Councils

There are city councils for the **five** most populous and important cities: Dublin, Cork, Limerick, Waterford and Galway (see Fig 21.3). These cities have played a major role in the development of the state, especially for their hinterlands (surrounding areas).

One of the critical problems for all city councils is that their administrative areas have not expanded enough to take account of suburbanisation (how large new housing estates

or suburbs are built, allowing the population to spread outside historic city boundaries).
Modern growth now occurs mainly outside town boundaries and in areas of
neighbouring county councils, for example Limerick city spreading into Co. Clare.

> Can you suggest any
> planning problems if a
> city expands into a
> different administrative
> region?

Limerick City Council offices and the River Shannon.

Fig. 21.3 Counties, city councils and borough councils in Ireland.

Borough and Town Councils

Borough councils administer the five medium-sized towns that come below the city
councils in Ireland's urban hierarchy, for example Kilkenny.

The third type of urban-based administrative unit are the 75 **town councils**, which
have their roots in the nineteenth century. These have some planning powers, but do
not play a vital role in the administrative framework of modern Ireland.

Regional Administration

There is no effective regional level of administration in Ireland. From the 1960s, some
efforts have been made to set up regional administration units to help planning within the
state. Different types of regional authority areas relating to issues of public concern have
been created, for example for regional development and health (see Figs. 21.4 and
21.5).

The central government does not give regional bodies important decision-making powers. Regional administrative units within Ireland are therefore not as important as in many other countries. In 1999, however, two new regions were created to more effectively administer Ireland's programme for national development and EU structural funds. These were the Border, Midland and West (BMW) and Southern and Eastern (S&E) regions (Fig. 21.4) and deal with local issues at a local level.

Fig. 21.4 Regional Authority Areas and two new planning regions for European Union (EU) funding.

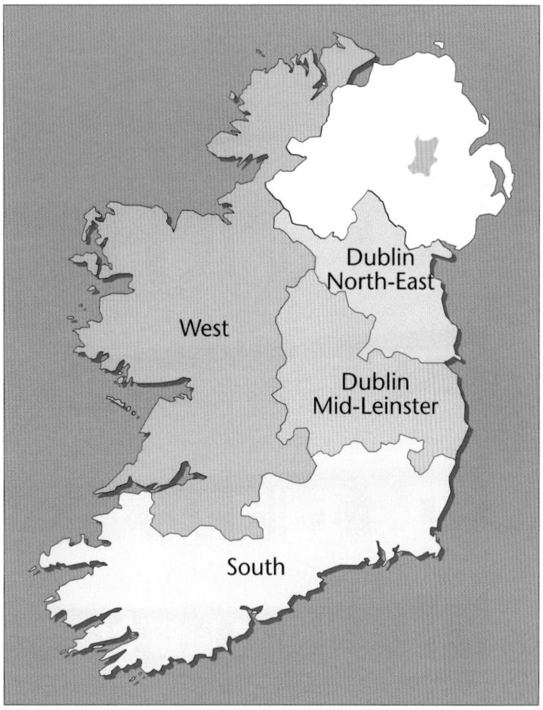

Fig. 21.5 Health Service Executive Areas.

Activity
Look at Figs. 21.4 and 21.5 and suggest some problems that can arise for effective planning because of differences in regional authority areas.

Local Government in Ireland

There are over 100 local authorities in Ireland. They form the country's system of local government.

As well as providing the community with essential services, such as housing, water supply and sewerage, local authorities have also taken on a development role. Local authorities have to draw up strategic **development plans** to meet the development needs of their areas. These must be updated every six years and are key documents in zoning land for different uses. They help shape transport, industry and housing developments in local authority areas.

Activity
Access the development plan of your local authority area. What are the main features of the plan for your community?

Local planning operates under **three** key principles:

- **Subsidiarity:** Decision-making should allow people to have a major role in governing their own affairs. This encourages self-reliance rather than depending on outside organisations to promote development.
- **Appropriateness:** Services and administration should be provided as close to the people as possible. This emphasises, where practical, local rather than regional or national levels of government.
- **Partnership:** This encourages local people to take part in government.

Local authorities have provided over 350,000 houses for people in Ireland who otherwise could not afford a house of their own.

Do you think providing housing is an important role for local authorities?

The *Départements* of France

France is one of Europe's largest countries, with a surface area of 551,000 km², a population of over 62 million and a wide variety of human and physical landscapes. Despite its size and diversity, government is centralised on Paris, although by the late twentieth century, regional administrations had a stronger role.

Much of the present regional administration in France can be traced to the French Revolution of 1789. After the Revolution, a new pattern of local government was based on the *département*. These were designed to be approximately the same size in terms of area and total population and, where possible, with some special cultural feature. There are 92 *départements* in present-day France (see Fig. 21.6).

The *départements* are responsible for a number of functions, including social services and co-ordinating urban and regional planning in their areas. The central government in Paris still has a powerful role and influence on local administration because it appoints the key administrative officer, known as the *préfet*, for each *département*. Also, as local administration was centred on the main town in each *département*, no regional centres developed enough in size and function to rival the dominance of Paris.

After the Second World War, there was some administrative reform and twenty-two regions were created in 1955 (see Fig. 21.6). These were, however, little more

Fig. 21.6 The regions and *départements* of France.

Activity

Which French region in Fig. 21.6:

1. Is linked most to Celtic culture?
2. Produces high-quality sparkling wine?
3. Includes the capital of France?
4. Is the location of the EU Parliament?

Départements are the equivalent of counties in Ireland.

than a collection of *départements* and had little authority. Pressure to decentralise (spread out) power from Paris increased in the 1970s, and a 1982 law gave the regions a new status.

French regions now have responsibilities for economic and cultural activities, such as job creation, tourism and heritage. They have become effective planning bodies and co-ordinate initiatives put forward by the *départements*. A region's population is also represented in regional assemblies through direct elections.

As each region is a large size and has a range of planning functions, some regional centres have now become more important. These include Lyons-St Étienne-Grenoble, Toulouse and Bordeaux. This is important to counterbalance the dominance of Paris.

The *départements* centred on Bordeaux have been linked to the production of high-quality wine for centuries.

- In which ways would the wine industry have helped the growth of Bordeaux as an important regional centre?

CHAPTER 22
CULTURAL REGIONS

KEY IDEA!

Language and religion are two major factors
that are used to define culture regions.

Defining a Culture Region

In constructing regions based on human rather than physical factors, **culture** is the most fundamental factor. Yet culture is a difficult concept to define. It involves many features, such as behaviour, attitude, learning and knowledge, and how these are passed on from one generation to the next.

These values, however, have an impact on the landscape. This can be through the ways in which people organise and adapt to their resources. In farming, it could be building stone walls and the field patterns in Co. Galway, or in a city it might be its special architecture and street layout.

By mapping cultural features, geographers create **culture regions**. Identifying culture is complex, but **two key factors** are often used to map cultural regions. These factors are **language** and **religion**.

Three different cultural landscapes from Ireland, Italy and India.

Language Regions

Language is central to cultural identity, as it is the main way of passing knowledge and ideas between people. It is seen as a powerful symbol of cultural identity, and many cultures strongly resist outside pressures to reduce the vitality of 'their' language.

In many national territories, there are often strong passions about keeping minority regional languages, such as the Basques in Spain and Bretons in France. Yet there are also cases in which different language groups can co-exist with little sign of stress. In Switzerland there are four official languages: French, German, Italian and Romansch. This causes little or no problem for the Swiss.

Case Study: Ireland and the Gaeltacht

In the Republic of Ireland, the Irish language has an important role in expressing Irish culture and identity. In the 2002 Census, 1.57 million people (40 per cent) in the Republic claimed some ability to speak and understand Irish. This is almost three times the number of people who claimed this ability when the Free State was set up, reflecting the efforts of government and voluntary bodies to promote the Irish language, especially within the education system.

Although more people claim to have some knowledge of Irish, Irish is used in everyday life only in relatively small and peripheral parts of the country. These are the **Gaeltacht regions,** and are the heartland of the Irish language and culture (see Fig. 22.1).

The Gaeltacht was defined in 1925 by a Commission for Irish-Speaking Districts. To qualify as an Irish-speaking district (*Fíor Gaeltacht*), 80 per cent of the population had to speak Irish. Partly Irish-speaking districts (*Breac Gaeltacht*) were defined as areas where 25 to 79 per cent of the population spoke Irish. Using District Electoral Divisions as a basic area for analysis, the Commission was able to create distinctive cultural regions based on the Irish language (see Fig. 33.2 on page 241).

At the start of the twenty-first century, the Gaeltacht is composed of a number of relatively small areas scattered along the west and south coast of the country from Donegal to Waterford. The total population of the Gaeltacht in 2002 was about 86,500. Of this total, 61,150 people over the age of three years spoke Irish. Although these Gaeltacht areas are small and have peripheral locations, they have a special importance for the Irish people and are strongly supported by government grants and incentives (see Chapter 33).

Fig. 22.1 The Gaeltacht areas.

Legend:
- less-developed western region
- Gaeltacht

How is Irish promoted as a language in the Irish education system? Is this a success?

In 2006, controversy arose over using only the official Irish place names for this important tourist centre in the Gaeltacht.

- *Why did many residents also want to keep the English version of the town's name?*

Activity

Look at Fig. 22.1 and answer the following.
1. In which counties are the Gaeltacht areas?
2. Why do you think the Gaeltacht is confined mainly to the less-developed West?

Belgium and Its Language Regions

Belgium was created as an independent state in 1830, following a revolution which led to this area separating from the Netherlands. Despite Belgium's relatively small size (30.5 million km², which is less than half the area of Ireland), the country has **three** official languages: Flemish, French and German (see Fig. 22.2). The Flemish language is a type of Dutch.

This Flemish-speaking area is culturally linked to the Netherlands. Historically, this was a poor region that lived from farming. Since the 1960s, this region has become more prosperous, attracting growth industries to places such as the port of Antwerp and its hinterland.

Brussels is the capital of Belgium. It is a bilingual city where French and Flemish are given the same status.

This small enclave of German speakers is territory ceded to Belgium by Germany after the First World War.

Fig. 22.2 The language regions of Belgium.

The southern part of Belgium is mainly French speaking because it is near France. During the 1800s, this region became prosperous, based on heavy industries that developed in the Sambre-Meuse and Liège coalfields. The collapse of these industries has seen the prosperity of Wallonia decline sharply.

This town near Brussels is located in Flanders, but has a majority of French-speaking people. Flemish language activists have crossed out the French place name, indicating the tensions between the two language groups.

Since the 1960s, tensions between the two main language-based communities (Flemish and French) have increased. Although Flanders has a majority of the national population and has attracted a lot of growth industries to become one of the EU's most prosperous regions, its Flemish-speaking community feels under threat from the more dominant international language of French.

As tensions grew and the different communities wanted to gain more autonomy (control) over their own affairs, fundamental reforms have been made to Belgium's constitution. There is now a federal-style government, which recognises three separate regions based mainly on language. These regions are Flanders, the Brussels-Capital Region and Wallonia (which is French speaking but includes a small German-speaking community).

The new political-cultural regionalisation has highlighted divisions within Belgium. The 'defensive' attitude of Flemish communities over the spread of the French language has led to the creation of a new political party called *Vlaams Belang*. This party is committed to protecting Flemish culture, with more extreme elements seeking an independent state. These language tensions make it difficult for Belgium to function as a single national state.

> If you were going to live in Brussels, would you choose to learn French or Flemish? Explain your answer.

Regions and Religion

If cultural regions were based only on language, they would be relatively easy to define. Systems of belief, which are key elements in defining culture, can cut across language barriers. The Islamic world, for example, is made up of many different language groups. Sometimes similar language groups can be divided through religious conflict, as in Northern Ireland.

Each of the world's major religions has a distinctive geography (see Fig. 22.3) and has had a key role in shaping individual and group identities. These include aspects such as attitudes to women, birth control, the environment and diet.

For example, in some traditional Islamic societies, women generally play an inferior role to men in daily life. A large number may be uneducated.

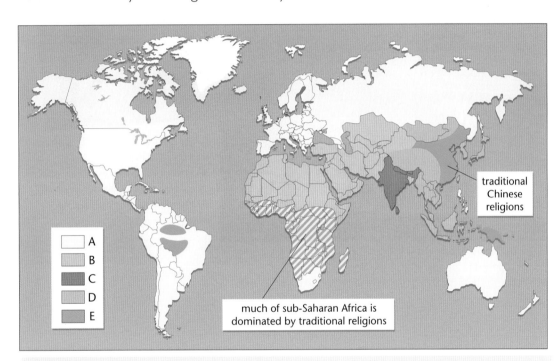

Fig. 22.3 The world's major religions.

Activity

Look at Fig. 22.3 and say which of the major world religions matches A to E on the map.

Choose from:

- Hinduism
- Islam
- Christianity
- Buddhism
- Traditional/regional religions

Which two religious groups clash in Palestine and Kashmir?

Most religions wish to convert non-believers to their faith. As a result, boundaries that define religions change over time and for varying reasons, such as the work of Christian missionaries. The passion of some religious groups is so strong that conflict zones occur along boundaries between different religions. Present-day examples include Israel and the neighbouring Arab countries; Islamic Pakistan and Hindu-dominated India, especially in Kashmir; and Christian and Islamic communities in the Balkans following the break-up of Yugoslavia.

Two examples we shall look at are regions associated with religion but on very different scales:

- Northern Ireland.
- The Islamic world.

An estimated 200 million cows roam the streets in the towns and cities of India. Since cows are regarded as holy creatures in the Hindu faith, they cannot be killed or mistreated.
- *What problems could this create?*

In the middle of Rome is the Vatican City. It is the centre of the Roman Catholic Church, where the Pope lives.
- *What regions of the world are dominated by the Christian faith?*

A woman in Afghanistan dressed in traditional Islamic style.
- *How does gender inequality affect development in Islamic countries? (Think about employment and population growth.)*

Religious Divide in Northern Ireland

The Irish Free State set up in 1921 did not cover the whole island of Ireland. After a referendum, six counties in north-east Ireland chose to remain part of the United Kingdom. This decision was associated with British colonial rule when large numbers of English and Scottish Protestant communities had been settled there. In contrast, the rest of the island was, and remains, dominated by the Catholic faith. Northern Ireland emerged as a distinctive cultural region based around its majority Protestant population.

Despite many changes in the Protestant and Catholic populations in Northern Ireland, the political divide separating the region from the Republic has not changed. In Northern Ireland, however, Catholic and Protestant communities became increasingly segregated (e.g. Catholic and Protestant children attend different schools), especially after the outbreak of violence in the region in 1968. Generally, the Catholic population tends to form the majority in more rural areas, while Protestants dominate in the larger urban centres. At the start of the twenty-first century, approximately 55 per cent of Northern Ireland's population was Protestant.

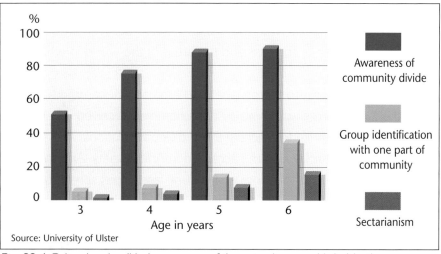

Fig. 22.4 Cultural and political awareness of three-to-six-year-olds in Northern Ireland (%).

Which six counties make up Northern Ireland?

● *What does this image and Figure 22.4 suggest about the cultural divide in Northern Ireland?*

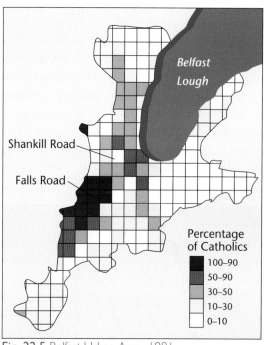

Fig. 22.5 Belfast Urban Area, 1981.

Within Belfast, there is religious segregation. After the outbreak of civil disorder in 1968, minorities of both religions who had chosen to live in a different majority community often had to retreat into their own communities. The result was Catholic-only and Protestant-only ghettos and a divided city.

A geographer named Paul Doherty drew up an interesting map of the Belfast urban area to show religious segregation in 1981 (Fig. 22.5). Using one-kilometre squares, Doherty shows that only nineteen out of 157 squares had a Catholic majority (for example, in the Falls Road). In contrast, there are large areas with a majority of Protestant residents (for example, in the Shankill Road).

What is a ghetto? Use a dictionary to find out.

The Islamic World

Islam is one of the world's great religions, with more than 1 billion believers. It is a religion that is expanding its number of converts and the areas of the world in which it is practised.

The Islamic religion traces its origin to the prophet Muhammad (Mohammed), who was born at Mecca in the Arabian Peninsula in AD 571. Muhammad received revelations from Allah (God) and committed his life to teaching these divine revelations. At first there was opposition, but his teachings quickly became accepted in Arab society. After his death in AD 632, the Islamic religion, its teachings and cultural landscapes spread quickly from its source area in the Arabian Peninsula (its cultural hearth) to the surrounding regions.

Islam was spread by powerful conquering armies that invaded other parts of the Middle East and North Africa, Spain and the Balkans. Arab traders travelled to distant markets, such as the Indian subcontinent and the islands of South-East Asia, taking their faith with them and converting local populations to Islam (see Fig. 22.6).

Today, the global region of Islam occupies most of North Africa and south-west Asia, with important outlying areas in the densely populated islands of South-East Asia, such as Indonesia. In these regions, religion is still a powerful influence on the lives of people and in shaping distinctive cultural landscapes, such as the design of towns, palaces and mosques. Also, women generally have less control over their lives in this more male-dominated culture and are allocated the roles of wife and mother.

The Alhambra palace is in Granada, which became the capital of Moorish Spain from the eleventh century until 1492.

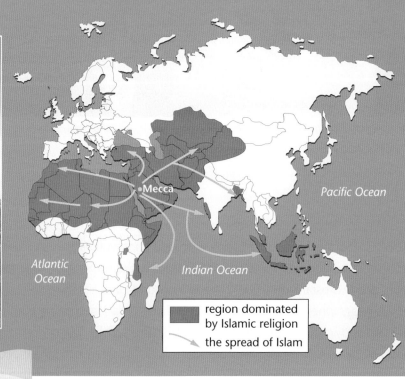

Fig. 22.6 Where Islam spread around the world.

Find the Arabian Peninsula on a map of the world.

Even in areas that were under the influence of Islam centuries ago, there are still impressions of the past in the present-day landscape, as in the case of **southern Spain.** When the Moors invaded Spain in 711, they spread the Islamic faith there. They were finally pushed out of Spain in 1492, but palaces like the Alhambra, in Granada, are a reminder of nearly 800 years of Moorish presence in Spain.

Mecca is the most sacred city in Islam. Up to 750,000 Muslims can gather to pray together at the Kaaba, or Sacred Mosque of Islam.
● *In which country is Mecca?*

Islam continues to expand as a global religion. For some, this is seen as a threat associated with **Islamic fundamentalism,** and conflict zones have emerged in places such as the Balkans and Kashmir. Yet Islam also expands along more peaceful avenues, often associated with migration into countries of the developed world. An increasing number of major cities in Western Europe, such as London, Paris and Amsterdam, and also in North America, now have mosques, reflecting their growing population of converts to Islam.

What do you know about Islamic fundamentalism? What is it?

For Muslims, making a pilgrimage to Mecca is one of the five pillars (or duties) of Islam.

Multi-part Questions

1. A. **CONCEPT OF REGION**

   i.   Define what is meant by the term 'region'.

   ii. Explain some factors that are common to all regions. [20 marks]

   B. **PHYSICAL REGIONS**

   i.   Name one **Irish** physical region and one **European** physical region.

   ii. In the case of one of the physical regions above, explain how it was formed. [30 marks]

   C. **CLIMATIC REGION**

   Describe and explain the climate of north-west Europe. [30 marks]

2. A. **SKETCH MAP**

   Use your atlas to draw a sketch map of Ireland. On it, mark and name the following:

   i.   two major rivers

   ii. two upland regions

   iii. one urban region. [20 marks]

   B. **ADMINISTRATIVE REGIONS**

   'Administrative regions exist at a variety of scales.' Explain this statement using examples from Ireland and one other European country that you have studied. [30 marks]

   C. **CULTURAL REGIONS**

   Explain the factors that define Gaeltacht areas as distinctive cultural regions. [30 marks]

3. A. **IRISH PHYSICAL REGIONS**

   i.   **Identify** the physical region at **each** of the locations A, B and C.

   ii. Name the counties in **each** case. [20 marks]

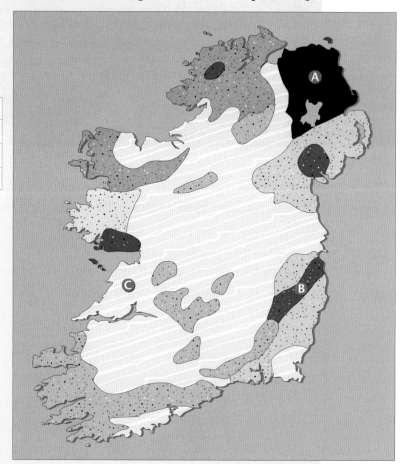

Physical Region	County
A:	
B:	
C:	

   B. **IRISH AND EUROPEAN REGIONS**

   With reference to one Irish language region and one European language region, explain the criteria that define these areas as distinctive cultural regions.

   [30 marks]

   C. **EUROPEAN OR NON-EUROPEAN REGIONS**

   With reference to one region you have studied, describe its regional extent and explain its growth over time.

   [30 marks]

CHAPTER 23
SOCIO-ECONOMIC REGIONS 1: CORES AND PERIPHERIES

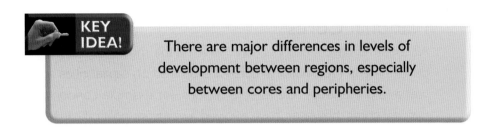

KEY IDEA!

There are major differences in levels of development between regions, especially between cores and peripheries.

Economic development does not affect all areas in the same way. Some regions develop strongly because there is a good combination of factors, including what raw materials are available or being a strategic location for trade. In contrast, regions without enough resources, unfavourable environments and poor access to trade routes and market centres usually fail to develop prosperous communities.

It is important to note that less-developed regions can occur within countries that are prosperous. In this case, the status of these regions is relative to the more prosperous regions in that country. For example, the West of Ireland is less developed compared to the eastern region centred on Dublin.

The core-periphery model is a simple model that divides an area into two types:

- Core.
- Periphery.

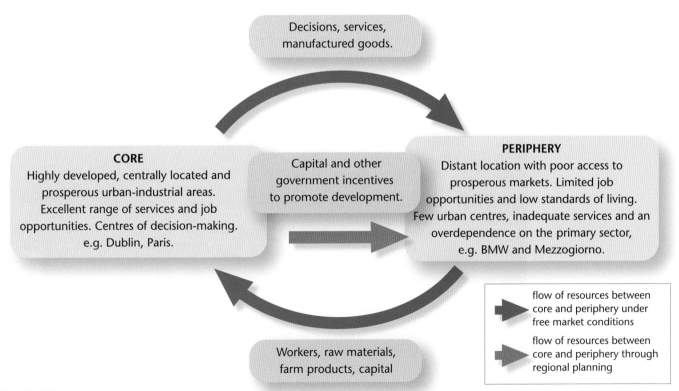

Fig. 23.1 The core-periphery model.

The difference between the core and periphery encourages resources to flow in a way that benefits the core, e.g. migration of young people. Some recent trends, however, have encouraged development in the periphery, but are linked directly to the flow of resources from the core: industrial investment, tourism and government incentives through regional planning. This is seen between the core region of northern Italy and the Mezzogiorno in southern Italy (see Chapter 27).

National Cores

All countries have a national core, which is the most important area for national development. Most national cores are centred on capital cities and have had a historic as well as a present-day role as core regions, for example London or Paris. Some important national cores, however, have evolved away from political capitals, such as the north-west region of Italy. Dublin is Ireland's national core.

The prosperity and growing economies of core regions create development in adjacent areas. This occurs through the overspill of jobs, people and investment via well-developed transport links, e.g. the expanding national cores of Paris (Chapter 28) and Dublin (Chapter 34).

An International Core in Western Europe

An international core has emerged in Western Europe as a number of national cores and growth regions have combined. They are usually located next to each other and are well connected through a variety of links. These links have become stronger throughout the last half of the twentieth century, as the European Union encouraged more international trade between its member states.

Fig. 23.2 shows the international core of the European Union, which has been given a variety of names, including 'European Dogleg' and the 'Hot Banana'. It also includes the four regions considered to be the 'motors' of the European Union. This is because of their powerful economies and their increasing role within the EU's single market.

Lyons on the River Rhône is one of four 'motors' of the European Union.

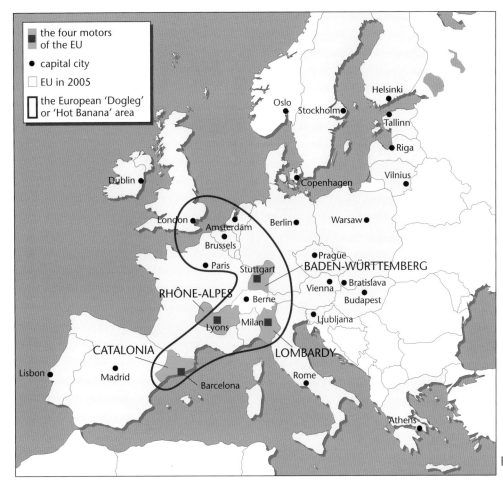

the four motors of the EU

● capital city

□ EU in 2005

⬜ the European 'Dogleg' or 'Hot Banana' area

Fig. 23.2 The core region of the EU.

Why do you think the core of the EU has been given the name 'dogleg' or 'banana'?

Peripheral Regions

Although core areas have socio-economic problems such as congestion, high land values and inner city decline, regions with the greatest development problems are in peripheries. There are a variety of problem regions, but two types can be highlighted:

● Rural underdeveloped, e.g. the West of Ireland and the Mezzogiorno.

● Regions of industrial decline, e.g. the Sambre-Meuse Valley in Belgium.

Problem Regions in the European Union

Since 1988, the EU has had a well-defined Common Regional Policy. Under this policy, large and increasing amounts of money have been made available through **structural funds** to assist development of its many problem regions.

Most of the structural funds have been spent in the regions that experience the greatest problems, such as low income per person, high unemployment and poor transport links to core regions. Examples include Ireland, the Mezzogiorno and the countries from Central and Eastern Europe that joined the EU in 2004. Until 2007, these problem regions were called Objective 1 Regions (Fig 23.3).

A village in the Mezzogiorno.

● *What evidence suggests that this is part of Europe's periphery?*

157

Fig. 23.3 Objective 1 Regions for the European Union, 2004–2006.

- *Do you think building new roads such as this in Spain is a good way to spend structural funds in Objective 1 Regions?*

Since 2007 the term 'Convergence Regions' has replaced Objective 1 Regions (see Fig 32.1 on page 237).

Up to 2007, structural funds were also available to help modernise the economies and environments of depressed and declining urban-industrial regions. These were called Objective 2 Regions and included declining coalfield economies such as the Sambre-Meuse area in Belgium (see Chapter 24).

● *Why is new international investment such as this modern chemical plant so important for depressed industrial regions such as Lorraine in north-eastern France?*

Ireland's Problem Region

Although the whole of Ireland was designated an Objective 1 Region in the EU, there were clear differences in levels of development between the east and the west of the country. This had been recognised as early as 1952 by the Irish government when it introduced the Undeveloped Areas Act. Under the Act, large areas of the West of Ireland received government funding to help promote this less developed 'half' of the country (see Fig 22.1 on page 147).

In 1999, the government adjusted this regional divide by creating two new regions. These are the Border, Midland and West (BMW) and the Southern and Eastern (S&E) regions (Fig 23.4). The BMW has major problems of rural underdevelopment and benefited least from the success of Ireland's 'Celtic Tiger' economy. As a result, this region continued to receive significant amounts of structural funding between 2000 and 2006. In contrast, the more prosperous Southern and Eastern Region was allocated a declining share of structural funds. By 2006, the S&E Region had lost its status as an Objective 1 Region.

● *Why is training or education so important for marginal groups?*

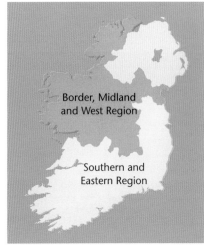

Fig. 23.4 The BMW and S&E regions in Ireland.

● *Refer to Chapter 26 for a more detailed account of these two regions.*

CHAPTER 24
SOCIO-ECONOMIC REGIONS 2: REGIONS OF INDUSTRIAL DECLINE

 **KEY IDEA!**

Once-prosperous regions based on coal mining and heavy industries have declined and face major problems.

The Industrial Revolution started in Western Europe during the late eighteenth century. This led to a new regional pattern of industrial development, based around coalfields. These became the growth regions of the nineteenth and early twentieth centuries.

Case Study: The Sambre-Meuse Coalfields

The Sambre-Meuse coalfields stretch about 150 km from the French border to Liège along the Sambre-Meuse Valley in Belgium (see Fig. 24.1). It was one of the first regions of continental Europe to experience large-scale industrialisation at the start of the nineteenth century. The region's development depended on reserves of coal, a location central to the major urban-industrial markets of north-west Europe and well-developed canal and railway networks.

> For well over 100 years, coalfield areas were the growth regions of Western Europe.

The Sambre-Meuse coalfields are located in Wallonia. Rising levels of prosperity and jobs in coal mining and heavy industries, such as iron, steel, engineering and chemicals, attracted large numbers of migrants, especially from Flanders. This made Wallonia the dominant cultural and economic region in Belgium.

After the 1950s, the economy of the Sambre-Meuse coalfields declined. This was due to a number of factors:

- **Alternative sources of energy** to coal.
- **Costs of production** were high and the industries were less competitive in world trade.
- **Cheaper imports**, especially from less developed economies.
- **Alternative products** became available, for example plastics replaced metals.
- **New technologies** reduced the number of jobs available for people in these industries.
- **New plants** were built to replace older units, but these were often in different regional locations, such as coastal sites rather than inland coalfields, e.g. the modern steelworks at Zelzate.

Steelworks at Charleroi surrounded by old, working-class housing for its labour force. Note also the coal tips in the background linked to a large coal mining industry.

As the heavy industries declined, so did the regions that depended on them. There were huge job losses and high levels of unemployment, out-migration and economic depression in these once proud and prosperous communities. **Deindustrialisation** is the term used to describe a large-scale decline in the industrial base.

By 1984, the last colliery in the Sambre-Meuse coalfields had closed (Fig. 24.2). This left many mining communities with a high level of unemployment and a scarred landscape, which was not attractive to modern industries.

The decline of the heavy industrial base meant that the coalfields and Wallonia emerged as major problem regions. Out-migration increased from these economically depressed communities to more dynamic growth centres, such as Brussels, and Antwerp and Ghent in Flanders. Flemish-speaking Flanders replaced French-speaking Wallonia as the economic core of Belgium.

Government and EU support has been essential for promoting development in this declining industrial region. Most of the coalfields were designated as an Objective 2 Region in the EU.

Collieries such as this once had a dominant role in the landscape and economy of the Sambre-Meuse Valley.

● *What impact did their closure have for this region's economy and quality of environment?*

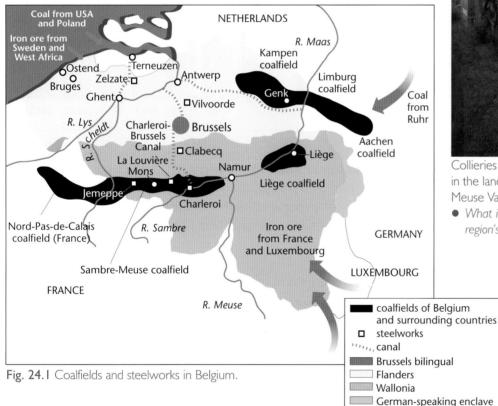

Fig. 24.1 Coalfields and steelworks in Belgium.

Map labels:
Coal from USA and Poland
Iron ore from Sweden and West Africa
NETHERLANDS
R. Maas
Kampen coalfield
Ostend
Terneuzen
Antwerp
Zelzate
Bruges
Ghent
Genk
Limburg coalfield
Coal from Ruhr
Vilvoorde
R. Lys
Charleroi-Brussels Canal
Brussels
R. Scheldt
La Louvière
Mons
Clabecq
Namur
Liège
Aachen coalfield
Liège coalfield
Jemeppe
Charleroi
Nord-Pas-de-Calais coalfield (France)
R. Sambre
Iron ore from France and Luxembourg
GERMANY
Sambre-Meuse coalfield
LUXEMBOURG
FRANCE
R. Meuse

Legend:
■ coalfields of Belgium and surrounding countries
□ steelworks
''''' canal
▨ Brussels bilingual
☐ Flanders
▥ Wallonia
▤ German-speaking enclave

Which languages are spoken in Wallonia and Flanders? See Chapter 22.

Activity

Look at the map in Fig. 24.1 and answer the following.

1. In which Belgian region are the Sambre-Meuse coalfields?
2. Do you think rivers and canals have been an important factor influencing the location of Belgium's steelworks? Explain your answer.
3. How does the Belgian steel industry source its main raw material inputs even though the country now produces no coal or iron ore?
4. Is this a disadvantage for steelworks in the Sambre-Meuse area compared with Zelzate? Explain your answer.

Fig. 24.2 Whereas the coal industry of the Sambre-Meuse Valley ended in 1984, investment in the region's steel industry allowed for increased productivity.

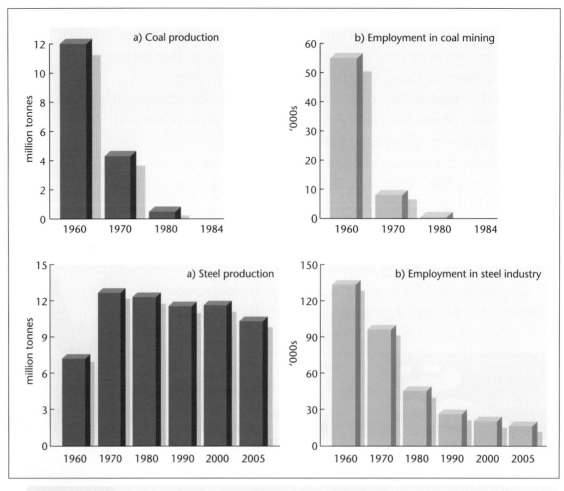

Activity

Look at Fig. 24.2 and study the caption to answer the following.

1. What is the trend for employment and production of coal from 1960 to 1984?
2. Why is the loss of jobs in mining an important problem for the Sambre-Meuse Valley?
3. Contrast the trends for steel production and employment from 1960 to 2005. Explain these different trends.

This Objective 2 Region has had a large amount of investment from the Belgian government and the EU to change its image and make it more attractive for private investment. Of special importance have been:

- Investment in transport infrastructure, especially new motorways that link the region to neighbouring growth regions, e.g. Paris, Ruhr, Randstad.
- New industrial estates located along the motorways and near larger urban centres such as Charleroi and La Louvière.
- Upgrading the airport at Charleroi, mainly for Ryanair, to improve international access.
- Cleaning up the derelict landscape to improve the image of the local environment and take away an impression of economic depression.

The results have been quite positive, and a large number of new industries, such as Caterpillar at Charleroi, have been attracted to the region. Despite this, the Sambre-Meuse area remains a problem region in Belgium and has a long way to go before it becomes as prosperous as it was in the early twentieth century.

Case Study: The Greater Cork Area

When Ireland joined the European Union in 1973, Cork was the country's dominant centre for large-scale, port-related industries. These included Ireland's only:

- Steelworks (Irish Steel).
- Shipyard (Verholme).
- Oil refinery (Irish Refining).
- Car assembly plant (Ford).

Cork also had a number of large chemical plants and a range of more traditional Irish industries, such as food processing, clothing and textiles.

These industries had been attracted to Cork by a combination of location factors linked to the city and its main physical asset: Cork Harbour (see Fig. 24.3).

Up to the 1980s, these industries provided the Greater Cork Area with good employment prospects. Cork was considered a **growth centre** for the national economy.

At the start of the 1980s, an international recession and growing competition in European and world markets caused major problems for Cork's industrial base. The local industrial plants were mostly small, relatively inefficient and high-cost producers by international standards. Decisions were taken to close or run down most of Cork's long-established industries.

Before the 1980s, Cork had built its economy around a limited number of large but slow-growing or declining industries.

Cork Outer Harbour is an ideal location for a growing number of port-related industries, especially chemicals.

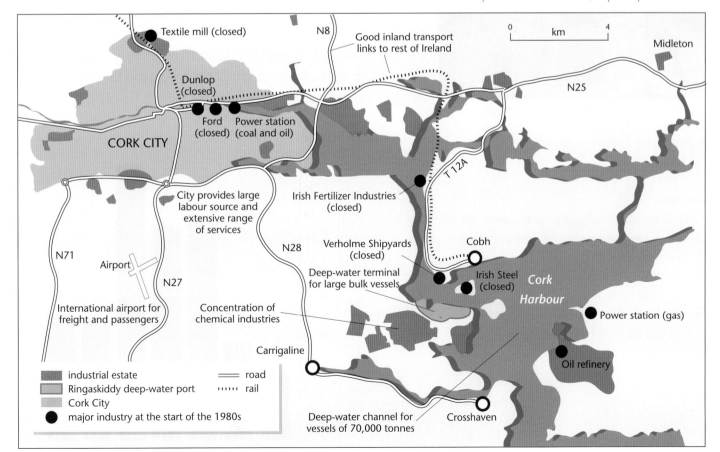

Fig. 24.3 Industrial development in the Greater Cork Area. Cork is the nearest port to continental Europe. This and access to shipping routes are important for import/export.

163

By 1985, the shipyards, Ford and Dunlop had been closed, with a loss of about 3,000 jobs. Cutbacks at other plants added another 2,500 job losses. Most of these jobs had been thought of as well paid and secure. Losing these jobs led to huge social problems for communities that had depended heavily on these industries. Cork had experienced **deindustrialisation,** becoming a region of industrial decline and a 'blackspot' for national unemployment.

> How many jobs in manufacturing did Cork lose from 1980 to 1985? Note that this was almost a third of the industrial base.

During the 1990s, Cork's industrial economy was revived, and a large number of new growth sectors were attracted to the city region.

- Chemical and pharmaceutical companies have located here, mainly around Cork's Outer Harbour and especially near the deep-water terminal at Ringaskiddy (see Fig. 24.3), e.g. Pfizer, Novartis. Cork is now regarded as the 'chemical capital of Ireland'.
- A growing number of electrical, IT (information technology) and health-related companies have set up in the 'necklace' of industrial estates that have been built around the edge of the city, e.g. Apple, Boston Scientific.

Government and regional planning have been vital in achieving this change of fortune for Cork. A large investment has been made in modernising the region's infrastructure, including education institutions, port facilities, airport, roads and urban renewal. This has changed the image and attractiveness of the region for growth industries.

At the start of the twenty-first century, Cork can no longer be described as a region of industrial decline. The change was not easy to achieve, but shows the importance of effective national and regional planning. In spite of this, the effects of a recent global recession have caused unemployment to rise from the low levels of 2000. It also shows the problem of depending too heavily on foreign investment.

The inner quays of Cork were the site of early industrial development in the city.
- *Do you think these areas remain attractive for manufacturing?*

Activity

Look at the chart in Fig. 24.4 and answer the following.
1. What were the years of lowest and highest unemployment?
2. Do the figures support the idea that unemployment became a major problem in the early 1980s?
3. Do trends for the late 1990s suggest that Cork benefited from a significant increase in new jobs?

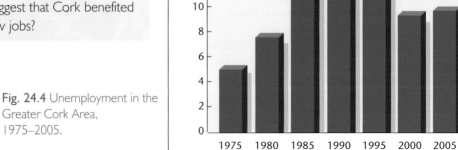

Fig. 24.4 Unemployment in the Greater Cork Area, 1975–2005.

CHAPTER 25
URBAN REGIONS

KEY IDEA!

Urban regions (regions centred on urban areas) have become more important in modern development.

What Is an Urban Region?

An urban region is an area that surrounds a human settlement and is linked to it by interactions such as shopping, the journey to work and supplying farm produce. The area linked to the urban centre is called the **hinterland** of that centre. An urban region is also called a nodal or city region. It is important because:

- More and more of the world's population lives in towns and cities.
- The lives of people are increasingly organised by an urban-based environment.
- Urban areas can be seen clearly in the landscape. These built-up areas can be easily mapped.

European City Regions

By the start of the twenty-first century, about 80 per cent of the population of Western Europe was living in towns or cities.

The well-developed countries that border the North Sea have the highest levels of urbanisation. In Belgium, 95 per cent of the population lives in urban centres (Netherlands 89 per cent and Britain 87 per cent). Peripheral countries with underdeveloped economies usually have lower levels of urbanisation. In Portugal, for example, only 30 per cent of the population lives in towns and cities (Ireland 60 per cent).

Fig. 25.1 shows that there are three major zones of urban settlement in Western Europe:

- The **Manchester-Milan axis** is the most important area of concentrated urban development. It is based on the historic trading corridor of the **River Rhine** that links the North Sea lowlands and the Mediterranean.

Köln (Cologne) on the River Rhine has long been a major trade and religious centre.
- *What evidence in the photo supports this statement?*

Fig. 25.1 Major urban centres and axes where population is concentrated in the European Union.

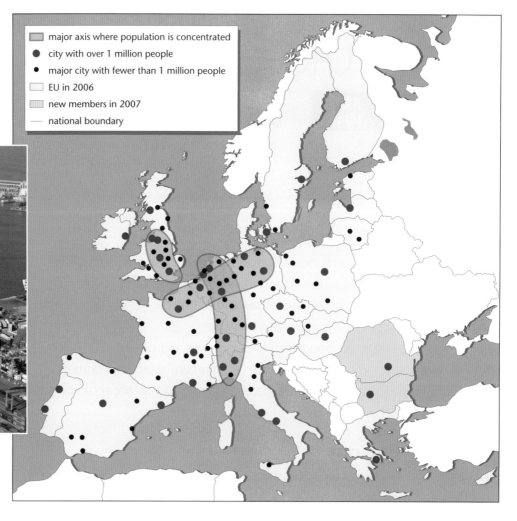

Barcelona is one of the four 'motors' of the EU. Its prosperity is mainly due to its historic and present role as a major port.

Map legend:
- major axis where population is concentrated
- city with over 1 million people
- major city with fewer than 1 million people
- EU in 2006
- new members in 2007
- national boundary

- The **Paris-Berlin axis** links the capitals of France and Germany across the North European lowlands.
- The **coastline of Western Europe:** Many of Europe's largest cities are ports. This is linked to its long tradition of maritime (sea) trade and colonial empires of states such as France, Spain and Britain.

The **core** region for urban development in Europe occurs where the Manchester-Milan axis intersects with (crosses) the Paris-Berlin axis. Two **polycentred** urban regions have emerged here: Randstad Holland and the Rhine-Ruhr.

In Europe, it is more common for a single city to spread out to swallow up surrounding smaller settlements, as happened with London and Paris. These large areas of almost continuously built-up areas are called **conurbations.**

> A polycentred urban region is made up of several closely located cities which interact strongly. No single city dominates.

Advantages for Urban Development in Europe's Core Region
- Centrality (central position).
- Access to major trade routes within Europe.
- Access to global markets through major ports and airports.
- Rich agricultural environment.
- Near coalfields and early industrialisation.

Ireland's Urban Regions

Ireland is one of the least urbanised societies in Western Europe. This reflects its past as a colony, its underdeveloped economy, peripheral location in Europe and its dependence on the primary sector. In 2002, 60 per cent of the country's population lived in urban centres.

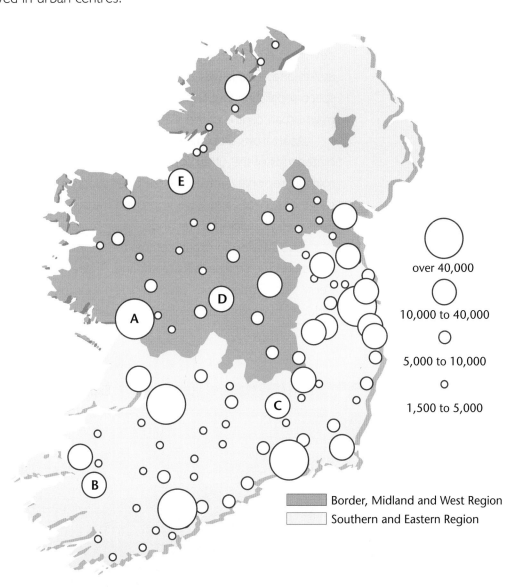

Fig. 25.2 Cities and towns in Ireland by the size of population.

over 40,000

10,000 to 40,000

5,000 to 10,000

1,500 to 5,000

Border, Midland and West Region
Southern and Eastern Region

In Ireland, the eastern and southern parts of the country are the most urbanised. More market towns grew up on the richer agricultural land, while its ports were developed to trade with Britain. In contrast, the West of Ireland is in a more peripheral location and has difficult environmental conditions for productive farming. There are fewer towns and they are more dispersed across the region (see Fig. 25.2). In the Southern and Eastern (S&E) Region, almost 75 per cent of the population lives in urban areas (areas with a population larger than 1,500), while the Border, Midland and West (BMW) Region has only a third of its population in towns and cities.

Activity

Look at Fig. 25.2 and answer the following.
1. Name the towns marked A, B, C, D and E on the map.
2. Why are there so few towns in Connaught?
3. Why are the largest ports along the east and south coast?

Fig. 25.3 shows the hinterlands of Irish cities and towns suggested by planners as growth centres for national development. It also highlights the large area influenced by Dublin. This stretches both north to south and east to west.

The north-south coastal corridor that links Dublin to Belfast is becoming an important area for economic development. To the west, Dublin's influence goes as far as Athlone. This leaves only a narrow strip of more rural space separating Dublin's hinterland from Galway, the main urban centre of the West of Ireland.

Apart from Dublin, you can see the important urban hinterlands of the other four main cities, which also have roles as regional centres. These cities supply a wide range of services and have improved transport links to their well-populated hinterlands.

The smaller an urban centre, the fewer services it offers and the smaller is its hinterland. Tralee, in Co. Kerry, and Castlebar, in Co. Mayo, are examples of reduced hinterland areas of smaller market towns in rural Ireland (Fig. 25.2).

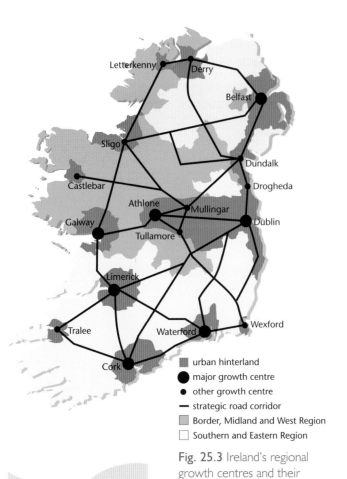

Key
- urban hinterland
- ● major growth centre
- • other growth centre
- — strategic road corridor
- Border, Midland and West Region
- Southern and Eastern Region

Fig. 25.3 Ireland's regional growth centres and their hinterlands.

A growth centre is a town that is chosen for development, so that growth will spread out into its hinterland.

Explain the word 'hinterland'.

Apart from Dublin, what are Ireland's four other cities?

Kilkenny (left) and Clifden, Co. Galway (right) are examples of smaller urban centres that have developed in different physical environments.
- *Do these photographs suggest ways in which their locations influenced the scale and nature of their development?*

Case Study: Dublin

Ireland has one dominant city – Dublin. Since the foundation of the town by the Vikings in the ninth century, it has grown into a sprawling urban region. The population of the Greater Dublin Area is over 1.3 million, which is 35 per cent of Ireland's total population. It is therefore a primate city.

The growth and importance of Dublin is due to:

- **Site:** The original settlement occupies a low-lying site on either side of the River Liffey where it enters Dublin Bay. It is the lowest bridging point on the river and has a long tradition as a trade, administrative and military centre.

- **Situation:** The deep, sheltered waters of Dublin Bay allowed Dublin to become the most important harbour on the east coast. In addition, the valley of the River Liffey provides a natural route into the Central Lowlands (see Fig 26.1 on page 172). As a result, Dublin had easy connections to the rest of the country, while the short sea crossing to Britain enabled the city to dominate trade with Ireland's most important trading partner. These advantages are emphasised by the fact that Dublin is the focus of the country's road, rail and canal networks, and possesses the main airport and port facilities.

- **Capital:** Dublin is the capital city. Most of the national government and administration offices are located here, as well as the headquarters of many national and international companies.

- **Agriculture:** The hinterland of Dublin has some of the richest farmland in Ireland. Dublin became the main market for this region.

- **Industry:** The size of the market, efficient transport systems, labour force and a range of high-quality services, such as finance, education and legal, have attracted a large number of industries. This has been emphasised by the Celtic Tiger economy and the preference of high-tech growth industries to locate in this urban region. (See also Chapter 26, page 180.)

> A primate city is one that contains a large proportion of a country's population. Other examples include Paris and London.

As the capital and primate city of Ireland, Dublin has expanded greatly from its original site on the River Liffey.

For further information on the expansion of the Dublin urban region, see Chapter 34, pages 245–9.

Chapter 28 provides a case study of the Paris urban region.

Multi-part Questions

I. A. SKETCH MAP

Draw a sketch map to show the main physical characteristics of relief and drainage of a European region you have studied.

[20 marks]

B. MANUFACTURING

Examine the development of manufacturing in one Irish region. [30 marks]

C. CULTURAL DIVISION

Examine two factors which have influenced the development of distinct cultural divisions within a European region.

[30 marks]

2. A. EUROPEAN REGION

'A region may be identified by one or more characteristics.' Draw a sketch map of a European region that you have studied to illustrate/explain this statement.

[20 marks]

B. SOCIO-ECONOMIC EUROPEAN REGION

Describe one socio-economic region in Europe that has suffered economic difficulties over time. In your answer, refer to:

i. the causes of these difficulties

ii. attempts to solve these difficulties. [30 marks]

C. IRISH REGION

Account for the distribution and growth of Ireland's urban regions. [30 marks]

3. A. EUROPEAN REGIONS

Examine this map of Europe. In your answer book, associate each of these descriptions with the letters A, B, C, D:

- an administrative region
- a region defined by language
- an economic core region
- a geomorphological region.

[20 marks]

B. INDUSTRIAL DECLINE

Explain, with reference to an example you have studied, the decline of one socio-economic core region in Europe.

[30 marks]

C. IRISH REGION

Explain the factors that have led to the growth of Dublin's city region.

[30 marks]

CHAPTER 26
REGIONAL CONTRASTS IN IRELAND

The way human and physical processes interact gives rise to major contrasts between the east and west of Ireland.

Ireland is a relatively small island economy off the west coast of continental Europe. It forms part of the European Union's underdeveloped Atlantic periphery. Traditionally, there have been strong differences between the more prosperous eastern part of Ireland and the more marginalised western regions.

These differences are reviewed by contrasting the Border, Midland and West (BMW) Region and the Southern and Eastern (S&E) Region.

PHYSICAL PROCESSES

The relief, climate, soils and drainage of Ireland have a strong impact on the country's economic development and patterns of human activities, such as urban settlement. If you look at the **relief,** it is something like a saucer shape: a broad central lowland area surrounded by a broken rim of higher land (see Fig. 26.1).

The **climate** is influenced mainly by its island location and onshore south-westerly winds, which bring mild temperatures all year round and annual precipitation (rainfall) that is well distributed around the country. While these patterns are general to Ireland, there are important differences between the west and east of the country (see Table 26.1 on page 173).

Glacially eroded mountains in Connemara.
- *Do such areas provide a good basis for prosperous farming?*

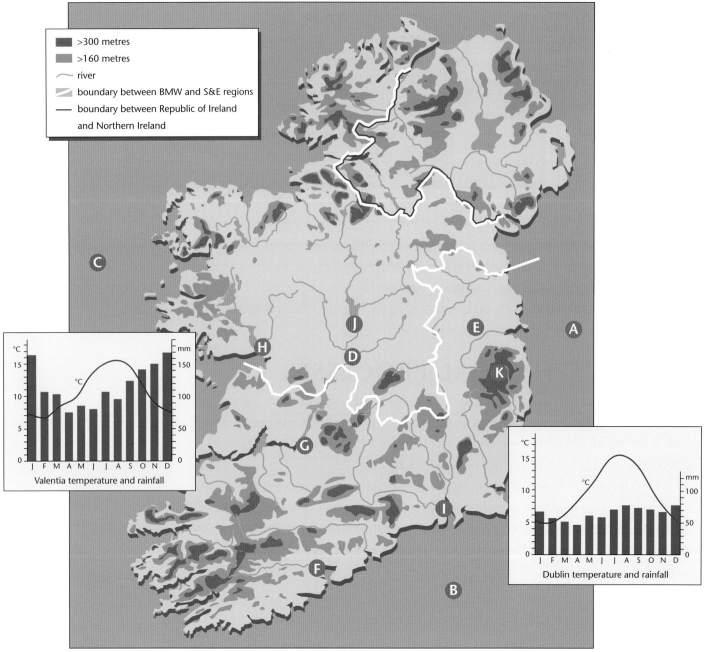

Fig. 26.1 Relief and drainage map, showing the height of land above sea level.

Activity

Look at the map in Fig. 26.1 and answer the following.

1. Name the:
   a. sea areas A, B and C
   b. rivers D and E
   c. towns F, G, H, I and J
   d. upland area K.

2. Why is 'saucer shape' a useful way to describe Ireland's physical relief?

3. Why is drainage so poor in the Central Lowlands?

4. Does Dublin have a greater temperature range than Valentia? Explain your answer.

5. Explain why Valentia has higher levels of rainfall than Dublin.

Relief, Climate, Soil and Drainage

Border, Midland and West Region	Southern and Eastern Region
Relief Much of the region has bleak, rugged upland areas, especially along the western seaboard where glacially eroded mountain ranges rise higher than 300 m. Inland areas form the western part of the undulating Central Lowlands (50–150 m). In general, the region has a submerged coastline that gives rise to a deeply indented coastal zone.	**Relief** The Central Lowlands generally have a larger area of low-lying and undulating landscapes. There is a mountainous area in the Leinster chain, centred on the Wicklow Mountains. The coastline tends to be less indented (jagged) and is more low-lying than the west coast.
Climate The climate is relatively mild, but very wet and windy. This is directly linked to the prevailing south-westerly winds and frontal depressions, which are forced to rise over the mountainous western coastline. Precipitation levels can be higher than 1,500 mm, with more than 250 days of rain in the year. The North Atlantic Drift has a moderating influence that keeps winter temperatures mild, while average summer temperatures do not rise much above 15°C.	**Climate** The lower relief and the rainshadow effect of the western mountains (when rain-bearing winds blow towards mountains and less rain falls on the other side of the mountains away from the wind) result in much lower levels of precipitation (less than 1,000 mm). Rainfall is also more evenly distributed through the year than in the West, where most rain falls in winter. The south-westerly winds have less of an effect. Winter temperatures are slightly colder, while summer temperatures and average amounts of sunshine per day are higher.
Soils The upland relief and high year-round precipitation give rise to large areas of peaty and waterlogged soils. These have low fertility, with blanket bog in many areas.	**Soils** Most of the region has brown soils, derived mostly from the limestone glacial drift that covers the Central Lowlands. These include some of the most fertile soils in the country.
Drainage Large areas of the West of Ireland have poor drainage. There are many lakes and poorly drained river floodplains, leading, for example, to flooding along the Shannon River. Apart from the Shannon, few major rivers reach the west coast.	**Drainage** This is a well-drained region with a number of large rivers that flow through the region into the Irish and Celtic Seas. These provide natural routeways and, at their mouths, important urban centres and ports have developed, e.g. Dublin, Waterford and Cork.

Table 26.1

ECONOMIC PROCESSES

The Industrial Revolution had little impact on Ireland, and its economy depended on the primary sector for much longer than most countries in Western Europe. During the 1960s, the country began its own industrial revolution based mainly on attracting a lot of foreign industries. This was a key factor in the take-off of the Celtic Tiger economy in the 1990s. Employment in services has also grown rapidly (see Fig. 26.2), although the level of development varies between the west and east of Ireland.

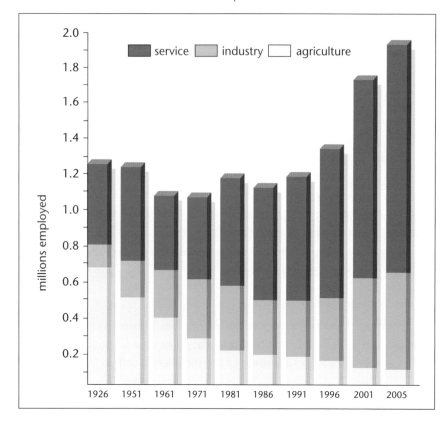

Fig. 26.2 Ireland's employment structure, 1926–2005.

Activity

Look at Fig. 26.2 and answer the following.

1. What was the most important sector in 1926?
2. What has been the trend for this sector since 1926?
3. Which sector was most important for employment in 2002?
4. Why has this sector grown so strongly since the 1960s?

The Primary Sector

Agriculture

Although agriculture is very important for Ireland, the trends and types of farming vary within the country. The way land is used highlights how physical factors can shape the agricultural geography of Ireland (see Fig. 26.3).

Traditional farming in the West of Ireland provides only low income to most farmers. This contrasts with intensive farming in eastern Ireland.
- *Do the photographs support this contrast?*

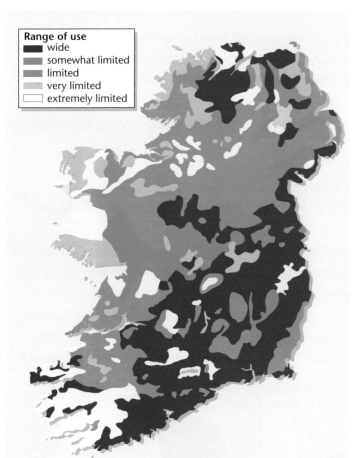

Range of use
■ wide
■ somewhat limited
■ limited
■ very limited
□ extremely limited

Fig. 26.3 Land use capability in Ireland.
● *Which regions in general can support the widest choice and most productive farming?*

Activity

Look at Table 26.2 and Fig. 26.3 and answer the following.
1. What causes income levels to be so low in the West of Ireland?
2. Why is average income so high in eastern Ireland?
3. Why is the West of Ireland not suitable for arable farming?

What is the difference between intensive and extensive farming?

Agriculture in Western and Eastern Ireland	
Border, Midland and West Region	**Southern and Eastern Region**
● Difficult environmental conditions limit how productive the land can be for agriculture (see Fig. 26.3). Despite this, 63 per cent of Irish farms are located in the BMW Region. ● The average farm size is small, levels of mechanisation are low and a high proportion of farmers are older. ● Tillage is not suitable for most of the region. Grazing is dominant, with beef cattle and sheep rearing. ● Farming is widespread, but income levels are low. Poor prospects in the sector add to problems of rural depopulation and underdevelopment. ● Average farm income is only 50 per cent of that of the eastern region, and only 14 per cent of farms can be considered viable, full-time units.	● A favourable natural environment encourages a wide range of productive agriculture. ● Although the region is more urbanised, farming remains an important economic activity. ● To be competitive, farms are more mechanised, larger and have a higher percentage of younger, more innovative farmers. ● Highly productive arable and pastoral activities occur throughout the region. Sheep and cattle reared in the West are often fattened on these lowland pastures. ● Farming is intensive and specialised, giving better income levels and prospects for rural communities. ● Average farm income is 40 per cent above the national level.

Table 26.2

Forestry

About 50 per cent of Ireland's land can be classified as marginal for agriculture. Environmental conditions are, however, more suitable for forestry. A long growing season, well-distributed rainfall and mild temperatures give an average growth rate of trees estimated at three to five times as high as in continental Europe.

Despite this favourable environment, only 10 per cent of the country is forested. The reasons for this are:

- Irish farms are generally small.
- In the past, farmers have not been keen to give up land for trees.
- Forestry involves high costs at first and requires a long-term view while trees are growing.

Since the 1980s, both state and private interests in forestry have increased. This has been aided by the EU, which sees forestry as a profitable, alternative enterprise for farmers, especially in more marginal agricultural areas. The environmental benefits of forestry (including drainage control, wildlife habitat and scenic qualities) have also been highlighted to help promote a stronger 'tree culture' within Ireland. State policy is to have 15 per cent of land under forestry, with most of the extra areas planted to be in the western regions.

New forested area in Connemara.
- *What benefits will new forest areas like this have? (Think about tourism, raw materials, jobs and environmental protection.)*

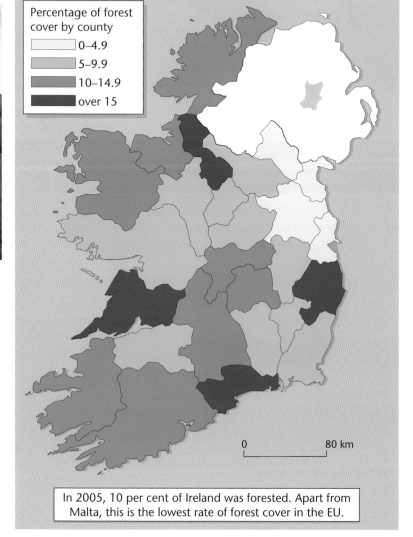

Percentage of forest cover by county
- 0–4.9
- 5–9.9
- 10–14.9
- over 15

0   80 km

In 2005, 10 per cent of Ireland was forested. Apart from Malta, this is the lowest rate of forest cover in the EU.

Fig. 26.4 Forest cover distribution in Ireland by county, 2005.
- *Why do you think forestry is a more important land use in the West of Ireland?*

Fishing

Although the continental shelf around Ireland is an extremely rich fishing area, the country's fishing industry is underdeveloped.

The importance of fishing as an industry that creates jobs and wealth for regional development has, however, increased recently with the growing market demand for fish products. Unfortunately, problems of overfishing and restrictions under the EU Common Fisheries Policy have reduced the opportunities for large-scale development of this industry in Ireland.

Despite problems of overfishing and EU fishing quotas, the quantity of fish landed at Irish ports has increased. There is also more aquaculture (fish and seafood farming) around Ireland's coastline, bringing more jobs and income from the fishing industry.

Do you remember how Ireland's continental shelf formed? These relatively shallow waters are a major fishing zone.

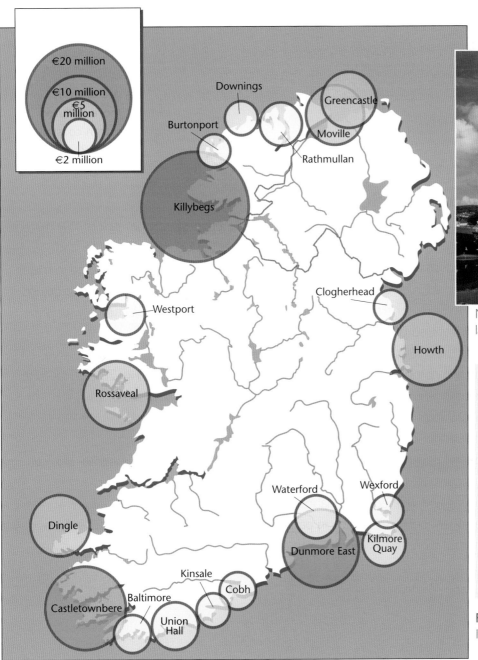

Modern fishing vessels in Killybegs, Ireland's largest port.

Activity

Look at Fig. 26.5 and answer the following.

1. Which is Ireland's most important fishing port?
2. How many of the top twenty fishing ports are on the west and south-west coast?
3. Why is the fishing industry concentrated along the western rather than the eastern coast of Ireland? (See Table 26.3.)

Fig. 26.5 The value of fish landings at Ireland's top twenty fishing ports in 2005.

Fishing in the Border, Midland and West and Southern and Eastern Regions	
Border, Midland and West Region	**Southern and Eastern Region**
• The deeply indented coastline provides sheltered harbours and faces onto the large fishing grounds of the North Atlantic. • Most of Ireland's fishing ports and fish processing plants are along the western seaboard. • 80 per cent by value of fish caught is landed at western ports. Killybegs is Ireland's largest fishing port by far, followed by Castletownbere. • Aquaculture is a growth industry. The deeply indented, sheltered and pollution-free waters along the western seaboard are an ideal environment for this industry, for example south-west Ireland and the Connemara coastline. • The lakes and rivers of western Ireland provide a good basis for inland fishing and add to the tourist potential of the region.	• Boats from ports on the Irish Sea have to travel further to access deep-water fishing grounds. • Smaller number of fishing ports as the industry concentrates on larger, specialised ports in the West. • Dunmore East and Howth are the two major fishing ports along the eastern seaboard. • The more polluted waters, especially along the coastline of the Irish Sea, limit opportunities for large-scale aquaculture. • Greater urbanisation and pollution along major rivers have had a negative impact on inland fishing. The clean-up of inland waters is helping to improve the tourism potential of these resources.

Table 26.3

> Why are eastern waters more polluted than western coastal waters?

The Secondary Sector

Ireland's colonial history, peripheral location on the edge of Europe, lack of raw materials (such as iron ore) and a small population meant that the country was a late starter in the process of industrialisation. Most of the country's limited industry was located in major urban centres, such as Cork and Dublin, due to their large populations, infrastructure and access to ports for trade. **By 1961** over half of Ireland's manufacturing was in the east region, centred on Dublin.

During the 1960s, Ireland began its modern industrial revolution with a large increase in the number and range of manufacturing activities (see Fig. 26.6). The factors that account for the country's successful programme of industrialisation are:

- Membership of the EU (1973).
- Improved transport and communication systems.
- Larger and developing urban areas to provide a better range of essential services, such as banking, education and marketing.
- A growing and well-educated labour force.
- Government policy to attract, in particular, foreign companies to locate in Ireland, e.g low corporation tax.

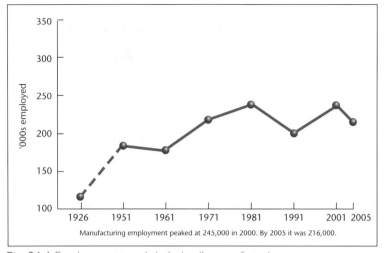

Manufacturing employment peaked at 245,000 in 2000. By 2005 it was 216,000.

Fig. 26.6 Employment trends in Ireland's manufacturing industries, 1926–2005.

In the 1960s and 1970s there was rapid growth in manufacturing employment. Branch plants of foreign multinationals were attracted to rural areas in particular where the costs of land and labour were lower than in the more developed urban areas. Government policy also encouraged a dispersal of industry from the Dublin region to the underdeveloped western periphery. This resulted in significant gains for the BMW Region (see Fig 26.7).

One of the first major foreign chemical companies attracted to Ireland was Pfizer. The US multinational established a large manufacturing plant in Cork Harbour in 1969.

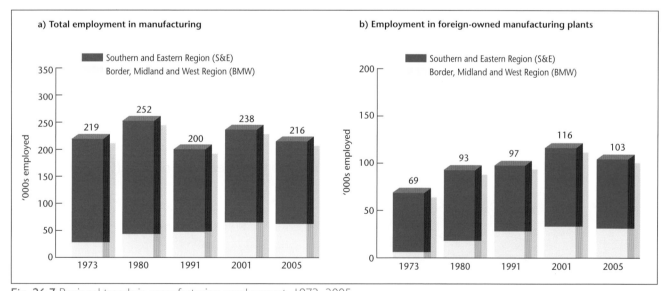

Fig. 26.7 Regional trends in manufacturing employment, 1973–2005.

Activity
Look at Fig. 26.7 and answer the following.
1. Which of the two regions is most important for manufacturing?
2. Have jobs in foreign industries increased?
3. What differences do you note between the two regions between 1980 and 1991?
4. Why did the S&E Region gain many more jobs than the BMW Region in the 1990s?
5. Can you suggest why employment in manufacturing has declined since 2001?

> A branch plant is a factory set up by foreign multinationals to produce large quantities of a basic product.

Closure in 1984 of the Dunlop tyre factory in Cork led to the loss of almost 1,000 jobs. Derelict industrial sites, lost jobs and high unemployment were common features of Ireland's major cities in the 1980s.

During the 1980s, an international recession affected Ireland. Older and more traditional Irish industries, such as textiles and clothing, experienced heavy job losses. These industries were mainly located in the larger urban centres of the S&E Region. This, together with the relative failure to attract growth industries, meant that unemployment became a major problem for urban regions such as Dublin and Cork (see page 164). The BMW Region continued to grow, but at a much slower rate, as some branch plants were closed or reduced their workforce (Fig. 26.7).

From the early 1990s, employment growth has been impressive as many high-tech industries (especially electronics and pharmaceuticals) located and/or expanded production in Ireland. These include Dell, Intel, Boston Scientific and Wyeth. This is a vital factor for the Celtic Tiger economy, which changed Ireland from a peripheral and underdeveloped country to one of the most prosperous economies in the EU.

High-tech industries are strongly attracted to large urban centres. Good communications, access to universities and educated workers, international transport links and high-quality recreational facilities are key locational factors. The S&E Region, therefore, gained most from the Celtic Tiger economy. For the BMW Region to become more attractive for modern growth industries, access to EU structural funds and continued government support are vital to improve this region's infrastructure and urban services.

One problem common to both the BMW and S&E regions is the **high level of dependency on foreign companies.** Almost 50 per cent of Ireland's manufacturing employment is controlled by foreign companies. This leaves the country open to potential problems. For example, if there is a global or US recession, the headquarters of the foreign company may decide to close or run down the Irish plant. In addition, costs of production in Ireland have significantly increased, and some companies have **relocated** their production to cheaper countries, such as India and Poland. The result has been a **decline in employment in manufacturing** from the peak year of 2001 (Fig. 26.6).

In the 1990s, 60 per cent of Ireland's net growth in manufacturing was in the Dublin region.

Intel factory.
● *Why do you think companies like this prefer to locate in the S&E Region rather than the BMW?*

The Tertiary Sector

The tertiary sector is made up of activities that provide services rather than producing goods. Since the Second World War (1939–45), the service sector has become more important and now forms the main economic activity in all developed economies.

Growth in Ireland's service sector has been slower than in most other developed economies. This was linked to the country's underdeveloped economy and having many people with low income levels, which reduced the demand for services. Since the 1960s, however, Ireland's successful economic take-off and the higher living standards of a growing population have encouraged rapid growth in services. In 1981, for the first time, Ireland had more than half of its working population employed in the tertiary sector. By 2005, approximately 67 per cent of all employment was in services (Fig 26.8).

Developments in services have been different depending on the region. Service industries prefer major urban centres, which have good access to large and prosperous markets. The country's western regions have therefore benefited less than the more urbanised eastern regions in developments within the service sector (see Table 26.4).

> Why are service industries located mostly in larger towns and cities?

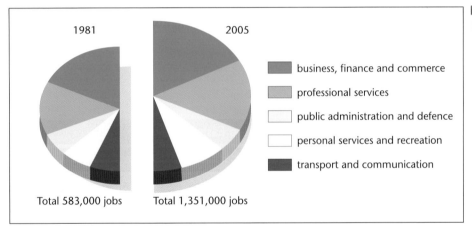

Fig. 26.8 Changes in Ireland's service sector, 1981–2005.

- business, finance and commerce
- professional services
- public administration and defence
- personal services and recreation
- transport and communication

1981 — Total 583,000 jobs
2005 — Total 1,351,000 jobs

Activity

Look at Fig. 26.8 and answer the following.
1. Calculate the growth of jobs in services between 1981 and 2005.
2. Which service sector had the most jobs in 1981 and in 2005?
3. Why are business, finance, commercial and professional services so important for a modern economy?
4. Why do you think that there has been a large increase in the number of people working in personal services and recreation?

During the 1990s, 80 per cent of all new jobs were in services. This sector was therefore the main driving force behind the Celtic Tiger economy. Of particular importance was the growth of internationally traded services (ITS), which include:

- Computer software development.
- Data processing (including telesales).
- International financial services.

Since its development in the 1980s, the IFSC (International Financial Services Centre) has become a major employer and landmark of the modernisation of inner city Dublin.

Each of these sectors has received large inflows of foreign money. By 2005, over 71,000 jobs were available in ITS. This was an increase of almost eight times in twelve years. Ireland has also emerged as second only to the US in exporting computer software.

Greater Dublin has benefited most from ITS. One of its most notable developments has been the **International Financial Services Centre (IFSC),** which has rejuvenated Dublin's inner city.

> Although the capital has problems, do you think it is easy to get civil servants to leave Dublin and relocate to the West of Ireland? Explain your answer.

Services in the Border, Midland and West and Southern and Eastern Regions	
Border, Midland and West Region	**Southern and Eastern Region**
• Dependence on the service sector for employment (60 per cent) is less than the national average. • The more rural society, agricultural economy and lower average levels of prosperity are less attractive for large-scale developments in services. • Apart from Galway, most towns in the BMW Region do not provide a good range of high-quality services. Many people commute to cities such as Cork, Limerick and Dublin to access services. • Decentralising service jobs, especially in government departments, has aided growth in some regional centres, e.g. moving the Department of Education to Athlone. • The underdeveloped services sector is an important factor for future development. Improving quality of life for the region's population requires easier access to essential services.	• Almost three-quarters of Ireland's service jobs are in this region. Dependence on service employment is 70 per cent. • The region's well-developed urban areas and infrastructure and a large, relatively prosperous population are attractive for this high-growth sector. • Dublin is the key centre for many services. It is the country's capital and decision-making centre for many public and private enterprises. It is the dominant shopping centre, with a range of major education, health and recreational facilities, and is the hub of the country's transport system. • Planners have tried to decentralise service jobs from Dublin because of problems of higher costs and traffic congestion. In spite of this, the attractions of the capital city region mean it is still growing strongly. • The service economy of regional centres and larger market towns must be built up to act as more effective counter-poles to Dublin.

Table 26.4

Tourism

Tourism is part of the service sector and is one of Ireland's main growth industries. In 2005:

- 6.8 million foreign tourists visited Ireland.
- There were also 7.2 million trips by Irish tourists.
- Total foreign earnings were €4.8 billion.
- Total tourist revenue was €5.4 billion.
- Tourism provided the equivalent of 200,000 full-time jobs.

Some 75 per cent of tourist revenue is spent in the **Southern and Eastern Region.** This is linked to its international access (over 90 per cent of scheduled air flights to Ireland go to Dublin and all ferry ports are in this region). Dublin benefits from this gateway function, and with its cultural and historic attractions accounts for a quarter of all tourist revenue.

The **Border, Midland and West (BMW) Region** has many advantages for tourism: scenic landscapes, historic monuments and cultural tradition. Despite this, the industry remains underdeveloped and grew less in the 1990s than the Southern and Eastern Region. While the BMW Region has almost half of tourist bed capacity, it generates less than 40 per cent of the country's tourist revenue.

There are **two problems** for tourism in **the BMW Region:**

- **Direct access** to the region for foreign visitors is limited and more expensive than for the S&E Region.
- While **seasonality** of tourism in Ireland is high, it is especially strong in the BMW Region. Most visitors come in July and August.

Major efforts are needed to improve access to the BMW Region and provide facilities for tourists that would generate a greater year-round industry, for example conferences, leisure activities (golf, fishing) and cultural events.

- *Use this photo of Doolin in Co. Clare to suggest why tourists are attracted to the West of Ireland, and what benefits they might bring to the local economy.*

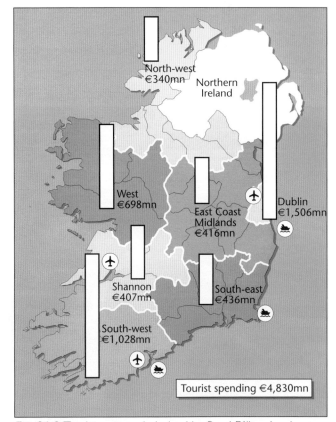

Fig. 26.9 Tourist revenue in Ireland by Bord Fáilte planning regions (in euros).

Activity

Look at Fig. 26.9 and answer the following:

1. Which region generates the most revenue from tourism? Why?
2. What advantages does the West of Ireland have for tourism?
3. Why is the tourism revenue so low in the north-west?

> What is meant by seasonality? Why is it high in the BMW Region?

Transport

Successful socio-economic development depends, to a large extent, on an efficient transport system. Until the 1980s, Ireland's internal and external transport infrastructures were poorly developed. This added greatly to the country's problems of being a periphery and its difficulty in accessing EU and world markets. With the help of structural funds from the EU, the country's transport systems have been improved.

Ireland's National Development Plan (2000–06) allocated €10 billion to improve transport systems, while the more recent NDP (2007–13) proposes to spend a further €33 billion on transport. Strategic road corridors receive highest priority as they effectively link Dublin to all other major urban centres. In addition, a north-south Atlantic corridor from Derry to Cork and on to Waterford will provide better links within the West of Ireland.

The Southern and Eastern Region has more developed transport systems than the BMW Region (see Fig. 26.10):

● Apart from the Shannon Estuary, it has all of the country's major ports.

● It has two of the three major international airports.

● The national rail network converges on Dublin.

● The national road network and strategic corridors focus on Dublin.

● Despite severe congestion in Dublin's transport system, the S&E Region has a greater choice, a lower-cost and more efficient transport system than that which operates over most of the BMW Region.

The M50 ring road and the Red Cow interchange in Dublin.

● *Use the photo to suggest how such road improvements have assisted the development and expansion of the city. (Think of housing, industry and services.)*

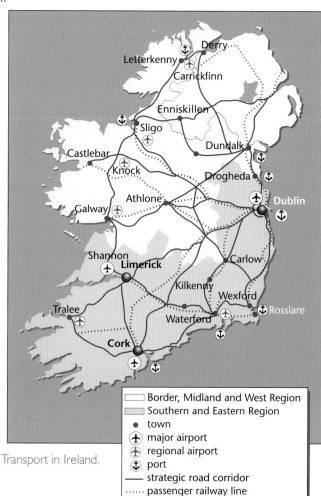

	Border, Midland and West Region
	Southern and Eastern Region
●	town
✈	major airport
✈	regional airport
⚓	port
——	strategic road corridor
⋯⋯	passenger railway line

Fig. 26.10 Transport in Ireland.

Human Processes

Differences in population dynamics, the rural-urban divide and levels of development occur within Ireland (see Table 26.5 and Fig. 26.11).

Table 26.5

Human Factors in the Border, Midland and West and Southern and Eastern Regions	
Border, Midland and West Region	**Southern and Eastern Region**
• Population has declined for most of the twentieth century. • Although it covers 47 per cent of the country, it has only 27 per cent of the country's population. • There are few large towns. Two-thirds of the population live in rural areas. Galway is the only urban centre with more than 50,000 people. It is the region's dominant town. • A lot of people have migrated from the region to the rest of Ireland and abroad. Since the 1990s, there has been a net inflow of migrants and retirees. • Only one of Ireland's seven universities is in the region. Most students have to leave for further education, and only 13 per cent of students graduating find a job in the region. This could be called a 'brain drain' and is an important problem for the BMW. • Low rates of natural increase (especially low birth rates) and an ageing population. • The region is the heartland of Irish culture, with most of the Gaeltacht areas located in the region (see Chapter 22, Fig. 22.1 on page 147).	• Throughout the twentieth century the region has increased its size and share of national population (see Fig. 26.11). • A densely settled region: the density of population is three times that of the BMW Region. • It has a well-developed and balanced distribution of urban centres. Almost three-quarters of people live in urban areas. Dublin is the dominant city, with 1.3 million people. Cork, Limerick and Waterford have populations over 50,000. • It receives a lot of migrants from the rest of the country and from abroad who are attracted by the job opportunities in Dublin. • An estimated 86 per cent of Ireland's third-level places are in the region. Almost all students wishing to enter further education can find a place in their home region. A variety of good-quality jobs also means that almost 90 per cent of graduates find employment in the Southern and Eastern Region. • Relatively high rates of natural increase (higher birth rates and inmigration) and a younger age profile are advantages for development. • A much more cosmopolitan society and culture shows more openness to outside influences.

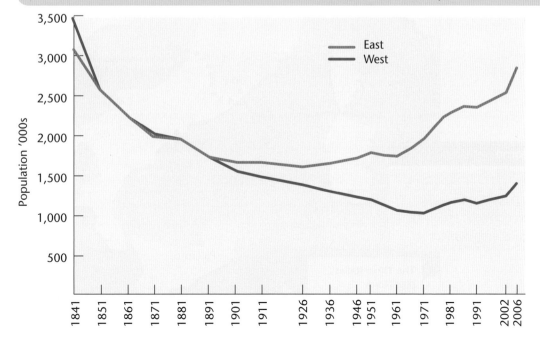

Fig. 26.11 Population changes in eastern and western Ireland, 1841–2006.

Activity

Look at Fig. 26.11 and answer the following.

1. Before the Famine, which region had the biggest population?
2. Contrast the trends for both regions before and after 1926.
3. Briefly explain these different trends and how they affect prospects for development.

185

CHAPTER 27
THE MEZZOGIORNO

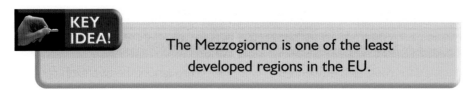

KEY IDEA!

The Mezzogiorno is one of the least developed regions in the EU.

Italy is a country of almost 60 million people and is one of the founding states of the EU. Today, it is one of the world's largest economies. It is also a country of great contrasts.

Some of Europe's most prosperous regions – centred on the cities of Milan, Turin and Genoa – are in northern Italy (see Fig. 27.1). Since the 1960s, growth has spilled over into nearby regions. The result has been a surge in prosperity and optimism in the centre of the country. The south of Italy, or the Mezzogiorno, however, is one of the poorest regions of the EU. It is an example of a **peripheral region**.

The Mezzogiorno (meaning 'land of the midday sun') is the part of the Italian peninsula south of Rome (see Fig. 27.1), and includes the islands of Sicily and Sardinia. This region has a long history of widespread poverty and underdevelopment and contrasts strongly with northern Italy.

Fig. 27.1 Italy's three main regions (The Three Italies).

The Mezzogiorno

- 40 per cent of Italy's territory.
- 36 per cent of the country's population.
- 25 per cent of its GDP (gross domestic product).
- 50 per cent of Italy's agricultural employment.

Milan
Turin
Genoa
0 km 160
Corsica (France)
Rome
northern limit of the Mezzogiorno
Naples
Cagliari
Palermo

The Three Italies
- North
- Centre
- Mezzogiorno

PHYSICAL PROCESSES

Relief, Drainage and Soils

Southern Italy is dominated by the steep slopes of the Apennines, the mountain chain that stretches 1,050 km down the Italian peninsula (Fig 27.2). About 40 per cent of the land in the Mezzogiorno is mountainous and too steep for crops to be grown. Another 45 per cent is hilly, and there are problems with soil erosion. The hilly soils have few nutrients.

The rich, fertile soils are mostly on narrow, coastal plains and valley floodplains that follow rivers flowing down from the Apennines to the coast. These include alluvial soils from river deposition and rich volcanic soils from weathered lava. Calabria, in the 'toe' of Italy, is mostly granite plateaus with poor-quality soils.

The largest river is the Tiber, which enters the sea south of Rome. The remaining rivers are small, fast-flowing streams from the Apennines that often reach the sea through narrow, gorge-like channels, especially in the west. To the east, along the Plain of Apulia, there are few rivers. The bedrock is porous limestone that allows little surface drainage. The high Apennines and some other uplands are karst landscapes, where no rivers flow on the surface. Where there are rivers, water levels can be very low during the hot, dry summers in June, July and August.

> Why does summer rain fall in heavy downpours? (Think about the type of rainfall.)

Climate

Summer

High pressure dominates in summer. Winds are hot and dry, and blow as north-easterly winds from the continent of Europe. These winds blowing off the land bring drought from June to September. Temperatures are high, with averages of between 28°C and 30°C throughout the summer (see Fig 27.3). Any summer rain usually falls in heavy downpours. This runs off the steep, sun-baked slopes, causing problems of gullying, soil erosion and mudflows.

> Get to know the Mezzogiorno by learning the features of southern Italy on the map. Look at your atlas as well.

Winter

Winters are mild, about 17°C, and moist. South-westerly winds that blow from the Atlantic and across the Mediterranean bring moisture that falls as relief rain over the Apennines. Amounts vary from 900 mm to 500 mm. The lower amounts fall along the Adriatic coast because it is in the rain shadow of the Apennines.

Activity

Look at Fig. 27.2 and use an atlas to identify:
a. where the main lowland areas are located
b. sea areas A and B
c. island C
d. mountains D
e. river E
f. cities F to I.

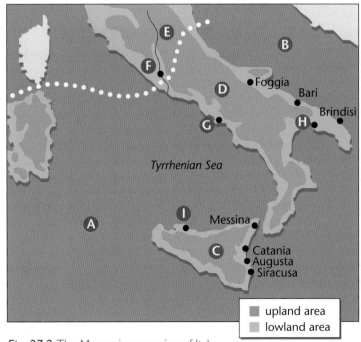

Fig. 27.2 The Mezzogiorno region of Italy.

upland area
lowland area

Tyrrhenian Sea

Foggia
Bari
Brindisi
Messina
Catania
Augusta
Siracusa

187

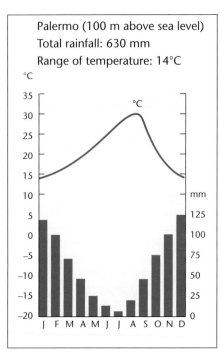

Palermo (100 m above sea level)
Total rainfall: 630 mm
Range of temperature: 14°C

Fig. 27.3 Temperature and rainfall in Palermo, Sicily.

Activity
Look at Fig. 27.3 and answer the following.
1. Which months have less than 25 mm of rain?
2. What is the temperature of the hottest month?
3. Contrast the climograph of Palermo with the one for Valentia (see Fig. 26.1, page 172).
4. Explain the reasons for the differences.

ECONOMIC PROCESSES

The Primary Sector

By the start of the 1950s, the Mezzogiorno was something like an underdeveloped country. Because people depended on a primary sector which was weak and in a difficult environment, most of the population was poor (see Fig 27.4)

Activity
Look at Fig. 27.4.
1. In which sector of the economy did most people work in 1950?
2. What have been the main changes in the Mezzogiorno economy since 1950?

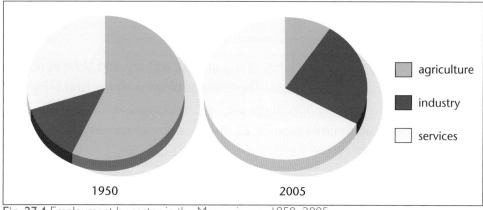

agriculture
industry
services

1950   2005

Fig. 27.4 Employment by sector in the Mezzogiorno, 1950–2005.

Animals grazing on the poor and relatively arid landscape of the Apennines.
● *Would you describe this as subsistence farming?*

Agriculture

Until 1950, most of the land, and especially the more productive lowland areas, in the Mezzogiorno was owned by landlords, most of whom lived outside the region (absentee landlords). To work their large estates, large numbers of peasants were hired as day workers. Land was also leased to peasants for grazing animals (sheep or goats) or growing some cereals. Many peasants paid their rent with a share of their farm produce (this is called sharecropping).

This form of farming was extensive. Levels of productivity and total output were low, especially given the difficult natural environment, e.g. summer drought and mountainous relief. It was very inefficient and gave low income to the people. This system of land use is called *latifundia*.

With most land owned by landlords, there was not enough land available to make farms big enough to provide a reasonable income to the large rural population. In addition, since the average family size was large, farm holdings were usually subdivided between family members. By 1950, therefore, 70 per cent of land holdings in the Mezzogiorno were less than 3 hectares.

To support large families, these tiny holdings had to be worked intensively. This led to overgrazing and overcultivation, causing soil erosion and declining soil fertility. The result was even lower levels of output and increased levels of rural poverty.

By 1950, the Italian government realised that it was necessary to try to deal with the many problems of the Mezzogiorno's primary sector. To promote development, the Italian government introduced the **Cassa per il Mezzogiorno** (Fund for the South). This was also supported by the European Union. At first, about 80 per cent of funding went to modernise farming, and this had some success.

> The Cassa per il Mezzogiorno operated until 1984. After that the Mezzogiorno received structural funds as an Objective 1 Region of the EU.

Solutions to the Agricultural Problems

To introduce a more productive and intensive form of farming, a number of important changes were necessary.

- **Land reform** was vital to give the peasants access to their own land. Most of the large estates were bought by the state and the land redistributed to landless peasants. New holdings of approximately 5 hectares were created in the lowlands, but larger units (up to 50 hectares) were formed in the upland.

- On the new, family-owned farms, **farmers were trained** to use more intensive farm methods. This involved both growing **new cash crops,** such as citrus fruits and vegetables, and producing **traditional crops more intensively.** These traditional crops included olives, vines and cereals.

- The success of intensive farming in the region depends on a **regular supply of water** to compensate for summer droughts. Large amounts of money were spent on developing reservoirs, wells and **irrigation systems.**

- **Improved transport,** such as the *autostrada* (motorway) system, was needed to allow high-value but more perishable crops to gain access to major markets, such as north-west Italy and Germany.

- When the new family farms were created in the lowlands, many people moved from hilltop villages to **new farmhouses or villages,** which were built to act as new service centres. These villages had schools, health care, leisure facilities and other services, which helped raise the **quality of life** for people living in the countryside. Processing and packaging factories were also built in larger towns, and these provided more jobs.

A hilltop village in the Mezzogiorno. Note the scarcity of suitable farmland near the village to support the rural population. Farmers travelled to nearby lowland areas to work their small holdings.

> What is quality of life? Why is it important for regional development?

The most prosperous farming in the Mezzogiorno usually occurs in the coastal lowlands.
- *Use this photograph and the one on page 189 to contrast lowland and upland farming, e.g. relief, settlement type, land use and transport.*

Intensive growing of citrus fruits, such as oranges, provides a much higher income for family farms in the irrigated areas of the Mezzogiorno.

Present-day Farming Activities

> Why has it been more difficult to change farming in the Apennines? (Think about environment and location.)

Dependence on agriculture has gone down dramatically. Today, only one in ten of the region's workforce works in farming (Fig 27.4). The move to more intensive farming has also increased rural prosperity. The Mezzogiorno is a now a major supplier of citrus fruits, vegetables and olives to European markets.

The successful transformation of farming in the South occured mainly in the coastal lowlands and river valleys, where irrigation is available. In the mountain areas inland, less successful traditional and extensive forms of farming are still used. Low incomes and continued out-migration from the region are typical of the more difficult conditions in Europe's most problematic farming regions.

The Secondary Sector

Industry

> Briefly explain why **each** of these factors limits the development of industry.

By the early 1950s, only 17 per cent of Italy's industrial workforce and output were located in the Mezzogiorno. This was due to:

- Few sources of raw materials and energy supplies.
- Peripheral position and high transport costs.
- Unskilled and poorly educated labour force.
- A large but poor rural population.
- Few large towns to provide services, such as banking or legal services.

As with agriculture, government intervention was needed to encourage industrial take-off. From the 1960s, there was help from the Cassa per il Mezzogiorno and EU funding. Among the key incentives for promoting industrial growth in the South were:

● Generous grants and tax relief.

● Major improvements to the physical infrastructure, such as building an *autostrada* (motorway) system (see Fig. 27.5) and modernising key ports, such as Naples, Taranto and Siracusa.

● State-controlled companies had to make 80 per cent of new investment in the South.

● Across the South, a number of industrial development areas were created to act as a basis for regional growth.

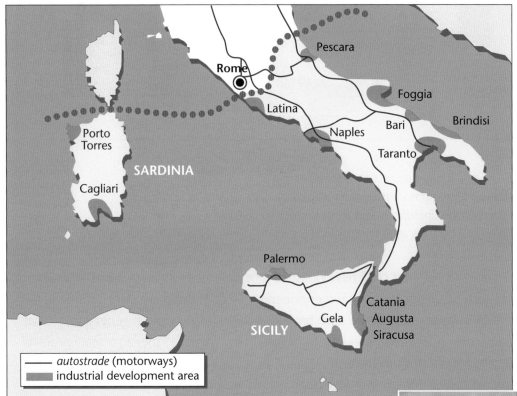

Fig. 27.5 Industrial development areas in the Mezzogiorno.

● *Why are there almost no growth zones in the central spine of the Mezzogiorno?*

Industrial development in the Mezzogiorno has had successes and failures. Many new jobs have been created. Between 1960 and 2000, the region's industrial workforce almost tripled to 1.4 million. This has reduced dependence on agriculture and encouraged growth in the service sector. Overall, the region's economy became more diversified. Despite this, the economy of the Mezzogiorno remains less well developed than northern Italy (Fig 27.6).

Capital-intensive projects such as this coastal oil refinery in Sicily were the basis for economic development in the Mezzogiorno.

Fig. 27.6 Employment and prosperity contrasts between northern and southern Italy.

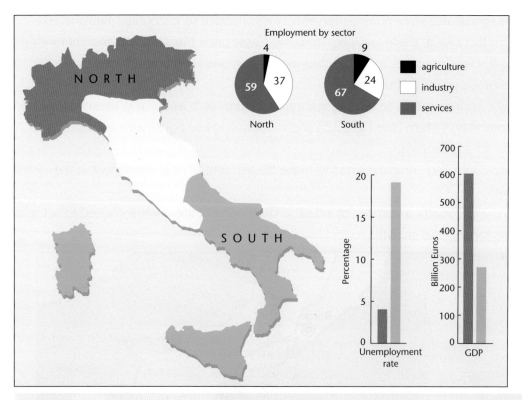

Activity

Look at Fig. 27.6 and answer the following.

1. Is the Mezzogiorno less dependent on industry? Suggest why.
2. Estimate the unemployment levels in the two regions.
3. Why do you think total wealth (GDP) is much lower in the Mezzogiorno?

Why are the giant new plants called 'cathedrals in the sun'?

Almost 75 per cent of all new industrial jobs have been in large, capital-intensive sectors such as steel, chemicals and engineering. Most of these are state controlled and need a lot of investment. While each project provides many jobs, in general they have failed to create many spin-off industries or jobs. This has led to the large-scale projects being called **'cathedrals in the sun'**.

While coastal zones have developed, inland areas remain depressed economically, so differences in levels of prosperity in the Mezzogiorno have increased. Some growth zones have been very successful in attracting industries. One of the best is the Bari-Brindisi-Taranto industrial triangle, where oil refining, chemicals and steel form the basis of a major industrial zone.

Suggest why there is a difference in prosperity levels between the coast and inland areas.

The Tertiary Sector
Transport

A key problem for the South is its peripheral location. To offset this, a major investment in transport infrastructure was needed to link the region to distant markets.

The *autostrada*, Italy's motorway system, was developed (Fig 27.7). The backbone of the system is the **Autostrada del Sole** ('sunshine motorway'). It starts near the Swiss border and runs along the western side of the country, ending in Calabria in the 'toe' of Italy. This, and another *autostrada* that runs along the east coast, provide fast, efficient links between northern and southern Italy.

As well as upgrading the road system, large investments were made to modernise key ports. Several of the ports have become a focus around which successful growth centres have developed. These include the deep-water port at Taranto (essential for the country's largest iron and steel plant) and port developments along the east coast of Sicily, which has one of the largest oil and chemical complexes in Western Europe.

Fig. 27.7 Italy's *autostrada* (motorway) system.
● *Why do you think the main routes are north to south in direction rather than east to west across the peninsula?*

The Autostrada del Sole was constructed through a very difficult landscape.
● *Why was this motorway vital for the development of the Mezzogiorno?*

See how the major cities are linked by the Autostrada del Sole.

Tourism

Located within the Mediterranean Basin, the Mezzogiorno has much to offer tourists, including a hot, sunny climate, beautiful scenery, beaches and historic cities. It also tends to be cheaper and less crowded than the more commercialised tourist resorts of northern Italy and southern France.

As tourism is an international growth industry, planners for the Mezzogiorno have made great efforts to promote tourism as a basis for economic development. To achieve this, transport has been improved for easier access to the region, and tourist facilities, such as hotels and recreation areas, have been upgraded.

This has been successful and the region has become more popular as a tourist destination. Over 12 million tourists visit the South, although three-quarters of these are from the rest of Italy. More has to be done to raise the profile of the region with international tourists.

Sorrento in the Bay of Naples is an important tourist centre in the Mezzogiorno.
● *What attractions does this area have for visitors?*

HUMAN PROCESSES

The Mezzogiorno is similar to the rest of Italy in its language and religion. Italian is the language people speak and almost all of them are Roman Catholic. Rome, the centre of the Catholic religion, is located between the Mezzogiorno and the more developed northern region.

The major differences in human processes between the North and South of Italy are in population trends.

Population Processes

In the 1960s, the population in northern Italy greatly increased, while people continued to leave the Mezzogiorno. From the 1980s, these roles began to be reversed. Five key factors that explain these trends are:

- Economic development.
- Natural increase in population.
- Internal migration.
- Emigration.
- Immigration.

Economic Development

Think of how the Cassa per il Mezzogiorno and economic planning helped the South.

Up until the 1980s, the underdeveloped and rural-based economy of the South did not experience population growth. This contrasted with the industrial region of northern Italy. In the 1980s, traditional industries, including textiles, vehicle assembly and shipbuilding in cities such as Milan, Turin and Genoa began to decline. This meant fewer job prospects and population growth rates in northern Italy were reduced. From this time, however, the South began to experience far more positive economic trends, linked to modernising agriculture and attracting new industries.

Natural Increase in Population

What does 'natural increase' mean?

For a long time, a high rate of natural increase was associated with Italy because the birth rate was high. The situation has changed, especially in northern Italy, where not enough babies are being born and the population is not replacing itself naturally. In the Mezzogiorno, however, birth rates continue to be higher than death rates. The result is a natural increase of population in the Mezzogiorno (Fig 27.8). If these trends continue, the region's total population will soon be greater than northern Italy.

Activity
Look at Fig. 27.8 and answer the following.
1. Why is the natural population change positive for the Mezzogiorno?
2. Is population growth higher in the North or South of Italy?
3. Does this provide advantages for the Mezzogiorno for economic development (think of labour force, market)?

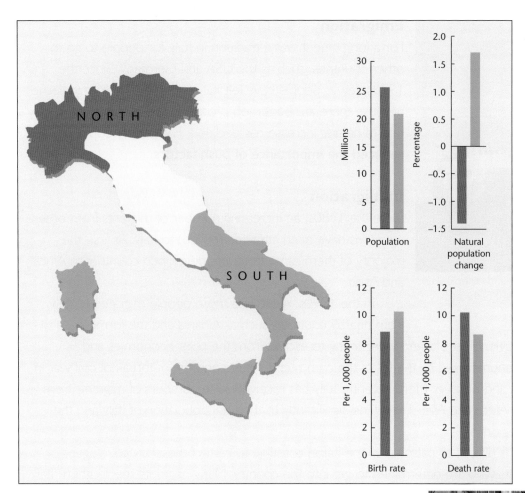

Fig. 27.8 Population indicators for the Mezzogiorno and northern Italy.

What are push and pull factors? List three push and three pull factors that influence migration from south to north in Italy.

Internal Migration

Internal migration has generally involved a flow of people from the countryside in the poor South to the richer cities of northern Italy. Between 1951 and 1981, over 4 million migrants left the South (**out-migration**) because of a number of **push factors.** Most of the people who left were attracted to cities (in-migration), such as Milan, Turin and Rome, by a variety of **pull factors.**

The out-migration to northern Italy continued up to the 1990s, with over 1 million people leaving the Mezzogiorno in the 1980s. The pull factors of northern cities have now been greatly reduced, while **modernisation of the South has reduced the push factors** that encourage people to leave. Better job prospects in growth zones of the Mezzogiorno have reduced out-migration. A 'trickle' of out-migration continues from the Mezzogiorno because unemployment levels are higher and prosperity is lower than in northern Italy.

The underdeveloped economy of the Mezzogiorno meant that large numbers of people migrated from overcrowded urban centres such as Palermo in Sicily.

195

Large numbers of refugees from Albania and other Balkan countries have tried to gain entry into the EU through Italian ports, such as Bari. Why?

Emigration

For a long time it was a tradition in Italy for people to go to other countries, such as the USA and Germany. Since the 1970s, fewer people have left Italy (including the Mezzogiorno) because there are better job prospects in the country, and Italy's rate of natural increase has declined. For Italian people, this has **reduced the importance of push factors.**

Immigration

Since the 1980s, an increasing number of migrants from other countries have been attracted (pulled) to Italy. At first, the majority of them came from less developed countries in Africa and Asia.

In the 1990s, more and more people migrated to Italy from nearby countries such as Albania and the former Yugoslavia. Most of them were trying to escape from the poor economies and devastation caused by the fall of the communist system and the outbreak of civil war in Bosnia and Kosovo. More recently, Italy has received large numbers of migrants from North Africa and Asia. These add significantly to the total population of Italy and the Mezzogiorno

It is difficult to patrol all of the Italian coastline to restrict the entry of refugees or migrants who are determined to get into the country. Many migrants see southern Italy as an easy way to enter the EU, believing that these coastal areas are less controlled than other parts of the EU. The east coast of the Mezzogiorno could be called the 'Achilles heel' for migration into the EU (Fig. 27.9).

In 2004, Italy received 560,000 migrants, which adds significantly to the country's total population.

Fig. 27.9 Migration into Italy through the Mezzogiorno.

As well as legal migration, up to 50,000 illegal migrants are estimated to enter Italy each year.

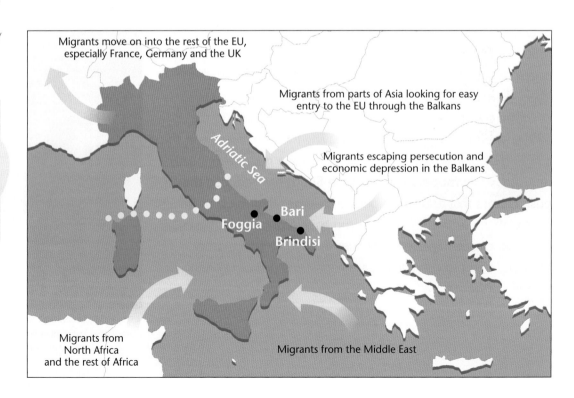

Migrants move on into the rest of the EU, especially France, Germany and the UK

Migrants from parts of Asia looking for easy entry to the EU through the Balkans

Migrants escaping persecution and economic depression in the Balkans

Adriatic Sea

Bari
Foggia
Brindisi

Migrants from North Africa and the rest of Africa

Migrants from the Middle East

CHAPTER 28
THE PARIS REGION

KEY IDEA!

The Paris Region is one of the most important core regions in Europe

France, one of the largest and most important countries in Europe, has a well-defined **core region**. This is the **Paris Region.** It is made up of the city of Paris, its sprawling suburbs and the four *départements* that surround the city (see Fig. 21.6 on page 145).

As is typical of cores, the Paris Region occupies only a small area of the country, but it dominates the economic, political and cultural life of France (Table 28.1). This dominance has caused many people to describe the rest of France as a periphery of this powerful national core.

There are several reasons why the Paris Region is such a powerful core region. These involve a combination of **both** physical and economic/human processes.

The Paris Region is also referred to as the Ile de France.

Paris is one of Europe's most important cities.
● *Name the river on which it is located.*

Fig 28.1 France and the Paris Region.

2 per cent of area of France but:
● 19 per cent of population.
● 21 per cent of employment.
● 29 per cent of GDP.

Table 28.1. The economic importance of the Paris Region to France.

Activity
Review the core-periphery model on page 155 (Fig 23.1) to understand the dominant relationships between a core and its periphery.

Remember what the meaning of a primate city and core region are.

197

PHYSICAL PROCESSES

Relief

The Paris Region is located at the heart of the much larger Paris Basin (Fig 28.2). This is an extensive, saucer-shaped depression, which is composed of a series of different landscapes where different sedimentary rocks reach the surface. The central area, or Ile de France, is a low-lying and gently undulating plateau which favours agricultural and urban development.

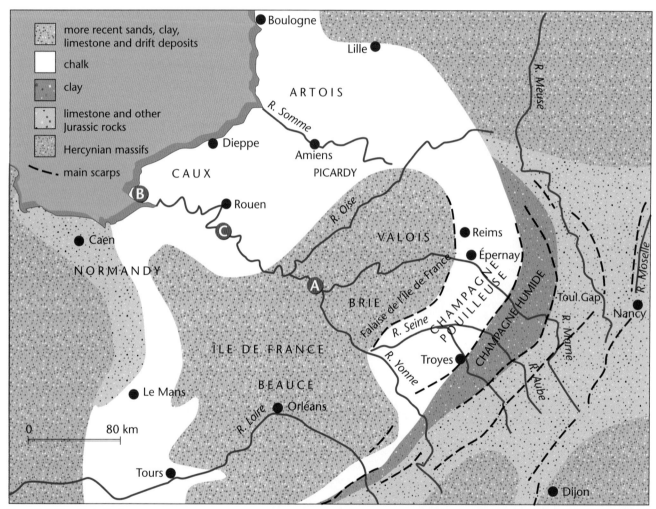

Fig. 28.2 The Paris Basin.

Activity

Study Fig 28.2 and answer the following.
1. Name urban centres A and B.
2. Name river C.
3. Why do rivers increase the centrality of Paris?

Soil

Most of the Ile de France region is covered by fertile **limon** (loess). This originated during and after the last Ice Age as windblown dust. Strong winds blowing south off the retreating ice sheets were able to pick up and transport large amounts of small, glacially eroded debris. These were then deposited in the Paris Basin, and elsewhere across the North European Plain, as deep layers of fertile and easily worked soil.

198

River System and Drainage

The Paris Region and Basin is drained by the **River Seine** and its tributaries. These form **natural routeways** which link Paris to other parts of France. The Seine also links Paris to the deep-water port of Le Havre.

The Seine and its tributaries have helped Paris improve its accessibility to a large hinterland.

The broad valley of the Lower Seine provides Paris with a natural routeway to the ports of Rouen and Le Havre.

Climate

The climate of Paris is one of **transition** between Cool Temperate Oceanic and Cool Temperate Continental (see Fig 19.1 on page 135). Summer temperatures are quite high (25°C) and although rainfall is well distributed throughout the year, a maximum occurs in summer (Fig 28.3).

Onshore westerly winds maintain relatively high rainfall totals in winter, although temperatures fall to near freezing point. This can give rise to some winter snowfall.

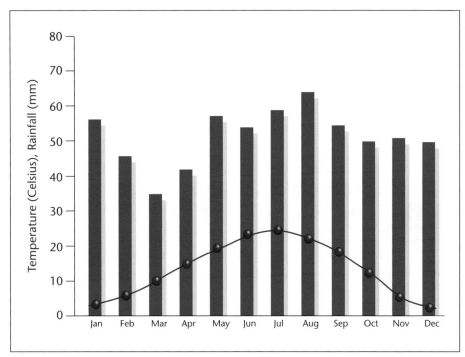

Fig. 28.3 Temperature and rainfall in Paris (Orly Airport).

Activity

Look at Fig 28.3 and answer the following.

1. What months have the highest temperature and rainfall?
2. Explain these observations (think about distance from area and type of rainfall).
3. Why is this climate suitable for intensive cereal farming?

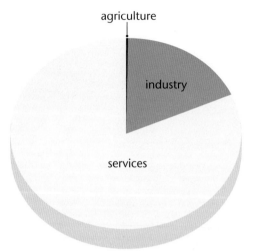

Fig. 28.4 Employment structure of the Paris Region.

ECONOMIC AND HUMAN PROCESSES

The Paris Region is a highly dynamic and prosperous core region in terms of both France and the EU. Output from its diverse and modern industries (especially services) makes Paris the fifth-most prosperous city in the world, and one of the most competitive regions in the EU. In total, some 5.1 million people are employed in this region (Fig 28.4).

Activity
Look at Fig 28.4.
1. Which sector is dominant? Why?
2. Why would you expect core regions to have such a small primary sector?

The Primary Sector

Although dominated by the large urban landscape of Paris, the city's rural hinterland includes some of the most prosperous and productive farming in Europe (see Table 28.2).

Activity
Use Table 28.2 as a basis to contrast farming in a core region with that found in a periphery, e.g. the Mezzogiorno (Chapter 27) or West of Ireland (Chapter 26).

Physical and Human Factors Influence Farming in the Paris Region	
Physical	**Human**
• Relief: Low-lying/undulating and favours large, mechanised farms. • Soil: Fertile (limon). • Drainage: Good. • Climate: Seasonal temperature and rainfall patterns favour cereals.	• Market: Near the large Paris market (high demand). • Land prices: High due to competition from other land uses – intensive farming. • Food prices: High due to CAP and good market- high returns (profits) encourage investment in farms. • Farmers: Young and educated – farms operated as a business.

Table 28.2

Cereal farming in the Paris Basin.
● *Why does the rich agriculture of the Paris Basin add to the growth of Paris?*

A key characteristic of the region is that different areas **specialise** in different forms of intensive farming. Some examples include:

● The fertile (limon-covered) limestone plateau of **Beauce**, to the south of Paris, devotes 80 per cent of its land to large-scale, mechanical farming of **cereals** (especially wheat and maize). It produces some of the highest cereal yields in the EU.

● **Market gardening** is practised on many small plots of land **adjacent to large urban centres**. High-value products, such as vegetables and flowers, are produced for the regional market.

● **Dairying** occurs in areas of clay soils in **Brie,** to the east of Paris. These damp soils favour pasture, and farmers concentrate on supplying liquid milk and dairy produce, such as butter and cheese (Brie), to the Paris market.

The Secondary Sector

Industry

The development of Paris as a **core industrial region** is due to a number of factors:

- **Market:** The large and prosperous market of over 11 million people attracts a wide range of consumer industries, such as cosmetics, vehicles and electrical goods.
- **Centrality and excellent transport systems:** Paris is the hub of the country's transport system and has good links to other major markets in the EU (see Fig. 28.5). Navigable waterways also link Paris to the rivers Rhine and Rhone, and to the deepwater port of Le Havre. These allow for the efficient and low-cost import of raw materials and export of products.
- **Labour supply:** The Paris Region provides a large and varied supply of workers. This is vital, especially for labour-intensive industries, such as clothing.
- **Services:** A wide range of services, such as banks, legal and marketing, supports industrial development. A large number of high-quality universities and research centres also encourages research and development, which is essential for high-tech industries.
- **Environment:** The beauty of Paris and its cultural facilities attract investors.

> Within three hours from Paris, 380 million people are accessible by air or high-speed rail.

The modern design of the Paris City of Science and Industry Park illustrates the role of Paris as a major centre for scientific research and development.

Employment in vehicle assembly in Paris fell from 185,000 in 1975 to only 37,000 in 2005. This Renault factory on the banks of the Seine near Paris once employed 30,000 people. It closed in 1992.

From the 1970s, however, **deindustrialisation** has affected the core region. Employment in manufacturing was more than halved between 1975 and 2005 (see Table 28.3). By 2005, only one in eight jobs in the Paris Region was in manufacturing.

Manufacturing Employment in the Paris Region			
	Employment (000s)	% total Paris Region workforce	% of French industrial workforce
1955	1,370	29	25
1975	1,360	29	22
2005	600	12	12

Table 28.3

Activity

Study Table 28.3.

1. Describe the trend in industrial employment.
2. Has Paris become more or less important for industrial employment? Explain your answer.

Deindustrialisation in Paris, and most other core regions, has been due to several reasons:

Remember the meaning of deindustrialisation? See page 161.

- Increasing cost of labour.
- High cost of land for factories.
- Congestion, which increases the time and costs of transport.
- Cheaper sites and labour costs in peripheral regions.
- Government policy to decentralise industry to help develop peripheral regions.

Despite the decline in industrial employment, Paris remains important, especially for high-tech and high-value products, for example electronics and fashion goods. In addition, it has increased its role as a **decision-making centre for industry,** as most major French manufacturing companies have their headquarters in the city.

The Tertiary Sector

Paris is the **capital** of France and the seat of the country's government. This, together with its central location, large population, excellent transport systems and an attractive city environment, has encouraged the growth of a huge variety of high-quality services. Today, over 80 per cent of the region's workforce is in services (see Fig 28.4).

As a national and EU core, many French and other international organisations have located their headquarters in Paris. This makes Paris a major decision-making centre and one which influences development in the rest of the country, especially the periphery.

Paris is the headquarters location of:
- 38 per cent of all French companies.
- 96 per cent of French banks.
- 70 per cent of French insurance companies.
- A variety of international organisations, e.g. UNESCO, OECD.

The French multinational Renault is one of the world's major vehicle manufacturers and is headquartered in Paris.

Transport

A well-developed and modern transport system is essential for core regions. It allows core regions, such as Paris, to extend their influences over large areas of a country – and even across international boundaries.

Paris is the **focus of the national transport systems,** as well as being an important **international hub** for road, rail and air traffic. This emphasises the **centrality** of Paris and allows for the efficient movement of people and goods to and from other parts of France and Europe.

A good example of the centrality of Paris is its emergence as a major European hub for high-speed railways (HSR). The EU has put an increased emphasis on HSR because of:

- Its energy efficiency.
- More environmentally friendly than road or air.
- Fast and efficient transport of passengers from city centre to city centre.

France was the first European country to invest heavily in HSR. It now has a number of HSR lines connecting Paris to other regions of France and on to neighbouring countries (see Fig 28.5).

Paris has two international airports which process over 70 million passengers a year.

A modern high-speed train in one of the main railway stations in Paris. These trains provide an efficient link from Paris to many regional centres in France and elsewhere.

Tourism

Core regions are generally considered to be **sources** of tourists. Increasingly, however, they have also become **destinations**. Paris is no exception to this.

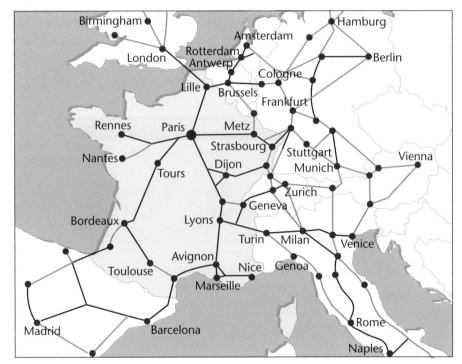

A HSR travels at over 250 km/hr. Travel time from Paris to Brussels is now only 1 hour 20 minutes and to London via the Channel Tunnel is only 2 hours 35 minutes.

Fig. 28.5 The high-speed rail network of France and the EU.

Activity

Study Fig 28.5 and answer the following.

1. Does the high-speed rail system highlight the centrality of Paris?
2. With what countries does it provide cross-border links?

The cathedral of Notre Dame is the top tourist attraction in Paris, receiving 13 million visitors each year.

Attractions of Paris for Tourists

- Beautiful and well-planned city, for example Eiffel Tower and parks.
- Rich array of historic churches, art galleries and museums, for example Notre Dame, the Louvre.
- Extensive range of high-quality shops and restaurants.
- Exciting night life and theatres.
- The 'atmosphere' of this historic city.

As a result of its attractions, Paris is the **most visited city in the world.** It receives over 30 million tourists a year, and 7 per cent of the city's workforce is involved in the tourist industry. This adds greatly to the wealth and international image of Paris.

Activity

Discuss the attractions of Paris for a holiday as opposed to the West of Ireland and the Mediterranean.

HUMAN PROCESSES

Population

The population of the Paris Region doubled between 1921 and 2004, and the area is now home to 11.3 million people (see Table 28.4). Such a large-scale increase could not be accommodated within the restricted administrative boundaries of the city of Paris. Huge suburban housing areas were built, and a series of new towns were planned to take the overspill of people (and jobs) from the city. The result is a sprawling urban region about 100 km in diameter.

> Almost 70 per cent of total employment in the region is located outside the city.

Population Change in the Paris Region (000s)					Table 28.4
	1921	1975	1999	2004	
City of Paris	2,907	2,317	2,125	2,145	
Rest of Region	2,976	7,570	8,827	9,201	
Total	5,883	9,887	10,952	11,346	
% in city	49	23	19	19	

Refer to pages 205–206 to note the problems and plans that encouraged large-scale dispersal of people and jobs from the city.

Activity

Look at Table 28.4.
1. Describe population trends in the city.
2. Explain the growth of population in the city's hinterland.

Natural Increase in Population

Core regions are especially attractive for young adults. As a result, some 30 per cent of the Paris Region's population is aged between twenty and thirty-nine years, with a further one-quarter being under twenty. This helps explain the region's **high birth and low** death rate as compared with both national and EU averages (see Table 28.5). Natural change is now the major factor in the continued growth of population in Paris.

Migration

Core regions, such as Paris, have traditionally attracted large numbers of migrants who seek jobs and a better standard of living.

Although foreign migrants continue to be attracted by the pull factors of Paris, the **rate of immigration** has declined because of fewer job prospects and stricter laws on immigration. In addition, since the 1980s, there has been a **strong out-migration** of French people from Paris to other regions of France. This involves a large number of retirees, as well as younger people looking for cheaper housing and/or an improved quality of life. This form of **internal migration,** especially to nearby regions, greatly exceeds foreign in-migration to Paris. The result was a **net migration loss** of 490,000 in the 1990s.

Population Change in the Paris Region (000s)		
	Birth rate	Death rate
Paris Region	15.2	6.8
France	12.3	9.1
EU	10.2	10.0

Table 28.5

Some Facts on Migration to Paris
- 40 per cent of all foreign migrants in France live in the Paris Region.
- 13 per cent (1.5 million) of the region's population are migrants.
- The largest migrant groups are from Portugal and former colonies in North and West Africa.
- One-third of the migrant population is from the rest of France.

Planning for the Paris Region

Despite their growth and prosperity, core regions are also faced with **problems** that require careful planning. In Paris, these problems are generally due to the **scale and rapid growth** of the region. Its problems have effects at three spatial levels.

1. Within the City

Planners in Paris have reacted to these problems by a variety of **urban renewal** projects, including demolishing poor-quality housing and replacing it with modern buildings, and improving transport systems.

Out-migration from Paris is less likely to involve foreign populations. As a result, the number and importance of foreign populations will increase within the Paris Region. This may add to racial tensions.

Approximately 200,000 commuters come into the city of Paris each day.

Problems in the City
- Inner city housing is often old and in poor condition.
- Overcrowded living conditions.
- Traffic congestion linked to large-scale commuting.
- High costs of housing and property.
- Deindustrialisation and out-migration of people.

The La Défense node is located 6 km from the centre of Paris. This former undeveloped site of 640 ha now houses 200,000 residents and employs over 100,000 people in Europe's largest office complex.

The main element of the plan, however, involved the creation of **eight large nodes** (centres) within Paris (Fig. 28.6). These include modern housing, employment opportunities and improved services. They are designed to reduce commuting and improve quality of life and therefore maintain people and employment **within the city.**

2. Within the Paris Region

Problems for the Region
- Uncontrolled urban sprawl.
- Traffic problems as commuting levels increase.
- Environmental decline.
- Dominance of the city prevents other urban centres from providing a good range of services and jobs.

To help control the overspill of population and employment from the city, **five new towns** have been created along two axes to the north and south of the River Seine (see Fig. 28.6). These towns have been a success, and each has a population of over 100,000, as well as a good range of services and job opportunities.

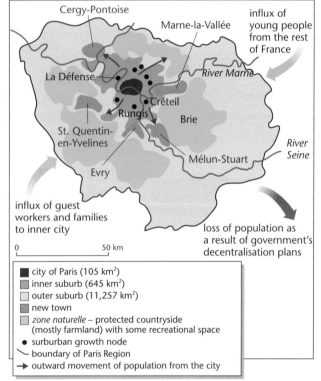

Fig **28.6** New towns around Paris.

Modern urban layout at Marne-la-Vallée, one of the five new towns designed to accommodate dispersal of people and employment from the city of Paris.

3. Within the Rest of France

The dominance of Paris within French politics, culture and economics reduced the prospects for regional capitals to grow and to compete with Paris. French national planning has therefore selected a limited number of provincial cities, such as Lyons, Marseilles and Bordeaux, to act as **national growth centres**. A large amount of investment has been targeted on these centres to upgrade their infrastructure and make them more competitive for economic development.

Although this has had some success, Paris remains the dominant core region of France.

Multi-part Questions

1. State Examinations 2006 (Higher Level)
   A. NON-IRISH EUROPEAN REGIONS
      Examine the development of primary activities in one non-Irish European region of
      your choice.   [20 marks]

   B. CONTINENTAL/SUBCONTINENTAL REGION
      Describe how any **two** of the following have influenced human activities in a
      continental/sub-continental region that you have studied:
      – climate
      – soil
      – relief
      – drainage.   [30 marks]

   C. CULTURE
      'Culture is an important factor in defining some regions.' Examine this statement with
      reference to any region you have studied.   [30 marks]

2. State Examinations 2006 (Higher Level)
   A. IRISH REGIONS
      Draw an outline map of Ireland. Show and name the following on it:
      i.   any one Irish region that you have studied
      ii. any two physical features in the region
      iii. one urban centre in the region.   [20 marks]

   B. EUROPEAN UNION EXPANSION
      Examine the impact of European Union expansion on Ireland's economy and/or
      culture.   [30 marks]

   C. THE TERTIARY SECTOR
      Account for the development of tertiary activities in one non-Irish European region of
      your choice.   [30 marks]

3. Example State Examination Paper 2005 (Higher Level)
   A. IRISH REGIONS
      Draw a sketch map of Ireland. On it, mark and name two contrasting regions.
                                                                                         [20 marks]

   B. EUROPEAN REGION
      Select a non-Irish European region and explain how (i) relief and (ii) climate have
      influenced the development of its agriculture.   [30 marks]

   C. NON-EUROPEAN REGION
      Examine **one** of the economic challenges facing a non-European region of your choice.
                                                                                         [30 marks]

4. State Examinations 2006 (Ordinary Level)
    The figures below show the tourist regions of Ireland visited by domestic tourists in 2004.

2004 – Regions Visited – Domestic Holidays (%)	
Dublin	13.9
Midlands-east	12.5
South-east	15.9
South-west	20.4
Shannon	11.3
West	17.9
North-west	8.1

A. IRELAND – DOMESTIC HOLIDAYS

Use graph paper to draw a graph that shows the data in the table above.

[30 marks]

B. EUROPEAN REGIONS

With reference to any **one** European region which you have studied, give and explain in detail **two** reasons why tourists might visit the region. [40 marks]

C. NON-EUROPEAN REGIONS

Describe the influence which **either** climate or the physical landscape has on the development of tourism in any non-European Continental or Sub-Continental region which you have studied. [30 marks]

5. State Examination 2006 (Ordinary Level)

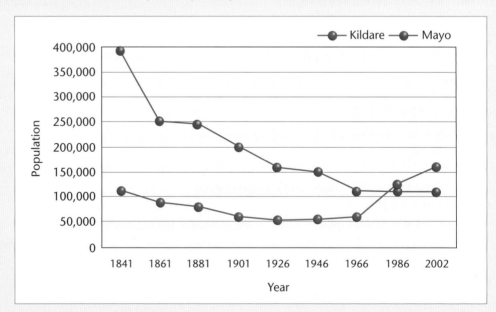

A. POPULATION TREND

Examine the above graph, which shows the populations of Mayo and Kildare since 1841.

i.   After which census year did Kildare show a significant change in trend?
ii. In which census year did the population of Kildare first exceed that of Mayo?
iii. Explain briefly **two** causes of the rise in population in core areas such as Kildare.

[30 marks]

B. EUROPEAN REGIONS

With reference to **two** contrasting European regions, explain the differences between them under **one** of the following headings:
– climate
– population patterns
– energy sources
– manufacturing industry.   [40 marks]

C. NON-EUROPEAN REGIONS

In the case of a non-European Continental or Sub-Continental region which you have studied, briefly describe **two** factors which have influenced the development of agriculture or industry in the region.   [30 marks]

6. State Examination 2006 (Ordinary Level)

A. IRELAND – REGIONS

Draw a sketch map of Ireland. On it mark and name:
i.   **two** contrasting regions
ii. **one** major city or town in each region.   [30 marks]

B. EUROPEAN REGIONS

Explain the importance of one of the primary industries listed below to the economy of any European region studied by you.
– Agriculture
– Forestry
– Fishing
– Mining/energy   [30 marks]

C. NON-EUROPEAN REGIONS

With reference to any non-European, Continental or Sub-Continental region you have studied, describe **two** factors which have influenced its industrial development.
                                                                          [40 marks]

CHAPTER 29

INDIA

> **KEY IDEA!** India is part of the world's most populated and poorly developed global regions. Its human and physical geographies have a strong effect on each other.

The vast, triangular-shaped country of India stretches from approximately 36°N, along its mountainous northern borders, almost to the Equator. It divides the northern Indian Ocean into the Arabian Sea and the Bay of Bengal (see Fig. 29.1).

India is home to 17 per cent of the world's population. Its population exceeds 1 billion and will soon overtake China to become the most populous country in the world. India is a part of the less developed world and faces huge problems of poverty and underdevelopment. The average daily income per capita (per person) is only a little over US$1 (see Table 29.1). Despite this, India has recently developed strongly and has become a more important global economy (see pages 218–19).

Some Comparative Indicators of Development (2005)				
	Ireland	Italy	France	India
Area (000 km²)	70	301	552	3,287
Population (million)	4.1	58.5	62.3	1,015
Density (per km²)	58	194	113	324
Percentage of urban population	60	68	77	28
GNP (gross national product) per capita (US$)	40,150	30,010	34, 841	720

Table 29.1

Activity

Look at Table 29.1 and answer the following.

1. What percentage of the Indian population is rural?
2. In Europe, rural economies usually support only low densities of population. Is this true in India?
3. How prosperous is the average person in Ireland compared to India?

PHYSICAL PROCESSES

A country the size of India has a great variety of natural environments. This is a key factor in shaping the human geography of India, since almost three-quarters of the population live in rural communities and work mainly in agriculture.

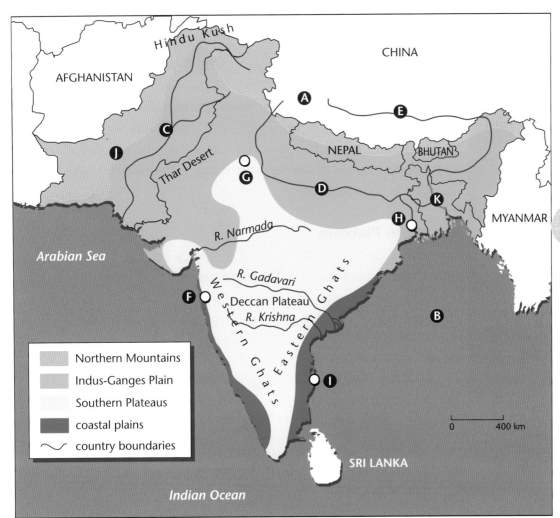

Fig. 29.1 The relief regions of the Indian subcontinent.

Locate the three major river valleys in Fig 29.1.

Activity
Look at Fig. 29.1 and at an atlas and name:
a. mountain area A
b. sea area B
c. rivers C, D and E
d. cities F, G, H and I
e. countries J and K.

Relief and Drainage

There are three main landform regions in India (see Fig. 29.1):

- Northern Mountains.
- Indus-Ganges Plain.
- Southern Plateaus.

Learn a simple sketch map that includes the major relief features and rivers of India.

Northern Mountains

These towering mountains form India's northern boundary zone. They extend from the Hindu Kush in the north-west, through the Himalayas to the extreme north-east of the country. The world's highest mountain ranges (including Mt Everest) came from the collision of two great tectonic plates, which compressed the earth's crust and resulted in the uplift of these fold mountains. They form one of the earth's most dramatic physical features and are the source of many rivers that flow south into India.

Indus-Ganges Plain

The Indus-Ganges Plain follows the Indus River Valley from Pakistan through the Ganges Valley to end with the double delta of the Ganges and Brahmaputra rivers in Bangladesh. The earth movements that created the Himalayas also caused the Indus-Ganges Plain, a major depression to the south of the mountains. The main drainage of northern India and the nearby states is directed to this depression. It includes India's three most important rivers (Indus, Ganges and Brahmaputra).

These rivers and their many tributaries are swollen by summer meltwaters from the surrounding mountains and, with monsoon rains, flood extensive areas of the lowlands. Large quantities of material eroded in the upper courses of the rivers are deposited along their lower courses as highly fertile alluvial soil.

Southern Plateaus

Peninsular India (the southern part that projects into the ocean) is made up of a number of plateaus. The **Deccan Plateau** is the largest of these and is tilted from west to east. Drainage flows from the higher elevations in the west across and out into the Bay of Bengal. The **coastal lowlands** are relatively narrow, rising abruptly along both west and east coasts to form the Western and Eastern Ghats. Both of these coastal mountain ranges have an effect on onshore winds and rainfall distribution for peninsular India.

The mountain ranges of the Himalayas form a northern boundary to the Indian subcontinent.

Climate

Most of India is in tropical latitudes. Only the mountainous zones of the north and north-west have frost. Temperatures year-round are relatively high, so the main climatic variable is precipitation and the **monsoon.** This shapes the patterns of development and livelihoods of the majority of people in India.

The monsoon is a reversal of winds over the Indian subcontinent and elsewhere in South-East Asia. The monsoon in India can be divided into **two** main seasons: **the dry and wet monsoon.**

Dry Monsoon

The dry monsoon occurs from October to June. It is caused by north-east winds that blow out from a high-pressure area in the continental interior, north of the Himalayas (see Fig. 29.2). From October to February, these are very cold winds that bring freezing temperatures and snow to the mountains of northern India. From March to June, the winds become warmer and, by June, temperatures in the Ganges Valley exceed 40°C. Coming from the continental interior, these winds are usually dry. Where these winds cross the Bay of Bengal and have to rise over the Eastern Ghats, this part of India receives a winter maximum of rainfall. The rest of India is dry.

> Why do these winds become warmer? (Think about the sun overhead.)

Wet Monsoon

From mid-June to September, warm ocean air is sucked into an intensive low-pressure area created in the continental interior (see Fig. 29.3). There are two branches to this monsoon.

One branch flows as a south-west monsoon across the Arabian Sea. Where these moist, warm winds are forced to rise over the Western Ghats, intense rain falls (more than 2,500 mm). A **second branch** crosses the Bay of Bengal and veers north to move along the Ganges. Torrential rain falls in the delta areas of the Ganges and Brahmaputra. In the hillier areas of north-east India, there can be more than 10,000 mm of rain in a period of six to eight weeks.

As these winds move westwards through the Ganges Valley, rainfall totals decline. In the extreme north-west of India there are areas not affected by the monsoon. Here desert conditions occur, as in the Thar Desert.

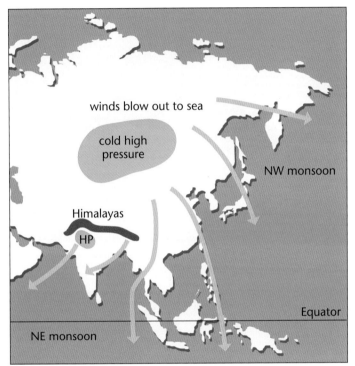

Fig. 29.2 October to June monsoon season.

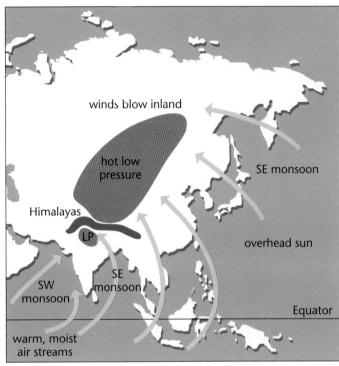

Fig. 29.3 June to October monsoon season.

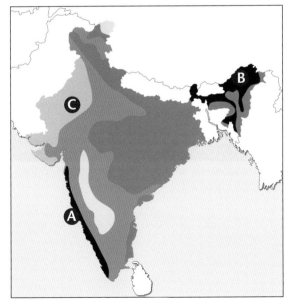

Fig. 29.4 Annual rainfall in India.

millimetres
- 200 to 600
- 600 to 1,000
- 1,000 to 2,000
- 2,000 to 3,000
- above 3,000

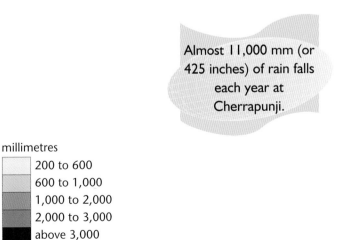

Almost 11,000 mm (or 425 inches) of rain falls each year at Cherrapunji.

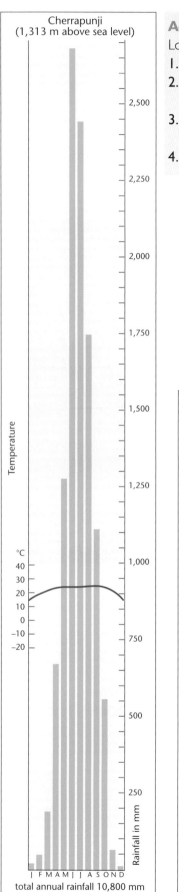

Cherrapunji
(1,313 m above sea level)

total annual rainfall 10,800 mm

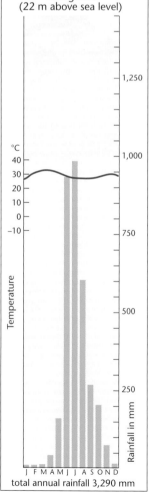

Mangalore
(22 m above sea level)

total annual rainfall 3,290 mm

Fig. 29.5 Annual rainfall in Cherrapunji and Mangalore.

Activity
Look at Figs 29.1 to 29.5 and answer the following questions about the Indian monsoon.
1. Does Fig 29.2 or 29.3 illustrate the dry monsoon? Explain your choice.
2. Look at where Mangalore (A) is located on Fig. 29.4. Explain why its region is so wet and why there is a high summer rainfall.
3. Look at where Cherrapunji (B) is located on Fig. 29.4. Explain why this is one of the wettest places on the earth.
4. Give reasons for the desert region at C on Fig. 29.4.

While the monsoon rains are vital for agriculture in India, they also cause major problems and damage through flooding.

The regular monsoon rains provide for a rich vegetation cover on the Western Ghats, including tea plantations in the south.

Why Are Monsoon Rains Essential for India?

The people of the Indian subcontinent wait anxiously for the sudden burst of the summer monsoon. The timing and the intensity of the monsoon are very important for the livelihoods of hundreds of millions of people:

- **Delay in the monsoon's arrival** affects the planting of crops and the efficient use of irrigation systems. Harvesting can also be delayed.
- If the monsoon brings **low rainfall totals**, it has an adverse effect on growing crops such as rice, which needs waterlogged conditions. Low yields and poor harvests can lead to starvation for millions of farmers and their families who depend on the rice crop.
- When monsoon rains are **too heavy,** extreme flooding can occur and can wash away seeds, destroy villages and cause landslides.
- **A reliable, regular monsoon** is essential for India's agriculture and rural society. If the monsoon fails, it is disastrous for India. In 1987, a great famine followed the partial failure of the monsoon.

There is no social welfare system in India. What does this mean if there is a poor harvest?

ECONOMIC PROCESSES

India's economy is dominated by agriculture. To understand the country's problems, it is important to know about the nature and patterns of this sector.

The Primary Sector
Agriculture

The cultivated area of India (138 million hectares) almost equals the total area of land under cultivation in the European Union. A lot of the land has good agriculture potential, especially where water supplies are available. Only in the high mountains and dry areas, such as the Thar Desert along India's western border with Pakistan, are conditions too extreme for productive farming. Arable farming, especially cereals, is the main type of farming.

The Type of Farming

The dominant type of farming throughout much of India is intensive subsistence. It is used especially in rural areas with high population density, where people depend on being able to feed themselves. Rice is the chief crop for this type of farming, especially in the floodplains of the Indus and Ganges rivers. Other cereals, such as wheat and millet, are grown in drier parts of peninsular India (see Fig 29.6).

Almost all planting, weeding and harvesting is done by hand, with all family members being involved. Since plots of land are usually very small, no land is wasted. Roadways are narrow, and there are no field boundaries. Double cropping is also practised to make sure enough food is produced during the year to feed the farmer's family. While rice is grown in the wet monsoon season, alternative crops such as wheat and millet are grown in the drier months.

Trade in farm produce plays a vital role in the life of most rural communities. Most produce is usually sold locally. Why?

Plantation farming is important in some areas. The crops grown include tea, coconuts and cotton. Tea plantations of north-east India, especially in Assam, are major suppliers to the world tea trade. Coconuts are a speciality of the south-west coast, while cotton is important in parts of central India and north of Mumbai.

Wheat is the main crop in the drier north-west of India. Crop yields are quite high, especially where land can be irrigated. The Green Revolution has helped increase productivity levels. Corn (maize) and chick peas are also grown in some parts of this zone.

- rice dominant
- maize and chick peas
- plantation agriculture (including tea, cotton and coconuts)
- groundnuts
- wheat dominant
- millet dominant
- herding, subsistence and shifting agriculture

Millet is a cereal grown in the west of India and in large areas of peninsular India. It is well suited to drier conditions in the rain shadow of the Western Ghats.

More land is planted to rice than in any other country. This is India's main crop and covers 25 per cent of all farmland.

Areas with heavy and reliable monsoon rains, such as the Ganges Valley, eastern India and places near the Eastern and Western Ghats, are major rice-growing areas.

Fig. 29.6 Agricultural areas of India.

Preparing the land for growing rice.

Planting the rice.

Harvesting rice.

Maintaining water levels for the rice crop.

Activity
Do these photographs and those on page 216 support the view that the successful planting and cultivation of rice depend on the natural environment, and especially the wet monsoon?

Modernising Agriculture

India is a country that has benefited from the **Green Revolution.** This refers to the development and introduction of genetically modified, high-yield varieties of staple crops, such as rice and wheat. These 'miracle crops' produce high yields and are resistant to many diseases and pests. This has helped India meet its needs for food production, and by the late 1990s the country became a net exporter of food.

Yet there are **many problems** linked to the Green Revolution:

- It depends on large inputs of chemical fertilizers and pesticides.
- Labour is often replaced with machinery, so rural unemployment goes up and more people leave the land and go to towns, increasing rural-urban migration.
- Larger fields and farms are needed, so the number of farms is reduced.
- A well-educated farm population and capital (money) for investment are needed.
- It only benefits comparatively few, larger-scale farmers; large numbers of small-scale farmers are not able to participate in this process.
- There is environmental damage, for example water and ground pollution from chemicals.

For a large number of Indian farmers, a better solution to their problems involves a more effective programme of land reform. This would redistribute land from large estate owners to landless peasants.

In the 1990s, however, almost half of rural families had farms of less than 0.5 hectares, or no land at all. In contrast, a quarter of India's agricultural land was owned by less than 5 per cent of farm families. Most small farms are also broken up into tiny and scattered parcels of land. This reduces productivity even more and makes introducing modern farm practices, such as mechanisation, difficult. Land reform is therefore an urgent need.

Review the benefits and problems of the Green Revolution. Are you in favour of this approach? Explain your answer.

The failure to modernise India's agricultural sector and raise levels of productivity for many key crops remains an important issue. The country's growing population places more demand on the food supply. If the farming sector fails to meet this demand, it can lead to large-scale famine.

The Secondary Sector
Industry

When India became independent in 1947, it only had a limited range of industries, especially textiles and food processing. Only 2 per cent of the working population was employed in industry, which was concentrated mainly in the major cities: Bombay (now Mumbai), Calcutta (now Kolkata) and Madras (now Chennai).

On gaining independence, the new government was determined to encourage industrial development. The aim was to reduce India's dependence on imported industrial goods and to promote greater wealth and employment across the country.

Two key factors helped India's programme of industrialisation:

Jute is used to make mats and rope.

- The size of India's population provided a large home market.
- The country has some important natural resources, e.g. minerals such as coal and iron ore, a large and cheap labour force and outputs from agriculture (cotton, jute). Mineral resources encouraged the government to develop heavy industries, such as iron and steel, shipbuilding and chemicals.

Despite these advantages, progress was relatively slow and helped only a small number of preferred growth centres. In addition, by the 1980s, many heavy industries were in decline. Industrial policy has therefore been changed to emphasise:

- **Agri-industries:** These include fertilizers, machinery and food processing, which can benefit rural communities.
- **Consumer goods industries and small-scale craft industries:** These are more labour intensive than large-scale, heavy industries, so more jobs are created. They also benefit from low labour costs and traditional skills, which make them competitive in export markets. Examples include jewellery, clothing and leather goods.
- **Development in the countryside rather than the cities:** With more than 70 per cent of India's population living in rural areas, jobs need to be taken to these people, rather than encouraging migration to urban centres. This involves support for **community-based developments and self-help schemes** to improve facilities like basic health care and drinking water. Education schemes to improve skill levels are also important.

Major deposits of iron ore and coal near Kolkata gave rise to an important iron and steel industry. This was important for national development.

Do you think that small-scale industries and rural-based development are better for rural communities than trying to set up large branch plants owned by multinational corporations?

A rural family works together and uses traditional skills to make carpets which are mostly for export.
- *Do you think the development of such industries is important for India?*

Although large-scale industries have developed in India and provide employment, many workers are paid low wages and continue to live in poverty.

- **High-technology industries:** These are attracted to India by the country's growing population of skilled workers, low costs and improved communication systems. These high-value-added industries present a new and modern 'face' of India. They also suggest a brighter future for the country's industrial base.

India has emerged as a growing and significant manufacturer of computer software. Many major multinationals, such as IBM and Texas Instruments, have located in the country. Large numbers of locally owned companies have also been set up to supply software components to Western markets.

India's new policy of industrial development, its large and growing market and relatively cheap costs of production (especially labour) have attracted a lot of foreign investment. Many multinational companies have located factories and office activities in the country. **India is a newly industrialising country (NIC)** and has a growing share of world production and trade in industrial goods and services. In the new future, India (and China) will be a major competitor for the EU and USA in the world economy.

> Give examples of high-technology industry.

India's Science Graduates
Although many people in the countryside are poorly educated, India has invested heavily in a well-developed education system, based largely in the cities. India now produces more university graduates than Canada and the USA combined, and 40 per cent of these are in science and engineering. A supply of skilled, English-speaking workers is attractive to international companies, especially as the cost of labour is low by Western standards. While a circuit board designer in California can earn between US$60–100,000, the salary in India averages about US$10,000.

Where Industry is Located
Although the government has tried to spread industry across the country, this growing sector remains concentrated in a small number of key city regions (see Fig. 29.7). The most important are Kolkata, Mumbai and its hinterland in the state of Maharashtra, and Chennai-Bangalore.

> Note that the key city regions are the same as in 1947.

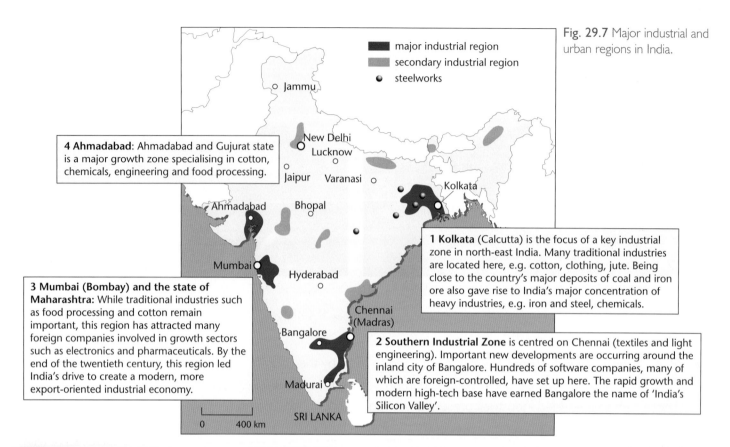

Fig. 29.7 Major industrial and urban regions in India.

major industrial region
secondary industrial region
● steelworks

4 Ahmadabad: Ahmadabad and Gujurat state is a major growth zone specialising in cotton, chemicals, engineering and food processing.

1 Kolkata (Calcutta) is the focus of a key industrial zone in north-east India. Many traditional industries are located here, e.g. cotton, clothing, jute. Being close to the country's major deposits of coal and iron ore also gave rise to India's major concentration of heavy industries, e.g. iron and steel, chemicals.

3 Mumbai (Bombay) and the state of Maharashtra: While traditional industries such as food processing and cotton remain important, this region has attracted many foreign companies involved in growth sectors such as electronics and pharmaceuticals. By the end of the twentieth century, this region led India's drive to create a modern, more export-oriented industrial economy.

2 Southern Industrial Zone is centred on Chennai (textiles and light engineering). Important new developments are occurring around the inland city of Bangalore. Hundreds of software companies, many of which are foreign-controlled, have set up here. The rapid growth and modern high-tech base have earned Bangalore the name of 'India's Silicon Valley'.

0   400 km

SRI LANKA

Modern textile factories provide opportunities for many workers, especially women.

One of an increasing number of high-technology parks in Bangalore which provides high-quality jobs for India's growing and educated workforce.

SERVICES

The Tertiary Sector

India's service sector remains underdeveloped. About 70 per cent of the country's population lives in rural areas. As so many people are poor and depend on a subsistence economy, they do not have the money for services. Many basic services are provided through self-help schemes and informal co-operation.

In India's cities, where most tertiary employment is located, there are **two types** of service activities.

- Large populations and more people with good incomes create demand for a full range of services. In the larger cities, there are increasing job opportunities in services, such as government administration, finance and banking, retailing and education.

- There is a second type of service activity in Indian and other cities of the less developed world. These services are in the **informal sector** (known before as the 'black economy'). Many people work as unlicensed sellers, offering a range of homemade goods and services. These services include street vendors, shoeshine boys and car repairs. Sometimes to survive, the urban poor are forced to take part in illegal activities such as drug dealing and prostitution.

Services in most urban centres remain underdeveloped, reflecting the poverty of the population. Here a woman's group has organised a co-operative bank to help improve the quality of life and development prospects for women.

Informal services are common throughout India. Here, a street typist works on a document for a customer.

Transport

Developing a country as large as India successfully needs an efficient transport system, but the government is not always able to find the money for improving transport. Transport systems in rural India are especially underdeveloped. One report suggested that by the late 1990s, half of the country's 600,000 villages did not have access to tarred roads suitable for motor vehicles. These communities use dirt-track roads and carts drawn by animals (usually oxen). It is unlikely that the transport networks in these areas will be modernised, especially in the short term.

Tourism

The size, history and variety of natural and cultural landscapes in India offer major attractions for the international tourist trade. International transport links to India have also improved in recent years, bringing more and more tourists to the country. For an underdeveloped economy, tourism offers many advantages, and the government actively promotes this industry.

Activity
What advantages does tourism have for a country like India, especially for its less developed regions?

The Taj Mahal is one of India's most famous tourist attractions. Over 3 million tourists visit this site each year.

Among India's attractions for tourists are:

● The spectacular mountain ranges of the Himalayas.

● The vast number of palaces and fortifications that reflect the history of India.

● Many religious temples, highlighting the variety of religions – Hindu, Buddhist, Sikh and Muslim.

● Cultural landscapes that are not familiar to many people from the developed world.

● The great rivers and varied physical landscapes.

To succeed in promoting tourism as a basis for development, a lot of investment has to be made in upgrading internal transport links and tourist facilities, such as accommodation. Another aspect to consider is that some tourists may be put off by the sheer pressure of population and the obvious poverty of many people in India.

HUMAN PROCESSES

Population

The size and especially the rate of population growth in India is the key factor behind many of the problems facing the country. At the start of the twenty-first century, the national population was more than 1 billion. India also has a comparatively high rate of natural increase (1.6 per cent a year) and its population could double to more than 2 billion by 2040.

The main reason for the rapid growth in India's population is natural increase (see Table 29.2 and Fig. 29.8). The country has only recently entered the third stage of the demographic transition model, whereas more developed countries, such as Ireland, Sweden and France, are in the fourth, or like Italy may have entered a fifth stage of this model. In India, while death rates have gone down a lot due to better health care, the birth rate remains high. The result is a high rate of population increase.

India has a large and rapidly growing population. In many rural areas children are often educated in open-air schools.

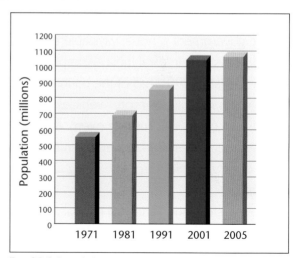

Fig. 29.8 Population growth in India from 1971 to 2005.

Some Demographic Indicators for India, Ireland, Italy and France				
	Birth rate (per 000)	Death rate (per 000)	Annual rate of natural increase (per 000)	Doubling time for population (years)
India	24	8	16	1.2
Ireland	16	7	9	1.9
Italy	9	10	−1	−0.4
France	13	9	4	0.3

Table 29.2

The Indian government recognises the problems caused by the country's large and expanding population. These include:

- Pressure on farmland.
- Making sure there is enough food.
- Rural-urban migration.
- Finding jobs for a growing labour force.

In the 1970s, the government started a campaign to reduce birth rates. They offered incentives to encourage people to use birth control (for example, a transistor radio for a vasectomy) and reduce average family size.

While the campaign had some success, it has been difficult to quickly educate large numbers of the population to the advantages of family planning. It is especially difficult in remoter rural communities, where large families are still seen in a positive way (for example, a sign of virility, help to work the land). Even with a slowdown in the rate of natural increase since the 1970s, the sheer size of the population and its young age profile have resulted in ever-greater numbers being added to India's total population. As urbanisation continues, it is thought that the birth rate will decline and help slow down the country's rate of natural increase.

> Remember the demographic transition model shows the stages a country with high birth and death rates goes through until it has low birth and death rates.

> Why will urbanisation cause birth rates to go down?

India has traditionally had a high birth rate. Here, a female health worker explains the importance of general health care and the use of contraceptives to women. Targeting women is thought to be especially important to reduce birth rates. Why?

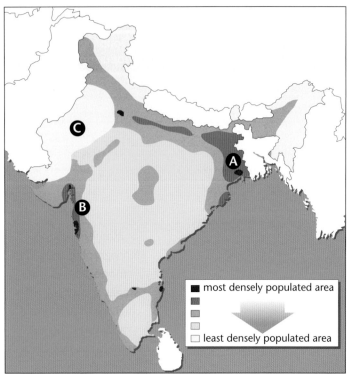

Fig. 29.9 Population density in India.

most densely populated area

least densely populated area

Population Distribution

India's population is not evenly distributed. There are many areas of very dense concentrations of people in the major river valleys, narrow coastal plains and hinterlands of major cities (see Fig. 29.9). These include:

● The major river valleys of the Indus, Ganges and Brahmaputra, where reliable water supplies and fertile alluvial soils provide the basis for intensive subsistence farming.

● The narrow coastal plains along the Eastern and Western Ghats also provide a rich agricultural environment. Areas of commercial farming mixed with intensive subsistence activities give a lower population density than in the major river valleys.

● The hinterlands of major cities, such as Kolkata (formerly Calcutta), Chennai (formerly Madras) and Mumbai (formerly Bombay). Growth of these and other large cities has attracted industrial development and a lot of immigrants.

● Less densely settled parts of India include the drier desert areas of north-west India, such as the Thar Desert, and the mountainous zones on the northern border.

Culture

India's large population is made up of many different culture groups. **Three major outside influences** have complicated India's cultural make-up, especially in language and religion:

● Early Indo-European influences.
● The spread of Islam.
● British colonialism.

Languages

The population of India does not speak a common language. A wide variety of different languages is spoken:

● The Constitution of India recognises eighteen languages.
● There are 1,600 minor languages and dialects.
● Schools teach in up to sixty languages.
● National newspapers are published in ninety languages.
● Radio programmes are broadcast in over seventy languages.

This creates communication problems between different language groups and for effective government in India.

Activity

Look at Fig. 29.9 and answer the following.

1. Why are population densities so high in the region marked A?

2. Why do coastal areas such as B have a high population density?

3. Why is the population density in area C so low?

What problems can be created by having many different languages in one country?

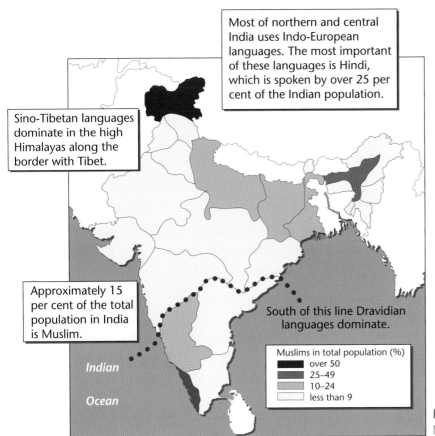

Most of northern and central India uses Indo-European languages. The most important of these languages is Hindi, which is spoken by over 25 per cent of the Indian population.

Sino-Tibetan languages dominate in the high Himalayas along the border with Tibet.

Approximately 15 per cent of the total population in India is Muslim.

South of this line Dravidian languages dominate.

Indian

Ocean

Muslims in total population (%)
- over 50
- 25–49
- 10–24
- less than 9

Activity
Look at Fig. 29.10 and answer the following.
1. What is the most-used language of India?
2. What is the main religion in most of India?
3. Does the high concentration of Muslims in the far north-west of India give rise to problems? (See Chapter 36.)
4. Can you suggest why a relatively high number of Muslims live in a zone going west to east across northern India? (Think about trade routes.)

Fig. 29.10 Language regions and main areas where Muslims live in India.

The various languages of India are based on three language families. The **Indo-European language** group dominates in India. This can be traced to migrants who entered the north-west of India from Europe. **Hindi** is the largest and single most important language and is spoken by over 250 million people. It is the official language of India. **Dravidian** languages are spoken by about 200 million people, who live mainly in the south (see Fig. 29.10).

Although only 2 per cent of the population speaks **English**, it is an important language. Introduced under British colonial rule, it remains the language of business and the educated classes.

Although Hindi is the official state language, this is resented by many cultural groups. Bitter and often violent rivalries exist between language groups. Language is clearly a powerful expression of cultural differences and, as well as religion, often emphasises the divisions within India rather than the unity of the state. This is a major problem for the development of India.

Remember the language differences between Flanders and Wallonia in Belgium?

Hinduism

Indo-European influences also shaped the basis of **Hinduism.** This is the dominant religion in India and shapes much of the social and political life of the country and its people.

Hinduism introduced a multi-layered social system (or caste system). Individuals are grouped into a caste according to their job. At the top of the caste system are the priests (Brahmins) and other high-ranking officials or professions. At the bottom are the low castes that do menial and dirty tasks. They are said to be 'unclean' and 'untouchable'.

This street sweeper is one of the millions of 'untouchables' who live in extreme poverty in India.

- *Explain some of the reasons for this.*

Belonging to a caste is mainly decided by being born into the caste. This shapes the social prospects of an individual because members of a caste can only marry, associate or even eat within a narrow range of groups.

In urban centres, the caste system is breaking down and allowing for some social mobility, but it is still very strong in rural India. Many 'untouchables' are limited to a life of poverty and have little prospect for improving their status under the caste system of Hinduism.

For Hindus, the cow is a sacred animal, so it cannot be killed. While the cattle provide milk, dried dung for fuel and pull carts, they are an under-used resource. Many poorly bred, undernourished cattle roam the countryside. For many, these animals could be considered to be a parasite on the economy, rather than an advantage for development. This is a good example of the impact of culture on development.

Minority Religions in India

People who practise the Islamic religion are Muslims.

Although dominated by Hinduism, India also contains several important religious minorities, for example Islam. Many people living on the Indo-Ganges Plain were converted to Islam long ago. This was due mainly to Muslim traders who travelled to the area from Arabia (see Fig. 22.6 on page 152).

There are now over 200 million Muslims in India, and most live in the north of the country. One of the major attractions of Islam for the low castes and 'untouchables' was that it rejects a rigid caste system and that all converts are considered equal.

Other examples of religious minorities are Buddhism, Sikhism and Christianity.

Muslim men at prayer in northern India, where this religion is concentrated.

Political-Religious Divides in India

India was a colony of Britain for centuries. After independence in 1947, two states were created. These were based on religious divides. India became a Hindu state, while Pakistan was Islamic.

Drawing political boundaries on the basis of a majority religion was very difficult, and large numbers of minority religious groups were left in both countries. This led to rioting and large-scale migration. More than 15 million people moved, as Muslims went from India to Pakistan, and Hindus from Pakistan to India.

Pakistan was based on the majority Muslim population living in the Indus and Ganges river systems. As a result, this state was split into two parts, separated by a long distance with northern India in between. This was not practical and, in 1971, Pakistan broke up into two distinctive states: Pakistan (around the Indus Valley) and Bangladesh (associated with the lower Ganges Valley – Fig. 29.1). Tensions between India and Pakistan remain high, especially over the disputed territory of Kashmir (see Chapter 36).

Hinduism is the dominant religion in India. Here, Hindus bathe in the holy river of the Ganges.

Do you see any similarity over religious divides between India and Ireland?

Urban-Rural Development

The process of **urbanisation** is continuing strongly in India, especially because of large-scale rural to urban migration. Large numbers of people move (pushed) from poor rural communities by hope (pulled) of better prospects in growing cities.

While urbanisation has a long tradition in India, the present patterns of urban development are linked to **two processes:**

- **British colonialism:** This emphasised the development of key ports and centres of administration such as Mumbai, Kolkata and Chennai.
- **National planning:** Following independence, national planning recognised the importance of modern urban centres for promoting industrial development. Large-scale investment was made to upgrade the infrastructure (e.g. transport) of key centres. A new capital was also set up at New Delhi (near Delhi).

While towns and cities occur throughout India, there are **four main urban regions** (see Fig. 29.9):

- On the west coast around Mumbai (population 18.1 million).
- The southern tip of the peninsula linked to Chennai (6.6 million) and Bangalore (5.5 million).
- Kolkata (12.7 million) in the north-east.
- Delhi – New Delhi (11.7 million).

These four urban regions have grown rapidly and have attracted many manufacturing and service industries. They also have huge problems of **squalor and poverty** linked to large-scale in-migration. The government faces major challenges in dealing with the urban poor, including housing, employment, health and education.

Although urbanisation is growing, about 760 million people still live in **rural areas**. Studying the villages of rural India is important in understanding India's problems of development. Villages in rural India:

- Have a very conservative and traditional society; they resist change.
- Have a rigid caste system, which limits people's social and economic progress.
- Are very dependent on the natural environment (especially the monsoon rains) and can be exposed to problems of famine.
- Have a subsistence economy, which means a hand-to-mouth existence for the people living there.
- Are self-sufficient. They make goods and supply services for themselves, with little surplus for trade and interaction with outside areas.
- Are often overpopulated, especially as there is a limit to the amount of land available.
- Lack the money (capital) to invest in basic facilities.

Rural poverty and other related issues, such as rapid population growth and a reluctance to adopt more modern farming practices, are major issues for the government of India.

Over 275 million people live in India's urban centres.

World's apart. Prosperity in the modern centre of Mumbai contrasts with slum housing on the city's outskirts.

CHAPTER 30
ECONOMIC, POLITICAL AND CULTURAL ACTIVITIES IN REGIONS

KEY IDEA!

The study of regions highlights how complex the ways that economic, cultural and political processes act on each other are.

Regional identities are usually developed through **complex interactions** both within a region and between that region and its surrounding areas. In this chapter, the Republic of Ireland and Northern Ireland are used as an **example** to show how economic, cultural and political activities affect each other to make a region's special identity.

IRELAND'S CHANGING RELATIONSHIPS ON THE ISLAND OF IRELAND

At the start of the twentieth century, the two islands of Britain and Ireland were controlled by a powerful and centralised government in London. In 1922, Ireland gained political independence from Britain. Six north-eastern counties, however, remained part of Britain, and a new political boundary was created to separate what is now the Republic of Ireland from Northern Ireland (Fig. 30.1). This division of Ireland has strong historical roots and has had major implications on North-South relationships on the island of Ireland.

Ireland Before Independence and Partition

The population of the north-eastern part of Ireland had historically built up a culture and economy that was very different from the rest of the island. For example, large numbers of English and Scottish settlers were brought to the region during the **Ulster plantation** of the seventeenth century. These settlers had a different culture and religion to the local Catholic population.

The north-eastern region was also the only part of Ireland to experience large-scale industrialisation in the nineteenth century. At the time of partition in 1921:

- Two-thirds of Northern Ireland's population were Protestant, while the rest of Ireland was overwhelmingly Catholic.
- Northern Ireland was a prosperous industrial economy with strong trade links to Britain.
- The rest of Ireland was a depressed rural economy.
- The Protestant majority benefited from links with Britain, while the rest of Ireland associated British rule with poverty, migration and the suppression of Gaelic culture.

Activity

Look at Fig. 30.1 and at an atlas and answer the following.

1. Identify the six counties that form Northern Ireland.
2. Name the counties marked X, Y and Z that are part of the historic province of Ulster but not in Northern Ireland.
3. What effect do you think the border has had on towns like Dundalk and Derry?

The majority of Ireland's population saw political independence from Britain as essential for their economic and cultural development.

Fig. 30.1 The political divide in Ireland.

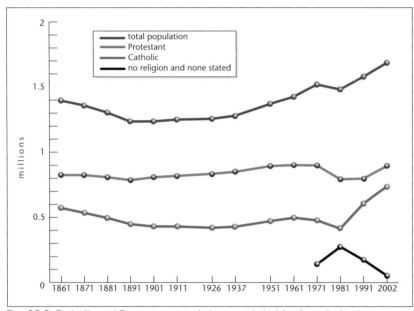

Fig. 30.2 Catholic and Protestant population trends in Northern Ireland.

Activity

Look at Fig. 30.2 and answer the following:

1. Estimate the proportion of Northern Ireland's population that was Catholic in 1926 and 2002.
2. What do you note about trends in Catholic and Protestant totals after 1981?
3. Why is this a concern for the Unionists?

Changing Relationships between the Republic and Northern Ireland

The creation of the political boundary between the Republic and Northern Ireland emphasised long-standing political, economic and cultural differences. Since the 1960s, however, these differences have been reduced. Much of this has been due to the **modernisation** of the Republic's economic, cultural and political systems.

Economic Trends

From the 1960s, the Republic has attracted many foreign industries and has built up a large and modern manufacturing economy (Chapter 26, pages 178–80). In contrast, most of Northern Ireland's old, traditional industries, such as textiles and shipbuilding, declined. Furthermore, the period of civil disturbances (the Troubles) that began in 1968 and continued into the 1990s discouraged foreign investors. The result was a depressed regional economy in the North as opposed to the prosperous Celtic Tiger economy of the South (Fig. 30.3 and Table 30.1). Since the Belfast Agreement of 1998, however, the economy of the North has improved.

Fig. 30.3 Manufacturing jobs in the Republic of Ireland and Northern Ireland.

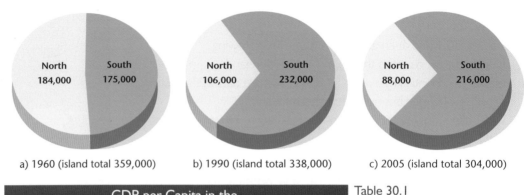

a) 1960 (island total 359,000)   b) 1990 (island total 338,000)   c) 2005 (island total 304,000)

Table 30.1

GDP per Capita in the Republic of Ireland and Northern Ireland as a Percentage of GDP in the EU		
	Republic of Ireland	Northern Ireland
1973	59	79
1980	63	62
1990	68	74
2000	126	82
2005	139	93

Activity

Look at Fig. 30.3 and Table 30.1 and answer the following.

1. Describe the trends in manufacturing employment in the Republic and Northern Ireland from 1960 to 2005.
2. Estimate the proportion of manufacturing jobs in the Republic in 1960 and 2005. Explain the change.
3. When Ireland joined the EU in 1973, which part of the island was the most prosperous?
4. In terms of personal prosperity, is the Republic still 'the poor relation of the North'?

Cultural Changes

While there are still cultural differences between the North and South, they are now less marked. Much of this has been linked to changes to more modern attitudes and ways of life in Ireland, especially in the Republic.

How has greater prosperity and urbanisation, together with the Catholic Church having less influence in shaping people's lives in the Republic, helped reduce the sense of difference **between** North and South?

Political Interaction on the Island of Ireland

Political tensions between the Republic, Northern Ireland and Britain have been harder to resolve. This was especially the case during the 'Troubles', when a state of almost civil war existed between extreme nationalist and unionist groups (see Chapter 22, pages 150–51).

During the 1990s, significant efforts were made to improve the political situation. In 1998, a major step forward occurred with the signing of the **Belfast Agreement** (also called the Good Friday Agreement). This created **three** new political bodies to act as the basis for what are called **strands** (see Fig. 30.4). These strands are designed to link together the political capitals of Belfast, Dublin and London. **In this way, inter-relationships are stressed rather than political division.**

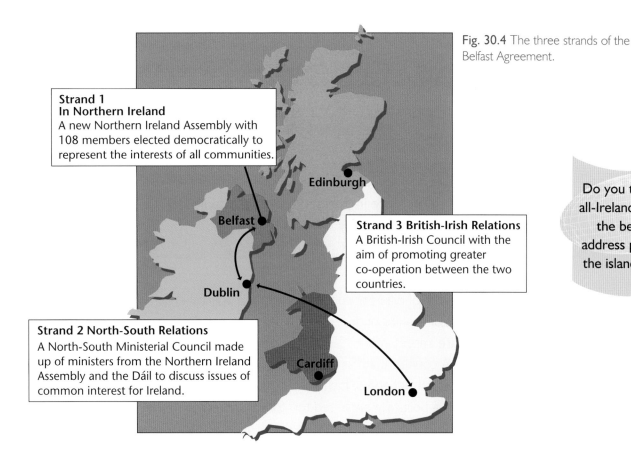

Fig. 30.4 The three strands of the Belfast Agreement.

Strand 1
In Northern Ireland
A new Northern Ireland Assembly with 108 members elected democratically to represent the interests of all communities.

Edinburgh

Belfast

Strand 3 British-Irish Relations
A British-Irish Council with the aim of promoting greater co-operation between the two countries.

Dublin

Strand 2 North-South Relations
A North-South Ministerial Council made up of ministers from the Northern Ireland Assembly and the Dáil to discuss issues of common interest for Ireland.

Cardiff

London

Do you think that an all-Ireland approach is the best way to address problems on the island of Ireland?

A street mural in the Republican Falls Road commemorating the 1916 Easter Rising. The current movements to integrate must combat deep historic and cultural divisions.

CHAPTER 31
CULTURAL GROUPS AND POLITICAL REGIONS

 **KEY IDEA!**

Cultural groups and regional identities are becoming more important in the political life of many countries.

> A sovereign government is one with supreme power within its territory.

Europe is a patchwork of different cultural groups and political units. The interaction between these is essential for understanding Europe as a distinctive region. There are three terms that are important:

- **Nation state:** A country that has political boundaries containing a population with a high level of cultural sameness. It should also have a sovereign government.
- **State:** A state is a politically organised territory that is administered by a sovereign government.
- **Nation:** A group of tightly knit people who have a common culture – language, ethnicity, religion and other cultural values. Many nations have gained political recognition and have become nation states, for example the Irish Republic following independence from Britain. Other nations, however, have not yet established their own sovereignty, for example Wales and Scotland.

Although most of Europe's countries are considered to be nation states, they all have cultural minorities. Generally, these groups identify with the state they live in and add to the strength and character of the state; for example, Switzerland with its four language groups.

There are, however, some examples of minority culture groups, especially those with strong identities, who feel their interests are ignored or threatened by the dominant culture group. In such cases, the links that tie the state together become weakened. **Nationalist groups** can emerge to represent their interests and **begin to look for greater powers of self-government.**

Basques marching in San Sebastian in 2006 in support of an imprisioned leader of the ETA, the Basque separatist group.

The process by which regions within a state seek greater autonomy (political control) over their own affairs while reducing the powers of the central government is called **devolution**. A more extreme form of devolution is **separatism.** In some cases, national governments have accepted the demands for greater self-government and regions have been given more autonomy. Examples include Scotland and Wales in Britain.

In other cases, central governments cannot accept the levels of self-government some nationalist groups demand. This is especially the case where these groups demand independence and the break-up of an existing country. Where this happens, cultural and political relationships between a region and central government can become violent. The result may be extremist groups leading terror campaigns against the official government, as in the Basque Country in Spain.

Case Study: Cultural Groups and Devolution in Spain

In Spain, the government has been centred on the capital, Madrid, for centuries. Although the central government is still powerful, Spain has several well-defined cultural groups that have their own language. The best-known groups are probably in the Basque Country and Catalonia.

Each of these regions has been given powers by the central government to administer a range of key functions, such as cultural affairs, education, economic development and the environment. Both regions have their own parliaments. Their distinctive languages, Basque (called Euskera in the Basque language) and Catalan, are co-official languages with Spanish.

The Basque Country is perhaps the Spanish region that is best known for demanding independence from Spain. As a people, the Basques form a distinctive cultural group that occupies an area on each side of the Pyrenees in northern Spain and south-west France. The core of the Basque area is in northern Spain and has a population of 2 million. Bilbao is the largest city in the region (Fig. 31.1).

The Basques in northern Spain:
- Have lived in the area for about 10,000 years, so they have developed their own special cultural identity.
- Are a distinctive ethnic group.
- Speak a language (Euskera) that is not like any other European language.

Above all, it is **because the Basque language has survived that this is a distinctive cultural region.** Under past Spanish governments, the Euskera language was declared illegal, and large numbers of Basque nationalists were put in prison for calling for independence and for their cultural roots to be recognised.

One reaction to government repression was the extremist nationalist group called ETA (Euskadi ta Askatasuma), which declared war on the Spanish state. ETA became involved in a large number of bombings and assassinations in its drive to gain independence from Spain.

'Ethnicity' means belonging to a group that has certain common traits, e.g. race, language or religion.

Separatism sees devolution as a stepping stone to independence and the emergence of a new nation state.

Fig. 31.1 The location of the Basque Country and Catalonia in Spain.

In 1979, the Basque Country in Spain was granted a high level of autonomy. This weakened public support for ETA because it seemed that democratic means were working to gain self-government for the region. Although the cultural strength of this region has been the basis for gaining the Basques a more equal relationship with the national government in Madrid, a weakened ETA continues to fight for independence.

Catalonia is another Spanish region that has gained a lot of regional autonomy because it has a distinct cultural identity. Centred on the major industrial and trading city of Barcelona, the Catalans have a strong sense of nationalism. They have their own language, Catalan, and have a very prosperous economy.

Although it has only 6 per cent of the Spanish population, Catalonia accounts for nearly 40 per cent of Spain's industrial exports. It attracts high-technology industry, has strong trading traditions, and Catalonia has emerged as one of the four motors of the EU (see Fig. 23.2, page 157).

With Catalonia's economic success, its pride in its cultural distinctiveness and the strength of feeling to achieve independence from Spain, it is not surprising that the Spanish government has devolved an increasing amount of political power to Catalonia to keep this important region within Spain.

In their attempts to gain independence from Spain, ETA has used violent tactics such as car bombs.

Do you see any similarities between Ireland and the Basques in their efforts to achieve autonomy or independence?

The Catalan demands for greater political autonomy are supported by a much stronger economic basis than in the Basque region.

The modern cathedral of Sagrada Familia in Barcelona stands as a symbol of a strong and growing Catalan identity and culture.

CHAPTER 32
THE FUTURE OF THE EUROPEAN UNION

KEY IDEA! Future developments in the European Union will have a major influence on the economies, politics and sovereignty within Europe.

In 1957, the Treaty of Rome brought together six countries to form an economic union to better promote development in Europe. The process was successful and, by 1995, the **European Union** had expanded to fifteen member states.

The process of enlargement was relatively easy because:

- Each enlargement involved no more than three countries.
- All new members were within Western Europe with similar cultural characteristics and were relatively well developed.

The enlargements in 2004 and 2007 were less easy. Proposals for further enlargement will also add to EU problems.

- **Ten countries** were admitted in 2004, and two more in 2007. Such a large number of new members has increased the **scale of impact** within the EU.
- Most new and proposed members are from **Central and Eastern Europe,** and were formerly part of a **communist system** dominated by the USSR. Their economies were less developed and the governments were not democratic. This made it hard to adjust to the EU.

The recent and ongoing process of enlargement will have major impacts on the future of the EU.

Look at Chapter 35 to learn more about how the European Union was formed and when different countries joined (enlargement).

Activity
Look at Table 32.1 and suggest some of the advantages and problems of the recent and future enlargements to the EU.

Table 32.1

Some Development Indicators of New and Proposed Member States of the EU					
	Area in sq. km (000s)	Population (million)	GDP per person (euros)	Unemployment (%)	Agriculture as % of total employment
EU (15)	1,317	380	24,250	7.8	4.0
Ten new states (2004)	736	74	9,550	14.9	13.2
EU (25)	2,053	454	22,300	9.0	5.4
New members (2007)					
Bulgaria	111	8	6,800	18.2	9.6
Romania	238	22	7,000	8.4	36.8
Applicant states					
Croatia	57	5	9,300	18.7	15.5
Turkey	780	70	5,600	10.1	36.0
Montenegro	14	0.6	2,850	28.0	2.0

Workers producing car engines for Audi in a major new investment in Hungary.

In Romania and Bulgaria, much farming remains underdeveloped.

Since Poland joined the EU in 2004, large numbers of Poles have migrated to countries such as Ireland to find work, e.g. in construction, agriculture and catering.

The Future of Economic Union

- **Prospects for economic development** have and will increase. This is linked to the increased population of the EU, which improves the market for goods and services (Table 32.1). The EU will become a larger and **more important power in world trade.**

- The **increasing area** of the EU provides more sources of raw materials and a **greater choice of location** for factories and offices. Newer member states have **lower costs of production** (especially labour) and this has and will encourage employers to **relocate production** to Central and Eastern Europe.

  Competition for foreign direct investment (FDI) is increasing. This has major implications for 'older' member states, such as Ireland, which rely heavily on FDI.

- New member states have a much **higher dependency on agriculture** than the EU of fifteen member states (see Table 32.1). The potential for increasing output by modernising their underdeveloped farming communities is huge. Reforms to the Common Agricultural Policy are therefore encouraging farmers to produce less but to **increase quality of production.** Farmers are also encouraged to **protect the environment** and to look for alternative sources of income, e.g. forestry, agritourism.

- Opportunities for international migration have and will increase in an enlarging EU. The **higher levels of unemployment** and **lower levels of prosperity** in newer member states create **push factors** than have caused many people to migrate to the countries of the EU 15.

  As the economies of newer member states improve, however, outward migration will be reduced.

- A **large new eastern periphery** will dominate EU regional policy and demands for structural funds. Most EU funding for 2007–13 is allocated to the problem regions (now called Convergence Regions) in Central and Eastern Europe (see Fig. 32.1). This means:
  - **Less money** will be available to aid development in long-established problem regions, such as the Mezzogiorno.
  - Some long-established **problem regions have been removed** from the list of regions that will receive significant support from structural funds. One example is Ireland, which is no longer classed as a problem (or convergence) region.

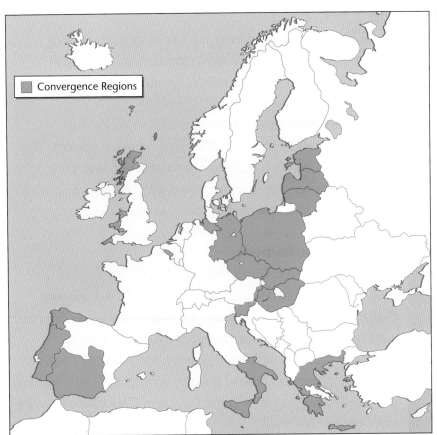

Fig. 32.1 Convergence Regions of the EU 25, 2007–13.

Legend: Convergence Regions

The Future of Political Union

In the 1990s, the EU became committed to **increasing political union** so it could play a stronger role in world affairs. This was prompted by the need for the EU to respond in a united way to events that were happening in nearby regions, for example the wars in (former) Yugoslavia and the Middle East.

Some progress has been made. The EU now has a **Foreign Minister**, who represents the views of member states at conferences that discuss important global issues, e.g. world trade and global warming. In addition, the EU has accepted a greater **peace-keeping role** in several conflict zones, e.g. Afghanistan, Bosnia.

Some key problems confront further political union:

- Persuading the populations of member states to accept an **EU constitution** to act as a political 'blueprint' to guide further development.
- Member states often have **different political agendas,** especially in foreign policy. As a result, states are reluctant to allow the EU to take policy decisions for them; an example of this is the different altitudes to the US invasion of Iraq in 2003.
- Neutral countries, such as Ireland, have major problems over suggestions of a **bigger military role** for the EU.

A lot of work has to be done before the EU can progress to a political union which matches what has been achieved for economic union.

The Future of Sovereignty

A key feature of the Treaty of Rome (1957) is that member states **have to give up some degree of sovereignty** (decision-making power) to this international organisation.

There are **three** main institutions that affect the sovereignty of member states.

European Commission

This is the main administrative body of the EU. Although it has no decision-making power, it is the only EU institution that can propose new legislation. It is located in Brussels and is divided into twenty-five directorate generals (government departments), each headed by a **commissioner.**

Currently, each of the twenty-five member states has a commissioner. It is proposed, however, to reduce this number to make administration more efficient. This will mean, especially with further enlargement, that **member states will lose their automatic right to have a commissioner.** For member states with no commissioner it will mean a loss of prestige and scope to shape developments in the EU.

The European Parliament building in Strasbourg.

European Parliament

This is the key forum for democratic debate. Since 1979, voters in all EU countries directly elect **members of the European Parliament** (MEPs) for five years. In 2007, there were 785 MEPs who represent 490 million people of the EU.

Although initially having limited powers, the parliament has increased its decision-making powers significantly. It now has joint decision-making power with the European Council in a growing number of policy areas.

It is proposed to reduce and cap the number of MEPs at 750 in the 2009 elections. This, and further enlargements, will reduce the number of MEPs allocated to individual countries (Ireland will lose one of its thirteen MEPs).

For small countries (such as Ireland) to be able to shape policy decisions in the European Parliament, it is essential that their MEPs **form effective political alliances** with other like-minded political parties from other member states.

Council of the European Union

This is the main decision-making institution in the EU. Each member state sends to the Council its minister responsible for the policy area to be discussed (for example, the minister for agriculture discusses agricultural policy).

To make decision-making more efficient, it is proposed that for a vote to pass in the Council, it must be supported by:

- 55 per cent of member states, and which represent
- 65 per cent of the total EU population.

To block a vote, at least four countries must support the block.

This proposal is designed to prevent a small number of large states dominating policy. It also means, however, that **smaller states that want to shape policy will have to form effective alliances with other member states.**

The EU has significantly increased its decision-making powers. As a result, member states have fewer decision-making powers. The issue of sovereignty will be an important element on any agenda for the future direction of the EU.

CHAPTER 33
CHANGING BOUNDARIES IN LANGUAGE REGIONS

 **KEY IDEA!**

The size and shape of language regions can change over time.

The regional boundaries of human activities change a lot over time. This is due mainly to **two processes:**

- Push-pull forces of migration.
- The effect of strong external forces.

The **push-pull forces of migration** cause people to move from one region to another. When more people move into a region than leave it, the region usually expands its boundaries. For example, rural-urban migration (when people move from the country into towns) often creates population pressure in the urban area, which then expands outwards into suburbs and rural areas around the town.

On another scale, the widespread migration of Islamic people to areas outside the Middle East has resulted in a large increase in the regions influenced by the religion of Islam (see Fig. 22.3 on page 149).

Strong external forces affect a region's identity. Stronger and more aggressive cultural forces can work to reduce the importance and regional patterns of minority cultures. For example, modern communication systems (radio, television and the Internet) have allowed the importance of major world languages, especially English, to increase. This often reduces the status of minority languages.

The decline of Irish and Welsh are examples of how both processes have changed the regional boundaries of these ancient Celtic languages.

An emigrant family leaving Cobh for the USA in 1953.
- *Why did so many Irish people migrate for more than 100 years after the Famine?*

Boundary Changes of Gaeltacht Areas

In 1851, the census of Ireland recorded 1.5 million people as speaking Irish. Large areas along the southern and especially the western coastline kept Irish as their majority language (see Fig. 33.1).

Fig. 33.1 The Irish-speaking population in 1851.

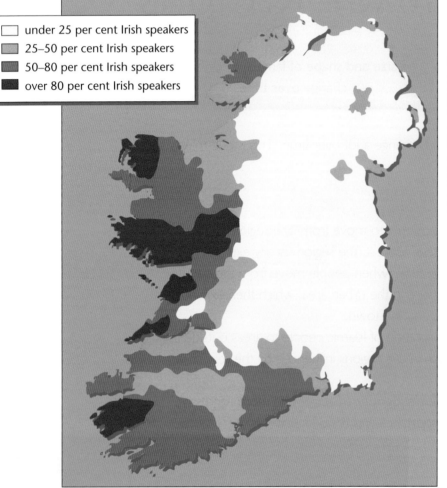

under 25 per cent Irish speakers
25–50 per cent Irish speakers
50–80 per cent Irish speakers
over 80 per cent Irish speakers

Activity

Look at Fig. 33.1 and answer the following questions.

1. Which parts of Ireland in 1851 show more than 50 per cent of the population speaking Irish?
2. Why was so little Irish spoken in eastern and northern Ireland?

The Irish Language from 1861 to 1926

In the period from 1861 to 1926, the number of Irish speakers declined to 544,000. The changes were greatest in Munster and Connaught, provinces that traditionally had the most Irish speakers (see Figs. 33.1 and 33.2). Decreases in these core regions for the Irish language were so strong that many people felt that the Irish language would become extinct in the twentieth century.

The decline in the area and numbers of Irish speakers was due to:

- Large-scale emigration.
- The growing dominance of English.

The Irish Language from 1926 Up to Now

On gaining independence from Britain, the new government committed itself to supporting the Irish language as an essential part of national identity. This support took several forms:

- Irish became the official language of the state, and being able to speak Irish was essential for many jobs, especially in government administration and public services.

- Irish was included as a compulsory subject in the school syllabus.
- An official Gaeltacht area, set up in 1926, has been strongly supported by the government.

These measures were aimed at reducing the dominance of the English language. Irish would be the majority language in the Gaeltacht and this would act as the core region to preserve and promote the Irish language.

At one level, the measures to support the Irish language appear to have been very successful. The numbers of people claiming to speak Irish in Ireland have increased from 589,000 in 1946 to some 1.57 million today. Interestingly, the largest numbers are located in Leinster. This reflects, perhaps, the fact that some knowledge of Irish is needed to work in government and administration, which is concentrated in Dublin.

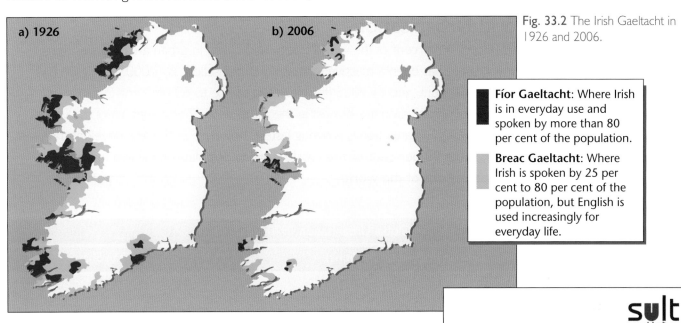

a) 1926   **b) 2006**

Fig. 33.2 The Irish Gaeltacht in 1926 and 2006.

Fíor Gaeltacht: Where Irish is in everyday use and spoken by more than 80 per cent of the population.

Breac Gaeltacht: Where Irish is spoken by 25 per cent to 80 per cent of the population, but English is used increasingly for everyday life.

Activity

Look at Fig. 33.2 and answer the following.

1. In 1926, which counties were identified most with the Fíor Gaeltacht?
2. What major changes took place to the boundaries of the Irish-speaking region from 1851 to 1926?
3. Where would you locate the core areas of the current Irish-speaking population?
4. In what ways are these different to 1926?

The boundaries of the Gaeltacht have changed. Various initiatives, such as the launch of the club SULT for young Irish speakers in Dublin, are being made to increase the use of Irish in non-Gaeltacht areas.

- *How effective do you think these will be in reviving the Irish language?*

While a growing number of people in Ireland claim an ability to speak Irish, relatively few are fluent and use Irish on a daily basis. English is by far the dominant language of Ireland's population.

This is highlighted by the big change in the **boundaries of the Gaeltacht**, where Irish is the majority language (see Fig. 33.2). Compared to 1926, the present Gaeltacht has been reduced to relatively small and isolated areas that occupy the peninsulas of the west coast of Ireland (see also Chapter 22, page 147). Even these areas face an uncertain future because the English-language culture is so strong.

CHAPTER 34
URBAN GROWTH AND CITY REGIONS

 **KEY IDEA!**

The growth of urban areas and the expansion of city regions are key features of development.

World Urbanisation

Urbanisation measures the proportion of a total population living in an urban area.

In 1950, only 6 per cent of the world's population lived in urban areas. Since then, however, there has been a massive increase in urbanisation. By 2000, this figure had risen to 48 per cent, and by 2025 it is expected to rise to 65 per cent.

Levels of urbanisation are highest in the more developed countries of the world (see Table 34.1). Urbanisation is growing fastest, however, in the less developed regions. **By 2025, some 80 per cent of the world's urban population will live in less developed regions of the world.**

Trends in Global Urbanisation 1970–2025						
Region	Urban Population (millions)			Urban Share (%)		
	1970	1995	2025	1970	1995	2025
More developed regions:	677	868	1,040	68	75	84
Europe	423	532	598	64	73	83
North America	167	221	313	74	76	85
Japan	74	97	313	71	78	85
Less developed regions:	676	1,653	4,025	25	37	57
Africa	84	240	804	23	33	54
Asia	428	1,062	2,615	21	32	54
Latin America	163	349	601	57	74	85

Table 34.1

Activity

Study Table 34.1 and the newspaper extract on the next page and answer the following.

1. In 1970, Europe and Asia had almost the same total urban population. Contrast the trends for these regions for 1970 to 2025.
2. Which continents will be dominated by conurbations (very large cities) in the future?
3. What problems will these large cities be exposed to?

Half the World Heads for Life in the Big City

Within six years more than half of humanity will live in cities for the first time in history. Increasing urbanisation will see growing concentration in the largest cities, with more than a quarter of people in settlements of more than 1 million by 2025.

The world will be increasingly dominated by vast conurbations in Asia and Africa. The populations of new giant cities such as Lagos (23.2 million) in Nigeria and Mumbai (26.1 million), plus twenty-five other cities, will pass 20 million. Such cities will prove increasingly difficult for poor countries to maintain. The poor will increasingly be concentrated in their own neighbourhoods characterised by high rates of crime, violence and social disaster.

Despite this, from 2015 the bulk of population growth will occur in urbanised areas, thus guaranteeing that the human future will be an urban one.

Sunday Times, 2 September 2002

Urbanisation in the European Union

The EU has many large and important cities, and 80 per cent of its population lives in urban areas (see Fig. 25.1 on page 166). Most of these cities continue to grow in population, and their built-up areas now extend well beyond their administrative boundaries. This is called **urban sprawl.**

In addition, modern transport and communication systems allow cities to have an important influence over an extensive area or hinterland (for example, travel to work and shop). This is called the **daily urban system.** For large cities like London, this can extend to about 150 km, while for Dublin it is some 80 km.

Two case studies are introduced to illustrate the growth and expansion of city regions in the EU:

- Randstad.
- Dublin.

> Car ownership has been a key factor in enabling large-scale urban sprawl to develop.

> **Activity**
> Look at Fig. 25.1 on page 166 and describe the patterns of urban development in the EU. Suggest reasons for the expansion of the urban axes in the directions shown.

Case Study: Randstad Holland

The western part of the Netherlands is one of the most urbanised regions in Europe. Most of the country's major cities are in this area, which has a radius of about 50 km. The growth and expansion of the towns and cities in this small area have resulted in a sprawling urban region called Randstad Holland.

The **Randstad** is shaped like a horseshoe, with an open end in the less populated east. It is a **polycentric city** region, which means it is made up of a number of major cities, with no single city being dominant. At its centre is an important agricultural and recreational area. This is the **Greenheart** of the Randstad (see Fig. 34.1).

Since the end of World War II, the Randstad has grown rapidly. This has been due to the region's strategic location within the core of the EU, its excellent transport systems and Rotterdam, the EU's largest port.

As this urban region developed, competition for land increased and caused urban sprawl to occur around the Randstad cities. In particular, it put huge pressure on the Greenheart.

> The Randstad contains 40 per cent (6 million) of the Dutch population living on only 17 per cent of the country's land area. Locate the Randstad on Fig. 34.1.

The town of Zoetermeer in the Randstadt is separated from other urban centres by the green belt in the background.

Planning for the Randstad

Planners face many difficulties in trying to overcome problems in the Randstad. The focus has mainly been placed on trying to limit urban sprawl.

At the **national level,** five regional centres have been designated for major investment in infrastructures such as transport and housing. Planners hope that these regional centres will become a stronger attraction for people and economic development, and reduce pressure on the Randstad (see Fig. 34.1).

In the **Randstad,** some high-density development will be allowed close to the major cities, but urban sprawl will be strongly controlled by using **buffer zones,** also called green belts. Urban developments will also be encouraged along the eastern edge of the Randstad to close off its 'open' edge.

> Green belts are special areas where no new urban development is allowed. It therefore protects the existing natural environment and rural countryside.

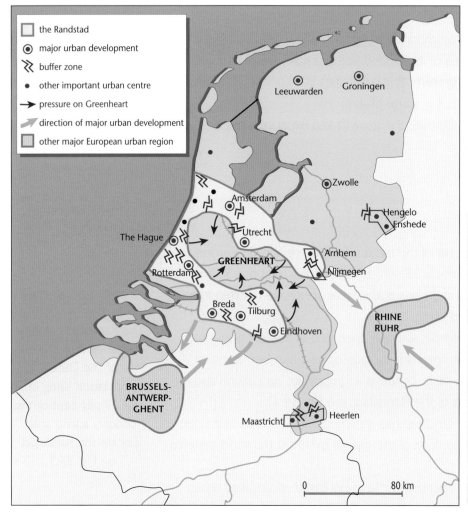

Legend:
- the Randstad
- major urban development
- buffer zone
- other important urban centre
- pressure on Greenheart
- direction of major urban development
- other major European urban region

Leeuwarden
Groningen
Zwolle
Amsterdam
Hengelo
Enshede
Utrecht
The Hague
Arnhem
GREENHEART
Nijmegen
Rotterdam
Breda
Tilburg
RHINE RUHR
Eindhoven
BRUSSELS-ANTWERP-GHENT
Maastricht
Heerlen

0   80 km

Fig. 34.1 Planning for Randstad Holland.

Activity

Look at Fig. 34.1 and answer the following.

1. What planning tools are being used to reduce the amount of urban sprawl in the Randstad?
2. If there are no strict planning controls, which two major urban regions could spread and merge along the Rhine Valley?
3. Is urban sprawl putting pressure on the Greenheart?
4. Why is it important to ensure that the Greenheart remains as a significant area in the Randstad?

EU Concerns about Randstad Growth

For the EU, controlling the expansion of the Randstad is also important. If uncontrolled urban growth is allowed eastwards along the Rhine River, the Randstad could eventually join up with the expanding cities of the Rhine-Ruhr (see Fig. 34.1). To the south, unplanned expansion could link up with the Brussels-Antwerp-Ghent growth zone of Belgium.

The result would be a **West European megalopolis,** with a huge concentration of population and economic activities in one vast and almost continuous urban sprawl. This would be an environmental disaster and will require strong planning controls to keep open spaces between these expanding urban regions.

> Increased demand for housing, industry, transport and recreation all contribute to the problems of congestion and urban sprawl.

Case Study: **Dublin**

Ireland's urban system is dominated by Dublin, which is a **primate city.** Since the 1960s, its built-up area has expanded rapidly. In addition, Dublin's zone of influence has increased strongly to create an urban region (or daily urban system) that extends some 80 km from the city centre.

Three factors in particular have contributed to the expansion of Dublin's urban region:

- Focus of the country's transport network.
- Dominant employment centre.
- High cost of land in the city.

Before World War II, Dublin was a compact city. The built-up area did not extend more than 5 km from its centre (see Fig. 34.2a). In the 1960s a period of significant growth began. Most of this expansion occurred within 8 km of the centre. It involved the relocation of inner city populations to large new housing estates and apartment complexes, such as Ballymun. By the 1980s, this zone was almost entirely built up (see Fig. 34.2b).

Urban expansion continued in the 1970s into the zone 8 to 16 km from Dublin's centre. Most of the growth here was due to the development of three new towns: Blanchardstown, Clondalkin and Tallaght. About 40 per cent of the population of Dublin's urban region now lives in this zone.

As competition for land and the cost of living continues to rise in Dublin, more people are encouraged to look for homes further from the city. Many small towns and villages more than 16 km from the centre of Dublin have therefore increased in size, especially if they are located on or near a transport route to the city. For many people living in such places, **long-distance travel to work** to Dublin has become an accepted part of their daily routine (see Fig. 34.3). This has been an important factor in the way the boundaries of Dublin's urban region have been extended.

Expansion of the Dublin urban region has led to a great increase in journeys to work and therefore more traffic congestion at peak times.

- *Suggest how this problem can be resolved.*

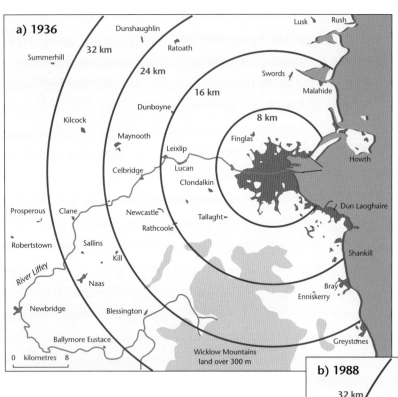

a) 1936

Lusk
Rush
Dunshaughlin
Ratoath
32 km
Summerhill
24 km
Swords
16 km
Malahide
Kilcock
Dunboyne
8 km
Maynooth
Finglas
Leixlip
Howth
Celbridge
Lucan
Clondalkin
Dun Laoghaire
Prosperous
Clane
Newcastle
Tallaght
Rathcoole
Robertstown
Sallins
Shankill
Kill
River Liffey
Naas
Bray
Enniskerry
Newbridge
Blessington
Ballymore Eustace
Greystones
0   kilometres   8
Wicklow Mountains
land over 300 m

Fig. 34.2 Built-up areas in the Dublin region.

Activity

Look at the two maps in Fig. 34.2 and answer the following.

1. In which direction has the urban area expanded the most? Why is further major expansion to the south of Dublin likely to be difficult?
2. Give examples of towns that have grown significantly because they are located on or near major roads that converge on Dublin.
3. Why are improved transport links important in extending Dublin's urban region?

Long-distance travel to work involves a journey of more than 16 km.

b) 1988

Dunshaughlin
Rush
Ashbourne
Lusk
Ratoath
N2
N1
32 km
N3
Portrane
Swords
24 km
Dublin
Airport
16 km
Malahide
Dunboyne
Portmarnock
N4
M4
Kilcock
8 km
Blanchardstown
Maynooth
Leixlip
Lucan
Phoenix
Park
Celbridge
Howth
Clondalkin
Clane
Newcastle
Dun Laoghaire
Prosperous
Rathcoole
Sallins
Tallaght
N7
Kill
River Liffey
Shankill
Naas
Bray
Newbridge
Enniskerry
Blessington
N11
Ballymore
Eustace
Greystones
0   kilometres   8
Wicklow Mountains
land over 300 m
Kilcoole

Blanchardstown is one of the three new towns built in the 1970s to accommodate Dublin's increasing population.

● *What evidence do you see in this photo to suggest that it is a planned settlement?*

Fig. 34.3 Long-distance commuting from towns with a population of more than 5,000 in the Dublin urban region in 1981 and 2002.

Activity

Look at Fig. 34.3 and answer the following.

1. Which three towns in 1981 had 50 per cent or more of their resident workforce commuting long distance?

2. Compare the percentage figures for all towns for 1981 and 2002. What do they tell you about trends in long-distance commuting?

3. As you travel from Naas to Portlaoise along the N7, what do the percentages show about the relationship between levels of commuting and the distance from Dublin?

4. Do railways as well as roads have an influence on commuting and the growth of towns in Dublin's urban region? Explain your answer.

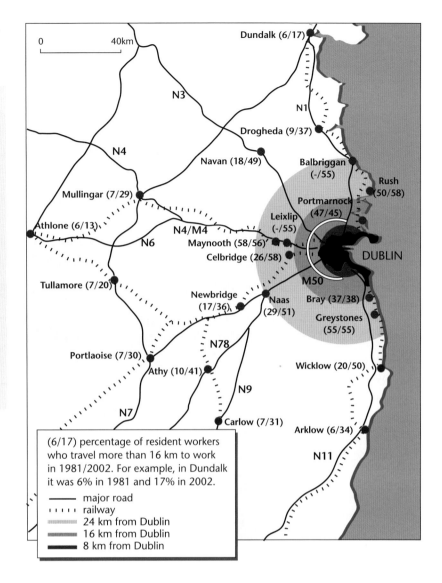

A Solution to Dublin's Continued Expansion?

The rapid and large-scale expansion of the Dublin urban region has raised concerns for both the city and country. These are highlighted in the following article.

Don't Let Isolated Rural Areas Become Ghost Towns

Dublin will continue to suck life out of major areas of the country unless there is a meaningful government intervention aimed at beefing up other regions.

It appears Ireland's lopsided development is destined to continue apace. Relentlessly, the population explosion of the capital and its sprawling hinterland along the east coast will accelerate unless urgent measures are introduced to redirect development from areas already mushrooming out of control.

The reality is that thousands of people in outlying regions have yet to hear the Celtic Tiger purring. While other cities and towns have benefited, the Tiger's economic impact is concentrated in and around Dublin.

Based on CSO figures, the population of the capital will tip 1,500,000 by 2020. That means traffic gridlock and a serious erosion of quality of life. The repercussions will reverberate right across the city, rippling outwards to greater Dublin and into the neighbouring counties already being turned into commuter dormitories.

Unless the trends are reversed, large areas of the country will be turned into reservations and stripped of people who are the lifeblood of Ireland's future.

Irish Examiner, 19 June 2001

247

A solution to the problems of Dublin's continued expansion appeared in the **National Spatial Strategy** (2002). This proposed large-scale developments in a series of **gateways and hubs** to encourage dispersal of population and employment out of the Dublin region (see Fig. 34.4).

- **Gateways:** Large urban centres with well-developed infrastructure that offer the best prospects for countering the dominance of Dublin.
- **Hubs:** Smaller urban centres that will help disperse development from gateways into their regions.
- **Strategic road corridors:** Important for providing efficient links between gateways, hubs and Dublin.

These developments will receive a significant amount of support from the government's €184 billion National Development Plan (2007–13).

Fig. 34.4 Ireland's National Spatial Strategy, 2002.

Activity
Do you think this system of gateways and hubs can produce more balanced urban and regional development?

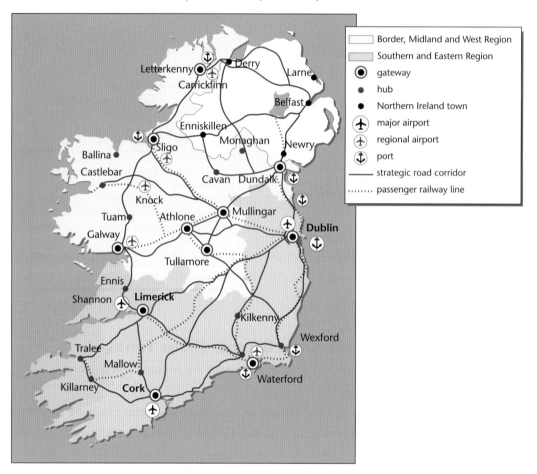

Administration Reform in Dublin

An important result of the increasing population and urbanisation within Dublin City and County has been the need to reform its local authority structure. Until 1994, the local authorities responsible for delivering essential services in Dublin were Dublin County Borough, Dun Laoghaire Corporation and Dublin County Council.

In 1971, two-thirds of the total population of Dublin City and County lived in the city (see Table 34.2). The dominance of the city declined as more of Dublin's population chose to live in the county's growing towns and rural communities. It proved increasingly difficult to serve the needs of such a large population growth, which was spread out across the county. As a result, it was decided to abolish Dublin County Council and Dun Laoghaire Corporation.

Three new counties were created: Fingal, South Dublin and Dun Laoghaire-Rathdown (see Fig. 34.5). These, together with the newly named Dublin Corporation, provide a more evenly distributed area and population for more efficient administration of Dublin's changing population patterns.

Population Trends in Dublin's Administrative Areas					
	1971 ('000s)	1981 ('000s)	1991 ('000s)	2002 ('000s)	2006 ('000s)
Dublin County Borough/Corporation	568	545	478	496	506
Dublin County	284	–	–	–	–
South Dublin	–	165	208	239	246
Fingal	–	115	153	196	240
Dun Laoghaire-Rathdown	–	178	185	192	194
Total	852	1,003	1,025	1,123	1,186

Table 34.2

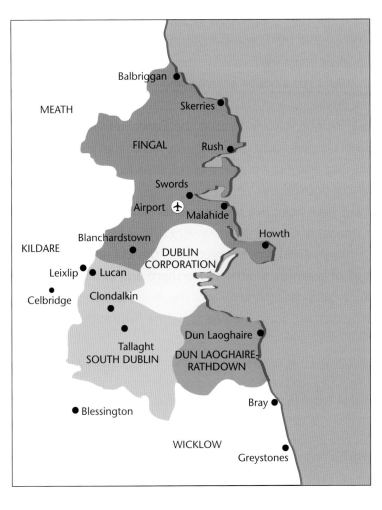

Fig. 34.5 Local government reform for County Dublin.

Between 1996 and 2002, Fingal was the fastest-growing county in Ireland.

Activity

Look at Table 34.2 and Fig. 34.5 and answer the following.

1. What share of the total population lived in the Dublin Corporation area in 2006 compared to 1971?
2. Do you think it was necessary to reorganise the local administration in Dublin? Explain your answer.
3. Which of the new counties has the largest and fastest-growing population? Explain your answer. (Think about new towns.)

CHAPTER 35
DEVELOPMENT AND EXPANSION OF THE EU

 **KEY IDEA!** The European Union has expanded from six to twenty-seven member states and is now the world's largest trade bloc.

Following the destruction that occurred during World War II, prospects for development within Europe seemed limited.

- The economies of most countries were devastated.
- A new political boundary, called the Iron Curtain, divided a democratic Western Europe from a communist-dominated Eastern Europe.

From this uncertain time, a new, confident and prosperous Europe emerged. The basis for this began in Western Europe and involved a **process of economic integration.**

In 1957, the **Treaty of Rome** created the European Economic Community (EEC). This was a small, compact group of six countries located in the core region of north-west Europe (see Fig. 35.1a). Its main aims were to increase trade between member states and their level of economic development. This was successful and it encouraged other European countries to seek membership. As a result, the **European Union,** as it is now called, has become the world's largest and most prosperous trading bloc. It is an excellent case study of a region that has expanded its international boundaries.

> The EEC has now become the EU.

There have been **five enlargements** of the EU. As a result, the boundaries of the EU are now very different from those in 1957. Through a series of enlargements, **the EU now covers almost all of western, southern, northern and eastern Europe.** Its boundaries stretch from the Arctic to the Mediterranean, and from the Atlantic to the Russian border.

> In 1990, East Germany was reunited with West Germany (see Chapter 36). This did not increase the number of countries in the EU. It was seen only as an existing member increasing its territory. The reunification of Germany increased the population of the EU by 17 million.

Activity

Look at Fig. 35.1 and Tables 35.1 and 35.2, and with the help of an atlas answer the following.
1. Locate the member states listed in Table 35.1 on the maps of the EU in Fig. 35.1.
2. In the first enlargement, which new member state was responsible for the large increase in population and GDP?
3. Why did enlargements in the 1980s and in 1995 result in a decline in average population density for the EU? (Think about growth in area compared to population.)
4. Why do you think the enlargement in the 1980s was troublesome for the EU?
5. What evidence supports the view that the 2004 and 2007 expansions added to the problems of regional development in the EU?

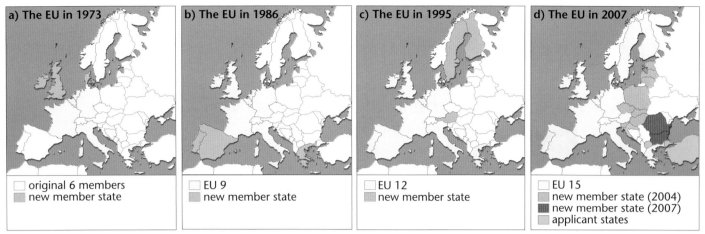

Fig. 35.1 Enlargements of the European Union.

Enlargements of the European Region		
1957	Belgium, France, (West) Germany, Italy, Luxembourg, Netherlands	The original six members, mainly from the **economic core** of north-west Europe.
1973	Britain, Denmark, Ireland	A **westward** enlargement of the economic core.
1981	Greece	These **southern** enlargements into Mediterranean
1986	Spain, Portugal	Europe were considered to be troublesome due to their underdeveloped economies.
1995	Austria, Finland, Sweden	Mostly a **northern** expansion into Scandanavia. It also included some of Alpine Europe. All were well-developed economies.
2004	Cyprus, Czech Republic, Estonia, Hungary, Latvia, Lithuania, Malta, Poland, Slovak Republic, Slovenia	The largest single expansion, involving ten countries. This **eastern** enlargement is difficult due to its scale and the underdeveloped economies of the new members.
2007	Bulgaria and Romania	This adds to the problems of an underdeveloped periphery.

Table 35.1

Selected Data for the Enlarging EU				
European Union	Increase in area (%)	Increase in population (%)	Increase in GDP (gross domestic product) (%)	Change in GDP per person (%)
EU 6 to EU 9 (First enlargement)	31	32	29	−3
EU 9 to EU 12 (Second and third enlargements)	48	22	15	−6
EU 12 to EU 15 (Fourth enlargement, including German reunification)	43	11	8	−3
EU 15 to EU 27	34	29	9	−16

Table 35.2

CHAPTER 36
CHANGING POLITICAL BOUNDARIES AND CULTURAL GROUPS

 **KEY IDEA!**

Changes in political boundaries can have an important effect on cultural groups.

> How do you think the lives of people living in Northern Ireland have been affected by the creation of a border separating it from the Republic?

Changes in political boundaries often have major impacts for people who, as a result of boundary changes, find themselves living under a different political system. Their economic prospects, cultural experiences (language and religious beliefs) and human rights can all be affected by these changes.

This chapter will present **two case studies** to show how changing political boundaries affect cultural groups:

- **Kashmir:** An example of a violent clash of cultures after British India broke up and new political boundaries were drawn up.
- **A reunified Germany:** The peaceful reunification of East and West Germany.

Case Study: The Problem of Kashmir

In Chapter 29, important religious and other cultural differences in India were highlighted. These led to the partition of the subcontinent into three independent states, based primarily on religion: India, Pakistan and Bangladesh.

The differences are still strong and continue to give rise to tensions between different cultural groups. Nowhere is this more marked than in the Kashmir region, where India and Pakistan have fought three wars to settle their claims to this disputed border zone (see Fig. 36.1).

On gaining independence from Britain in 1947, the states of the Indian subcontinent had to choose whether to form part of Pakistan, dominated by Islam, or India, where Hindu was the majority religion.

In the Kashmir Valley, violent conflict broke out between the minority (25 per cent) Hindu population and the majority (75 per cent) Islamic population (see Fig. 29.10, page 225). The Hindu minority looked to India for support, while the Islamic population was supported by Pakistan. This resulted in war between the two newly independent states. Many civilians were killed and large numbers of people fled from areas where they were of the minority religion.

> India is a country dominated by Hinduism, while Pakistan is an Islamic state.

The United Nations negotiated a ceasefire line to end the conflict. This **Line of Control** was to be temporary, but it has remained as the dividing line between the two cultural groups.

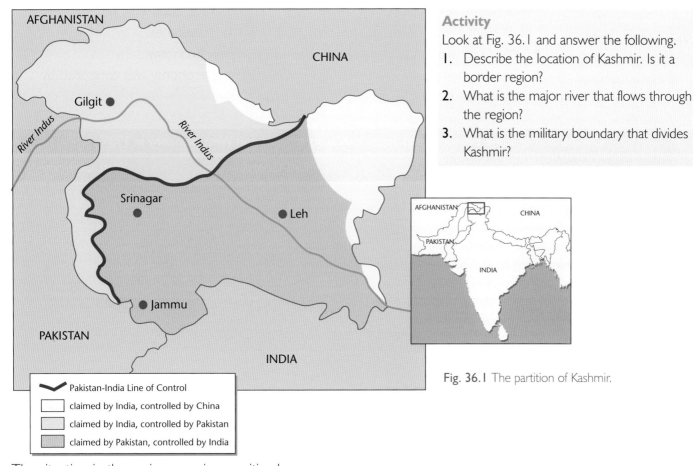

Fig. 36.1 The partition of Kashmir.

Activity

Look at Fig. 36.1 and answer the following.

1. Describe the location of Kashmir. Is it a border region?
2. What is the major river that flows through the region?
3. What is the military boundary that divides Kashmir?

Map legend:

- Pakistan-India Line of Control
- claimed by India, controlled by China
- claimed by India, controlled by Pakistan
- claimed by Pakistan, controlled by India

The situation in the region remains sensitive because:

- India controls about 80 per cent of the Kashmir population, including large numbers of Islamic people.
- Pakistan and the majority Islamic population do not accept this. They want to integrate Kashmir into Pakistan.
- The Indus River and several of its large tributaries originate in Indian-controlled Kashmir. Pakistan wants to gain control over this essential water resource (for irrigation and industrial development).
- In the 1990s, an increase in Islamic fundamentalism has led to more fighting in the region.
- Both India and Pakistan have nuclear weapons. It is therefore a potentially dangerous situation when both countries come into conflict in this contested cultural and political border region.

Case Study: Reunified Germany

Changes in political boundaries not only have impacts on different cultural groups, such as in Kashmir and Northern Ireland. They can also create new conditions which affect a single cultural group. Germany is a good example of this with the changes in its political boundaries following World War II.

At the end of World War II, the victorious allies (USA, USSR, UK and France) were determined that a strong and united Germany would never again threaten the peace of Europe. As a result, a new political boundary was drawn which created **two Germanies** (Fig. 36.2).

Why is India more willing than Pakistan to make the Line of Control a permanent boundary?

Bill Clinton, a former US president, described Kashmir as 'the most dangerous place on earth'. Why?

253

From 1949 to 1990, Germany was divided into two separate states.

These two new states operated under different political and economic systems, which had different effects on German people living in the two countries.

- **West Germany** was a democracy and a free market economy.
- **East Germany** was a communist regime where the economy was controlled by centralised planning.

Comparison of Some Economic and Social Indicators for East and West Germany in 1989		
	East Germany	West Germany
Gross domestic product (billion Deutschmarks)*	353	2,111
Per capita GDP (Deutschmarks)*	21,500	33,700
% unemployment	–	6.9
% children under 3 years cared for in crèches	56	2
Doctors per 10,000 people	24	29
Hospital beds per 10,000 people	24	110

*The Deutschmark was the currency in Germany before it changed to the euro in 2002.

Table 36.1

Images of the two Germanies. Prior to reunification, drab state-built worker apartments and underdeveloped services in the east (top) contrast with the prosperity of cities in West Germany.

- *How did 'Ossies' react to such differences?*

West Germany's economy developed strongly and became the largest and most powerful in the EU. Its industries were very competitive and the population enjoyed a high standard of living. Population totals also increased from 50 million to 62 million between 1950 and 1989. Much of this increase was due to large numbers of migrants, from countries such as Turkey, who were attracted to this prosperous country (see Table 36.1).

In contrast, the East German economy was relatively inefficient, quality of life was poor and personal freedom was limited. Although the state provided its people with basic services, such as housing and health care, most East Germans looked with envy at those living in West Germany. Their population declined from almost 20 million to 17 million between 1950 and 1989.

Activity

Look at Table 36.1 and answer the following.

1. Which of the two Germanies was the largest and most prosperous economy?
2. Why did the East German population have relatively good access to a range of basic services?
3. Which of the two Germanies would migrant workers find more attractive?

A REUNITED GERMANY

In 1989, the communist government in East Germany collapsed, and in 1990 the political boundary that had separated the two Germanies was removed. Although now a single country, forty years of separate national identities had given rise to major differences between the **Ossies** (people from former East Germany and pronounced oss-sees) and **Wessies** (West Germans and pronounced vess-sees).

At first, there was considerable optimism that a reunited Germany would succeed in reducing east-west divisions. This has not occurred. In particular, the expectations of the Ossies that their standard of living and job prospects would rise quickly to those of the Wessies have not been met. Two main factors are responsible for this:

- **Free market forces** have meant that many of the older, less efficient industries located in East Germany were closed due to competition. Unemployment increased rapidly.
- **Freedom of movement** meant that large numbers of young East Germans migrated to Western Germany, leaving behind an ageing and economically depressed community.

East Germany became an Objective 1 Region in the EU and receives large amounts of financial support from structural funds and the German government. This contrasts with the prosperity of West Germany (see Fig 36.2). Therefore, rather than becoming equals within a united Germany, **Ossies felt that they were being treated as second-class citizens in their own country**. Meanwhile, many Wessies felt that Ossies were ungrateful given the high costs the West German government and citizens paid for reunification.

Ask your teacher about:
- Democracy.
- A free market economy.
- Communism.
- Centralised planning.

In 1990, Germany was reunited, with its capital in Berlin.

Fig. 36.2 East and West Germany before reunification.

The upper photograph shows Berlin citizens protesting in November 1989 on top of the Berlin Wall, which symbolised the divisions in Germany. This was torn down in 1989. The lower photograph is of the same location today, showing free movement through the Brandenburg Gate. This symbolises the unity of Germany.

Following reunification, an unprecedented consumer and construction boom, boosted by aid from the west, produced modern roads, sleek office buildings and shopping malls throughout East Germany. Easterners discovered the joys of fast cars and designer clothes. Their communist-era apartment blocks were given more colourful facades. For a while they seemed happy.

The merger, however, meant that western employment policies were extended to the east, where industries soon lost their competitive edge to Poland and the Czech Republic. Unemployment in eastern Germany has grown to 18 per cent, more than twice the western level and higher than in most of Eastern Europe.

'Just look out there,' said Manfred Geiger, behind the counter of his empty café in Reichenbach's central square. 'There are no young people here any more. They've gone. The east is dying.'

The German government has done nothing even while a 'brain drain' was depriving some eastern towns of doctors and dentists. Migration westwards, at more than 200,000 people a year, is greater now than in the years after the fall of the Wall.

'A collective depression has set in,' says Karen Retzel, the mayor of Cottbus, whose population is shrinking by 7 per cent a year. 'The promises of reunification have not been fulfilled.'

Sunday Times, 8 September 2002

Activity

Look at the newspaper extract and answer the following.

1. Is unemployment higher in eastern or western Germany? Suggest reasons why.
2. Is migration from eastern to western Germany a problem? Why?
3. If you were an Ossie, would you agree that the promises of reunification have not been met?

Multi-part Questions

1. **A.** EUROPEAN UNION UNEMPLOYMENT

   Examine the table below, showing selected unemployment statistics for 2004.

Country	Unemployment Rate (% of Adult Population)
Austria	3.8%
Estonia	9.7%
France	9.5%
Latvia	14.6%
Poland	16.1%
Spain	10.5%

   Using graph paper, draw a graph suitable to illustrate these data.

   [20 marks]

   B. MANUFACTURING INDUSTRY

   Examine some of the factors that have influenced the development of one economic activity in a non-Irish region that you have studied.

   [30 marks]

   C. URBAN GROWTH

   'The boundaries of city regions have expanded over time.' Discuss this statement, with reference to one example you have studied.

   [30 marks]

2. **A.** EUROPEAN REGIONS

   i. Examine the map of Europe. In your answer book, associate each of these descriptions with the letters A, B, C.
      - Peripheral economic region.
      - Cultural (language) region.
      - Climatic region

   ii. Name **two** characteristics of the above climatic region. Explain **one** factor that influences the climate of the region.

   [20 marks]

   B. LANGUAGE REGIONS

   Examine, with reference to an example or examples you have studied, the causes and consequences of changes in extent of language regions.

   [30 marks]

   C. URBAN REGIONS

   With reference to one region you have studied, examine the growth in the extent of urban regions and the efforts to control this growth.

   [30 marks]

257

3. **A.** EUROPEAN UNION

Examine the map of Europe showing labelled political regions, then complete the following table, which refers to the European Union.

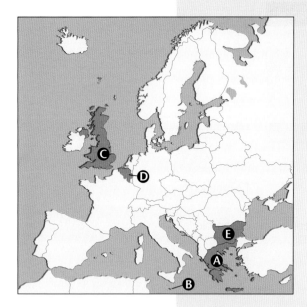

Description	Letter	Country
Member since 2007		
Member since 1981		
Member since 1957		
Member since 2004		
Member since 1973		

B. POLITICAL BOUNDARIES

Examine, with reference to **one** example, the impact of changes in political boundaries on cultural groups.

[30 marks]

C. CULTURAL REGION

Examine **two** factors which give rise to cultural identify or distinctiveness in a European or non-European region you have studied.

[30 marks]

4. **A.** REGIONS

'A region is an area which may be identified by one or more characteristics.' Briefly explain this statement, using a sketch map to illustrate an example or examples.

[20 marks]

B. CULTURAL REGIONS

Examine **two** factors which have influenced the development of distinct cultural divisions in a European region which you have studied.

[30 marks]

C. BOUNDARY CHANGES

Explain, with reference to **one** example, the causes and consequences of change in the boundaries of a region over time.

[30 marks]

5. **A.** NON-IRISH EUROPEAN REGION

Draw a sketch map of a non-European region you have studied. Mark the main relief and drainage features on the sketch map.

[20 marks]

B. IRISH REGION

'The physical environment affects human activities.' Examine this statement with reference to **one** primary activity in an Irish region you have studied.

[30 marks]

C. INDUSTRY

Examine the importance of the tertiary sector in a non-European country of your choice.

[30 marks]

6. A. AN IRISH REGION

Draw a sketch map to show the main physical characteristics of **one** Irish region you have studied.

[20 marks]

B. EU POLICY

Examine the influence of one EU policy on the development of a region you have studied.

[30 marks]

C. MANUFACTURING INDUSTRY

Select a non-European region and explain two factors that have influenced the development of manufacturing in the region.

[30 marks]

MAPS AND PHOTOGRAPHS

CHAPTER 37
ORDNANCE SURVEY MAPS

How to Locate Places on Ordnance Survey Maps

Can you remember how to locate a place on a map by a four-digit or six-digit grid reference? Remember **LATAS**: letter, across the top, then along the side.

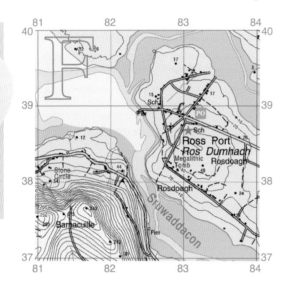

Activity

On the map extract, use:
a. a four-digit grid reference and
b. a six-digit grid reference to locate the post office.

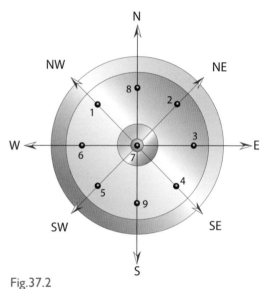

Fig.37.2

The National Grid

A	B	C	D	E
F	G	H	J	K
L	M	N	O	P
Q	R	S	T	U
V	W	X	Y	Z

Fig. 37.1 Remember, the national grid divides the whole country into twenty-five boxes, called sub-zones. Each sub-zone is identified by a letter of the alphabet.

How to Find Direction on Ordnance Survey Maps

Activity

1. Use Fig. 37.2 and look at the example given in (a), then answer the following:
   a. The number 3 is <u>east</u> of number 6.
   b. The number 2 is _____ of number 5.
   c. The number 8 is _____ of number 9.
   d. The number 7 is _____ of number 2.
   e. The number 1 is _____ of number 4.
   f. The number 7 is _____ of number 9.

2. In which direction would you travel when going from:
   a. 1 to 4   b. 5 to 2   c. 8 to 9   d. 7 to 1
   e. 7 to 3   f. 7 to 6   g. 9 to 3   h. 6 to 8

3. Carefully study the map extract at the top of this page. In which direction is:
   a. the megalithic tomb F 827 384 from the stone circle F 812 383
   b. the stone circle F 812 383 from the post office F 832 389
   c. the post office F 832 389 from the megalithic tomb F 827 384?

SCALE ON ORDNANCE SURVEY MAPS

Scale is the relationship between a distance on a map and its corresponding measurement on the ground. For example:

Remember what scale means. What does 1:50,000 mean?

SCÁLA 1:50 000	1 KILOMETRES 0 1 2 3 4
SCALE 1:50 000	1 STATUTE MILES 0 1 2
	2 ceintiméadar sa chiliméadar (taobh chearnóg eangal) 2 centimetres to 1 kilometre (grid square side)

Fig. 37.3

Measuring Distance on a Map

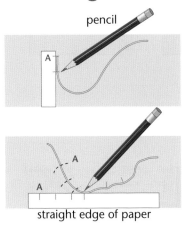

pencil

straight edge of paper

Fig. 37.4 Measuring a curved line.

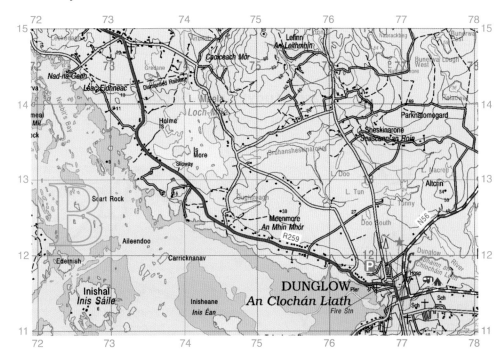

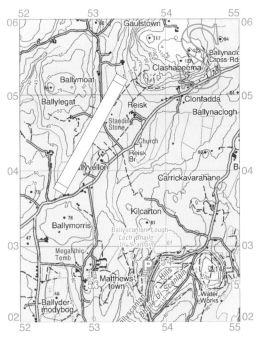

Measuring a straight line.

Activity

Find grid reference B 728 150 and measure the distance along the R259 between where the road enters the map at this point to where it meets the N56 at Dunglow. Then measure the distance between both places 'as the crow flies'. What is the difference in distance between these measurements?

- Small-scale maps show large areas in little detail.
- Large-scale maps show small areas in greater detail.

Some small and large-scale maps include:

Street map of a city for tourists	1:2,500
Rural place maps	1:15,000
National motoring map	1:250,000
World atlas map	1:100,000,000

Types of Slopes on Ordnance Survey Maps

Activity

Look at Fig. 37.5 and for A, B, C and D, find the numbers and descriptions that go together.

Fig. 37.5

Description:

- Concave
- Convex
- Stepped
- Even

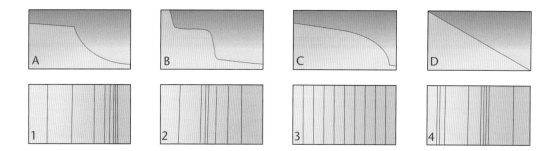

Case Study: Cross-Section

From spot height 397 m at grid reference T 012 730 to T 044 696 looking north-east.

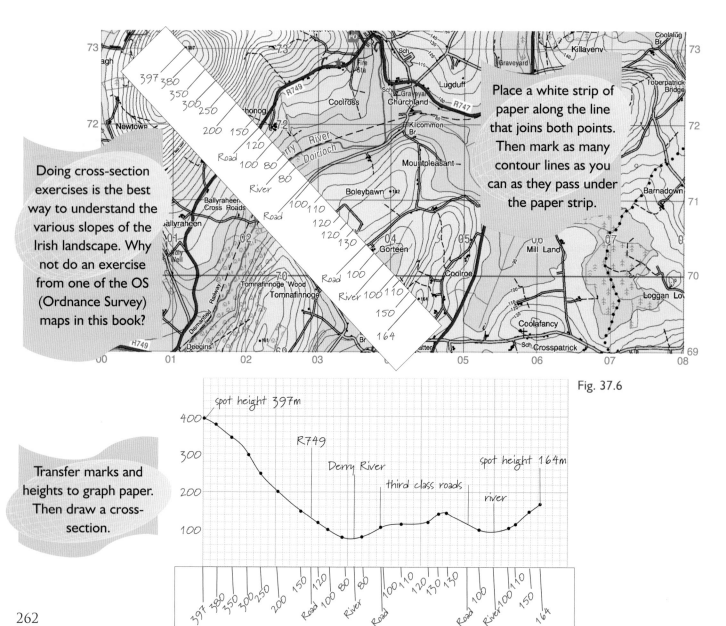

Place a white strip of paper along the line that joins both points. Then mark as many contour lines as you can as they pass under the paper strip.

Doing cross-section exercises is the best way to understand the various slopes of the Irish landscape. Why not do an exercise from one of the OS (Ordnance Survey) maps in this book?

Fig. 37.6

Transfer marks and heights to graph paper. Then draw a cross-section.

Gradient

Activity
Look at Fig. 37.7. What are the gradients of slopes A and B?

Fig. 37.7

Gradient refers to a slope expressed as a ratio. A gradient of 1 in 5 means that the ground rises or falls one unit for every five units travelled horizontally.

Calculating Areas on Maps

To Calculate Regular Areas

1. Count the number of grid squares across the base of the area that you wish to calculate.
2. Count the number of grid squares up the side of the area.
3. Multiply the number across by the number up the side. This gives you the area in square kilometres (km²).

For example:
- The number of grid squares across the base = 7.
- The number of grid squares up the side = 3.
- Area = 7 x 3 = 21 km².

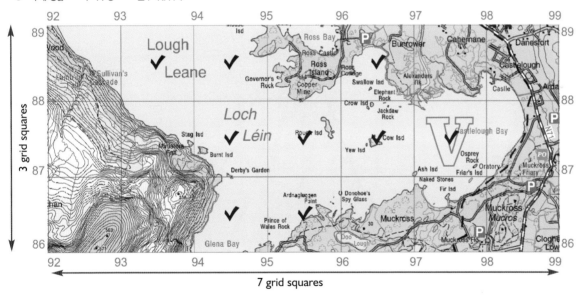

To Calculate Irregularly Shaped Areas

Each grid square on a 1:50,000 map is one square kilometre. By using these grid squares, we can easily find the approximate area of an irregularly shaped region, such as a lake or sea region.

Count all the squares that are at least half-filled by the features that you wish to measure. This number is the approximate area of the feature in km². For example, to calculate the approximate area of Lough Leane:
- The number of squares at least half-filled with water = 9.
- Approximate area of lake = 9 km².

Drumcliff Bay

Drumcliff Bay

Portcurry Point
Cullenamore Strand
Culleenamore
Carrowdough
Garrowburnaum
Midden
Standing Stone
Megalithic Tomb

Sligo Airport
STRANDHILL
An Leathros
Larass
Rinn
Tully

Maeve's
Cairn
Knocknarea
Cnoc na Riabh
Megalithic Tomb

Grange North
Rathcarrick
Lecarrow
Carton
Drinaghan
Scardan
Rathonoragh
Barnasrahy
Slieveroe
Tobernaveen
Carrowmore
Megalithic Tomb Cemetery
Ballydoogan
Standing Stone
Barrow
Knappagh More
Finisklin
Gibraltar Point
Barroe
Derrydarragh
Derrydarragh

Killaspug Point
Maguins Island
Church
Coney Island
Inishmulclohy
Dorrins Strand
Cummeen
Cummeen Strand

Sligo Harbour

Black Rock
Deadman's Point
Rosses Point
Bomore Point
Metal Man
Midden
Mound
Pier
Beacon
Oyster Island
Rosses Point
An Ros
Rosses Lower
Ballinphunta
Ballyweelin
Beacon
Bunowen Lough
Curraghmore
Fulacht Fia
Doonierin
Cregg
Castle
Springfield
Ballincar
Ballinvoher
Lisnalurg
Shannon Oughter
Shannon Eighter
Rathbraghan
Farranacardy
Bellanode

SLIGO
Sligeach
Garavoge River
Racecourse
Cleaveragh Demesne
Magheraboy
Abbeyquarter
Magheraboy
Afarmachaire Bui
Cartragh
Ballyquarter
Cleaverragh River
Hazelwood Demesne
Cairns
Barroe
Faughts
Doonally

Drumcliff
Droim Chliabh
Beacon
Finned Point
Finned
Camey
Fearann Uí Chearnaigh
Cullagh
Milltown
Cartronmore
Coolbeg
Castle
Ballygilgan Strand
Ballyweelin
Kintogher
Teesan
Carncash
Killycooly
Rahaberna
Tully
Rathcormack
Clooneen
Cloonderry
Drum
Collinsford
Listoney
Ballynagalliagh
Ballynagalliagh
Drumcliff River
Yeats' Grave
Drumcliff
Round Tower
Cross Megalithic Tomb
Lissadell
Ballygilgan Strand
Lissadell Strand
Clogbor
Tomb
Megalithic Tomb

Multi-part Questions

Case Study: The Sligo Region

1. Carefully study the Ordnance Survey map of Sligo, then draw a sketch map of the region. Mark and label the following features on it:

   i.   two upland regions
   ii. one urban region
   iii. a sea region
   iv. one recreation region.

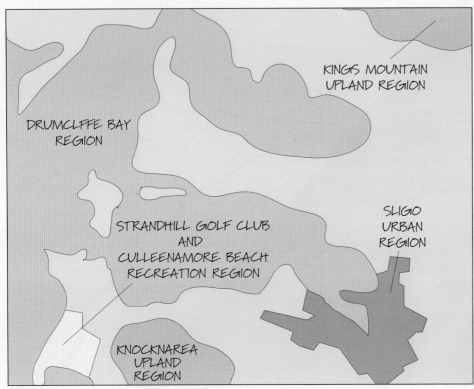

KING'S MOUNTAIN
UPLAND REGION

DRUMCLFFE BAY
REGION

STRANDHILL GOLF CLUB
AND
CULLEENAMORE BEACH
RECREATION REGION

SLIGO
URBAN
REGION

KNOCKNAREA
UPLAND
REGION

Fig. 37.8

2. **Class Activity 1**

   Draw a sketch map of the Sligo region. Mark and label the following features on it:

   i.   the coastline
   ii. one upland region
   iii. one urban region (not Sligo town)
   iv. two national primary roads
   v.   one regional road
   vi. one river.

3. **Class Activity 2**

   i. Calculate the area of the seawater region on the map.
   ii. Use the national grid map on page 260 to locate this region in Ireland.

265

Trail Master Activities

Carefully study the Ordnance Survey map and photograph images of the Twelve Bens and Maumturk Mountains in Connemara, then answer the following questions.

1. LANDFORMS

Identify the glacial landforms A to D and identify the process of erosion or deposition that formed them.

	Landform	Processes	Erosion/deposition
A			
B			
C			
D			

2. LANDFORMS

Identify the river landforms E to H and identify the process of erosion or deposition that formed them.

	Landform	Processes	Erosion/deposition
E			
F			
G			
H			

3. DIRECTION

i. In which direction would you be travelling if moving from (use the gridlines to find direction):
   a. landform D to landform E
   b. landform C to landform H
   c. landform B to landform E?

ii. In which direction would you be travelling if moving from the Cillín at L 843 496 to the Crannóg at L 845 519?

iii. Identify the trend of Sleíbhte Mhár Tóirc.

4. SCALE

i. Is this image of the map and photograph 'true to scale'? Explain.

ii. Use a paper strip and the gridlines to estimate the following distances:
   a. the distance from where the R344 enters the map in the south to the park and picnic site at L 845 538
   b. the distance between the letter K at L 800 496 and the Cillín at L 843 496.
   What does the comparison between both of these measurement methods tell you about scale on this image? Explain.

5. LAND USES

Identify the land uses at:
i. I
ii. J.

CHAPTER 38
UNDERSTANDING PHOTOGRAPHS

Types of Aerial Photograph

There are two types of aerial photograph:

- **Vertical photographs**, which are taken when the camera is pointing directly on the area being photographed.
- **Oblique photographs**, which are taken when the camera is pointing at an angle to the area being photographed. A **high** oblique shows **horizon**. A **low** oblique shows only **ground** surface.

Locating Places or Features on an Aerial Photograph

For easy reference, a photograph may be divided into nine areas, as shown below.

Vertical

Oblique

left   centre   right

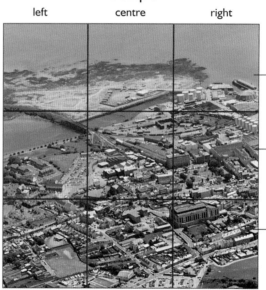

background covers a large area but background features appear small

— middle

— foreground covers a small area but features appear large

A north sign is given on a vertical photograph, so locations, such as the **north-west** or the **south-east** or the **east**, should be used.

For easy reference on an oblique photograph, nine divisions, such as **right background** and **left foreground**, should be used.

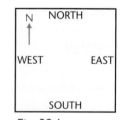

Fig. 38.1

Scale on aerial photographs

- All the features on a vertical photograph are in the same proportion to each other as they are on the ground. In other words, scale remains true throughout the photograph.

- Features which are located in the background of an oblique photograph appear small because they are far from the camera.
- Features which are located in the foreground of an oblique photograph appear large because they are nearer the camera.

Finding Direction on Oblique Photographs

An arrow indicating north is sometimes printed on a photograph. From this arrow we can find other directions. If an arrow is not given, we can find direction if we have an Ordnance Survey map of the same area.

Aerial view showing Limerick city and the Shannon River.
- *Which direction was the camera lens pointing when this photograph was taken?*

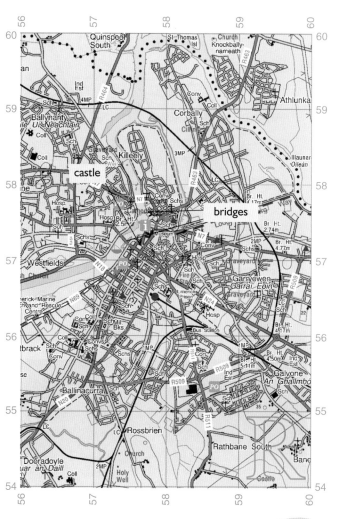

Finding Direction Using a Photograph and Map
Orientate Your Map or Photograph

1. Draw a line through the centre of the photograph from the foreground to the background (from the bottom to the top). This line represents the direction the camera was pointing when the photograph was taken.

2. Identify some important features through or near which your line passes, such as a church, a railway or a road.

3. Identify these same features on the Ordnance Survey map. Then draw a line on the map that corresponds to the line you drew on the photograph.

4. On the line, place an arrow near the feature on the map located in the background of your photograph.

5. Identify the direction of this line from the map. This represents the direction of the camera when the photograph was taken.

Match the features on the photograph with the ones marked on the map to find direction.

Time of year
Name all the features on a photo that may help identify the four seasons.

Sketch Maps from Photographs and Maps

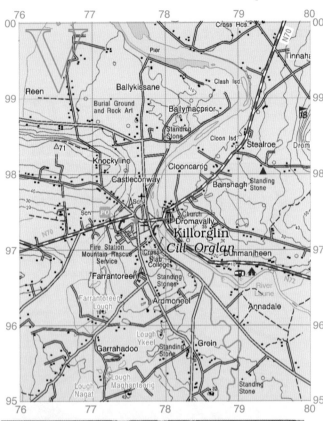

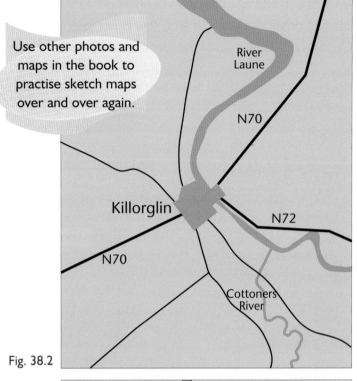

Use other photos and maps in the book to practise sketch maps over and over again.

Fig. 38.2

Roscommon town.

Mark in only those features that are asked for specifically.

Fig. 38.3

Activity

1. Draw a sketch map of the region shown on the Ordnance Survey map. Mark and name the following on it:
   a. Killorglin town
   b. two national secondary roads
   c. five third-class roads
   d. two rivers. (30 marks)

2. Draw a sketch map of the region shown in the photograph. Mark and name the following on it:
   a. a river
   b. the street pattern
   c. the main street
   d. a housing estate
   e. an area of on-street parking
   f. a church
   g. an industrial area. (30 marks)

GEOGRAPHIC INFORMATION SYSTEMS

A **geographic information system** (GIS) is a system for creating, storing, analysing and managing spatial data. In the strictest sense, it is a computer system capable of integrating, storing, editing, analysing, sharing and displaying geographically referenced information. In a more general sense, GIS is a tool that allows users to create interactive queries (user-created searches), analyse the spatial information and edit data.

Geographical information science is the science underlying the applications and systems.

Geographic information systems technology can be used for:

- Scientific investigations.
- Resource management.
- Asset management.
- Environmental impact assessment development planning.
- Cartography (map-making).
- Route planning or town planning.

For example, a GIS might allow emergency planners to calculate emergency response times in the event of a natural disaster, or a GIS might be used to find wetlands that need protection from pollution.

GIS is used in digital mapping of various kinds. Digital maps can hold lots of information about a particular region. All this information can be superimposed so that a greater understanding of a region may be achieved. This information is stored in digital form and can be updated or modified at any time.

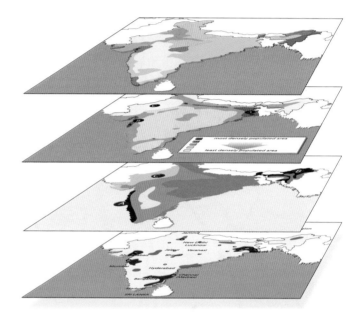

Fig. 38.4

Superimposition of information helps present maps in different layers. Each layer holds information about a particular topic, such as rainfall, hydrology (groundwater), housing, streets and drainage systems. Such related topics present a more complete three-dimensional understanding of pollution control, surface run-off and likely flooding points. The relevant information can be modified and projected outcomes can be viewed. For example, increased rainfall and waterlogging can be inserted to view likely outcomes.

GIS has been increasingly used by commercial bodies in recent years and this demand has funded the rapid growth of this new system of information. New urban developments, such as urban renewal projects, may use GIS to fully understand the factors involved in the building of large multi-storey structures that may house different commercial uses within a central business district in a major city. The manipulation of data allows for the interpretations of different outcomes or may highlight difficulties that may be faced during construction.

This is a three-dimensional computer map of Mt Shasta volcano in California, USA. The image was produced by the shuttle *Endeavor* mapping mission.

271

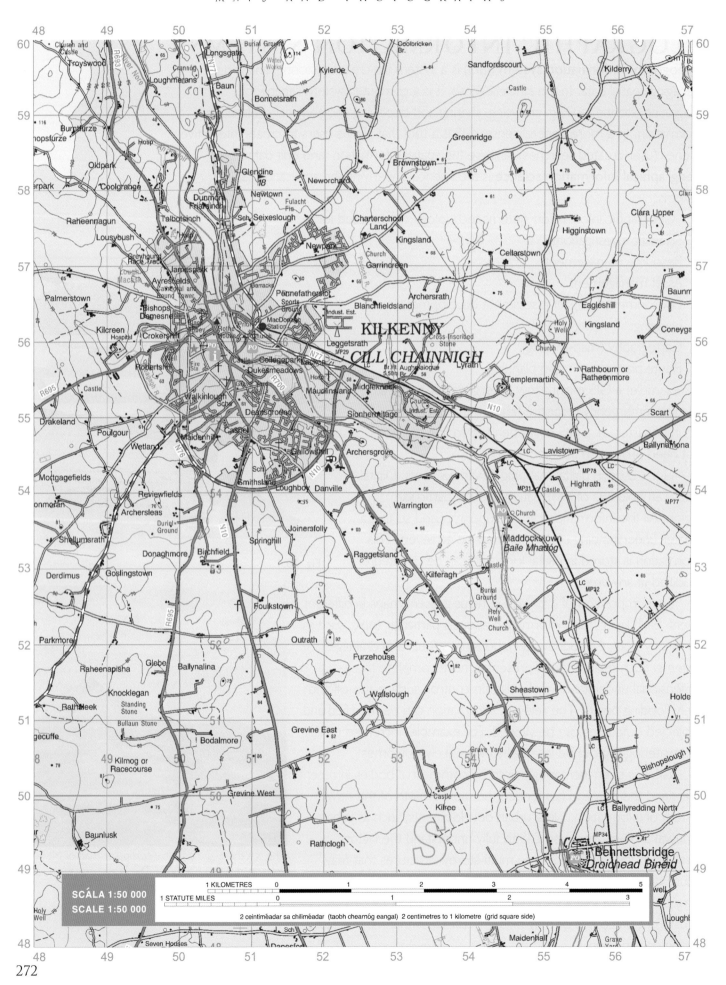

SCÁLA 1:50 000
SCALE 1:50 000

1 KILOMETRES   0   1   2   3   4   5

1 STATUTE MILES   0   1   2   3

2 ceintiméadar sa chiliméadar (taobh chearnóg eangal) 2 centimetres to 1 kilometre (grid square side)

Activity

Ordnance Survey Map

1. Identify by grid reference a suitable site for a major shopping centre. Using map evidence to support your answer, explain two reasons why you chose this site. [20 marks]

2. Describe:
   i. the location of Kilkenny (20 marks)
   ii. the location of Bennettsbridge. [20 marks]

3. The urban region of Kilkenny in the map extract shows evidence of historic development over time. Identify this evidence and explain its importance for the town's development. [30 marks]

4. 'The area shown on the map extract indicates evidence of a wide variety of historic settlement.' Examine this statement using map evidence, with reference to any three aspects of settlement. [30 marks]
   [Leaving Certificate 2006]

5. Draw a sketch map of the region shown on the Ordnance Survey map extract. On it, mark and name:
   i. one national primary route
   ii. one national secondary route
   iii. two regional routes
   iv. a railway
   v. the Nore River
   vi. the urban region of Kilkenny
   vii. one region of coniferous woodland. [20 marks)

Photograph: A Multi-part Question

A. Examine the aerial photograph **and** Ordnance Survey map of Kilkenny, then draw a sketch map of the photograph region. On it, mark and name:
   i. a large river
   ii. any five different land uses. [20 marks]

B. 'Much of Kilkenny's urban region was developed in the twentieth and twenty-first centuries.' Discuss this statement, using evidence from the photograph. [30 marks]

C. 'Kilkenny's urban street pattern poses many traffic problems for urban planners.' Discuss this statement, using evidence from the photograph. [30 marks]

273

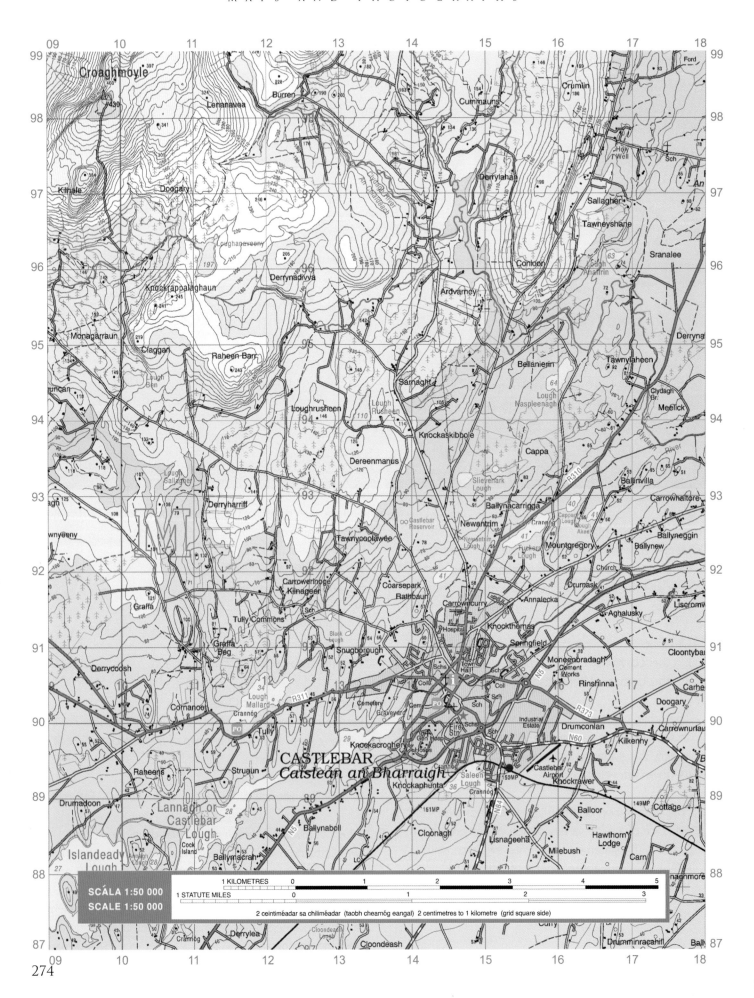

SCÁLA 1:50 000
SCALE 1:50 000

1 KILOMETRES

1 STATUTE MILES

2 ceintiméadar sa chiliméadar (taobh chearnóg eangal) 2 centimetres to 1 kilometre (grid square side)

Ordnance Survey Map

A. Draw a sketch map and on it mark and name the following:

   i.   one major river

   ii. two lakes

   iii. the urban region of Castlebar

   iv. a railway

   v. one national primary route

   vi. one regional route.   [20 marks]

B. 'The urban region of Castlebar shows evidence of many types of services.' With reference to your studies of central place theory and evidence on the photograph, discuss this statement.   [30 marks]

C. The map region of Castlebar displays examples of a number of physical landforms. Name four of these landforms and state whether they are landforms of erosion or deposition.   [20 marks]

D. Use evidence from the map to identify, locate and explain any two types of drainage patterns.   [20 marks]

E. Draw a sketch map of the region. On it, mark and label the major drainage features of the area.   [20 marks]

Photograph and Map

A. Draw a sketch map. On it, mark and label:

   i.   a lake

   ii. a river

   iii. four main streets of Castlebar

   iv. regions of different urban land uses.   [20 marks]

B. Identify the following features on the photograph:

   i.   the lake in the left background

   ii. the route in the right background.   [20 marks]

C. In which direction was the camera pointing when this photograph was taken?   [5 marks]

D. What evidence in the photograph suggests that Castlebar was a planned town? Explain your answer.

     [30 marks]

E. 'The shape and height of many large urban buildings may suggest their functions.' Examine this statement using evidence from the photograph.   [30 marks]

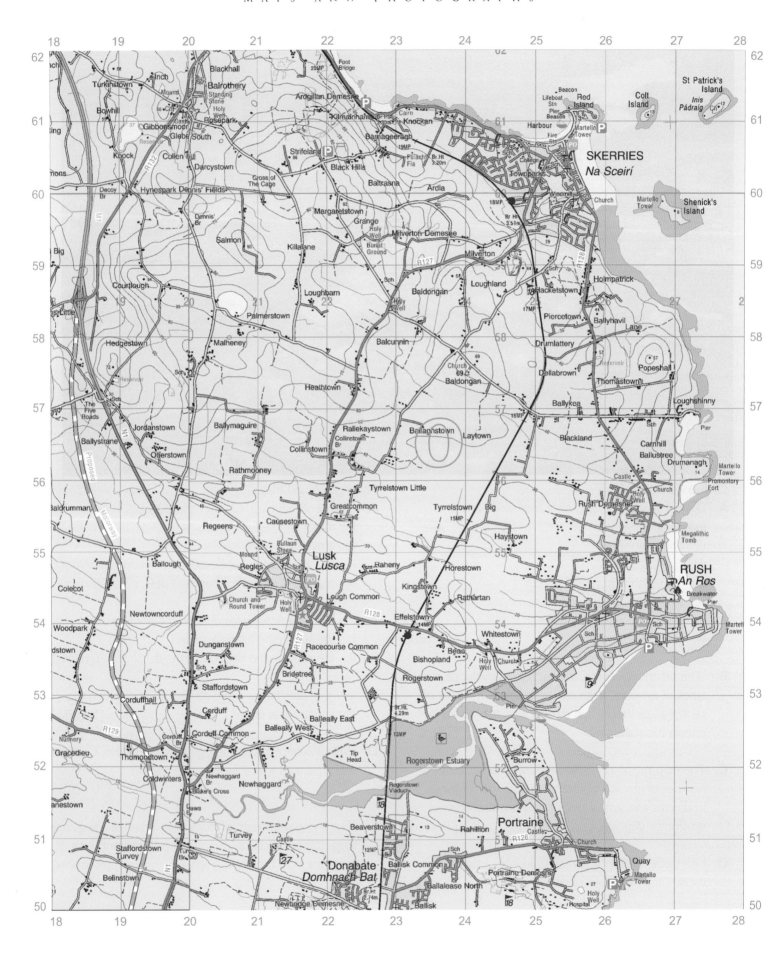

Ordnance Survey Map: North Dublin Region

A.
i. Calculate the approximate area of sea on this map. [10 marks]

ii. Calculate the distance from Lusk at 0 217 544 to the post office at Skerries at 0 251 606. [10 marks]

B. Draw a sketch map of the region. On it mark and label (name) the following:
i. the coastline
ii. one region of coastal deposition
iii. one region of coastal erosion
iv. a nature reserve region
v. one urban region
vi. one motorway
vii. one regional route. [20 marks]

C. Use evidence from the map to explain why the major industrial development in parts of this rural environment could lead to serious environmental pollution of the region. [30 marks]

Photograph of Bray

Carefully examine the photograph of Bray. Then do the following:

a. Draw a sketch map of this region. On it mark and name the following:
i. the coastline
ii. a greenbelt area region
iii. a harbour region
iv. a factory
v. any two other different land uses. [30 marks]

B. Identify two neighbouring land uses where a conflict of interest could arise in future years. Explain any two factors that might cause this conflict. [20 marks]

C. 'Urban planners have tried to create a balance in the pattern of urban development in Bray.' Discuss this statement with reference to evidence on the photograph. [30 marks]

CHAPTER 39
PATTERNS OF ECONOMIC DEVELOPMENT

 **KEY IDEA!**

Economic activities and wealth are unevenly distributed over the earth.

THE MEANING OF ECONOMIC DEVELOPMENT

Almost everyone is in favour of **development**. People may disagree, however, on what development actually means.

Some people feel that development is concerned simply with continued economic growth for the individual and a country. **Economic development** of a region or country is therefore measured in terms of the overall **strength of its economy** and **prosperity of its people**.

Most people, however, now point out that development must also involve **improving the quality of life of all people**, especially those who are poor and weak. This involves issues such as access to good medical care, education and a healthy diet. In effect, a country experiencing high levels of economic development uses its wealth to ensure a good quality of life for most of its population.

Today, economic development is also identified as needing to be **sustainable**. This means that development must not damage the environment or use up the world's resources in such a way that it would interfere with the future development of our planet (see Chapter 63).

Activity
Study the photographs and use the images to explain the meaning of **economic development** and **quality of life.**

The domestic possessions of the Yadev family in India.

The domestic possessions of the Calvin family in the USA.

MEASUREMENT OF ECONOMIC DEVELOPMENT

Gross National Product

The single indicator that is used most frequently to illustrate levels of economic development is the **gross national product per head for population** (GNP per person). It is usually measured in US dollars ($).

Since the price of goods and services differs greatly between countries, the purchasing power of a dollar can vary significantly. For example, in a country such as Ethiopia, one dollar will buy far more than in the United States. In order to take this into account, and to make international comparisons in income levels more effective, we use the term **purchasing power parity** (PPP). This converts a national income to its equivalent in the USA. We note this as **GNP per person (PPP)**. This is the preferred way to illustrate international differences in income.

Economic development can also be measured by a number of other indicators, such as:

- Infant mortality rate.
- Life expectancy.
- Percentage employed in agriculture.
- Literacy rate.

> The GNP of a country is the total value of all output produced by that country's economic activities, including any net income from abroad. Dividing this value by total population provides the average GNP per person.

> The GNP per person in 2005 for Ethiopia was $110. When this is converted to PPP, its value in terms of purchasing power is increased to $810.

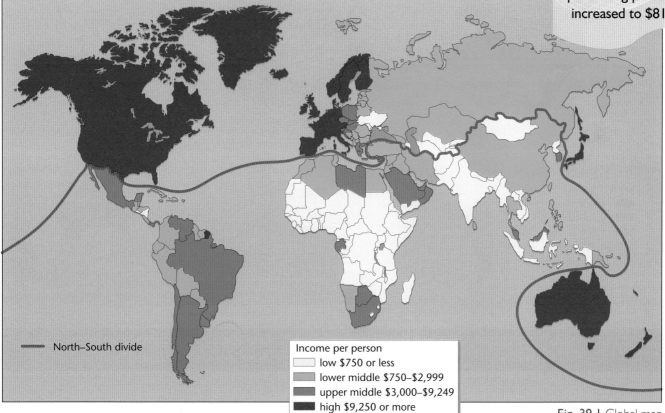

North–South divide

Income per person
- low $750 or less
- lower middle $750–$2,999
- upper middle $3,000–$9,249
- high $9,250 or more

Fig. 39.1 Global map of GNP per person.

Activity

Study Fig. 39.1 and answer the following.

1. Identify the **three** global regions of high income located in the northern hemisphere.
2. What global regions have the lowest levels of income per person?
3. Does GNP per person justify the use of a North-South dividing line to illustrate differences in levels of global development? Explain.

Human Development Index

Economic development is a complex process and involves a number of demographic and social conditions as well as economic factors. As a result, most people think that no single indicator is adequate to illustrate different levels of economic development.

The United Nations has devised a way to measure the complexity of development through its **Human Development Index (HDI)**. This combines **three** different indicators of development:

- Life expectancy (demographic factor).
- GNP per person (PPP) (economic factor).
- Adult literacy rates and enrolments in school (social factor).

By combining these three factors, the HDI is considered to be an effective measure of development. The index has a range of values from 0.0 to 1.0. The higher the value of the HDI, the more developed the national economy (Fig. 39.2 and Table 39.1).

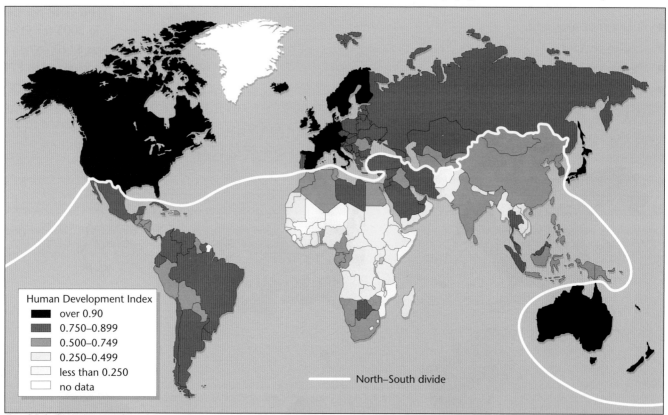

Human Development Index
- over 0.90
- 0.750–0.899
- 0.500–0.749
- 0.250–0.499
- less than 0.250
- no data

—— North–South divide

Fig. 39.2 Global map of the Human Development Index.

	GNP per Person ($PPP)	Infant Mortality Rate 1	Literacy Rate 2	Poverty Rate 3	HDI
USA	41,950	6	100	–	0.941
Ireland	34,720	5	100	–	0.946
India	3,460	55	61	35	0.602
Ethiopia	810	110	41	31	0.367

Table 39.1 Sample indicators of development in selected countries.

Rate 1: Per 1,000 live births.
Rate 2: Percentage of relevant age group enrolled in secondary education.
Rate 3: Percentage of population living on less than $1 a day.

Activity

Study Fig. 39.2 and Table 39.1 and answer the following.

1. What global regions have the lowest levels of HDI?
2. Why are the levels so low in these regions?
3. Which global regions have the highest levels of HDI?
4. Compare Fig. 39.2 with Fig. 39.1. Do you see a relationship between levels of HDI and GNP per person?
5. Use Table 39.1 to discuss differences in levels of economic development between Ireland, India and Ethiopia.

UNEVEN ECONOMIC DEVELOPMENT

For geographers, perhaps the most important characteristic of global development is its uneven distribution (Table 39.1 and Figs. 39.1 and 39.2).

The majority of people living in countries in the northern hemisphere have relatively high incomes and a good quality of life. This contrasts with the extreme poverty that affects large numbers of people living in the tropical zone and southern hemisphere.

The scale of the problem is illustrated by the number of people living on less than one dollar a day (Fig. 39.3). This suggests that a huge effort will be necessary by richer countries if economic development is to take off in regions such as sub-Saharan Africa and south Asia, and their large populations are to begin to enjoy the benefits of a higher quality of life.

> Eighty per cent of global wealth is produced by 15 per cent of the world's population living in a small group of countries located mainly in the northern hemisphere.

> Approximately 20 per cent (1.2 billion) of the world's population lives on less than one dollar a day.

> The world's richest 1 per cent of people receive as much income as the poorest 57 per cent.

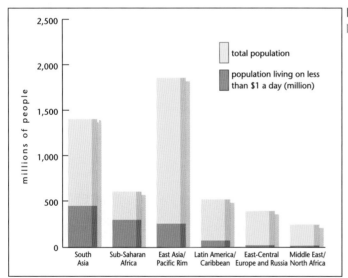

Fig. 39.3 Distribution of population living on less than US$1 a day.

Activity

Study Fig. 39.3 and answer the following.

1. What global regions have the greatest number of people living in extreme poverty?
2. Estimate the percentage of people living on less than one dollar a day in sub-Saharan Africa.
3. Suggest some reasons as to why so many people are living in extreme poverty in this region. (See Figs. 39.4 and 39.5.)

In India, an estimated one-third of the population lives on less than a dollar a day.

● *Suggest why this is a problem for the development of this country.*

281

UNEVEN PATTERNS OF AGRICULTURAL AND INDUSTRIAL ACTIVITIES

The wealth of a country is strongly influenced by its levels of:

● Agricultural development.

● Industrial development.

> Over 50 per cent of all workers in the world are engaged in agricultural activities.

The Role of Agriculture

Despite being recognised generally as a declining economic sector, especially in terms of job opportunities and wealth creation, agriculture has a powerful influence on patterns of development.

The role of agriculture is particularly important in influencing low levels of income and quality of life within less developed countries (see Fig. 39.4). This is related to:

● Few alternative prospects for employment – large numbers of people are forced to remain in farming.

● Severe population pressure on a limited land area means that subsistence farming dominates most areas.

● Difficult environmental conditions, such as drought, low soil fertility and soil erosion, add to the problems of productive farming.

● Low levels of education make it difficult to introduce new farming skills and techniques.

● Poor access to markets.

● The price of cash crops, such as coffee and rubber, is unstable in world trade and profits are often low.

Farming in Ethiopia, in sub-Saharan Africa, and the Paris Basin in France.

● *Describe the contrasting farming activities and environments, and explain which provides a higher standard of living.*

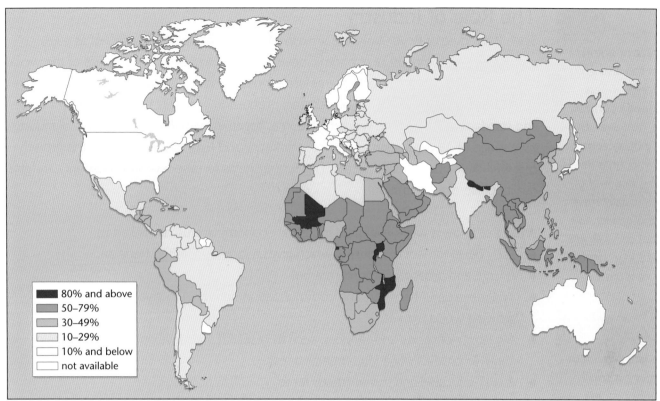

Fig. 39.4 World map of employment in agriculture.

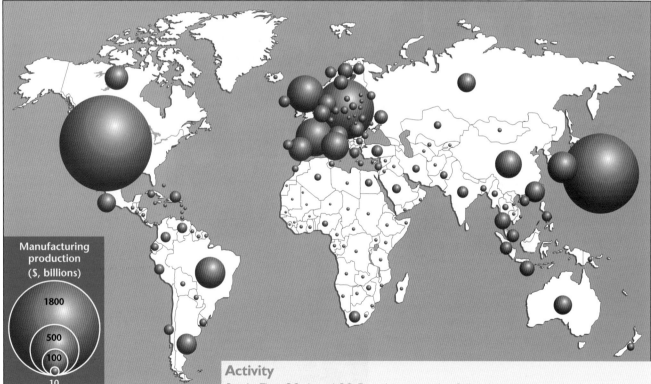

Fig. 39.5 World map of industrial production.

Activity

Study Figs. 39.4 and 39.5 and answer the following.

1. Identify the global regions that have the lowest and highest dependency on agricultural employment.
2. Identify the global regions that dominate industrial production.
3. Which continent shows the lowest levels of industrial production? Explain.
4. What general conclusions do you make when comparing the maps in Figs. 39.4 and 39.5 with those in Figs. 39.1 and 39.2?

The Role of Industry

Since the Industrial Revolution, the growth of industry has been recognised as a key sector for the promotion of economic development. However, not all areas of the world have been successful in attracting large-scale industrialisation (see Fig. 39.5).

Countries with high levels of industrial production generally benefit from high wages and standards of living. The workers' income, together with the requirements of industry for a range of services, such as finance, marketing and legal, also encourage the growth of a well-developed service sector. This further helps to raise levels of prosperity and the quality of life of a population.

Areas that show a well-developed industrial economy are usually linked to:
- Early development of industry, which gives a long-established tradition.
- A large and prosperous home market.
- Well-developed transport and communication networks to give access to the growing world market.
- Availability of capital and services, such as research and development, which help improve productivity and competitiveness.
- A well-educated and skilled labour force.

Employment in services has also grown strongly in less developed countries. Here, however, the poor industrial base and low income levels for the majority of people usually mean that the quality and range of services are limited, e.g. street vendors.

In the late twentieth century, a small number of less developed countries significantly increased their industrial economy. This was based on strong government support and a relatively cheap but flexible labour force. These are called newly industrialised countries (NICs). Examples include Singapore, South Korea and Mexico.

Industrial development in many less developed countries often involves large numbers of females and children who work for low wages in sweatshops.
- *Why do you think they are called sweatshops?*

The busy trading port of Pusan in South Korea illustrates the success of this country's recent industrial development. South Korea is termed a newly industrialised country.

UNEVEN DEVELOPMENT IN THE EUROPEAN UNION

Although the European Union (EU) is one of the three most developed global regions, considerable differences in levels of economic development exist within its boundaries. These differences occur between countries and within each of the member states (see Fig. 39.6).

At the EU level, a well-defined axis of urban-industrial development can be identified from Manchester to Milan. Increasingly, however, the core of prosperity is centred around the Alps in southern Germany and northern Italy. This contrasts with an extensive area of low income levels in the EU's Mediterranean periphery and, more especially, in its new eastern periphery.

Each country of the EU has its core and periphery, and significant differences in economic development exist between them. One of the best examples of this is between the well-developed north of Italy and the country's underdeveloped Mezzogiorno in the south (see Chapter 27).

> Greater London, the richest region in the EU, is almost ten times as prosperous as the poorest regions located in central and eastern Europe.

> Recall the meaning of core and peripheral regions.

Milan forms part of the core of the EU.
● *What evidence can be seen in the photograph which supports the fact that this is one of the richest cities in the EU?*

The peripheral location and difficult environmental conditions, especially in the Apennines, continue to make the Mezzogiorno one of the least developed regions in the EU.
● *Refer to the photograph to justify this statement.*

Ireland was once an underdeveloped and peripheral economy of the EU. In the 1990s, however, Ireland's economy developed strongly and now its GDP per person is well above the EU average. Most development occurred in the more prosperous S&E Region. Although the BMW Region remains relatively underdeveloped in an Irish context, its levels of prosperity are well above those found in the new member states.

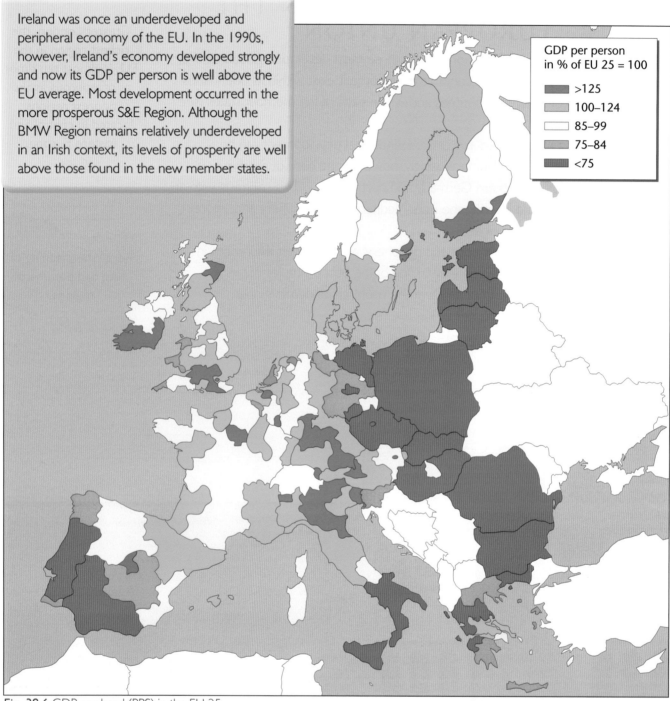

GDP per person
in % of EU 25 = 100

- \>125
- 100–124
- 85–99
- 75–84
- \<75

Fig. 39.6 GDP per head (PPS) in the EU 25.

Activity

Study Fig. 39.6 and answer the following.

1. What countries or regions form the underdeveloped Mediterranean periphery of the EU? Justify your selection.
2. Identify the Manchester–Milan axis. Suggest reasons why this axis is so wealthy.
3. What is the dominant characteristic of member states that joined the EU in 2004 and 2007? Will this be a problem for the EU?

CHAPTER 40
CHANGING PATTERNS OF GLOBAL ECONOMIC DEVELOPMENT

 **KEY IDEA!** Economic development is not only unevenly distributed, but levels of development also change over time.

Economic development should not be seen as being static. It is, above all, **a dynamic process that results in significant changes in levels of development over time.** Generally, **five changes** are considered important for a region to become economically developed:

- **Change in the structure of the economy:** This usually involves a shift from dominance of the primary sector (especially agriculture) to a greater role for industry and services. This creates a greater range of well-paid jobs and generates high-value manufactured goods and financial services.

- **Changes in the use and levels of technology:** High productivity levels are often linked to the successful introduction and promotion of new technology. This can involve the use of new machinery, computers and other labour-saving practices. It helps regional and national economies to be more competitive in trade and increases prosperity.

- **Changes in the forms of economic organisation:** This involves a shift away from a relatively localised and simple way of life (subsistence) to one that demands more complex management. These tend to be larger-scale organisations that operate in the more competitive national or international market, e.g. big businesses replacing small family workshops, and large shopping centres, which can cause the closure of small, community-based shops.

> Economic development is a process of change that affects the make-up of a region's economy, together with its levels of prosperity.

Large areas of India continue to depend on agricultural practices that have changed little over the centuries.

- *Describe the farming activity and suggest the crop being planted.*

An automated assembly line using robots at a Ford vehicle plant in Germany.

- *Do such plants result in an increase in productivity and employment?*

287

Economic development in less developed countries often involves multinational companies.
- *In what ways can such companies help economic development?*

Changes to the economic well-being: Economic development is expected to bring an improvement to the quality of life of a region's population. This involves improvements in services such as health care, education and housing. It is also expected to upgrade a region's transport systems and energy supplies to improve prospects for development.

A school classroom in Uganda in sub-Saharan Africa. Here, there are 100 pupils to each teacher and six pupils to every textbook.
- *Why is education important for economic development?*

Changes in the volume and composition of trade: Economic development is strongly influenced by a country's ability to increase the volume and value of its trade. This is particularly important in terms of exports in order for a country to achieve a positive balance of trade. Through this, money flows into a country and this can be used to promote economic development. To raise the value of exports, it is important for a country to shift its dependency from relatively low-priced primary goods, such as foodstuffs and raw materials, to higher-valued industrial goods and services.

What is meant by balance of trade? Why is a positive balance of trade important for economic development?

CHANGES TO GLOBAL PATTERNS OF ECONOMIC DEVELOPMENT

Since the end of the Second World War, the world economy has grown strongly. This has led to an increase in levels of development for most countries. Fig. 40.1 illustrates changes in four key indicators that are used to measure education, health and income.

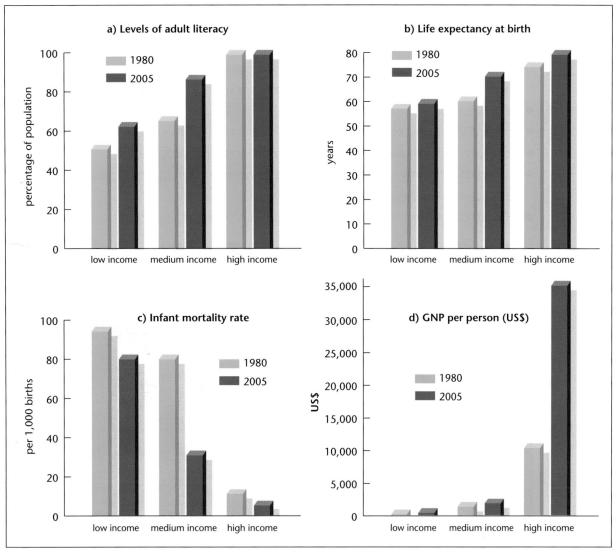

Fig. 40.1 Changes in economic development in high-, medium- and low-income regions of the world economy, 1980–2005.

Activity

Study Fig. 40.1 and answer the following.

1. Describe the development trends shown by the indicators.
2. Apart from GNP per person, why does the high-income region show relatively small improvements in quality of life indicators?
3. Explain the link between income levels and quality of life indicators in the low-income region.

While most countries have shared to some extent in the process of economic development, the richer countries have shown a remarkable ability to capture most of the increases in wealth. In this way, the prosperity gap between the richest and poorest countries and regions of the world has increased over time. Clearly, many countries in the less developed world, and especially those in sub-Saharan Africa, have experienced major difficulties in advancing their levels of economic development.

SUB-SAHARAN AFRICA – THE WORLD'S PROBLEM REGION

Fourteen of the twenty poorest countries in the world are located in sub-Saharan Africa. Many of these countries have become poorer since the 1990s. This can be linked to:

- Warfare and civil disturbances.
- Political instability, which deters investment from multinational companies (MNCs).
- Environmental problems, e.g. droughts and increasing desertification.
- Failure to industrialise and reduce overdependency on the primary sector for employment and export earnings.
- Health crisis linked to AIDS (almost one in ten of the adult population has the virus).

> Sub-Saharan Africa means the part of Africa that is south of the Sahara.

Many wars have broken out within and between countries in sub-Saharan Africa.

- *Why do you think these have a negative impact on development?*

	1990	2004
Population (millions)	418	726
GNP (US$, billions)	161	440
GNP per person (US$)	385	606
Life expectancy	50	46
Infant mortality (per thousand all births)	104	101
Literacy rate (%)	45	62
Debt total (US$, billions)	63	235
Debt as % of GNP	39	53
Poverty (% population living on <$1 a day)	48	46

Table 40.1 Selected development indicators for sub-Saharan Africa, 1990–2004.

Activity

Use the information in Table 40.1 to justify the belief that sub-Saharan Africa is the world's problem region.

At the start of the twenty-first century, levels of global inequality continue to increase. By 2000, the United Nations Report on Human Development described inequalities in income and living standards as having reached grotesque proportions. Clearly, much work needs to be done if we are to experience a more balanced distribution in global economic development.

Activity

Study the cartoons above and answer the following.

1. Discuss what messages the cartoonist presents in trends in world development.
2. In what ways do you think inequalities in world development are grotesque?

CHAPTER 41
ECONOMIC DEVELOPMENT AND REGIONAL CHANGE IN IRELAND

 **KEY IDEA!**

East–west differences in economic development in Ireland have changed since political independence in 1922.

Regional development in Ireland is uneven. In particular, a **strong east–west divide between a more developed east and an underdeveloped west highlights the human geography of the country.** The nature and the extent of this divide have, however, changed since independence. This can be seen in terms of both manufacturing and service industries.

> Review Chapter 26 to recall the major contrasts between the east and west of Ireland.

MANUFACTURING INDUSTRIES

Before independence in 1922, few industries were located in Ireland. Since then, however, the number and type of industries have grown substantially through four periods. These periods have had different impacts on the east and west of Ireland.

1922–61

In 1926, only 10 per cent of Ireland's workforce was employed in manufacturing. Over one-third of these were in Dublin.

> A policy of protection means placing tariffs on imports. This raises their costs and allows less efficient Irish industries to compete in the home market.

To promote development, the government adopted a policy of protection. This meant protecting the country's few industries from cheaper imports, and allowed Irish industries, such as clothing, shoes, food and drink, to grow.

These industries all showed a strong preference to locate in Dublin. Apart from some growth in other major cities, such as Cork, the rest of Ireland showed slow growth or decline in manufacturing employment (see Fig. 41.1).

From 1926 to 1961, the east–west divide increased as Dublin dominated industrial development.

1961–81

> See Chapter 47 for a fuller explanation of branch plants and multinational corporations.

During this period, the policy of protection was replaced by one of **free trade** and attracting **multinational companies** (MNCs). This was successful and many branch plants of multinational companies located in Ireland.

These new branch plants were **footloose industries**. Their main concern was to find **low-cost locations** to mass-produce basic industrial goods. As a result, they showed a strong preference to locate their factories in rural areas and small towns. The result was large employment gains for western Ireland (see Fig. 41.1).

In contrast, Dublin and other large cities, such as Cork, proved less attractive for MNCs. **From 1961–81, the manufacturing gap between east and west was therefore reduced.**

Factories, such as this one located outside Charleston in Co. Mayo, show the attraction of rural environments for footloose industries.

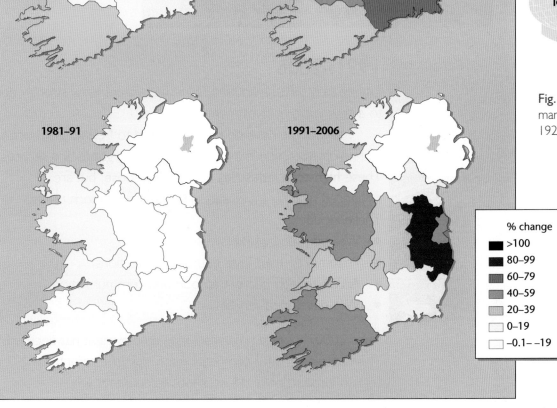

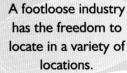

A footloose industry has the freedom to locate in a variety of locations.

Fig. 41.1 Regional trends in manufacturing employment, 1926–2006.

% change	
■	>100
■	80–99
▨	60–79
▨	40–59
▨	20–39
□	0–19
□	–0.1– –19

1981–91

As a result of economic recession in the 1980s:

- Fewer MNCs were attracted to Ireland, while many branch plants were closed or reduced their workforce.
- The closure of many traditional Irish industries caused large job losses.

Although growth of industrial employment in the West of Ireland slowed down compared to 1961–81, it performed better than the urban regions. Cork, and especially Dublin, experienced significant declines in their industrial workforce.

In the 1980s, therefore, the industrial divide between east and west was further reduced.

The site of the Ford and Dunlop factories along the inner quays of the port of Cork and close to the city centre. Both factories closed in 1984 with the loss of 2,500 jobs.
- *Suggest reasons why this inner city location became less attractive by the 1980s.*

Activity
Use the four location factors listed as important for the period 1991–2006 to explain why the industrial divide between east and west increased during the Celtic Tiger economy.

1991–2006

During the 1990s, manufacturing employment grew strongly due to a new wave of investment by MNCs.

Many of the new industries attracted to Ireland use modern technology to produce a range of high-value goods and services. These **high-tech industries** are also **footloose**, but are influenced by different locational factors from branch plants. These include:

- Well-educated workers.
- Proximity to third-level education institutions.
- Access to high-quality transport and communications.
- Well-developed services.

Since 2000, however, manufacturing employment has declined. This is due to greater competition for new investment, rising costs of production and loss of jobs to countries where labour costs are lower.

Park West Industrial and Business Park in Dublin.
- *Use the photograph to suggest reasons for its development at this location.*

SERVICE INDUSTRIES

1922–61

Service industries show a strong preference to locate in large urban centres. As a result, service employment in Ireland focused on the more urbanised eastern region. Dublin in particular dominated the country's service sector.

The **West of Ireland**, therefore, not only failed to attract manufacturing industries during this period, but also **failed to develop an effective services sector**. This widened the east–west development gap.

1961–91

Employment in services grew rapidly in this period due to:

- Increasing population.
- Industrial development.
- Increasing income levels.

Dublin is the centre of government and most key services. This dominance has restricted the growth of strong regional centres.
- *Can you locate the new International Financial Services Centre (IFSC) on the left bank of the Liffey and the growing complex of high-rise office blocks on the right bank?*

Although services employment increased in all regions, the East region, centred in Dublin, benefited the most (see Fig. 41.2). In addition, Dublin and other key cities, such as Cork, Galway and Limerick, attracted most of the high-value office employment, e.g. banking and financial services. Dublin, above all, gained from this **centralisation of services** and increased its role as the **dominant decision-making centre in Ireland**.

In contrast to manufacturing, therefore, **trends in services did not result in a narrowing of the development gap between the east and west of Ireland**. Large areas of the West of Ireland depend on Dublin for many high-value services.

> Almost 40 per cent of all new service jobs created in Ireland between 1991 and 2006 were located in the eastern region, centred on Dublin.

1991–2006

All regions benefited from a strong growth in services (see Fig. 41.2). The high-value and well-paid office employment continues, however, to prefer locations in major cities, especially Dublin. By 2006, almost 50 per cent of Ireland's total service employment was located in Dublin and the adjoining Mid-East region (Fig. 41.2).

During the 1990s, a new factor emerged to influence the regional pattern of services. This was the inward investment of **footloose international service industries.** One element of this has been the relocation to Ireland of routine **back-office functions** of large international companies.

The vast majority of these back offices are located in Dublin because of its large pool of educated workers and excellent telecommunication systems.

Therefore, in addition to its national dominance, **Dublin has gained a new international role within the global economy.** This emphasises the historical development gap between the east and west in Ireland. It furthermore suggests that the gap may widen in the future.

Back-office functions involve routine work and require little face-to-face contact, e.g. processing insurance claims and ticket reservations through the use of modern telecommunications.

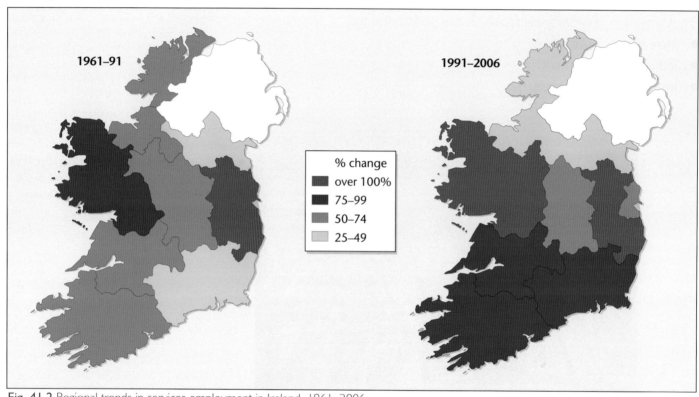

Fig. 41.2 Regional trends in services employment in Ireland, 1961–2006.

1961–91

1991–2006

% change
over 100%
75–99
50–74
25–49

Activity

Study Fig. 41.2 and answer the following.

1. Which region has shown the greatest growth in services employment? Suggest reasons for this.
2. Suggest a reason why the West region showed relatively high growth rates for services during both periods.
3. In general, do rural regions prove to be more attractive locations than urban centres for services? Why?

The city of Galway, with its attractive urban environment, university and growing number of high-tech industries, has emerged as a major growth centre for services in the West of Ireland. Note the new ring road and the expanding urban developments beyond this ring road.

Case Study: Services in Dublin

Two good examples of the rapid growth and centralisation of services in Dublin are customer contact centres (call centres) and the International Financial Services Centre (IFSC).

Customer Contact Centres

Since the 1990s, a growing number of international customer contact centres have been attracted to Ireland. Strong government support, high-quality telecommunications and a cheap but well-educated workforce have been vital for this development (see Fig. 41.3).

By 2005, some sixty of these centres had located in Ireland, employing over 20,000 people. **Approximately half of these jobs are located in Dublin.**

Customer contact centres have located outside Dublin. However, concerns over access to enough qualified workers, especially with language skills, as well as less developed services in smaller towns, have caused most of these centres to select the larger regional centres.

IFSC

In 1988, the IFSC was opened. This was the centrepiece of a major scheme aimed at revitalising a large area of underutilised or derelict land along Dublin's inner quays.

By providing generous financial incentives, the plan was to attract footloose international financial services to Dublin. The scheme has been remarkably successful. Dublin is now an important financial centre within the EU. This further adds to its international image to attract more high-quality service employment.

> A customer contact centre is a central location from which services, such as technical support and sales, are provided to a dispersed customer base through the use of the telephone and the internet.

> In 2005, some 12,000 of the 25,000 jobs in international financial services in Ireland were located at the IFSC in Dublin.

Fig. 41.3 Ireland: the call centre of Europe.

The IFSC is located on the site of the inner quays in the old port of Dublin.
- *Use this photograph to suggest how the IFSC has helped to change the image, function and types of employment in this historic area.*

Activity

What do you think this Industrial Development Agency (IDA) advert is suggesting in order to attract inward investment of call centres?

297

CHAPTER 42
CHANGING PATTERNS OF ECONOMIC DEVELOPMENT IN BELGIUM

KEY IDEA! The core region of Belgium's economy has changed from Wallonia to Flanders.

In 1953, there were 123 coal mines in Wallonia, employing 120,000 miners. The last mine closed in 1984.

Since the 1950s, Belgium's core region for economic development has shifted from Wallonia in the south to Flanders in the north (Fig. 42.1). This is due to three processes which have affected each region differently:

- Decline of mining and heavy industries.
- Changing locational preferences of modern, footloose industries.
- Increasing importance of services as a growth sector.

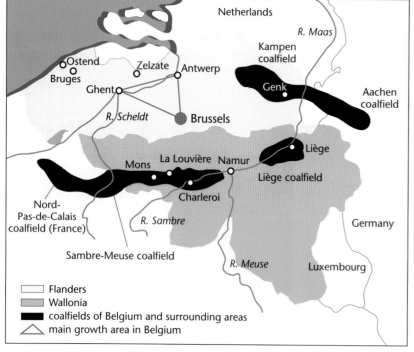

Fig. 42.1 Belgium, Flanders and Wallonia.

Activity

Study Fig. 42.1 and answer the following.

1. Which region possessed the major Belgian coalfields?
2. In which region is the present growth area located?
3. What three towns form Belgium's growth triangle?

Wallonia: The Historic Core Region

Belgium's main coalfields are located in Wallonia. This led to the large-scale development of mining and heavy industries throughout the Sambre-Meuse Valley and around Liège. The coalfields enjoyed great prosperity from about 1800 to the 1950s.

Since the 1950s, exhausted coal seams, falling productivity and rising costs meant that the region's coal and heavy industries could not compete against cheaper imports. For communities dependent on these industries, closure of the mines and decline of the steel industry resulted in large-scale unemployment.

Wallonia has become a depressed region at the heart of the EU.
Without Belgian and EU funding, decline would have been greater. Support was given to:

- Modernise the region's declining steel industry to protect some jobs.
- Retrain workers, improve transport systems and clean up the despoiled environment.
- Attract new industries and services.

In spite of this, industrial employment has been more than halved since 1975, while the depressed regional economy has been less attractive than Flanders for high-value services (see Fig. 42.2). One important result has been a large and continuous movement of people from Wallonia to Flanders and Brussels. This further depresses the economic and cultural position of Wallonia.

> Revise the development and decline of the Sambre-Meuse Valley in Chapter 24.

One of the many large coal mines that closed in the Sambre Meuse Valley in the 1980s.
- *Use the photograph to suggest some consequences of closure for local communities and the environment.*

> After 150 years of dominance, Wallonia's core status has been replaced by Flanders.

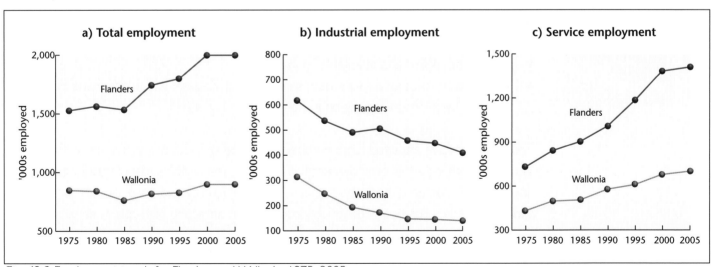

Fig. 42.2 Employment trends for Flanders and Wallonia, 1975–2005.

Antwerp is the third-largest port in the EU and has been a critical factor in attracting a large amount of industrial investment to Flanders.

Along with Antwerp and Brussels, the historic city of Ghent forms Belgium's triangle of growth.
- *Compare this photograph with that on page 299.*
  Why is Ghent more attractive for modern service industries and tourism?

Flanders: Belgium's Modern Core Region

Before the Second World War, small traditional industries in Flanders could not compete with the large-scale factories of Wallonia. Many were closed and large numbers of Flemish people were forced to migrate to the prosperous coalfields of Wallonia.

Since the 1960s, however, Flanders has experienced significant economic growth. This is due to:

- Its central location and excellent transport networks to access major markets in Belgium and the EU.
- Its access to Antwerp, Europe's third-largest port and the most important industrial centre in Flanders.
- Its attractive environment and many historic towns as locations for high-quality service sectors.
- Its growing, skilled and adaptable workforce.
- The decision to open a major new steelworks at Zelzate, which has made Flanders the main steel-producing region in Belgium (see Fig. 42.1).

These factors have attracted large numbers of modern, footloose industries to Flanders. Thus, although industrial employment has declined, the region's manufacturing base is now mainly made up of growth sectors such as electronics and pharmaceuticals. In addition, Flanders has been remarkably successful in attracting high-quality service jobs, especially those in business and financial services. This suggests that **prospects for continued growth and prosperity in Flanders are strong, and it will remain a core region of the EU.**

Between 1975 and 2005, 90 per cent of the net gain in total employment for both Wallonia and Flanders was located in Flanders.

CHAPTER 43
COLONIALISM AND DEVELOPMENT

 **KEY IDEA!**

Colonialism led to the exploitation of large areas of the world in the interests of a small number of powerful countries.

Historically, **colonialism** is linked to a small number of European states which extended their economic and political control over large areas of the world (Fig. 43.1). In this way, **colonialism had a major impact in changing the patterns of world development**.

The Objectives of Colonialism

Name some colonial powers in addition to Britain.

- To control and exploit the **raw materials and food produce of colonies**. These were vital to supply the growing economies and populations of colonial powers.
- Colonies would provide **markets** for goods manufactured by the colonial power.
- Control over large areas of the world and the growing trade patterns linked to colonialism would increase the **political importance and wealth of colonial powers**.

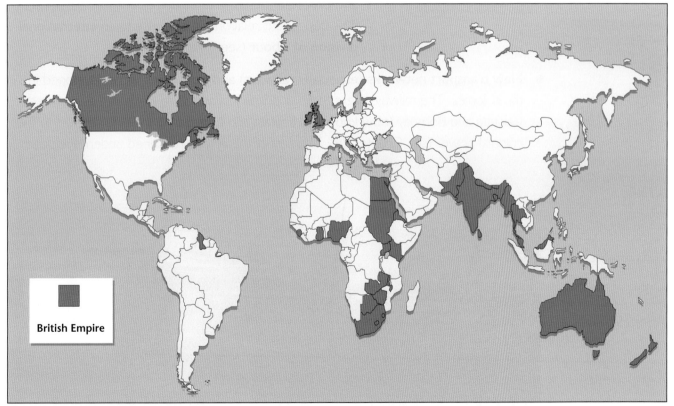

British Empire

Fig. 43.1 Britain's colonial empire in 1914.
- *At this time, the British Empire controlled 25 per cent of the world's population and land area. Why was it described as an empire 'on which the sun never sets'?*

An advertisement c.1860 for the British tea company, Lipton. Note the images used to illustrate work on the tea plantation and trade links to Britain.

The Impacts of Colonialism

- Most colonies changed from being generally self-sufficient to **specialising in a narrow range of primary products**. For example, local food crops were replaced by plantation farming, and cash crops, such as bananas, coffee and rubber, were exported to meet the needs of the colonial power.

- Before colonialism, countries now considered to be underdeveloped dominated global manufacturing output (see Table 43.1). Under colonialism, however, their **domestic industries were run down**. This was done to remove competition from industrial goods made in countries like Britain, which were exported to their colonies. By the First World War, manufacturing activities in the colonies had almost ceased. **Colonialism, therefore, contributed to major changes in patterns of global manufacturing.**

- Colonialism created **a new and dependent pattern in world trade**. Colonies **specialised in producing primary goods for export** to colonial powers. In contrast, countries like Britain specialised in industrial production and exported these higher-valued goods to their colonies. This dependent relationship gave rise to an **international division of labour** (see Chapter 51).

- **New transport networks (especially railways) and port cities** were developed in the colonies. The railways were to bring primary products to key port cities, such as Calcutta and Bombay (now known as Kolkata and Mumbai) in India, for export to their colonial power (see Chapter 29). The rest of the colony remained underdeveloped.

British sailing ships and local fishing boats crowd into Calcutta Harbour (c. 1860).

- *What role did such ports play to allow colonial powers to dominate these colonies?*

	1750	1830	1913
Developed market economies	27	40	93
e.g. Britain	2	10	14
USA	–	2	3
Underdeveloped economies	73	60	7
e.g. India	25	18	1

Table 43.1 Changing patterns of world manufacturing output (%).

Activity

Study Table 43.1 and answer the following.
1. What part of the world economy dominated manufacturing before the Industrial Revolution?
2. In what ways do the 1913 patterns differ from 1750?
3. Suggest reasons for the different trends for Britain and India.

● Colonialism is an **exploitative process** by which colonial powers dominate their colonies. This increases the wealth of the colonial power, but results in the underdevelopment of the colonies.

Case Study: India – A Changing Colonial Economy

Before independence in 1947, India had long been exploited as a British colony. Such was its importance for Britain's empire that it was known as 'the jewel in the British Crown'.

Until the early 1800s, India's large population and raw material base supported a variety of important craft industries, especially textiles. These were all run down to allow British goods to gain access to a large, new market. So, as India's population increased, its industrial economy collapsed under colonialism (Table 43.1).

India specialised in exporting primary commodities such as cotton, tea, jute and spices to Britain. Taxation of the large population also added greatly to Britain's wealth. Key port cities such as Bombay, Calcutta and Madras (now known as Chennai) developed under colonialism, although most of India remained underdeveloped and dependent upon a poor, subsistence economy.

Do you think these impacts of colonialism can be applied to Ireland, which was a colony of Britain until 1921?

'[British rule] has impoverished the people [of India] by a system of progressive exploitation . . . It has reduced us politically to serfdom.'
M. Gandhi, 1930

CHAPTER 44
DECOLONISATION AND ADJUSTMENTS TO THE WORLD ECONOMY

 **KEY IDEA!** Despite gaining political independence after the Second World War, most former colonies remain underdeveloped and economically dependent on core economies.

Find out more on the debt crisis in Chapter 45.

Interest repayments on debt amounts to over $260 billion. This is a huge loss of much-needed money for developing countries.

After the Second World War, most colonies gained political independence. This is a process called **decolonisation**. To help newly independent states adjust to the new world economy, a number of strategies have been used. These include:

- Borrowing in order to finance development.
- Attracting new industries.
- Trade policies.

Borrowing

Colonialism left most colonies with little capital for development. Borrowing large sums of money from developed countries to help modernise their infrastructures, such as transport and energy systems, seemed an easy option. However, because of high interest rates, less developed countries have been unable to pay back their loans. This is called the **debt crisis** (Table 44.1).

Bono of U2 has become a major campaigner to reduce world poverty. This involves cancelling the debt and increasing aid to less developed countries.

- *Do you agree with these proposals?*

To help meet repayments, most less developed countries have reduced their spending on important social programmes, such as health care and education. The result has been a decline in the quality of life for many people in less developed countries.

Large-scale borrowing has further increased their dependency on core economics.

	Total Debt ($ billion)	Debt as % of GNP	Interest Repayments as % of Export Earnings
Sub-Saharan Africa	235	53	10
Brazil	235	49	47
India	113	20	19

Table 44.1 Examples of the scale of world debt, 2005.

Activity

Study the information in Table 44.1 and answer the following.
1. Why do countries in Sub-Saharan Africa need to borrow?
2. Does the final column suggest Brazil faces a major problem in repaying its debt?
3. Do you think India has a major debt problem?

Attraction of New Industrial Development

From the 1960s, large multinational companies (MNCs) emerged as a powerful force for industrial development. As part of their plans to serve the growing and more competitive world market, MNCs began to invest in low-cost locations in less developed countries.

Branch plants of MNCs therefore became an important new element in the economies of some developing countries. These rely on low-cost labour to produce basic goods which require few skills. This led to a **new international division of labour** (see pages 337–9). It also allowed developing countries to increase their share of world manufacturing output (see Fig. 47.3 on page 321).

A small number of less developed countries, however, have created a strong industrial sector. These are called **newly industrialising countries (NICs)**. However, the vast majority of less developed countries remain underdeveloped and continue to depend on the export of primary products (see Fig. 44.1). **Sub-Saharan Africa** in particula has found great difficulty in attracting new industries due to wars, corruption and poverty.

Recent decisions by the world's richest countries have cancelled large amounts of debt and have reduced the problem of repaying debts in the world's poorest countries.

For a fuller account of MNCs in global development, see Chapter 47.

Eighty per cent of all manufactured exports from developing countries are sourced in only ten NICs.

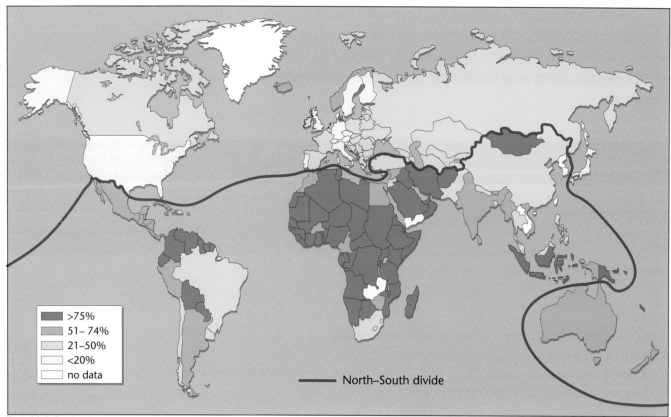

Fig. 44.1 Percentage share of exports held by primary goods.

Legend:
- >75%
- 51–74%
- 21–50%
- <20%
- no data

North–South divide

Activity

Study Fig. 44.1 and answer the following.

1. Which world region is most dependent on the export of primary goods? Suggest reasons why.
2. Why is dependency on the export of primary goods so low in developed countries?
3. What level of dependency does India have on the export of primary goods? Do you expect this to fall?

Farm workers in Honduras cleaning their crop of coffee beans. Many developing countries remain highly dependent on exporting primary products such as coffee.

- *Why is this a problem for their economic development?*

Trade Policies

On gaining independence, many countries placed taxes, called tariffs, on imported goods. This was to protect home industries from cheaper imports. Today, however, **free trade** dominates the global economy.

Free trade removes restrictions for international trade and **encourages the export of goods for which a country has a comparative advantage**. This has helped increase trade for most less developed countries. Their comparative advantage, however, remains in the production of primary goods and low-value, basic industrial products.

After some fifty years of political independence, most less developed countries continue to depend on core economies. This favours rich, core economies and is termed **neo-colonialism**.

The modern face of development is seen in this pharmaceutical plant in Mumbai in India.

- *Does this suggest that India is showing signs of adjusting well to the new world economy?*

Case Study: Post-Independent India

Since independence, India has adopted elements of all three strategies to help adjust to the new world economy.

Until 1990, India followed a policy of **protection**. Its large population and resource base provided both a strong home market and the inputs needed for industrial development, e.g. textiles, steel, food processing. Since 1990, however, it has adopted **free trade**, as the country looked to benefit more from expanding world trade. This has been successful.

India also **borrowed wisely** and is not faced with a debt crisis (see Table 44.1). Investments were made to modernise the economy and upgrade infrastructure and education. In addition, India has **attracted a lot of new foreign investment.**

- Many MNCs have been attracted by its large market and low-cost but well-educated workforce.
- Large amounts of high-tech goods and services are now produced in India.
- The value of industrial exports has increased significantly, and India is classed as an NIC.
- As exports of higher-value industrial goods and services increased, India's dependency on exports of primary goods decreased. (Why should this help promote development in India?)

CHAPTER 45
GLOBAL ISSUES OF JUSTICE AND DEVELOPMENT

 **KEY IDEA!** Large numbers of people have failed to benefit equally from the growing world economy.

Previous chapters have shown that global development is uneven. Less developed countries in particular have generally failed to adjust successfully to new patterns of world trade. As a result, large numbers of the world's population feel a deep sense of injustice in that they have not been treated fairly by global development. This chapter introduces three areas of injustice:

- World trade.
- Health.
- Gender discrimination.

World Trade

Many developing countries continue to depend mainly on the export of primary commodities, such as coffee and copper. This trade, however, is controlled by powerful MNCs which often work against the interests of less developed countries.

- **Commodity prices** for goods such as coffee and copper have generally fallen since 1980 (see Fig. 45.1 and Table 45.1). As a result, less developed countries have to export more of a commodity simply to maintain their income levels. This can, however, flood the market and cause prices to drop even further. **Consumers in developed countries benefit from this, while producers suffer a major decline in incomes and standards of living.**

- **Terms of trade** have added to the problems of less developed countries. While prices of primary commodities have declined, the prices of manufactured goods exported from developed countries have increased significantly. This is unfair, and is seen as an exploitation of populations in the developing world.

- Producers of primary commodities **receive only a small proportion of the final value of a manufactured product**. Most of the profits are made by companies, which process the raw material inputs, and by retailers.

World trade is therefore far from being fair. It has generally worked against the interests of most people in less developed countries. This economic injustice has to be addressed to achieve a fairer world economy.

In 1972, Uganda had to sell 6 tonnes of cotton to import a truck made in Europe. By 2002, the import of a similar truck needed 35 tonnes of cotton.

For more information on world trade and global exploitation, see Chapter 49.

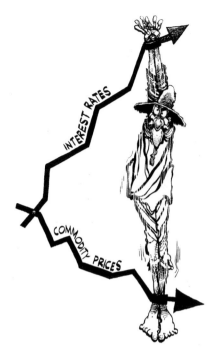

	1970	1980	1990	2000	2004
Cocoa (cents/kg)	240	330	122	93	147
Coffee (cents/kg)	330	412	118	94	75
Copper ($/tonne)	5,038	2,770	2,662	1,866	2,724
Cotton (cents/kg)	225	260	182	134	130
Rubber (cents/kg)	145	181	86	69	124

Table 45.1 Price changes for a sample of primary commodities, 1970–2004.

Fig. 45.1 Experience of less developed countries being torn between high interest rates on debt repayments and falling commodity prices.

Activity

Study Fig. 45.1 and Table 45.1 and answer the following.

1. What are the dominant price trends for primary commodities?
2. Contrast these trends with those for interest rates on loans made to developing countries.
3. What message does the cartoon suggest for producers of primary commodities?

One approach to bringing about fairer conditions of trade has been the establishment of **fair trade organisations**. These promote fairer international trade by ensuring that producers in less developed countries:

- Are paid a fair price for their product.
- Work in safe and decent conditions (are not exploited).
- Respect the local environment (sustainable development).

Products that meet the above objectives can be awarded a Fairtrade label. In Ireland this is the **Fairtrade** logo (Fig. 45.2).

Guarantees a **better deal** for Third World Producers **FAIRTRADE**

Fig. 45.2 The Fairtrade logo.
- *In what ways does Fairtrade guarantee a better deal for Third World producers?*

Health: A Matter of Life and Death

A fundamental human right is the right to life. Central to this is good medical care, which can help cure sickness, improve quality of life and increase life expectancy. This, however, is not equally available and results in major differences in health-related issues between populations in developed and less developed countries (Fig. 45.3).

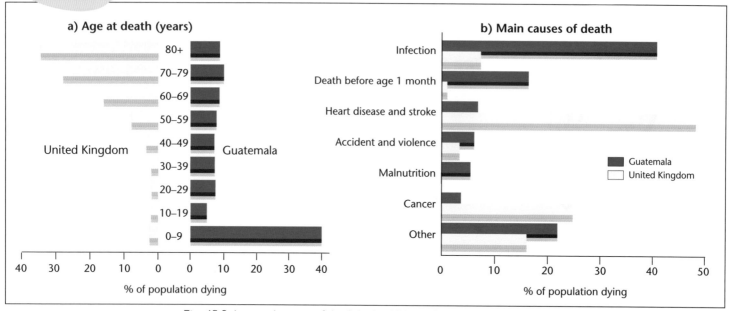

Fig. 45.3 Ages and causes of death in the UK and Guatemala.

Activity

Study Fig. 45.3 and answer the following.

1. What age group shows the highest death rates in Guatemala? Compare this with the UK.
2. Contrast the main causes of death in Guatemala with those in the UK.
3. What do these trends tell you about health care and quality of life in both countries?
4. Does this suggest equal social justice for both populations?

People in developed countries, such as Britain, are generally well fed, even though much of the food we eat is not considered to be healthy.

Many people in less developed countries, such as these children in Guatemala, live in poverty and are undernourished. They are forced to scavenge for food from garbage dumps or gather discarded items to sell or to use for themselves.

Activity

What do these two images tell you about the health of people in Britain and Guatemala?

AIDS: A Disease of the Poor?

Since it first appeared in the late 1970s, over 25 million people have died from AIDS/HIV. Although considered to be a disease that can occur throughout the world, 90 per cent of all cases are in the less developed world (Fig. 45.4).

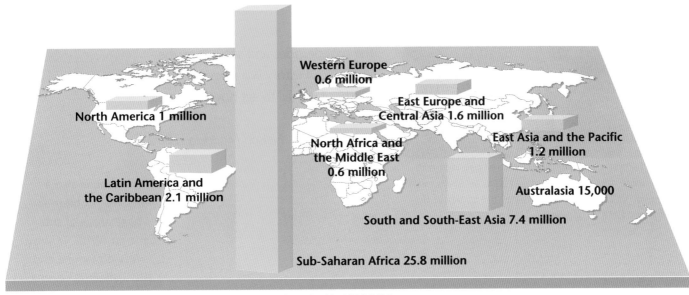

Fig. 45.4 Estimated world distribution map of people infected with AIDS/HIV.

Activity

Study Fig. 45.4 and answer the following.

1. Which world region dominates the AIDS problem?
2. Discuss the ways in which AIDS can affect development in sub-Saharan Africa.
3. Do you think the developed world should take more responsibility in helping to reduce the AIDS crisis?

Sub-Saharan Africa: The AIDS 'Hot Spot'

Of the 42 million people in the world living with AIDS or HIV, more than 60 per cent are in sub-Saharan Africa. In 2005, 3.2 million new cases were reported in this region. All of the twenty countries of the world with the highest levels of AIDS or HIV cases are located in sub-Saharan Africa.

Given the scale of the AIDS crisis, especially in sub-Saharan Africa, it is both unfair and impractical to expect the poorest of world regions to deal with this health problem. Developed countries must commit more resources to such regions to combat AIDS. This would help reduce the huge inequalities in health care experienced by so many people in sub-Saharan Africa.

Access to low-cost and effective medicine would be a major help to combat AIDS in sub-Saharan Africa.

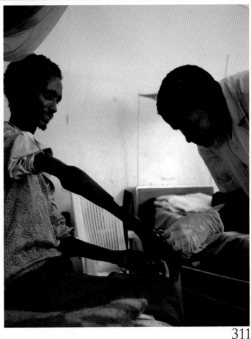

An AIDS/HIV patient receiving treatment in Ethiopia. Throughout sub-Saharan Africa, the AIDS crisis has put a huge strain on health services and has caused life expectancy to fall and infant mortality rates to rise.

Starving children wait for food aid at a refugee centre in Somalia. Here and elsewhere in sub-Saharan Africa, wars, famine and AIDS have greatly reduced the quality of life for large numbers of people.

'AIDS today in Africa is claiming more lives than the sum total of all wars, famines, and floods, and the ravages of such deadly diseases as malaria … AIDS is clearly a disaster, effectively wiping out the development gains for the past decades and sabotaging the future . . . History will judge us harshly if we fail to act now, and right now.'

Nelson Mandela, 2000

Famine is also a massive problem for large areas of sub-Saharan Africa. In what ways do famine and AIDS affect economic development?

Discrimination: An Issue of Gender

Injustice in the world extends to gender. Despite the ideal that all people are equal, women have long been discriminated against in favour of men. This has important implications for development and cannot be justified for half of the world's population.

Women face **discrimination** in various ways:

- In some societies, the **law discriminates against women**. For example, in certain Muslim societies women do not have equal rights in marriage and face restrictions in working outside of the home.

Activity

Study Fig. 45.5 and answer the following.

1. Do women or men account for most of the world's illiterate population?
2. Do girls or boys have a better chance of becoming educated?
3. Why should these figures be a cause of concern?

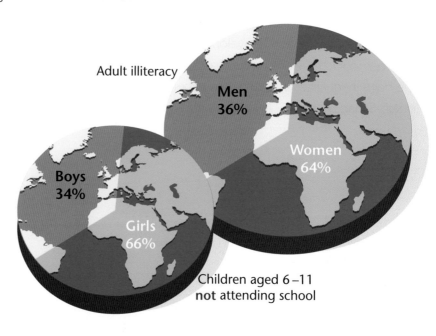

Adult illiteracy

Men 36%

Women 64%

Boys 34%

Girls 66%

Children aged 6–11 **not** attending school

Fig. 45.5 The gender gap in education.

312

- Although the situation is improving, males **generally are given easier access to education** than females. This reduces the opportunities for females to improve their employment prospects and quality of life (see Fig. 45.5).
- **The preference for male children/heirs**, especially in traditional rural societies, is strong. This has resulted in selective abortion, or even the killing of girl babies.
- **Arranged marriages** often force young women into unsatisfactory relationships.
- Women are identified as **a cheap source of workers**, especially in developing countries.

Refer to the description of women workers in developing countries on page 340.

Activity
In what ways do these images of women suggest discrimination against women in less developed countries?

Woman wearing traditional dress (burqua) in Syria.
- *Does this contrast with the clothes of her husband and two boys?*

In less developed countries, women are identified as a major source of cheap labour. Here, large numbers of women work long hours for low pay on a production line in Indonesia.
- *Can you pick out a male worker? What job do you think he is doing?*

Slaves of the Twenty-first Century

An extreme form of human injustice occurs in the form of slavery of millions of men, women and children. Today, an estimated 27 million people in the world have been bought, sold, held captive and brutally exploited for profit.

In India, for example, millions of poor people have been caught in a debt trap leading to slavery. Unable to repay loans to moneylenders, they are forced to sell themselves in a form of slave labour. An estimated 15–20 million people are debt slaves in India, Pakistan, Bangladesh and Nepal.

For women, prostitution has long been a form of slavery. Today, criminal gangs illegally traffic in women. For example, more than 100,000 women have been moved illegally into Europe from Eastern Europe, Africa and the Middle East. They end up mostly as prostitutes in Europe's major cities. In India, some 50,000 prostitutes work in Mumbai, more than half trafficked illegally from Nepal. Their life expectancy is less than forty years.

CHAPTER 46
GLOBALISATION

The world has become a smaller place in which decisions and events in one part of the world can have major impacts on people living in other parts of the world.

The world today appears to be changing more dramatically and more quickly than ever before. Furthermore, our lives seem to be increasingly influenced by events and decisions that occur far from where we live and work. The term '**globalisation**' is used to define such processes.

Globalisation is a process by which events, actions and decisions in one part of the world can have significant consequences for communities in distant parts of the globe. In effect, this means **we are living in an increasingly and highly interconnected world**.

CAUSES OF GLOBALISATION

The process of globalisation, which allows people and places located throughout the world to interact strongly, is influenced by **five** main factors.

- **Improvements in transportation** have reduced the costs and time involved in moving large amounts of raw materials, goods and people over longer distances, e.g. bulk shipping, containerisation, air travel.

The twin towers of the World Trade Center in New York were a symbol of US economic and political power. Their destruction in a terrorist attack on 11 September 2001 had major consequences for the world.
- *Can you think of any of these consequences?*

Supertankers of up to 500,000 tonnes play a major role in globalisation by transporting vast amounts of oil from oil fields to markets throughout the world.
- *Why is this important for global development?*

- **Advances in telecommunications**, such as electronic mail (e-mail), communications satellites and fax machines, link people and places more efficiently than older systems, such as the telephone and telegraph. Furthermore, the internationalisation of television, such as CNN, Sky and MTV, allows images of other places, events and cultures to be transmitted directly into our homes.

- **The reorganisation of business** has seen the emergence of very large international companies, e.g. Ford, Microsoft, Sony, Nike, which are termed multinational companies (MNCs). They invest large amounts of money (termed foreign direct investment, or FDI) to set up mining operations, factories and offices in different countries. As a result, they purchase inputs, produce goods and services, and sell them at a global level.

- **Global banking and integrated financial markets**: Using new technologies to move capital through the world, about US$100 billion worth of currencies are traded daily. To control this trade, international banking and financial institutions have emerged, with headquarters in world cities such as London, New York, Frankfurt and Tokyo. Stock exchanges in these financial capitals have a key role to play in shaping development trends throughout the world.

- **A more liberal world trading system** has been strongly promoted by MNCs and richer capitalist countries. These and the World Trade Organization (WTO) encourage the movement to free trade by removing or reducing barriers that limit trade, such as tariffs and quota restrictions. More and more goods and services can therefore be sold in the markets of other countries. This makes it easier for MNCs and rich countries to increase their dominant role in trading goods and services at a global level.

> Look at your TV guide to see the origin of your favourite programmes. How many are produced in Ireland?

Financial dealings inside the London Stock Exchange involve traders moving vast amounts of money. This influences the economies of companies and countries throughout the world.

Fig. 46.1 A cartoonist's view of the process of globalisation.
- *Study the cartoon. How many US products can you identify? What do you think is the main message illustrated by this cartoon?*

315

CHAPTER 47
MULTINATIONAL COMPANIES

KEY IDEA!

Multinational companies invest in foreign locations to reduce their costs of production and increase profits.

- Some 45,000 MNCs operate globally.
- These control about 400,000 subsidiary companies in foreign countries.
- They account for one-third of the value of global exports.

Since the 1960s, **multinational companies** (MNCs) have emerged as one of the most important elements shaping the global economy. As part of their strategy for growth, they undertake investments in countries that are outside their home country. This is termed **foreign direct investment (FDI)**. Through these investments and using improved transport and communications systems, MNCs can co-ordinate their production and sales as part of a **single global system**. As a result, MNCs control increasing amounts of global trade, production and employment. They therefore have a major influence in the development prospects for most countries, including Ireland.

THE GROWTH OF MNCs AND FDI

Foreign investment by MNCs began to show a major increase since the mid-1980s, and now amounts to $1,000 billion.

At the start of the twenty-first century, some of the largest MNCs had reached a scale of business which made them economically more powerful than many countries (Tables 47.1 and 47.2). The business of Exxon-Mobil, the MNC with the largest sales in 2006, equalled the GNP of Belgium, and was almost half that of India, the second-most populous country in the world. Compared to the poverty-stricken countries of sub-Saharan Africa, these powerful MNCs have sales values that greatly exceeded their national GNPs.

A multinational company is a company with production and service activities located in more than one country.

The international headquarters of Royal Dutch/Shell in Amsterdam. This is the largest non-US MNC in the world (see Table 47.1).

USA	Sales ($ billion)	Employment ('000s)
1 Exxon-Mobil	378	106
2 Walmart	349	1,800
3 Chevron	205	59
4 General Motors	193	327
5 Ford Motors	160	328

Rest of the World	Sales ($ billion)	Employment ('000s)
1 Royal Dutch/Shell	319	112
2 BP	262	96
3 Toyota Motors	179	286
4 Total	154	111
5 DaimlerChrysler	150	383

Table 47.1 Sales and employment levels in the five leading MNCs in the USA and rest of the world.

GNP of Selected Countries (US$ billion)			
Germany	2,852	Ireland	167
India	793	Hungary	101
Belgium	374	Ethiopia	11
Denmark	257	Zambia	6

Table 47.2 GNP of selected countries.

The combined GNP of the thirty-six countries with the lowest values on the UN Human Development Index amounts to only $265 billion. Most of these countries are in sub-Saharan Africa.

Activity
Study Tables 47.1 and 47.2 and answer the following.
1. Name the MNCs with:
   a. the largest sales
   b. the highest employment.
2. What are the main products associated with each of the MNCs?
3. Why do you think these products are so dominant?
4. Identify the countries of origin of the MNCs listed under 'rest of the world'.
5. Do you think countries such as Ethiopia and Zambia can influence the investment strategies of MNCs? Explain.

Reasons Why MNCs Locate Activities in Different Countries

MNCs benefit significantly from investing in foreign locations. This is linked to **four** main reasons.

Access to Raw Materials

Historically, this was the most important reason. Colonial powers, such as Britain and France, invested heavily in their colonies to access raw materials, such as copper, coffee and rubber. MNCs continue to invest strongly in **securing supplies of critical raw materials**, such as oil and mineral ores. Many of these raw materials are sourced in less developed countries, and MNCs use bulk shipping to transport them to processing plants, often located in more developed countries. Good examples include oil and iron ore shipped to refineries and steelworks located around the coasts of Western Europe.

Access to Cheap Labour

As mechanisation of production has reduced the importance of skilled labour, MNCs search for locations that offer **cheaper and more flexible sources of labour**. Many less developed countries have large numbers of people who are prepared to work long hours for low wages. Movement of production of basic or simple goods and services to less developed countries therefore generates considerable savings for MNCs through lower labour costs. This **relocation of production** has given rise to what is termed a **new international division of labour** (see Chapter 51).

A large oil terminal in the Niger Delta, Nigeria. MNCs, like Royal Dutch/Shell, have major interests in this oil-rich region. Most of the oil is exported for refining in Western Europe.

- *Do you think these activities are of major benefit to less developed countries?*

Large numbers of female workers and children are prepared to work for very low wages in less developed countries. In this garment factory in Bangladesh, up to 300 employees work under sweatshop conditions up to 80 hours a week and for $15 a month.

Access to New and Expanding Markets

In today's world, three global markets dominate. These are North America (especially the USA), Japan and the European Union. To ensure **access** to these **prosperous markets**, most MNCs have a strategy of locating major production and servicing facilities in each of these regions.

Flexibility of Location

By having economic activities located in a number of different countries, MNCs are able to **move production between plants** if it is considered profitable to do so. If, for example, labour costs rise too rapidly in Ireland and/or another country provides higher grants, a MNC may decide to relocate part or all of its production from Ireland to the cheaper location. This gives MNCs considerable bargaining power with national governments.

The large Nissan car plant at Sunderland in England opened in 1986. Since then, €3 billion has been invested in this plant, which produced 400,000 cars in 2006 for the EU market.

The Product Cycle and Changing Locations of MNCs

The reasons that influence MNCs to invest in foreign locations can be viewed as part of the **product cycle**. This suggests that products evolve through **four** stages, and that each stage is influenced by a different set of location factors. As a product evolves from its first stage, when it is being researched and developed, to the final stage when it is mass-produced as a basic good, the preferred locations change (see Table 47.3).

By relocating production at different stages of the product cycle, MNCs benefit from the locational advantages of both core and peripheral regions.

The Product Cycle		
Stage	**Location Factors**	**Preferred Location**
1. Development of new product	Access to scientists, technology, investment money	Core urban regions, e.g. London, Boston, Tokyo
2. Early growth	Skilled workers, good regional market and infrastructure, e.g. business services, finance, marketing	Growth regions such as the Manchester–Milan axis, Catalonia
3. Rapid growth/ maturity	Less-skilled and lower-cost labour, cheaper land and good transport systems to access world market	Peripheral areas of more developed countries or NICs, e.g. South Korea, India
4. Old age or stagnation	Low labour costs, flexible workers, cheap land, government grants and access to world markets	Less developed countries in peripheral world regions such as south and east Asia

Table 47.3 The product cycle.

Activity

Study Table 47.3 and answer the following.

1. Why are new products usually developed in core locations?
2. In what stages would you expect to find branch plants? Why?
3. In the 1960s, Ireland was in Stage 3 but also attracted Stage 4 products. Now it is in Stage 2, although the Dublin region has elements of Stage 1. Can you explain this evolution of Ireland through the product cycle?

THE GLOBAL ASSEMBLY LINE

The production of a book, such as this, is an example of the global assembly line. The author in Cork writes the text, while editorial and graphic design work is located in London. Basic typesetting and production of the book occurs in South-East Asia. Books are shipped in bulk to the headquarters and sales offices of the publisher located in Dublin for distribution within Ireland and other parts of Europe.

The product cycle can also be seen to be a part of the global assembly line. This is a term used to describe the global production and sales systems of MNCs. In effect, MNCs locate different activities in different places to achieve the lowest costs/highest profits. Generally:

- Decision-making and the more skill-demanding and higher-value elements of the production system are located in highly developed countries. Over 90 per cent of MNCs have their headquarters in developed countries, such as the USA and Japan.
- Basic production and services are relocated to less developed countries where costs are lower.

The main locational advantages in attracting MNCs to less developed economies are the low costs and the flexible attitude of the workforce.

INVESTMENT AND LOCATIONS OF MNCs

MNCs are attracted to **two** main types of location:

- Major industrialised regions.
- Peripheral regions.

Major Industrialised Regions

Although MNC investment in less developed countries has been increasing, most remains concentrated in industrialised countries, such as the USA, Japan and Western Europe. This shows the powerful attraction of their prosperous markets for goods and services. Some 70 per cent of total MNC investments are located in the industrialised countries that contain only 15 per cent of the global population.

Why do you think sub-Saharan Africa attracts little multinational investment? Refer to page 290 to help you with your answer.

Peripheral Regions

Investment in less developed countries has historically been low and was focused mainly on the exploitation of raw materials. Since the late 1980s, however, investment in such countries has increased significantly (see Fig. 47.1). By 2005, some 30 per cent of the world's manufacturing production was located in developing countries. This compares with less than 10 per cent until the late 1960s.

This is due to the dispersal of **branch plant activities** to cheaper locations in the global periphery. One important result has been to help industrialise a growing number of less developed countries. Where this has been particularly successful, such as in Brazil, India, South Korea and Thailand, the term **newly industrialising country** (NIC) is used.

Some countries and world regions, however, continue to attract little MNC investment. This is seen clearly in sub-Saharan Africa, which remains the least industrialised global region (Fig. 39.5, page 283).

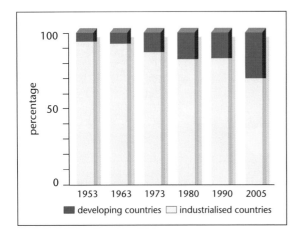

Fig. 47.1 The changing distribution of world manufacturing production between industrialised and developing countries, 1953–2005.

Activity
Study Fig. 47.1 and answer the following.
1. Have developing countries increased their share of world manufacturing production since the Second World War?
2. Briefly explain what factors encouraged the growth of manufacturing production in developing countries.

A branch plant economy is one with a high dependency on branch plants for employment and wealth creation. These economies tend to be unstable and show limited potential for longer-term growth and development.

BRANCH PLANTS OF MNCs

One of the main strategies of MNCs for remaining competitive is to establish branch plants in peripheral regions of the world.

Branch plants can bring a variety of benefits to countries (see Table 47.4). As a result, many governments, including that of Ireland, offer significant incentives, such as cash grants and tax benefits, to encourage MNCs to locate branch plants in their country.

Branch plants can also bring problems to host countries. This is particularly the case if **dependency** upon branch plants for employment and prosperity is too high. When this occurs, we use the term '**branch plant economy**'.

Probably the most significant problem is linked to the loss of control over decision-making. Decisions are often made at the headquarters of an MNC with little or no consultation with the workforce and government of the host country. Branch plants can therefore be closed or run down if the MNC considers other locations to be a more profitable option. Overdependency on branch plants is not regarded as an effective basis for sustainable development.

Advantages	Disadvantages
1. They provide many jobs.	1. Wage rates are often not high (late stages of product cycle). Job losses can also occur as local firms can be put out of business by more competitive MNCs.
2. They introduce new skills to the workforce and new technologies.	2. Focus on basic production requires relatively low skill levels – repetitive and often boring work.
3. They can help increase demand for other goods and services located in the country (the multiplier effect).	3. Linkages with national suppliers of goods/services can be poor. Many key goods and services are purchased from other units of the MNC and in other countries (poor multiplier effect).
4. They bring a lot of investment and stimulate exports.	4. A lot of the profits are lost through repatriation to headquarters and shareholders outside of the country.
5. They diversify the economy and help integration into the global economy.	5. Instability – the type of work and the possession of branch plants by the MNC in other countries can cause a plant to be run down/closed and production transferred to cheaper and more profitable locations.

Table 47.4 Advantages and disadvantages of branch plants.

A Fruit of the Loom factory at Buncrana in Co. Donegal. Note the new housing developments that were directly linked to the jobs and prosperity provided by the factory.

● *Describe some of the consequences of the factory's closure on this community.*

A good example of the problems of branch plant dependency is Fruit of the Loom. In 1987 this US MNC opened the first of a number of branch plants in Donegal to manufacture T-shirts and other items of clothing. At its peak, the MNC employed 3,500 people in this peripheral region and many communities depended on these factories for their economic well-being.

Since 2000, however, rising costs of production and increasing competition caused the MNC to gradually close all of its plants in Ireland. Production was located to Morocco, where labour costs are 90 per cent lower than in Ireland. This has left major problems of unemployment in many communities in Co. Donegal and Derry.

CHAPTER 48
MULTINATIONAL COMPANIES IN THE EUROPEAN UNION AND IRELAND

KEY IDEA!

Large-scale investments by MNCs in both the EU and Ireland have given rise to complex trading patterns and helped increase economic development.

Multinational companies from the EU, especially its core countries in north-west Europe, have a long tradition of foreign direct investment (FDI). Most EU investment is directed to other prosperous and developed world regions. An increasing amount, however, is used to open branch plants and service activities, such as back offices, in NICs in South-East Asia and Latin America. Former colonies of EU countries also attract investments.

The European Union also attracts large amounts of FDI. This is mainly due to its large, prosperous and growing market. Almost 90 per cent of this comes from US and Japanese MNCs. Britain receives the highest national share of this investment, although peripheral countries, such as Ireland and Spain, and, increasingly, countries in Central Europe, also benefit significantly.

> Almost 50 per cent of MNC investment from the EU is directed to the USA.

> Up until enlargement of the EU in 2004, Ireland, with only 1 per cent of the population of the EU, received 8 per cent of MNC investment in the region.

Case Study: Ford Europe
Ford is one of the largest MNCs operating within the global economy (see Table 47.1, page 317). It organises its worldwide production system in terms of global regions. **Ford Europe,** for example, controls manufacturing and sales throughout Europe.

Name of company: Ford Europe
Headquarters: Cologne
Total sales: $30 billion
Employment: 66,000

Ford has a long history of producing vehicles in Europe. Initially, most of the Ford plants were located in core locations, such as near London and in Cologne. This was due to their large and prosperous markets, availability of skilled labour and good transport systems.

This MNC still has some plants in core regions. More recently, however, Ford Europe has invested heavily in opening several large vehicle assembly plants in peripheral countries such as Spain and Turkey (see Fig. 48.1). This is due to:

- Increasing costs of production in core locations.
- Cheaper labour and land costs in peripheral regions.
- Government grants to help open new plants.
- Improved transport to link cores to peripheries.
- Less need for skilled workers as vehicle assembly becomes more automated.

In addition, Ford Europe's strategy for vehicle assembly is for its major plants to concentrate on one or only a limited range of models (see Fig. 48.1). This allows the plants to benefit from the lower costs associated with the specialisation of production. The finished vehicles are distributed to its customers through Ford sales offices, which are located in all European countries.

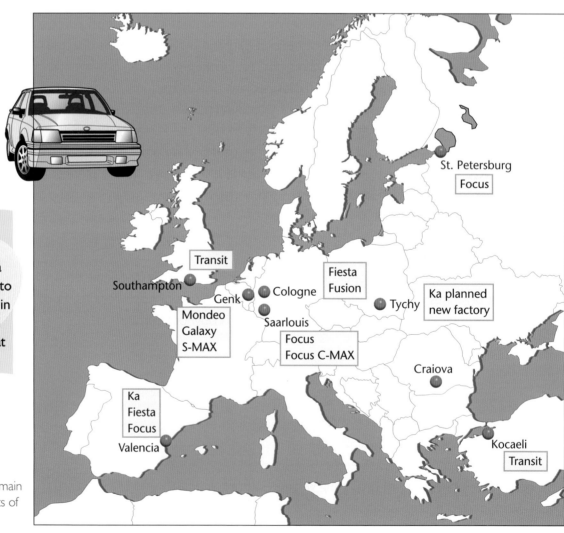

Ford plans to take production of its Ka model from Valencia to a new plant at Tychy in Poland, and to take over another plant at Craiova, Romania.

Fig. 48.1 Location of main vehicle assembly plants of Ford Europe.

The production of vehicles is complex and involves assembling many component parts and materials. Rather than producing most of these inputs themselves, Ford Europe subcontracts work to specialist suppliers located mainly within Europe (see Fig. 48.2). In this way, costs can be reduced. Suppliers, however, have to be able to guarantee the quality of supplies and delivery on time. This requires good transport links between assembly plants and suppliers.

The most specialised and higher-value components are generally sourced in core countries, since they have the skilled workers and technology necessary to manufacture inputs such as engines or braking systems. In contrast, lower-value components can be sourced in peripheral regions where costs are lower, e.g. wheel caps, metal panels.

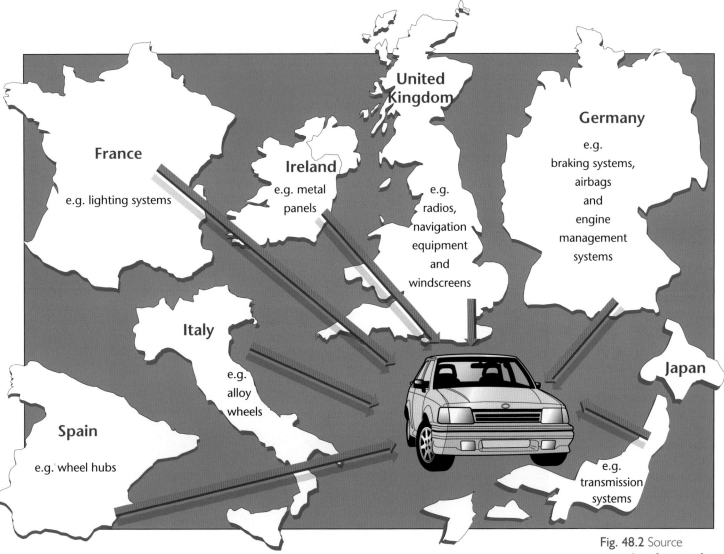

Fig. 48.2 Source countries of some of the major components for Ford Europe.

Activity

Study Figs. 48.1 and 48.2 and answer the following.

1. In how many countries does Ford Europe have a vehicle assembly plant?
2. How many countries in Europe provide major supplies of component parts for Ford Europe?
3. Suggest locational advantages of peripheral countries such as Spain and Poland for vehicle assembly.
4. Why are good transport systems so important for MNCs such as Ford Europe?

Ford's major car production plant at Valencia in Spain.
● *What would attract Ford to this location rather than developing its plants in the core of Europe?*

Since Ford closed its car assembly plant at Cork in 1984, all Ford cars sold in Ireland are imported through the port of Cork from its plants elsewhere in Europe.

Multinational Companies in Ireland

Of all EU countries, Ireland has benefited most from the inward investment of MNCs as a basis for economic development. From the 1960s, the government focused on attracting MNCs to increase national wealth and provide much needed-employment. This policy of **industrialisation by invitation** has been successful.

Refer to pages 292–4 and Chapter 41 for further information on industrial development in Ireland.

The Dell computer manufacturing plant at Raheen, Limerick opened in 1991. This and a second Limerick plant employ 3,300 people. Dell is the largest employer in Limerick and is the company's main production centre for Europe, Africa and the Middle East.

From the 1960s to the 1980s, large numbers of **branch plants** were attracted to Ireland (Table 48.1). Ireland became a **branch plant economy.**

Recession and increasing competition for branch plants in the 1980s, however, resulted in MNCs closing factories or reducing employment in Ireland, and looking for even lower-cost locations in the less developed world. This highlighted the problem of dependency on branch plants and on decision-making at headquarters of MNCs located outside Ireland.

Branch Plants 1960s–1980s	High-tech Plants 1990s – Present
• Plenty of cheap but unskilled labour	• Large supply of well-educated and young workers
• Cheap land (rural areas)	• Access to good-quality research institutions and universities
• Government grants	• Low taxation rates for industry
• Access to EU market	• Access to expanding EU market
• Basic services and adequate transport systems	• High-quality environment, e.g. housing, recreation

Table 48.1 Factors attracting branch plants and high-tech MNC investment to Ireland.

Activity

Use Table 48.1 to explain why:

1. More recent MNC investment locates mainly in larger urban centres, especially Dublin.
2. Branch plants can be closed and production relocated to less developed countries.
3. Higher-tech plants are less likely to be closed or relocated to less developed countries.

In the 1990s, a **new wave of MNC investment** was attracted to Ireland. Many of these differed from earlier branch plant operations and were a vital factor in developing the Celtic Tiger economy.

- Most investment is concentrated in **growth sectors**, such as electronics, pharmaceuticals and internationally traded services.
- The focus is on producing **high-value goods and services** rather than mass production of low-value goods in branch plants.
- New plants include **more key decision-making functions,** such as research and development, marketing and finance.
- MNCs are **less likely to close** their newer plants than branch plants. Why?

> In 2005, US investment in Ireland amounted to $73 billion with 600 American firms employing over 90,000 workers.

Today, more than one in every two industrial jobs in Ireland is provided by foreign-owned MNCs. The Dublin urban region in particular has benefited most from this new wave of high-tech investment.

Case Study: Wyeth in Ireland

The following are some **basic facts about Wyeth**, a multinational company with factories in Ireland.

Name: Wyeth
Headquarters: Madison, New Jersey, USA
Importance: The tenth-largest pharmaceutical (medicines) company in the world
Main product: Pharmaceuticals; veterinary medicines; vaccines; biotech; health care products (such as baby milk formula)
Global involvement: Has plants located across the globe, including Ireland
Global workforce: 50,000
Global sales: US$20.4 billion

Fig. 48.3 The location of Wyeth headquarters.

327

Fort Dodge Laboratories Ltd (1990) makes animal vaccines in Sligo. It employs about 100 people.

Wyeth Pharmaceuticals and Consumer Health Care operates sales, marketing and product support for Wyeth in Ballymount, Dublin.

Wyeth Biotech (2005) makes pharmaceuticals, biotech and vaccines at Grange Castle, Co. Dublin. It employs 1,250 people.

Wyeth Nutritionals (1974) manufactures baby milk formula at Askeaton, Co. Limerick, where it employs 550 people. It is Wyeth's oldest Irish venture.

Wyeth Medical Ireland (1992) employs 1,300 people at a large complex at Newbridge, Co. Kildare. It manufactures a range of pharmaceutical products.

Fig. 48.4 Locations of Wyeth's Irish enterprises.

Wyeth opened its first plant in Ireland in 1974. Since then, its investments in the country have increased significantly. This reflects the advantages of Ireland for pharmaceutical MNCs (see below). Currently, Wyeth manufactures a wide range of products from its facilities in Ireland (see Fig. 48.4). It also employs more than 3,000 people, which makes Wyeth the largest pharmaceutical employer in Ireland.

Wyeth Medica at Newbridge, Co. Kildare is one of the largest pharmaceutical plants in Ireland. It is an example of the new wave of high-tech companies that have been attracted to Ireland since the 1990s.

● *Why are such companies important for regional development?*

Of the top twenty pharmaceutical companies in the world, sixteen have significant operations in Ireland.

Reasons for Wyeth Locating in Ireland

● The high-quality education system, especially at third level, provides a large number of **well-qualified and skilled workers**.

● **Financial incentives**, such as government grants and a favourable corporation tax rate.

● As a member of the EU, Ireland provides easy access to a large and prosperous **EU market**.

- **Well-developed transport and communications systems** to help export finished products and to import raw materials.
- **Other world-class pharmaceutical companies**, such as Pfizer, have located in Ireland. This creates a larger pool of skilled labour and encourages research and development for companies to remain competitive.
- American companies find it easier to locate in **English-speaking** countries, such as Ireland.

Wyeth Medica Ireland, Newbridge

This is one of Wyeth's major investments in Ireland. It opened in 1992 on a 40-hectare site at Newbridge, Co. Kildare and employed fifty people. Today, the plant employs over 1,300 people on a 120-hectare site, showing the degree of success of this location.

The plant manufactures an extensive range of high-quality pharmaceutical products, such as antibiotics and hormone replacement drugs. In addition, the company has invested heavily in promoting research and development and increasing the skills of its workforce at this site. This is to ensure the company remains competitive and can develop new pharmaceutical products to meet evolving market demands.

- **Source of material inputs**: Wyeth Medica sources most of its key inputs, such as active chemical ingredients. These are obtained mainly from companies in Europe, such as Germany, and are imported mainly through the port of Dublin. The only input sourced from within Ireland is packaging.
- **Markets**: The extensive range of products manufactured at Newbridge are exported to more than 100 countries across Europe, Latin America, Asia and Africa. This occurs mainly through the port of Dublin, with small quantities also exported through Dublin Airport.

CHAPTER 49
PATTERNS OF WORLD TRADE 1: MERCHANDISE TRADE

 **KEY IDEA!** World trade in merchandise goods has increased strongly since the Second World War, although much of this trade is focused on three dominant global regions: the global triad.

Since the end of the Second World War, the volume and value of world trade has increased dramatically. Three key factors have encouraged this growth and have emphasised linkages between different regions of the world economy.

Remember the five factors that influence globalisation. See pages 314–15.

- **The growing number and power of MNCs** that organise production at a global level. This has led to an increasing trade in goods and raw materials, and flows of information and services, between different countries and regions of the world.
- **Innovations in transportation and communications** have been vital to accommodate the growth in global trade flows.
- **The more liberal trade policy of the World Trade Organization (WTO)** and its member countries have reduced or removed many barriers to world trade, such as tariffs and quotas.

Large sea ports, such as Le Havre, made the EU the most important world region for merchandise trade.

- *Why are sea ports so important for world trade in merchandise goods?*

MERCHANDISE TRADE

Merchandise trade has grown rapidly as different countries specialise in producing goods for which they have a comparative advantage.

Not all regions, however, have shared equally in the increases in world trade (see Table 49.1). Some world regions, such as sub-Saharan Africa and South Asia, remain marginal to this process. This is because of:

- Their **late development**, linked to their colonial history.
- Their concentration on **products with relatively low value**, e.g. raw materials and/or mass-produced and basic goods manufactured in branch plants of MNCs.
- The **prices of most primary commodities**, which have declined compared to prices of higher-value goods produced in developed world regions (see the injustice of world trade on pages 308–309.

> Merchandise trade involves trade in goods that have a physical form, such as food products, raw materials and manufactured goods.

Region	1990	2004
East Asia and Pacific	240	968
East Europe and Central Asia	189	623
Latin America and the Caribbean	169	463
Middle East and North Africa	134	171
South Asia	34	104
Sub-Saharan Africa	80	144
Low-/middle-income countries	834	2,473
High-income countries	3,418	6,672
World total	**4,252**	**9,145**

Table 49.1 Merchandise exports by global region, 1990–2004 (US$ billion).

Activity

Study Table 49.1.
1. Which two regions show the lowest involvement in merchandise exports? Suggest some reasons for this.
2. Which world region has increased its merchandise exports the most? Suggest reasons for this. (Think of China.)

Perhaps the most outstanding feature of world trade in merchandise goods is the dominance of high-income regions. In effect, **three core economies** organise and control this trade. These are the EU, the USA and Japan. Together, these are termed the **global trading triad** (see Figs. 49.1 and 49.2).

The global trading triad controls well over half of the value of world merchandise trade. The EU is the most dominant trading partner within the triad. In addition, trade between its member states exceeds total EU trade with both the USA and Japan.

Activity

Study Fig. 49.1 and answer the following.
1. What percentage of world exports is sourced in these three regions?
2. Which core region is the largest exporter?
3. Between which two core regions does the greatest trade occur? Suggest reasons for this.

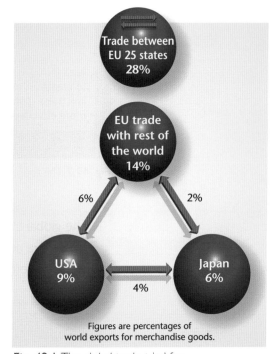

Figures are percentages of world exports for merchandise goods.

Fig. 49.1 The global trade triad for merchandise goods.

The Global Trading Triad

The development gap between the world's rich and poor regions remains large. At the heart of these **'two worlds'** are the three core regions that form the **global trading triad**. These core economies have become more strongly linked through trade, investment and improvements in transport and communication systems. In addition, they have used trade and investment to increase their influence over poorer regions of the world.

Fig. 49.2 shows the three core regions of the global trading triad and their preferred areas of extended influence.

Some 75 per cent of merchandise trade is sourced in high-income regions. These regions contain only 15 per cent of the world's population.

The growing economic strength and trade of India and China may upset this triad in the future.

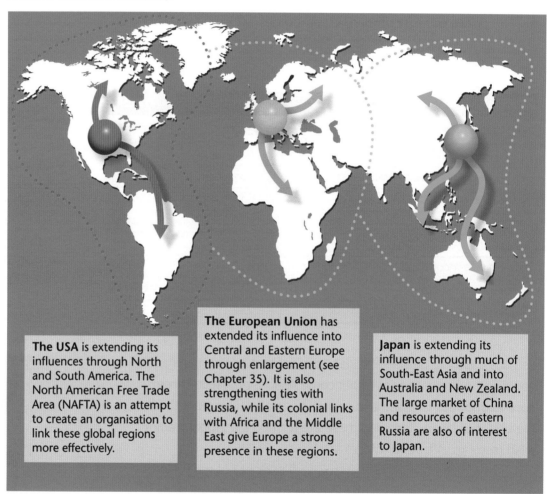

The USA is extending its influences through North and South America. The North American Free Trade Area (NAFTA) is an attempt to create an organisation to link these global regions more effectively.

The European Union has extended its influence into Central and Eastern Europe through enlargement (see Chapter 35). It is also strengthening ties with Russia, while its colonial links with Africa and the Middle East give Europe a strong presence in these regions.

Japan is extending its influence through much of South-East Asia and into Australia and New Zealand. The large market of China and resources of eastern Russia are also of interest to Japan.

Fig. **49.2** The three core regions of the global triad and their areas of preferred global influence.

The global trading triad is, in effect, 'sucking in' more and more of the world's productive activity, trade and investment. The triad sits astride the global economy like a modern three-legged colossus. It constitutes the world's megamarkets.

CHAPTER 50
PATTERNS OF WORLD TRADE 2: SERVICES

 **KEY IDEA!**

Globalisation has increased demands for a wide range of services, and international trade in services has become a vital element for an efficient global economy.

The globalisation of industrial production and the growing importance of MNCs have increased the demands for a wide range of services. Demand is especially high for **quaternary services**. These are recognised as the global growth sector and are responsible for an increasing amount of employment and wealth creation. As a result, the services sector and trade in services have become an increasingly important element in world development and trade.

Innovations in communication systems have been vital for the large-scale and rapid developments in global services. The telephone, fax, satellite communication links and, above all, the internet allow large volumes of information to be transmitted around the world. At the same time, efficient computer systems are able to store and process such data. These innovations have been developed and are used most in core world regions. This has allowed these regions to further extend their control over the world peripheral regions.

> Quaternary services involve the collection, processing and transmission of information and knowledge and therefore generally require a well-educated workforce. Examples include legal and financial services, marketing and research and development.

> Almost 80 per cent of internet users live in the USA and Europe.

● *Do you have e-mail? Why are internet cafés becoming increasingly popular?*

333

An employee at a customer contact centre in Bangalore, India, answering questions from customers in the USA and the UK.
- *What advantages does India have for these centres?*

As the importance of services has increased throughout the world, service industries have internationalised their activities. In a similar way to branch plants, a growing number of service companies are relocating some of their **back-office functions** to peripheral regions. If their communication systems are adequate, this allows them to take advantage of lower labour costs.

The decentralisation of services has tended to benefit only those countries which have invested in upgrading their telecommunications and education systems. These are vital for the successful take-off of this sector. Examples include India and Ireland.

For most countries in the global periphery, the costs and levels of education needed to support office-related functions remain an effective barrier to their development. As a result, **the relocation of international service functions to the less developed countries is much less extensive than it is for branch plants of manufacturing industries**.

OFFSHORE FINANCIAL CENTRES

As part of globalisation, vast amounts of money circulate through the world economy. While traditional banking centres deal with the majority of these flows, they are less able to meet the needs of clients who look for secrecy and/or shelter from taxation and other forms of regulation. The result has been the growth of **offshore financial centres**.

These are generally islands, or microstates, such as the Isle of Man and Andorra in Europe, which have become specialised centres for trade in international finance. Vast amounts of capital flow through these centres and create significant wealth and employment. One concentration of such centres occurs in and around the Caribbean. Examples include the Cayman Islands (population 36,000), which have 600 banks with deposits estimated at over $450 billion. Furthermore, over $900 billion passes through the financial institutions in the Caymans, making this small group of islands the most successful of all offshore centres.

> Remember the definition of back-office functions, see page 296.

The Cayman Islands are a major centre for offshore banking.
- *Use the photograph for evidence to suggest another important international industry that occurs in these islands.*

Although some relocation of services to the global periphery has occurred, the dominant characteristic of this sector is its continued focus on the largest international cities in core regions. These cities are called **geographical centres of control**, and include London, New York and Tokyo (Fig. 50.1).

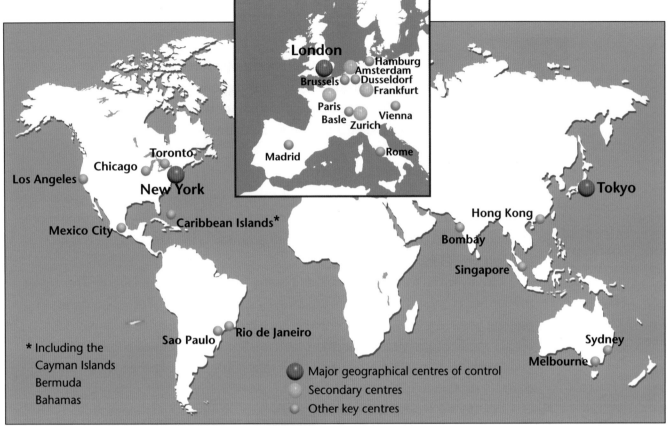

Fig. 50.1 Locations of major centres of international finance.

Geographical centres of control are major world cities that dominate international flows of finance, information and decision-making. The headquarters of many MNCs are located in them.

New York, with its powerful stock exchange, large number of business headquarters and excellent communications networks, is one of the world's major geographical centres of control.

● *What does geographical centre of control mean?*

335

CHAPTER 51
THE INTERNATIONAL DIVISION OF LABOUR

 **KEY IDEA!** The workforces of different countries tend to specialise in producing particular goods and/or services. This international division of labour is an essential part of globalisation.

> The more familiar a worker becomes with a task, the easier it is for the worker to perform that task. Productivity rises, while costs fall.

All economic activities require labour. Furthermore, development theory suggests that if workers are allowed to specialise in certain tasks or products, they can become more efficient. Productivity rises, while the costs of production fall. This concept is known as the **division of labour**.

Closely linked to this concept is that of the **spatial division of labour**. This argues that further economic benefits can be gained if specialisation of production occurs in different areas. It allows the workforce in such areas to concentrate on the production of certain goods and services. In addition, land use and infrastructures become closely linked with the specialised production. This raises productivity further, while lowering costs.

In a city, for example, the CBD (central business district) provides specialist services, such as banking, legal and insurance, the retail area provides major shopping facilities, while manufacturing activities are often located on industrial estates adjacent to ring roads around the edge of the city.

> Can you identify specialist areas of employment in your home area?

Henry Street in Dublin.
- *What is the main employment provided in areas such as this?*

At the national level, the spatial division of labour provides many benefits. Economic development and productivity increases as a country focuses on producing goods and/or services for which it has a **comparative advantage** over other areas. This allows that country to export these goods or services. The profits made from export trade allow it to import those goods or services that the country does not produce, or can produce only at costs higher than in other countries. Specialisation of labour at this level is called the **international division of labour**.

> Comparative advantage means that a region possesses some advantage, such as raw materials or a specialised labour force, which allows it to produce particular goods more cheaply than other regions. This is vital for success in world trade.

A refinery at one of the most remote oilfields in Saudi Arabia. It produces over 500,000 barrels of oil each day, which are piped to the coast for export.
- *Is this an important comparative advantage for Saudi Arabia?*

The Evolving International Division of Labour

The idea of an evolving international division of labour is central to the emergence of the global economy. In particular, it is linked to the two key features which have driven the process of globalisation:
- MNCs and their investments in branch plants and services.
- Increased levels of global trade.

> In Phase I, workforces in the core specialised in the secondary sector, while the primary sector dominated in the global periphery.

Since the start of the Industrial Revolution, the international division of labour has gone through three phases, with a fourth phase just beginning.

Phase I: The Traditional International Division of Labour

This began with the Industrial Revolution and continued until the 1960s. It involved the core economies of Western Europe, and later the USA, in exporting manufactured goods to the global periphery. In turn, countries of the global periphery specialised in producing food and raw materials for the core economies. This phase was influenced strongly by colonialism (see Chapter 43).

Farm workers on a sugar cane plantation.
- *Which phase of the international division of labour does this best illustrate? Why?*

The Microsoft Research and Development complex in Seattle, USA. Microsoft occupies 10 million square feet of office space and employs almost 30,000 people in the Seattle area.

- *Why are the headquarters and main research and development units of most MNCs still located in core countries?*

Phase 2: The New International Division of Labour

From the 1970s, in order to reduce production costs and remain competitive, many MNCs relocated branch plants to countries in the global periphery. At the same time, MNCs in core economies reduced their industrial workforces to concentrate on higher-value goods and services.

Phase 3: The Newer International Division of Labour

From the 1990s, a growing range of service functions has been relocated from core to peripheral countries. As with the earlier relocation of branch plants, these are basic service activities for which low labour costs are vital. Development of what are called **back-office functions** has created a new form of labour specialisation in the global periphery.

The core region had to respond to this relocation of both branch plants and back-office functions. As a result, their labour force increasingly specialises in high-tech industries and the growing quaternary sector.

Low costs of labour allowed peripheral countries to increasingly specialise in branch plant production of industrial goods. This led to an increase in the world trade in merchandise goods.

Employees work in one of the growing number of customer contact centres that have been relocated to India. Almost 1 million people are now employed in such centres in India.

- *What phase of the international division of labour does this photograph represent? Explain.*

Phase 4: The Most Recent International Division of Labour

A fourth phase of the international division of labour has begun, and its importance is expected to grow. In effect, MNCs are **outsourcing,** or subcontracting, an increasing number of key functions from their high-cost locations in core countries to locations in the world periphery (Fig. 51.1).

In India, an engineer with an MSc designs computer chips for $1,000 a month. A counterpart in the USA demands $7,000 a month.

This involves a significant number of high-value and skill-demanding jobs, such as research, chip design and financial analysis. These new jobs have been attracted to countries in the world periphery by a combination of push and pull factors:

- Costs in core countries are very high, due mainly to high wages and salaries.
- Employees in peripheral countries, such as India and the Philippines, are becoming more educated but wages remain low. Improved communication systems also allow easy access to customers in the developed world.

Rather than well-educated workers in peripheral countries migrating to core economies, work is now coming to the workers. **This reverses the long-established pattern of a brain drain from less developed countries.** It also increases their export of higher-value goods and services. Do you think this is a positive step in promoting development?

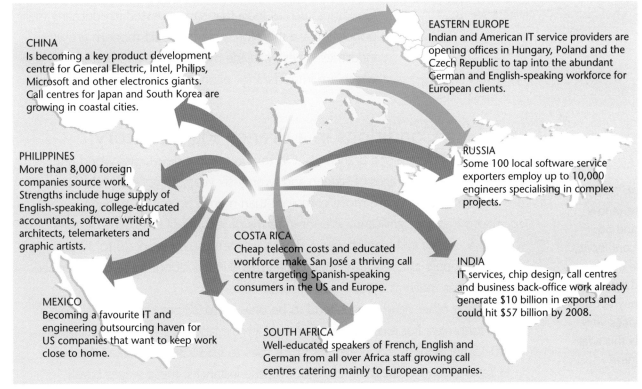

CHINA
Is becoming a key product development centre for General Electric, Intel, Philips, Microsoft and other electronics giants. Call centres for Japan and South Korea are growing in coastal cities.

PHILIPPINES
More than 8,000 foreign companies source work. Strengths include huge supply of English-speaking, college-educated accountants, software writers, architects, telemarketers and graphic artists.

MEXICO
Becoming a favourite IT and engineering outsourcing haven for US companies that want to keep work close to home.

COSTA RICA
Cheap telecom costs and educated workforce make San José a thriving call centre targeting Spanish-speaking consumers in the US and Europe.

SOUTH AFRICA
Well-educated speakers of French, English and German from all over Africa staff growing call centres catering mainly to European companies.

EASTERN EUROPE
Indian and American IT service providers are opening offices in Hungary, Poland and the Czech Republic to tap into the abundant German and English-speaking workforce for European clients.

RUSSIA
Some 100 local software service exporters employ up to 10,000 engineers specialising in complex projects.

INDIA
IT services, chip design, call centres and business back-office work already generate $10 billion in exports and could hit $57 billion by 2008.

Fig. 51.1 A world of outsourcing.

LABOUR SUPPLIES IN THE GLOBAL PERIPHERY

The type of labour supply has been central to attracting branch plants and service functions to countries of the global periphery. Four features are critical for the evolving international division of labour.

Chinese women sew garments in a clothing factory for export to the USA and Europe.

- **Costs of labour:** This is the most significant factor. Compared to core economies, costs of labour are low and are therefore very attractive to companies wishing to reduce costs of production (see below).

- **Numbers of workers:** The high growth rate in the population, together with an underdeveloped economy, mean that a large supply of workers is available for basic tasks in most countries of the global periphery.

- **Flexible workers:** The protection of workers' rights is generally weak. As a result, employers are often able to exploit their workforce through low wages, long hours of work and poor working conditions (see below).

- **Education:** Initially this was not significant, especially for branch plants. By Phase 4 it had become very important. Countries such as India that have invested in educating their population are therefore able to attract modern growth industries. These provide more secure and better-paid jobs, which are important for economic development.

Because of low wages and poor working conditions, people in the developed world are able to buy goods and services very cheaply. Is this a fair system?

Working Conditions in a Branch Plant Factory

The typical employee of a branch plant factory in the less developed world is a woman between the ages of sixteen and twenty-six years. In general, MNCs prefer women as they are more compliant than men in accepting working conditions that are significantly inferior in terms of security of employment, safety, shift work, wages and fringe benefits. These women usually work 20 to 30 per cent more hours per year than their counterparts in the labour force of developed countries – as much as 50 per cent in some cases.

On the other hand, wages tend to be only 10 to 20 per cent of those paid in core economies. For example, experienced female labour can be paid as little as US$0.15 per hour in Indonesia; this figure rises to US$0.36 in Thailand, US$0.57 in El Salvador and US$0.89 in Mexico. In some instances, these wages barely provide for the basic necessities of life. In spite of these working conditions, however, the productivity per worker tends to be only slightly below that of developed countries. (The minimum wage in Ireland in 2005 was the equivalent of almost $10.00 per hour.)

Activity

1. Describe the typical worker in a branch plant in the less developed world.
2. Why do MNCs prefer to employ women?
3. If you were the owner of a company in Western Europe and were concerned about your wage costs, why would Indonesia or Thailand be attractive for a new investment?
4. Do you think this type of employment is a good basis for development? Why?

Case Study: Nike

Nike, the US sports footwear and clothing company, provides a good example of globalisation and taking advantage of geographical differences between countries and the international division of labour. This is vital for their success.

Headquarters: Bevertown, Oregon, USA
Annual sales: $13.8 billion
Direct employment: 16,000 (mostly in global management, design and marketing)
Indirect employment: 500,000 (essentially production)
Original locations: Core economies such as the USA, UK and Ireland. These production plants have all closed, since they were uncompetitive due to high labour costs.
Relocated to: South-East Asia, where Nike subcontracts production to companies located in over thirty countries. Manufacturing was originally focused in countries such as South Korea and Taiwan. However, as labour costs increased in these NICs, production was relocated to cheaper labour-cost locations in countries such as Indonesia. Now, as costs rise in these countries, Nike seeks out even cheaper locations, such as China.

Indonesian shoe workers protest at Nike's plans to stop ordering sports shoes from Indonesia. Such a decision would result in the loss of 7,000 jobs.

Protests against what was seen as the company's 'sweatshop' working conditions in peripheral countries led Nike to join the Fair Labour Association. This global organisation promotes the ideal of a basic minimum wage to meet the daily needs of a worker and his/her family. Despite this, decisions made by Nike headquarters in the USA to seek low-cost locations still have major consequences for thousands of workers in less developed countries.

CHAPTER 52
TRADING PATTERNS OF THE EUROPEAN UNION

 **KEY IDEA!**

The European Union is the world's largest trading bloc, with extensive internal and external trading links.

Refer to Chapter 43 to review the importance of colonialism and trade.

The countries of Western Europe have a long and important tradition in world trade. This is linked historically to their roles as **colonial powers** which enabled them to dominate world trade. Even following their loss of colonial empires, much of the growing world patterns of trade continue to focus on Western Europe.

The EU forms the world's largest trade bloc. In 2006, the then 25 member states accounted for over 40 per cent of all trade in goods and services. The development and patterns of EU trade, however, can be divided into two types:

- Trade between its member states, called intra-EU trade.
- EU trade with the rest of the world (extra-EU trade).

Intra-EU Trade

Prior to the signing of the Treaty of Rome in 1957, which established the European Economic Community (now called the European Union), trade between countries in Western Europe was limited. This was due, in part, to the great rivalries that existed between countries, such as France and Germany.

Following the Second World War, Europe's economy was devastated and was in urgent need of redevelopment. The Treaty of Rome was central to this process and created a free trade area, or **Common Market,** between member states. This meant the removal of barriers to trade and encouraged growth in trade and prosperity for all member states.

Growth in trade between member states has increased dramatically (see Fig. 52.1). Following slow growth in the 1960s, intra-EU trade has expanded rapidly. By 2005, approximately two-thirds of EU trade flowed between its then 25 member states.

- *Why is the River Rhine important for EU trade?*

342

This growth and the scale of intra-EU trade is due to:

- The Treaty of Rome (1957), which established the **principle of free trade** between member states.
- A number of **enlargements**, which have increased the number of countries in the EU.
- Well-developed **transport and communication networks** to link member states.
- The **size and prosperity of the EU market**, which encourages trade.
- The creation of the **Single European Market** in 1993, which further helped trade flows within the EU.

Germany is the most important member state in terms of intra-EU trade. This is due to its well-developed economy, central location and excellent transport networks. Germany, together with the other top four trading countries of the EU, accounts for 70 per cent of intra-EU trade.

Refer to Chapter 35 to review enlargement of the EU.

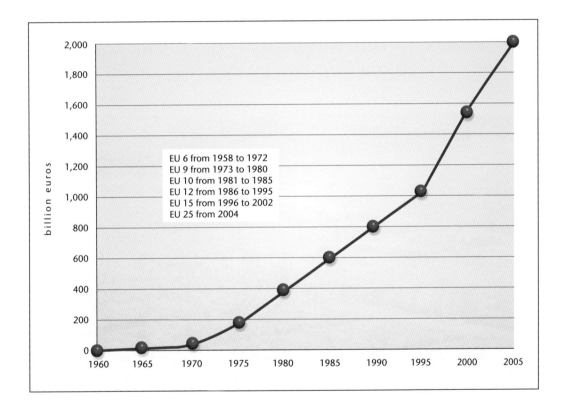

EU 6 from 1958 to 1972
EU 9 from 1973 to 1980
EU 10 from 1981 to 1985
EU 12 from 1986 to 1995
EU 15 from 1996 to 2002
EU 25 from 2004

Fig. 52.1 Growth in intra-EU trade.

- *Explain why enlargements have been important for influencing trends in intra-EU trade.*

EU TRADE WITH THE REST OF THE WORLD (EXTRA-EU TRADE)

Due to its size, levels of wealth and its historic role in global development, the EU has extensive trade links throughout the world (see Fig. 52.2). **The USA and Japan are its most important trade partners and account for 30 per cent of the value of its external trade.**

The EU also has important trade links with many less developed countries. These can be traced to the region's former colonial empires located throughout the world, e.g. the British and French colonial empires.

Remember the global trading triad? It is composed of the three global core regions that dominate world trade (see Fig. 49.2 on page 332).

Rotterdam is the European Union's largest port.
- *From the photograph, suggest a product and a region of the world which are particularly important for Rotterdam's trade.*

One of the most significant agreements to encourage trade and development with less developed countries was the **Lomé Convention**. This originated in 1963 and established formal economic links between the EU and countries in **Africa, the Caribbean and the Pacific** (termed **ACP countries**). Most of these countries are former colonies of EU member states.

In an effort to encourage development, members of the Lomé Convention, now replaced by the **Cotonou Agreement**, are granted duty-free access for all industrial goods and for most agricultural commodities exported to the EU. While this has assisted some economic growth in ACP countries, they contribute a very small proportion of total EU trade (see Fig. 52.2). This is especially the case for sub-Saharan Africa, which includes some of the poorest countries of the world economy.

In addition to its formal links with ACP countries, the EU has increased its trade with countries in **Asia and Latin America**. This relates to the attraction of these world regions (especially NICs) for branch plants and office-related activities.

Why would duty-free access for goods exported to the EU help development in the ACP?

Large numbers of containers line the quayside of the port in Barcelona before being loaded on special container ships for export to markets around the world. Such trade is vital to the continued prosperity of the EU.

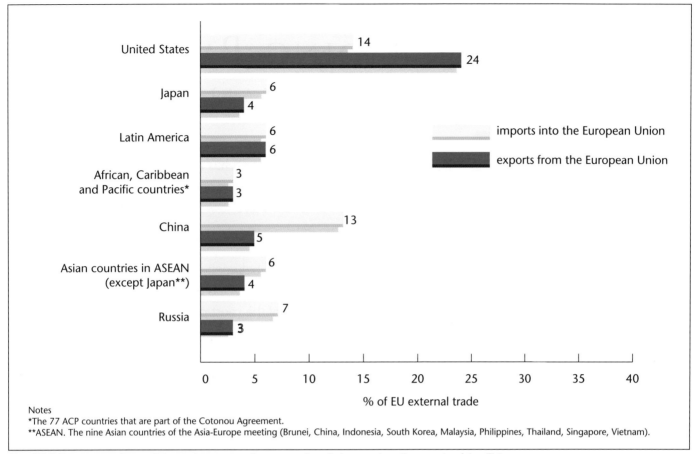

Fig. 52.2 Percentage share of the main partners for external trade in merchandise goods of the EU.

Activity

Study Fig. 52.2 and answer the following.

1. Which country is the dominant trading partner of the EU? Suggest some reasons for this.
2. What global region has the lowest trade with the EU? Why?
3. Why has EU trade, especially imports, increased strongly with Asia (including China)?

CHAPTER 53
IRELAND'S TRADING PATTERNS WITHIN THE EUROPEAN UNION

KEY IDEA! Membership of the European Union has had a major impact on the value, content and patterns of Ireland's trade.

A main aim of the EU is to promote free trade between its member states. In this, Ireland has done well. From being, in effect, a protected economy with limited foreign trade before the 1960s, Ireland is now one of the most open trading economies in the EU. **Since 1973, development of the country's economy has been driven largely by exports.**

Irish trade may be examined under three headings:
- Changes in the value of trade.
- Changing patterns of trade.
- Changes in the make-up of trade.

Free trade within the EU has been crucial for Ireland's successful development.

Dublin Port.
- *Suggest reasons why Dublin is Ireland's most important port for trading with the rest of the EU.*

CHANGES IN THE VALUE OF IRISH TRADE

Before joining the EU in 1973, the total value of Irish trade was relatively small (see Fig. 53.1). EU membership resulted in a steady growth in trade, although the value of imports continued to exceed exports until the mid-1980s. This negative balance of trade was due to:

- High costs of imported energy supplies, especially oil.
- Ireland's new branch plants involved the processing or assembly of imported raw materials and component parts.
- The mass-produced goods manufactured in branch plants for export did not generally have high value.

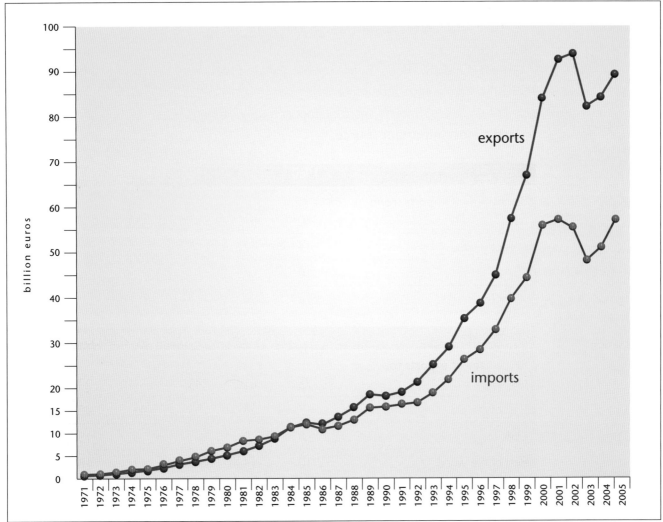

Fig. 53.1 Import and export trade of Ireland, 1971–2005.

Activity

Study Fig. 53.1 and answer the following.

1. What is the main trend for both imports and exports?
2. Do these trends suggest membership of the EU has been good for Ireland's economy?
3. In what year did Ireland begin to show a positive balance of trade?
4. Briefly explain why Ireland's balance of trade has been so positive since 1990.

From the mid-1980s, Ireland's trade increased rapidly. In addition, the value of exports began to exceed imports (see Fig. 53.1). These new trends became especially marked in the 1990s, and were due mainly to changes from a branch plant economy to the production of higher-value goods and services. The net result was a growing surplus in Ireland's balance of trade. This provided the government with resources to invest in upgrading critical infrastructures like telecommunications and education. **The strong trade performance from the 1990s is therefore a critical factor behind the success of the Celtic Tiger economy.**

> The manufacture of computer software requires few, if any, imports. In addition, international services depend mainly on the skilled and educated workers located in Ireland.

THE CHANGING PATTERN OF IRELAND'S TRADE

Historically, Britain has been Ireland's largest trading partner for both imports and exports (see Table 53.1). An important reason for joining the EU was to reduce this level of dependence.

Until the early 1980s, Britain supplied at least half of Ireland's imports. However, as MNC branch plants located in Ireland began to source their imports from other EU and non-EU countries, Britain's share of import trade declined. Despite this, **Britain remains Ireland's most important source**.

> Ireland's diversification of trade links points to its increasing involvement in the process of globalisation.

	1960	1972	1980	1990	2000	2005
Percentage of imports from:						
UK	50	51	51	42	36	32
Rest of the EU	14	17	20	25	23	26
USA	10	8	9	15	15	14
Rest of the world	26	24	20	18	26	28

	1960	1972	1980	1990	2000	2005
Percentage of exports to:						
UK	75	61	43	34	24	17
Rest of the EU	7	16	33	41	40	46
USA	8	9	5	8	18	19
Rest of the world	10	14	19	17	18	18

Table 53.1 Changing patterns of Ireland's trade.

Activity

Study Table 53.1 and answer the following.
1. Which country traditionally dominated Ireland's import and export trade?
2. Describe trends in Ireland's trade with the rest of the EU. Did exports grow at a faster rate than imports?
3. Suggest reasons why Ireland's trade with the rest of the EU and the world has increased.
4. Suggest reasons for the declining importance of the UK for Ireland's trade since 1973.

Changes in Ireland's export trade have followed the general trends for imports. However, **the changes in the geography of the country's export markets have been more dramatic** (see Table 53.1).

One of the main attractions of Ireland for MNC investment was its access to the large, prosperous and growing market of the EU. In effect, MNCs used Ireland as a **production platform** to gain free access to the EU. The net result has been a relative decline in Britain's dominant role and a marked increase in exports to the rest of the EU (see Table 53.1).

As these MNCs began to adopt a more global marketing strategy, exports to both the USA and the rest of the world began to rise. The role of MNCs from the USA is of particular importance, since they account for almost two-thirds of Irish manufacturing employment in MNCs.

● *Suggest reasons why companies such as Liebherr, a German MNC located in Killarney, Co. Kerry, influence Ireland's changing pattern of trade.*

CHANGES IN THE COMPOSITION OF IRELAND'S EXPORT TRADE

As part of Britain's colonial economy, Ireland's exports were dominated by agricultural goods. Despite gaining political independence in 1922, fifty years later, food and live animals still accounted for 43 per cent of the total value of Irish exports (see Fig. 53.2).

Ireland's membership of the EU and its growing attraction for MNCs led to a major change in the make-up of the Irish export trade. Despite the benefits to farming of the Common Agricultural Policy (CAP), the share of exports provided by farm produce fell dramatically to only 6 per cent by 2005.

The dominance of agricultural goods in Ireland's export trade was rapidly replaced by a range of manufactured goods (Figs. 53.2 and 53.3). Multinational companies attracted to Ireland have invested mainly in **international growth industries such as electronics and chemicals**. As a result, two-thirds of the total value of manufacturing exports is accounted for by these two industrial sectors. This has been vital for the modernisation of the country's economy.

In addition, since Ireland is such a small market, **almost all MNC production is for export**. Membership of the EU is therefore crucial for the long-term success of these industries in Ireland.

For the influence of the EU and CAP on Irish farming, see Chapter 54.

Over 90 per cent of most chemicals and electronic equipment produced in Ireland is exported.

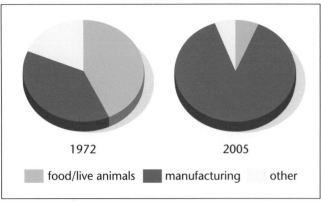

Fig. 53.2 Irish merchandise trade, by main sectors, 1972–2005.

food/live animals ▪ manufacturing ▪ other

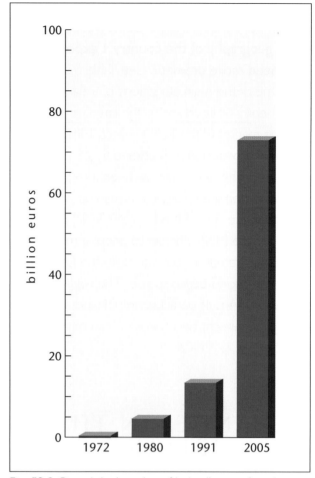

Fig. 53.3 Growth in the value of Ireland's manufacturing exports.

Activity

Study Figs. 53.2 and 53.3 and Table 53.1 and answer the following.

1. What was the most important export sector in 1972? Suggest reasons why.
2. What sector dominated Irish export trade by 2005? Why?
3. In what period did the value of industrial exports increase the most? Why?

Most industries located around Cork Harbour have contributed strongly to the growth in Ireland's trade.

● *Suggest reasons for this.*

CHAPTER 54
THE COMMON AGRICULTURAL POLICY AND ITS IMPACT ON IRELAND

KEY IDEA!

Since 1973, trends in Irish agriculture have been influenced mainly by the CAP.

In 1962, a Common Agricultural Policy (CAP) was introduced to guide the development of agriculture in the EU. Two of its main objectives were to:
- Increase production and productivity.
- Provide a fair standard of living for all farmers.

These required two key policy decisions:
- Creating a common tariff barrier (tax) around the EU to protect its farmers from cheaper imports.
- Establishing an agricultural fund made up of guarantee and guidance sections to finance the CAP.

The **Guarantee Fund** was to maintain high prices for farm produce. It did this by intervening in the market to buy up any surplus output that would cause prices to fall from a high level, fixed each year by the EU. Prices were not allowed to fall below what was called the **intervention price**. To help reduce surpluses, the Guarantee Fund also subsidised exports to allow them to be sold in the world market.

The **Guidance Fund** provides money to help modernise farm buildings and machinery, and encourages increases in farm size. Through these supports, productivity levels are increased.

The CAP had a number of positive and negative impacts on EU farming (see Table 54.1).

The Common Agricultural Policy is called the CAP.

The intervention price is the minimum guaranteed price farmers can expect for their output.

Under the original CAP, the more a farmer produced, the more income was made. This benefited larger, productive farmers and encouraged surplus output. Why?

Positive	Negative
• High prices and guaranteed markets	• Build-up of large, costly surpluses
• Modernised farming	• Larger and richer farmers benefited most
• Increased productivity (intensive farming)	• Environmental impacts such as soil and water pollution

Table 54.1 Some positive and negative impacts of CAP.

In 1992, the first of a number of reforms was made in the CAP. These:

- **Reduced price levels** guaranteed to farmers.
- **Diversified farm activities** to provide additional income, especially for small farmers, e.g. farm-based tourism, forestry, craft industries such as cheese-making.
- Tried to make farmers **more competitive** in the EU and global market for food.
- Provided more **direct income support** for small-scale farmers.
- Stressed the role of the farmer in **protecting the environment**.

IRELAND AND THE CAP

In 1973, agriculture was vital for Ireland. It accounted for 24 per cent of employment, 43 per cent of the value of exports and almost 50 per cent of the population lived in rural areas.

Membership of the EU was strongly supported by Irish farmers. They saw many important advantages from the CAP:

- Free access to a large and growing market.
- Reduced dependency on Britain's low-priced food market.
- Increased and guaranteed farm prices in the EU.
- Large transfers of money via high prices and funds to modernise farming.

Although agriculture has declined in importance since 1973, it still dominates the landscape over much of the country.

Impacts of the CAP on Ireland
Farm Output

Initially, farm output increased under the influence of higher guaranteed prices and access to the large EU market (see Table 54.2). Farms were modernised and productivity increased.

Reforms of the CAP aimed at reducing costly surpluses had a less positive impact on output trends in the 1990s. Furthermore, Ireland's important dairy sector had been affected as early as 1984 when a **milk quota** was introduced to reduce milk output. This caused many small-scale dairy farmers, especially in the West of Ireland, to change emphasis in the 1980s from dairying to sheep (see Table 54.2).

- *What does this cartoon suggest to you about Ireland's view of the CAP?*
- *Do you agree with this view?*

	1970	1980	1990	2000	2005
Product					
Cereals (000 tonnes)	1,408	1,711	1,965	1,986	1,934
Milk (million litres)	3,629	5,425	5,268	5,400	5,500
Veal and beef (000 tonnes)	337	434	515	540	524
Animals (millions)					
Cattle	5.9	6.9	6.8	6.5	6.2
of which:					
Dairy	1.8	1.9	1.4	1.2	1.2
Sheep	4.1	3.3	8.5	5.1	4.3

Table 54.2 Output in selected farm products and animal numbers, 1970–2005.

Activity

Study Table 54.2 and answer the following.

1. Which ten-year period showed the greatest increases for most products or animals? Why?
2. What has been the dominant trend for dairy cattle and milk from 1980 to the present? Explain this.
3. Contrast trends in sheep and dairy cattle. Suggest reasons for the differences.

Overstocking of sheep in upland areas has caused overgrazing and soil erosion. These environmental problems and lower prices led to a decline in sheep numbers since the early 1990s (see Table 54.2).

Activity

Review Fig. 54.1.

1. Estimate the value of exports in 1970 and 2005.
2. Suggest reasons for this growth.

Farm Exports

The EU has provided a large and guaranteed market for Irish farm output. It resulted in **a major increase in the value of Ireland's food exports** (see Fig. 54.1). This has been an important contribution to the country's positive balance of trade.

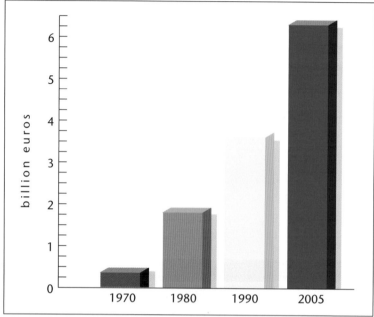

Fig. 54.1 Value of export trade in food and live animals, 1970–2005.

Farm Income

Farm incomes have increased as they benefited from the higher prices and better market prospects in the EU. Despite this, farmers' incomes remain about 70 per cent of the average industrial wage.

- Under the CAP, the more farmers produced, the more they earned. This favoured large and efficient farms, especially in the Southern and Eastern Region.
- Large numbers of farms, especially in the Border, Midlands and West Region, are too small to produce enough output to earn a reasonable income.
- Inequality between small- and large-scale farmers and between the east and west of Ireland has therefore been increased by the CAP.
- Reforms to the CAP since the early 1990s, however, have provided more income support for small-scale farmers. This has helped improve their standards of living.
- Funding from the CAP is vital for Irish farmers. In effect, the vast majority of them depend on subsidies in order to survive.

In 2005, 80 per cent of Irish farm income was provided by CAP subsidies. Does this suggest Irish farming is competitive?

Reform of the CAP

Reform of the CAP in 2004 has changed the system of farm income support. In effect, it has broken the link between production and farm income; to increase income, a farmer no longer has to produce more. This is termed **'decoupling'**. Farmers are now given a single annual payment based on the average income they received from the EU between 2001–04. With this guaranteed income, farmers are now encouraged to:

- Produce farm products for which there is a **market demand** (reduce surpluses).

● *Suggest regions of Ireland in which these farm environments are located. Which of these regions benefited most from the CAP? Explain why.*

● Focus on *quality* and not quantity of output (**higher-value** farm products and **safer** food products).
● **Diversify** farm activities to achieve additional income.
● **Protect their environment** to gain additional income (see page 354).

Numbers of Farmers and Farms

It had been expected that the benefits of CAP would slow down the **long-established decline in agricultural employment**. However, this did not occur (see Fig. 54.2a). While farmers declined in number, the **average size of farms increased** (see Fig. 54.2b). This was important to raise levels of income and productivity. Farms also became more specialised.

> Part-time farming has increased in importance for many small-scale farmers who want to stay on the land.

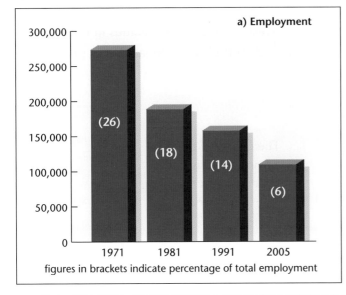

figures in brackets indicate percentage of total employment

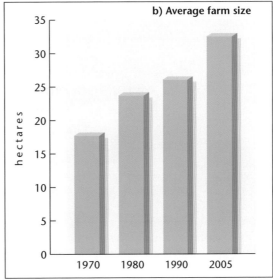

Fig. 54.2 Changes in employment and average farm size, 1970–2005.

Activity

Study Fig. 54.2 and answer the following questions.

1. Estimate the numbers employed in agriculture in 1971. How many agricultural jobs were lost by 2005?
2. Is the trend for farm size the same as for employment?
3. Is there a relationship between trends for employment and farm size? Explain.

● *Alternative farm enterprises, as suggested in this photograph, have increased in importance, especially for smaller-scale farms. Why? Can you suggest any other enterprises farmers can use to increase their income?*

Farming and the Environment

To increase income under the original CAP, farmers were encouraged to use intensive farming methods. While output increased, this was often at the expense of the environment:

● Increased chemical fertilizers gave rise to soil and water pollution.

● Traditional field boundaries such as hedgerows and dry stone walls were removed to increase field size – this meant a loss of habitat for flora and fauna and a decline in scenic quality.

● Overstocking of the land – overgrazing and soil erosion, especially in uplands.

● Replacement of attractive and traditional farm buildings by modern structures.

Since the 1990s, the CAP has focused attention on reducing the environmental impact of intensive farming. Farmers are now given payments to maintain and restore the quality of their farm environments. In Ireland, this works mainly through the **Rural Environmental Protection Scheme (REPS)**.

This commitment to the environment has been emphasised further since the 2004 CAP reforms. Now, all farmers are required to maintain or improve the quality of their farm environments if they are to receive financial support from the EU. **The future of the majority of Irish farmers is now linked more to their abilities in managing a clean environment than their traditional role as producers of food.**

> The quality of the rural environment is crucial for Ireland's tourist industry.

● *Describe what this farmer is doing as part of the Rural Environmental Support Scheme. Why is this important for rural development in Ireland?*

CHAPTER 55
THE EUROPEAN UNION AND IRELAND'S FISHING INDUSTRY

 **KEY IDEA!**

The Common Fisheries Policy (CFP) of the EU has undermined development of the full potential of Ireland's fishing industry.

Ireland has control over a large area of the sea around its coastline. These **territorial waters** provide opportunities to exploit natural resources, such as natural gas and fishing (see Fig. 55.1).

The shallow waters of the continental shelf, warmed by the North Atlantic Drift, are ideal conditions for the growth of plankton. This is the main food for fish.

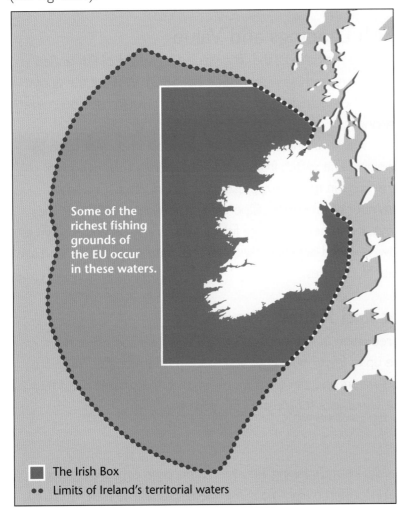

Fig. 55.1 Ireland's territorial waters.

Some of the richest fishing grounds of the EU occur in these waters.

☐ The Irish Box
•• Limits of Ireland's territorial waters

For further information on Ireland's fishing industry and overfishing in the EU, see Chapter 61.

Despite its growth within the EU, the introduction of a **CFP in 1983 has restricted the full potential of Irish fishing**. This is directly linked to the growing problem of overfishing and the need to conserve fish stocks. In addition, a strong feeling has emerged that Ireland undervalued its rich fishing resources in return for ensuring continued benefits from the CAP.

THE CFP AND ITS IMPACT ON IRELAND

Free Access to Ireland's Territorial Waters

One of the main concerns of the CFP is to prevent overfishing and the destruction of this renewable natural resource.

This exposed the country's underdeveloped fishing industry to increased competition from other EU states for its valuable fish resources. Spain in particular was seen as a major threat, but Ireland has succeeded in preventing most of the Spanish fishing fleet from gaining access to the Irish Box until 2010. This will help to conserve fish stocks in this important fishing zone (see Fig. 55.1).

Fish Quotas

For other measures to restrict fishing in EU waters, see Chapter 61, page 389.

Despite possessing 16 per cent of the territorial waters of the EU, Ireland receives a quota of only 11 per cent of the total allowable catch (TAC). This has restricted the development of the Irish fishing industry and has meant the creation of fewer jobs and less wealth, especially along the west coast. **Overfishing** of some valuable species, such as cod, has seen the TAC drop dramatically and has further affected the industry (see Fig. 61.1, page 390).

Total Allowable Catch (TAC)

In its attempt to prevent overfishing, each year the EU fixes an upper limit on a total allowable catch for each member state. A TAC is also fixed for each species of fish within EU territorial waters. Each country is given a quota or percentage of the overall TAC and for each species of fish.

Fish Landings and Value

Despite restrictions, the total value and weight of fish landed have increased significantly (See Fig. 55.2). Without the quota and other restrictions, however, growth would have been even stronger.

Mackerel and herring were the most important catch by weight. The switch from overfished species such as cod to mackerel in the 1990s presented opportunities for a small number of fishermen. Operating mainly out of Killybegs, they invested in new and large fishing vessels and became known as mackerel millionaires. Now, reduced quotas for such fish has meant that fishermen have to look for other, more plentiful species.

The Fishing Fleet and Fishermen

Free access and a small quota means that only 20 per cent of the value of fish caught in Irish waters is by Irish boats.

The CFP has called for a reduction in numbers of fishing vessels. Ireland's fleet has declined and is now made up of fewer but larger and more modern boats. These are able to fish in more distant waters and can catch more fish than the smaller boats they replaced, but they provide fewer jobs for Ireland's fishermen.

Fishing Ports

With fewer but larger vessels, Ireland's fishing industry has become concentrated on a small number of major ports located mainly along the western coastline (see Fig. 26.5).

These provide the essential services for such vessels. In addition, the fishing vessels provide a large and regular supply of fish for the processing industries, which also locate at the main ports. Killybegs and Castletownbere account for one-third of the value of Ireland's total catch.

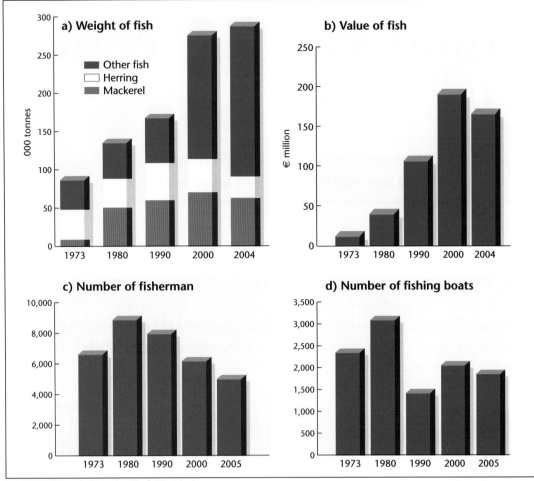

Fig. 55.2 Trends in Ireland's fishing industry.

Irish fishermen continue to argue for higher, not lower, TACs and greater protection of their fishing grounds from other member states, such as Spain.

Activity

Review the bar charts in Fig. 55.2 and answer the following.

1. What is the trend for weight and value of fish landed in Ireland?
2. In what ways do trends for fishermen and boats differ from those for weight and value of fish landed?
3. Suggest reasons why the weight of fish landed has increased even though numbers of boats have declined.

A REVISED COMMON FISHERIES POLICY

The CFP was revised in 2003 to deal with the growing problem of overfishing. Greater stress continues to be placed on reducing total catch, and large areas have been closed or restricted for fishing. Therefore, growth prospects for Ireland's fishing industry do not appear to be strong.

CHAPTER 56
THE COMMON REGIONAL POLICY OF THE EU AND IRELAND

KEY IDEA!

Large transfers of structural funds from the EU have been vital for Ireland's development.

Remember the expected benefits for trade, agriculture and industrial development?

When Ireland joined the EU in 1973, it was the least developed of the then nine member states. Membership of the large and prosperous EU, therefore, held many advantages. Not least was the expectation of a large transfer of funds to help national development. In this context, the introduction of a **Common Regional Policy** (CRP) became a key benefit for Ireland.

Structural funds have been important in raising prosperity levels in Ireland. Despite a lot of investment, however, large areas remain underdeveloped in the Border, Midlands and West Region.

In 1975, a CRP was introduced in the EU. This included the establishment of a **European Regional Development Fund** (ERDF). The ERDF became one of four funds used by the EU to support development in problem regions of the EU. Collectively, these are known as **structural funds**.

Structural Funds

These refer to four funds that are co-ordinated by the EU to support development in problem regions.

- The **ERDF**, the main fund of the CRP, focuses on aiding industrial development and upgrading infrastructures, such as roads.
- The **European Social Fund** (ESF) supports the training or retraining of workers and addressing problems of marginal communities, such as the unemployed and minority groups.
- The **Guidance Section of the Agricultural Fund** aids the improvement of farm structures.
- The **Financial Instrument of Fisheries Guidance** (FIFG) focuses attention on supporting the fishing industry and regions dependent on this sector.

> Gross domestic product (GDP) is another way to measure national wealth. It is the total value of output produced in a country, but excludes net income from abroad. Contrast this with GNP on page 279.

Support from the CRP

To qualify for support under the CRP, a region should have:

- A GDP per person below the EU average.
- A high dependency on agriculture or another declining sector, such as textiles or coal mining.
- High and persistent unemployment.

Ireland qualified on all points and was designated as a single problem region. Between 1975 and 1988, the country received €3.2 billion in structural funds to help national development (see Fig. 56.1). This involved promoting new industrial activities and improving the country's transport systems, especially roads.

In spite of this, levels of prosperity in Ireland compared to those in the EU changed little (see Fig. 56.2). This was because:

- The amount of money was too little.
- There was inefficient use of funding.

> By 1988, Ireland's GDP per person remained less than two-thirds the EU average.

1989–99: A Reformed CRP and the Celtic Tiger

The CRP was reformed in 1988 and had a more positive impact on Ireland. In particular, it addressed the two problems that had limited its impact from 1975 to 1988.

Increased Structural Funds

The EU realised that if inequalities were to be reduced, structural funds had to be increased and targeted on the most depressed regions. This benefited Ireland.

Ireland was designated an **Objective 1** Region. This recognised the severe problems of its peripheral location and underdeveloped economy. As a result, **the country was given high priority for structural funds**.

In the ten years to 1999, Ireland more than trebled its amount of structural funds (see Fig. 56.1). **This was a major source of money for the government to invest in industrial development, modernise the infrastructure and improve the skills of its workforce.**

> Objective 1 Regions are defined as the least developed in the EU. They have a GDP per person of less than 75 per cent of the EU average. See also Chapter 23, page 157.

Between 1993 and 2006, Ireland also received €2 billion from the EU Cohesion Fund. This was used to improve transport and the environment. From 2006, Ireland is no longer eligible for such funding.

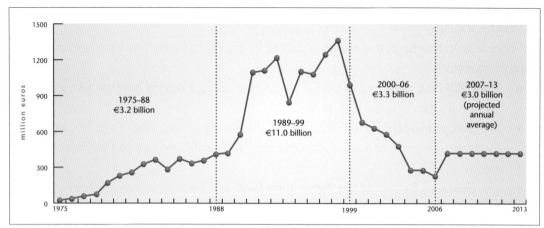

Fig. 56.1 Structural funds to Ireland, 1975–2013.

On a per-person basis, from 1975 to 1999, Ireland received more structural funds than any other problem region.

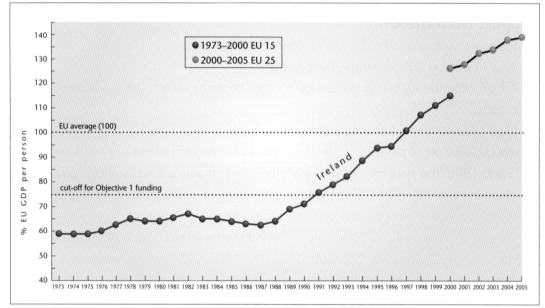

Fig. 56.2 GDP per person in Ireland.

Activity

Study Figs. 56.1 and 56.2 and answer the following.

1. Use the four periods shown in Fig. 56.1 to describe and explain trends in structural funds allocated to Ireland.
2. Estimate Ireland's GDP per person in 1973, 1988 and 2005.
3. Describe the trends for Ireland's GDP per person.
4. Is there a link between the trends shown in Figs. 56.1 and 56.2?
5. In what year did Ireland's GDP per person exceed 75 per cent of the EU average? What should this mean for an Objective 1 Region?

The Wyeth pharmaceutical plant at Grange Castle, near Clondalkin.

- *Use these photographs to illustrate the three interlinked components of development under Ireland's NDPs.*

FÁS is the government body funded in part by the EU and charged with training and retraining workers in Ireland.

National Development Plans

To ensure structural funds are used effectively, Ireland has to submit National Development Plants (NDPs) to the EU. These have forced the government to plan strategically over a number of years and are programmes for sustainable development.

Ireland's NDPs have invested heavily in three key and **interlinked** components of the economy:

- Modernising the productive sectors, such as high-tech industry.
- Improving infrastructures, such as transport and communications, to reduce the costs of a peripheral location.
- Increasing labour skills and flexibility to meet the needs of modern growth industries.

So far Ireland has produced four NDPs: for 1989–93; 1994–99, 2000–06 and 2007–13.

Structural funds and NDPs have been central to the country's remarkable economic recovery. From being one of the poorest member states, Ireland's economic boom has transformed the country into one of the richest in the EU (see Fig. 56.2). This is the Celtic Tiger economy.

2000+: THE CRP AND A PROSPEROUS IRELAND

By 2000, Ireland's level of prosperity meant that it should no longer remain an Objective 1 Region. In spite of this, the government argued strongly that the country's peripheral location and large gaps in its infrastructure justified a continued inflow of structural funds. The government was successful, and structural funds continued to flow into the country. Three important differences, however, are to be noted.

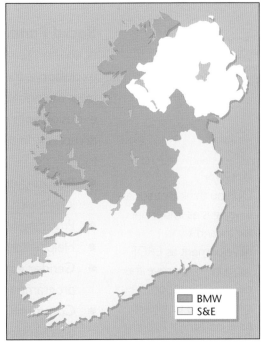

Fig. 56.3 Ireland's planning regions for structural funds, 2000–06.

363

Despite increasing prosperity in Ireland, many people continue to live in poverty. Why is social funding important to help combat poverty?

- The amount of **structural funds has been significantly reduced** (see Fig. 56.1). To compensate for this, Ireland has had to provide the money for most of its development. Thus, for example, under the current NDP (2007–13), the EU is providing only €3 billion of a total planned expenditure of €184 billion.

- Although Ireland retained its Objective 1 status in 2000, the Irish government recognised that the BMW Region had not benefited as much as the S&E Region under the Celtic Tiger economy. As a result, structural funds were **increasingly focused on promoting development in the BMW Region**.

- Ireland's continued economic growth and prosperity mean that the **country lost its Objective 1 status for 2007–13** (now called Convergence Regions; see Fig. 32.1, page 237). Even the BMW Region no longer receives priority funding from the EU. So, while Ireland continues to receive some financial support, this will be marginal for its future development needs. In addition, given Ireland's prosperity, the country **will now pay more in the EU budget than it receives**.

NDPs and structural funds have been a success story for Ireland. The country's productive sectors, infrastructure and human resources have all benefited enormously. This is essential for a peripheral economy like Ireland to compete in a future EU of twenty-seven or more member states.

Social Funding

In addition to regional inequalities, significant social inequalities also exist in Ireland. **Social exclusion** is the term used to define the process whereby some people are excluded from the benefits of development. A key aim of the NDPs, therefore, is to replace social exclusion with **social inclusion** to ensure that all people can benefit from increasing prosperity. In this, the **European Social Fund** (ESF) has a vital role by providing money for:

- Reducing unemployment through **training and retraining schemes** (especially for long-term and youth unemployment).
- Providing more **affordable housing** for the poorest members of society.
- Helping to **integrate minorities**, such as Travellers and refugees, into society.
- **Gender equality** by improving work opportunities for women, e.g. crèches, training programmes.
- **Community support schemes** to help improve the quality of life for people living in disadvantaged areas, e.g. high-density working-class housing areas in inner cities.

Activity

Do you think that social funding is as important for Ireland's development as ERDF support to improve the country's transport systems and to attract new industries? Explain.

CHAPTER 57
RENEWABLE AND NON-RENEWABLE RESOURCES

 **KEY IDEA!** The use of renewable and non-renewable resources, especially energy resources, has been vital for economic development.

Natural resources include mineral deposits (e.g. iron ore, copper), fossil fuels, such as coal and oil, water, air and soil. They can be subdivided into renewable or non-renewable resources.

Renewable resources can be replaced through natural processes. If they are used at a faster rate than they are replaced, these resources can be run down to levels at which they become of little or no use to people, e.g. forests, fish, soil.

Non-renewable resources such as coal, **oil and iron ore** are available only in a **finite amount**. They cannot be replaced once they have been used. The availability of these resources can be extended, however, through careful planning, e.g. recycling and more efficient use.

> Natural resources are used by people to meet their needs, such as food, and as inputs for industrial production, e.g. iron ore.

ENERGY RESOURCES

Energy resources have been, and remain, vital for economic development. For example, the Industrial Revolution, which was centred on Western Europe throughout the nineteenth century, was based on the cheap and large-scale availability of coal. Coalfields, therefore, became major industrial regions; for example, the Ruhr and Sambre-Meuse. Since the Second World War, however, coal has been increasingly replaced by other energy sources, especially oil and natural gas.

The European Union and Energy Resources

The EU has a large and varied range of energy resources. As demand for energy has increased, so has production (see Fig. 57.1).

The main sources of energy production from within the EU have, however, changed significantly (see Fig. 57.2). While **fossil fuels** continue to dominate energy production, oil and natural gas have replaced coal as the main sources of supply. This has primarily been due to the discovery and exploitation of large **oil and gas resources in the North Sea**. In addition, rising costs and pollution from burning coal led to the closure of many coalfields.

Production of **nuclear power** has increased rapidly since the 1970s. It has become especially important for some countries which lack alternative domestic energy resources (for example, Belgium following the closure of its coalfields). **Renewable energy** sources, such as hydroelectric power, are important in Alpine Europe and Scandinavia.

Consumption of energy has also increased within the EU (see Fig. 57.1). This reflects the region's continued economic development. Production inside the EU is unable to meet this demand. As a result, almost half of the region's energy needs have to be imported.

> Coal provided 90 per cent of EU energy supplies in 1950 but only 22 per cent in 2005.

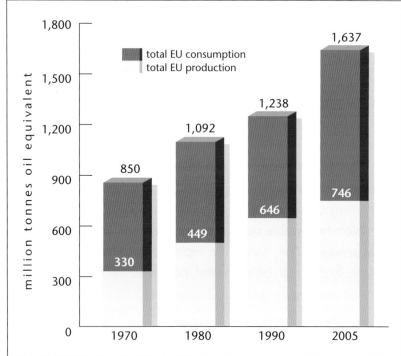

Fig. 57.1 Production and consumption of energy in the EU, 1970–2005.

Despite difficult environmental conditions and high costs, large quantities of oil and natural gas have been produced from production platforms in the North Sea.
● *Britain and Norway have benefited most. Why?*

Activity

Study Figs. 57.1 and 57.2 and answer the following.
1. Describe the trends for energy production and consumption.
2. Is the EU self-sufficient in energy supplies?
3. Describe the main changes in production of energy within the EU between 1970 and 2005. Can you suggest reasons for these changes?

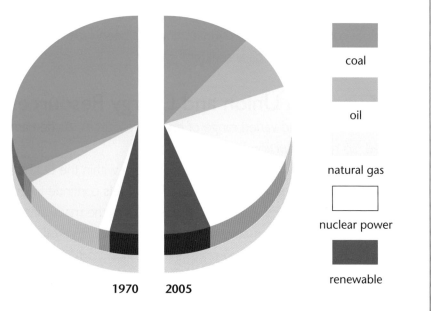

Fig. 57.2 Changing sources of energy production in the EU.

National Energy Resources

Countries such as Britain that possess a large range of domestic energy resources have important advantages for economic development.

In contrast, where national energy resources are poor, as in Ireland, energy has to be imported. This adds to production costs and exposes the economy to the risks of disruption to supplies of energy, as in the oil crises of the 1970s and, more recently, due to conflicts in the Middle East.

Different countries in the EU depend on different resources to meet their energy needs (see Fig. 57.3). Most, however, are not self-sufficient in domestic energy supplies and are **dependent on imports**.

Although production of coal in the EU has declined, the port of Fos, near Marseilles in the south of France, imports large amounts of coal for its large steelworks and coal-fired power plants. Oil is also imported through this port.

> **List some advantages for a country that has a good range of energy resources.**

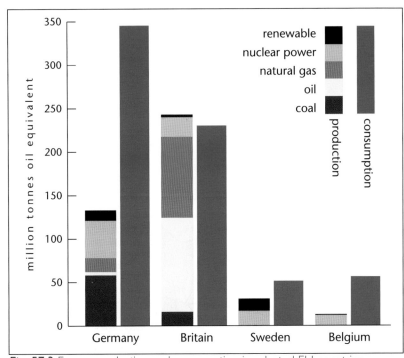

Fig. **57.3** Energy production and consumption in selected EU countries.

A large nuclear power plant in the Loire Valley. France has the largest nuclear power industry in the EU. This energy sector was developed since France now has few alternative sources of energy.

Activity

Study Fig. 57.3 and answer the following.

1. Which country is the largest producer of energy in the EU and a net exporter of energy? Can you explain this?
2. Which country is most dependent on renewable energy? What type of renewable energy?
3. In which country does nuclear power dominate the domestic production of energy? Why?
4. Which country imports most energy? Suggest a problem for such a high dependency.

The relatively small and inefficient peat-fired power station at Bellacorrick, Co. Mayo, was closed in 2005. Note the area of machine-cut turf around the plant.

- *Can you locate another form of energy being developed in this area?*

Ireland and Energy Resources

Ireland has relatively few energy resources (see Fig. 57.4). On gaining independence from Britain, the government attempted to increase the use of its limited sources of energy supply. This has involved both renewable and non-renewable forms of energy.

Through Bord na Móna, the government exploits large areas of bogland. These provide a low-grade fossil fuel in the form of **peat**. This is used for domestic heating and supplying three large, modern peat-fired power stations located in the Midlands (Fig. 57.4).

Renewable energy supplies involve **hydroelectric power stations** on some of Ireland's major rivers. More recently, there has been growing interest in trying to harvest **wind power**, given the strong and regular wind flows that cross the country (see page 137).

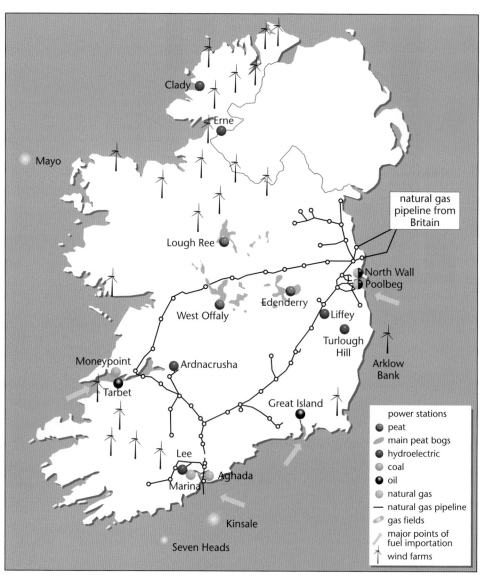

Fig. 57.4 Energy resources of Ireland.

368

Offshore exploration for oil and gas in the 1970s led to the discovery and exploitation of a significant **gas field** off the Cork coast. This gas (and imported gas from Britain) is redistributed through an extensive system of gas pipelines. More recently, a large gas field has been found off the Mayo coastline. This should have major implications for this peripheral region.

Consumption of energy has increased rapidly since the late 1950s (see Fig. 57.5). Since domestic production accounts for about 10 per cent of the country's energy needs, **Ireland is very dependent on imports of energy to promote national development**.

> Natural gas accounts for two-thirds of Ireland's domestic production of energy.

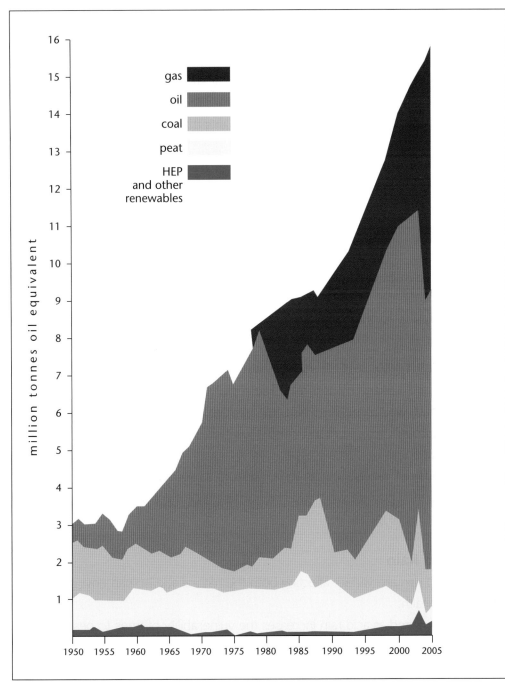

Fig. 57.5 Pattern of energy consumption in the Republic of Ireland.

Activity
Study Figs. 57.4 and 57.5.
1. Why are Ireland's largest power stations located near major ports?
2. Describe the trends in total energy consumption. Suggest why they increased strongly after the 1950s.
3. Which energy source has dominated consumption since the 1960s? Is this a domestic resource?
4. Which two fossil fuels are produced in Ireland? Suggest reasons for the different trends in their consumption.
5. Describe and account for the location of wind farms.

> In 2007, Ireland committed to greatly increase its renewable energy. By 2020, one-third of electricity is to be from renewable sources of energy.

CHAPTER 58
THE ENVIRONMENTAL IMPACT OF BURNING FOSSIL FUELS

KEY IDEA!

Acid rain and declining air quality are two important consequences of burning fossil fuels.

Fossil fuels include coal, lignite or brown coal, peat, oil and natural gas. Since the Industrial Revolution, these natural resources have dominated the energy markets of developed urban and industrial regions. To release their stored energy for human use, fossil fuels have to be burned. This takes place in homes (domestic heating), factories (e.g. iron and steel plants) and especially in power plants that burn fossil fuels to produce electricity.

Burning fossil fuels has increased enormously over the last 100 years and has had a major impact on the environment. This chapter outlines two impacts: acid rain and air quality.

> **Burning fossil fuels also releases large amounts of carbon dioxide (CO_2). They are called greenhouse gases and give rise to global warming (see page 383).**

ACID RAIN

Burning fossil fuels releases large quantities of sulphur dioxide (SO_2) and nitrogen oxides (NO_x) into the atmosphere. These gases react with water vapour to form weak acids. Precipitation then falls to earth as **acid rain.**

The Geography of Acid Rain

> **Remember acid rain from your Junior Certificate studies?**

All parts of Europe are affected by acid rain. The regions with the largest fall-out from acid rain form an east–west zone stretching from Britain to Poland (see Fig. 58.1). This includes most of Europe's major urban-industrial centres and are the sources for most SO_2 and NO_x pollution.

Prevailing winds can cause acid rain to fall far from its source region. As a result, large areas of peripheral Europe which do not burn significant amounts of fossil fuels are affected by acid rain (see Fig. 58.1).

Impacts of Acid Rain

The impacts of acid rain are varied, affecting both the natural and human environments, as well as human health.

- **Forests are damaged** as acid rain increases the vulnerability of trees to pests and disease. Tree growth is stunted, leaves become discoloured and drop early. In extreme cases, the tree dies. An estimated one in four of Europe's trees is affected by acid rain (see Fig. 58.2).

370

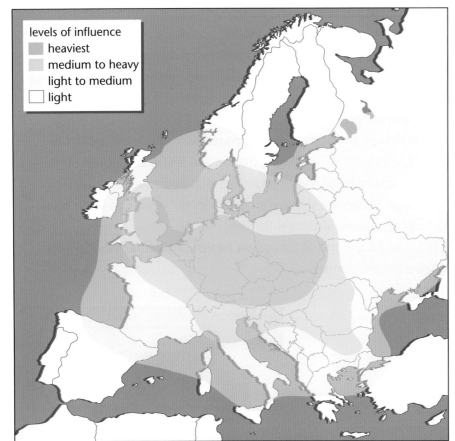

Fig. 58.1 Levels of influence from acid rain.

We turned off the road into a rough track. 'Climb up there,' he said, 'then you'll understand what acid rain is all about.' On the way up I nearly fell into a deep gully gouged out of the mountainside by water rushing down the treeless slopes. From a high ridge I saw a forest of stark, grey, dead tree trunks extending as far as the eye could see. The feeling of desolation was overpowering. If the chimney smoke has had this effect on trees, what could it be doing to human health, I wondered.

A description of the effects of acid rain in south-west Poland
National Geographic Magazine, June 1991

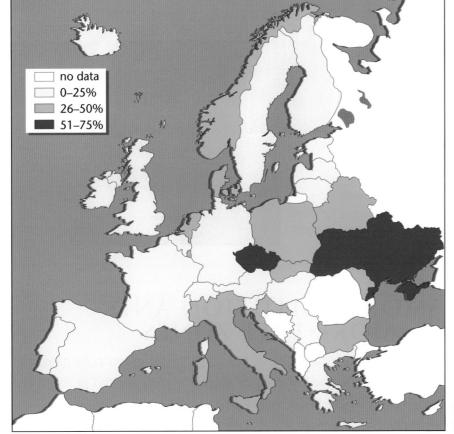

Activity

Study Figs. 58.1 and 58.2.

1. Why are core regions of Europe major sources of acid rain?
2. Explain the high proportion of damaged trees in:
   a. Norway
   b. Central/Eastern Europe.
3. Do you see a relationship between acid rain and damage to trees?

Fig. 58.2 Proportion of trees in Europe damaged by acid rain.

371

- **Lakes and rivers** have their acid levels increased. This affects both fish life and plant growth. In southern Norway and Sweden, the fish populations in a majority of lakes have declined. Lime is being deposited in the most badly damaged lakes to counteract the influence of acid rain. This is an expensive process.

- **Leaching of soils** increases. This removes essential nutrients for plant growth and also causes toxic minerals to enter rivers and lakes.

- **Many important buildings and statues are damaged** as acid rain increases the weathering process, especially of limestone, marble and some sandstones. This can cause a considerable loss of detail to stone carvings that decorate the outside of many historic buildings. When the stonework is sufficiently weakened it can break away from the building, causing structural damage.

- High levels of SO_2 and NO_x in the air can **cause health problems**, especially for people with respiratory problems.

Forest destruction caused by acid rain.

Weathering of stonework increases through acid rain, causing significant damage to many historic buildings.

One of the most severe winter smogs occurred in London in December 1952. Over 4,000 deaths through respiratory and heart problems were linked to the smog. This led to the 1956 Air Pollution Act which quickly helped clean up air quality in British cities.

SMOKE POLLUTION AND SMOKE-FREE ZONES

The burning of solid fuels, such as coal and peat, not only releases greenhouse gases into the air, but also large quantities of solid particles, **or smoke.** Historically, this problem was greatest in major urban areas where heavy industries and large numbers of people burned coal as their main form of energy and domestic heating. In the absence of strict air pollution controls, the larger the city is, the poorer the quality of air.

Smoke and air pollution are generally highest in winter and can cause **winter smogs**. These occur especially in combination with low temperatures (which increase the burning of coal for domestic heat), low wind speeds and temperature inversions (which prevent the dispersal of the pollution).

Case Study: Dublin

Throughout the 1980s, the main air quality problem in Ireland was the occurrence of winter smog. This resulted from the widespread use of coal, particularly in Dublin (see Fig. 58.3).

By the mid-1980s Dublin was producing an average of 55 tonnes per km² per year of smoke-based pollution. This was six times the average amount produced in London. It was claimed that **Dublin was probably the most smoke-polluted city in Europe**.

In 1987, some twenty years later than in Britain, Ireland introduced its Air Pollution Act. As a result, in 1990 a 'coal ban' was introduced in Dublin to prevent the marketing, sale and distribution of bituminous coal in the Dublin area. This created a smoke-free zone for the capital city.

The ban on using 'dirty' coal resulted in a dramatic fall in levels of smoke pollution in Dublin (see Fig. 58.3). In effect, the city is now almost smoke-free. This has had a major impact on air quality within the city. Medical research has also shown that the ban has resulted in fewer respiratory deaths and fewer heart-related deaths per year in Dublin.

Smog over Ballymun before the 'coal ban' was introduced in Dublin in 1990.

● *Has air quality improved in the city since that date?*

Bituminous coal gives off relatively high levels of smoke and SO_2 when burned. This has been replaced by smokeless coal. Access to natural gas by pipeline from the Kinsale Head gas field also helped reduce levels of smoke pollution.

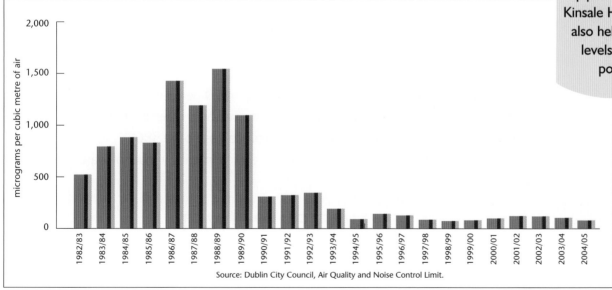

Source: Dublin City Council, Air Quality and Noise Control Limit.

Fig. 58.3 Highest daily black-smoke levels in Dublin City, 1982–2005.

Activity

Study the graph in Fig. 58.3 and answer the following.

1. Describe and account for the trend in smoke pollution in the 1980s.
2. In what year was the highest level of smoke pollution?
3. In what year was there a dramatic fall in levels of smoke pollution? Why?
4. What has been the trend in levels of smoke pollution since the early 1990s?

CHAPTER 59
RENEWABLE ENERGY AND THE ENVIRONMENT

KEY IDEA!

Renewable energy sources are effectively a clean source of electricity, although there are some environmental impacts.

What do the terms biomass, geothermal and solar energy mean?

Sources of renewable energy include biomass, geothermal, solar, tidal, wave, water and wind. Most have been used on a small scale for thousands of years. Today, about 20 per cent of global energy is supplied by renewable energy, mostly in the developing world. In developed countries, however, renewable energy sources generally supply only a small proportion of total energy consumption, e.g. 6 per cent in the EU and 2.5 per cent in Ireland in 2005.

Since the 1980s, there has been increasing interest in renewable energy.

- Improved technologies allow for more efficient production of electricity from renewable resources.
- With effective management, they will not be exhausted (like fossil fuels) and so can provide a long-term solution to global energy needs.
- They are generally clean sources of energy and do not pollute the environment.
- There is greater government support for renewable energy.

In 2007, the EU indicated that it plans to increase to 20 per cent by 2020 the share of renewable energy in the total energy supply. This will help meet its promises to reduce greenhouse gas emissions under the Kyoto Protocol (see page 386).

This chapter reviews the development and environmental impact of water and wind power.

WATER POWER

Remember from your Junior Certificate studies how HEP is generated?

The use of flowing water to create **hydroelectric power (HEP)** is seen by many as an important alternative energy source to fossil fuels. In spite of this, several problems prevent its growth and greater use:

- Most of the **best sites** for HEP have **already been developed**.
- **High costs of construction** of the dams and reservoirs of large HEP stations – this is especially important for developing countries.
- Large HEP stations can cause **some environmental problems**.
  These include:

- Loss of land due to flooding to create the reservoir.
- Resettlement of people displaced by the reservoir.
- Changing environmental qualities for plant, animal and fish life.
- Reduction in the visual quality of the landscape caused by the building complex and transmission lines to distribute electricity.

The larger the HEP scheme, the greater the problems become. Why?

Ireland and HEP

Water power was the first domestic energy source developed to generate electricity in Ireland after independence. The first of the country's HEP schemes was opened at Ardnacrusha in 1929. In the 1930s, it became a vital source for extending electricity supplies throughout rural Ireland.

Most of Ireland's HEP capacity has now been tapped. It is unlikely that any large new HEP station will be built. By 2005, only 2 per cent of Ireland's electricity was provided by HEP.

The Ardnacrusha HEP site on the River Shannon.
- *Do you think the environmental problems linked to the development of HEP were an important consideration for this project?*

A wind farm is a group of wind generators which feed electricity into the national grid.

WIND ENERGY

Wind is one of the most underdeveloped renewable energy resources. However, many countries are now investing in wind power as an effective and clean source for generating electricity.

Preferred sites for wind farms cover large areas, have low population densities, and are exposed to regular winds. Coastal lowlands with onshore winds, or hilltops or mountaintops, provide suitable locations. Offshore areas are also becoming attractive options for wind farms.

Western Denmark and northern Netherlands are important regions for wind power. Why?

A wind farm in Co. Donegal.
- *Why are such sites suitable for wind farms? Do you think they are unattractive features in the landscape?*

By 2010, three-quarters of Ireland's renewable energy will come from wind power.

Service boats are dwarfed by the giant turbines on the Arklow Bank wind farm.
- *Do you think such offshore locations are suitable sites for wind farms? Why?*

Although a clean source of energy, there are some **environmental impacts** linked to wind farms:

- Noise caused by the rotating wind blades.
- The visual impact of the large wind turbines – especially as they are often located in attractive uplands or coastal lowlands.
- The large areas covered, although farming can be continued around the turbines.
- Birdkill.

Wind Power in Ireland

The focus of Ireland's recent national policy for renewable energy is wind. This is linked to the country's large and regular flow of onshore, south-westerly winds (see Fig. 57.4, page 368).

The first wind farm project commenced in 1992, but despite good site conditions, only 2 per cent of Ireland's electricity supply in 2005 was produced from wind. It is planned, however, to greatly increase the number of wind farms in order for Ireland to meet its **target of 33 per cent of electricity demand from renewable resources by 2020.**

In 2002, the Irish government gave planning permission to begin construction of the world's largest offshore wind farm. This is on the Arklow Bank, a sandbank 7 km off Arklow, Co. Wicklow. This project began generating electricity in 2004 and currently there are seven large wind turbines in operation. This development is regarded as a success and there are plans to increase the number of turbines to 200 in total. If this happens, this offshore wind farm could supply almost 10 per cent of Ireland's electricity and serve the power needs of 500,000 people along the east coast. In addition, this will help Ireland meet its Kyoto Treaty obligations by reducing the need to burn fossil fuels to produce electricity.

For renewable energy sources to become a major source of power and thereby reduce environmental pollution from fossil fuels and nuclear power, far greater government investment is necessary. Also, consumers will have to change their attitudes to energy supply. **Are we prepared to pay more for our energy in order to have a cleaner environment?** What are your thoughts on this subject?

CHAPTER 60
ENVIRONMENTAL POLLUTION

KEY IDEA! Pollution knows no boundaries and can impact on the environment at local, national and global scales.

Since the Industrial Revolution, improved technologies and a rapidly increasing population have placed huge pressures on natural resources. Not only are non-renewable resources depleted, but the by-products of development also create major problems of **pollution**.

Furthermore, **pollution knows no boundaries**. As a result, pollution is rarely confined to the area in which it originates.

> Pollution means the release of substances, primarily from human activities, in amounts which cannot be absorbed naturally by the environment.

POLLUTION AT A LOCAL/ NATIONAL SCALE

Waste Disposal in Ireland: What a Load of Rubbish!

There has been a massive increase in the build-up of solid waste, or rubbish, in Ireland. As our levels of prosperity have increased, we have become a 'throw-away society'.

The preferred option, to date, for waste disposal in Ireland has been to use the thirty or so local authority authorised landfill sites (rubbish dumps) located around the country. This, however, is not sustainable, especially as most of these sites are nearing their capacity.

In addition, most local communities are strongly opposed to any planning application to enlarge or open a new landfill site in their locality.

This is often referred to as the NIMBY (not in my back yard) attitude. As a result, there is an urgent need to find an alternative solution for the country's growing mountains of waste.

Each person in Ireland generates a heap of rubbish similar to this every year.
● *Does this create problems for our environment?*

> What is meant by NIMBY? Identify three pollution problems linked to landfill sites.

> Remember acid rain in Chapter 58. Is this an example of 'pollution knows no boundaries?'

Incineration of Waste: A Burning Issue!

This is a recent means of disposing of solid waste. It involves burning waste in large incinerators. The process, however, is very controversial between supporters and those who oppose it, especially in terms of environmental pollution (see Table 60.1).

Table 60.1 Arguments for and against incineration.

In Favour of Incineration	Opposed to Incineration
• Takes up little space	• Air pollution concerns
• Deals with large volumes of waste	• Incineration releases dioxins into the air which can cause cancer
• Generates heat, which provides an additional source of energy	• Residue ash contains toxic materials which have to be disposed of
• Technology ensures only limited pollution	

At least six major incinerators are planned to deal with waste on a regional basis in Ireland. For example, one planned for Poolbeg in Dublin could treat 600,000 tonnes of the city's waste and generate power for 35,000 homes.

Opposition to incineration has been especially strong in Ringaskiddy in Cork Harbour. Here, a toxic incinerator is planned to deal with all of the country's toxic waste. Residents in this area are strongly opposed to the development on the grounds that their local environment and health will be badly damaged by such a venture.

Local residents oppose the construction of an incinerator in their community.

• *Do you think incinerators are a good solution to the country's waste problem?*

Recycling: The Sustainable Solution to Waste?

The volume of waste and its pollution of the environment in Ireland is not sustainable. **A National Waste Management Strategy,** therefore, calls for local authorities and communities to become more committed to recycling or reusing waste materials.

Currently, however, Ireland is one of the least committed to recycling within the EU (see Fig. 60.1). This has to change, and the government aims to recycle 35 per cent of waste by 2013.

Recycling bins for people to deposit their renewable waste are becoming an increasingly common sight in Ireland.
● *Do you support the recycling of waste?*

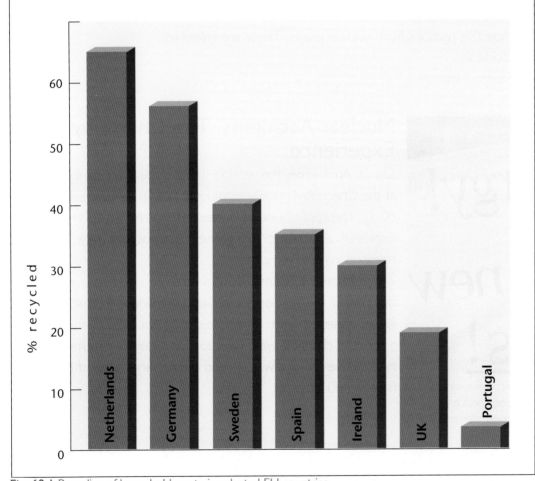

Fig. 60.1 Recycling of household waste in selected EU countries.

One estimate suggests that 100 per cent of household waste can be recycled.

Activity

Study Fig. 60.1 and answer the following.

1. What percentage of Ireland's waste is recycled?
2. What countries show the highest percentage? Does this surprise you?
3. What is Ireland's target percentage for recycling in 2013?
4. Suggest ways in which this target can be met. Do you think this target is reasonable?

RADIOACTIVE POLLUTION: AN INTERNATIONAL PROBLEM

The nuclear power industry uses small amounts of uranium to generate electricity. In the process, radioactive particles are created. These are dangerous to all living organisms. Radioactive particles also remain contaminated for up to 30,000 years. The threat of radioactive pollution to the world's environment will not be resolved quickly.

There are three sources of concern over radioactive pollution:

- **Discharge**, or the escape of radioactive particles from nuclear plants, which pollute the water, air and soil.
- **Disposal** of radioactive water created by the need to cool nuclear reactors.
- **Decommissioning** nuclear plants after their normal lifespan of about thirty years. Isolating and guarding large sites which contain contaminated buildings and material will be difficult, expensive and a long-term commitment.

International concerns over nuclear pollution mainly relate to the **discharge** and **disposal** of radioactive particles from nuclear plants. These are linked to:

- Accidents.
- 'Normal' leakages.

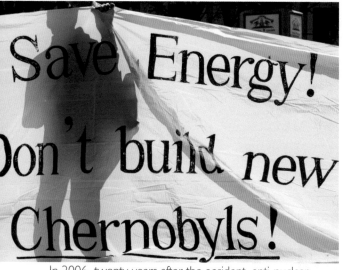

In 2006, twenty years after the accident, anti-nuclear demonstrators still use the Chernobyl experience to protest against building new nuclear power stations.

- *What messages does this banner highlight?*

Nuclear Accidents: The Chernobyl Experience

On 26 April 1986, the world's worst nuclear accident occurred at the Chernobyl nuclear plant near Kiev in the Ukraine (see Fig. 60.2). The roof of one of its reactors was blown off in an explosion. As a result, 190 tonnes of radioactive material were released into the atmosphere.

Radioactive material continued to be released over a ten-day period. While most fall-out occurred close to Chernobyl, lighter materials were transported long distances by the wind. As a result of changing wind directions and rainfall patterns, **the radioactive fall-out was spread over a large area of Europe** (see Fig. 60.2).

The Local Effects of the Chernobyl Nuclear Accident

- The area around Chernobyl is the most radioactive environment in the world.
- Two thousand towns and villages remain uninhabited.
- Large areas of farmland and forest remain contaminated. Food produced in these areas has higher than normal levels of radiation and are a health risk.
- Seven million people have been affected by radioactive pollution.
- Cancer cases are abnormally high, especially in children.

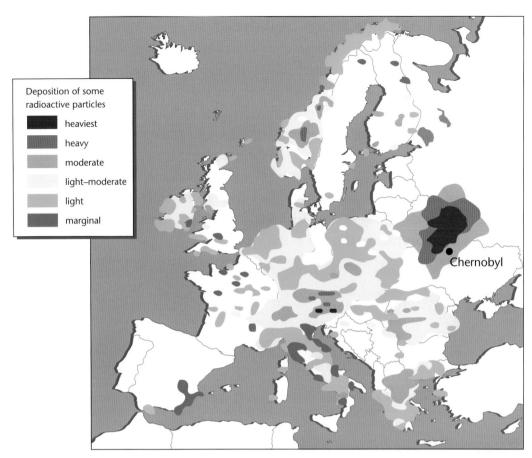

Fig. 60.2 Distribution of some radioactive material from the Chernobyl accident.

Deposition of some radioactive particles

- heaviest
- heavy
- moderate
- light–moderate
- light
- marginal

Chernobyl

Activity

Study Fig. 60.2 and answer the following.

1. What country is Chernobyl in?
2. Where did the heaviest radioactive pollution occur? Why?
3. Describe the overall pattern of radioactive pollution.
4. Does this pattern support the view that 'pollution knows no boundaries'?

A cemetery of highly contaminated and radioactive vehicles used by the Ukranian government in the attempted clean-up operation following the Chernobyl nuclear accident.

Radioactive Leakage from Sellafield

The Sellafield nuclear power plant is located on the north-west coast of Britain (see Fig. 60.3). This extensive operation is concerned with the **storage** and **reprocessing** of nuclear waste.

Sellafield reprocesses both British nuclear waste and used nuclear fuel imported from countries such as Germany and Japan. The end products are plutonium and enriched uranium, which can be used as a fuel for nuclear power plants.

This reprocessing plant has a long history of '**minor accidents**' which have resulted in the **leakage of radioactive materials** into the environment. Much of this involves liquid waste which finds its way into the **Irish Sea**. Largely as a result of this, the Irish Sea is regarded as the **most radioactive sea in the world**.

> Importing highly toxic nuclear waste by ship through the Irish Sea is a cause of great concern. A shipping accident would result in massive pollution of the Irish Sea.

The Sellafield nuclear reprocessing plant in north-west England, located on the coastline of the Irish Sea.

- *How does this plant pollute the Irish Sea? Is this of concern to Ireland?*

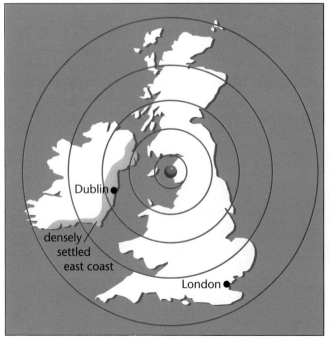

Fig. 60.3 Location of the Sellafield nuclear plant.

Activity

1. Is Dublin located closer to Sellafield than London?
2. What influence do you think this distance factor has on decision-making regarding Sellafield?
3. How could a nuclear accident at Sellafield affect Ireland's densely settled east coast?

Pollution at the Global Scale: Global Warming

The world is gradually growing warmer. Glaciers are receding in the Alps and Andes, while the permafrost of Alaska and the Canadian Arctic is slowly getting thinner and arctic sea ice is melting. The 1990s were the warmest decade, and 1999 was the warmest year of the twentieth century. Most scientists agree that by increasing the greenhouse effect, humans are responsible to a large extent for this global warming (see Fig. 60.4).

How the Greenhouse Effect Works

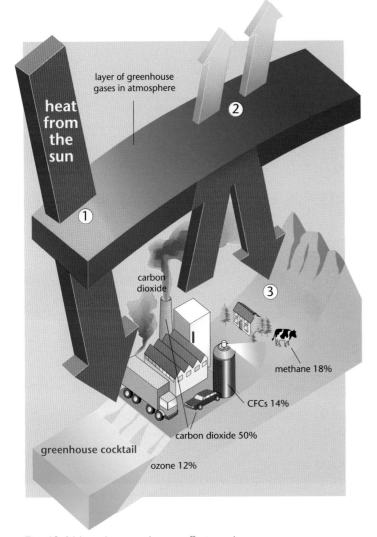

1. The sun heats the earth with **solar radiation** (visible light). This is **short-wave radiation** and **passes in** easily through the earth's atmosphere.

2. The earth converts solar radiation into **infrared heat radiation**, which it sends back into space. But some of this **long-wave radiation cannot easily pass out** through the greenhouse gases in our atmosphere. The principal greenhouse gas is carbon dioxide (CO_2), while others include ozone (O_3) and methane (CH_4). They are called 'greenhouse gases' because they hold in the earth's heat radiation, rather like glass retains warmth in a greenhouse.

3. The greenhouse gases are essential for human survival. Without them, our planet would be a frozen wasteland with temperatures of about 30°C colder than at present. The problem is that the **greenhouse effect has been steadily growing** in recent times as increasing amounts of carbon dioxide and methane are being released into the atmosphere. This causes our planet to gradually become warmer and is likely to have severe human and ecological consequences.

Fig. 60.4 How the greenhouse effect works.

Some Causes of Global Warming

- **Burning of fossil fuels**, such as wood, coal, oil and gas, is the principal human cause of global warming. When these fuels are burned, carbon dioxide is released into the atmosphere, which increases the greenhouse effect.

- **Economically developed countries** are overwhelmingly responsible for the excessive use of fossil fuels. This is directly linked to large-scale industrialisation, intensive agriculture and increased vehicle traffic (See Figs. 60.5 and 60.6 on page 385).

The USA, with only 5 per cent of world population, discharges 25 per cent of global CO_2 emissions.

383

- **Spread of industrial and urban development:** Less developed world regions are copying the development trends of richer countries. The result has been a major increase in the use of fossil fuels (see Fig. 60.5). This is especially the case in India and China.

- **Rapid population growth:** In 1850, total world population was 1.2 billion. Now it stands at over 6 billion. This has increased the demand for fossil fuels, especially for heating and cooking. Since future population growth will occur mainly in the less developed world, the problem of continuing and large-scale emission of CO_2 may be difficult to stop (see Fig. 60.6).

Burning wood for heating and cooking in less developed countries adds to CO_2 emissions.

- *At present the amounts are relatively low, but this will increase rapidly if these people follow the example of the developed world. Why?*

The large-scale use of fossil fuels in core countries of Europe and North America is a major cause of global warming.

For further information on deforestation, see Chapter 63.

- **Deforestation:** Trees are able to absorb carbon dioxide and can help offset the effect of global CO_2 emissions. The destruction of forests, especially large areas of dense, tropical rainforests, is therefore a major concern. Furthermore, the destruction of these forests by burning releases carbon dioxide (which is stored in the wood) into the atmosphere. Through both processes, deforestation adds significantly to the increased greenhouse effect.

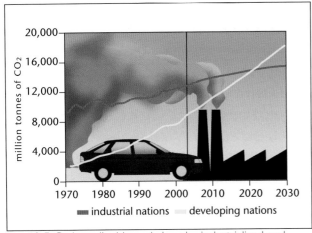

Fig. 60.5 Carbon dioxide emissions by industrialised and developing countries, 1970–2030.

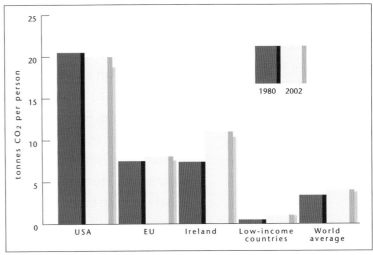

Fig. 60.6 Average amount of CO$_2$ emitted per person.

Activity

Study Figs. 60.5 and 60.6 and answer the following.
1. Describe and account for the trends in CO$_2$ emissions since 1950.
2. Suggest reasons why CO$_2$ emissions from developing countries will soon overtake those from industrialised nations.
3. Why are emissions per person so high in high-income countries?
4. Why are emissions per person so low in low-income countries?

Some Impacts of Global Warming

If greenhouse gases continue to accumulate at their present rate, the earth's temperature could rise by possibly 3°C in the twenty-first century. This could have several dramatic effects on our planet.

- **Sea levels will rise** as melting of the polar ice caps will accelerate. This could result in the **disastrous flooding** of several highly populated coastal and low-lying regions of the world. In Europe, this would include the Netherlands, while in India millions of people living in the Ganges Delta would be affected. In Ireland, more than 19,000 ha of lowlands around the Shannon Estuary could be at risk in the next forty years.

- **Agricultural changes** will occur as global warming causes climate changes. Increased droughts, crop failures and **desertification** could, for example, affect **sub-Saharan Africa**. This would result in famine and mass migrations from this poverty-stricken region to other parts of Africa. In more temperate, mid-latitude countries such as **Ireland**, a rise in global temperatures could result in longer growing seasons and an **increase in agricultural production**. Grass yields could increase by 20 per cent, while crops such as vines and peaches could be grown on a commercial basis.

- **Ocean currents** could change their direction and intensity. This is of particular concern in Western Europe, where oceanographers fear that the melting polar ice caps might cause the **North Atlantic Drift** to take a more southerly course than at present. If this happened, it is likely that **Norway**'s ice-free ports would freeze in winter, with disastrous results for its fishing industry. In **Ireland**, onshore winds blowing off colder seas could result in lower temperatures and wetter winters.

385

Sea levels could rise by at least 50 cm this century.

- **Human health problems** could increase in temperate latitudes as tropical diseases, such as **malaria**, might spread to these regions due to higher summer temperatures. More intensive sunshine could also increase cases of **skin cancer**.
- **World tourism** could be radically altered. While warmer summers might encourage more tourists to visit **Ireland**, many **Mediterranean resorts** are likely to suffer serious decline. For example, it is estimated that by 2050, Crete could be too hot for tourism in the peak tourist months of July and August. Winter ski resorts will also be affected, especially those found at relatively low elevations, such as Splügen in Switzerland. Here, less reliable and lower amounts of snow will not be able to sustain tourism based on skiing.

A Solution to Global Warming: The Kyoto Protocol

For Ireland's commitments and response to Kyoto, see Chapter 75.

Throughout the 1990s many countries recognised the need to combat the dangers of global warming. As a result, an international conference was held at Kyoto, in Japan, in 1997 to discuss this issue. Arising from the conference, an agreement, called the **Kyoto Protocol, set a target of reducing the 1990 global level of greenhouses gases by 5 per cent by 2012**.

This was to be achieved by:
- Reducing the burning of fossil fuels.
- Promoting the greater use of clean, alternative fuels.
- Reducing the process of deforestation, especially in the less developed world (see pages 399–404).

In 2007, the EU pledged to cut its greenhouse gas emissions by 20 per cent, rather than the 10 per cent agreed under Kyoto.

Despite the initial optimism and goodwill for Kyoto, progress has been limited. This reflects the huge problem of trying **to break the direct link between economic development and increasing use of fossil fuels**. For example, the USA has abandoned its commitment to Kyoto because a reduction in greenhouse gas emissions would 'harm the American economy'. Without the active co-operation of the world's leading polluting country, it is generally recognised that the targets set by Kyoto will not be achieved. This is a matter of serious concern for the future of planet Earth. In addition, the rapidly expanding economies and growing populations of India and, especially, China are releasing large and increasing amounts of CO_2 into the atmosphere (see Table 60.2). Without greater and immediate commitment to limit CO_2 emissions, the Kyoto targets will not be achieved. This is a matter of serious concern for the future of the planet.

	CO_2 Emissions (billion tonnes)		Annual Rate of Increase (%)
	2003	2004	2003–2030
North America	6.8	9.7	1.3
Developing Asian countries	5.8	16.0	3.6

Table 60.2

CHAPTER 61
SUSTAINABLE ECONOMIC DEVELOPMENT AND THE ENVIRONMENT

 **KEY IDEA!** Sustainable economic development takes a long-term view of development and reduces its negative impact on the earth's natural resources.

Economic development has brought many benefits for humanity. It has also brought problems for past, present and future generations. Our overuse of non-renewable resources, such as fossil fuels, has polluted the environment (e.g. acid rain, global warming) while also reducing the reserves available for future generations. In addition, misuse of renewable resources limits their potential for long-term development.

An alternative model of development is needed. It should take a long-term view of development and reduce the negative impact of economic growth on the environment. This is the model of **sustainable economic development.**

> Sustainable economic development means meeting the needs of the present without limiting the ability of future generations to meet their own needs.

ASSESSING THE ENVIRONMENTAL IMPACT OF ECONOMIC DEVELOPMENT: THE IRISH EXPERIENCE

A major problem for planning sustainable development in Ireland is a lack of knowledge of the global environment and the potential impacts that development projects can have on the environment. To overcome this problem, the **environmental impact statement** (EIS) has been introduced.

The EIS now forms a vital part of national and county development plans in Ireland. Before any major development project can proceed, an EIS has to be undertaken. This:
- Is made by independent researchers.
- Assesses and reports on the state of the environment.
- Evaluates the costs and benefits of the project.
- Assesses its likely impacts on the environment.

All major infrastructure projects, such as this new road and bridge over the Boyne River near Drogheda, must undergo an EIS.
● *Do you think the EIS is important to regulate development?*

The EIS therefore evaluates the likely environmental impacts of a project **before** the project is allowed to start. As a result, modifications or restrictions can be imposed on developers in order to reduce any future negative impacts on the environment.

The Role of the Environmental Protection Agency (EPA)

To further promote sustainable economic development in Ireland, the **Environmental Protection Agency** (EPA) was established in 1993. The EPA closely monitors the state of Ireland's environment and advises the government on matters of environmental policy.

One of the main purposes of the EPA is to **licence and control all large-scale activities that have the potential to cause significant environmental pollution**. So, for example, any industry or waste-disposal site wanting to operate in Ireland must apply for an **integrated pollution control licence**. This details the levels of pollution within which they can operate. Industries must report their ongoing emission levels to the EPA, which monitors them to ensure they stay within their limits. In this way, economic development should proceed with only limited impacts on the environment.

> The mission statement of the EPA is to promote and implement the highest practical standards of environmental protection and management for sustainable and balanced development.

Cork Harbour is the chemical capital of Ireland. All these chemical plants must have an EPA licence to operate.
● *Why is this important?*

Sustainable Development and Ireland's Fish Stocks

Ireland's territorial waters (see Fig. 55.1 on page 357) include some of the richest fishing grounds in the European Union. For a long time, this natural resource remained underdeveloped. Since the 1970s, however, pressures on fish stocks have increased rapidly. The causes of this have been:

> Maintaining a clean environment in Ireland is vital for 155,000 jobs in farming, forestry, fishing and tourism.

● **Unrestricted access to Irish waters** for fishing fleets from other EU countries is the **main cause**.

- The **increased size and efficiency of Irish fishing vessels** that allowed more than a fourfold increase in the weight of fish caught by Irish boats (see Fig. 55.2a on page 359).

The result has been **overfishing** and the **depletion of fish stocks**. This is **not sustainable economic development**.

As a natural resource, fishing can sustain a reasonable rate of exploitation, providing there is **no prolonged overfishing**. Fish stocks can be sustained in two ways:
- Allow the spawning stock to reproduce at an effective level.
- Allow young fish to mature to add to the breeding population.

The Common Fisheries Policy (CFP) of the EU has tried to encourage this in four ways:
- Establishing a **Total Allowable Catch (TAC)** for each species of fish to be caught in EU waters (see page 358).
- **Conservation measures** to protect the young and spawning fish. These include preventing fishing in certain areas, called fishery exclusion zones, minimum mesh sizes of nets to prevent catching young fish, and restricting the number of days a fishing boat can be at sea.
- **Reducing the size of the fishing fleets** of each member state.
- **Controlling and enforcing** the TACs and conservation measures by fishery protection vessels and monitoring landings of fish at ports.

> Foreign vessels account for 80 per cent of the value of all fish caught in Irish waters.

> An early example of overfishing occurred in the 1970s when herring stocks in the Celtic Sea were almost wiped out. Between 1977 and 1982 all herring fishing in this area was suspended to allow herring stocks to recover.

> Remember the impact of the CFP on Irish fishing in Chapter 55.

An arrested Japanese fishing vessel at anchor in Castletownbere. This trawler was caught fishing illegally within Ireland's territorial waters. Such activities reduce fish stock for Irish fishing boats.

These measures have not been successful. National governments and fishing organisations have argued successfully to increase the size of TACs. These have therefore been set at too high a level for fish stocks to replace themselves (see Fig. 61.2). Control and enforcement of conservation measures have also been difficult. In addition, most governments (including Ireland) have tried to resist demands to reduce the size of the fishing fleets.

The result has been continued overfishing and depletion of fish stocks in EU and Irish waters.

Most fish species in Irish waters are now under threat. For an industry which depends on a renewable resource, this is not sustainable. **Unless much stronger and more effective policies are put in place and are accepted by the fishing industry, one of Ireland's richest renewable resources will be lost.** This will be a disaster for the environment and for coastal fishing communities.

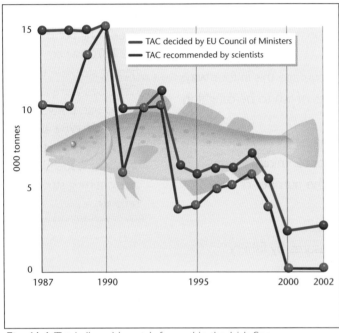

Fig. 61.1 Total allowable catch for cod in the Irish Sea.

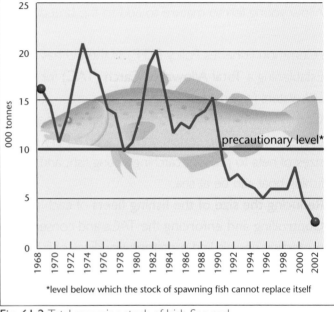

*level below which the stock of spawning fish cannot replace itself

Fig. 61.2 Total spawning stock of Irish Sea cod.

By 2000, two-thirds of fish stocks in EU waters were approaching commercial extinction.

Activity

Study Figs. 61.1 and 61.2 and answer the following.
1. Describe the trend for the TAC in cod. Why did this occur?
2. How do TAC levels compare with scientific recommendations?
3. What has been the main trend for spawning cod since the early 1980s?
4. In what year did Irish Sea cod fall below its precautionary level?
5. What do the trends shown in both graphs mean for the future of fishing in the EU?

Mining and Environmental Impact

Mining refers to the activity of digging, generally below ground level, to extract non-renewable mineral resources, such as coal and copper. In the past, this activity gave rise to major problems for the environment around the mine site. These include:
- A huge build-up of waste which litters the landscape.
- The pollution of rivers and groundwater.
- Large amounts of dust in the atmosphere.

In addition, mining generally requires large numbers of workers. Communities are therefore built up in close proximity to the mine and become dependent on it for their livelihood.

When mineral resources become exhausted or too costly to extract, the mine closes. This leaves:

- **A despoiled landscape**.
- Mining communities with **high unemployment**.
- Governments needing to invest large amounts of money, through **regional planning,** to restore or rehabilitate the environment and encourage new industries to relocate to mining communities.

This is not sustainable economic development.

Since the 1970s, however, the mining industry in developed countries has become more aware of its environmental impacts. The industry is required to reduce pollution levels and restore the quality of the environment if pollution occurs. In this way, mining now has a less negative impact on the local environment and communities. **This is more sustainable economic development.**

Communities in the South Wales coalfield usually developed around a local coal mine. Waste material from the mines gave rise to polluted environments.
- *Why was regional planning important for such areas?*

> Remember the problems of the Sambre-Meuse coalfields in Chapter 42?

Case Study: Tara Mines

In 1977, Europe's largest zinc and lead mine began production near **Navan**, Co. Meath. **Tara Mines** extracts ore from extensive underground workings and processes it into almost pure zinc and lead called **concentrate**. The concentrate is transported by rail to Dublin Port for export.

By the 1970s, planning restrictions were in place in Ireland to reduce the environmental impact of mining operations. This was particularly important for Tara Mines since it was sited near urban centres and in a rich agricultural region. It was also close to the Blackwater River, one of the country's prime fishing rivers. The **planning conditions** included:

- The mining site was to be screened by trees to reduce the visual impact.
- Noise and air pollution were closely monitored.
- Large quantities of mining waste, or tailings, were carefully managed.
- Water used in the operation was purified before being released into the Blackwater.

> Some 7 per cent of the costs of development were given to conservation measures.

The site of Tara Mines, the largest zinc and lead mine in Europe, processing over 2.5 million tonnes of ore a year.

● *Use evidence from this photograph to discuss whether the development of Tara Mines has had a large-scale and negative impact on its environment. Then compare the photo of Tara Mines with the photo on page 391. Which suggests more sustainable economic development?*

The waste from processing the ore is called tailings. It is a mixture of water and solid particles.

Tara Mines has an integrated pollution licence from the EPA.

Disposal of waste is the main problem for Tara Mines (see Table 61.1). Each year, 1 million tonnes is returned underground to backfill areas that have been mined. Most waste, however, is piped to a tailings pond located 5 km from the mine. Here, the solid particles settle to the bottom of the pond, leaving clear water above.

Total Production at Tara Mines, 1977–2005	
Ore processed	60 million tonnes
Zinc concentrate	8 million tonnes
Lead concentrate	1.5 million tonnes

Table 61.1

Activity
Study Table 61.1. What do these figures tell you about the waste problem for Tara Mines?

The water from the tailings pond is recycled for use in the mine. Over time, the level of solid tailings builds up. Eventually, the water is drained off the tailings, leaving new land. This **rehabilitated land** can then be used for grassland or left as a natural wetlands.

In the ways described above, the surrounding environment is not extensively damaged. The environment is rehabilitated so that it will not repel new developments when the mine closes. This is important for the 650 workers and communities that depend on the mine. As a result, **modern mining practices and concerns with environmental impact can be seen as a form of sustainable economic development**.

CHAPTER 62
ECONOMIC DEVELOPMENT OR ENVIRONMENTAL PROTECTION: A CAUSE FOR LOCAL CONFLICT

 **KEY IDEA!**

Conflicts of interest can occur within local communities over the extent to which their natural environments should be exploited for economic gain or protected to maintain their quality.

Economic development is generally viewed positively by most people, especially if their quality of life is improved. It can, however, cause a conflict of interests within local communities. This generally focuses on the priority that should be given to protecting the environment as opposed to promoting its use for immediate economic gain.

This chapter reviews local conflicts of interest that have arisen in Ireland over:

- Large-scale development of fish farming.
- Peat extraction or bogland preservation.

> Another example would be the conflict over developing heritage tourism in the Burren, such as the Mullaghmore Visitor Centre.

FISH FARMING IN IRELAND

Fish farming has developed rapidly in Ireland since the early 1980s (see Fig. 62.1). This recent growth has been due to:

- Restrictions placed on total fish catch at sea under the CFP of the EU (see Chapter 55 and pages 177–8).
- Increasing market demand for fresh fish and fish products.
- Excellent environmental conditions for fish farming, especially along Ireland's western coastline. These include:
  - Pollution-free water due to the absence of large-scale, urban-industrial development.
  - Many sheltered bays and estuaries.
  - Regular tidal flows to help keep the water clean.

> Fish farming is the cultivation of fish under controlled conditions, for example in large fish cages.

Fish farming in Killary Harbour, which forms the border between Co. Mayo and Galway. Here, workers at transport cages bring salmon to the surface for harvesting.

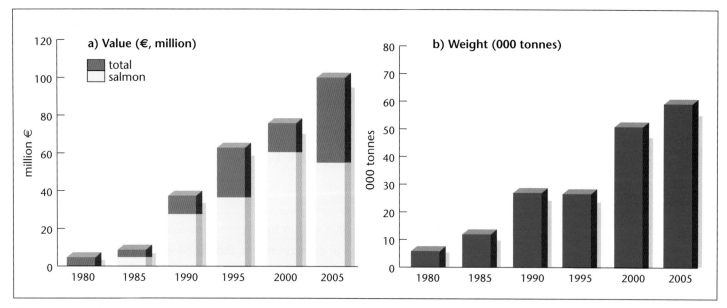

Fig. 62.1 Growth in the output of Irish fish farming, 1980–2005.

Activity

Study Fig. 62.1 and answer the following.

1. Describe and explain the trends shown in both graphs.
2. What is the most important type of fish by value?
3. Do you think development has been good or bad for coastal communities? Explain your answer.

Economic Interests Promoting Fish Farming

Several economic arguments have been used to justify the large-scale development of fish farming along Ireland's western seaboard.

- Remote coastal communities have **high rates of unemployment and emigration**. The introduction of fish quotas and conservation measures under the EU fishing policy reduced one of the main natural advantages possessed by small fishing communities.

- These **coastal communities need to be supported**, and both the Irish government and the EU identified fish farming as having good prospects for development. **Generous incentives** are offered to help set up fish farming operations. Most are located along the western coastline, especially in counties Donegal, Mayo, Galway, Kerry and Cork (see Fig. 62.2).

- The **natural environments** of these areas are very good for fish farming. In addition, the **fishing tradition** and use of local, renewable resources help to **reduce costs** of production.

- Despite government support, the costs of setting up large fish farms are high. Companies are therefore encouraged to **rear as many fish as possible** to offset costs and make a good profit.

- The **creation of new jobs and wealth** remain the main argument for developing fish farming. By 2005, over 1,800 jobs had been provided in fish farming.

The Irish government is committed to further development of fish farming and to double its output in 2003–08.

- The success of fish farming also generates **spin-off industries**, and therefore more jobs and wealth for these coastal communities, e.g. building fish cages, preparing fish feed, processing the fish.

Environmental Objections to Fish Farming

Initially, there were few objections to the development of fish farming in Ireland. However, as the scale of its development increased, objections have been raised regarding the impact of fish farming on **local environments**.

- **Water quality** declines due to the large-scale use of chemicals to help combat the spread of parasites and disease among the high concentrations of fish. Chemicals are also used to clean the fish cages. These chemicals are dispersed throughout the water bodies in which the fish farms are located.

- **Water pollution** levels also increase as excess fish food, faeces and dead fish fall and build up below the cages. This build-up of material pollutes the water, which was a major initial attraction for fish farming in that area.

- **Diseases** can break out and spread quite easily through the fish in the high-density environments. **Sea lice** in particular are a major problem and kill large numbers of fish.

- **Escaping farm-bred fish** can interbreed with native wild fish species. Also, diseased fish and the spread of sea lice, mainly from salmon farms, have caused a **massive decline in native sea trout and in wild salmon**. As a result, there are now far fewer native sea trout and wild salmon found in Ireland's main fishing rivers. (Is this good for angling tourism?)

- The overdevelopment of fish farming can affect the **scenic qualities** of the coastal environments in which they locate. For example, fish cages and pollution washed up on the shoreline can be unsightly.

areas of large-scale fish farming

Fig. 62.2 Locations of large-scale fish farming in the West of Ireland.
- *Why are such locations suitable for fish farming?*

Most environmental concerns are linked to the scale of fish farming, especially salmon, where many thousands of fish are confined in cages within relatively small areas.

The Conflict of Interests

The economic interests of fish farmers and the government are to develop the industry further. This, they argue, will bring more jobs and prosperity to coastal communities.

Many local communities, however, fear that large-scale fish farming has negative impacts on their environment. They say this affects the development prospects of other activities that depend on the local coastal environment and that could help to diversify their economy. These include:

- Tourism.
- Other forms of fishing, both coastal and inland.
- Water sports.

Integrated Coastal Zone Management: A Solution?

There is an urgent need for effective planning to help resolve this conflict of interests. This should involve an Integrated Coastal Zone Management scheme. These schemes try to ensure that various interest groups, such as fish farmers, tourists and anglers, are able to use the coastal environment **without** damaging it for others. In this way **both the economic and environmental interests** of local communities are protected, and allow for long-term sustainable development.

> The Federation of Irish Salmon and Sea Trout Anglers has suggested that Ireland's stocks of native sea trout and wild salmon have become victims of ethnic cleansing. What do you think this means?

IRELAND'S BOGLANDS: AN ISSUE OF HERITAGE?

At one time, Ireland's **boglands** covered large areas of the country (see Fig. 62.3). They were an important natural resource, providing peat, which could be used as a source of fuel.

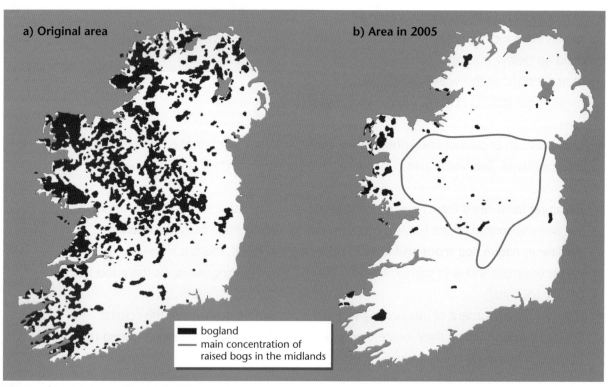

a) Original area   **b) Area in 2005**

▬ bogland
— main concentration of raised bogs in the midlands

Fig. 62.3 Changing area of boglands in Ireland.

While peat extraction from Ireland's boglands has occurred over many centuries, the rate of removal increased markedly following the 1950s. **Exploitation of peat was seen as important for the country's economic development.** Before the development of its natural gas resources, Ireland had no alternative energy supply, apart from some HEP.

Dependency on imported energy sources was therefore extremely high. This was an economic disadvantage, highlighted by the oil crises of the 1970s, and encouraged the large-scale development of boglands for peat.

Most peat is extracted by Bord na Móna from the large **raised bogs** of the Midlands. Here, the more level terrain and deep layers of peat allow for strip mining of peat by large machines. Most of the peat is used as a fuel source for peat-fired power stations. This **helps the national economy and also provides many jobs** for communities that have become dependent on the peat industry.

On the large areas of **blanket bog** in the West of Ireland, peat is also harvested as an economic resource. Farmers cut the peat as a source of domestic fuel and sell the surplus as a cash crop. It is therefore an essential resource for many marginal communities.

As a result of the economic exploitation of peat, less than 20 per cent of Ireland's original boglands remain (see Fig. 62.3).

This loss of boglands is a source of concern for many people interested in the environment. Ireland's boglands are regarded as one of Europe's last wilderness areas, possessing many unique qualities. As a result, **they need to be protected as part of our heritage** and not lost for the production of peat.

- Boglands support a great range of rare plants and animals.
- They are important as bird sanctuaries.
- Many archaeological sites and cultural relics are preserved in the boglands.
- They are attractive natural environments which can be promoted to attract tourists.

> The state established Bord na Móna in 1946 to develop the economic potential of peat.

Machine-cutting of peat from raised bogs, such as the Bog of Allen in the Midlands, removes large amounts of this natural resource for burning in power stations.
- *Do you think this is the best use for this declining natural resource?*

- *Traditional hand-cutting and drying of peat on blanket bogs in the West of Ireland remains an important part of the land use for many upland farmers. Why? Would forestry be an acceptable alternative and renewable land use in these areas?*

Areas of blanket bog in the West of Ireland.
- *Do you think such wilderness areas should be protected?*

A **conflict of interest** has emerged over the conservation or exploitation of boglands. The interests of communities that are dependent on peat extraction have to be protected, but equally the loss of Ireland's boglands will leave the country's natural environment in a poorer state.

> Preservation of boglands will create some new jobs and wealth through eco-tourism, e.g. bird watching, rambling. Will this help communities adjust to job losses in the peat industry?

Farmers Enraged as EU Orders Ban on Turf-Cutting

More than 6,000 farmers have been ordered to stop cutting turf on their land. The move follows criticism from European Union partners over Ireland's failure to enforce laws protecting about 200,000 acres of bog as special areas of conservation. Farmers' representatives say the crackdown is the latest attack on a way of life already under siege.

Because of their unique chemical properties, the wetlands are home to rare flora and fauna, which environmentalists are anxious to protect. They are among the last remaining wildernesses in Europe and have been proven to serve a historical purpose by preserving tools and even human remains for thousands of years.

For the farmers, however, the wetlands are a source of fuel. Turvey rights, allowing families to harvest turf from local bogs for use during winter, have been passed down from generation to generation.

Turf provides cheap fuel and additional income to farmers around Galway, Roscommon, Mayo, Kerry, Donegal and large parts of the Midlands. Those who do not use their rights often sell them on to professional turf cutters.

The farmers' association says it can understand why the government is trying to clamp down on industrial harvesting by Bord na Móna and the ESB. However, a spokesperson added: 'I cannot see in what way the harvesting of small amounts of turf on a hillside bog can be especially harmful to the environment. It has been going on for hundreds of years and the wildlife has prospered.'

Sunday Times, 15 September 2002

Activity

Read the newspaper extract above, then answer the following.
1. How many acres of bogland are to be conserved?
2. Why are the bogs to be conserved?
3. Why do farmers object to the loss of turf-cutting?
4. Do you support the farmer or the EU over the issues of cutting turf? Why?

CHAPTER 63
ECONOMIC DEVELOPMENT OR ENVIRONMENTAL PROTECTION: GLOBAL CONCERNS

 **KEY IDEA!**

At the global level, large-scale exploitation of sensitive environments creates major problems, such as deforestation and desertification.

The previous chapter introduced conflict of interests at a local level between people favouring economic exploitation of the environment as opposed to those favouring its conservation and a more sustainable form of development. This chapter reviews similar conflicts, but on a much larger scale and giving rise to major global concerns. Two examples of global conflict are highlighted:

● Deforestation.
● Desertification.

> Deforestation means the large-scale cutting and clearing of forests for wood products and to create new land for agriculture and other land uses.

DEFORESTATION

The cutting of trees has long been a characteristic of development, as people create more land for farming and settlement, and wood for fuel.

For example, large areas of Europe have been cleared of trees, as in Ireland, where forests now cover only 10 per cent of the landscape. Developed countries, however, now recognise the significant economic and environmental benefits of forests if they are developed in a sustainable way. As a result, **reforestation** rather than deforestation is more typical in the developed world (see Fig. 63.1).

Deforestation continues to occur on a vast scale in the less developed world, where one half of the world's forests are located. **This is especially the case in tropical regions**, where exploitation of these valuable natural resources is seen by many people as offering important economic benefits. Opposed to this view, however, are a growing number of people who see **large-scale deforestation of the tropics as not only a natural, but also a global, environmental disaster**.

> Can you think of any economic and environmental advantages of increasing forest areas?

About 2 billion people living in developing countries still rely on wood and dung for fuel. This contributes significantly to deforestation and desertification.

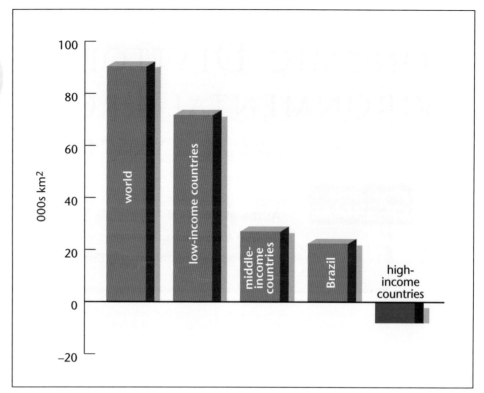

Fig. 63.1 Average annual deforestation, 1900–2000.

Activity

Study Fig. 63.1.

1. Which global region shows the greatest rates of deforestation? Why?

2. What is unusual about trends in high-income countries? Explain.

Case Study: Deforestation in the Amazon River Basin

Most of the Amazon River Basin consists of a vast area of equatorial rainforest, or *selva*, situated in north-west Brazil (see Fig. 63.2). This *selva* makes up one-third of the planet's tropical rainforest. Until the 1960s, interference with this vast ecosystem was minimal. Since then, however, increasing numbers of people have moved into the Amazon rainforests. The result has been **massive deforestation**.

The Amazon River meanders through extensive areas of tropical rainforest. Overexploitation of this major natural resource will have serious consequences for the future development of our planet.

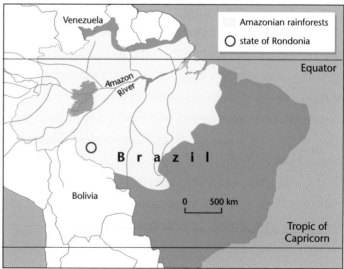

Fig. 63.2 The extent of the Amazon rainforest in relation to Ireland.

400

Economic Interests and Deforestation in the Amazon Basin

Economic interests of decision-makers who usually live **outside** the region are **not** focused primarily in sustainable development. As a result, they have a major role in the large-scale deforestation of the Amazon Basin.

- The general cause of rapid deforestation is the **concept of development** which views the *selva* as a wilderness to be conquered for profit. This view is shared by profit-hungry **domestic and multinational logging, mining and other companies**, and also by successive **Brazilian governments**. For these organisations, deforestation allows for a range of products, such as wood, minerals and food, to be exploited. Most of these products are **exported** to earn income for the government and profit for the companies.

- **Cattle ranching** is one of the most important but environmentally damaging land uses within Amazonia. Some large ranches, set up with government aid, were devoted to supplying American fast-food outlets with cut-price beef burgers. Most of these new grasslands were farmed in an unsustainable manner. The land loses its fertility and degenerates into scrubland within a decade of the forest being cleared (see Fig. 63.3). This reults in more land having to be cleared by farmers.

- **Land ownership patterns** throughout Brazil have been extremely uneven and unjust, with just 2 per cent of the population owning more than half of the country's agricultural land. This gave rise to demands for land redistribution by millions of land-hungry peasants in the south and east of the country. The government saw the Amazon Basin as an **'easy solution' to the land problem**. Poor Brazilians were lured into Amazonia with promises of free land (which needed to be cleared of trees) and a more prosperous future.

- **Consumers in the developed world** provide a major market for the products of Amazonia, e.g. wood, minerals, cheap food.

- **International monetary bodies** have played major roles in Amazonian deforestation. The **World Bank**, for example, has invested heavily in the region since 1981 and has funded developments such as the Polonoroeste Project. This huge settlement and farming project was responsible for widespread deforestation in the Amazonian state of Rondonia (see Fig. 63.2).

Extensive areas of the Amazon rainforest are being cleared for farming and wood products. In 2005, over 26,000 km² of the Amazon was deforested. This type of exploitation is unsustainable.

401

Economic and Environmental Interests Opposing Deforestation

A growing body of 'local' and global opinion opposes large-scale deforestation in areas such as the Amazon Basin. This reflects a variety of economic, environmental and cultural reasons.

Within the Amazon Basin

- **Loss of productive land**. In its natural state, the tropical rainforest is a **rich but finely balanced ecosystem**. When this ecosystem is upset by deforestation, the land can become a barren wasteland (see Fig. 63.3). Deforestation, combined with unsuitable farming practices (such as ranching), quickly reduces soil fertility. Farmers (and loggers) then have to clear more forest. This is **not a sustainable form of economic development**. It also contributes to the growing problem of **desertification** (see pages 404–406 for a more detailed account of this process).

The ecosystem ...

1. Trees **intercept** precipitation and so protect the soil from heavy tropical rain.
2. The tree canopy provides **shade** for animals and small plants.
3. Soil nutrients and water are taken up by the tree roots and gradually released through the leaves by the process of **transpiration**. This reduces the amount of water in the ground and helps to regulate rainfall.
4. Trees shed leaves and other plant litter, which bacteria in the soil turn into **humus**. This compensates for the soil nutrients taken up by the trees.
5. Leaching (washing down of soil nutrients) is limited.

high rainfall and temperatures

Destroyed ...

1. Heavy rain beats on the soil, causing **erosion**. The upper soil layers, which contain the most nutrients, are the first to be washed away.
2. With less shade, the hot sun can harden the soil and make it less permeable. This increases **gully erosion** by surface water.
3. More groundwater means swollen rivers and **flooding**.
4. Reduced plant litter causes the soil to become barren and eventually **desertified**.
5. Heavy leaching washes soil nutrients below the reach of surviving plant roots.

Fig. 63.3 A rainforest ecosystem and some of the consequences of its destruction.

It is calculated that in the Amazon Basin, one or more species is now becoming extinct every day!

- **Loss of plant and animal species:** Tropical rainforests cover only 6 per cent of the earth's surface, but contain over 50 per cent of its plant species. Deforestation destroys the environment that supports such a rich variety of plants, as well as the extensive range of animals that survive in this habitat. This decline in **biodiversity** is not only a disaster for the Amazon Basin, but is also of major concern for the global environment.

- **Loss of cultural diversity:** Forest peoples face cultural and human extinction because of Amazonian 'development'. One such people is the **Yanomami** who live on both sides of the Venezuelan-Brazilian border (see Fig. 63.2). These people lived independently for centuries by hunting, fishing and subsistence farming in a manner that did not upset the delicate balance of the forest ecosystem. Since the 1970s, however, the Yanomami have seen their territories invaded by 'developers' and their culture diluted by Western influences. 'Outside' diseases, such as measles, have killed up to **90 per cent** of the people in some Yanomami villages. Traditional social life has been shattered, with many survivors being forced to adopt a squalid roadside existence as beggars and prostitutes.

Yanomami with vine for basket making. Tribal peoples like the Yanomami have lived in harmony with their environment through hunting and food gathering.

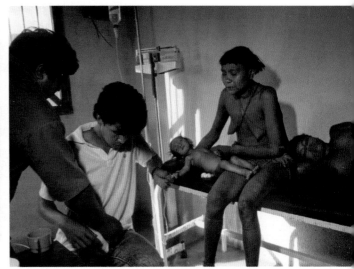

For the Yanomami, deforestation destroys their subsistence way of life, while migrant workers expose them to disease they have no resistance to. Here, a Yanomami mother brings her child dying from a disease brought to their territory by migrant workers to a field hospital.

Activity
Use the two photographs above to discuss the influence of outside development on traditional tribal cultures.

Deforestation and Global Concerns

- **Human health and development:** Many pharmaceutical drugs have originated from research conducted on plant and animal species found only in tropical rainforests. Great potential exists for many more discoveries, especially since only 10 per cent of these species have been studied. It is very important, therefore, that we protect these vital global ecosystems.

- **Desertification:** Deforestation and unsustainable farming result in a growing area of barren and desertified landscapes within the Amazon Basin. As a result, deforestation is contributing to the global spread of desert conditions or desertification (see pages 404–406).

403

Remember the causes and threats of global warming in Chapter 60, pages 383–6.

- **Global warming and climate change:** This is perhaps the most important global issue linked to deforestation. Tropical rainforests are considered to be the 'lungs of the world'. This is because these vast forests absorb large amounts of CO_2 from the atmosphere and convert it into oxygen. Deforestation reduces this natural process. Furthermore, the burning of trees adds more CO_2 to the atmosphere. **Conserving the rainforests therefore has a vital role to play in reducing the threat of global warming and associated climate changes.**

Possible Solutions for Sustainable Development

The short-term economic exploitation of tropical rainforests, as in the Amazon Basin, has to be replaced by approaches that encourage more long-term, sustainable development. These could include:

- Promoting the renewable resources of the rainforests as a source of wealth and employment, e.g. harvesting food and medicinal products, selective cutting of trees and replanting.
- Establishing national parks in the rainforests to attract high-income tourists to visit these exotic environments.
- Reward developing countries that conserve large areas of rainforests in the interests of protecting the global environment. For example, the **Debt for Nature Scheme** allows less developed countries to offset some of their debts by protecting large areas of tropical rainforest.

DESERTIFICATION

Desertification is a process involving the spread of desert conditions, usually into adjacent semi-arid environments. Once the process of desertification begins, it is extremely difficult (and expensive) to stop.

This is a large-scale and growing global problem and affects virtually every semi-arid region of the world. It is even occurring in the Amazon Basin linked to deforestation. The global region **worst affected by desertification**, however, lies along the southern edge of the Sahara Desert. This is called the *Sahel* (see Fig. 63.4).

Causes of Desertification: The Sahel

Scientists believe that desertification is caused by **three** factors that work together.

- **Rainfall totals** are very low and unreliable in the Sahel. Since the 1960s, it has experienced a period of prolonged drought.
- Human actions in other parts of the world contribute to **global warming**, which influences climate change.
- **Increased population** in the Sahel forces more people into marginal environments, especially as the most productive land is usually given over to cash crops for export. As a result, people **overgraze**, **overcultivate** and **deforest** the land in order to survive.

These processes have occurred as a result of conflict between local and more global interests over the use of this region's land resource. In effect, **national and global economic interests have overridden local and more traditional land uses** (see Table 63.1). The result is desertification.

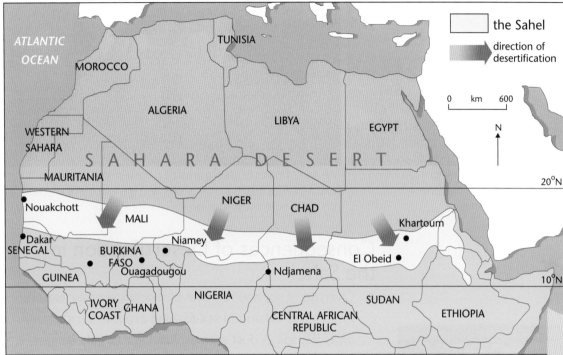

Fig. 63.4 The Sahel. This region stretches for 6,000 km east to west along the southern edge of the Sahara Desert.

Some estimates suggest that in the Sudan, for example, the desert frontier has been advancing at 5.5 to 9 km a year.

Global and National Economic Interests	Local and Traditional Interests
• Global demand for primary products, such as groundnuts (peanuts) and cotton, encourages intensive farming.	• Concentration on a variety of food crops grown on a rotation basis, and including a fallow period, prevents soil exhaustion. No overcultivation.
• National governments promote cash crops for export to help finance development and repay global debt.	• Nomadic herders graze a variety of animals over extensive areas to avoid overgrazing.
• Falling world prices demand a further increase in output. This pushes intensive farming into more marginal environments, which cannot support intensive farming.	• Traditional land uses are therefore well adapted to the difficult environment.

Table 63.1 Economic versus environmental interests in the Sahel.

Many children of the Sahel die from diseases due to malnutrition. For example, Kwashiorkor results in wasted limbs, swollen stomachs and an almost complete lack of energy.

The size of herds of grazing animals in most of the Sahel has increased. This results in overgrazing and the herding of animals into even more marginal areas.

Financial aid and improved education are vital to stop desertification. Here, women are building small stone walls to help prevent further soil erosion.
- *Why does this, and the planting of trees, help stop desertification?*

Consequences of Desertification in the Sahel

- Overuse of soil and removal of vegetation cover expose the dry and exhausted soil to wind erosion. Winds carry away the soil as **dust storms, leaving a largely barren landscape** to become part of the advancing Sahara Desert.

- Failure of the land to provide adequate harvests and grazing, especially in years of drought, results in **large-scale famine**. Millions die of **hunger or disease** as the health of the population declines.

- As the Sahel fails to support its population, millions are **forced to migrate southwards**. This can lead to overpopulation in reception regions. One result is an overuse of land to feed these people, which encourages the **further spread of desertification**.

- Many migrants move to cities, such as Niamey in Niger (see Fig. 63.4). These cities become **overpopulated** and demand for firewood causes deforestation of the limited trees that grow in the urban hinterland. This adds further to desertification.

At the global level, one estimate suggests that desertification threatens 35 per cent of the earth's land and 20 per cent of its population. The future well-being of the earth and its population cannot afford to lose such a vast renewable resource if sustainable economic development is to occur.

CHAPTER 64
MODELS OF DEVELOPMENT

KEY IDEA!

We must critically examine contrasting models of development.

Almost everybody is in favour of human and economic development. People may disagree, however, on how development can best take place. This has given rise to different approaches to development. These approaches are called 'development models' and each has its own strengths and weaknesses. Three contrasting development models are discussed in this chapter.

Model 1: The Determinist Approach

A theory called **environmental determinism** was popular among some European and other Western geographers in the nineteenth and early twentieth centuries. This approach to development is now regarded as being oversimplistic.

Theory

The determinist approach is centred on the idea that **human development is determined by** (depends on) **environmental factors** such as climate, relief and soils. It argues, for example, that some countries in tropical regions are destined to be underdeveloped because of negative environmental factors, such as deserts, natural disasters or tropical diseases. It also proposes that people in some 'temperate' mid-latitude countries tend to be high achievers because of the presence in these countries of climatic conditions that suit mental and physical activity. In the past, some supporters of the determinist model used the above arguments to justify as 'natural' the domination of Third World countries by European empires in the nineteenth century.

Strong Points

There is no doubt that environmental factors can have considerable influence on human development. This is especially so in places which, because of their physical geography, suffer from extreme climatic, agricultural or human health problems.

High, steep slopes and poor soils (see photo above) can discourage economic development in parts of the West of Ireland, but it is often possible for people to develop these areas, as can be seen from the bottom photo. This shows the weakness of determinism as a theory of development.

- Mountainous areas, such as some of those in the **West of Ireland,** find economic development difficult, because high land and steep slopes hinder agriculture and transport.
- **Niger** and **Mali** are countries that are situated on the fringes of the Sahara Desert. Dry conditions there discourage agriculture, so that rural population densities are very small. This in turn means that these countries lack the population and infrastructure needed for significant economic development.
- Extremely hot and humid conditions can discourage human activity and therefore human development in places such as the **Congo or Amazon Basins**, where heavy convectional rainfall is common and where midday temperatures normally exceed 30°C.

Weaknesses

The great weakness of the determinist approach is that it ignores the fact that **environmental conditions are not the only factors that influence development.** It also overlooks the fact that people can overcome environmental difficulties in developing their regions.

- The **Inca** people once developed a great and prosperous civilisation in the high Andes mountains of Peru. They built terraces in order to farm steep slopes and used suspension bridges to cross deep gorges.
- **Mali,** a country at the edge of the Sahara Desert, was once a great and prosperous centre of trade. Timbuktu in Mali was an important university centre before Oxford University was established in Britain.
- **The Swiss Alps** largely consist of high mountains with steep slopes and thin soils. They are without significant mineral resources and have no port. Yet, largely through the clever adaptation of the Alpine region to industry and tourism, Swiss people have developed this region into one of the most prosperous in Europe.
- The southern part of the Central Valley of **California** has an extremely dry climate. Irrigation schemes have, however, turned this region into one of the most agriculturally prosperous in the United States.

Most geographers now agree that human or economic development is not determined solely by economic conditions, but can be **made possible by human activity.** This general idea is called **possibilism.**
There are many **possibilist** models of development. They include:
- **Modernisation** and **Free Enterprise Model.**
- **Centrally Planned Model.**

Model 2: Modernisation and Free Enterprise

At present, this development model **dominates** most of the world. Typified by the **United States,** it now holds sway in a great number of countries ranging from **Brazil to Ireland to Nigeria.**

The Irish economy has grown enormously as part of a modernised global economy. Many modern factories, such as the computer plant shown here, are owned by foreign multinational companies. They produce high-value, low-bulk products for export.

Theory

This model's aim is to provide a **global economy** in which all barriers to trade will be removed and in which **private enterprise or capitalism** would be allowed to operate with minimum interference from governments or people. The theory of this model is that countries should make **exports** the priority for development. Wealth created by exports could be used to pay for imports and (especially in the case of Third World countries) to pay back international debts. The theory of this model is that free international competition will result in continued economic growth. The benefits of economic growth will eventually 'trickle down' even to the poorest people, making everybody better off than before.

Good Points

The principal positive result of this approach to development has been the **massive creation of wealth**. The world's leading economy – the USA – is the cornerstone of capitalist development. The Irish economy, too, has grown enormously as an export-driven economy. The economies of some Third World countries, such as South Korea and Brazil, have also grown significantly. A minority of people have amassed great personal wealth. A vast variety of consumer and luxury goods and services are readily available for those who can purchase them.

A young child worker in an Asian carpet factory. The exploitation of child labour has been a feature of free enterprise development in some parts of the world.

Weaknesses

The modernist, free-market approach has, in its purest form, given rise to several concerns, especially of a social, cultural or moral nature.

- This model sees development only in terms of economic growth. It tends to value **profit above people**. In developing countries especially, some free-market wealth has been created through the abuse of poor women and children who are forced to work in very bad conditions for low pay (see the photograph).
- The free-market model emphasises the creation of wealth but pays little heed to its fair **distribution**. This has contributed to grave and widening economic inequalities, both between and within countries. The world's seven richest people now own more personal wealth than it would take to provide basic water supplies, health and education facilities for all the poor of the world.
- The modernist model tends to discourage state involvement in running social services such as public transport, water supplies and even public health. Instead it favours the privatisation of public services so that they can be run 'efficiently' by private companies for profit. In countries such as the United Kingdom, privatisation

409

Ireland's wealthy Celtic Tiger economy was achieved through the modernisation and free enterprise development model. Yet throughout the height of the Celtic Tiger economic boom, many social services have been funded inadequately. In 2006, for example, Ireland's public health care was found to be among the worst in all of Europe.

Gross national product (GNP) is the total value of all output produced by a country's economic activities in a year.

has resulted in the decline of many public services. This has adversely affected the quality of life of many poorer people and so has led to increased inequality between rich and poor.

● This model of economic modernisation was semi-imposed on countries such as Russia, Nigeria and Mexico as part of the **structural adjustment programmes** prescribed by the International Monetary Fund. These programmes, while often increasing the **gross national product** of the countries involved, brought many hardships for workers and poorer people:

　– **Unemployment increased** dramatically as formerly state-supported industries were 'slimmed down' to make more profits for their private owners.

　– Enforced **devaluation** of local currencies made exports easier to achieve, but they also greatly **increased** the **costs** of imported oil and other essentials.

　– The governments of developing countries were not allowed to subsidise the price of basic foodstuffs because this might hinder 'international free trade'. The resulting **increases in the costs of basic foods** pushed many poor people to the brink of hunger.

　– Third World countries were encouraged to greatly increase exports so that they could better pay their debts to foreign bankers. Nigeria, for example, was encouraged to give more and more land over to the production of cocoa. This resulted in less basic food being grown for local consumption and so led to increased **malnutrition**.

Model 3: Centrally Planned Development

This development approach was broadly based on the communist ideas of Karl Marx. It was originally developed in the former USSR (Russia) and China, but was practised in various forms throughout the 1960s and 1970s in a number of Third World countries. Central planning is still practised (with recent modifications) in Cuba and China.

Theory

The aim of this approach to development is to create **greater equality** in the distribution of national wealth and to provide for the **principal human needs** of every citizen. It follows Marx's belief that the state should give 'to each according to his needs' and receive 'from each according to his ability'.

This model seeks to develop an economy by means of **planned industrialisation**. Factories, land, banks and other commercial entities were **nationalised** and managed by the state on behalf of the people. Profits were invested in **social services** and in **producer goods** (such as steel) for further production, rather than in consumer goods and personal 'luxuries'.

Good Points

The positive results of many centrally planned states lay mainly in **social gains** for all people. Cuba, for example, enjoyed tremendous improvements in health care, education, the equality of women and sporting achievements following the socialist revolution led by Fidel Castro. In the socialist-controlled Kerala region of India, over 90 per cent of girls as well as boys receive a formal education and the average life expectancy is nineteen years higher than in the rest of the country.

Weaknesses

Problems associated with central planning include the **discouragement of individual initiative and political choice**. Strict government control over production severely limited private enterprise. Some monopolistic state industries began to produce shoddy goods or provide inefficient services. Consumer and 'luxury' goods, not being widely produced, were generally in short supply. Each of these factors combined to severely limit economic growth. In politics, too, individualism was frowned upon, leading to rather rigid one-party political systems. Largely because of its **failure to bring about prolonged economic growth**, this model has been abandoned in most of the countries that once practised it.

Cuba in 2007: Centrally planned development in this Third World island-nation has not stimulated the production of a great deal of personal wealth. It has, however, succeeded in distributing wealth to provide high standards of education and other social services for all.

411

The **Human Development Index** measures development by taking into account a combination of **life expectancy** rates, literacy rates and **GNP per person**.

Summary: The Need for an Appropriate Development Model

No major model fully answers the needs of human development. The **determinist** approach is seriously flawed because it does not even adequately recognise the potential of people to develop themselves. The **modernist/free enterprise** model is generally good at producing wealth, but poor at distributing it. The **centrally planned model**, on the other hand, is good at distributing but poor at producing wealth. Countries that follow the free enterprise model are more likely to enjoy high GNP levels. Countries that follow socialist models, on the other hand, might enjoy relatively high adult literacy and life expectancy rates and so score relatively well on the **Human Development Index**.

Perhaps what really matters in development is for the people of an area to be able to meet their own needs, solve their own problems, guarantee the ecological survival of the area and enjoy life at a satisfactory pace. That is what we might call **appropriate development**, because it is appropriate to the real needs of ordinary people in any given locality.

Appropriate development requires people to participate, co-operate and take control of their local communities. With appropriate development, the individual is liberated both from the tyranny of endless competition as well as from the bureaucracy of the state. He or she is free to develop in the only way that really matters – as part of a caring, tightly knit and viable group.

Activity

Read the summary above and discuss the following.
1. Outline the faults of three major development models referred to in this chapter.
2. Define the concept of appropriate development in your own words.
3. Do you think that appropriate development, as described above, is desirable and achievable? Explain your point of view.

Fig. 64.1
- *What point does this cartoon make about development?*
- *Which development model is the cartoon referring to? Explain your answer.*

Activity

Critically examine any two development models of your choice.

CHAPTER 65
DESCRIBING A DIVIDED WORLD

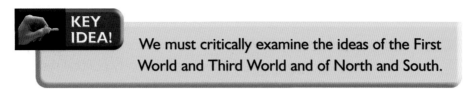

KEY IDEA! We must critically examine the ideas of the First World and Third World and of North and South.

We are aware that great divisions exist between the rich and poor countries of the world. Over time, two different models have been used to describe these broad divisions:

● **The three-world model.**

● **The two-world or North-South model.**

The Three-World Model

In the 1960s to the 1980s, people described inequality between countries in terms of a threefold division of the planet into the First World, the Second World and the Third World (see Fig. 65.1).

● **The First World** was made up of countries in Western Europe and North America, but also included Australia, New Zealand and Japan. These were the richest countries in the world and had capitalist, free-market economies. Many First World countries, such as Britain and France, became wealthy when they were centres of powerful empires. Today, they are ruled under systems of parliamentary democracy in which two dominant political parties usually compete for power.

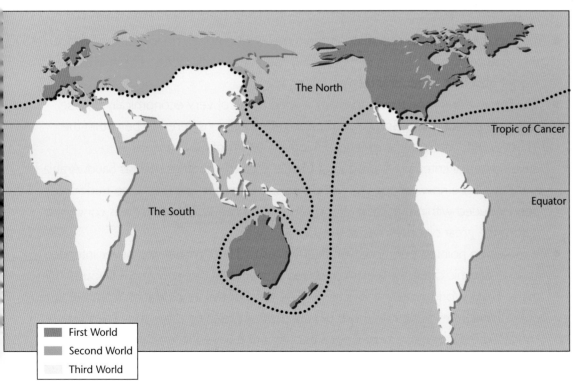

Fig. 65.1 The First, Second and Third Worlds. It also shows the world divided into 'North' and 'South'.

(a) This map is known as the **Peter's Projection**. It shows the correct sizes but not the correct shapes of landmasses. Contrast this map with the Mercator map shown on page 417.

(b) This map is similar to one produced in a textbook for schools in Australia. In what way does its 'world view' contrast with that presented by most maps used in Ireland?

(c) Make three separate lists of ten countries in each of the First, Second and Third Worlds.

The term 'Latin America' refers to Central and South America. Most people there speak Spanish or Portuguese, both of which are known as Latin languages.

- **The Second World** was comprised of communist and socialist countries with centrally planned economies. Second World countries consisted mainly of Eastern European states, such as Poland, Hungary and the former Soviet Union. While Second World countries were not nearly as rich as many First World countries, their people generally enjoyed adequate diets and good life expectancy rates. They also enjoyed good social services, such as health and educational facilities. Second World countries were typically ruled under a one-party political system, with the Communist Party holding all power.

- **The Third World** included most countries in Africa, Latin America and Asia. In general, these were the poor countries of the world. The Third World contained 75 per cent of the world's people, but earned only 20 per cent of the world's wealth. Most Third World countries were once colonies of First World powers, such as Britain, France or the United States. Many are still dominated economically or politically by such powers. Most but not all Third World countries follow the capitalist model of development. Some are governed under a system of parliamentary democracy, but many are controlled by powerful, single leaders.

Several **objections** have been raised to the continued use of the division of our planet into the **three-world model**.

- Many people see it as a product of **Eurocentric** and Western thinking. They see the threefold division as unacceptable on the grounds that it implies some kind of order of priority or superiority between the world's nations, with our Western societies being thought of as having achieved the highest rates of human development.

- Many people object to the term 'Third World' because they feel it can be associated in people's minds with 'third rate'. They therefore argue that the term is an insulting one.

- The Second World, as described in the three-world model, no longer exists since the collapse of communism in Eastern Europe in the early 1990s. This makes the model **obsolete in general terms**.

- The three-world model puts together a wide range of very economically diverse countries. Ethiopia and Brazil, for example, are each considered to be within the Third World, yet Brazil far exceeds Ethiopia in terms of GNP and other developmental criteria. Oil-producing Middle Eastern countries such as Saudi Arabia and Kuwait are now among the world's richest countries, yet they have traditionally been included within the Third World, since the three-world model was conceived before the great oil price rises of the 1970s.

- It should be pointed out, however, that the term 'Third World' was never intended as an economic category. It was conceived as a political category and is favoured by many Third World writers and activists. The term draws its inspiration from the time of the French Revolution. In those days, a political grouping called the 'Third Estate' contained the vast majority of French people, but enjoyed little political power or influence. The term 'Third World' **refers to the lack of real political power** enjoyed by poor countries in today's world. From that point of view, it is a term that is acceptable to most geographers and political commentators.

Eurocentric thinking is explained in Chapter 66.

The Two-World Model

In the 1970s, an Independent Commission on International Development met to discuss poverty, famine, unfair trading and other global problems. In 1980, this commission issued the **Brandt Report**.

The Brandt Report ignored the three-world model of world development and instead divided the planet into the two-world model of North and South (see Fig. 65.1):

- **The North** comprises the world's richer and more powerful countries and contains the First and Second Worlds together. It is referred to as 'the North' because it generally lies on the northern part of the planet, north of the Tropic of Cancer.
- **The South** is the equivalent of the Third World. It is so called because it generally lies to the south of the richer North.

Look back at Fig. 65.1. What difficulty does it suggest with the terms 'North' and 'South'?

The North-South model has two **advantages** over the older three-world model:

- The two-world model is more up to date in **omitting reference to the 'Second World'**. The communist 'Second World' disappeared as a separate category with the collapse of communism in the USSR (Russia) and in Eastern Europe in the early 1990s.
- By merging the First World and Second World into the North, the two-world model emphasises the fact that **political and military power** over the planet have been shared in the past between First and Second World countries.

Despite the above advantages, the two-world model displays the following **weaknesses**.

- Not all northern countries lie in the northern hemisphere. Fig. 65.1 shows that Australia and New Zealand, each part of the North, lie deep within the southern hemisphere.
- **The term 'South'**, like the term 'Third World', puts together many countries that contrast greatly with each other in terms of human development. South Korea and Mali, for example, are both in the South. In reality, however, South Korea's position is far superior to that of Mali in terms of development indicators such as GNP, life expectancy, infant mortality and literacy levels.
- **The term 'North'** also bundles together countries that contrast greatly in terms of power and wealth. It equates powerful countries such as the United States with much less powerful countries such as Bosnia. It groups together rich countries such as Switzerland with much less wealthy countries such as Poland.
- The North-South model suggests that countries of the North are all more **economically developed** than countries of the South. This is not so. Kuwait, for example, is in the South, while Romania is in the North. Yet GNP per capita (per person) in oil-rich Kuwait stands at $22,000, which is three times higher than Romania's GNP per capita of $7,300.
- The North-South model might also suggest that countries of the North are all more **socially developed** than countries of the South. This is also incorrect. Cuba, for example, is in the South, yet it exceeds 'Northern', European countries such as Bulgaria or Romania in terms of life expectancy, infant mortality and literacy levels.

A school in Cuba (above). An urban area in Romania (right).
- *What do these photographs suggest about terms such as 'First World' and 'Third World', or 'North' and 'South'?*

A Problem with All Geographical Models

A geographical model is used to present complicated information in a simplified way. The problem with geographical models is that they tend to impart generalised information that seldom reflects the precise truth of any particular situation.

The three-world and North-South views of the world are examples of geographical models. They categorise the countries of the world in a way that is logical and fairly easily understood. But they present generalised pictures of large areas of the world without recognising that every country (and sometimes every region within a country) is unique in its own level and type of development. Ireland and Poland are each part of the North, yet their levels of development are quite different. Argentina is considered part of the Third World. Culturally and economically, however, Argentina is closer to some European countries, such as Spain, than it is to some Third World countries, such as India.

Activity

1. Critically discuss the First World-Third World and/or the North-South models of world economic development.

2. **a.** 'Classifications such as "First World" and "Third World" can be both useful and misleading.' Discuss.

    OR

    b. 'Terms such as "First World" and "Third World" should be examined critically rather than accepted without question.' Discuss.

CHAPTER 66
EUROCENTRIC THINKING AND IMAGES

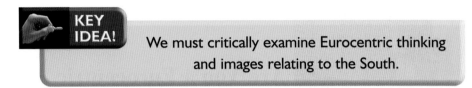

KEY IDEA! We must critically examine Eurocentric thinking and images relating to the South.

EUROCENTRIC THINKING

With the rise of the British, French and other European empires, Europeans were presented with the notion that they were more 'developed' and therefore somehow superior to the peoples of European colonies.

Many Europeans, influenced by these notions, began to think **Eurocentrically**. They began to regard Europe as the cultural and developmental centre of the world. Some adopted hostile and blatantly racist attitudes towards colonised peoples. Others came to believe that it was 'the white man's burden' to 'civilise' colonised peoples by encouraging them to adopt the languages and cultures of their European conquerors. Many simply believed that the European way of life was the 'natural' one and that it ought to be copied in other parts of the world.

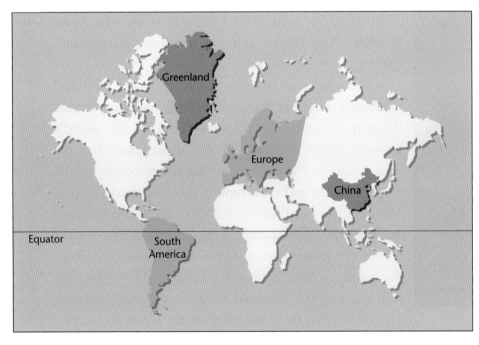

Fig. 66.1 The world according to Mercator. The following points illustrate some of the misleading Eurocentric messages portrayed by the Mercator map:
- **Fact:** China is about four times larger than Greenland. (Which seems to be larger on the map?)
- **Fact:** South America is twice the size of all of Europe. (Which seems to be larger on the map?)
- **Fact:** Half of the world lies south of the Equator. (What does the map suggest?)

Messages of supposed European superiority were also presented in more subtle forms. Up to recent times, the principal wall map used in European schools has been **the Mercator Projection**, from which European children learned the locations of places

417

throughout the world. But the Mercator map (while accurately showing the shapes of land masses) presents a very **Eurocentric** view of the world. It exaggerates the importance of Europe by placing it at the centre of the map and so, by inference, at the centre of the world. The Mercator projection also exaggerates the sizes of places in high and mid-latitudes in comparison to places in low latitudes. European children thus began to believe that their own mid-latitude countries were much bigger on a world scale than is really the case (see Fig. 66.1).

Female construction workers in Bangladesh.

A typical African farmer.

● *How do the images above differ from Eurocentric images of workers?*

Are You a Eurocentric Thinker?

When you think of the word 'farmer', do you think of a man? When you think of 'businesspeople', do you think in terms of people in smart suits with briefcases in office buildings? If the answer is yes to either of those questions, you may be suffering from a bout of Eurocentric thinking.

The fact is that the majority of farmers in the world are women. In the Third World, where most of the world's farmers live, women carry out most agricultural work. In most traditional African societies, for example, men clear and plough the land. Women, on the other hand, plant, weed, hoe, reap and save the crops. As most Westerners cannot quite get used to the concept of female farmers, Western aid to Third World farmers is often given to men, who are seen as the 'heads of families'. The female farming majority is frequently ignored.

The image of businesspeople in smart suits and inhabiting large office buildings is another largely Western concept. The most powerful of the world's business sector certainly fit this description. But the image does not extend to most businesspeople in the world's largest and most rapidly growing cities, such as Mexico City, Sao Paolo or Kolkata. There you will find millions of businesspeople without suits. These are the tailors, the sellers, the repairers, the cleaners, the shoe-shiners and a host of other self-employed entrepreneurs who make up the 'informal' business sector of business. The wealth that these people generate is not counted by us Europeans as part of a country's GNP, yet these 'barefoot businesspeople' are as much a part of capitalism as any European in a pinstripe suit.

MEDIA IMAGES OF THE THIRD WORLD

Most Irish people rely on television, newspapers and radio reports for information on world affairs, yet the following facts show that our media can sometimes present us with inadequate and distorted views of people and events in Third World countries.

- The Majority World contains more than two-thirds of our human family. It receives **less than one-tenth of all Irish news coverage**.

- Wars, famines and other disasters directly affect the daily lives of a very small proportion of Third World inhabitants, yet almost all our Third World **news coverage focuses on** such **disasters**. Bad news sells news items.

- Where disasters do happen, it is usually local people who do most to alleviate the hardships caused, yet local relief efforts are often under-reported and most of our news items emphasise the importance of Irish or other foreign emergency aid in alleviating suffering. **Local people are often inaccurately stereotyped as inactive, helpless victims** who are dependent on Westerners for survival. This image can reinforce prejudice and attitudes of superiority among us towards peoples of the Third World.

- **News items often trivialise** even the most serious of disasters, seeking 'human interest stories' in the midst of appalling human suffering. In the late 1990s, serious flooding devastated large areas of Mozambique. These floods killed thousands of people and made hundreds of thousands homeless, yet many TV and newspaper images focused attention on a young Mozambican woman who, fleeing the floods, gave birth to her baby in a tree before being rescued by a foreign helicopter crew.

- Most news items are **shallow and unquestioning**. Few reports investigate the root causes of Third World poverty – causes that often relate to unjust world trading systems from which First World countries benefit.

- Even 'serious' news items often depend on visiting journalists and Western 'experts' for commentaries on complex local Third World issues. They **seldom seek the views of local people**, who are usually the real experts on their own affairs.

- *To what extent might the image given in this photograph distort our view of the South and of North-South relations?*

Aid Agency Images

Irish and other non-governmental agencies (NGOs) do a great deal of excellent development work in Third World countries. Many such agencies also work hard to present us with accurate images of the Majority World.

However, NGOs may sometimes feature images of starving children or other suffering people in their appeals for public subscriptions. The advantage of these images is that they stimulate human pity and so entice people to contribute to the alleviation of poverty. On the other hand, such images can present the following problems:

- They may reinforce a stereotypical view of Third World people as helpless and dependent on Westerners.
- They may portray the message that 'charity' rather than justice is the answer to developmental problems.
- If repeated too often, such images tend to have diminishing visual impact. This may lead to 'donor fatigue' and reduced donations.

Activity

Study the photographs below, each of which could be used to advertise the work of aid agencies.

1. Contrast the images of Third World people presented by these photographs.
2. For each picture, write a paragraph to describe the Third World people shown. Choose your language carefully to suit the images given in each picture. Use adjectives such as some of the following: lazy, greedy, dependent, hard-working, oppressed, pathetic, successful, independent, helpless, powerful, weak, noble, clever, inferior, equal, superior, capable, bright, dull.
3. Should aid agencies ever produce advertisements featuring starving people? Explain your point of view.

Activity

'Eurocentric thinking and images can affect our understanding of and attitudes towards the South.' Discuss.

CHAPTER 67
SOME IMPACTS OF MULTINATIONAL CORPORATIONS

KEY IDEA!

We live in an interdependent global economy. Actions taken in one area have an impact on other areas.

We now live in a global economy in which relatively few powerful companies control more and more of the world's trade and industry. These companies are called **multinational or transnational corporations** (MNCs or TNCs) because they each operate in more than one country. Over 70 per cent of world trade is now controlled by approximately 500 of these giant companies.

Multinationals provide much-needed **investment and employment** in the economies of Ireland and other countries. That is why our government and the Irish Trade Board offer financial incentives to MNCs that set up branch factories in Ireland. Our Celtic Tiger industrial boom owed much of its production to the involvement of overseas-based companies.

The world's multinational companies thrive under a system of **global free trade,** which is encouraged and policed by a powerful international body called the **World Trade Organisation.** There is no doubt that free trade has stimulated the creation of a vast array of relatively **low-cost goods,** which services the consumer societies of Ireland and other First World countries.

However, there are serious downsides to the MNC-driven global economy in which we live.

Find out more about branch plants of MNCs on pages 321–2.

- Multinational companies destroy as well as create employment. Their operations are often capital intensive rather than labour intensive and their arrival can often cause **serious job losses** by putting local firms or small farmers out of business. As some MNCs chase lower and lower production costs in different parts of the world, their creation of employment in one country frequently comes at the cost of job losses in another (see **The Global Hunt for Cheap Labour** on the next page). The employment that multinationals provide may therefore be quite temporary, as any branch factory can be closed down suddenly by a financial decision made at a far-away MNC headquarters. For example, employees at the Packard multinational plant in Tallaght, Co. Dublin arrived home from work one evening in April 1996 to learn on the RTÉ news that their factory was to close with a loss of 800 jobs. If the economy of an area relies too much on a single multinational branch factory, the closure of that factory could cause an economic and social crisis in the area.

- In some instances, economic globalisation can **undermine** local **democracy**, workers' rights to form trade unions and even national independence. Multinationals are often wealthier than the countries in which they operate and this can make it difficult for national governments to control MNC activities. Shell, which operates oil interests in Nigeria, has annual sales which are three times the total annual income of Nigeria's 100 million people.

- Much of the profits made by MNCs return to the corporations' home countries. It is estimated that such **'profit flight'** allows US multinationals to take hundreds of millions of dollars more out of Africa each year than they invest or leave there.

The Global Hunt for Cheap Labour

Environmentalist Dave Phillips recently told a story about the tuna industry which illuminates the globalisation process.

'In the old days,' he said, 'California had the largest tuna-canning industry in the world, but today the wages in California are about $17 an hour. So the industry moved, first to Puerto Rico, where wages are about $7 an hour, and then, when they decided that was too much, to American Samoa, where wages are about $3.50 an hour. From there it moved to Ecuador, where workers are paid about $1 an hour and then on to Thailand, where a great deal of the industry is today and wages are about $4 a day! And now, amazingly enough, there is some movement to Indonesia, where wages are as low as a couple of dollars a day.'

Wages in Indonesia are so low, of course, because union organisation there is weak under military dictatorship and working conditions are therefore poor.

New Internationalist

Activity
1. Read the extract about the tuna industry and discuss the impacts on the workers and regions involved in the production of canned tuna.
2. Do you think that consumers of canned tuna should support the activities described? Explain your point of view.

Case Study: Wyeth Nutritionals Ireland, Askeaton

See the Wyeth case study in Ireland on pages 327–9.

Ireland is now Europe's largest producer of infant formula (manufactured baby milk). The country's largest infant formula plant is that of **Wyeth Nutritionals Ireland**, situated near the village of Askeaton, Co. Limerick (see the photograph and map on the next page).

The Wyeth plant at Askeaton is a large branch factory of Wyeth, a multinational corporation with its headquarters in Madison, New Jersey, USA.

Wyeth Nutritionals Ireland

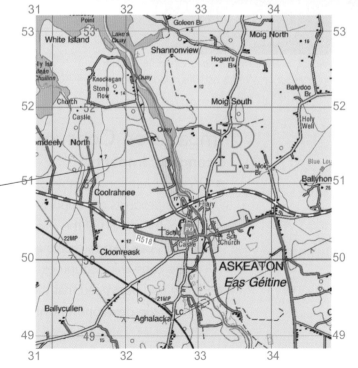

Activity

1. Study the photograph and the OS map and describe the site and situation of the Wyeth plant.

2. Do you consider the location of the plant to be a suitable one? Explain your answer.

423

Impacts on Producer Regions

The establishment of Wyeth Nutritionals Ireland has had significant **positive impacts** on Ireland as a producing region of infant formula.

- More than 600 people are **directly employed** at the Askeaton plant. The employees can avail of contributory pension schemes, free life assurance and subsidised health insurance. Outside of the factory, indirect employment is fostered in transport, engineering and other companies that service the Wyeth plant.

- The Wyeth company contributes more than €150 million to the Irish economy each year. Much of this goes to the co-operatives and farmers of Munster's dairy sector. Some goes to Smurfit of Cork, which provides packaging, and to supporting services such as construction, energy and engineering. Some of the wages earned by Wyeth employees are circulated in the Askeaton and Limerick areas. This **multiplier effect** assists the general economies of these areas.

- *What is meant by the term 'multiplier effect'? How does the multiplier effect of Wyeth's Askeaton plant influence this creamery in the Golden Vale?*

However, it must be remembered that in a world of globalised manufacturing, **the prosperity of one producing area can mean the depression of another**. The main aim of most multinational companies is to seek greater and greater corporate profits for themselves. To achieve this aim, they frequently switch their production units from one geographical area to another. The opening or expansion of a plant in one area might therefore be accompanied by the closure of a plant in another area.

In 1992, Wyeth's Askeaton plant expanded to double its production. Hand in hand with this came the closure of a Wyeth plant in Havant, southern England, with the loss of hundreds of jobs. The expansion of the Askeaton plant in 2000 was similarly accompanied by the closure of alternative factories in Australia and Colombia and of a supply plant in South Africa.

Impacts on Consumer Regions
Economic Impacts

- Wyeth Nutritionals' baby formula products are exported to many parts of the world. These products are imports to such countries and, like all imports, must be paid for out of the wealth of the consuming countries. If not balanced adequately by exports, imports can help to create a **trade deficit** which can ultimately harm the economies of the consuming countries.

- It can also be argued that the imported products of large multinational companies can **hinder the development of alternative products** in the consumer countries themselves. Large multinationals are so immensely wealthy that they can package and sell their products at a low cost to stifle any potential competition from within the consuming countries. They may therefore have a negative effect on native economic enterprise within consuming countries.

Social and Health Impacts

- It is an established fact that breastfeeding is nutritionally and emotionally best for infants. But when a mother cannot or chooses not to breastfeed her baby, and when sanitary conditions are adequate, baby formula provides a second-best alternative to breastfeeding. It is clear, therefore, that baby formula provides some mothers in **economically developed countries** with a convenient though usually inferior alternative to breastfeeding.

- The export of baby formula to **Third World countries** is a controversial issue because the sanitary and economic situations of many families may render the use of baby formula dangerous. The United Nations' Children's Fund (UNICEF) has calculated that every thirty seconds, a child dies in the Third World because they are not breastfed and that Third World babies are twenty-five times more likely to die if they are bottle-fed.

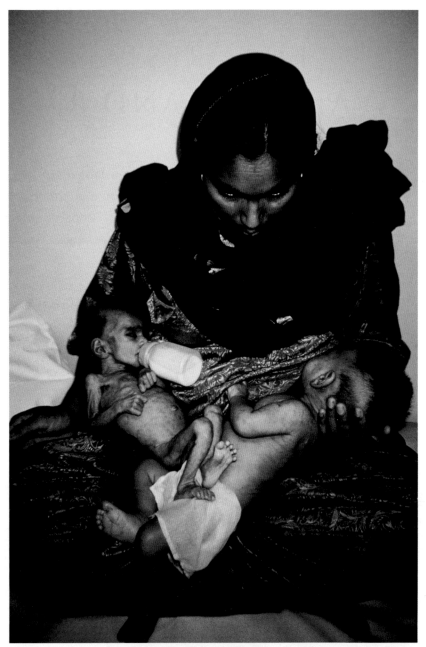

These infants are twins. The baby girl was bottle-fed and died the day after this photograph was taken, but her breastfed brother thrived. This young Pakistani mother was told that she might not have enough breast milk to feed both babies, so she bottle-fed the girl.
- *Why might the mother have chosen to breastfeed the boy?*
- *Why do you think the baby girl did not survive?*

How Powdered Baby Milk Formula Can Kill in Third World Countries
- Unclean water supplies and difficulties in keeping bottles and teats sterile can cause **diarrhoea**, which is the world's biggest killer of infants.
- Because baby milk is expensive, poor mothers may **overdilute** the powder to make it go further. This can cause the baby to be malnourished.
- Some mothers feed milk formula to their babies on trial bases. But when the mothers stop breastfeeding, they soon stop producing their own milk. They must then continue to try to feed their babies on expensive artificial milk.

CHAPTER 68
DEFORESTATION, GLOBAL WARMING AND DESERTIFICATION

In an interdependent world, actions or decisions taken in one area can have environmental impacts on other areas.

Global Warming
See the case study already covered on pages 383–6.

Deforestation
See the case study already covered on pages 399–404.

Desertification
See the case study already covered on pages 404–6.

Activity

Examine the impacts of any two of these global environmental issues:
- Global warming.
- Deforestation.
- Desertification.

(Leaving Certificate 2006)

CHAPTER 69
THE MOVERS

 **KEY IDEA!** Social and political decisions may result in:
- Human migration patterns.
- Economic and political refugees.
- Human rights issues.

Some Useful Terms Relating to Human Migration

- **Migration:** The movement of people from one administrative area to another for the purpose of living over a long period of time. 'Administrative unit' usually refers to a country, city or other region. 'A long period of time' usually refers to a year or more.
- **Internal migrant:** A migrant who moves within a country.
- **International migrant:** A person who moves from one country to another. Such a person would be an **emigrant** from the country from which he/she leaves, and an **immigrant** in the country into which he/she enters.
- **An economic migrant:** Someone who migrates for economic reasons, such as to improve one's standard of living or to escape poverty.
- **A refugee:** Someone who, for fear of persecution, has left his/her country and is afraid to return.
- **An asylum-seeker:** Someone who, on grounds of being a refugee, formally requests permission to live in another state.
- **An illegal immigrant:** Someone who has entered a country without permission.
- **Push factors:** Circumstances (such as unemployment) that encourage people to **leave** their areas of origin.
- **Pull factors:** Circumstances (such as the prospect of employment) that encourage people to **move into** an area.
- **Racism:** The false idea that some ethnic groups are naturally superior to others, implying that those of a 'superior' group might be entitled to dominate or otherwise abuse those of an 'inferior' group.

> Revise what you learned about migration in your Junior Certificate Geography textbook.

SOCIAL AND POLITICAL DECISIONS RESULTING IN HUMAN MIGRATION

Social Decisions and Economic Refugees
Rural-to-Urban Migration in the Third World

Colonial governments in the past and powerful international bodies such as the World Trade Organization (WTO) of today have used their influence to increasingly **'westernise'** and **globalise world agriculture.** As a result, more agricultural production is being controlled by a few powerful landowners rather than by numerous peasant smallholders. This trend has contributed to increasing mechanisation, landlessness and unemployment in rural areas. Rural unemployment has been a major factor in rural to urban migration, which is the greatest single form of human migration in the world today.

Rural to urban migration takes place all over the world. It is most common, however, in the Third World, where agriculture dominates employment and where the populations of large cities are growing dramatically. Rural-to-urban migration has resulted in massive urban growth in Third World cities such as Mexico City, Sao Paulo in Brazil and Kolkata (Calcutta) in India.

The Use by Some Employers of Economic Immigrants

Businesspeople sometimes seek to reduce labour costs so as to increase their profits and their competitiveness with rival low-cost companies. To achieve this, some businesses replace local employees with cheaper foreign workers. This has led to the migration of workers into countries such as Ireland, Britain and the United States.

Pavement people in Kolkata. The population of Kolkata has now grown to 16 million people.

- *Explain how decisions taken in other areas have contributed to the growth of Kolkata.*
- *How has rapid urban growth affected living standards in Kolkata? Why are some of the people shown here called 'pavement people'?*

- Between 2004 and 2006, the **Irish Ferries** company let go more than 600 Irish employees on its ships and replaced them with workers from Latvia and other Eastern European countries. The Latvians worked for as little as €3.50 per hour, which was much less than had been paid to the former local staff. This move caused great controversy in Ireland and led to massive demonstrations against Irish Ferries.
- While the use by **Irish Ferries** of overseas workers was legal, **some businesses also use illegal immigration** as a source of cheap labour.
  - Poor people migrate regularly **from Mexico into the United States,** where they form a source of cheap labour in Californian vegetable and fruit farms. This migration is illegal and the United States authorities use fences, sensory detectors and armed patrols to keep the migrants out. But some people suspect that the US authorities overlook the abuse of illegal immigrants by large agribusiness companies. Child labour, for example, is forbidden in the United States, yet thousands of immigrant children can be found working on large US farms during harvest time.
  - Poor **Chinese immigrants** have been smuggled into Britain by traffickers called 'snakeheads'. There, held by gangmasters in a position of semi-slavery, they work long hours for small pay and often in dangerous conditions. In 2004 the plight of some illegal immigrant workers was dramatically highlighted on the coast of Lancashire. In February of that year, nineteen abandoned Chinese cockle pickers were drowned by rising tides on the sandbanks of Morecambe Bay.

A massive protest in Dublin against the importing of cheap labour by Irish Ferries

- *Why do you think so many people opposed this Irish Ferries policy?*

Political Actions and Political Refugees
The Creation and Collapse of Yugoslavia

Throughout the 1990s, more than 5 million people fled from Bosnia, Kosovo and other regions of what was formerly the state of Yugoslavia. These were mainly **political refugees,** who were fleeing discrimination, persecution and armed conflict in the region. Some had been victims of 'ethnic cleansing', whereby minority groups were driven from their homes by hostile majorities. Most refugees migrated within the territory of former

Yugoslavia, while others fled to neighbouring European countries such as Italy. Over 1,000 Bosnians found their way to Ireland, where they sought asylum.

The eruption of conflict and population movements in the former Yugoslavia resulted partly from a series of **political decisions and events that took place outside the Balkan region** in which Yugoslavia was situated.

- The state of Yugoslavia was established at the end of World War One, largely in order to deprive the defeated Austrian empire of its territories in the Balkan region. But Yugoslavia was essentially **an artificial state**. It contained many different ethnic groups who were deeply suspicious of each other. These groups included Orthodox Christian Serbs, Catholic Croatians and Muslim Bosnians.

- In 1941, **Nazi Germany invaded Yugoslavia** and, with the help of some Croats, set up a puppet state in northern Yugoslavia. Communist partisans and Yugoslavian nationalists resisted Germany. In the four years that followed, one-tenth of Yugoslavia's population was killed, mostly in fighting between fellow Yugoslavians. At the end of World War Two, Yugoslavia was reunited and civil strife was halted under the strong communist leadership of Marshal Tito, but the events following the German invasion created **lasting enmity** between different sections of Yugoslavia's population.

- With **the collapse of Eastern European communism** in 1990, the last threads holding Yugoslavia together were broken. Almost immediately, the country disintegrated into small and often mutually hostile states (see Fig. 69.1). The conflict and persecutions that followed resulted in widespread forced migrations from Bosnia, Serbia, Croatia and other new states.

Mexican children harvest the fruit of American farms.
- *What are the causes and effects of child labour such as this?*

Fig. 69.1 Former Yugoslavia.
- *Identify the states that make up the former Yugoslavia. Why might Yugoslavia be described as 'an artificial state'?*

Political refugees fleeing armed conflict after the break-up of Yugoslavia.

429

Patterns of Movement

Migration is usually a result of political, social or economic decisions taken either by governments or by individuals. While migratory patterns are extremely complicated, some general patterns are outlined in Table 69.1.

Patterns	Some Causes and Examples
1. Rural to urban (internal migration)	Most migrants are in search of **employment** and better **social and cultural infrastructures**, such as hospitals, colleges and sources of entertainment. Examples include migrations from *rural India into Kolkata* and from the *West of Ireland to Dublin*. A flight from **ecological disasters**, such as desertification in the Sahel region of Africa, is another cause of internal migration. An example would include *rural migration into Niamey*, the capital city of Niger. Some migrants flee from areas of conflict. In 2006, 1 million people were made homeless by an Israeli invasion of southern Lebanon. Many fled towards their capital city of Beirut.
2. International migration between Third World countries	Over 80 per cent of all international migration is between Third World countries. A principal cause of such movement is the search for **employment**, as from *Mozambique to neighbouring South Africa*. Flights from **ecological disasters** also cause such migration, as from the *Sahel region* in Niger into nearby Nigeria. Other people migrate to neighbouring countries to avoid **war or persecution**, as in the case of the flight of refugees from *Rwanda into the Democratic Republic of Congo* in 1994.
3. International migration from Third World to First World countries	The main migratory trends under this category are from **Central and South America to North America and from Africa, the Middle East and China to the EU and the USA. Poverty and unemployment** in these source regions, coupled with a **demand for labour** in the EU and USA, have been the principal causes of this migratory trend.
4. Migration from Eastern to Western Europe	The collapse of communism in Eastern Europe in the early 1990s was followed by social and economic upheavals in much of the region. This has contributed to large-scale migration to Germany and other Western European countries. Most migrants move for **economic** reasons, but some gypsies have been forced to flee from **discrimination**. It is estimated that between 2001 and 2006, 2 million people migrated from East to West.
5. Migration from peripheral to core regions within the EU	Searches for **employment and higher living standards** have been the principal causes of this migratory pattern, while the desire for better **social and cultural infrastructures**, ranging from education to nightlife, is a contributory cause. Examples include the movement of people from **southern to northern Italy** and from the **West of Ireland to the Greater Dublin Area**.

Table 69.1

International Migration Trends and Ireland

- From the Great Famine of 1845–49 up to the 1990s, Ireland was one of the world's most persistent suppliers of economic **emigrants**. During that period, millions of Irish people left our shores to seek employment in industrial countries such as England, the United States and Canada. Others went in search of adventure or 'the bright lights' of foreign cities. Smaller numbers were political refugees at a time when Ireland was dominated by Britain.

- In the mid-1990s, Ireland's Celtic Tiger economy began to blossom and to provide plentiful employment. The flow of international economic migration was then reversed, as people began to move into the Republic in search of work. Many of these **immigrants** were returning Irish people who had once emigrated. Most others came from other EU states, such as Britain and especially from Eastern European countries such as Poland and the Czech Republic.

- Among immigrants to our shores are small numbers of **refugees and asylum-seekers** from outside the EU (see Table 69.2). Some of these are economic immigrants who, like our Irish ancestors, fled from extreme poverty in their home countries. Others are political immigrants who seek asylum from war or persecution in countries such as Sudan or Somalia.

Year	Number Entering Ireland	Number Granted Refugee Status
1997	3,883	231
1998	4,626	114
1999	7,724	441
2000	10,938	605
2001	10,325	940
2002	11,634	1,992
2003	7,900	1,173
2004	4,766	1,138
2005	4,323	996

Activity

1. Describe the trends in the numbers of asylum-seekers entering Ireland between 1997 and 2005.

2. Comment on the proportions of asylum-seekers who have succeeded in obtaining refugee status in Ireland.

Table 69.2

- *What point is this cartoon making about Ireland's attitude towards asylum-seekers?*

IMMIGRATION AND HUMAN RIGHTS ISSUES

Immigrants are sometimes vulnerable to various forms of racist abuse.

Racist Attitudes

- A minority of Irish people have displayed racist attitudes towards immigrants whose culture, colour or religion differs from their own. It has been assumed by many that anti-immigrant attitudes are most common among people who are themselves economically deprived or poorly educated, but this is not always so. A survey of Irish **third-level students** in 2001 showed that one in five students felt that illegal immigrants should be sent home to their countries of origin without exception.

- Some **establishment figures** have also contributed to racism. In the late 1990s, when the numbers of asylum-seekers in Ireland began to rise, sections of the media went on a spree of alarmist and exaggerated reports of Ireland being 'swamped' by 'bogus' refugees and other 'undesirables'.

Racist Abuse

Racist attitudes have sometimes led to the racist abuse of immigrants in Ireland and elsewhere.

- Racist attacks on black people (most of them British citizens) have been well documented in **Britain,** where extreme right-wing political groups have encouraged racism.

- **Italy** considers itself to be less racist than most other countries in Europe, yet in 1997, immigrants were being murdered in Italy at a rate of more than two a week.

- In 1995 and 1996, a spate of violent racist attacks on Chinese and Polish people took place in parts of **Northern Ireland.**

- A survey by a Catholic organisation called the Pilgrim House Community found that 95 per cent of African asylum-seekers in the **Republic of Ireland** had suffered verbal racist abuse, mostly on a daily basis. More than one in five of those abused had been physically assaulted.

Activity
Discuss Mr Luyindula's views on Irish people. Do you think they are well founded?

The Case of Mr Luyindula

Mr Luyindula is a journalist from Zaire (now Democratic Republic of Congo) who has sought asylum in Ireland. He escaped from Zaire having been imprisoned for criticising its then dictator, Mr Mobutu.

Life in Ireland has not been a happy experience for Mr Luyindula. He was beaten up by a group of thugs in Temple Bar in Dublin. Nobody stopped to help him. An anonymous racist letter was then sent to 'The African' at his flat, and he has been told to 'go back to Africa' several times by people in the street.

'When I came here everyone seemed friendly,' said Mr Luyindula, 'but since the attack I have started to see some Irish people in a new light. Many of them think it's all right to have one or two black people living in Ireland. However, more than that irritates them. Older people are usually nice, but younger people are sometimes nasty and become particularly aggressive when they are drunk.'

Human Rights and Refugees, Trócaire

Racial Discrimination

Racial discrimination has been evident or suspected in many European countries.

- **Britain** appears to discriminate in favour of white people and against Africans and Asians who request settlement in the United Kingdom. A survey shows that fewer than one in 500 Australians and fewer than one in 200 Americans requesting settlement in the United Kingdom were refused. For people from India and Ghana, the refusal rate was almost one in three.

- The Irish **Employment Equality Act** of 1999 makes it illegal to discriminate unfairly in job recruitment or promotion. Yet some people feel that people from ethnic minorities tend to benefit little from promotion in **some Irish professions.** In 2000, for example, more than a third of our junior doctors, but less than 1 per cent of our senior hospital consultants, were from ethnic minorities.

Professionals from ethnic minorities play a vital role in Irish hospitals, but they tend to be employed overwhelmingly in the more junior ranks of the medical profession.

Human Trafficking

It is suspected that more than 100,000 economically poor young women and girls are trafficked illegally into Europe and America each year for the purpose of **sexual exploitation**. Many of these women come from Eastern European countries such as Russia and Ukraine. They are held in conditions of virtual slavery. If discovered by Western authorities, the women sometimes may be treated as criminals, while little effective focus is given to apprehending the criminal networks that traffic them.

The Irish Government and Refugees

Positive and negative aspects exist in the Irish government's attitude towards asylum-seekers and refugees. Some of these are outlined below.

Table 69.3

Positive Aspects	Negative Aspects
• All arrivals to Ireland have the **right to apply for refugee status** and cannot be deported until that application is heard. If their application is refused, they have the right to appeal the decision. • Asylum-seekers have the same rights as Irish citizens to **public health care.** • Those who are given refugee status have the same rights as Irish citizens to employment, education, social welfare, etc. **Refugees** may apply for Irish citizenship after three years.	• Asylum-seekers are **forbidden to work** in Ireland or to leave the country while their application for refugee status is being processed. They are usually accommodated in hostels with full board and receive a living allowance of €19 per adult per week. It is very difficult for people to survive in Ireland on that allowance. • Asylum-seekers have **no right to education, training, free legal aid or access to language interpreters.** • Asylum-seekers who are **parents** of children born in Ireland do not themselves have the right to stay in Ireland and may be deported to their countries of origin. • Some asylum-seekers have had to wait years for their applications for refugee status to be heard. Only a **tiny proportion** of applicants are granted refugee status (see Table 69.2 on page 431).

• *Discuss the message of this cartoon.*

The Irish Government and Refugees
Ways of Improving the Treatment of Immigrants

It is important that our education system and our media should actively support **enlightened and humane principles** relating to immigration. These principles might include the following:

- The principle that all human beings are essentially part of a single human family. This belief carries with it the assumption that each member of the human family has an obligation to help other, less fortunate members.
- A realisation that the 'asylum-seeker problem' in Ireland stems partly from Ireland's difficulty in moving from a situation of cultural insularity to a state of interculturalism. Instead of focusing solely on the treatment of asylum-seekers, we should also focus on what can be done to assist Irish society in making this transition.
- We must accept that immigrants to Ireland possess and are entitled to traditions that are different from those already existing in Ireland. We should also realise that blending the best of new and existing traditions is likely to enrich rather than weaken our cultural identities as Irish people.

Assistance for Voluntary Bodies

More state support could be given to assist voluntary bodies such as the Irish Refugee Council and Trócaire, which play positive roles in Ireland's response to immigration. **The Irish Refugee Council,** with the help of unpaid volunteers, provides asylum-seekers with advice on law, housing and social welfare services. Organisations such as **Trócaire** do much to educate Irish opinion on the issues associated with immigration and on the needs of asylum-seekers and other immigrants.

Activity
1. With reference to places and situations that you have studied, explain how social and political decisions can lead to large-scale human migration.
2. 'Various human migratory patterns exist over time and space.' Discuss.
3. Explain how migration can raise important human rights issues in European countries such as Ireland.

An asylum-seeker being assisted by an Irish Refugee Council volunteer.
- *Why is such assistance important?*

CHAPTER 70
INTERNATIONAL DEBT
AND CYCLES OF POVERTY

 **KEY IDEA!**

International debt increases Third World poverty.

One of the greatest **obstacles to human development** is the large financial debts that developing countries owe to international private banks and to international world bodies such as the World Bank. The payment of these debts has placed an intolerable burden on Third World governments and unbearable hardships on many Third World people.

Find out more about borrowing in Chapter 44.

Third World Debt and Its Impact on Third World Poverty

In 1973, there was a big **rise in the price of oil**. This resulted in greatly increased import bills for all oil-importing countries. It also triggered an almost worldwide **economic recession.**

Leaders and big businesspeople of oil-producing countries such as Saudi Arabia and Kuwait became hugely wealthy. They deposited vast amounts of oil profits in **Western banks**. The banks found it hard to reinvest this money in Europe and America because of the economic recession.

In desperation, the banks offered big **loans** at very low interest rates to the governments of Third World countries that sought capital for development. The banks chose countries that were considered relatively safe places to invest. Some of these 'safe' countries were ruled by dictators who were considered 'pro-Western'.

Borrowed money was used wisely by some Third World governments to help develop their countries and empower their peoples. Tanzania, for example, invested in health and education programmes. But in other countries, **money was wasted** on weapons or on useless 'prestige' schemes or was simply stolen by dictators. President Mobutu of Zaire embezzled enough cash to purchase several mansions in Europe. President Marcos of the Philippines invested in a nuclear plant on the site of a volcano! (The plant was never used, but cost $2.2 billion of borrowed money.) The bankers did not care much, as long as their Third World investments appeared to be secure.

Debt Facts
- For every €1 the South receives in international aid, it pays €9 in debts to the North.
- Each person in the Third World 'owes' several hundred euro to international banks. This is more than many earn in an entire year.
- The government of Pakistan spends twice as much on servicing its debts as it does on health and education combined.
- A child dies in the Third World every three seconds because of hardship related to international debt.

On the surface, at least, all went well until the early 1980s. Then disaster struck. The United States had been spending far more than its income, particularly on military equipment. It therefore needed to attract capital from abroad. To do this, it raised its interest rates sharply. When the United States increased its interest rates, other Western countries did the same. **World interest rates soared**.

Rising interest rates made it virtually impossible for poor Third World countries to manage their debts. The national **debts** of many Third World countries grew quickly and soon went **out of control**. In 1982 Mexico declared that it simply could not repay its debts. Some other Third World countries began to say the same.

Western banks and governments began to panic, fearing that non-payment of Third World debts might result in the collapse of the banking systems of the West. They joined together with the **International Monetary Fund** (IMF) to ensure that international debts would be 'rescheduled' rather than not paid.

The banks agreed to delay repayments, provided that Third World debtor countries agreed to **IMF structural adjustment programmes**. These programmes forced debtor countries to 'restructure' (change) their economies so that they could earn more money from exports and so more easily pay their debts. The programmes typically entailed the following:

- **Increased production of cash crops for export:** This usually resulted in less land being used to produce food crops for local people. Food shortages became more common.

- **Reduction in 'unprofitable' public spending:** This meant less money for schools and health care for poor people.

- **Abolition of price controls** so that prices could rise or fall to 'market values': This meant that governments such as that of Zimbabwe could no longer subsidise the price of maize, which is the staple diet of poor people. The price of such commodities rose dramatically.

Poor-quality public health and education facilities in the Third World.
- *How has international debt contributed to poverty such as this?*

- **Free movement of capital out of Third World countries:** This enabled foreign multinational companies and investors to move profits more easily, but it resulted in 'capital flight' from Third World countries and reduced the control of Third World governments over the economies of their countries.

- **Devaluing of Third World currencies:** This favoured exporting by making Third World exports cheaper, but First World imports cost more to buy and this increased living costs.
- **Implementing wage restraint and wage freezes:** This reduced inflation but made economic survival more difficult for working people. Civil unrest followed in countries such as Zambia and Zimbabwe.

Structural adjustment programmes helped to protect international banks from the threat of unpaid international debts, but they also resulted in falling living standards for the poor of the Third World and in an even wider gap between the rich and the poor of our planet.

International debt has thus helped to keep Third World people and governments poor. **Debt has therefore contributed to an ongoing cycle of poverty in the Third World.**

> Discuss the merits or demerits of the structural adjustment programme solutions to Third World debt.

- *What is the message of this cartoon?*

What Should Be Done About Third World Debt?
International debt is now recognised as a major problem facing humanity. There is disagreement as to how the problem should be solved.

- Many people argue that debt repayments should be reduced to a **sustainable level.** This is a level which Third World countries can reasonably afford to pay while still having enough money to meet the basic development needs of their peoples.
- Some people point out that some international loans were given to military dictators who held Third World people in bondage. They argue that Third World people cannot be responsible for debts incurred by unelected oppressors and that these debts should therefore be **scrapped.**
- Other people say that Third World debts should be **retained.** They argue that the widespread scrapping of Third World debts could bring about the collapse of the world's banking system. They fear that this might plunge the world into a recession that would ruin First World and Third World countries alike.
- Some people call for a **conditional reduction** of debt. They believe that debts should be reduced for countries that undertake to protect their natural environments, respect individual human rights or satisfy other conditions.

Activity
Describe the role of international debt in the cycle of Third World poverty.

CHAPTER 71
THE AID DEBATE

The 'aid debate' – who benefits?

Aid is the transfer of money, food, skills or technology from developed nations to developing nations. When properly applied, it can help to empower people by stimulating economic growth and human development in the Third World. Fig. 71.1 shows how international aid works.

Fig. 71.1 How international aid operates.

| GIVERS OF AID | ▶ | Individuals | ▶ | (tax) | ▶ | Governments in richer countries |

SOURCES OF AID ▶

Non-governmental Aid
This aid is **given by voluntary non-governmental organisations** (NGOs) such as Trócaire, Concern and Oxfam.
Aid given by NGOs is small compared with the aid given by many rich First World governments. NGOs, however, can operate flexibly and so they sometimes succeed well in helping those most in need. NGOs such as Trócaire and Oxfam also do valuable work in raising awareness within First World communities of Third World problems.

Bilateral Aid
This is **given directly by the government of one country to the government of another.** About 56 per cent of Irish ODA is bilateral.
An advantage of this type of aid is that, being transferred directly from the donor to the recipient country, less of it is likely to be swallowed up in administration costs.
Bilateral aid can, however, be used by donor governments to exert undue political influence over the governments of receiving countries.

Multilateral Aid
This is government aid that is **given indirectly** to recipient countries **through international institutions,** such as the United Nations or the Red Cross. About 15 per cent of Irish ODA is multilateral.
This might seem to be a more cumbersome (and therefore more costly) way of distributing aid. It does, however, reduce the possibilities of donor countries gaining too much direct political influence over Third World countries.

TOTAL AID

TYPES OF AID ▶

Development Aid
This is aid spent over a period of time for improving agriculture, health services, educational facilities, etc.
It could come in the form of **personnel** (nurses, engineers, teachers, etc.) or **technical aid** (tractors, medical equipment, etc.).
The overall purpose of development aid should be to empower Third World people to help themselves.

Emergency Aid
This aid is given in times of crisis to prevent people from dying. It could include food, clothing, temporary shelter or medicine and might be given in response to emergencies such as that caused by the earthquake in El Salvador in January 2001.

| RECEIVERS OF AID | ▶ | Governments and individuals in poorer countries | 439 |

AID – WHO BENEFITS?

Arguments for Aid

Emergency Aid

Emergency aid in the form of food, fresh water, medicines and temporary shelter has **saved countless lives** in situations such as famine in Ethiopia in 1984, floods in Mozambique in 1999 and earthquakes in El Salvador and India in 2001. Modern communications and transport have made the delivery of emergency aid faster and more effective than ever before.

A survey by the **Save the Children Fund** investigated the effects of emergency aid during a particularly severe drought in Ethiopia. The survey found that food aid had saved thousands of lives, that it reached even the most remote regions and that it did not damage the livelihoods of local food producers, as many people had predicted it would. The survey concluded that the ability to deliver food and other emergency aid was now so great that, apart from hunger owing to wars, there need never again be a famine in the world.

Food aid must, however, **be carefully administered** so that it does not harm Third World economies in non-famine situations. Care must be taken that aid does not depress the price of locally produced food and thus threaten the livelihoods of Third World farmers. It is important, for example, that food aid is not used as a means of dumping surplus First World farm produce on the South. Surplus-dumping helps to boost farm production in the North, but it reduces the demand for local produce in receiving Third World countries. It is also important that food aid does not create a taste-dependency for First World foodstuffs among people in the South. To avoid this, food aid to the South should ideally take the form of wholesome, locally produced or familiar foods.

Emergency food aid being delivered to people in Uganda.

● *Discuss the advantages and possible problems associated with this type of aid.*

Development Aid

'Give me a fish,' says a Chinese proverb, 'and you feed me for a day. Teach me to fish and you feed me for a lifetime.' Development aid usually tries to follow the guidelines of this proverb. It plays an important role in permanently **empowering** people in the South by helping them to help themselves.

Development aid can assist Third World countries to set up vital infrastructure such as water, supplies, sanitation and roads. In that way it can give a 'quick start' to countries where sufficient funds for development are lacking. Most Irish official aid to developing countries is in the form of developmental aid (see text box below).

Ireland Aid

By 2007, Irish governmental aid (known as Ireland Aid) had grown to more than €700 million. A positive point about Irish aid is that (unlike EU official aid) it is focused on poverty reduction in the world's **least developed countries** (LDCs). Ireland Aid finances programmes in six LDCs in Africa and in Vietnam and East Timor in Asia.

Most Irish government aid programmes are carried out in accordance with local Third World wishes and with the active involvement of local people and governments. The Ireland Aid office in Northern Zambia, for example, is staffed and managed entirely by Zambians.

Irish Aid concentrates on developing facilities that will cater for the long-term, basic **needs** of the poorest people. It also focuses on aid that will help to make people **self-sufficient** in catering for these needs. It funds projects such as clean water schemes in Lesotho, farm livestock improvement in Tanzania and primary education and adult literacy courses in Ethiopia. Several of those schemes serve to **empower** local people. Aid such as this is referred to as **'appropriate aid'** because it serves the real needs of local people and can be successfully operated by them.

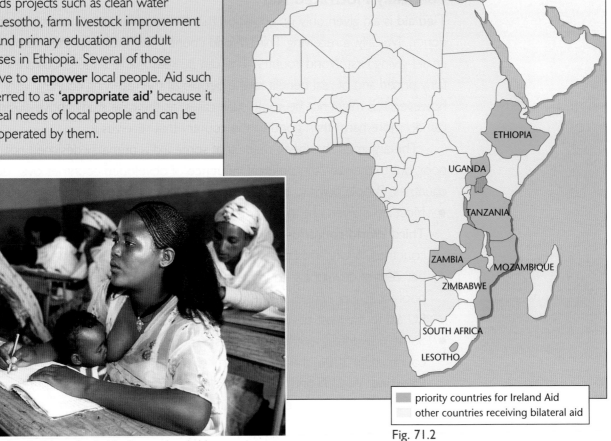

priority countries for Ireland Aid
other countries receiving bilateral aid

Fig. 71.2

An adult literacy class in Eritrea funded by international aid.

● *Contrast this type of aid with the aid shown in the photo on page 440.*

441

Arguments against Aid

The Dam and the Hawks – A Story of Tied Aid

In 1996, the then Conservative government of the United Kingdom gave $100 million of tied aid to the government of President Suharto of Indonesia. This aid was used to build a big hydroelectric power station at Samarinda. The power station would provide electricity for those Indonesians who could afford to buy it, but it would also cause large-scale deforestation in one of South-East Asia's last remaining rainforests and would result in the local Dayak people being driven from their forest homes.

In return for this 'developmental' aid, President Suharto agreed to purchase twenty-eight Hawk jet fighters which Britain needed to sell in order to finance its arms industry. Suharto was a dictator who suppressed small nations such as East Timor, where his forces murdered up to one-third of all East Timorese. The jet fighters were of potential use to the Indonesian government in its oppression of the Timorese people.

Politically Motivated Aid

Tied aid is aid given only on condition that the receiver carries out some service for the donor. Typically, a receiving Third World country might be expected to buy goods from an aid-giving First World country. This can be reasonable if the goods are of good quality, fairly priced and of real benefit to the people of the receiving country. Very often, however, this might not be so. In such cases, as the case study above illustrates, tied aid can do more harm than good to the country that receives it.

The argument has been made that some aid is primarily designed not to help the poor, but to maintain the **political influence** of developed countries over developing countries. People point to the following facts to support this belief:

- Most aid is given not to the countries most in need of it, but to relatively **better-off Third World countries** which might serve the political or economic needs of donor countries. A United Nations Development Programme revealed that the richest 40 per cent of developing countries got over twice as much aid per person as did the poorest 20 per cent of developing countries. Between 1986 and 1997, the share of EU aid to the least developed countries (LDCs) fell from 40 per cent to 28 per cent.

- Some powerful countries use aid as a means of political control over weaker countries. In 2006, the Hamas party was swept to power in democratic elections in **Palestine**. Vital US and EU aid to Palestine was then promptly cut off, leaving many Palestinian people without basic human needs.

- During the Cold War, Western aid was used to block the spread of communism and socialism. When the Chilean people elected a socialist government in the early 1970s, the United States stopped all aid to Chile. The elected Chilean government was later overthrown by an anti-communist but violently oppressive military dictatorship under General Pinochet. US aid to Chile was then immediately resumed.

- Since the end of the Cold War, aid has been frequently used to encourage **global free trade**, which opens the markets of poor countries to the products of rich nations. This can further enrich the richer nations, but may have devastating effects on the local industries of poor countries. Mozambique, for example, was recently granted aid only on condition that it

- When this military coup (takeover of the state) overthrew the elected government of Chile, the United States provided aid for the new dictatorship. Why?

lowered its import tariffs (taxes) on imported goods. The aid was welcomed in this poor country, but the lowering of tariffs meant that many Mozambican businesses were unable to survive and many thousands of Mozambicans lost their jobs.

False Aid

Some aid can actually do more harm than good to the peoples of the countries that receive it, as the following points illustrate.

- Much international aid is in the form of loans. Some of these are soft loans, which can be paid back over long periods and at small rates of interest. Other loans, however, are given on standard commercial terms and contribute to the crippling national debts of many Third World countries. Zambia has to spend four times as much on servicing its international debts than it can on primary education or health care. For every €1 that flows from North to South in the form of aid, €9 goes from South to North, largely in the form of debt repayments. In that sense, aid in the form of loans can contribute to the poverty rather than to the development of Third World countries.

- Describe the message of this cartoon.

- Aid in the form of military assistance has caused death, destruction and oppression in the South. In the mid-1970s, for instance, the USSR was hoping to gain political influence in East Africa, so it offered military aid to Somalia in its war with neighbouring Ethiopia. For similar reasons, the United States gave military support to Ethiopia. In 1977 the American-backed emperor of Ethiopia was overthrown and replaced by a communist government. The Russians and Americans quickly changed sides, with the Americans now arming Somalia and the Russians assisting Ethiopia. Such 'aid' allowed the war to continue without interruption. Hundreds of thousands of people died in an 'aid-fuelled' conflict between countries that could barely feed their citizens.

Not Enough Aid

Many people believe that one of the main problems with international aid is that there is simply not enough of it. The United Nations recommends that if Majority World poverty is to be combated effectively, developed countries should set aside **0.7 per cent of their annual GNP** for this purpose. Less than 1 per cent of GNP might seem like a modest price to pay for the reduction of world poverty. Yet **only four countries** – Denmark, Norway, the Netherlands and Sweden – have so far answered the UN's call. Ireland's aid, for example, falls well short of the UN target. Aid from the US, which is the world's richest and most powerful country, stood at a mere 0.1 per cent of its GNP in 2000. Official Third World aid from many EU member states has **declined** in recent times. This decline is partly owing to a belief among European decision-makers that private investment and global free trade can solve the social and economic problems of developing countries. This belief seems to ignore the fact that as world trade has grown, so has world poverty.

Fig. 71.3 Aid as a percentage of GNP of selected countries in 2001.
- *Analyse and comment on the information in the chart.*

In 2000, EU financial assistance to Ireland was more than ten times greater than official Irish aid to the Third World.

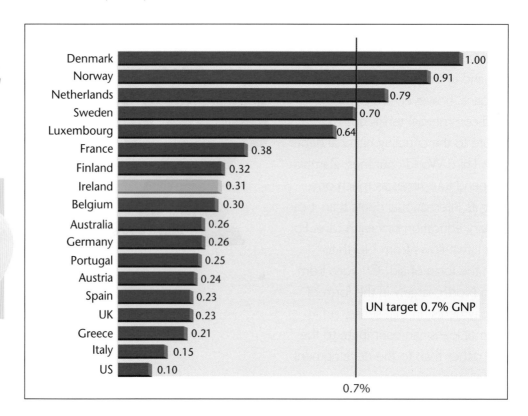

Country	Aid % GNP
Denmark	1.00
Norway	0.91
Netherlands	0.79
Sweden	0.70
Luxembourg	0.64
France	0.38
Finland	0.32
Ireland	0.31
Belgium	0.30
Australia	0.26
Germany	0.26
Portugal	0.25
Austria	0.24
Spain	0.23
UK	0.23
Greece	0.21
Italy	0.15
US	0.10

UN target 0.7% GNP

0.7%

The Role of NGOs

Non-governmental agencies (NGOs) are private organisations that provide aid to developing countries. NGOs operating in Ireland include **Trócaire, Concern, Oxfam and Afri.**

Voluntary agencies usually adopt a combination of the four following approaches to aid:

- **Relief aid,** which is devoted to saving lives in emergency situations.
- **Development aid,** which funds long-term development projects. Irish NGOs spend most of their money on development aid.
- **Empowerment** helps to fight the **causes** of poverty by enabling people to claim their rights, to challenge injustice and to question inequality.
- **Education** is vital to bring about a more just social and economic world order. NGOs actively encourage such education in Ireland through activities such as **Concern Debates** and other inter-school activities.

Some Strengths of NGOs

- The private nature, **flexibility** and willingness of NGOs to take political risks often enable NGOs to get more directly in touch with needy people in the Third World.
- NGOs usually involve themselves in locally driven, small-scale **appropriate aid** that bset serves the real demands of Third World communities.
- NGOs often work for political change by **challenging injustices** that are among the root causes of world poverty. The campaign against world debt is an example of this work.

Some Weaknesses of NGOs

- The amount of funds at the disposal of voluntary organisations is usually very small compared with the funds that governments can invest in aid.
- Some NGOs have used the **'starving Third World baby' image** in order to raise funds. This image distorts the First World view of Third World people.

Activity

'Aid to developing regions often fails to improve the lives of those for whom it is intended.' Examine this statement with reference to examples you have studied.

A Dáil na nÓg session being held in Croke Park.
- *How do activities such as these contribute to world development?*

CHAPTER 72

EMPOWERMENT THROUGH LAND OWNERSHIP, CO-OPERATION AND PARTICIPATION

 **KEY IDEA!**

Land ownership and co-operative decision-making processes are important to human empowerment and development.

Land ownership patterns often play a key role in rural development. If the people who work the land have a level of control over it, they will have a much better opportunity to develop, both economically and humanly.

Case Study: Land Ownership and Empowerment in Nineteenth-Century Ireland

During the mid-nineteenth century, land was Ireland's main source of wealth. Most of the land was owned by a relatively small number of wealthy landlords. However, a large number of **tenant farmers** and labourers worked the land. This pattern of land ownership created several social and economic difficulties for the tenants who rented the land.

- Some landlords charged rents that were so high that they made the economic lives of tenants difficult. Such 'rack rents' were especially hard on tenants with small holdings.

Evicted tenants in nineteenth-century Ireland.
- *How did the land ownership system affect social and economic development?*

- In the mid-nineteenth century, up to a third of all landlords did not live on their country estates. These **absentee landlords** normally took little interest in farming improvements. In some cases, tenants who improved their holdings were met with demands for higher rents. Such situations worked against economic development and human initiative.

- Tenants usually held their farms by verbal agreement and on a year-to-year basis. They were referred to as **'tenants at will'** because they could be evicted from their homes and holdings at the end of any yearly letting. In 1849 (the final year of the Great Famine), over 13,000 families were evicted.

- Many landlords were fair to their tenants, but tenants were largely **powerless** in the hands of ruthless landlords. In 1861, landlord John Adare of the Derryveagh Estate in Co. Donegal threw sixty farmers and their families out of their homes in the depths of winter because he suspected that some of them might have been involved in the murder of one of his agents.

446

The Land War

In October 1879 Michael Davitt, supported by Charles Stewart Parnell, set up the **National Land League**. The long-term aim of the Land League was to win ownership of tenant farms for the tenants. The struggle that ensued between the Land League and the tenants on one side and the government and the landlords on the other became known as the **'land war'**. It ultimately led to government Land Acts which were to wrest ownership of the land from landlords to tenants.

Tenants at a Land League protest. Activity in Land League affairs was in itself an empowering process that helped the human development of many tenants.

The Land Acts

Between 1885 and 1905, successive UK governments passed a series of **Land Acts** that essentially transferred ownership of most tenant holdings to tenant farmers. The basic principle of the Land Acts was to set up land **purchase schemes** for the transfer of land. The government would give loans to the tenants to enable them to purchase their holdings (farms) from the landlords. The tenants would then repay the loans through a system of annual payments or 'annuities'.

There were several Land Acts, including the Ashbourne Act (1885), the Balfour Act (1891) and the Wyndham Act (1903). The final Land Act, passed in 1909, made it compulsory for the remaining landlords to sell holdings to tenants who wished to buy. This marked the final phase of a land ownership revolution in Ireland. Ireland's land was now firmly in the hands of Irish farmers.

In the 1880s, Danish farmers began to organise themselves into co-operative societies. These voluntary organisations operated mainly at local level and were usually owned and democratically controlled by the farmers themselves.

The co-operative principle spread quickly to all branches of agriculture, so that most farmers became members of several co-operatives.

- Some co-ops set up shops to **bulk-buy** seeds, machinery and other items and then sell them cheaply to the farmer-members.
- Other co-operatives established **dairies and bacon factories** in which they processed their own produce. These plants accepted only top-quality produce and made sure that finished products only of uniform standard and high quality were released onto the market. Danish farm products soon earned such a high reputation for quality that they sold widely and at high prices in countries such as Britain.
- **Machinery co-ops** rented and sold the latest farm machinery.
- Some co-ops organised **agricultural research.**
- Other co-ops specialised in **marketing** farm products and in providing agricultural **education, advice, bank loans** and even **insurance** to farmer-members.

The efficiency of the co-ops played a vital role in the success of Danish farming. Most of all, the co-operative movement empowered Danish farmers by helping them to maintain ultimate control over and some level of active participation in their own industry.

Empowerment and Development through Teamwork and Participation
The Co-operative Movement in Ireland

Land ownership gave a degree of empowerment to Irish farmers, but it was not sufficient in itself to lead to significant economic development. Each farmer controlled an isolated economic unit and enjoyed no support network in the formidable task of agricultural improvement. Individual farmers suffered from a lack of capital, technology and agricultural education. The standards of farm produce, such as home-produced butter, varied greatly. The transport and marketing of produce created great difficulties.

Sir Horace Plunkett set about helping Irish farmers to overcome these difficulties. By this time, Denmark had displaced Ireland as the main supplier of butter and bacon to the British market. Plunkett saw that the secret of Denmark's success was that Danish farmers had used co-operation as a key to economic development (see the case study on this page).

Plunkett founded the **Irish Co-operative Movement** on the Danish model. In 1889, he started the first co-operative in Doneraile, Co. Cork.

Plunkett's movement developed rapidly so that by 1914 it embraced over 1,000 co-operatives. As the twentieth century progressed, the influence of 'co-ops' continued to increase. Co-operatives became fewer in number and larger in size, as small units amalgamated or were taken over by larger co-operatives. These grew into big, successful businesses that now run numerous creameries, processing plants, marts and co-op superstores throughout Ireland and that export products such as cheese and butter to many parts of the world. The development of co-operatives has played a vital role in empowering farmers to participate actively in the economic growth of agriculture.

European Case Study 2: Changes in Land Ownership and Farming in Southern Italy

Prior to 1950, the systems of land ownership and farming operating in southern Italy were very unjust and inefficient. Most of the land was owned by a small number of rich landlords, many of whom did not even live on their *latifundia,* or estates. The estates were divided into tiny plots that were rented out to the poor peasants. Many of these tenants were **sharecroppers,** who paid the landlords up to 60 per cent of their crops in rent. Forty-five per cent of those who worked on farms possessed no land at all. They were the *braccianti,* or day labourers, who toiled for tiny wages on a day-by-day basis. Farm production was very poor and poverty was rife.

> Southern Italy is often called the **Mezzogiorno**. This word means 'midday' and it refers to the warm climate of the region.

In 1950, the Italian government set up the **Cassa per il Mezzogiorno** ('Fund for the South') to develop agriculture and other sectors of the Mezzogiorno's economy. It also set up land reform agencies called **enti di riforma**. These bodies introduced many much-needed agricultural changes, including the following:

- Many *latifundia* were purchased from the landlords and divided into small farms, which were **redistributed** to 100,000 peasants. Houses and sheds were built on the farms. The new owners paid for their land and buildings over a twenty-five-year period.

- **Co-operatives** were set up to provide seeds, fertilizers, pesticides and machinery to farmers. Co-operatives also provided money, technical support and training to farmers. They encouraged farmers to irrigate their land and to grow 'new', well-paying crops such as fruit and vegetables.

Farming in the Mezzogiorno is still not as prosperous as in other parts of Italy, but it has **improved** considerably as a result of the reforms. The ownership of land and the support of co-operatives gave peasants the opportunity and the drive to increase agricultural production. Poor-yielding extensive farming was replaced in many areas by high-yielding intensive farming.

☐ The Mezzogiorno

An intensive, irrigated farm in the Mezzogiorno.

Revise Chapter 27.

449

Local Enterprise Boards – Assisting Local Empowerment in Irish Communities

During the 1990s, the government encouraged the establishment of **local enterprise boards** (LEBs) throughout the country as a means of helping local people to develop their own areas, both economically and socially. The LEBs usually take the form of private limited companies managed by representatives of local interest groups such as community councils, chambers of commerce and farmers, as well as by representatives of state bodies such as FÁS and Teagasc. Many LEBs are active in the following two areas of local development:

- They manage the **Leader Project**, an EU-funded rural development initiative which operates across the European Union. 'Leader' funds up to 50 per cent of capital investment and up to 100 per cent of training costs for local development projects. Some of these schemes are community-driven and might involve, for example, the refurbishment of community halls. Most projects, however, are privately run and are designed to create private wealth. Critics of the Leader Project might claim, therefore, that the project uses taxpayers' money to enrich those who are already well-off and to further empower those who are already empowered.

- Many LEBs also administer nationally funded **local development programmes**. These programmes, unlike most Leader projects, are focused on empowering marginalised groups within our society. They include schemes such as those to train disabled people, Travellers or long-term unemployed people for the workplace. They offer practical assistance to these groups in the form of child care facilities, advice on interview techniques and assistance in the preparation of CVs. Activities such as these assist the human development of marginalised people. They also foster economic growth by preparing much-needed workers for employment.

This computer and TV recycling plant at Monasterboice, Co. Louth was partially funded by the Leader Project.
- *Describe an advantage and a disadvantage of the Leader Project.*

Activity
Explain how land ownership and decision-making processes have contributed to human development. Refer to Irish and other European case studies that you have studied.

CHAPTER 73
HUMAN EXPLOITATION

 **KEY IDEA!** Human exploitation takes place at global and at local scales.

One of the biggest obstacles to human empowerment is the exploitation of vulnerable people by powerful people. This exploitation can happen at global and local levels.

WORLD TRADE AND GLOBAL EXPLOITATION

The purpose of trade is to increase prosperity. Some people argue, however, that world trade in its present form has increased world poverty. They point to the following problems experienced by many Third World countries.

Reliance on Unprocessed Commodities
Since colonial times, countries of the South have been used to provide commodities such as coffee, tea, sugar and cotton for the manufacturing nations of the North. These products are usually in their cheapest, raw state and up to 90 per cent of the profit comes from the processing, marketing and retailing of the products – activities that are usually carried out in First World countries. Prices are usually controlled by powerful multinational corporations (MNCs), such as Chiquita (bananas) and Nestlé (coffee), whose headquarters are all in rich First World countries.

Some Third World countries are so **reliant on a single commodity** that a fall in the price of that commodity can have disastrous economic results.
- The economy of **Cuba,** for example, has been over-reliant on sugar, while that of **Sri Lanka** depended too much on tea.
- **Zambia** relied on copper for 83 per cent of its export earnings. The country went bankrupt when the price of copper halved between 1973 and 1975.
- The island of Negros in the **Philippines** has been so dependent on exporting sugar to the United States that it suffered widespread famine when the US suddenly slashed its sugar imports in 1985.

Unfair Terms of Trade
In recent times, the prices of developed countries' exports to the South have risen enormously owing to inflation. But Third World countries have not received corresponding price rises for their products. Desperate to sell their goods at almost any price, they have sometimes found themselves having to produce more and more in order to pay for the same amount of manufactured goods from the North. In 1972, for example, Uganda had to sell 6 tonnes of cotton to purchase one European truck.

Do the Prices of First World Commodities Fluctuate as Much as Those of Third World?
No. First World governments are the main promoters of free global trade. But they have no hesitation in distorting free trade to protect the prices of their own commodities. The US and the EU, for example, subsidise domestic agriculture to prevent fluctuation and boost the prices of their own farm products. Third World governments cannot afford subsidies like these.

By 2002, more than 35 tonnes of cotton were needed to buy a similar truck. These **terms of trade** (as the relationship between the price of goods being bought and sold is called) are unfair and contribute to the economic exploitation of Third World peoples.

Fluctuating Prices

The prices of most Third World commodities, as well as generally being low, have been allowed to fluctuate wildly according to supply and demand on the world market. This has made it almost impossible for Third World countries to plan their economies. The price of sugar, for example, actually fell below its cost of production in March 1992. This resulted in hunger and hardship in the Philippine island of Negros. The World Trade Organization (WTO) has sometimes contributed to fluctuating prices by encouraging the overproduction of commodities in the South. Between 1980 and 1992, the WTO encouraged some West African countries to increase cocoa exports in order to pay international debts. The resulting increase in exports created a 'glut' (surplus) in the world market and this resulted in the collapse of world prices. Consequently, countries such as Ghana doubled their exports, but actually earned less foreign exchange.

Cheap Manufacturing Labour

Manufactured products, such as clothing and footwear, are now being produced increasingly in Third World countries such as China, the Philippines and Indonesia. The emergence of MNCs and of new technology have been responsible for this trend. New technology has reduced the need for highly paid, skilled labour. It has allowed MNCs to abandon expensive First World manufacturing locations in search of less skilled but **cheap labour** in the South.

Female workers in a Third World clothing factory. These women are paid as little as 30 cents for making a garment that would sell for €100 in Irish shops.

MNCs bring much-needed employment to some Third World communities, but most of the money they make returns to the First World countries where MNCs have their headquarters.

Some MNCs make huge profits on the backs of poorly paid and **badly treated workers.** Indonesia, for example, produces increasing numbers of trainers, jeans and other fashion clothing for some of the West's leading brand names. Some such fashion items have been produced in sweatshop conditions where workers, 80 per cent of whom are women, work for as little as 50 cents a day. In some factories, workers are fined if they go to the toilet without permission. Pregnancy means instant dismissal. A normal working week is 50 hours and there is no pay for overtime. Workers who protest can be interrogated and tortured by the military.

EXPLOITATION AT LOCAL LEVEL

Case Study 1: Sex Slaves Reach Ireland

It is estimated that criminal gangs have illegally trafficked more than 100,000 women into Europe, and a small minority of these women into Ireland. These women come from Eastern Europe, the Middle East and Africa. They start off as economic migrants who hope to secure better lives in Europe, not originally understanding that this is legally impossible without proper visas and work permits. The immigrant women are then made to live in circumstances of extreme exploitation, as described below.

Gang members confiscate their victims' passports and hold the women under threats of violence. Lacking legal documents, local knowledge and language skills, the frightened women find it almost impossible to resist or escape from their 'minders'. They essentially become **slaves**.

A prostitute in Amsterdam, the Netherlands. A minority of female prostitutes in Europe have been virtually enslaved by criminal gangs that traffic them into Western Europe from Third World or Eastern European countries.

About one-third of the slave-women become locked into **prostitution**, for example in the Netherlands and Belgium. Approximately another third are trafficked into **'domestic service'** in which they work for a pittance for rich European families. Most of the rest end up working in **illegal sweatshops**, particularly in the textile industry in Italy.

Development agencies such as Trócaire and the Rahuma Women's Project estimate that hundreds of female sex slaves, some as young as fourteen, have ended up **in Ireland**. They are believed to be virtually imprisoned in 'closed' houses that function as brothels. Some are believed to have become mentally deranged because of the beatings, threats and exploitation that they suffer. A few have escaped or have been rescued by bodies such as the Rahuma Women's Project. They live in fear of being deported to their home countries, where they could be in danger from the mafia gangs which originally trafficked them.

Case Study 2: **The Boys at Letterfrack**

An imposing and remote building in Co. Galway once housed up to 200 boys at any one time. They were the inmates of Letterfrack Industrial School, which had been set up in 1887 to discipline and mould unruly boys, generally from poor families. The boys were aged from six to sixteen. At the reform school they were supposed to receive the education and training needed to make them productive and responsible members of society.

Local people remember Letterfrack as a self-sufficient industrial entity with its own farm, bakery, carpenter, blacksmith and tailor. The letterhead on the school's stationery proudly announced 'Orders Received in Tailoring, Bootmaking, Carpentry, Bakery, Cartmaking, Smithwork' and other services.

Behind this image of good order and moral reform lurked another side to the industrial school. Boys as young as six were made to work long hours and for no pay at the various 'industries' that made up to €16,500 annual profit for the school. Formal education took second place to forced labour. Discipline was rigorous and beatings were common and allegedly severe. Between 1996 and 2001, more than 150 allegations of physical and sexual abuse were made against the institution by former inmates who lived at the school until its closure in 1974.

Even allowing for the bygone educational belief that 'to spare the rod is to spoil the child', it would appear that institutions such as Letterfrack wittingly or unwittingly took part in severe human exploitation at local level.

Activity

1. Discuss the contention that world trade has contributed to human exploitation and poverty.
2. 'Exploitation exists at local as well as at global levels in today's world.' Discuss.

- *Why were schools such as Letterfrack called industrial schools?*

Case Study 3: **Bonded Labour in Pakistan**
See pages 475-6 in Chapter 77.

CHAPTER 74
GENDER ROLES

KEY IDEA! Positive gender roles are needed to empower people.

Discrimination

Poverty, injustice and tradition have often conspired to place females in subservient positions to males. This discrimination against women has seriously hindered development, particularly in many Third World societies. It has taken many forms in different parts of the world.

Revise **Discrimination: An Issue of Gender** on pages 312–13.

- Some women suffer **discrimination under the law**. In certain Muslim societies, daughters have been allowed to inherit only half as much as sons. In others, women have been forbidden to initiate divorce against husbands, while men can quite easily divorce their wives. Throughout the 1990s, the Taliban government in Afghanistan compelled women to veil themselves heavily when appearing in public. It also forbade women to attend schools or work outside the home, where they might mix with men. 'If women want to study,' declared one Taliban follower, 'they can do so at home under their husband's supervision.'

- In some parts of the world, females are discriminated against at birth or even before it. In China, the government's encouragement of 'one child per family', together with an old Chinese preference for boys who continue 'the family name', has led to the **selective abortion** of many unborn baby girls. In the Madurai district of southern India, some parents feel that they cannot afford to bring up daughters and provide them with marriage dowries and other traditional support. In such cases, desperately poor parents have been known to **kill their baby daughters** within hours of birth.

A woman in Afghanistan under the Taliban government.
- *Discuss why rulers might want women to dress like this.*

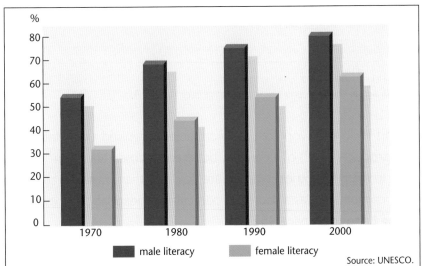

male literacy   female literacy
Source: UNESCO.

Fig. 74.1 The literacy gap between males and females in the Third World, 1970–2000.
- *Describe the gaps and trends shown.*

455

- Throughout childhood, discrimination against females often continues. Where scarce **educational facilities** present economic challenges for poor people, boys tend to be given priority over girls. Fig. 74.1 shows that although the global literacy gap between the genders is closing, males are still more likely than females to be able to read and write.

- While Third World boys are given at least some basic education, girls are often prepared for marriage and motherhood. In some areas of the Ivory Coast, girls as young as eleven years of age are still forced into **arranged marriages** with distant relatives who may be two or three times their age. These marriages are arranged by parents to strengthen clan relationships and to 'protect' girls from the romantic 'adventures' that they might otherwise encounter in single life.

- As wives and mothers, women are often burdened with a traditional **triple workload** of caring for children, managing the household and working at tasks such as subsistence farming. While such women work very hard indeed, their efforts are usually **unpaid and even unrecognised** as 'real work'.

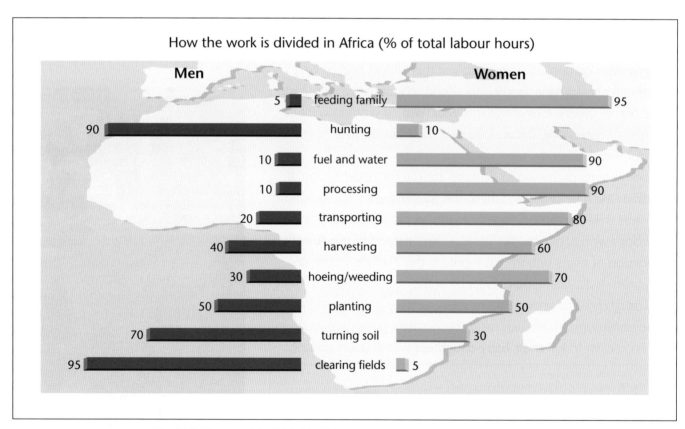

Fig. 74.2 How work is divided in Africa.
- *What does the information shown in these graphs suggest about gender roles in Africa?*

More than 70 per cent of the world's poorest people are women. Can you explain why?

- Many women take part in 'formal work' of the kind that is recognised as contributing to the gross national product (GNP) of a country, but these women are often discriminated against. In many countries, women are paid less than men and are used by multinational corporations as a source of particularly **cheap labour** (revise **Cheap Manufacturing Labour** on page 452).

Ways of Changing Gender Roles
Self-Help

Self-help is a vital key in the struggle to achieve equal rights for women. The best self-help initiatives have usually been carried out at **local levels by women working in co-operation** with each other. An example has been the Kassassi Women's Agricultural Development Association.

Sierra Leone

> ### Kassassi – A Case Study of Women's Self-Help
>
> Kassassi is an isolated village in the African country of Sierra Leone. It is a poor area. The main economy is subsistence farming, and the main 'export' has been young people who migrate to far-away towns and cities.
>
> In an effort to create a better future for their children and to improve their own economic situation, a group of women got together to drain and clear a nearby swampland. Calling themselves the **Kassassi Women's Agricultural Development Association**, they joined forces to reclaim and farm about 100 acres of land. The harvests of this land are owned communally and sold to members at a fair price during the 'lean' season when no crops grow.
>
> Although the project is run by the women, it benefits the entire local community. Boys and girls, for example, earn money to pay for school fees by working on the Association's land. For the women involved, the benefits have not only been economic. They have grown in self-confidence and now take part much more in decision-making within the village. Men, too, have benefited from the growing realisation of the organisational and economic capabilities of their womenfolk. Progress for the women's co-operative has been progress for all in Kassassi.

Education

Many Third World families tend to spend their limited resources on educating their sons. Girls may be kept at home to help their mothers, who themselves have already been denied education. These situations create cycles of female illiteracy, which in turn reduce female self-esteem and socio-economic expectations.

Harvesting crops at Kassassi.
- *What are the benefits of this women's self-help project?*

- **Improved educational facilities** for females are needed to break such cycles of illiteracy and passivity. Many developing countries have made big efforts to provide education for girls as well as for boys. Vietnam is one of the world's poorest countries, yet over 80 per cent of its females are literate.

- Some countries such as Kenya have offered scholarships and reduced school fees to females, but the education that girls receive often lacks the **vocational elements** required to enter skilled employment. This situation needs to be changed, as it severely limits women's capacity to enter the workplace on an equal footing with men.

457

- **Adult education** is very important to the human and economic development of women who in their youth were denied the benefits of an adequate formal education. Mothers who learn to read and write or to master other educational skills often discover new levels of awareness and empowerment. They in turn encourage education for their daughters, thus breaking the cycles of illiteracy and impotency of earlier generations.

- Social education aimed at **men** is another vital element in the struggle for gender equality. In developed as well as developing countries, males still control most positions of political and financial influence. For example, men control 97 per cent of the senior positions in the United Nations and more than 97 per cent of the world's property. It is important for men themselves to realise that this situation is illogical and unjust and then to act to change the situation.

> Throughout the world, boys receive up to ten times more training than girls in 'vocational' subjects, such as carpentry and plumbing.

Empowerment through appropriate adult education – these Bolivian women are learning to read and write.

Fig. 74.3 What are the messages of this cartoon regarding gender issues and education?

- *Is the cartoon itself fair and appropriate? Explain your viewpoint.*

PLANTU
LE MONDE
Paris
FRANCE

CARTOONISTS & WRITERS SYNDICATE http://CartoonWeb.com

458

Workplace Reforms

The creation of strong trade unions for all workers has in the past protected many people in Europe from the worst elements of economic exploitation. The spread of effective trade union activity would greatly help to empower female as well as male workers throughout the world. Such activity, however, is not always easy to achieve. Some Third World governments work hand in hand with powerful employers to discourage effective trade unionism. China, for example, permits workers to join only 'official' trade unions that demand little from multinational employers.

Many multinational companies avoid having to negotiate with any trade unions at all by subcontracting their work to generally non-unionised subcontractors. The subcontractors who can produce at the lowest costs (usually by paying the lowest wages) tend to win the contracts. The American sportswear company Nike, for example, has manufactured some of its products through subcontractors in Asia.

Revise **Cheap Manufacturing Labour** on page 452.

Nurses demanding improved hospital conditions in Ireland.
- *Discuss the importance of and problems facing trade unions in today's 'global economy'.*

Since the Employment Equality Act of 1997, equal pay for equal work has become the norm in Ireland, yet an average gender pay gap of 15 per cent still exists. This occurs partly because men are more likely than women to seek promotion within the workplace. Women might feel better empowered to seek work promotions if **maternity leave and crèche facilities** were more generously and evenly available throughout the country.

Lingering **cultural conceptions** of what constitutes 'male' and 'female' work roles also help to account for the gender pay gap. Some Irish men and women have yet to be fully liberated from notions such as those that tend to equate women with housework and men with jobs in carpentry or plumbing. Formal and informal education, ranging from classroom lessons to television advertisements, could do much to achieve this cultural liberation.

Fig. 74.4
● *What is the cartoon's message?*

Gender-Appropriate Aid

In the past, even international aid tended to discriminate against women in developing countries. The traditional European notion of the male 'breadwinner' and the female 'housewife' affected many development projects in the 1960s and 1970s. Many aid agencies assumed that if the head of a family (who was almost always assumed to be male) received aid, its beneficial effects would 'trickle down' to the women of the receiving household. Most farmwork in countries such as Kenya and Zambia is carried out by women, yet agricultural assistance to these countries, in the form of educational programmes and technology, almost always went to men. Such aid merely cemented already existing tendencies towards male domination, since education in all its forms tends to empower the receiver.

During the 1980s, **development aid became more associated with gender issues**. By 1995, the world's principal aid donor – the EU – passed a resolution that 'women should participate in and benefit from the development process and that the economic empowerment of women … must be strengthened.' By 2005, development aid had focused to a larger degree on the economic empowerment of women.

Activity
1. To what extent do gender roles and discrimination affect human development?
2. Describe specific ways in which the empowerment of women could alter existing gender roles in society.
3. 'Despite ongoing improvements in the status of women, social and economic discrimination against females continues to exist.' Discuss.

CHAPTER 75
THE SUSTAINABLE USE
OF RESOURCES

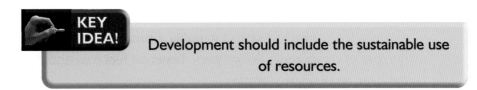

KEY IDEA! Development should include the sustainable use of resources.

Economic development has often been achieved at great cost to our global and local environments. As described in Chapter 68, it has contributed to deforestation, desertification and the threat of global warming. A **preferred model for future economic and human growth must lie in the sustainable use of economic resources.**

The Sustainable Use of Fossil Fuels

The overuse of fossil fuels, especially in economically developed countries, is the main cause of global warming. It follows, therefore, that the reduced use of fossil fuels is vital to sustainable development.

The Kyoto Protocol

A UN conference was held in Kyoto, Japan in 1997. At this conference the industrialised countries of the world agreed that, by the year 2012, they would reduce greenhouse gas emissions by an average of 5 per cent on their 1990 figure. This agreement, called the **Kyoto Protocol,** is seen as vital in the battle against the perils of global warming.

A lack of commitment by some countries has put the agreement in doubt. In March 2001, the United States shocked other countries by announcing that it was abandoning its Kyoto commitments because a reduction in its greenhouse emissions would 'harm the American economy'. The US is the world's leading producer of greenhouse gases and without its co-operation the Kyoto Protocol is unlikely to be effective. Yet the Protocol would appear most important to the sustainable global use of fossil fuels.

Ireland and Kyoto

Ireland agreed at Kyoto to keep its 2012 emissions to just 13 per cent above its 1990 level. However, the Irish economic boom had already pushed Ireland's emissions to 5 per cent above the 1990 figure by the year 2007. It seems highly unlikely, therefore, that Ireland will keep its Kyoto commitment. Nevertheless, the government has set out the following **plan of action** in an effort to keep our fossil fuel usage and our greenhouse gas emissions to sustainable levels.

- It is planned to convert the big coal-burning ESB power station at **Moneypoint** on the Shannon Estuary to natural gas. It is also intended that in the future, more of our energy will come from 'clean' and renewable sources such as wind. A large wind farm is being planned on the Moneypoint site.

Definition
The sustainable use of economic resources means meeting the needs of the present without compromising the needs of the future. In using the resources of the earth, we must respect the rights of all its inhabitants and not squander resources that will be needed by future generations.

Revise the **Kyoto Protocol** on page 386.

- In 2007, the government announced plans to produce one-third of our energy needs from 'clean', renewable energy sources (such as wind and wave power) by 2020. It is hoped that wind farms can be built at sea, thus avoiding the visual impact of too many land-based windmills.

- Efforts will be made to reduce the huge amount of carbon dioxide being produced by our ever-increasing **road traffic**. The **Vehicle Registration Tax** favours vehicles that use less fuel, while the **National Car Test** weeds out old fuel-hungry engines. There will be more investment in **public transport** in an effort to reduce the number of car journeys being taken. **Taxes on fuel** may also be raised to discourage the overuse of private vehicles.

- Our **homes** will also have to change. **New building regulations** are reducing energy consumption in new houses. The government plans to introduce **Energy Efficiency Certificates** for houses that were built before 1991. People wishing to sell a pre-1991 house will have to obtain such a certificate in order to do so.

- **Trees** help to reduce the amounts of carbon dioxide in the atmosphere. In the early 1990s, the Department of Forestry pursued a policy of increasing **new forest planting** in Ireland by 50 per cent. **Grants** and other encouragements are now being offered to farmers to grow more trees on their farms.

Fig. 75.1 Carbon dioxide emissions in the principal carbon-dioxide producing countries, set against Kyoto targets.
- *What does the graph reveal?*

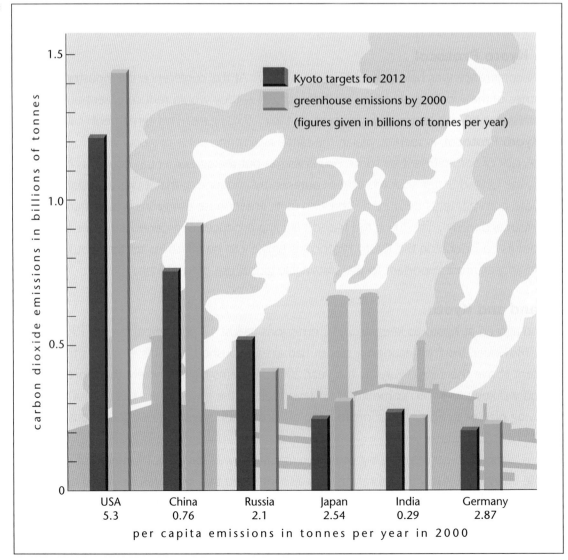

- **Cattle** produce a greenhouse gas called **methane** when they digest grass. A 10 per cent reduction of Ireland's herd size is being planned. This will help to reduce greenhouse emissions in agriculture, which now produces more greenhouse gases than any other activity in the state.

The Use of Alternative Energy Sources

The use of energy alternatives to fossil fuels can play a major role in the sustainable use of resources. Sustainable energy sources should ideally be clean and **renewable,** which means they can be used again and again without becoming depleted.

Solar Energy

Solar energy is an ideal sustainable energy source for places that receive large amounts of dependable sunshine. Renewable and completely clean, solar panels of various sizes can be used to generate or to supplement electricity for buildings ranging from large factories to tiny outhouses. Installation costs are, however, relatively expensive.

Wind Farms

Wind farms are being increasingly used to produce energy in windswept areas such as the West of Ireland. Wind power is clean and renewable, but wind turbines can be visually ugly and somewhat noisy. They also depend on unpredictable wind speeds and may pose a danger to bird life.

Geothermal Energy

Countries such as Iceland, Japan and New Zealand enjoy the benefits of geothermal energy. They make use of underground volcanic heat to generate electricity and domestic heating.

Wave and Tidal Power

Wave and tidal power can also be harnessed for clean, renewable energy.

- The use of **wave-powered turbines** is still in its infancy and the occurrence of sea waves is unpredictable. It is believed, however, that exposed coastal areas off the West of Ireland could generate enough power to meet a large portion of Ireland's electricity requirements.
- **Tidal power** is based on the flow of tidal currents, rather than on the turbulence of sea waves. A tidal energy turbine has been installed in Strangford Lough, Co. Down, where strong tidal currents in and out of the lough generate enough energy for about 800 homes.

A solar-powered chicken house in the Swiss Alps.

An artist's impression of the tidal energy turbine at Strangford Lough, Co. Down.

463

Revise sustainable development and Ireland's fish stocks on pages 358 in Chapter 55.

The Sustainable Use of Fish Stocks

Improved technology and larger fishing vessels have led to serious **overfishing** and to a dangerous **depletion** of fish stocks in many parts of the world. By 2000, for example, two-thirds of the fish stocks in EU waters were approaching commercial extinction.

Traditionally, the governments of developed coastal nations have encouraged their fishing fleets to expand in size and 'efficiency'. It is now widely recognised that such unbridled expansion may destroy the fish stocks on which fishing depends. The priority must now be to ensure that fishing is carefully managed so that it allows fish stocks everywhere to replenish themselves. Fishing, like other commercial activities, must be carried out in a **sustainable** manner.

Protecting Herring in the Celtic Sea

By the 1970s, overfishing by Irish and foreign trawlers had almost wiped out herring stocks in the Celtic Sea. Between 1977 and 1982, all herring fishing had to be suspended to allow stocks to recover. The following conservation measures are now used in an attempt to manage stocks and so prevent future stock depletion.

- The European Union sets upper limits or **quotas** on the quantities of fish that each of its member states may catch. Each year, a **total allowable catch** (TAC) is agreed for each species of fish. Each member state is allocated a **national quota** or percentage of the TAC. An **individual fishing vessel** is then licensed to catch a small part of their country's national quota.
- **Fishery exclusion zones** have been set up to limit international fishing on rich coastal fishing grounds. Waters within 10 km of the Irish coast may be fished by Irish boats only. Waters between 10 and 20 km off our coasts may be fished by Irish and other EU vessels only. The boats of non-EU countries must limit their activities to outside the 20-km zone.
- The EU proposes to reduce the size of its **fishing fleet** by 40 per cent to lessen the pressure on fish stocks. This proposal has drawn criticism from the fishermen and government of Ireland and some other EU member states.

A Spanish trawler being arrested for fishing illegally in Irish waters. Poaching (illegal fishing) by foreign trawlers presents a threat to fish stocks in Irish waters. It is difficult to prevent poaching, as the Irish navy has only eight fishery protection ships to police our waters.

What About Third World Fish Stocks?

Declining stocks and more rigorously policed coastal exclusion zones have now greatly reduced fishing opportunities in temperate waters. This has caused the world's larger fishing nations to look to Third World fish supplies to maintain unsustainable fishing practices. The EU has made **'Third Country Fishing Agreements'** whereby it can purchase the right to fish in their coastal waters from the governments of developing countries. Greenpeace and the Worldwide Fund for Nature describe these agreements as little more than bribes to poorer countries to allow the pillaging of the world's fish stocks. Some developing countries agree. The governments of Morocco and Chile have each complained that Third Country Fishing Agreements, to which they have been party, have resulted in serious overfishing within their territorial waters.

> Are large factory ships such as the *Atlantic Dawn* an advantage to or a problem for the world's fishing industries?

The *Atlantic Dawn* – Europe's largest fishing vessel – was enthusiastically launched by Ireland's Minister for the Marine in February 2000. This 145-metre-long ship cost €63 million to build and was financed by a syndicate of Irish banks. The ship originally fished off the shores of Mauritania in West Africa. The *Atlantic Dawn* can catch more than a tonne of fish every five minutes and is capable of holding enough fish to make 18 million meals. The ship has now changed from Irish to Dutch ownership.

A Senegalese fisherman. Over half a million people in the West African country of Senegal depend on fishing for their livelihoods. Some of these people complain that local fish stocks are being depleted and their livelihoods are being threatened by the large European boats. Under the terms of an EU Third Country Fishing Agreement, European vessels have been permitted to fish off the coast of Senegal.

465

Waste Management

Irish people now live in a consumerist, 'throw-away' society. Each Irish person produces an average of 1 tonne of rubbish per year, most of which is buried in ever-growing dumps called **landfill sites**. This situation is clearly unsustainable and needs to be addressed.

Learn more about **recycling waste** on page 477.

Revise **incineration** on page 378.

Multinational waste companies, such as **Indaver Ireland,** have called for waste to be burned in huge **incinerators** that have been planned for sites such as Ringaskiddy in Cork Harbour and Poolbeg in Dublin. But environmental experts point out that the incineration of waste produces dioxins and other poisons which can cause deadly air pollution. They argue that incineration, while reducing the volume of waste in existence, merely changes it into ash that is far more toxic and dangerous than the original waste. The plans to build incinerators in places such as Ringaskiddy have therefore met with fierce local opposition.

It appears that the only sustainable way of dealing with waste can be summed up in the slogan **'reduce, reuse, recycle'**. This method, which is outlined below, demands that we radically modify the 'throw-away' lifestyle that has now established itself in Ireland.

- The key to sustainable waste management is to **produce less waste.** To do this, manufacturers need to **reduce** the amount of unnecessary packaging that helps to fill our garbage bins each week.
- Many products that we throw away after a single use can be **reused** numerous tines. For example, good but unwanted clothing can be given to charity shops for resale.
- Many used products can be separated from other waste and collected for **recycling**. These items include clothing, paper, glass, aluminium cans and even domestic appliances.

Activity

1. With reference to examples that you have studied, examine how natural resources can be exploited in a sustainable way. (*Leaving Certificate 2006*)
2. Write a critical analysis of the statement that 'Irish society has yet to commit itself realistically to the sustainable use of resources'. (*Leaving Certificate Sample Examination 2005*)

CHAPTER 76
FAIR TRADE

KEY IDEA!

Fair trade would impact positively on sustainable development.

The globalisation of world trade has created much employment in China, Brazil and other parts of the Majority World, but as discussed in Chapter 72, globalised trade has also tended to increase inequalities between rich and poor and has led to exploitation and misery within many Third World communities.

The problem is that at present trade tends to be driven almost solely by the desire to make ever greater profits for a select few, rather than by the need to achieve human, community and environmental development for all. Fair globalised trade could play a major role in achieving the sustainable development of peoples of all nations.

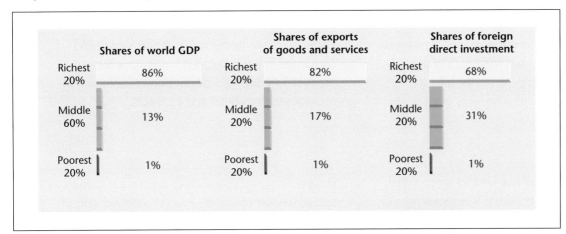

	Shares of world GDP		Shares of exports of goods and services		Shares of foreign direct investment
Richest 20%	86%	Richest 20%	82%	Richest 20%	68%
Middle 60%	13%	Middle 20%	17%	Middle 20%	31%
Poorest 20%	1%	Poorest 20%	1%	Poorest 20%	1%

Fig. 76.1 Disparities in trade and investment.
● *Describe the disparities in global opportunity shown here and outline some likely effects of these disparities on human development.*

Fig. 76.2 Aspects of North-South trade.
● *List the faults of existing world trade that are referred to in this cartoon.*

WHAT IS FAIR TRADE?

Fair trade might be taken to include the following elements:	The present situation:
1. The means to enable all producers and their families to earn adequate livings. This implies commodity **prices that are fair and that do not fluctuate too much** on the world market. It also implies long-term, fair relationships between the costs of First World and Third World goods. These relationships must include **fair terms of international trade**. This ensures that prices paid for Third World products will be in some way index-linked to the prices charged by developed countries for the manufactured products that they sell to the South.	The prices of Third World commodities such as coffee still fluctuate considerably on the world market. Multinational companies (MNCs) and First World countries have generally resisted the concept of index-linking the prices of Third World products to those of First World goods.
2. **Fair wages and working environments** which do not harm producers physically, psychologically or socially.	Some products sold in the West are made in countries such as China and Indonesia by people who work for very low wages in 'sweatshop' working environments.
3. Production which is both economically and ecologically **sustainable** – one which meets the needs of this generation without damaging the needs of future generations.	Some beef and hardwood (mahogany and teak) consumed in the developed world have been produced through the destruction of rainforests in countries such as Brazil and Indonesia.
4. **Fair access to international markets** for all countries and products. This would entail the free movement of products from producers to consumers without involving the unnecessary use of speculators or trade middlemen.	Powerful countries sometimes erect trade barriers against weaker countries, even in contravention of international trade regulations. The United States has conducted a politically motivated trade blockade against neighbouring Cuba since 1961.
5. A reasonable degree of **control** for Third World governments over the resources of their own countries. This would imply some degree of control over First World multinational companies that operate in the South.	Third World governments exert almost no influence or control over MNCs.
6. A preference for working with small-scale producers and marginalised workers so that trade would better support poor people.	Big MNCs dominate world trade, 70 per cent of which is controlled by MNCs.

The Fairtrade Network and Its Activities

Fairtrade is a worldwide network of trading organisations that are working to create more justice and equality in international trade. Products that meet the standards of the Fairtrade network are allowed to display the Fairtrade Mark (Fig. 76.3). This is a guarantee that Third World producers are paid a fair price for the products, that workers work in a safe environment and that production respects the local environment.

Fig. 76.3 The Fairtrade Mark.

How Fairtrade Works

Fairtrade can work in a simple but effective way, as shown by the following example of Fairtrade involving Nicaraguan coffee producers:

- The First World **importers** deal directly with the producers. This saves money because it eliminates the use of costly and unnecessary middlemen. The producers are offered a guaranteed minimum price higher than the international market price. Some money is paid in advance. Credit terms are arranged if needed. An extra premium is offered to fund local community projects, such as those providing water pumps or building community halls.

- The **producers** agree to provide safe and decent working conditions and to pay their workers above the normal rate. They pledge to respect the local environment by ensuring that the land is cared for properly.

- Fairtrade certifies that the coffee has been produced meeting Fairtrade standards.

- The consumer pays about two US cents extra per cup in the knowledge that the coffee they drink has been produced in a way that does not exploit the people or the environment of the producing region.

- Many consumers have shown themselves willing to pay a little extra for products that they know have been produced and traded fairly. As a result, Fairtrade labels can now be found on some brands of coffee, cocoa, chocolate, honey, sugar, tea, fresh fruit and sports balls. Their combined international sales account for more than €200 million. Fairtrade Mark products can increasingly be found in most of our main supermarkets, as well as in specialist Fairtrade shops, such as Oxfam Ireland shops.

Two sides of fair trade. Members of this co-operative in Nicaragua (top) provide Fairtrade coffee for this Irish customer (bottom).

Fairtrade activities help to finance community projects such as this water pump in Tanzania.

- *Why are schemes such as this important to people in the Third World?*
- *Describe some other benefits which fair trade would bring to the South.*

How Might Fair Trade Affect Development?

Social and economic equality – including the fair distribution of wealth – are key ingredients of **sustainable development**. Fair trade would be likely to play a major role in the creation of such equality. Fair trade is important, therefore, to the creation of sustainable development on a global scale.

- Fair international trade would result in higher prices for Third World goods. This would deliver more wealth to Third World communities and countries and would create more **economic equality** between North and South.

- Extra wealth would help Third World communities to achieve **economic sustainability**. As Third World people and countries became more prosperous, there would be less need for First World aid to the South. Some Third World countries might also be able to reduce the international debts that now cripple their economies.

- Fair trade would seek to ensure that the wealth it creates is shared by poor as well as by rich people. Existing Fairtrade organisations already finance health care, education and housing projects among the poor of the Third World. Global trade could result in a mushrooming of such projects and so would lead to increased **social sustainability** in Third World countries.

- Fair trade would avoid the destruction or the unsustainable use of soil, forests, energy, fish stocks or other resources. Fair trade would therefore lead to increased **environmental sustainability**, which is vital to the well-being of our planet.

- North as well as South would be likely to enjoy long-term benefits from fair trade. First World people would have to pay more for Third World products, but increasingly prosperous Third World countries would provide well-paying **markets** for many First World exports. This would further stimulate trade and so increase prosperity in the North as well as in the South.

- As equality and partnership grew between North and South, so too would mutual trust and respect between different peoples. This might contribute to world **peace**.

Activity

1. What is fair trade and how might it contribute to sustainable global development?

2. With reference to an area or trading example that you have studied, explain how fair trade contributes to human development.

470

CHAPTER 77
JUSTICE AND MINORITY GROUPS

KEY IDEA!

The just treatment of minority groups is an aspect of sustainable development.

The level of development of any society can be measured by the degree of justice with which that society treats its weakest members. These members are usually poor and are often members of distinctive minority groups or cultures. The unjust treatment of minority groups is unsustainable, because it leads to alienation within these groups and eventually to civil unrest.

This chapter will focus in particular on justice issues relating to **Travellers** in Ireland and to **bonded labourers** in southern Asia.

Case Study 1: Travellers in Ireland

Who Are the Travellers?

There are about 30,000 members of the Traveller community. Travellers are native Irish people with a separate identity, culture and history from the majority of people in Ireland.

- **Nomadism** is a central characteristic of the Traveller community. Travellers earn their livings and carry out important social and cultural activities in a way that requires frequent, planned movement. Members of an entire extended family may leave their usual halting places at any time and come together to be closer to a sick relative or to celebrate a wedding.

Many Travellers who live in trailers or caravans remain in one place for the winter so that the children can attend school. They use the fine summer period to move from place to place to work as casual traders.

- Strong **family ties and religion** are important to Travellers. A member of the Travelling community is expected to be loyal to his or her extended family.

- **Music** plays an important part in Travellers' lives and many Travellers are highly skilled musicians and singers. A distinctive Travellers' **language** called 'cant' still survives. **Traditions of arts and crafts** are also strong and these skills are handed down for generations within families.

In Search of Justice

Prejudice and discrimination have been widespread against Ireland's Travelling community. Our Travellers have been identified by a European Parliament Inquiry as **'the single most discriminated-against ethnic group'** within the European Union.

Racism

Injustices	Moves Towards Justice

Travellers have long suffered from **prejudice and racism**.

- An ESRI (Ireland's Economic and Social Research Institute) report from 1986 revealed that **'Irish Travellers are ... often despised and ostracised.'** A survey in 2000 found that 93 per cent of Irish people would not accept a Traveller as part of their families.
- A law of 2002 makes it a criminal offence for Travellers to halt for a night on the roadside. Offenders can be fined, jailed and have their property confiscated. This law makes nomadism a crime and so has a huge, negative impact on Travellers.

It is essential that the law and its enforcement should be used to stamp out racism against our Traveller minority. Limited progress has already been made in this regard.

- **The Prohibition of Incitement to Hatred Act** of 1991 forbids incitement to hatred of Travellers. By the year 2000, however, not a single case had been successfully brought under this Act.
- **The Equal Status Legislation** of 2000 offers most hope in the struggle against anti-Traveller discrimination. This law outlaws discrimination in the provision of all services. It means that a Traveller refused service in a hotel, for example, can seek retribution in the courts. Travellers' groups have complained that later amendments to this legislation now make it more difficult for Travellers to make claims.

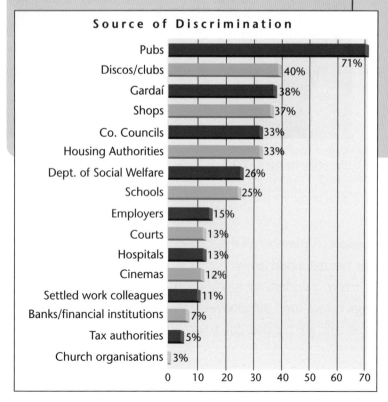

Source of Discrimination

Source	%
Pubs	71%
Discos/clubs	40%
Gardaí	38%
Shops	37%
Co. Councils	33%
Housing Authorities	33%
Dept. of Social Welfare	26%
Schools	25%
Employers	15%
Courts	13%
Hospitals	13%
Cinemas	12%
Settled work colleagues	11%
Banks/financial institutions	7%
Tax authorities	5%
Church organisations	3%

Fig. 77.1 Sources of discrimination against Travellers in Ireland.

- *Comment on the information provided here. Are you surprised by the information? Explain.*

Education

Injustices	Moves Towards Justice
• There has been a tradition in some primary schools to **segregate** Traveller children into special classes, sometimes with separate lunchtimes from other children. Traveller support groups such as **Pavee Point** believe that this practice stemmed from the hostility of some settled parents to the inclusion of Travellers in their children's classes.	• In 1995, a government White Paper called for the full participation in school life by Traveller children by means of fully integrated classes that respected Traveller culture. This White Paper marked the beginning of a new **intercultural educational policy**, which can help to reduce suspicions and misunderstandings between the Traveller and settled communities.
• Education was sometimes used in the past to **'take the Traveller out of the child'** (see text box). This created cultural confusion, inferiority complexes and resentment among many Traveller children.	• There has also been a modification of the education system to meet the **special needs** of Travellers. The Department of Education and Science funds a visiting service in which teachers act as intermediaries between the Traveller communities and schools. These teachers visit halting sites and try to encourage Travellers to stay in school.
• Almost all Traveller children attend primary schools, and 85 per cent of those transfer to post-primary education. But Travellers traditionally leave school at the age of fifteen. Fewer than 100 Travellers take the Leaving Certificate and fewer than thirty attend third-level education each year. This **relative lack of higher education** contributes to a widening prosperity gap between Travellers and settled people.	

'I first became aware that being a Traveller meant being treated differently when I went to school. I was put in a Traveller-only class. We were also given a separate playtime. Our teacher looked upon us as a problem. She told us we were settled people "gone wrong". She told us that if we moved into houses we'd be "all right again".'

Mr P. McDonagh, February 2001

Accommodation and Living Conditions

Injustices	Moves Towards Justice
By 1998, 24 per cent of Travellers still lived in **unserviced sites** by the sides of roads.	The particular **accommodation needs** of Travellers ought to be met more fully. In doing this, key features of Traveller culture must be respected. Account must be taken, for example, that extended families often share a house and that Traveller families are usually larger than those of the settled community. It must also be remembered that some degree of nomadism is an important part of Traveller tradition. For these needs to be met, a range of options including well-serviced halting sites, group housing schemes and conventional housing must be made available to our Traveller community.
• These sites have no running water, toilet facilities, refuse collections or electricity. Such conditions **reduce life expectancy** among Travellers, only 3 per cent of whom live to sixty-five years or more.	
• They result in **untidy and unsanitary conditions,** which in turn creates hostility towards Travellers on the part of the settled community.	
• The poor living conditions that they provide make it almost impossible for Traveller children to succeed in **school**.	

Health

Injustices	Moves Towards Justice
Infant mortality among Travellers is nearly four times higher than that among the settled community, while **life expectancy** among adult Travellers is at least ten years less than among the average adult of the majority community.	• The creation of **national medical cards** for Travellers would also greatly contribute to improved Traveller health. A medical card is at present valid only for a single health board area. This means that if a Traveller moves – or is moved – to another area, a new medical card will have to be applied for and a new general practitioner found to accept the Traveller as his/her patient. • The creation of **medical liaison officers** with Travellers would also be of benefit. These officers could visit Travellers' halting sites, informing people on sickness prevention and advising people on the health services available to them.

Travellers from the Pavee Point support group discuss the importance of primary health care with other Travellers. Travellers themselves now play leading roles in organisations that work to achieve full empowerment and equality for the Traveller community in Ireland.

Case Study 2: Bonded Labour in Pakistan

Slaves can be described as people whose movements and choice of work are severely restricted and who do not have any bargaining power with the people who 'employ' them.

The United Nations estimates that there are approximately 72 million slaves in the world today. This is possibly more than at any other time in human history. Bonded labour is the most common form of modern slavery.

How Bonded Labour Works

A poor person in the Third World may need some money urgently, perhaps to purchase medicine for a sick child. Such a person will find it almost impossible to obtain loans from banks, so he/she may resort to borrowing from an unscrupulous moneylending landlord or businessperson. The borrower 'bonds' (agrees) to work for the moneylender until the loan is paid off.

Bonded labourers often lack even basic formal education and have no idea how interest is calculated. Wages paid by the moneylender may be so low and the rates of interest may be so high that the loan can never be paid off through the borrower's labour. The bonded labourer is then persuaded that he/she must work indefinitely and without wages for the borrower. Other members of his/her family may also have to work against the loan, which may even be handed down from generation to generation. In 1984, a poor family in Pakistan took a loan which was the equivalent of €90. By 2001, this 'debt' had grown to the equivalent of €890, despite the fact that a family of six had spent fifteen years working to pay it off.

Slaves of our time.
- *Explain how people like these become bonded labourers.*

The Search for Justice in Pakistan

The Pakistani government has banned the practice of bonded labour within its territory. This ban has not, however, always been vigorously enforced.

- Moneylending landlords or businesspeople are usually influential within their localities, and few of them are ever charged with using bonded labour.
- The Pakistani government has been in official denial of the level of bonded labour within its state. The government claims that no more than 7,000 bonded labourers exist within Pakistan. Human rights organisations estimate that the figure is close to 4 million.
- Pakistan has no system of identifying and providing alternative work for those bonded labourers who have been fortunate enough to be released from their slavery.

475

Solidarity in Ireland
Irish bodies such as Trócaire have drawn attention to the plight of bonded labourers and campaign for an end to bonded labour.

Voluntary bodies, such as the **Bonded Labour Liberation Front** of Pakistan, have battled to liberate bonded labourers and to hold governments and slaveholders accountable for the abuses of slavery. The interventions of such groups have led to High Court rulings which have resulted in 12,000 bonded labourers being freed over the past ten years.

The Catholic Bishops' Conference of Pakistan set up the **National Commission for Justice and Peace (NCJP)** in 1984. This human rights organisation has been to the fore in the struggle against bonded labour in the brick industry. The NCJP uses seminars and newspaper articles to create public awareness of the issue. These campaigns bore fruit when the Lahore High Court outlawed money being advanced in return for bonded labour in the brick industry. As a result, the debts of thousands of bonded labourers were written off.

Iqbal Masih – Child Labourer and Campaigner

When Iqbal's parents took a bonded loan of less than €18, Iqbal was enslaved at a carpet loom in Pakistan from the age of four until the age of ten. He was tied to his loom, tying tiny knots for twelve hours a day, every day. Six years later, when

he went to his boss to demand freedom, he was told that his debt had grown to approximately €470.

Iqbal was freed with the help of the Bonded Labour Liberation Front and soon became president of the youth wing of that movement. He travelled to Europe and the United States, urging support against the slavery of bonded and child labour in the carpet industry.

Back in Pakistan, he received several death threats in the spring of 1995. On 16 April of that year, he was shot dead while out cycling with two relatives. The Pakistani government reported his death as accidental.

Iqbal's murder caused a rapid growth in the international campaign to end bonded labour in the carpet-making industry. The RUGMARK label is the best assurance that no illegal child labour has been used to make a carpet or rug. The success of the brand in Europe has resulted in the freeing of thousands of slaves.

Activity
Discuss the view that a more just treatment of minority groups is a prerequisite for sustainable development in today's world.

CHAPTER 78
SELF-HELP DEVELOPMENT

 **KEY IDEA!**

Self-reliance or self-help is important for sustainable development.

Self-Help in the Irish Home

Global warming is one of the most worrying environmental problems of our time, while **waste disposal** poses a serious national challenge for Ireland. Yet even these large-scale problems could be reduced by greater degrees of self-reliance within Irish households. Each family can become a self-help environmental unit by adopting tactics such as those outlined below.

Revise **Waste Management** on page 466, in Chapter 75.

Global Warming

To help combat global warming, simply use less energy. Adopt as many of the following policies as possible:

- Conserve domestic energy. Use energy-efficient lights and appliances. Use thermostats and timers on heating systems. Lag hot water tanks and always turn off unused lights and appliances. Insulate your loft and walls, and make doors and windows draught-proof.
- When burned, natural gas emits less carbon dioxide than coal or oil. Carbon dioxide is a greenhouse gas, so where feasible, use natural gas in preference to coal or oil.
- Use public transport in preference to private vehicles. This helps to reduce fuel consumption as well as traffic congestion. Where feasible, walk or cycle to work. This saves energy and money and stimulates physical fitness. If you do take your car to work, try to organise a car pool with other workers.

Domestic Waste

The average Irish person now produces 1 tonne of domestic waste each year. Recycling is a more effective than waste disposal as a solution to our waste problem. More than half of the waste we produce could be usefully recycled instead of being incinerated, buried or dumped. Recycling is also good for the economy because it reduces energy costs and lessens the amounts of raw materials being used.

Some waste food can be recycled into useful compost for gardens. Glass, paper and metals can be left at separate public authority recycling bins which now exist in car parks or near supermarkets in many urban areas. Since 2001, Dublin City Council has been providing households with three different wheelie bins in which domestic waste can be separated for recycling.

Public authority recycling bins in Dublin.

- *Why is the use of these bins an important form of self-help?*

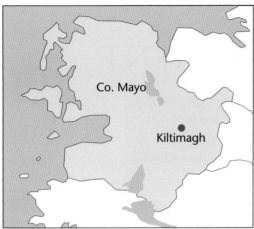

Fig. 78.1

A Kiltimagh scene before and after self-help development.
● *Describe the improvements over time shown in the photographs.*

Community Development in Kiltimagh, Co. Mayo

Throughout the 1980s, the small east Mayo town of Kiltimagh was in the throes of economic depression. Unemployment was rife, three-quarters of young adults had migrated out of the area and four out of ten buildings in the town were derelict. Since that time, local self-reliant activities have helped to change this situation radically.

In 1989, a group of self-reliant local people set up a body called **Integrated Resource Development (IRD).** This body went about transforming Kiltimagh into a prosperous and progressive town. In doing so, it was helped by larger outside bodies such as Mayo County Council, the ESB and FÁS.

● **Urban renewal** greatly improved the appearance and physical quality of the town. The town square was restored. Electricity cables were placed underground. Street lighting and shop fronts were redesigned in a more traditional manner.

● **Economic development** has been fostered by the building of two enterprise centres and the setting up of training courses for the unemployed. These initiatives have helped many new businesses to become established and so have promoted local employment.

● **Recreational and tourist facilities** have been improved. A wildlife and recreational park has been set up, as has a sculpture park, a museum and large indoor and outdoor playing facilities for children. Brochures have been published highlighting angling and other tourist attractions in the area. Improved tourism then led to the building of one hotel and the refurbishment of another.

Thanks largely to these self-help initiatives, Kiltimagh is now a vibrant town that has enjoyed a steady growth in population and employment.

Self-Help Houses in Lusaka, Zambia

The Zambian government cannot afford large public housing schemes for the many homeless people who have flocked from rural areas into Lusaka, the country's capital. Instead, the government and the World Bank have together encouraged local communities to organise the building of their own homes.

When a small group of twenty to thirty local people band together to organise homebuilding, they are given a plot of land of approximately 10 hectares with a water tap on it. The World Bank and the government then provide enough money to build simple homes and to lay water and drainage pipes, provided that the group itself digs the trenches and foundations needed. If the locals also build the shells of the houses, the money saved is used to add electricity and tarmac for the roads. A school or clinic might eventually be added using the same self-help formula.

Schemes such as this are a good example of how self-reliant groups can combine with outside bodies to achieve local development in an inexpensive manner that is **appropriate** to their resources and needs. The local people not only acquire homes for themselves, they also develop self-esteem, community spirit and useful skills.

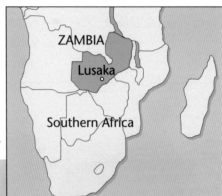

Fig. 78.2

Trócaire has assisted this self-help building project in Zambia.

Self-Reliance in Kerala, India

The people of Kerala in southern India (see Fig. 78.3) live on average more than ten years longer than Indians in general. They enjoy better health, education and transportation services, as well as lower inequalities between the sexes or castes than people in other Indian regions. The activities of grassroots self-help groups, supported by a wise regional government, have been largely responsible for this level of development and, in particular, for the following developmental activities.

- **Land reform** gave more than 1 million people direct access to land. Co-operative credit was arranged to allow people to purchase essential livestock and inexpensive hand tools. This allowed rural people to increase their incomes as well as their sense of self-reliance and self-worth.

- Community-based schemes helped to provide **clean water and primary health care** to many villages and rural areas. These projects combined to greatly increase public health in the region and to reduce disease and death rates among the people. This in turn helped to improve economic output in the region.

- As people became healthier and more economically secure, their need to have large families was reduced. Locally run **family-planning campaigns** helped them to reduce birth rates and population pressures in the region.

Activity

Referring to settings that you have studied, discuss the role of self-help in development.

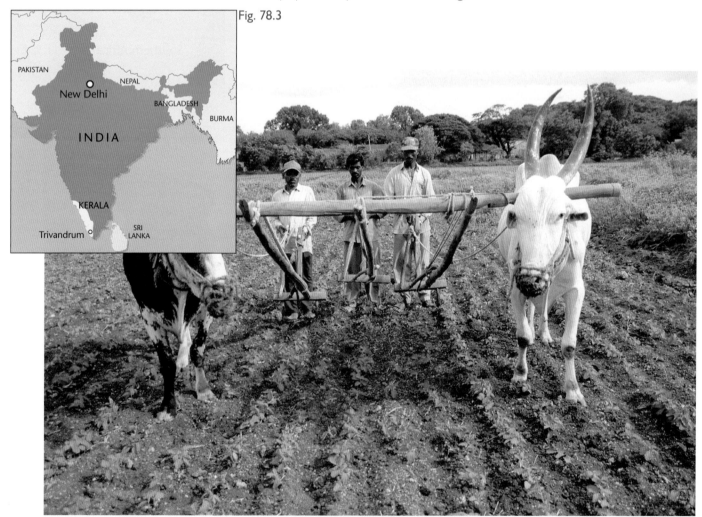

Fig. 78.3

- *Why has land reform been essential to development in India's Kerala region?*
- *Explain how the term 'appropriate development' might be applied to the scene in this photograph.*

CHAPTER 79
SOIL MAKE-UP AND CHARACTERISTICS

KEY IDEA!
Soil is made up of a mixture of various ingredients and has many characteristics.

THE COMPOSITION OF SOIL

A mixture of **mineral matter**, **organic matter**, **air** and **water** make up soil. These all combine together to make soil a fertile **natural resource**. The proportions are approximately as shown in Fig. 79.1, although they may vary from one soil type to another and even according to changes in weather.

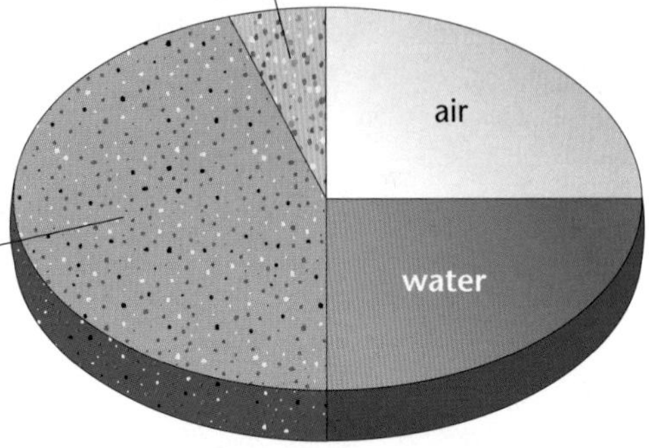

organic matter

air

mineral particles

water

Fig. 79.1

Mineral Particles

Mineral particles are the largest ingredient and usually make up about 45 per cent of the soil. Most minerals exist in the form of tiny particles. These particles were weathered or eroded from the soil's **parent rock** over a long period of time. The parent rock might be local or might have been broken up and carried from other regions by agents of erosion, such as moving ice.

Mineral particles contain **compounds**, which help to make the soil fertile. These compounds largely depend on the nature of the parent rock. Limestone, for example, provides particles with plenty of **calcium,** which helps the bone development of grazing animals.

Mineral **particles vary in size**. Those derived from sandstone may, for example, be large and coarse. Particles derived from clay, on the other hand, are very small and tightly packed.

Some minerals are **soluble**. They can dissolve in water and so take a liquid form. Soluble minerals are very important. They nourish plants because plant roots can absorb them.

Organic Matter

Organic matter includes the remains of plants and animals. Although it makes up only about 5 per cent of the soil, organic matter plays a vital role in soil fertility.

- Many **living creatures** live in the soil. Some of these, such as earthworms, are visible to the naked eye. They help to keep soil fertile while they live (see the photo on page 482) and contribute to organic matter when they die. But the vast majority of animals are too small to be seen without the aid of a microscope. These include

Activity
1. Rank the components (ingredients) of soil according to their proportions shown in Fig. 79.1.
2. How might each of the following processes alter the proportions of the soil components shown:
   a. a period of drought
   b. the laying of water-drainage pipes
   c. the addition of animal manure.

481

How Humus Increases Soil Fertility
- It **nourishes plants** with nutrients such as carbon and nitrogen.
- It **absorbs minerals** that might otherwise be washed down through the soil.
- It helps to **hold soil particles together** and so reduces the risk of soil erosion.
- It helps the soil to **hold moisture**.

bacteria and fungi and are called **micro-organisms**. They play a vital role in the production of organic matter.

- When plant litter (leaves or twigs) falls on the ground or when animals die, they are broken down by micro-organisms. This causes the plant and animal remains to decay into a dark, jelly-like substance called **humus**. Humus is found mainly near the surface of the soil, where it gives the soil a dark appearance. It is also helps to make the soil fertile (see the box on this page).

When earthworms burrow through the soil:
- They help air and water to pass through.
- They loosen the soil, which helps plant roots to penetrate it.
- They mix the soil.
- When earthworms die, their bodies decay into humus.

Soil micro-organisms under a microscope. These creatures are so tiny that millions of them can live in a teaspoonful of soil.

Air

Air is found in the spaces between soil particles. It usually makes up about 25 per cent of the soil's volume, though it is more plentiful in loosely grained, sandy soil than it is in tightly grained, clay soils. Air is essential for soil fertility. It supplies the **oxygen and nitrogen** that plants and micro-organisms need in order to live.

Water

Water typically makes up about 25 per cent of soil volume, though this would depend on climate. In desert areas, the amounts of water in soil can be so small that almost no vegetation can grow. In very wet areas, some soils can become waterlogged or filled with water.

A moderate amount of rainwater is usually good for soil fertility. As water moves slowly through the soil, it **dissolves soluble minerals**. It then distributes these minerals to plants that can absorb them in liquid form through their roots. The water and the dissolved minerals nourish the plants.

SOIL CHARACTERISTICS

Texture

Texture refers to the coarseness or smoothness of soil. It depends on the size of the particles that make up the soil.

Sandy Soils

Sandy soils have large particles and a **loose, coarse texture**. Large spaces between particles allow plenty of air and water to pass through sandy soils. This helps fertility. The loose texture makes sandy soils easy to cultivate.

On the other hand, water passing easily through sandy soils can leach nutrients out of the soils. This reduces fertility. There may also be a shortage of water in the soil during long spells of dry weather. That is why farmers may irrigate and frequently fertilize sandy soils.

Clay

Clay soils have very tiny particles that fit together very tightly. These **tight-fitting particles** prevent air and water from passing through them, and the soil can become waterlogged. Clay soils are heavy and sticky when wet and hard and cracked when dry. They are therefore difficult to plough and are more suited to grass. Farmers may add lime and use land drainage schemes to make clay soils more fertile.

Loam

Loam soils contain fairly even amounts of sand and clay particles. They contain sufficient air and allow enough drainage to make them **ideal for agriculture**.

Structure

The cementing action of water or humus causes individual particles of soil to cling together in small groups called **peds**. The structure of soil depends on **the shape of these peds**, which can vary from one soil type to another.

- **Crumb structure:** Soil is said to have a crumb structure if the peds form **rounded** shapes, looking something like breadcrumbs. Water and air can move through this kind of soil, which therefore tends to be fertile.
- **Platy structure:** The peds in platy soil tend to be **flat and overlapping**. This stops water from moving through the soil. This kind of soil is generally infertile and waterlogged.

The main characteristics of soil include:
1. Texture
2. Structure
3. Colour
4. Organic content
5. Water retention
6. Water content
7. pH value

A typical clay particle is about one-fivehundreth part of a millimetre in diameter!

Experiment to Test Soil Texture
- Take a screw-topped jar and fill three-quarters of it with soil.
- Pour water into the jar so that it is almost full.
- Shake the jar well for about 60 seconds.
- Leave to settle overnight.

Layers of different-sized particles will collect in the jar. The largest sandy particles will be at the bottom and the finest clay particles will be on top. Use the sizes of each layer to try to determine if your soil sample is sand, clay or loam.

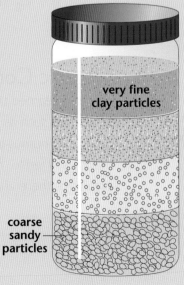

very fine clay particles

coarse sandy particles

Fig. 79.2

483

Colour

Soil types can vary in colour, which in turn can be a sign of the soil's level of fertility.

- **Black or brown soils are usually very fertile for the following reasons:**
  - They are dark because they contain a lot of **humus**, which makes the soil fertile.
  - Dark soils tend to be **warm**, because they absorb more sunlight than light-coloured soils. Warm conditions help organic material to break down into humus and help seeds to germinate (grow) more quickly.
- **Grey soils** are normally **infertile**. Their surface layers are grey because heavy rain has washed (**leached**) dark humus and other minerals down through the soils and often out of reach of plant roots.
- **Red soils** are common in regions of tropical or equatorial climates close to the Equator. A combination of high temperatures and plentiful rainfall creates intense chemical weathering, which causes iron in the rocks to break down into **iron oxide, or rust**. This is what gives **tropical red soil** its rusty, red colour.

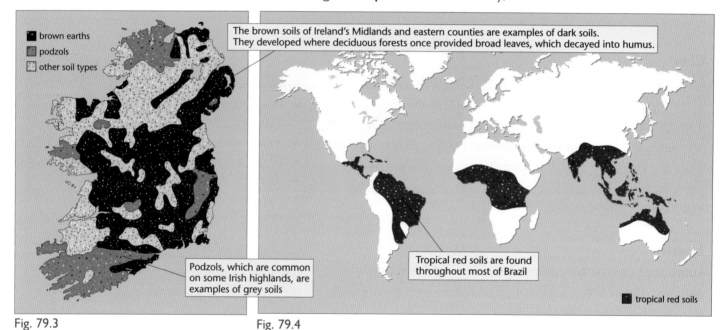

brown earths
podzols
other soil types

The brown soils of Ireland's Midlands and eastern counties are examples of dark soils. They developed where deciduous forests once provided broad leaves, which decayed into humus.

Podzols, which are common on some Irish highlands, are examples of grey soils

Tropical red soils are found throughout most of Brazil

tropical red soils

Fig. 79.3   Fig. 79.4

Organic Content

Revise **organic matter** on pages 481–2.

You have learned that the organic content of soil comes from **the remains of plants and of animals** such as earthworms, slugs and insects. Plant litter or dead animals are broken down into humus by micro-organisms, such as bacteria. Humus plays a vital role in making soil fertile. It follows, therefore, that the more plant litter, animals and micro-organisms there are in soil, the more fertile that soil is likely to be.

Water-Retention Properties

The degree to which soils hold water largely depends on their **structure** and **texture**.

- **Structure:** Soils with **crumb structures** allow water to move easily through them and so tend to be relatively dry. Soils with **platy structures** do not easily let water through and so tend to have a high water content.

- **Texture:** The photographs below show that soils of varying textures have different water-retention properties.

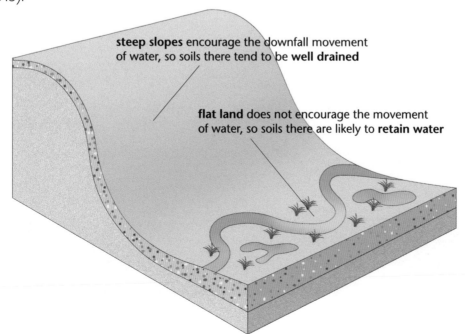

Coarse **sandy soils** have such large spaces between their particles that they retain little water. While these soils often favour the growing of vegetables, they may suffer from water shortages in times or places of little rainfall.

Smooth **clay soils** hold so much water that they may be poorly drained and even waterlogged. They often provide good grasslands for cattle, but are usually too heavy for tillage farming.

Loam soils have a texture between that of sand and clay. The loam soils tend to be well drained, while retaining enough moisture to maintain high levels of fertility.

- **Relief:** The shape of the land surface can also affect water retention in soils (see Fig. 79.5).

Fig. 79.5 How relief affects water retention in soil.

steep slopes encourage the downfall movement of water, so soils there tend to be **well drained**

flat land does not encourage the movement of water, so soils there are likely to **retain water**

485

Water Content

The amount of water in soil is influenced by the following factors:

- Water content in soil is affected by that soil's **water-retention properties**, as described previously.
- **Precipitation:** Soils in areas of **high rainfall**, such as in the mountains of Kerry or Connemara, tend to contain more water than soils in the relatively dry south-east of Ireland.
- **The nature of the underlying rock:** Soils overlying permeable rock tend to hold more water than soils on impermeable rock. Permeable rock, such as limestone, allows water to pass through it and so to escape more easily from the soil above. Impermeable rock, such as slate, blocks the downward movement of water and so tends to increase the water content in the overlying soil.
- **The presence of a hard pan:** Soils that are heavily leached sometimes contain an impermeable hard pan, which blocks the downward movement of water. The surface layers of this kind of soil often become saturated with water. (Leaching is explained fully on page 488.)

The pH Value of Soil

A soil's pH value measures its level of **acidity** or **alkalinity**. Soils with low pH values are said to be acid, while those with high pH readings are alkaline. Soils with a pH reading of about 7 are described as neutral. (See Fig. 79.6.)

- **Alkaline soils** contain a lot of calcium. They develop mainly on limestone or chalk landscapes.
- **Neutral or slightly acidic soils** encourage the growth of bacteria that break down organic matter into humus. These soils are best suited to farming.
- **Acid soils** often occur in areas of heavy rainfall, where rainwater leaches calcium (which is alkaline) out of the soil. Too much acidity discourages micro-organisms. This means that plant remains will not break down, so the soil is usually infertile. Lime may be added to reduce acidity.

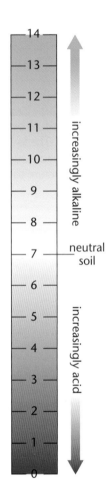

Fig. **79.6** The pH values of soil.

See questions 1 and 2 on page 524.

Infertile acid soils cover this mountain in the West of Ireland. Peat develops because plant remains have not broken down.

CHAPTER 80
PROCESSES THAT AFFECT SOILS

 **KEY IDEA!**

A variety of physical processes (happenings) may affect soil. No two soils are exactly the same.

We have already examined the general characteristics of soil, but soils vary and no two soils are exactly alike. This is partly because a variety of physical processes may affect any particular soil (see box on right). These processes may operate together, but not all processes will operate in any one soil.

> **Physical processes that affect soil:**
> - Weathering
> - Soil erosion
> - Leaching
>   – Podzolisation
>   – Laterisation
> - Calcification
> - Humification

Weathering

Weathering helps to break down parent rock into small particles, which are the main ingredient of soil.

- **Physical weathering** causes parent rock to shatter. It is carried out by agents such as frost action and temperature changes. **Frost action** is common on Irish mountainsides in winter. **Temperature changes** are very effective in hot deserts, where daytime temperatures are very high and night-time temperatures are often below freezing.
- **Chemical weathering** causes rock to decompose. This happens, for example, when carbonic acid in **rainwater** reacts with the calcium carbonate in **limestone**. Rainwater can also slowly dissolve **granite,** resulting in the formation of clay soil.

Soil Erosion

The agents of erosion not only break down parent rock, they also transport the resulting mineral particles and soil over great distances and deposit them in other areas.

Rivers, for example, grind down rock into fertile **alluvial soil**, which is deposited in the lower sections of **river valleys** such as those of the Shannon and the Liffey. **Wind** has deposited fertile **loess** soils in the Paris Basin of France. **Boulder clay** has been deposited in many parts of Ireland by **glacial ice** during the last Ice Age.

Existing soil is subject to attack by the agents of erosion. **Gully erosion**, caused by heavy rain, severely damages soil in those parts of the Amazon rainforest that have been cleared for agriculture. **Wind erosion** blows away topsoil from those areas of Africa's Sahel region that have been cleared of vegetation cover.

● *Describe this soil erosion in the Amazon Basin, Brazil.*

487

Leaching

In countries such as Ireland, rainfall exceeds evaporation. In such areas, rainwater will percolate (soak) down through the soil. This downward movement might be quite rapid in permeable, large-grained, loosely packed soils, such as sandy soils.

Water often dissolves minerals, humus and other plant nutrients on the upper horizons (layers) of the soil. **As the water seeps downwards, it carries these nutrients with it.** This process is called **leaching**. Severe leaching reduces soil fertility because it washes plant nutrients down beyond the reach of many plant roots.

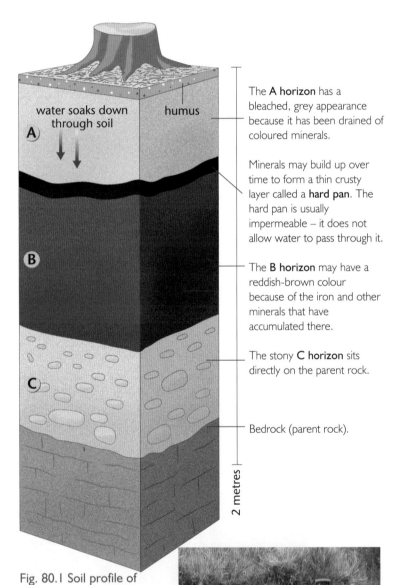

water soaks down through soil

A)

humus

B

C)

2 metres

The **A horizon** has a bleached, grey appearance because it has been drained of coloured minerals.

Minerals may build up over time to form a thin crusty layer called a **hard pan**. The hard pan is usually impermeable – it does not allow water to pass through it.

The **B horizon** may have a reddish-brown colour because of the iron and other minerals that have accumulated there.

The stony **C horizon** sits directly on the parent rock.

Bedrock (parent rock).

Fig. 80.1 Soil profile of podzols. A soil profile is a vertical section of the soil from surface to bedrock. It contains horizontal layers called horizons.

A podzol soil horizon.
● *Identify the A horizon, the hard pan and the B horizon.*

Podzolisation

Podzolisation is an **intense form of leaching**. It can occur in **cool areas of heavy rainfall**, such as on many of Ireland's highlands. It also occurs in areas of coniferous forest or moorland vegetation. This vegetation causes the rainwater seeping through it to become so acidic that it would dissolve most soil nutrients.

Podzols (the soils associated with podzolisation) have very distinct **soil profiles** (see Fig. 80.1).

Lateralisation

Lateralisation is a form of **extreme leaching** that happens in **tropical and equatorial regions**. **Heavy rainfall** is the main cause of this leaching. **High temperatures** also contribute by speeding up the chemical reactions of water on rock. High temperatures also break down iron in the rock into **iron oxide** or rust. The presence of iron oxide gives the soil a red, rusty appearance. That is why some soils in these regions are called **tropical red soils**.

Activity
1. With the help of an atlas and the map on page 491, name three countries where you would find:
   ● podzols
   ● tropical red soils.

Calcification

Calcification happens in places with dry climates, where evaporation exceeds precipitation. **Water seeps up through the soil by capillary action**, which is the opposite of leaching described on page 488.

Calcification results in calcium being built up close to the surface of the soil. This helps to make the soil very fertile, as in the **chernozem**, or the 'black earth' soils, of the **steppes** (grasslands) of Russia and the Ukraine. Chernozems are also found in the **prairies** of the United States.

Humification

Most soil contains **organic matter**, which consists of dead animal remains and plant litter. **Micro-organisms**, such as bacteria and fungi, work on the organic matter. They cause it to decay slowly into a black, jelly-like substance called **humus**.

Oxygen is also needed to assist the breakdown of organic matter into humus. Air in the soil therefore plays an important role in the process of **humification**. Humus makes the soil fertile. It converts nitrogen, calcium and other nutrients into soluble forms so that they can be easily absorbed by plant roots.

How Capillary Action Works
After rain, gravity causes water to sink through the soil. But following long periods of dry weather, the water is absorbed upwards through the dry soil. This acts something like water does on a wet surface when a dry towel is put over the water to soak it up.

Activity
1. Locate the chernozem soils of the steppes and prairies on the map on page 491.

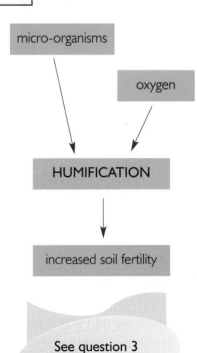

Ukraine

Rich black earth soils being ploughed in the Ukraine.
- *Why, in your opinion, is this soil so dark in colour?*
- *Describe two processes that you think help to make this soil fertile.*
- *For what type of farming is this soil being used?*

micro-organisms

oxygen

HUMIFICATION

increased soil fertility

See question 3 on page 524.

CHAPTER 81
THE GLOBAL PATTERN OF SOILS

KEY IDEA! Major soil types form global patterns owing to climatic and other factors.

Brown earth is Ireland's zonal (and most common) soil type.

Peaty, intrazonal soils are found in some poorly drained areas of Ireland.

Sand dunes provide an example of immature (not fully formed) azonal soil.

Learn any three of the examples given below.

HOW SOILS ARE CLASSIFIED

Zonal Soils

Climate is the most important factor affecting soil formation. Soils are therefore usually classified **according to the climate types** that help to form them. They are called zonal soils because they occupy large climatic zones or regions of the earth's surface. **Brown earth**, for example, is the zonal soil type in Ireland and other regions of cool temperate oceanic climate.

Zonal soils develop over long periods of time. They therefore have well-formed soil profiles with clear horizons.

Intrazonal Soils

Within zonal soil belts, strong **local factors** can sometimes create different types of soil in certain areas. These are called intrazonal soils. Poor drainage, for example, creates **peaty soils** in parts of Connemara.

Azonal Soils

Azonal soils are soils that are **not yet fully developed**. They do not have clear soil profiles. Recent deposits of **sand** – as in sand dunes – is an example of azonal soil.

How Zonal Soils are Related to Climate and Vegetation Zones		
Zonal soil	Climate zone	Vegetation zone
Tundra soil	Tundra	Tundra
Podzols	Cold Temperate Continental	Coniferous forest (taiga)
Brown earths	Cool Temperate Oceanic	Deciduous forest
Chernozems/grassland soils	Warm Temperate Rainy and Steppe	Grasslands
Desert and semi-desert soils	Desert	Desert
Terra rossa	Mainly Warm Temperate Oceanic	Mainly Mediterranean
Latosols/tropical red soils	Equatorial/Tropical	Rainforest
Mountain soils	Mountain climate	Mountain vegetation

The global pattern of soils is shown on the map in Fig. 81.1. This map shows only the **general locations** of the world's most common *zonal soils*. It does not show the many intrazonal and azonal soils that exist within each zone.

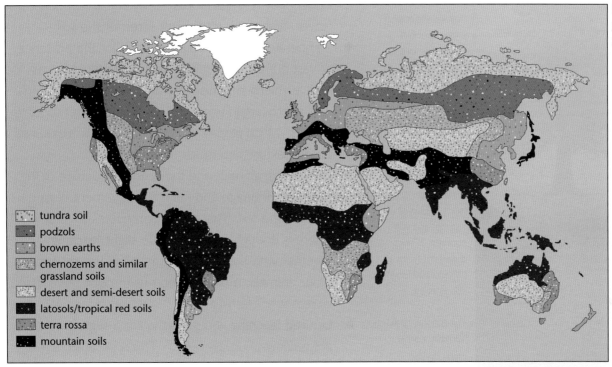

tundra soil
podzols
brown earths
chernozems and similar grassland soils
desert and semi-desert soils
latosols/tropical red soils
terra rossa
mountain soils

Fig. 81.1 The global pattern of zonal soils.

Activity

1. What zonal soil type occurs in each of the following areas?
   a. Italy
   b. Sweden
   c. The Sahara Desert
   d. The Amazon Basin
2. What zonal soil type is most common on the west coast of Europe? What climatic zone exists there?
3. Do you think the map in Fig. 81.1 shows precisely the soil type in any part of the world? Explain.

BROWN EARTHS
Sample Study of a Major Soil Type

You will see from Fig. 81.1 that brown earths are common in temperate latitudes (40° to 60° North) within the continent of Europe. They occur mostly in areas of Cool Temperate climate. They stretch from Ireland in the west to Russia in the east and from Scotland in the north to Portugal in the south.

Most brown earths:

- Have a **crumb texture** and are **well drained**.
- Are **slightly acidic**.
- Have a **dark brown colour** throughout their profile.
- Are usually very **fertile**.

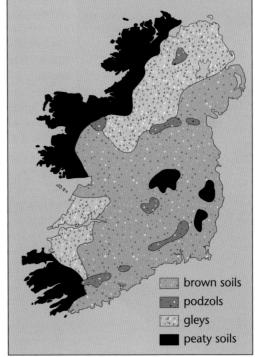

brown soils
podzols
gleys
peaty soils

Fig. 81.2 Ireland's principal soils.

Activity

1. Does the map in Fig. 81.2 show more or less detail than that in Fig. 81.1?
2. List in rank order Ireland's four most common soil types.

491

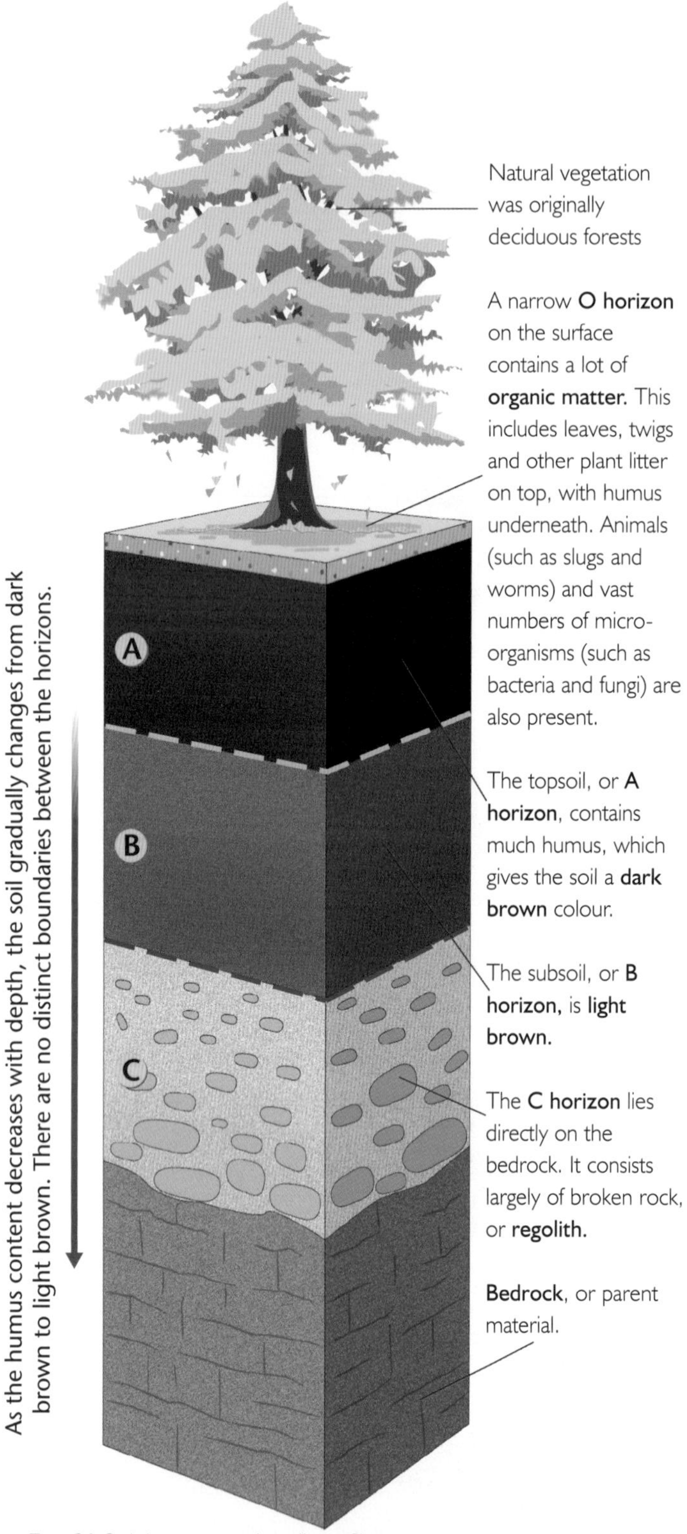

The causes of these characteristics are as follows:

- Brown earths developed in areas that were once covered in dense **deciduous forests**, with heavy undergrowth. These forests provided an abundance of leaves, twigs and other **plant litter** for the soil.
- Temperate climate is warm enough for the presence of vast numbers of animals such as earthworms as well as **micro-organisms**, such as bacteria and fungi. The micro-organisms break down plant litter to form **humus**, which gives the soil its dark brown colour, its crumb texture and much of its fertility.
- **Burrowing animals** and the **crumb structure** of the soil assist **drainage** and help the movement of **air** through the soil. This in turn contributes to fertility.
- There is enough rain to provide **slight leaching**. This, together with the burrowing action of worms and other **animals**, **mixes the humus** through the soil and increases soil fertility.
- **Limited leaching** also gives the soil a **slightly acidic** pH reading of usually 5 to 7. This is because rainwater absorbs carbon dioxide in the atmosphere and so becomes a very weak carbonic acid.
- **There is not enough leaching to create impermeable hard pans**, which would hinder drainage. Brown earths are therefore **well drained**.

You will see from Fig. 81.2 that brown earth is the principal but not the only soil type in countries such as Ireland. It is also worth noting that, even within a small country such as Ireland, there are different varieties of brown earths:

- **Acid brown soils** have formed on bedrocks such as granite or sandstone, which are low in lime.
- **Brown podzolic soils** have formed in areas where leaching is relatively high. The A horizons of these soils have a pale ashy rather than a brown colour.

Brown earths have been cultivated for centuries and now contain very few of the deciduous forests which once nourished them. Farmers now nourish the soils with artificial fertilizers, manure and lime. When properly maintained, these soils are very suitable for a wide range of agriculture, ranging from tillage to pasture to forestry.

As the humus content decreases with depth, the soil gradually changes from dark brown to light brown. There are no distinct boundaries between the horizons.

Natural vegetation was originally deciduous forests

A narrow **O horizon** on the surface contains a lot of **organic matter**. This includes leaves, twigs and other plant litter on top, with humus underneath. Animals (such as slugs and worms) and vast numbers of micro-organisms (such as bacteria and fungi) are also present.

The topsoil, or **A horizon**, contains much humus, which gives the soil a **dark brown** colour.

The subsoil, or **B horizon**, is **light brown**.

The **C horizon** lies directly on the bedrock. It consists largely of broken rock, or **regolith**.

Bedrock, or parent material.

Fig. 81.3 A brown earth soil profile.

See questions 4 and 5 on page 524.

CHAPTER 82
PEOPLE AND SOILS

 **KEY IDEA!**

People impact on soils.

PEOPLE AND SOIL EROSION

Soil is a renewable resource that can be used again and again. But it depends on vegetation cover for its fertility and health and sometimes even for its survival. People sometimes destroy or remove this vegetation cover. The soil can then be swept away by landslides or become exposed to **agents of erosion**, such as wind and running water.

- **Wind erosion** happens when wind removes dry, exposed topsoil from the land.
- **Sheet erosion** is the removal of a uniform layer of topsoil by rainwater washing evenly down a slope.
- **Gully erosion** happens when rainwater concentrates into small streamlets and carves gashes into the land's surface. It forms numerous grooves or gullies in the ground.

How Vegetation Protects Soil

- Plant leaves and other vegetation **intercept** raindrops. They stop heavy rain from pounding off the soil and loosening it. Some rain will evaporate off the plants without ever reaching the ground. This reduces the possibility of sheet or gully erosion in wet climates.
- Plant roots **absorb** water from the soil. This helps to prevent mudflows in wet climates.
- Plant roots **bind** the soil together. This helps to prevent it from being washed or blown away.
- Dead plant roots leave channels that help water to **percolate** through the soil. This assists soil drainage.
- Tree trunks help to **block** landslides and avalanches (snow slides) in mountain areas.
- Plant litter provides humus that **fertilizes** the soil. This allows more vegetation to grow and continue to protect the soil.

Activity

1. What kind of soil erosion can you identify in this photograph?
2. How might people help to cause this erosion?

How People Destroy Vegetation Cover

Human activities can destroy vegetation cover and help to cause soil erosion.

- **Overgrazing** happens when too many farm animals are allowed to graze the land. The animals can strip the soil of so much of its vegetation cover that the soil becomes exposed to landslides, mudflows or to the agents of erosion. Animals can also expose the soil by trampling vegetation with their hooves.
- **Overcultivation** happens when people grow crops year after year on the same patch of land without fertilizing the soil, resting it or practising crop rotation. This causes the soil to become deficient in minerals, so that crops eventually fail to grow. The soil is then left without protective cover and is exposed to erosion.
- **Deforestation** happens when people cut or destroy forests that protect the soil from landslides, mudflows, avalanches or the agents of erosion.

Case Study 1: The Burren

> You have already learned about the Burren on page 59.

The Burren is a karst area of largely exposed limestone in north Co. Clare. There are places where its almost bare rock surface supports very little farming or human habitation. Yet there is evidence that, from the Stone Age to Celtic times, this area was farmed successfully and was quite heavily populated (see Fig. 82.1 and the photograph below). The Burren then must have had sufficient soil and grass cover for agriculture.

Scientists believe that overgrazing by Ireland's cattle farmers of old might have exposed the Burren's soil to the elements. Rain may then have stripped the land of its soil, leaving the underlying limestone exposed.

The Burren
Co. Clare

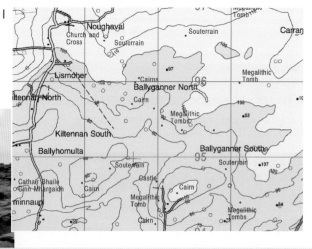

Fig. 82.1

Parts of the Burren, Co Clare.

Activity

1. How many square kilometres does the map fragment represent?
2. Count the number of antiquities (ancient buildings, etc.) on the map and calculate their density per square kilometre.
3. Count the number of present-day buildings on the map and calculate their density. (Note: Do not confuse buildings with spot heights on the map.)
4. Try to account for (explain) the contrast between the densities calculated in questions 1 and 2.

Case Study 2: Duncarton Hill

The night of 19 September 2003 produced a nightmare experience for the residents of Pollathomas in north-western Co. Mayo. With a terrifying roar, thousands of tonnes of mud, rock and earth swept down nearby Duncarton Hill. Roads and bridges were torn up. Holiday homes were destroyed. Parts of a graveyard were swept into the sea. An elderly woman was trapped in her home while mud ripped through her house. Miraculously, no one died in the terrible mudslide.

Prolonged heavy rain, which had saturated the soil, was the immediate cause of the mudflow, but human activities might also have contributed. Some locals believe that sheep had been allowed to overgraze Duncarton Hill. Others fear that rock-breaking work near the foot of the hill might have loosened peat and soil. More say that a road built to service an aviation tower at the top of the hill might have undermined topsoil and blocked the free drainage of water downhill.

Activity
In what way might the human activities shown here contribute to desertification?

Case Study 3: Desertification in the Sahel

Desertification is the spread of desert conditions, usually following the erosion of exposed topsoil. The world's worst instance of desertification is happening in the Sahel region of Africa. The Sahel is on the southern borders of the Sahara desert (see Fig. 82.2). Desertification is so bad there that desert conditions are spreading southwards into the Sahel at the rate of 5 to 10 km each year. You will see from this case study that human activities help to cause desertification in the Sahel.

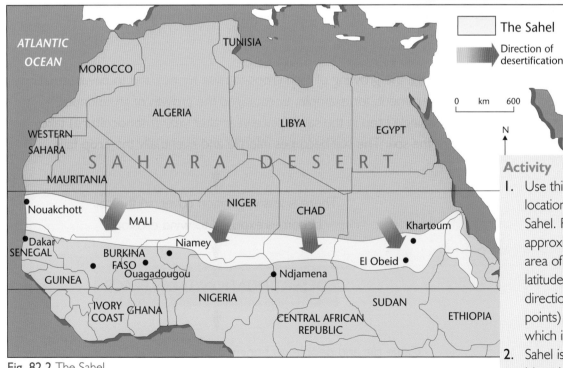

Fig. 82.2 The Sahel.

Activity
1. Use this map to describe the location and extent of the Sahel. Refer to the approximate length, width and area of the region. Refer to its latitude, its orientation (the direction in which its long axis points) and the countries which it partly occupies.
2. Sahel is an Arabic word for 'shore'. Why do you think the Sahel is so called?

Causes of Desertification

Climate Change

The excessive burning of fossil fuels, especially in rich First World countries, has contributed to global warming and other climate changes that affect the Sahel.

- Rising temperatures have caused **more evaporation** and less condensation. This has reduced rainfall levels.
- Over the past twenty years, **rainfall has decreased** by one-third.
- There have been several long and serious **droughts**, for example from 1968 to 1973.

Some **vegetation** that is not drought resistant **dies** as a result of these changes.

Population Growth

High birth rates have led to an annual population increase of nearly 2 per cent. Because of this:

- **More cattle** are needed. They overgraze the land and trample vegetation.
- **More food crops** are needed. The land is overcultivated.
- **More firewood** is needed. Trees and shrubs are cleared for firewood.

Local Customs

Peoples such as the **Masai** measure their wealth by the number of cattle they own. They keep so many cattle that the land is **overgrazed**.

Wells

Wells are sunk to provide water. The wells **use up groundwater** that took centuries to accumulate. This causes the water table to fall. Cattle herders come to live near wells, so that the areas surrounding the wells become **overgrazed and trampled**.

Cash Crops

Governments encourage the growing of cash crops to raise money and to pay international debts. The Niger government, for example, encouraged the growth of groundnuts.

The growth of a single crop in the same place year after year (**monoculture**) takes many nutrients from the soil. The soil becomes infertile and eventually the **crop fails**.

There is less vegetation cover, so the soil becomes exposed to wind erosion.

DESERTIFICATION TAKES PLACE

Cattle die and people go hungry. Famines occur. Millions of people migrate from the Sahel into the savannah grasslands further south. The overpopulation of the grasslands causes desertification there.

> The Sahel is also referred to on page 513.

Activity
Explain how the sinking of wells such as the one shown in the photograph might contribute to desertification in the Sahel.

The Sahel.

Case Study 4: The American Dust Bowl

In the 1930s, overcropping led to serious soil erosion in that part of the Midwest of the United States known as the Dust Bowl (see Fig. 82.3).

The Great Plains of the Midwest are windy, semi-arid (dry) areas of **natural grassland**. Throughout the 1920s, farmers **ploughed** the plains to plant wheat, which could be sold at a high price. In the early years, there was sufficient rainfall and the plains were golden with wheat.

Then, throughout the 1930s, the **rains failed**. The farmers continued to plough and plant, but nothing would grow. With no vegetation to protect it, the soil became dry, loose and dusty. Winds whipped across the barren fields, carrying away the soil in great clouds of dust. With their farms ruined by **wind erosion**, many farmers abandoned their homes. Like refugees, they headed west to California in search of work and survival.

You have already learned about the Dust Bowl on page 116.

The dust was everywhere. It piled up against walls, clogged machinery and even crept into houses where people struggled to breathe. Children wore dust masks going to and coming from school. Farmers watched helplessly as their farms blew away.

Fig. 82.3
The Dust Bowl.

Activity

1. Which six states of the USA were part of the Dust Bowl?
2. What enabled the wind to create the dust storm shown in the photo?

CONSERVING SOIL

Throughout the world, people employ different methods of preventing or reducing soil erosion. Some of these methods of **soil conservation** are as follows.

Improving Vegetation Cover

Revise **How Vegetation Protects Soil** on page 493.

You have learned that the removal of vegetation cover is a major cause of soil erosion. It follows that one of the best ways of combating soil erosion is to increase or improve vegetation cover. There are many ways of doing this.

Crop Rotation

Different crops remove and replace various minerals in the soil. Crop rotation is the planned growing of **different crops in the same place from one year to another** so that the soil does not become deficient in any particular mineral. This helps to keep the soil healthy and fertile so that it will always produce enough vegetation cover to protect it from erosion.

Regrassing

Wind erosion in regions such as the Sahel can be reduced by replanting tough drought-resistant grasses in places threatened by erosion. The grasses will trap wind-blown soil, while their roots will help to bind the surviving soil together.

A similar method of soil conservation is practised on Irish coastal sand dunes, where **marram grass** is used as a means of 'anchoring' dunes against wind erosion.

Afforestation

The planting of trees also combats erosion. Trees are even more effective than grass at trapping wind-borne soil. The shallow roots of conifers bind the soil together very effectively. Trees also intercept heavy rainfall and reduce surface run-off that might result in gully erosion. Tree roots absorb moisture from the soil and so reduce the possibility of mudflows in wet, hilly regions, such as in the West of Ireland. Fruit-producing trees are of added benefit in Third World regions such as the Sahel, because they produce nutritious food for local people.

Activity
Identify and describe the method of soil conservation shown in this photograph.

Shelter Belts

Well-separated lines of trees or shrubs break the force of the wind over the land between them. They can therefore act as shelter belts or protective barriers against wind erosion in places such as the Sahel or the Great Plains of the United States.

Reducing Surface Run-off

The surface run-off of water can result in gully erosion on hilly or even gently sloping areas. There are different methods of reducing surface run-off.

Stone Lines

Burkina Faso is a country that partly lies in the Sahel. This area suffers from very infrequent falls of heavy rain. People there place **lines of small stones across slopes** in order to reduce surface run-off. Rainwater gets trapped behind the stones, so it has a chance to soak into the ground. The stone lines also trap waterborne soil and prevent it from being removed from the area. Stone lines therefore replenish groundwater and reduce soil erosion. They work best on very gentle slopes, where they can result in a 50 per cent increase in crop yields.

See question 5 and 6 on page 524.

lines of stones built across slopes reduce run-off →

water trapped behind the stones can infiltrate into the ground

Fig. 82.4 Stone lines in Burkina Faso.

Contour Ploughing

In contour ploughing, **ridges run across rather than up and down a slope**. These ridges act like little dams that hold rainwater and give it time to infiltrate the ground. They therefore prevent gully erosion by stopping water from rushing down the freshly ploughed soil. Contour ploughing can reduce soil erosion by up to 50 per cent. It is practised in those parts of the **Midwest of the United States** where large-scale tillage farming is practised.

Terraces in China.

Terracing

Terracing prevents soil erosion in slopes that are too steep for contour ploughing. A series of **walls are built one above the other across a hillside**. Behind each retaining wall, a 'step', or terrace of land, is flattened and farmed. The tops of the retaining walls trap water that would otherwise flow rapidly downslope. Soil erosion is thus prevented. Terracing is common in **South-East Asia**, where water trapped behind terrace walls supports the growing of rice.

Activity
Describe how the use of terraces supports rice farming.

New Animals
Efforts have been made to reduce the large numbers of poor-quality cattle that overgraze much of the Sahel.

- **New breeds** of smaller, better-quality cattle are being introduced. They eat less, but produce more milk and meat than existing breeds.
- Limited numbers of **sheep and goats** are being introduced into areas where the only vegetation is poor-quality scrub. Sheep and goats can survive on such scrub.

CHAPTER 83
BIOMES

Biomes are large world regions in which climate, soils, natural vegetation and animal life are all interrelated. The desert biome is an example.

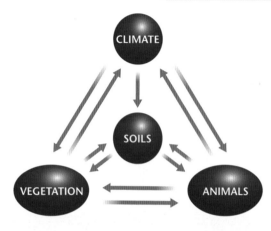

Fig. 83.1 Some interrelationships within a biome.

Biomes are large world regions in which climate, soils, natural vegetation and animal life are all interrelated (see Fig. 83.1). Vegetation and animals, for example, are adapted to the climate and soils of the biome in which they exist.

Biomes are usually named after the types of natural vegetation that occupy them. Ireland, for example, is within the **temperate deciduous forest biome**. This biome is so called because, under natural conditions, it was once covered with deciduous trees.

Geographers usually identify nine different biomes in the world. The map in Fig. 83.2 shows these biomes. It is, of course, a very simplified map, which gives only a very generalised idea of the location of biomes.

Fig. 83.2 World biomes.

Activity

Try to briefly explain each of the connections referred to in Fig. 83.1.

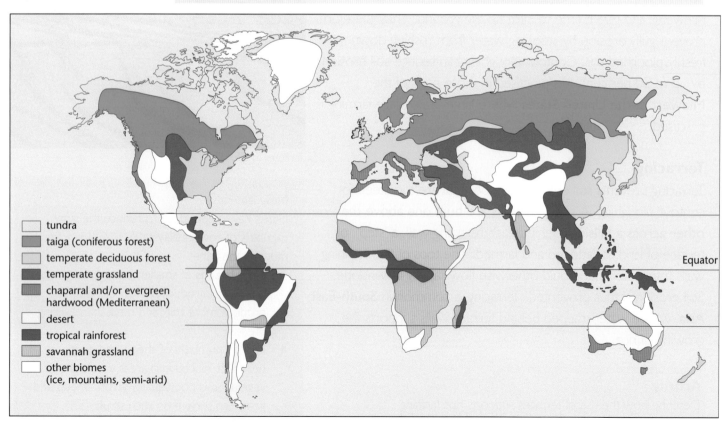

- tundra
- taiga (coniferous forest)
- temperate deciduous forest
- temperate grassland
- chaparral and/or evergreen hardwood (Mediterranean)
- desert
- tropical rainforest
- savannah grassland
- other biomes (ice, mountains, semi-arid)

Equator

Activity
Activity

Study Fig. 83.2, then answer the following.

1. Within which biome is each of the following places?
   a. Italy
   b. the Amazon Basin
   c. France
   d. Iceland
2. This map shows precise borders between different biomes. Do you think that these precise borders normally exist in reality? Explain your answer.

THE DESERT BIOME

The term 'desert biome' refers to the world's hot and mid-latitude deserts. This chapter will focus on the **hot deserts**, which are the most well-known and characteristic desert regions in the world.

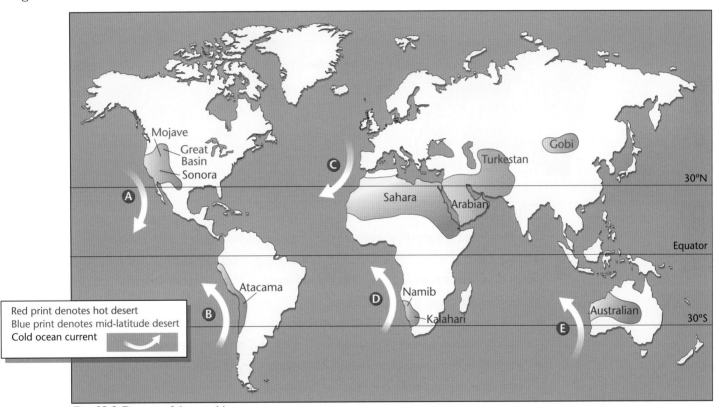

Red print denotes hot desert
Blue print denotes mid-latitude desert
Cold ocean current

Fig. 83.3 Deserts of the world.

Activity

1. Identify:
   a. two hot deserts in the Americas
   b. two hot deserts in Africa
   c. two hot deserts in Asia
   d. one hot desert in Australia.
2. Name three temperate desert areas. What do the locations of these deserts have in common?
3. Five cold ocean currents are shown and labelled A–E on this map. Match each of these letters with one of the following currents: West Australian Current; Benguela Current; Canaries Current; California Current; Peru Current.

501

THE DESERT BIOME

Where Are the Hot Deserts?

Fig. 83.3 reveals that hot deserts are generally situated in tropical and sub-tropical zones **between 15° and 30°** north and south of the Equator. Much of this zone is in the path of the **trade winds** and some of it lies on the **high pressure belt** that exists over landmasses about 30° from the Equator.

Most hot deserts lie on the **western side of great continents**, near **cold ocean currents**.

Some desert areas, for example in North America, lie on the **leeward side of mountains**, where a rain shadow effect results in very little rainfall (see Fig. 83.4).

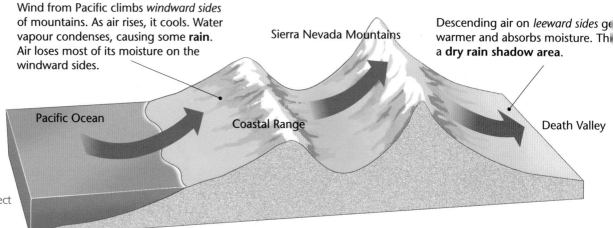

Wind from Pacific climbs *windward sides* of mountains. As air rises, it cools. Water vapour condenses, causing some **rain**. Air loses most of its moisture on the windward sides.

Sierra Nevada Mountains

Descending air on *leeward sides* g[e] warmer and absorbs moisture. Th[is] a **dry rain shadow area**.

Pacific Ocean

Coastal Range

Death Valley

Fig. 83.4 Rain shadow effect on Death Valley, a desert area in California, USA.

Climate

Desert climate is **very dry**, with a yearly rainfall of between 0 and 250 mm. Rainfall is as unpredictable as it is rare. When rain does occur, it usually comes in the form of short, heavy downpours, which may affect small areas. These **'desert storms'** are usually of limited use for plant growth because:

- The heavy rains do not have much opportunity to infiltrate the soil. Rainwater runs rapidly on the surface, causing flash floods and eroding deep gullies.
- High temperatures cause rain to evaporate very quickly off the surface. Some rain evaporates even before it reaches the ground.

Very limited precipitation can also occur in the forms of dew or fog. Sudden drops in temperature can cause night **dews** in parts of the Sahara. **Fog** sometimes brings limited moisture to narrow coastal areas where cold ocean currents flow offshore. Such fogs occur regularly on the coastal sand dunes of the Namib Desert in Africa.

Deserts have **hot** climates, especially in summer, when daytime temperatures can reach higher than 45° C. But temperatures can drop by up to 30° C within an hour of sunset and night temperatures can fall below freezing point in winter. This **diurnal (day/night) temperature range** is greater than the average summer/winter temperature range of between 20° C and 25° C. That is why some geographers say that 'night is the winter of the desert'.

Why Deserts Are So Dry

- Some hot desert areas lie on the 'horse latitudes, **high pressure** belts that run across much of the earth at about 30° north and south of the Equator (see Fig. 83.3). Air descends towards the earth along these high-pressure belts. As it does so, the air becomes warmer. Warm air holds more water vapour than cooler air, so the descending air absorbs moisture. That is why high pressure brings prolonged dry conditions.

- Most hot desert regions are in the path of the **trade winds** that blow over much of the earth from 30° latitude towards the Equator (see Fig. 83.5). As these winds blow towards the Equator, they become warmer. Warm air holds more water vapour than cold air can. The trade winds therefore absorb rather than emit moisture, and they are therefore dry winds.

- Occasionally, moisture-laden winds can blow in from the western seas towards the deserts, but these winds must pass over cold **ocean currents**. As they do so, they are cooled and lose almost all of their moisture – usually in the form of fog – before they reach the land.

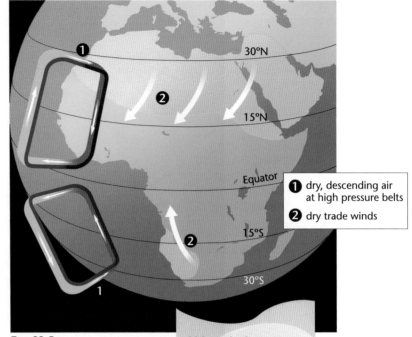

① dry, descending air at high pressure belts

② dry trade winds

Fig. 83.5

Although deserts are dry regions, very few desert areas are completely dry. Parts of the Atacama Desert in Chile are said to be the driest places on earth. They receive an average of less than 15 mm of rain per annum and sometimes receive no rain for years on end.

Why Deserts Are Hot by Day…

- Hot deserts are **within the tropics**, where the sun shines from almost vertically overhead in the summertime. These sunrays reach the earth's surface at almost right angles. They are therefore concentrated over small areas of ground and so give great heat.

- Another reason for high daytime temperatures is that the desert atmosphere contains little or **no cloud or humidity**, which would help to block sunrays. This, together with a general absence of vegetation or water bodies, allows sunrays to be absorbed rapidly into the desert surface. The surface then returns great heat to the atmosphere, giving rise to high atmospheric temperatures.

…And Cold by Night

- **Cloudless skies** allow daytime temperatures to rise rapidly. But with no clouds and little humidity to blanket it, the heat escapes quickly after nightfall.

A weather satellite photograph of Africa.

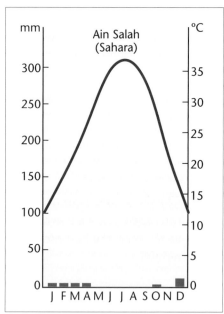

Fig. 83.6 Temperature and precipitation at Ain Salah, Algeria, in the Sahara Desert.

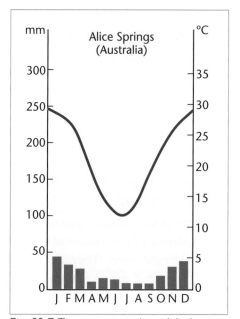

Fig. 83.7 Temperature and precipitation figures for Alice Springs in the Australian Desert.

Soils

Some hot desert areas have potentially fertile soils, which need only water to produce luxuriant plant life. Irrigation schemes, for example, have made deserts bloom in places such as southern California and parts of Libya. But soils in many desert areas **do not favour the growth** of a wide variety of plants. Some reasons for this are outlined below.

Little Soil Cover

Some desert areas have very deep soils. These limited areas are usually low-lying basins. Their soils were eroded from surrounding mountains and washed into the basins over tens of thousands of years by flash floods from occasional, torrential rainstorms. But most hot desert areas are rocky or stony, with very little soil cover.

Coarse Texture

Many regions have coarse-textured, gravelly soils. These occur where winds have blown away the finer dust and sand particles, leaving only heavier particles behind. Such soils are unable to retain moisture and so tend to be infertile.

Lack of Water and Humus

Very low precipitation results in desert soils being so dry (arid) that they are referred to as **aridisols**. Dry conditions cause vegetation to be very sparse and, in some areas, non-existent. Sparse vegetation leads to a shortage of plant litter, which in turn leads to a scarcity of humus. A scarcity of humus contributes to soil infertility. It can also result in soils being **grey** in colour.

Poor Development

Low precipitation also leads to a shortage of chemical weathering, which would contribute to the formation of soil. This, together with a shortage of humus, means that desert soils are often **poorly developed** and lack the clear horizons or the varied components that exist in most Irish soils. Soils in some desert areas consist of little more than a collection of broken-down mineral particles.

Fig. 83.8 The soil profile of a typical aridisol.

Activity
Contrast this profile with that of brown earth soil (Fig. 81.3) on page 492.

● *Describe this Sahara Desert scene.*

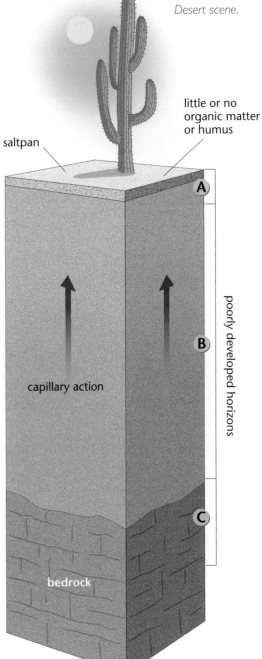

saltpan

little or no organic matter or humus

A

capillary action

B

poorly developed horizons

C

bedrock

Salinisation

Hot, dry conditions cause moisture to move up through the soil by **capillary action** (see page 489). This causes large quantities of dissolved salts, such as chloride and sodium, to move up close to the surface in a process called **salinisation**. These salts are poisonous to most varieties of plants. They also form an impermeable crust, or **saltpan**, on or near the surface. The saltpan impedes the development of plant roots.

Vegetation

Vegetation is **scant** in hot deserts, mainly because of **a shortage of water** and of **high rates of evaporation** owing to elevated daytime temperatures. Yet many plant species survive. They have different ways of adapting to desert conditions.

- Many desert plants use large **root systems** to find water.
  - Some plants have *taproots* that reach deep into the ground in search of water. The most famous of these is the *mesquite bush*. Its roots are up to 50 m long.
  - Some cacti and other plants have *shallow roots*, which spread outwards (rather than downwards) for great distances, so that they create a large moisture-collecting area in times of rainfall.

The desert in bloom: these ephemerals bloomed suddenly following a rare desert downpour. Their life cycles will span only a few weeks.

- Some plants adapt to short and very infrequent desert downpours by growing very quickly. These plants are called **ephemerals**. The seeds of many ephemerals have waxy surfaces, which allow them to retain moisture for long periods of time. These seeds remain dormant, sometimes for years, awaiting desert rain. When rain does fall, the seeds develop into mature plants, burst into flower and produce a new generation of seeds, all within a few weeks. The old plants then die, while the new seeds become dormant and wait for the next period of rain. *Desert poppies* and the *creosote bush* of North America are examples of ephemerals.

- Many plants are **succulents**. They store water for long periods in their impermeable, waxy stems, in their roots or even in underground bulbs. The *barrel cactus* and the *giant saguaro* (see page 507) are examples of succulents.

- Some plants produce **juicy fruits**, which are eagerly devoured and digested by birds. The digested fruit seeds are then spread in bird droppings over large areas.

- The leaves and barks of some shrubs contain **poisonous or unpleasant substances**, which protect them from most hungry animals. The *Sodom apple*, for example, cannot be eaten by goats or camels.

- Plants such as the cereus, or 'desert dandelion', **bloom only at night**, when evaporation rates are lowest. The flowers of the cereus remain closed during the day to escape the drying effect of the hot sun.
- Some plants adapt in several different ways to their hot desert environments. The giant cactus, or *saguaro*, of North America is an example of such a plant (see Fig. 83.9).

Despite its thorny skin, some animals manage to burrow holes in the saguaro. This hole was made by a woodpecker. It is now the home of the elf owl, which is the world's smallest owl.

Oases

An oasis is an area of desert that has been made fertile by the presence of surface water. The water and the sun's heat usually contribute to the lush growth of vegetables, cereals, fig trees and other types of vegetation. The date palm is popular among oasis dwellers because it provides welcome shade as well as fruit.

People and Hot Desert Vegetation
- People with large herds of cattle or sheep have **overgrazed** semi-desert areas, such as parts of the Sahel in Africa. This destruction of natural vegetation has contributed to desertification (the spread of desert conditions).
- People in areas such as southern California have used **irrigation** to produce high crop yields in hot deserts. But the rapid evaporation of irrigation water can result in **salinisation**, or the build-up of salt, near the surface of the land. Too much salt makes the soil toxic to plants.

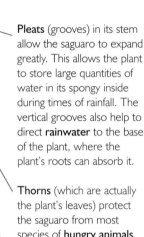

Pleats (grooves) in its stem allow the saguaro to expand greatly. This allows the plant to store large quantities of water in its spongy inside during times of rainfall. The vertical grooves also help to direct **rainwater** to the base of the plant, where the plant's roots can absorb it.

Thorns (which are actually the plant's leaves) protect the saguaro from most species of **hungry animals**. The thorns also create areas of **still air** around the plant, protecting it from the drying effect of desert winds.

Waxy, impermeable skin acts like a plastic wrapper around the plant. It helps to prevent moisture within the plant from escaping.

Fig. 83.9 The giant cactus and how it adapts to desert conditions.

The fennec fox.

Fauna (Animals)

Hot deserts can support numerous animal species, but only if these animals adapt to prolonged very hot and dry conditions. Desert animals have different ways of adapting to these conditions.

The Hiders

Many animals survive by avoiding the scorching heat of the sun.

- Some creatures are **nocturnal**. They hide away in cool places during the day and come out at night to hunt and to eat. Animals such as the *rattlesnake* and *kangaroo rat* (which live in underground holes and burrows) and the *elf owl* (which lives in holes burrowed out of cacti) are examples of nocturnal animals.

- Some animals survive long, dry conditions by **hibernating** for extended periods. They remain very still and underground during these long periods and emerge only when rain finally arrives to frantically eat, mate and breed. An example of this are the *toads* of the Arizona Desert in the United States. They hibernate, often for more than a year, to await a desert rainstorm. They then emerge quickly to the surface and immediately enter flood pools to mate. Within 24 hours of mating, the females' eggs will be fertilized and hatched. Within two days, the pools will be full of tadpoles. Within two weeks (if the flood waters have not evaporated) a new generation of toads will emerge from the pools.

- Some animals avoid the heat by simply *staying in the shadow* of plants. The *jackrabbit* of North America uses cacti for shade, while many desert *insects* avoid the sun's rays by staying on the shaded sides of twigs or plant stems.

The Non-drinkers

Some animals do not need to drink water, because they get all the liquid they need from the food they eat.

- Carnivorous (meat-eating) animals, such as the *fennec fox*, get much of the liquid they need from the blood of their prey.

- The *desert gazelle* gets all the liquid it needs from the vegetation it eats. It conserves moisture by never urinating. Instead, it passes uric acid in the form of small, dry pellets.

Big-eared Animals

Animals lose heat through their ears, which contain many veins and blood vessels. The *fennec fox*, the *jackrabbit* and the *desert hedgehog* all have very large ears. This helps to keep them cool in the heat of the day.

The Birds

Most birds need regular water supplies, so few bird species live in deserts. Those that do have novel ways of adapting to their environment. The **roadrunner** of the North American deserts runs from place to place because it can use less energy by running than by flying. The roadrunner also has a very large tail, which it often spreads over itself like a parasol during the heat of the day.

The Marvellous Camel

Few large animals can withstand excessive heat or can retain moisture well enough to survive in hot, dry desert conditions. The camel is a notable exception. Known for centuries as 'the ship of the desert', the camel is perfectly adapted to the desert environment.

The roadrunner.
- *Explain how this bird adapts to hot desert conditions.*

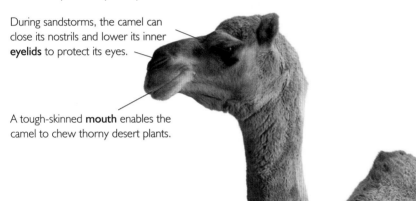

During sandstorms, the camel can close its nostrils and lower its inner **eyelids** to protect its eyes.

A tough-skinned **mouth** enables the camel to chew thorny desert plants.

Fat in the **hump** acts as a food reserve. Because fat is concentrated in one area, the rest of the camel's body can cool more easily.

Coarse hair protects the camel's **back** from the sun.

The camel can drink more than 100 litres of water at a time. By not sweating, it conserves body fluids. It can thus survive for up to several months **without water.**

Tough belly and kneepads enable the camel to lie on hot sand.

Wide, padded **feet** allow the camel to travel easily over soft sand.

See questions 7, 8 and 9 on page 524.

How the camel is adapted to desert conditions.

509

CHAPTER 84
HOW HUMAN ACTIVITIES HAVE ALTERED BIOMES

KEY IDEA!

Biomes throughout most of the world have been greatly altered by human activities.

In many places, natural biomes have been altered by human activities or have been replaced completely by 'created' rather than natural environments. In this chapter we will study the impacts of the following human activities on biomes:

1. Early settlement and the clearing of forests.
2. The felling of tropical rainforests.
3. Intensive agricultural practices.
4. Industrial development.

Limestone pavement in the Burren.

Activity
1. Explain how the surface shown here became so bare.
2. What evidence of former settlement can be seen in the photo?

Case Study 1: Early Settlement and the Clearing of Forests

From very early in human history, people have altered biomes by clearing forests to make homes. Since the invention of farming about 10,000 years ago, forests have also been cleared for agricultural purposes.

Ireland

Farmers first reached Ireland about 7,000 years ago, during **Neolithic** (New Stone Age) times. They mostly farmed upland areas because they could till the lighter, grittier soils of the uplands more easily than heavier lowland soils. Stone Age people could not, however, clear much of the existing deciduous forests with their stone tools. When the **Celts** arrived in Ireland around 500 BC, they brought iron tools with them. These allowed the Celts to clear more of Ireland's ancient forests of oak, ash and other broad-leaved species.

Stone Age and Celtic farmers did, however, have considerable impact on the biome in particular parts of Ireland. Archaeological evidence suggests, for example, that **the Burren** in Co. Clare was heavily populated during Stone Age and Celtic times (see Fig. 82.1 on page 494). Farmers at this time appear to have cut down existing trees in order to graze their farm animals. They probably exceeded the **carrying capacity** of the land by grazing too many animals on it. This resulted in **overgrazing**, which caused the grass cover to be almost all eaten and soils to be exposed to the weather. Rain and coastal winds then **denuded** (stripped) the land of its soil, leaving the underlying limestone exposed as it is today.

From the sixteenth century, as **English and Scottish planters** took over large parts of Ireland, the clearing of forests increased greatly. Tilled and other agricultural land replaced more and more of the old deciduous woodlands. Towns and roads also demanded more land. By 1921, at the end of English rule, less than 1 per cent of Ireland was covered in forest. Populations of forest animals, such as deer and foxes, had decreased greatly, while some species, such as the wolf, had become extinct. Today, only tiny fragments of our ancient Irish forest biome remain. These can be found near Killarney and Kenmare in Co. Kerry and near Lough Gill in Co. Sligo.

California

Before the mid-nineteenth century, California in the United States was very lightly populated by Native Americans and by the descendants of earlier Spanish settlers. These people did little to modify California's **Mediterranean forest biome**. Then, the discovery of gold and the resulting gold rush caused hundreds of thousands of people to flood into California.

The forest biome was altered as settlers cut down oak, pine and other native trees to provide fuel and to make houses and pit props for gold mines. But it was the coming of **the railway** that really heralded a massive modification of California's natural biome. As the population of the state soared, forests were cleared for farmland, roads and railway lines, as well as for rapidly growing cities, such as San Francisco. Timber was carried away by rail to be sold in other parts of the United States. Over time, California's natural forest biome came to be replaced in some areas by **chaparral** (scrubland) and in most areas by 'created' environments of farmland or towns.

Meanwhile, California's most famous tree species – **the giant redwood** – was cleared almost to extinction. With less than 5 per cent of the old redwood forests now remaining, some redwood areas have been placed under state ownership so that they can be preserved. They include trees 100 m tall and more than 2,000 years old. The preservation of the remaining redwoods also preserves the habitats of several species of endangered flora (plants) and fauna (animals). In this way, fragments of California's original biome have been preserved from the interference of settlers.

These majestic redwoods once formed part of the natural biome of California.

Activity

How and why did settlers alter the Californian biome since 1850?

Revise **How Vegetation Protects Soil** on page 493.

Original Mediterranean vegetation (above) and secondary growth (below).

Italy

The natural biome of the Italian peninsula is one of **Mediterranean forests** of pine, cypress and cork oak trees as well as myrtle, laurel and other shrubs. These trees and shrubs played vital roles in the survival and protection of this biome. They provided suitable habitats for Mediterranean fauna. The trees soaked up water from the ground during occasional heavy rainstorms and their roots helped to bind the soil together on steep hillsides. Tree trunks helped to block landslides on steep slopes.

For thousands of years, people have modified the natural biome of Mediterranean Italy. From before the time of ancient Rome, settlers have cleared forests for firewood and farming. Where forests were cleared, **secondary growth** usually replaced the original trees. In some areas, this secondary growth consists of what is called *macchia* in Italy. *Macchia* contains shrubs such as myrtle, together with sweet-smelling smaller plants such as rosemary and lavender. *Garrigue*, a secondary growth of thorny bushes and plants, often developed on poorer soils.

From early times, people damaged the Mediterranean forest biome by **overgrazing** land with sheep and goats. This resulted in the occurrence of deadly **landslides and mudflows** on some hill slopes. With the removal of tree roots, water built up in the soil following rainstorms. When the soil became heavy and saturated, mudflows or landslides occurred, especially in the absence of tree roots and tree trunks that would help bind the soil together and prevent the downward movement of mud or regolith (loose rock).

Mudflows happen to this day on Italian hillsides. In 1998, following a period of heavy rain, a sea of mud ripped downhill through overgrazed slopes into the town of **Sarno** near Naples in Southern Italy. That mudflow left 135 people dead and 1,500 homeless.

Activity
Compare the remaining fragment of Mediterranean forest (top photo) with the *macchia* vegetation (bottom photo).

The Sahel

In parts of the Sahel region of Africa, a savannah grassland biome has been replaced largely by a hot desert biome. This process is called **desertification** and it has been caused partly by human intervention in the region.

For more on the Sahel, revise pages 495–6.

Population increase, together with many years of wetter than usual weather, encouraged many people to move into the Sahel between the 1930s and the 1970s. The people, whose numbers increased by a third in that period, cut down more and more trees and shrubs for **firewood**. They also burned trees and shrubs so that they could graze cattle more easily on the land. The number of cattle in the Sahel doubled during this period, so that serious **overgrazing** took place. All this caused the gradual deterioration of the existing biome.

From the 1960s onwards, the rains began to fail. Decades of wetter than usual conditions were replaced by many years of **drought**. The overgrazed vegetation failed to reproduce itself. Soils became dry, dusty and exposed to the weather. **Winds** began to blow away the topsoil, leaving much of the land barren, like that of the Sahara Desert to the north. Human activities, together with climatic variations, had resulted in desertification.

See question 10 on page 524.

Activity

What effects did the human activities shown in these photos have on vegetation cover and on desertification in the Sahel?

Case Study 2: The Felling of Tropical Forests

This study will focus on the effects of felling the world's **equatorial forests**.

Fig. 84.1 Equatorial forests are located close to the Equator. They cover vast areas in places such as the Amazon Basin, the Congo Basin and Indonesia.

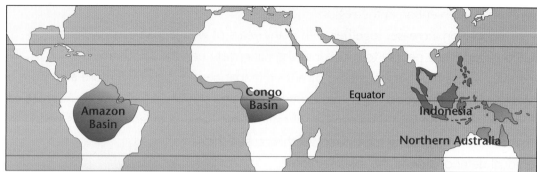

Equatorial climate provides high temperatures and plentiful rainfall all through the year. **The forest** is dense and luxuriant and its trees form an almost continuous canopy over the land. Beneath this canopy, a huge variety of smaller plants flourish. Millions of species of animals, ranging from tiny microbes to colourful birds, inhabit the forest. In their natural state, the equatorial forests contain the world's richest and most diverse biome.

Dense forest in an equatorial region.

The Impacts of Deforestation
Early and Later Forest Users

The Amazon Basin alone contains 40,000 different varieties of flowering plants. It is said that one square kilometre of the Basin contains as many plant and animal varieties as the whole of Europe.

The original inhabitants of the equatorial forests include peoples such as the **pygmies** of the Congo Basin and the **Yanomani** and other 'Indian' tribes of the Amazon. Living in small groups, some of these tribes have for centuries slashed and burned tiny patches of forest in order to grow food crops such as manioc. In the absence of plant litter from trees, the cleared areas become infertile within a few years. When this happens, the people clear other patches of forest, leaving forest vegetation to reclaim the originally cleared areas. The small-scale activities of these indigenous (native) peoples left no permanent, damaging mark on the forest biome. Their activities are examples, therefore, of the **sustainable** use of forests.

Since the middle of the twentieth century, **large-scale clearances** of equatorial forests have taken place, especially in the Amazon Basin in Brazil. These clearances are carried out by a variety of people who come from outside the forest. They include rich cattle ranchers, logging companies, mining corporations and road builders. Using bulldozers and other heavy machinery, they clear such vast areas that they cause a hectare of forest to be destroyed every 1.5 seconds. Such clearances are clearly **unsustainable** and cause immense damage to the rainforest biome.

Effects on Water and Soils

When the canopy of trees is cleared away, there is nothing to intercept (stop) heavy equatorial rains from hitting the ground directly. More rain then falls on the exposed ground and flows quickly into the rivers as surface run-off. This makes rivers bigger and more likely to **flood** nearby plains. Surface run-off also carries soil into rivers and some of this soil is deposited on riverbeds. This process causes river levels to rise and so contributes to flooding. Some floods have damaged the rainforest biome by destroying vegetation and animal habitats and by drowning countless animals. New settlements in the Amazon have also damaged the biome by **polluting** river water with everything from household waste to deadly mercury used in the process of gold mining.

When trees are cut, **soils** become exposed to the full force of equatorial rain. The rain sometimes erodes soil by **sheet erosion**, which is the even washing away of the soil's upper layers. More commonly, **gully erosion** takes place, as deep grooves are cut into the land surface. Without trees to soak up groundwater, **leaching** greatly increases, so that a great deal of soil nutrients are washed down below the reach of plant roots. The absence of trees also deprives soil of the plant litter that it needs to maintain fertility. **Infertility** develops rapidly, especially in the absence of artificial fertilizers being used by those who work the cleared land.

Destruction of Habitats

The habitats (homes) of forest peoples and of countless plants and animals are changed or destroyed by 'developers' who clear equatorial forests.

Forest peoples face cultural destruction and sometimes even human extinction at the hands of 'developers' in regions such as the Amazon Basin. The **Yanomani**, who live near the border between Brazil and Venezuela (see Fig. 84.2), are an example of such a people. For centuries the Yanomani lived off the forest in a sustainable way. They hunted, fished and practised subsistence* farming in a way that did not damage or upset the delicate balance of the tropical forest biome. Since the 1970s the Yanomani have seen their world disappear as rich cattle ranchers, miners and other 'developers' invade and deforest their territory. The Yanomani have little natural resistance against some of the **diseases** brought by outsiders. Illnesses such as measles have killed up to 90 per cent of the populations of some Yanomani villages. Those who survive are denied the human right to live undisturbed in their own environment. Their culture is diluted or destroyed by Western influences. Their traditional social life is shattered. Many are reduced to living miserable roadside existences as beggars or prostitutes.

Activity
Explain and describe the human impact on tropical forests shown in this photo.

*Subsistence farmers use most of the crops they grow and the animals they rear to feed themselves and their families.

515

The Amazonian rainforest is home to peoples like the Yanomani.

The world's rainforests contain up to 2 million species of plants and animals. One-quarter of all pharmaceutical drugs already owe their origins to rainforest species, despite the fact that up to now only about one-tenth of those species have been studied by people from outside the forests. But rainforest plants and animals survive in a finely balanced biome. When the biome is upset by deforestation, a multitude of **plant and animal species become extinct**. It is calculated that in the Amazon alone, one or more plant or animal species now becomes extinct every day.

Activity

1. Describe the size of the Amazon rainforest in relation to the size of Ireland.
2. How have the Yanomani been affected by the modern 'development' of the rainforest?

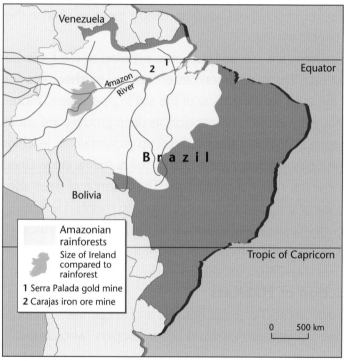

Fig. 84.2

Worldwide Impacts

The much-feared process of **global warming** is caused by the gradual build-up in our atmosphere of carbon dioxide and other 'greenhouse gases'. The burning of fossil fuels is the main cause of this build-up. But trees use up carbon dioxide and convert it into oxygen, which is why equatorial forests have been described as 'carbon sinks' and 'the lungs of the world'. Deforestation in places such as the Congo and the Amazon Basin therefore decreases the amount of oxygen and increases the amount of carbon dioxide in the atmosphere. The burning of trees during deforestation further adds to the build-up of carbon dioxide. All this plays a role in global warming and in associated climate change. One result of global warming might be a rise in sea level by up to 6 m during this century. Such a rise would flood many low-lying parts of the world, such as Bangladesh and the south-east coast of the USA.

Another global impact of tropical deforestation is **desertification**, or the spread of deserts. We have seen how deforestation is exposing land to the elements and how heavy rain then removes topsoil from the land. This leaves the land barren and open to the spread of desert conditions. Desertification is already widespread in the Sahel region to the south of the Sahara Desert in Africa. Early signs of desertification now also exist at the edge of the Amazon Basin in north-east Brazil.

See question 11 on page 524.

The polar bear is an endangered species.

Activity

How can the clearing of rainforests threaten the habitats of species such as the polar bear?

Case Study 3: Intensive Agricultural Practices

Intensive agriculture seeks to get the highest yield possible from the land. In doing so it sometimes leads to soil erosion, which alters and damages biomes.

Clearing Natural Vegetation

Intensive farming can lead to soil erosion when it involves **removing natural vegetation** from the land surface. A cover of natural vegetation usually protects soil from erosion. When farmers remove this protection, the soil is exposed to the elements and can be eroded by wind or surface water. There are many examples of this happening throughout the world:

1. **The Burren** in Co. Clare is now a karst area of mostly bare, exposed limestone. It is thought that this area enjoyed a covering of soil and natural vegetation during Neolithic (New Stone Age) times. Scientists believe that overgrazing by cattle farmers of old might have removed so much natural vegetation that the soil was exposed to the elements. Surface water following rain may then have stripped away the soil, leaving the underlying rock exposed.

2. In the 1930s, overcropping led to serious soil erosion in that part of the Midwest of the United States known as **the Dust Bowl**. Natural grasslands were ploughed to plant wheat. When the rains failed, the wheat failed to grow. The dry, exposed soil was then blown away by the wind.

3. Overgrazing has led to massive wind erosion of soil in parts of **the Sahel**, which lies just south of the Sahara Desert in Africa. The removal of soil has led to desertification – the spread of desert conditions – over vast areas of the Sahel. Plant and animal life have been greatly reduced and the local biome has been seriously altered.

Revise pages 494–7.

Cash Crops in the Third World

The intensive growth of cash crops in Third World countries has damaged biomes. An example of this has been the cultivation of **groundnuts (peanuts) in the African state of Niger**.

Niger was once a colony of France. In the 1960s, the French government encouraged the growth of massive quantities of groundnuts in Niger. These nuts would be exported to France as a source of cooking oil. The growth of these nuts was an example of **monoculture**, which means that no other crop was grown on the land. The monocultural growth of groundnuts exhausts soil so much that, after they have been grown for three years, the land needs to be left fallow (rested) for a six-year period in order to recover its fertility. Because most African farmers could not afford to rest their land for such long periods, the soil gradually became infertile. As the infertile soil produced smaller crops, the farmers tried to expand groundnut production to other areas in order to maintain their incomes. This in turn caused cattle rearing and millet cultivation to be pushed into 'marginal' semi-desert areas, which were not suited to agriculture. During particularly dry years, this cultivated marginal land produced little or no crops or grass, leaving the soil bare and exposed to wind storms. As the wind carried the dusty topsoil away, some land became part of the Sahara Desert. Intensive farming had thus caused desertification to take place and had altered the biome.

Exhausted soil as a result of the monocultural growth of groundnuts in Niger.

The Use of Fertilizers and Insecticides

Fertilizers are widely used to provide plentiful crop yields in modern intensive farming. But the overuse of fertilizers sometimes results in too many **nitrates and phosphates** entering the soil. These nutrients can then combine with groundwater and seep into our rivers and lakes. Too high concentrations of nitrates and phosphates cause the rapid growth of weed-like **algae** in rivers and lakes. The algae can use up so much of the water's oxygen supply that fish and other water creatures die. Some rivers and lakes in Ireland become so polluted in this way that their surfaces become completely covered with green algae.

Pesticides are chemicals that are sprayed on the land and are used often in intensive farms. They are designed to kill insects that eat crops or that spread disease among animals. Many pesticides are dangerous poisons that can cause serious pollution where they are not used properly. A pesticide once commonly used in Third World countries was DDT, a chemical that destroys mosquitoes and so helps to prevent malaria. The problem with DDT is that it is **cumulative**. It builds up to harmful levels in animals other than mosquitoes. When DDT was sprayed on land, some of it was washed into rivers and lakes, where it was absorbed by water plants. When fish ate the water plants, they too became contaminated with DDT. People or other animals that ate the fish then also became contaminated. In this way, the pesticide poisoned an entire food chain and so damaged the biome.

Disappearing Hedgerows

Hedgerows that separate fields have been a traditional and pleasant feature of the Irish countryside. These hedgerows can be described as 'uneconomic' because they may occupy a lot of land, especially where they separate small fields. But they also provide natural habitats (homes) for numerous species of birds, animals and insects.

Over the past fifty years, farmers have bulldozed many hedgerows. They do so in order to reduce 'non-profitable' space on their farms and to create bigger fields that are better suited to the use of harvesters and other modern farm machinery. The destruction of hedgerows has increased the amount of farmland available and has led to farms being used more intensively. But it has also resulted in the destruction of habitat for many birds, mammals, insects and traditional trees and plants. By damaging local ecosystems, hedgerow clearances alter our biome.

Hedgerow clearances may also ultimately contribute to a reduction, rather than an increase, in crop yields. Damage to soil and crops may occur in the absence of hedges that once protected them from the force of the wind.

Activity
Describe the cause and the consequences of the algae shown here.

Activity
Contrast photo A with photo B under the headings of intensity of land use and biodiversity (the richness and variety of plant and animal life).

See question 12 on page 524.

Case Study 4: Industrial Development

Manufacturing industry can damage biomes in a number of ways. These range from the creation of **greenhouse gases** and **acid rain** to an increase in **air and water pollution**.

Global Warming

See **Worldwide Impacts** on page 516.

Global warming is one of the most serious threats to biomes throughout the world. The main cause of global warming is the increased use of **fossil fuels**, especially in the world's more economically developed countries. Factories are major users of fossil fuels, such as oil and gas. When fossil fuels are burned, carbon dioxide (CO_2) is released into the atmosphere. Carbon dioxide is a greenhouse gas, which traps solar energy. As it increases, it causes the atmosphere to gradually become warmer.

Scientists believe that severe **droughts** being experienced in African countries such as Sudan and Ethiopia may be a result of increased evaporation caused by global warming. These droughts are resulting in the desertification of much of Africa's Sahel region. They are causing the biome of much of this region to change from one of savannah grassland to one of hot desert.

Global warming is causing **polar ice caps to melt** and this could have devastating effects on the world's biomes. Ice cap and tundra regions near the poles could be so altered that polar bears, Arctic foxes and other inhabitants of these regions might become extinct. The melting of ice caps would also cause sea levels to rise so that vast, low-lying areas in all parts of the world would be submerged. This would result in the widespread destruction of biomes in places ranging from Bangladesh to the Netherlands to the Shannon Estuary.

Global warming may already be altering **Ireland's biome**. Recent winters have been among the mildest recorded and birds of warmer climates, such as little egrets, are beginning to colonise our shores. If global warming causes Ireland's climate to become warmer, we might yet produce fruits like oranges, but catch tropical diseases like malaria. Global warming could also disrupt the flow of the North Atlantic Drift. If this happens, Ireland might become so cold that our harbours could freeze in winter.

The little egret.

Activity

Outline the connection between industrial activity and the increase in Ireland's little egret population.

Acid Rain

Industrial development has contributed greatly to acid rain, which has a major effect on biomes. As stated earlier, factories burn huge amounts of oil and gas. The burning of these fossil fuels causes **sulphur dioxide and nitrogen oxides** to be released into the air. These gases combine with moisture to form weak **sulphuric and nitric acids**, which fall as acid rain.

Acid rain causes soils to become gradually more acidic and to experience more leaching. This in turn alters plant life. **Coniferous trees** suffer so much that acid rain is sometimes called 'forest death' in Sweden. The roots of conifers are poisoned, so many trees stop growing or die. It is estimated that half of Germany's trees have been damaged by acid rain. Acid rain also causes sulphur to build up in soils. This kills some plants, such as certain types of mushrooms. It causes other plants, such as nettles, to spread at an alarming rate.

When forests, water supplies and soils are altered by acid rain, so is **animal life**. Woodland animals in Europe, for example, have died in their millions as a result of acid rain.

Acid rain can also damage **lakes**, many to the point that they no longer support fish life. An estimated 15,000 lakes have been damaged in Norway, which receives acid rain in south-westerly winds blowing from countries such as Britain.

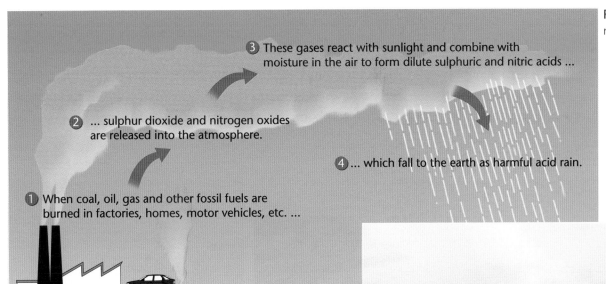

Fig. 84.3 How acid rain is caused.

③ These gases react with sunlight and combine with moisture in the air to form dilute sulphuric and nitric acids ...

② ... sulphur dioxide and nitrogen oxides are released into the atmosphere.

④ ... which fall to the earth as harmful acid rain.

① When coal, oil, gas and other fossil fuels are burned in factories, homes, motor vehicles, etc. ...

Activity
Describe the effects shown here of acid rain in the Black Forest, in Germany.

521

Death in Bhopal

This is an account of what happened after the gas leak in Bhopal.

'People simply started dying in the most hideous ways. The gases burned the tissues of their eyes and lungs and attacked their nervous systems. People lost control of their bodies. Urine and faeces ran down their legs. Women lost their unborn children as they ran. Some (people) vomited uncontrollably, went into convulsions and fell dead. Others choked to death, drowning in their own body fluids.'

Air Pollution

Some industries, such as smelters, steel mills and certain chemical plants, cause air pollution which harms animals and plants and so damages biomes. While industrial air pollution happens in all parts of the world, most of the worst examples happen in Third World countries, where governments are too weak or too poor to insist on high standards of environmental protection.

One of the world's worst examples of industrial air pollution happened in **Bhopal** in India (see Fig. 84.4). Union Carbide, an American-owned multinational company, operated a pesticide factory at Bhopal. The factory failed to make profit and was closed, but huge quantities of deadly chemicals continued to be stored in the abandoned plant.

On the morning of 3 December 1984, an explosion in the Union Carbide plant released a mixture of heavy, poisonous gases into the air. All the safety systems in the factory failed and the gases spread out across the ground, attacking the lungs, eyes and almost every other organ of the human body. Nobody knows how many people died of gas inhalation. Union Carbide estimated 3,800, while local people say that at least 15,000 perished. More people died slowly from poisoning, while up to 50,000 have not worked since then as a result of their injuries. The site of this accident has never been cleaned up properly. The remains of toxins from the explosion are now reported to have entered the soil and water in the area. These toxins kill plants and fish, poison animal and human food chains and so damage the biome.

Victims of Bhopal explosion.

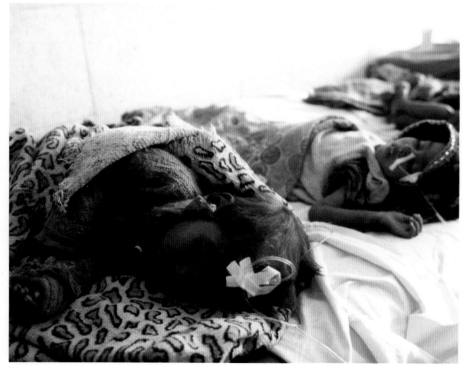

Fig. 84.4

Activity

1. How might an industrial accident like this effect a biome?
2. Why might disasters like this be more likely to happen in Third World countries than in economically developed countries?

Water Pollution

Water bodies, such as rivers and lakes, are important parts of our biomes. The water itself provides habitats for fish and other animals, while nearby land supports waterside creatures such as kingfishers, otters and water-loving plants. Industrial pollution may pollute water and so damage biomes in a number of ways.

Some industrial plants, such as thermal (heat-generating) power stations, use water for cooling purposes. This water becomes heated in the process and may then be released back into the rivers or lakes from which it was taken. **Warm water** does not contain as much oxygen as cool water. Heated water is therefore a pollutant in that it may result in the suffocation of fish or other water creatures.

Poisonous **chemicals**, such as lead, zinc and cyanide, are used in some manufacturing industries and may sometimes seep into rivers, lakes or groundwater. These chemicals are cumulative poisons. They build up gradually in animals until there is enough to kill the animals. Lake Erie in North America (see Fig. 84.5) once became so polluted that it had no animal or plant life at all. The River Cuyahoga, which flows into the lake through the old industrial city of Cleveland, once became so polluted with chemicals that experts feared it might catch fire!

Stricter anti-pollution laws have resulted in reduced industrial pollution of water in developing countries. But some industries still try to cut the costs of dealing safely with waste by illegally **dumping** chemicals when or where they think they will not be caught.

Fig. 84.5 Lake Erie and Cleveland.

See questions 13 and 14 on page 524.

Activity
How could the emission of warm water from this power station affect the biome of the area?

Examination Questions

1. Examine the factors that influence soil characteristics.

2. *'Soils can vary greatly in their make-up and characteristics.'* Comment on this statement with reference to some soils that you have studied.

3. With reference to soils that you have studied, discuss the view that soils are affected by a combination of different processes.

4. *'Different soil types predominate in different parts of the world by adapting to local biomes.'* Comment on this statement, with particular reference to Ireland's most common soil type.

5. *Examine how human activities can accelerate soil erosion.

6. Examine, with reference to European and non-European examples, the statement that people can conserve as well as destroy soils.

7. *Examine the main characteristics of a biome that you have studied.

8. *Illustrate the development of biomes, with reference to a specific example.

9. Explain how vegetation and animals are related to the physical geography of any biome that you have studied.

10. To what extent has early settlement and the clearing of forests altered biomes in European and non-European regions which you have studied?

11. *Assess the global implications of the continued felling of tropical rainforests.

12. Evaluate the view that intensive agricultural practices have had an impact on biomes in many parts of the world.

13. Describe some worldwide effects of industrial development on biomes.

14. *Assess the impact of human activity on a biome that you have studied.

* Denotes a question that has appeared in a Leaving Certificate examination or sample paper.

CHAPTER 85
FIELDWORK INVESTIGATION

Students should carefully read the guidelines set out in the syllabus for the geographical investigation.

THE GEOGRAPHICAL INVESTIGATION

The geographical investigation is a core area of study, and all students must carry out a fieldwork exercise and write a report on it. Field studies and investigations using primary and secondary sources are a very important part of studying geography. These practical investigations allow you to apply the core geographical skills you have studied and practised through all units of the syllabus. The investigation also encourages you to **experience and question relationships and issues in your own surroundings**.

To carry out the geographical investigation, you have to:
- Devise a strategy for it and **identify aims** and **objectives** to allow an effective investigation of the topic.
- **Select methods of gathering information** that are appropriate to the investigation topic.
- **Use suitable methods for gathering and recording information.**
- Write a report.
- Analyse and interpret results and draw valid conclusions.

Structuring and Organising the Investigation

You choose your investigation topic from a list put together by the Department of Education and Science. You have to complete your investigation by 1 December of Leaving Certificate year two. Although you may work in class groups, for assessment purposes each student must present their own full and complete report. No group projects are accepted.

Higher Level students are expected to write a report of 1,000 words or less. The investigation report must be presented in a reporting booklet provided by the State Examination Commission.

For your investigation you must use at least 60 per cent primary and up to 40 per cent secondary sources of information.

Primary sources give information that comes directly from the time or place that is being studied. These include original photographs, newspaper reports and maps of the time, and old buildings. Secondary sources are ones that may be written after the time period being studied but indirectly give us information about a time or place. These could include parish journals, historical accounts or interviews.

For further examples/information, refer to *Geographical Exploration, Investigating Ireland's Heritage* produced by the Heritage Council and edited by Tony Dunne. Copies have been issued to every school by CDVEC Curriculum Development Unit.

The **geography teacher** and **school principal** will **verify** that the investigation has been carried out by each Leaving Certificate candidate. The Geographical Investigation and Skills core unit allocates 20 per cent of marks at both Higher and Ordinary Level.

The table below shows the different steps of the geographical investigation and how many marks are allocated to each part. The different approaches to geographical skills for Ordinary and Higher Level students are shown in the way marks are allocated for each part of the investigation.

Stage	Activities	Proposed Assessment Weighting	
		Ordinary Level	Higher Level
Introduction: Posing the problems and devising a strategy	• Selecting a topic for investigation • Clear statement of the aim • An outline of the objectives • Identifying the types of information required	5%	5%
Planning and preparing the work to be carried out	• Selecting methods for collecting and gathering information • Designing a questionnaire or recording sheets • Deciding on locations for the investigation	5%	5%
Collecting data	• Using instruments to make measurements • Records of observations made in the field • Using questionnaires and surveys, as appropriate • Using a variety of secondary sources, e.g. documentary sources • Discussing the problems encountered	30%	30%
Preparing the report: Presenting results	• Organising data • Using illustrations, graphs, maps and tables • Using ICT, where appropriate, to prepare and present results and conclusions	40%	40%
Conclusion and evaluation for the report	• Analysis and interpretation of results • Drawing valid conclusions • Comparison of findings with established theory • Evaluation of the hypothesis • Examining the validity of the investigation and suggestions for improvements	20%	20%

FIELDWORK NO. 1

To Examine the Geomorphic Processes of Transportation and Deposition in a Coastal Environment

Use OSi Trailmaster to research and view your fieldwork locations.

The **first** task is to **choose a location** where coastal transportation and deposition is occurring. This location should be easily accessible to the students (access from a road) and it should be a place where activities can be carried out safely. This location should be within a reasonable distance of the school so that all the necessary activities can be carried out while students are fresh and enthusiastic.

The **second** task is to **prepare for this fieldwork** activity so that students understand what exactly they are expected to **observe**, **measure** and **record**. This would include some or all of the following:

- Identifying the objectives of the fieldwork.
- Recap on all coastal processes of transportation and deposition.
- Recap on all features/landforms of coastal deposition.
- Learn and practise all methods of measuring and recording coastal processes of transportation and deposition.
- Recap on all remedial work/interference by people in coastal environments.
- Create simple clinometers from large wooden protractors.
- Gather other instruments from other school departments, such as quadrats, ranging poles, measuring tapes, callipers, stopwatch for timing tasks.
- Creating a fieldwork worksheet for recording.

The **third task** is the fieldwork activity. This should involve the following activities so that the objectives of the fieldwork can be achieved:

- Observing coastal features and processes.
- Drawing sketch maps to identify and label the features/landforms of the coastal environment.
- Carrying out various measurements/calculations/tasks – these tasks should include:
  - finding the slope of the beach
  - measuring longshore drift
  - measuring the sizes of beach material.
- Recording the information from these tasks on a worksheet.

Some Instruments and Tasks to Find Height of Dunes

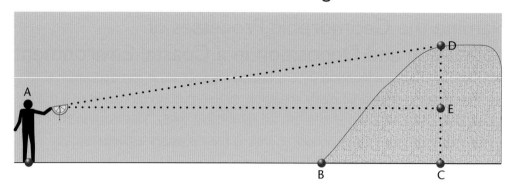

Task: To find height of sand dune

1. Find angle to top of dune.
2. Find length to base of dune. _____ ⎤ Combined answers give horizontal distance
3. Estimate length of BC. ⎦ to base of sand dune = AC
4. Height of DE = AE x tan DAE
5. Height of dune = DE + height of student (EC)

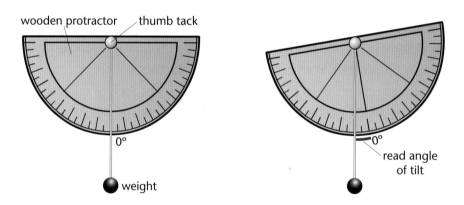

To find beach profile

- Use a clinometer to measure the beach profile.
- Get backsight and foresight for an average reading.

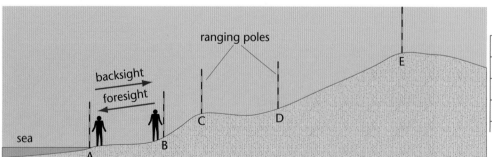

Recording Sheet

	A–B	B–C	
Dist.			
Angle			
Angle	B–A	C–B	

To find rate of longshore drift

This involves two measurements, i.e. time and distance.

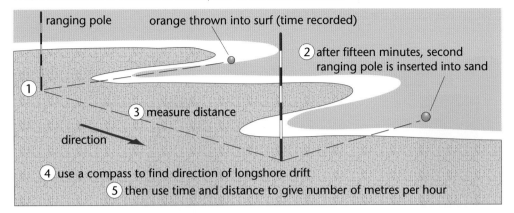

To find size of beach sediment up the beach

Throw the quadrant on sediment at three different locations from water to storm beach. At each location measure and record twenty rock samples within the quadrant. These measurements should help to prove that sediment size increases up the beach.

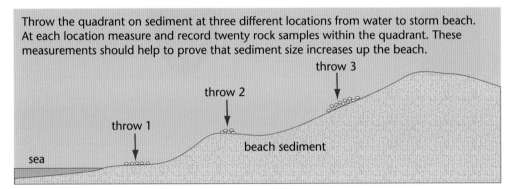

Beach Material Analysis
Presenting the Results

- Using graph paper, draw a bar chart to show the average size of the material at the three locations.
- The results can also be presented as a series of coloured circles drawn to a suitable scale.
- Get the average of all pebbles/stones found and draw a graph or chart or both to show these results.

If the type of rock is analysed, a percentage breakdown of rock type can be shown in chart form, e.g. a pie chart. This type of analysis may be justified in the case of proving transportation begins at a particular cliff face.

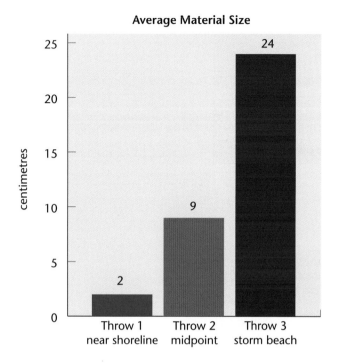

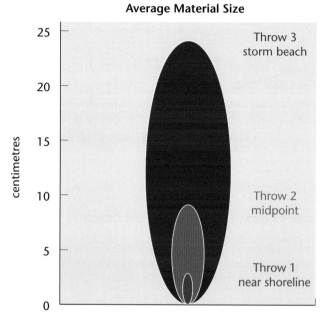

The fourth task is to write a report of the fieldwork. The report should be structured so that each task, result and conclusion should relate to each objective.

You should write up this report in a **booklet** similar to that presented by the Examinations Board. On it, sketch the various instruments and activities/worksheets you used during your fieldwork. This should be corrected and redone again until it is your best effort.

FIELDWORK NO. 2

Tips for a Fieldwork Exercise on River Study

A field study may include either erosion or deposition or both processes. Whichever is the case, a correct approach to the task must be carefully planned.

Aims and Objectives

- To understand the energy of running water and the factors that affect this energy.
- To identify landforms that result from variations in the energy of a river.
- To prove there is a relationship between sediment size, depth and speed of river.
- To prove that sediment shape is affected by transportation.
- To prove that certain features are associated with a particular stage in the course of a river.

When you do a fieldwork exercise, certain information must be gathered and recorded. There are four important points to remember:
- What information is needed and why.
- Where the information will be collected and why.
- How the information will be collected and why.
- When the information will be collected and why.

Make sure that you clearly identify the areas or activities of fieldwork that you take part in or contribute to.

Planning and Preparing for the Fieldwork

1. In class, review information on rivers, river features and river processes.
2. Choose a short section (about 200 m), or sections, of a shallow river suitable for the fieldwork. A shallow stretch of the river **with at least one bend** is usually the best choice for river study. This kind of river allows you to cross from one bank to the opposite side and makes precise measurement of depth, cross-section and pebble size easier.
3. Make copies of a map of the river section 1:2,500.
4. The class should work in groups. Initially:
   - Group A focuses on river bend(s).
   - Group B focuses on transportation by the river.
   - Group C focuses on the speed of river flow.
   - Group D focuses on the volume of river flow.

Remember, each group should carry out all tasks during the day.

With your teacher, make sure that the preparation is followed by co-ordinated activities to check that the fieldwork exercise goes according to plan.

Collecting Data

Group A

This group makes a cross-section of the river. You can practise this by making a simple cross-section of a slope in a grassy area or a slope in a field near the school buildings or schoolyard.

- Use measuring poles, line-levels, tape and cord to carry out this exercise.
- Indicate fast, medium and slow areas of the river by marking wide, medium and thin arrows on 'section line/tape'.
- Choose two points at A and B where there are significant bends in the river and follow through with skills learned in class or in a preliminary activity.

Group B

This group examines the material that the river carries. Bring to school samples of pebbles and stones taken from a riverbed near your home. Examine each sample and explain why they are rounded.

- Focus on cross-section skills and measuring poles, and find the depth of water at various points on the river at the location chosen. (This could be done in parallel to the cross-section line for Group A.)
- Measure and find the average diameter of stones and their minimum and maximum sizes. Use a quadrat to choose random samples.
- Create a chart with the following headings:
  - Section.
  - Depth.
  - Pebble Diameter.
- Create a graph using pebble size and depth to see if there is a relationship between the water depth and pebble size.

Group C

This group aims to identify factors that influence the speed of the river. The exercise can be done in the river at various points in a particular location. This could be a few yards upstream or downstream from the cross-section area of Group A or at a bend or another point.

- Research ways of measuring the speed of flow where the river is:
  - fast
  - slow
  - still.

This can be done using a drain in the schoolyard, a gallon or bucket of water, a cork, a stopwatch and a tape.

- Observe the size of pebbles at various speed locations and see if there is any relationship between speed and pebble size, or the width, speed and pebble size.
- Observe and debate factors, such as riverbed roughness, which might affect the speed of river flow.

Group D

This group aims to measure the cubic flow of water in a river. This can be done by:
- Finding the average depth and width across the river at the three crossing points chosen.
- Choosing the crossing points. Each crossing point should be about 5 m across.

To calculate the cubic flow of water of the river along each section chosen, use the formula:

volume = speed (metres/second) x depth x width.

All Groups

All groups should make photocopies of a map of the river from a 1:2,500 OS sheet.

- Mark each area being studied on the core map. (Your teacher may explain and practise map orientation with you.)
- Draw a sketch map of the river section. Use a viewfinder (with nine dimensions, as on a photograph).
- Note the direction of flow.
- Take photographs of the sections of the river needed for each group.
- Use a school video recorder, if available, to record the activities.

Results

- Each group should record their findings carefully on charts. A student can give a brief description of each fieldwork activity on site once each group has completed its work. This is to make sure that each group is aware of each other's work and its relevance for the fieldwork activity.
- Each group records and presents its findings so that results and conclusions can be drawn from the information gathered.

Conclusion and Evaluation

Each student should write a report that includes:

- Relevant and logical conclusions from the material gathered.
- Identify reasons for any changes in surveying methods.
- Identify skills you have learned.
- Identify areas that could be improved when carrying out a similar survey and fieldwork.

INDEX

PICTURE CREDITS

For permission to reproduce photographs the author and publisher gratefully acknowledge the following:

ALAMY: 13, 16B, 21T, 37, 48, 49, 57T, 58T, 59, 61B, 62T, 62B, 63, 70B, 71CB, 73, 75, 76, 81, 85B, 88, 99T, 100, 101, 102, 103, 104, 105, 107, 124T, 124B, 125, 126B, 127, 134R, 136, 141T, 156, 157, 160, 169, 174R, 176, 183, 188, 189, 190R, 191, 200, 201T, 206B, 222B, 226C, 231, 236T, 254T, 282L, 282R, 285R, 310L, 316, 318T, 335, 344T, 344B, 352, 355R, 356T, 356B, 367B, 367T, 368, 376T, 379, 382, 393, 397T, 397BL, 403L, 403R, 407B, 408, 409, 433, 440, 447, 469B, 477, 482L, 482R, 485R, 496, 507, 509B, 515, 516, 519T, 519B; BARRY BRUNT 391; CAMERA PRESS 314L; CHARLIE HAYES 463T; CORBIS: 19 © Karen Kasmauski, 20T © Roger Ressmeyer, 20C © Proteccion Civil de Colima/epa, 27T © Michael St Maur Sheil, 33, 416R © Reuters, 34 © epa, 35B © Yannis Behrakis/Reuters, 35T © David Smith/Sygma, 43C © Bill Ross, 43B © M. Angelo, 44T © Patrick Durand/Sygma, 67R, 116T © Corbis, 68B © Vince Streano, 71T © Corbis Sygma, 80 © Wolfgang Kaehler, 83 © Tom Bean, 121T © Les Stone/Sygma, 138, 197, 234B © Yann Arthus-Bertrand, 145 © Adam Woolfitt, 171 © George McCarthy, 193T © Sandro Vannini, 199 © Ted Spiegel, 202 © Patrice Latron, 234T © Abel Alonso/epa, 236C © Bogdan Croitoru/epa, 281© Reuters/Rupak De Chowdhuri, 284B© John Van Hasselt, 287T © Earl & Nazima Kowall, 288L © Michael S. Yamashita, 288R © Action Aid/Gideon Mendel, 302B © Hulton-Deustch Collection, 304 © Joe Castro/epa, 312, 419 © Peter Turnley, 337T © George Steinmetz, 338T © Dan Lamont, 387 © Geray Sweeney, 429B © Mladen Antonov/epa, 446 © Sean Sexton Collection; ESB 375; DEREK SPEIRS: 180T, 428B, 471, 474; DIGITAL PHOTO LIBRARY OF THE REGIONAL POLICY DIRECTORATE-GENERAL OF THE EUROPEAN COMMISSION 158; DUBLIN PORT 346; EC/ECHO SOUTH ASIA OFFICE 36; ECOSCENE: 488 © Peter Hulme, 512B © Andrew Brown, 519C © Frank Blackburn; EMPICS: 20B, 21C, 60, 147, 381, 389, 401, 476; FÁS 363R; FINBARR O'CONNELL: 163, 164, 179, 294T, 326R, 350, 388, 423; FLPA: 485C © Bob Gibbons, 490C © David Hosking, 490B © Terry Whittaker; FORD, SPAIN 326L; GARY O'NEILL 376B; GETTY: 302T, 454 © Hulton, 443T © AFP, 522 © Getty; GEOLOGICAL SURVEY OF IRELAND 69; HARALD FINSTER: 161, 299; IMAGEFILE: 16C, 26T, 28, 43T, 43B, 44C, 44B, 45, 53, 55T, 55B, 57C, 61T, 74, 78B, 85T, 85C, 89, 99C, 99B, 121B, 123, 126C, 130B, 146C, 146R, 150C, 152, 153, 165, 166, 167R, 177, 190L, 193B, 195, 203, 204, 206T, 212, 216R, 222T, 226B, 227T, 238, 254B, 285L, 300R, 342, 366, 372L, 372R, 400, 411L, 418B, 420L, 426C, 426B, 457, 465B, 470, 480, 485L, 486, 489, 494, 499, 505, 506, 508T, 510, 511, 512T, 514, 517, 520R, 520L, 521, 523; INPHO 141B; INTEGRATED RESOURCE DEVELOPMENT, KILTIMAGH 478; IRISH EXAMINER 239; IRISH IMAGE COLLECTION: 134L, 146L, 174L, 182, 354; IRISH TIMES: 151, 378, 459, 465T; KEVIN DWYER: 268R, 269; LIEBHERR 349; LIMERICK CITY COUNCIL 142; LONELY PLANET IMAGES: 58B, 360 © Eoin Clarke, 355L © Wayne Walton, 397BR © Grant Dixon, 407T © Richard Cummins; MARTYN GODDARD 377; NATIONAL CHILDREN'S OFFICE: 445 © Derek Speirs; NEIL WARNER 293; NISSAN 318B; NOAA 122; ORDNANCE SURVEY: 268L, 270; PANOS: 218 © Robert Wallis, 221B, 313R © Chris Stower, 226T, 364, 475 © Mark Henley, 236B © Piotr Malecki, 284T © Dieter Telemans, 290 © Martin Adler, 306, 469T © Sean Sprague, 310R © Dermot Tatlow, 311 © Pep Bonet, 315 © Mark Chilvers, 318C, 418T © Fernando Moleres, 406B © Giacomo Pirozzi, 437 © Tim A Hetherington, 441 © Stefan Boness, 452 © Liba

Taylor; PAT O'DWYER 115; PATRICK J MCKEEVER 68T; PETER BARROW: 167L, 180B, 184, 245, 246, 273, 275, 277, 294B, 295, 296, 322, 326B, 363L; PETER MENZEL 278R; PETER GINTER 278L; PHOTOCALL IRELAND: 144, 297, 336, 373, 410; REPORTDIGITAL.CO.UK: 159R © Paul Box, 435 © Howard Davies; REUTERS: 70T, 71CT, 116B, 117, 120, 148, 150L, 150R, 196, 205, 214T, 232, 255, 334T, 338B, 340, 341, 380, 384R, 416L, 420R, 426T, 455; SCIENCE PHOTO LIBRARY: 16TR, 16T, 18, 21B, 23, 26B, 27B, 31, 56, 57B, 67L, 71B, 78T, 86, 87, 90, 91, 93, 130T, 131, 271, 487, 490T, 497, 504, 527; SEAGEN 463B; SKYSCAN: 300L © Patrick Henderyckx, 330 © Ph. Guignard/air-images, 244 © Aerophoto Schiphol; STILL PICTURES: 159L © PHONE Rigel H, 201B © BIOS Brudieux Franck, 214B © Kevin Schafer, 215, 217L, 221T © Sean Sprague, 216L, 220R, 307, 313L, 428T © Joerg Boethling, 217R, 219L, 227B, 337B, 406TR, 498, 513T © Mark Edwards, 219R © Chris Caloicott, 220L, 513B © Ron Giling, 223 © Shehzad Noorani, 287B © Friedrich Stark, 314R © P&A McDonald, 333 © Jochen Tack, 384L, 479, 518 © Jorgen Schytte, 406TL, 453 © Hartmut Schwarzbach, 411R © ullstein – Gebhardt, 424 © PHONE Thiriet Claudius, 429T © Russell Gordon, 449 © A. Riedmiller, 458 © Achim Pohl, 493 © Charlotte Thege, 495 © Knut Mueller, 509T © Wyman Meinzer; SULT 241; TARA MINES: 392 © R Blakeman; THE DEFENCE FORCES 464; THE RECYCLING VILLAGE 450; UNICEF: 425 © Dr M. Khan; WARD SCOTT 334B; WYETH MEDICA 328.

Ordnance Survey Maps reproduced by permission of Ordnance Survey Ireland. Images produced using OSi Trail Master program, reprinted with permission of Ordnance Survey Ireland. © Ordnance Survey Ireland.

The author and publisher have made every effort to trace all copyright holders, but if any has been inadvertently overlooked we would be pleased to make the necessary arrangement at the first opportunity.